ATION PRESS GETS YOU

CCNP
CERTIFICATION PATH

Cisco Certified Network Professional
Recommended Training:

- ACRC – Advanced Cisco Router Configuration
- CLSC – Cisco LAN Switch Configuration
- CMTD – Configuring, Monitoring, and Troubleshooting Dial-up Services
- CIT – Cisco Internetwork Troubleshooting

EXAMS

(Candidates have two options to choose from based on preference, and candidates must have CCNA certification before they will receive their CCNP certification)

Test Option 1

- Foundation R/S Exam #640-409
- CIT Exam #640-406

Test Option 2

- ACRC Exam #640-403
- CLSC Exam #640-404
- CMTD Exam #640-405
- CIT Exam #640-406

CERTIFICATION PRESS STUDY GUIDES

CCNP Advanced Cisco Router Configuration Study Guide (Exam 640-403)

ISBN 0-07-211910-1

CCNP LAN Switch Configuration Study Guide (Exam 640-404)

ISBN 0-07-211906-3

CCNP Configuring, Monitoring, and Troubleshooting Dial-up Services Study Guide (Exam 640-405)

ISBN 0-07-211908-X

CCNP Cisco Internetwork Troubleshooting Study Guide (Exam 640-406)

ISBN 0-07-211912-8

CCIE
CERTIFICATION PATH

Cisco Certified Internetwork Expert
Recommended Training:

- CID – Cisco Internetwork Design
- IMCR – Installing and Maintaining Cisco Routers

For CCIE-ISP Dial Path, add recommended courses:

- MCNS – Managing Cisco Network Security
- AS5200 – Cisco AS5200 Universal Access Server

EXAMS

Routing and Switching Path:

- CCIE – R/S Qualification Exam #350-001
- CCIE – R/S Certification Laboratory

ISP Dial Path:

- CCIE – ISP Dial Qualification Exam #350-004
- CCIE – ISP Dial Certification Laboratory

CERTIFICATION PRESS STUDY GUIDES

CCIE Cisco Certified Internetwork Expert Study Guide (Exam 350-001)

ISBN 0-07-882486-9

For complete Cisco Certification details visit:
http://www.cisco.com/warp/public/10/wwtraining/certprog/index.html

CCNA Cisco Certified Network Associate Study Guide

(Exam 640-407)

Syngress Media, Inc.

Osborne/McGraw-Hill

Berkeley New York St. Louis San Francisco
Auckland Bogotá Hamburg London Madrid
Mexico City Milan Montreal New Delhi Panama City
Paris São Paulo Singapore Sydney
Tokyo Toronto

Osborne/**McGraw-Hill**
2600 Tenth Street
Berkeley, California 94710
U.S.A.

For information on translations or book distributors outside the U.S.A., or to arrange bulk purchase discounts for sales promotions, premiums, or fund-raisers, please contact Osborne/**McGraw-Hill** at the above address.

CCNA Cisco Certified Network Associate Study Guide (Exam 640-407)

1234567890 AGM AGM 901987654321098

ISBN 0-07-882487-7

Publisher
Brandon A. Nordin

Editor-in-Chief
Scott Rogers

Acquisitions Editor
Gareth Hancock

Editorial Assistant
Debbie Escobedo

Project Editor
Madhu Prasher

Technical Editors
Richard D. Hornbaker
Pamela Forsyth

Copy Editor
Kathleen Faughnan

Indexer
Jack Lewis

Proofreaders
Laurie Stewart
Karen Mead

Computer Designers
Jean Butterfield
Ann Sellers

Illustrators
Brian Wells
Lance Ravella

Series Design
Roberta Steele

Cover Design
Regan Honda

Editorial Management
Syngress Media, Inc.

FOREWORD

From Global Knowledge Network

At Global Knowledge Network we strive to support the multiplicity of learning styles required by our students to achieve success as technical professionals. In this series of books, it is our intention to offer the reader a valuable tool for successful completion of the CCNA Certification Exam.

As the world's largest IT training company, Global Knowledge Network is uniquely positioned to offer these books. The expertise gained each year from providing instructor-led training to hundreds of thousands of students worldwide has been captured in book form to enhance your learning experience. We hope that the quality of these books demonstrates our commitment to your lifelong learning success. Whether you choose to learn through the written word, computer-based training, Web delivery, or instructor-led training, Global Knowledge Network is committed to providing you the very best in each of those categories. For those of you who know Global Knowledge Network, or those of you who have just found us for the first time, our goal is to be your lifelong competency partner.

Thank you for the opportunity to serve you. We look forward to serving your needs again in the future.

Warmest regards,

Duncan Anderson
Chief Operating Officer, Global Knowledge Network

ABOUT THE CONTRIBUTORS

Syngress Media creates books and software for Information Technology professionals seeking skill enhancement and career advancement. Its products are designed to comply with vendor and industry standard course curricula, and are optimized for certification exam preparation. You can contact Syngress via the web at www.syngress.com.

Melissa Craft is a consulting engineer for MicroAge, a dynamic systems integration company in Phoenix, Arizona. Melissa handles internetwork systems design for complex or global network projects, concentrating on infrastructure and messaging. She has a bachelor's degree from the University of Michigan. During her career, she has obtained several certifications: MCSE, CNE-3, CNE-4, CNE-GW, MCNE, and Citrix. Melissa Craft is a member of the IEEE, the Society of Women Engineers, and American Mensa, Ltd.

Brian Mayo is a Microsoft Certified System's Engineer (MCSE), Microsoft Certified Professional + Internet, (MCP + Internet) and a Compaq Accredited Systems Engineer (ASE). He comes from a deployment and support background, and currently works as a systems engineer for CompuCom out of their Indianapolis branch.

John Pherson has more than 16 years of technical consulting and technical management experience in the computer industry, specializing in networking technologies and operating systems. He holds MCSE and MCT certifications, as well as Novell Master CNE and CNI designations, and a B.S. in business administration. John has been a member of several CompTIA (Computer Technology Industry Association) committees responsible for the growth and direction of the A + Certification, and has been a featured speaker at the computer industry's biannual System Support Expo. He is also a member of American Mensa, Ltd. He is currently employed as an instructional consultant with Global Knowledge Network in Dallas, and also provides independent consulting services to small and medium-sized businesses. His personal interests include spending time with his wife and four daughters, playing guitar and folk harp, biking, sailing, and photography.

Herbert Borovansky is a consultant with the Forté Consulting Group, based in Phoenix, Arizona. He gained his bachelor's degree in management information systems from the University of Arizona. He is currently leading the design and implementation of switched network infrastructures for two call centers for a large financial services company. His fields of expertise range from network operating systems to personal computer operating systems to internetworking using switching and routing.

Todd VanDerwerken is a senior network design engineer with First Data Corporation in Omaha, Nebraska. He has a strong background in Token Ring, Frame Relay, SNA, and IP. With more than 15 years experience in data communications, Todd began his career with the USAF as an in-flight maintenance technician instructor/evaluator. He is currently working toward his CCIE certification and is a contributor to the CCIEPrep Web page.

Darryl Luff is currently responsible for the day-to-day management of 90 routers spread across 20 sites. He handles maintenance of the existing infrastructure, as well as provides design services for new installations and upgrades. Darryl is also responsible for the provision of intranet web and proxy services. He has supported networks utilizing IPX, OSI protocols, IP, Appletalk and SNA. In the future, he hopes to continue his work in the network management area, and has a particular interest in web technologies and network security. Darryl can be reached via email at djluff@bigpond.com.

Irwin Overton has more than 14 years of experience in the complex computer information industry. Irwin has had extensive experience in system administration, minicomputers, and mainframes, and has worked with almost every type of network operating system and cabling topology available in the industry. He also has an extensive knowledge of Cisco products and software configuration. Irwin's technical expertise includes LAN, WAN, and MAN design, configuration and implementation, Cisco router design and configuration, system analysis and development, and network systems architecture. Irwin is a Certified Cisco Systems Instructor. He holds a B.S.E.E., and a J.D., and is a member of IEEE.

Prakash Ranade has more than ten years of experience in the application of state-of-the-art computer technologies to the solution of complex engineering problems. His expertise includes systems analysis and requirements definition, operation systems architecture, operations planning, software testing and conceptual modeling. Through his work at major American corporations, he has acquired broad experience in technical areas ranging from space science to telecommunications. He has taught computer science and chemical engineering courses at major academic institutions in the United States. Prakash holds an M.S. and a Ph.D. in chemical engineering.

Technical Review

Richard D. Hornbaker is a consultant with the Forté Consulting Group, based in Phoenix, Arizona. He specializes in large-scale routing and switching projects for Fortune 500 companies. Recent projects include a 12,000-node campus network using a combination of routing, switching, and ATM. Richard is currently designing the network for a major corporate merger. Richard has more than ten years of internetworking experience and holds several certifications: CCIE, MCSE, and MCNE. His skills are diverse, ranging from operating systems and software, to telephony systems and data networks. Protocol analysis and troubleshooting are among his strong suits.

Technical Review and From the Classroom Sidebars

Pamela Forsyth has been working in a technical capacity with digital electronics and computer systems for more than 20 years, and has been active in the networking field since 1989. Her certifications include CCIE (Routing and Switching), Certified Cisco Systems Instructor (CCSI), CNX, Master CNE, and MCSE. She is currently a senior network engineer with Wang Global in the Enterprise Transport Group, specializing in design and integration of large-scale routed networks and ATM networks based on Cisco WAN switching products. Pam can be reached via email at pforsyth@clark.net.

Special Thanks to the People at International Network Services

Robert Erani is a managing consultant for International Network Services in Iselin, New Jersey. He has a bachelors degree and masters degree in electrical engineering from Columbia University School of Engineering and Applied Sciences in New York, New York. Robert obtained his CCIE certification from Cisco Systems in September 1995.

Louis Bancalari is a senior network systems consultant for International Network Services in Iselin, New Jersey. He graduated *cum laude* from the Manhattan College in Riverdale, New York, with a B.E.E.E degree. In December 1997, Louis obtained CCIE certification from Cisco Systems. Louis is also a member of IEEE.

Helen Byrne is a network systems engineer for International Network Services. She has a bachelor's degree from Dowling College in New York and holds CCIE and CNE certifications.

Kenneth Bhanote is a consulting engineer for International Network Services in New York, New York. Kenneth has five years experience in the IT field, and has obtained CCIE, CNE, and MCP certifications.

Marwan Hennawi is a managing consultant for International Network Services in New York, New York. He has a bachelor's degree in electrical engineering from the University of Arizona. Marwan has been in the internetworking industry for more than 14 years and has obtained several certifications: CNI, MCNE, and CCIE.

Michael Murphy is a senior network systems consultant for International Network Services in Iselin, New Jersey. He has ten years of internetworking experience, predominantly with large banks and brokerage firms in the New York area. Since joining INS, Michael has been involved in the redesign and engineering of several large campus networks. He is regularly involved in the mentoring of other INS engineers, and has assisted in the creation of internal study material. He obtained his CCIE in Routing and Switching in the autumn of 1997.

Richard Ruiz is a network systems engineer for International Network Services in Iselin, New Jersey. He has 14 years experience in the computer field—the last eight being dedicated to WAN and LAN technologies. Richard is currently working on his CCIE certification and his Network Security Certification.

Christopher Sulentic is a Principal Consultant for International Network Services in Atlanta, Georgia. He has a Master's degree in Engineering from the University of Iowa and has been heavily involved in all aspects of network design. Chris maintains a CCIE certification and is a member of the IEEE.

ACKNOWLEDGMENTS

We would like to thank the following people:

- Ralph Troupe, Frank Musacchia, and Rob Erani of International Network Services (INS) for their invaluable support and their insight into real world Cisco networking.
- Richard Kristof of Global Knowledge Network for championing the series and providing us access to some great people and information. And to Shelley Clark, Marty Young, Patrick Faison, Brenda Thistle, Stacey Cannon and Chuck Terrien for all their cooperation.
- Imran Qureshi and Tina Dupart at Cisco for their time and insight.
- To all the incredibly hard-working folks at Osborne/McGraw-Hill: Brandon Nordin, Scott Rogers, and Gareth Hancock for their help in launching a great series and being solid team players. In addition, Madhu Prasher, Debbie Escobedo, Steve Emry, Anne Ellingsen, and Bernadette Jurich for their help in fine-tuning the book.
- For your constant support, thank you Eddie and Christopher; Vesna, Sasha, and Sam; Paul; and Thomas and Winston.

CONTENTS

PREFACE

This book's primary objective is to help you prepare for and pass the required CCNA exam so you can begin to reap the career benefits of certification. We believe that the only way to do this is to help you increase your knowledge and build your skills. After completing this book, you should feel confident that you have thoroughly reviewed all of the objectives that Cisco has established for the exam.

In This Book

This book is organized around the topics covered within the Cisco exam administered at Sylvan Testing Centers. Cisco has specific objectives for the CCNA exam: we've followed their list carefully, so you can be assured you're not missing anything.

In Every Chapter

We've created a set of chapter components that call your attention to important items, reinforce important points, and provide helpful exam-taking hints. Take a look at what you'll find in every chapter:

- Every chapter begins with the **Certification Objectives**—what you need to know in order to pass the section on the exam dealing with the chapter topic. The Certification Objective headings identify the objectives within the chapter, so you'll always know an objective when you see it!
- **Certification Exercises** are interspersed throughout the chapters. These are step-by-step exercises that mirror vendor-recommended labs. They help you master skills that are likely to be an area of focus on the exam. Don't just read through the exercises; they are hands-on practice that you should be comfortable completing. Learning by doing is an effective way to increase your competency with a product.

- **From the Classroom** sidebars describe the issues that come up most often in the training classroom setting. These sidebars give you a valuable perspective into certification- and product-related topics. They point out common mistakes and address questions that have arisen from classroom discussions.
- **Q & A** sections lay out problems and solutions in a quick-read format:

I entered a static route that I want to use as a last resort. We are using OSPF, but currently my route takes precedence over OSPF entries. How do I change the configuration?	Change the administrative distance for your static route to any number above 110, which is OSPF's default.
I am running RIP across a 64-kbps WAN link. The updates are taking up too much bandwidth. What should I do?	Change the update period to a slower amount than the default 30 seconds.

- The **Certification Summary** is a succinct review of the chapter and a re-statement of salient points regarding the exam.
- The **Two-Minute Drill** at the end of every chapter is a checklist of the main points of the chapter. It can be used for last-minute review.
- **Tables** are liberally sprinkled throughout the chapters. You'll find that these provide an easy way to look up information and show material you may find worthy of memorization:

Protocol	Familiar Name	Port
Trivial File Transfer Protocol	TFTP	69
Domain Name Service	DNS	53
Time Service	-	37
NetBIOS Name Server	-	137

Protocol	Familiar Name	Port
NetBIOS Datagram Server	-	138
Boot Protocol (Client and Server)	BOOTP	67 and 68
TACACS	TACACS	49

- The **Self Test** offers questions similar to those found on the certification exams, including multiple choice and true/false questions. The answers to these questions, as well as explanations of the answers, can be found in Appendix A. By taking the Self Test after completing each chapter, you'll reinforce what you've learned from that chapter, while becoming familiar with the structure of the exam questions.

Some Pointers

Once you've finished reading this book, set aside some time to do a thorough review. You might want to return to the book several times and make use of all the methods it offers for reviewing the material:

1. *Re-read all the Two-Minute Drills*, or have someone quiz you. You also can use the drills as a way to do a quick cram before the exam.
2. *Review all the Q & A scenarios* for quick problem solving.
3. *Re-take the Self Tests.* Taking the tests right after you've read the chapter is a good idea, because it helps reinforce what you've just learned. However, it's an even better idea to go back later and do all the questions in the book in one sitting. Pretend you're taking the exam. (For this reason, you should mark your answers on a separate piece of paper when you go through the questions the first time.)
4. *Complete the exercises.* Did you do the exercises when you read through each chapter? If not, do them! These exercises are designed to cover exam topics, and there's no better way to get to know this material than by practicing.

5. *Check out the web site.* Global Knowledge Network invites you to become an active member of the Access Global web site. This site is an online mall and an information repository that you'll find invaluable. You can access many types of products to assist you in your preparation for the exams, and you'll be able to participate in forums, on-line discussions, and threaded discussions. No other book brings you unlimited access to such a resource. You'll find more information about this site in Appendix C.

INTRODUCTION

How to Take a Cisco Certification Examination

by Richard D. Hornbaker (CCIE, CNX, MCSE, MCNE), Forté Consulting Group

Catch the Wave!

Congratulations on your pursuit of Cisco certification! In this fast-paced world of networking, few certifications compare to the value of Cisco's program.

The networking industry has virtually exploded in recent years, accelerated by non-stop innovation and the Internet's popularity. Cisco has stayed at the forefront of this tidal wave, maintaining a dominant role in the industry.

The rapid growth of the networking industry has created a vacuum of qualified people; there simply aren't enough skilled networking people to meet the demand. That's where Cisco certification programs come in.

Cisco started its certification program many years ago, offering only the designation of Cisco Certified Internetwork Expert, or CCIE. Through the CCIE program, Cisco provided a means to identify experts in the field. However, the CCIE tests are brutal, with a failure rate over 80 percent. (Fewer than 5 percent of candidates pass on their first attempt.) As you might imagine, very few people ever attain CCIE status.

In early 1998, Cisco recognized the need for intermediate certifications, and several new programs were created. Four intermediate certifications were added: CCNA (Cisco Certified Network Associate), CCNP (Cisco Certified Network Professional), CCDA (Cisco Certified Design Associate), and CCDP (Cisco Certified Design Professional). Two specialties were also added to the CCIE program for WAN Switching and ISP Dial-up.

Why Vendor Certification?

Over the years, vendors have created their own certification programs because of industry demand. This demand arises when the marketplace needs skilled professionals and an easy way to identify them. Vendors benefit because it promotes people skilled in their product. Professionals benefit because it boosts their career. Employers benefit because it helps them identify qualified people.

In the networking industry, things change too quickly to rely on traditional means of certification, such as universities and trade associations. Because of the investment and effort required to keep network certification programs current, vendors are the only organizations suited to keep pace with the changes. In general, such vendor certification programs are excellent, with most of them requiring a solid foundation in the essentials, as well as their particular product line.

Corporate America has come to appreciate these vendor certification programs and the value they provide. Employers recognize that certifications, like university degrees, do not guarantee a level of knowledge or performance; rather, they establish a baseline for comparison. By seeking to hire vendor-certified employees, a company can assure itself that, not only has it found a person skilled in networking, but it has also hired a person skilled in the specific products the company uses.

Technical professionals have also begun to realize the value of certification and the impact it can have on their careers. By completing a certification program, professionals gain an endorsement of their skills from a major industry source. This endorsement can boost their current position, and it makes finding the next job even easier. Often, a certification determines whether a first interview is even granted.

Today, a certification may place you ahead of the pack. Tomorrow, it will be a necessity to keep from being left in the dust.

Cisco's Certification Program

As mentioned previously, Cisco now has five certifications for the Routing and Switching career track. While Cisco recommends a series of courses for each of these certifications, they are not required. Ultimately, certification is based on a candidate passing a series of exams. With the right experience and study materials, each of these exams can be passed without taking the associated class.

Figure I-1 shows Cisco's Routing and Switching track, with both the Network Design and Network Support paths. The CCNA is the foundation of the Routing and Switching track, after which candidates can pursue either the Network Design path to CCDA and CCDP, or the Network Support path to CCNP and CCIE.

Table I-1 shows a matrix of the exams required for each Cisco certification. Note that candidates have the choice of taking either the single Foundation R/S exam, or the set of three ACRC, CLSC, and CMTD exams—four exams are not required.

You may hear veterans refer to this CCIE R/S Qualifying Exam as the "Cisco Drake test." This is a carryover from the early days, when Sylvan Prometric's name was Drake Testing Centers and Cisco only had the one exam.

FIGURE I-1 Cisco's Routing and Switching certification track

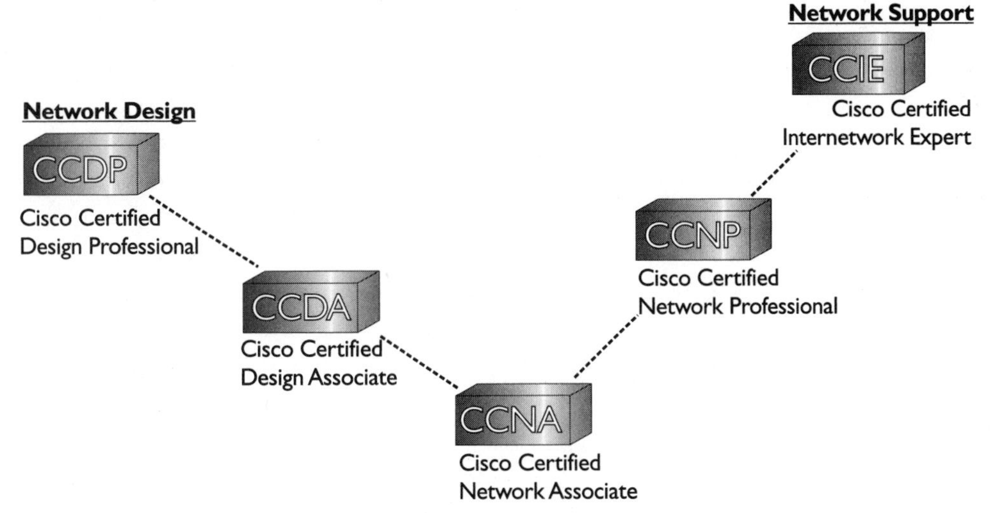

TABLE 1-1

Examinations Required for Cisco Certifications

Exam Name	CCNA	CCDA	CCNP	CCDP	CCIE
CCNA	x	x	x	x	
CDS		x		x	
Foundation R/S			x	x	
ACRC			x	x	
CLSC			x	x	
CMTD			x	x	
CIT			x		
CID				x	
CCIE R/S Qualifying					x
CCIE Lab					x

Computer-Based Testing

In a perfect world, you would be assessed for your true knowledge of a subject, not simply how you respond to a series of test questions. But life isn't perfect, and it just isn't practical to evaluate everyone's knowledge on a one-to-one basis. (Cisco actually does have a one-to-one evaluation, but it's reserved for the CCIE Laboratory exam, and the waiting list is quite long.)

For the majority of its certifications, Cisco evaluates candidates using a computer-based testing service operated by Sylvan Prometric. This service is quite popular in the industry, and it is used for a number of certification programs, including Novell's CNE and Microsoft's MCSE. Thanks to Sylvan's large number of facilities, exams can be administered worldwide, generally in the same town as a prospective candidate.

For the most part, Sylvan exams work similarly from vendor to vendor. However, there is an important fact to know about Cisco's exams: they use the traditional Sylvan test format, not the newer adaptive format. This gives the candidate an advantage, since the traditional format allows answers to be reviewed and revised during the test. (The adaptive format does not.)

To discourage simple memorization, Cisco exams present a different set of questions every time the exam is administered. In the development of the exam, hundreds of questions are compiled and refined using beta testers. From this large collection, a random sampling is drawn for each test.

Each Cisco exam has a specific number of questions and test duration. Testing time is typically generous, and the time remaining is always displayed in the corner of the testing screen, along with the number of remaining questions. If time expires during an exam, the test terminates, and incomplete answers are counted as incorrect.

At the end of the exam, your test is immediately graded, and the results are displayed on the screen. Scores for each subject area are also provided, but the system will not indicate which specific questions were missed. A report is automatically printed at the proctor's desk for your files. The test score is electronically transmitted back to Cisco.

In the end, this computer-based system of evaluation is reasonably fair. You might feel that one or two questions were poorly worded; this can certainly happen, but you shouldn't worry too much. Ultimately, it's all factored into the required passing score.

Question Types

Cisco exams pose questions in a variety of formats, most of which are discussed here. As candidates progress toward the more advanced certifications, the difficulty of the exams is intensified, both through the subject matter as well as the question formats.

True/False

The classic true/false question format is not used in the Cisco exams, for the obvious reason that a simple guess has a 50 percent chance of being correct. Instead, true/false questions are posed in multiple-choice format, requiring the candidate to identify the true or false statement from a group of selections.

Multiple Choice

Multiple choice is the primary format for questions in Cisco exams. These questions may be posed in a variety of ways.

"SELECT THE CORRECT ANSWER." This is the classic multiple-choice question, where the candidate selects a single answer from a list of about four choices. In addition to the question's wording, the choices are presented in a Windows "radio button" format, where only one answer can be selected at a time.

"SELECT THE 3 CORRECT ANSWERS." The multiple-answer version is similar to the single-choice version, but multiple answers must be provided. This is an "all-or-nothing" format; all the correct answers must be selected, or the entire question is incorrect. In this format, the question specifies exactly how many answers must be selected. Choices are presented in a check box format, allowing more than one answer to be selected. In addition, the testing software prevents too many answers from being selected.

"SELECT ALL THAT APPLY." The open-ended version is the most difficult multiple-choice format, since the candidate does not know how many answers should be selected. As with the multiple-answer version, all the correct answers must be selected to gain credit for the question. If too many answers are selected, no credit is given. This format presents choices in check box format, but the testing software does not advise the candidates whether they've selected the correct number of answers.

Freeform Response

Freeform responses are prevalent in Cisco's advanced exams, particularly where the subject focuses on router configuration and commands. In the freeform format, no choices are provided. Instead, the test prompts for user input and the candidate must type the correct answer. This format is similar to an essay question, except the response must be very specific, allowing the computer to evaluate the answer.

For example, the question

Type the command for viewing routes learned via the EIGRP protocol.

requires the answer

SHOW IP ROUTE EIGRP

For safety's sake, you should completely spell out router commands, rather than using abbreviations. In the above example, the abbreviated command SH IP ROU EI works on a real router, but might be counted wrong by the testing software.

Fill in the Blank

Fill-in-the-blank questions are less common in Cisco exams. They may be presented in multiple-choice or freeform response format.

Exhibits

Exhibits accompany many exam questions, usually showing a network diagram or a router configuration. These exhibits are displayed in a separate window, which is opened by clicking the Exhibit button at the bottom of the screen. In some cases, the testing center may provide exhibits in printed format at the start of the exam.

Scenarios

While the normal line of questioning tests a candidate's "book knowledge," scenarios add a level of complexity. Rather than just ask technical questions, they apply the candidate's knowledge to real-world situations.

Scenarios generally consist of one or two paragraphs and an exhibit that describe a company's needs or network configuration. This description is followed by a series of questions and problems that challenge the candidate's ability to address the situation. Scenario-based questions are commonly found in exams relating to network design, but they appear to some degree in each of the Cisco exams.

Exam Objectives for the CCNA

Cisco has a clear set of objectives for the CCNA exam, upon which the exam questions are based. The following list, taken from http://www.cisco.com, gives a good summary of the things a CCNA must know how to do.

1. Identify and describe the seven layers of the OSI model.
2. Describe key differences between connection-oriented and connectionless network services.
3. Describe the difference between network addresses and data link addresses.
4. Define the role of a MAC address.
5. Describe the three basic methods of flow control used in networking.
6. Differentiate between these key WAN services: Frame Relay, ISDN, PPP, and HDLC.
7. Log on to a router in both User and Privileged modes.
8. Use the router's context-sensitive command-line help.
9. Use the editing features of the router's command-line interface, including command history.
10. Examine router elements (RAM, ROM, CDP, IOS Version, show).
11. Manage router configuration files.
12. Control router passwords, banner notices, and identification.
13. Identify the main Cisco IOS commands for router startup.
14. Check an initial configuration using the SETUP command.
15. Manipulate and copy configuration files from Privileged mode.
16. List the commands to boot the router's IOS software from flash memory, a TFTP server, or ROM.
17. Prepare to back up, upgrade, and load a backup Cisco IOS software image.

18. List the key internetworking functions of the OSI model and how they are performed in a router.
19. Describe the two components of network addressing, and then identify these parts in specific protocol addressing examples.
20. List problems that each routing type encounters when dealing with topology changes, as well as techniques for reducing these problems.
21. Explain the services of separate and integrated multiprotocol routing.
22. Describe the different classes of IP addressing, plus the traditional and newer methods of subnetting.
23. Configure IP addresses.
24. Verify/validate IP addresses.
25. Prepare a router's initial configuration and enable IP.
26. Add the RIP protocol to a router's configuration.
27. Add the IGRP protocol to a router's configuration.
28. List the required IPX address and encapsulation type.
29. Enable the IPX protocol and configure router interfaces.
30. Monitor IPX operation on a router.
31. Recognize key Frame Relay terms and features.
32. List commands to enable Frame Relay, ILMI, protocol mappings, and sub-interfaces.
33. List commands to monitor Frame Relay operation in a router.
34. Identify PPP operations to encapsulate WAN data between routers.
35. Configure standard access lists to filter IP traffic.
36. Monitor and verify selected access list operations on the router.
37. Describe the features and function of ISDN networking.
38. Identify ISDN protocols, function groups, reference points, and channels.
39. Describe Cisco's implementation of the ISDN BRI interface.

40. Describe the advantages of LAN segmentation.
41. Describe LAN segmentation using bridges.
42. Describe LAN segmentation using routers.
43. Describe LAN segmentation using switches.
44. Name and describe two methods of switching.
45. Describe the difference between full-duplex and half-duplex Ethernet operation.
46. Identify at least three reasons the industry uses a layered network model.
47. Identify the functions of each layer in the OSI model.
48. Define and explain the five conversion steps of data encapsulation.
49. Identify the functions of the IP transport layer protocols.
50. Identify the functions of the IP network layer protocols.
51. Identify the functions provided by ICMP.
52. Configure extended access lists to filter IP traffic.
53. Configure IPX access lists and SAP filters to control basic Novell traffic.
54. Monitor and verify selected access list operations on a router.
55. Describe the network congestion problem in Ethernet networks.
56. Describe the benefits of network segmentation with bridges.
57. Describe the benefits of network segmentation with routers.
58. Describe the benefits of network segmentation with switches.
59. Describe the features and benefits of Fast Ethernet.
60. Describe the guidelines and distance limitations of Fast Ethernet.
61. Differentiate between cut-through and store-and-forward switching.
62. Describe the operation of the Spanning-Tree Protocol (STP) and its benefits.
63. Describe the benefits of virtual LANs.

Studying Techniques

First and foremost, give yourself plenty of time to study. Networking is an intricate field, and you can't expect to cram what you need to know into a single study session. It is a field best learned over time, by studying a subject and then applying your knowledge. Build yourself a study schedule and stick to it, but be reasonable about the pressure you put on yourself, especially if you're studying in addition to your regular duties at work.

Second, practice and experiment. In networking, you need more than knowledge; you need understanding, too. You can't just memorize facts to be effective; you need to understand why events happen, how things work, and (most importantly) how they break.

The best way to gain deep understanding is to take your book knowledge to the lab. Try it out. Make it work. Change it a little. Break it. Fix it. Snoop around "under the hood". If you have access to a network analyzer, like Network Associate's Sniffer, put it to use. You can gain amazing insight to the inner workings of a network by watching devices communicate with each other.

Unless you have a very understanding boss, don't experiment with router commands on a production router. A seemingly innocuous command can have a nasty side effect. If you don't have a lab, your local Cisco office or Cisco users group may be able to help. Many training centers also allow students access to their lab equipment during off-hours.

Another excellent way to study is through case studies. Case studies are articles or interactive discussions that offer real-world examples of how technology is applied to meet a need. These examples can serve to cement your understanding of a technique or technology by seeing it put to use. Interactive discussions offer added value because you can also pose questions of your own. User groups are an excellent source of examples, since the purpose of these groups is to share information and learn from each other's experiences.

And not to be missed is the Cisco Networkers conference. Although renowned for its wild party and crazy antics, this conference offers a wealth of information. Held every year in cities around the world, it includes three days of technical seminars and presentations on a variety of subjects. As you might imagine, it's very popular. You have to register early to get the classes you want.

Then, of course, there is the Cisco Web site. This little gem is loaded with collections of technical documents and white papers. As you progress to more advanced subjects, you will find great value in the large number of examples and reference materials available. But be warned: You need to do a lot of digging to find the really good stuff. Often, your only option is to browse every document returned by the search engine to find exactly the one you need. This effort pays off. Most CCIEs I know have compiled six to ten binders of reference material from Cisco's site alone.

Scheduling Your Exam

The Cisco exams are scheduled by calling Sylvan Prometric directly at (800) 204-3926. For locations outside the United States, your local number can be found on Sylvan's Web site at www.prometric.com. Sylvan representatives can schedule your exam, but they don't have information about the certification programs. Questions about certifications should be directed to Cisco's training department.

The aforementioned Sylvan telephone number is specific to Cisco exams, and it goes directly to the Cisco representatives inside Sylvan. These representatives are familiar enough with the exams to find them by name, but it's best if you have the specific exam number handy when you call. After all, you wouldn't want to be scheduled and charged for the wrong exam (for example, the instructor's version, which is significantly harder).

Exams can be scheduled up to a year in advance, although it's really not necessary. Generally, scheduling a week or two ahead is sufficient to reserve the day and time you prefer. When scheduling, operators will search for testing centers in your area. For convenience, they can also tell which testing centers you've used before.

Sylvan accepts a variety of payment methods, with credit cards being the most convenient. When paying by credit card, you can even take tests the same day you call—provided, of course, that the testing center has room. (Quick scheduling can be handy, especially if you want to re-take an exam immediately.) Sylvan will mail you a receipt and confirmation of your testing date, although this generally arrives after the test has been taken. If you need to cancel or reschedule an exam, remember to call at least one day before your exam, or you'll lose your test fee.

When registering for the exam, you will be asked for your ID number. This number is used to track your exam results back to Cisco. It's important that you use the same ID number each time you register, so that Cisco can follow your progress. Address information provided when you first register is also used by Cisco to ship certificates and other related material. In the USA, your Social Security Number is commonly used as your ID number. However, Sylvan can assign you a unique ID number if you prefer not to use your Social Security Number.

Table I-2 shows the available Cisco exams and the number of questions and duration of each. This information is subject to change as Cisco revises the exams, so it's a good idea to verify the details when registering for an exam.

In addition to the regular Sylvan testing sites, Cisco also offers facilities for taking exams free of charge at each Networkers conference in the USA. As you might imagine, this option is quite popular, so reserve your exam time as soon as you arrive at the conference.

TABLE I-2

Cisco Exam Lengths and Question Counts

Exam Title	Exam Number	Number of Questions	Duration (minutes)	Exam Fee (US $)
Cisco Design Specialist (CDS)	9E0-004	80	180	$100
Cisco Internetwork Design (CID)	640-025	100	120	$100
Advanced Cisco Router Configuration (ACRC)	640-403	72	90	$100

TABLE 1-2

Cisco Exam Lengths and Question Counts *(continued)*

Exam Title	Exam Number	Number of Questions	Duration (minutes)	Exam Fee (US $)
Cisco LAN Switch Configuration (CLSC)	640-404	70	60	$100
Configuring, Monitoring, and Trouble-shooting Dialup Services (CMTD)	640-405	64	90	$100
Cisco Internetwork Trouble-shooting (CIT)	640-406	69	60	$100
Cisco Certified Network Associate (CCNA)	640-407	44	60	$100
Foundation Routing & Switching	640-409	132	165	$100
CCIE Routing & Switching Qualification	350-001	100	120	$200
CCIE Certification Laboratory	n/a	n/a	2 days	$1000

Arriving at the Exam

As with any test, you'll be tempted to cram the night before. Resist that temptation. You should know the material by this point, and if you're too groggy in the morning, you won't remember what you studied anyway. Instead, get a good night's sleep.

Arrive early for your exam; it gives you time to relax and review key facts. Take the opportunity to review your notes and run through the Two-Minute Drill section in each chapter. If you get burned out on studying, you can usually start your exam a few minutes early. On the other hand, I don't recommend arriving late. Your test could be cancelled, or you may not be left with enough time to complete the exam.

When you arrive at the testing center, you'll need to sign in with the exam administrator. In order to sign in, you need to provide two forms of identification. Acceptable forms include government-issued IDs (for example, passport or driver's license), credit cards, and company ID badge. One form of ID must include a photograph.

Aside from a brain full of facts, you don't need to bring anything else to the exam. In fact, your brain about all you're allowed to take into the exam. All the tests are "closed book," meaning you don't get to bring any reference materials with you. You're also not allowed to take any notes out of the exam room. The test administrator will provide you with paper and a pencil. Some testing centers may provide a small marker board instead.

Calculators are not allowed, so be prepared to do any necessary math (such as hex-binary-decimal conversions or subnet masks) in your head or on paper. Additional paper is available if you need it.

Leave your pager and telephone in the car, or turn them off. They only add stress to the situation. Purses, books, and other materials must be left with the administrator before entering the exam. While in the exam room, it's important that you don't disturb other candidates; talking is not allowed during the exam.

Once in the testing room, the exam administrator logs onto your exam, and you have to verify that your ID number and the exam number are correct. If this is the first time you've taken a Cisco test, you can select a brief tutorial for the exam software. Before the test begins, you will be provided with facts about the exam, including the duration, the number of questions, and the score required for passing. Then the clock starts ticking and the fun begins.

The testing software is Windows-based, but you won't have access to the main desktop or any of the accessories. The exam is presented in full screen, with a single question per screen. Navigation buttons allow you to move forward and backward between questions. In the upper-right corner of the screen, counters show the number of questions and time remaining. Most importantly, there is a "Mark" checkbox in the upper-left corner of the screen—this will prove to be a critical tool in your testing technique.

Test-Taking Techniques

One of the most frequent excuses I hear for failing a Cisco exam is "poor time management." Without a plan of attack, candidates are overwhelmed by the exam or become sidetracked and run out of time. For the most part, if you are comfortable with the material, the allotted time is more than enough to complete the exam. The trick is to keep the time from slipping away.

The obvious goal of an exam is to answer the questions effectively, although other aspects of the exam can distract from this goal. After taking a fair number of computer-based exams, I've naturally developed a technique for tackling the problem, which I share with you here. Of course, you still need to learn the material. These steps just help you take the exam more efficiently.

Size Up the Challenge

First, take a quick pass through all the questions in the exam. "Cherry-pick" the easy questions, answering them on the spot. Briefly read each question, noticing the type of question and the subject. As a guideline, try to spend less than 25 percent of your testing time in this pass.

This step lets you assess the scope and complexity of the exam, and it helps you determine how to pace your time. It also gives you an idea of where to find potential answers to some of the questions. Often, the answer to one question is shown in the exhibit of another. Sometimes the wording of one question might lend clues or jog your thoughts for another question.

Imagine that the following questions are posed in this order:

Question 1: Review the router configurations and network diagram in exhibit XYZ (not shown here). Which devices should be able to ping each other?

Question 2: If RIP routing were added to exhibit XYZ, which devices would be able to ping each other?

The first question seems straightforward. Exhibit XYZ probably includes a diagram and a couple of router configurations. Everything looks normal, so you decide that all devices can ping each other.

Now, consider the hint left by the Question 2. When you answered Question 1, did you notice that the configurations were missing the routing protocol? Oops! Being alert to such clues can help you catch your own mistakes.

If you're not entirely confident with your answer to a question, answer it anyway, but check the Mark box to flag it for later review. In the event that you run out of time, at least you've provided a "first guess" answer, rather than leaving it blank.

Take on the Scenario Questions

Second, go back through the entire test, using the insight you gained from the first go-through. For example, if the entire test looks difficult, you'll know better than to spend more than a minute or so on each question. Break down the pacing into small milestones; for example, "I need to answer 10 questions every 15 minutes."

At this stage, it's probably a good idea to skip past the time-consuming questions, marking them for the next pass. Try to finish this phase before you're 50 – 60 percent through the testing time.

By now, you probably have a good idea where the scenario questions are found. A single scenario tends to have several questions associated with it, but they aren't necessarily grouped together in the exam. Rather than re-reading the scenario every time you encounter a related question, save some time and answer the questions as a group.

Tackle the Complex Problems

Third, go back through all the questions you marked for review, using the Review Marked button in the question review screen. This step includes taking a second look at all the questions you were unsure of in previous passes, as well as tackling the time-consuming ones you deferred until now. Chisel away at this group of questions until you've answered them all.

If you're more comfortable with a previously marked question, unmark it now. Otherwise, leave it marked. Work your way through the time-consuming questions now, especially those requiring manual calculations. Unmark them when you're satisfied with the answer.

By the end of this step, you've answered every question in the test, despite having reservations about some of your answers. If you run out of time in the next step, at least you won't lose points for lack of an answer. You're in great shape if you still have 10 – 20 percent of your time remaining.

Review Your Answers

Now you're cruising! You've answered all the questions, and you're ready to do a quality check. Take yet another pass (yes, one more) through the entire test, briefly re-reading each question and your answer. Be cautious about revising answers at this point unless you're sure a change is warranted. If there's a doubt about changing the answer, I always trust my first instinct and leave the original answer intact.

Rarely are "trick" questions asked, so don't read too much into the questions. Again, if the wording of the question confuses you, leave the answer intact. Your first impression was probably right.

Be alert for last-minute clues. You're pretty familiar with nearly every question at this point, and you may find a few clues that you missed before.

The Grand Finale

When you're confident with all your answers, finish the exam by submitting it for grading. After what will seem like the longest 10 seconds in of your life, the testing software will respond with your score. This is usually displayed as a bar graph, showing the minimum passing score, your score, and a PASS/FAIL indicator.

If you're curious, you can review the statistics of your score at this time. Answers to specific questions are not presented; rather, questions are lumped into categories, and results are tallied for each category. This detail is also printed on a report that has been automatically printed at the exam administrator's desk.

As you leave the exam, you'll need to leave your scratch paper behind or return it to the administrator. (Some testing centers track the number of sheets you've been given, so be sure to return them all.) In exchange, you'll receive a copy of the test report.

This report will be embossed with the testing center's seal, and you should keep it in a safe place. Normally, the results are automatically transmitted to Cisco, but occasionally you might need the paper report to prove that you passed the exam. Your personnel file is probably a good place to keep this report; the file tends to follow you everywhere, and it doesn't hurt to have favorable exam results turn up during a performance review.

Re-Testing

If you don't pass the exam, don't be discouraged—networking is complex stuff. Try to have a good attitude about the experience, and get ready to try again. Consider yourself a little more educated. You know the format of the test a little better, and the report shows which areas you need to strengthen.

If you bounce back quickly, you'll probably remember several of the questions you might have missed. This will help you focus your study efforts in the right area. Serious go-getters will re-schedule the exam for a couple days after the previous attempt, while the study material is still fresh in their mind.

Ultimately, remember that Cisco certifications are valuable because they're hard to get. After all, if anyone could get one, what value would it have? In the end, it takes a good attitude and a lot of studying, but you can do it!

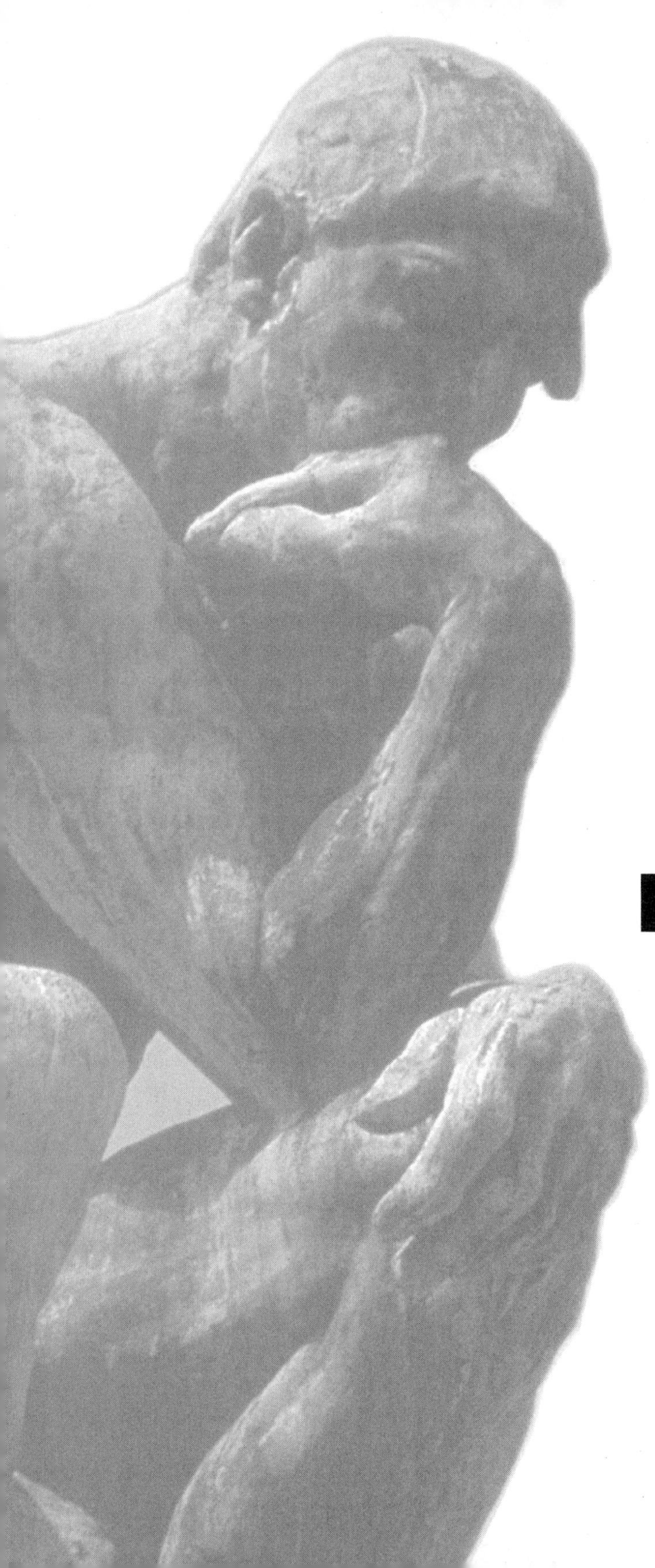

CCNA

CISCO CERTIFIED NETWORK ASSOCIATE

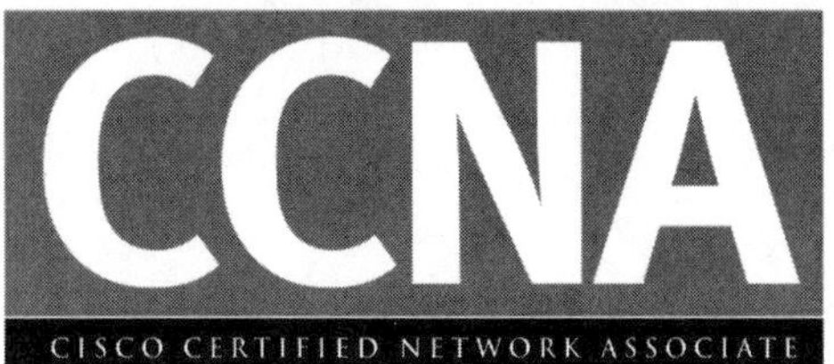

1

Introduction to Internetworking

CERTIFICATION OBJECTIVES

1.01 The Internetworking Model

1.02 Physical and Data Link Layers

1.03 Network Layer and Path Determination

1.04 Transport Layer

1.05 Upper Layer Protocols

1.06 Cisco Routers, Switches, and Hubs

1.07 Configuring a Cisco Switch and Hub

Cisco Certified Internetworking Engineers, or CCIEs, are recognized as some of the premiere internetworking professionals in the information systems industry. Their understanding of the intricacies of internetwork design and architecture stems from both dedicated study and experience. To attain the highest level of certification—the CCIE—one is required to be able to:

- Design new internetworks
- Document existing internetworks
- Locate the cause of internetwork problems
- Resolve bottlenecks
- Redesign existing internetworks
- Understand and be able to connect internetworks to the Internet
- Configure new Cisco routers, switches, and hubs
- Reconfigure existing Cisco routers, switches, and hubs
- Understand Cisco Internetworking Operating System software
- Upgrade and repair Cisco routers, switches, and hubs

To start you on your certification path, this book provides you with the information needed to become a Cisco Certified Network Associate (CCNA). A potential CCNA must have the knowledge to install, configure, and operate simple-routed LAN, routed WAN, and switched LAN and LANE networks.

This is the beginning of an adventure in knowledge. What this book can offer as both a reference and a learning tool can take an engineer to the heights of an internetworking career.

CERTIFICATION OBJECTIVE 1.01

The Internetworking Model

There is a distinction made between networking and internetworking. Networking is the process and methodology applied to connecting multiple computers so that they are able to exchange information. Internetworking is the process and methodology applied to connecting multiple networks, regardless of their physical topologies and distance. Internetworking has evolved with the rapid growth and change in networking. Because of this, the basic building blocks and reference models for networking are also used and applied to internetworking.

Network Evolution

Internetworks evolved from necessity. In the early days of computing (the 1950s and 1960s), internetworks did not exist. Computers were autonomous and proprietary. In the late 1960s, however, the United States Department of Defense (DOD), became interested in academic research being done on a packet-switched wide area network design. "Packet" referred to a small bundle of data. "Switched" referred to the use of a routing system similar to the switch-based telephone system. And "wide area network" (WAN) meant that the network would extend over sites that were physically distant from each other.

DOD wanted to use this technology for national defense, as a means to share radar data, and distribute control and commands in the case of a nuclear war. The agency within DOD that handled the network research was the Advanced Research Projects Agency (ARPA), which later prefixed "Defense" to the beginning of their name and became known as DARPA. The DARPA project included scientists and engineers from universities and the Bolt, Baranek and Newman company of Massachusetts, who faced the two challenges in this project: *interconnectivity* and *interoperability.*

- **Interconnectivity** the means of transporting information between the computers, inclusive of the physical media, the data packaging mechanism, and the routing between multiple network equipment pieces from the starting node until reaching the destination node.
- **Interoperability** the methodology applied to make data understandable to computers that use proprietary or simply different computer operating systems and languages.

The result of the DARPA project was ARPANET, which eventually became the Internet, and the evolution of the IP protocol suite, which was then included as part of Berkeley's version of UNIX. ARPANET grew into the Internet by including networks in other government and university campuses. And that grew even further with the inclusion of commercial enterprise networks.

Networks did not become prevalent in corporations until the 1980s when the personal computer (PC) became popular. After companies realized that sharing hard disk space on some of the earliest file servers enabled employees to share data easily and further boosted productivity, they implemented networks on a large scale. They created LANs (Local Area Networks) and then connected them into WANs (Wide Area Networks). After the Internet went commercial in the early 1990s, corporations began to connect to it as well.

The OSI Model

There are two standards to consider in internetworking: *de jure*, and *de facto*. De jure means by right or legal establishment. De facto means established by actual fact, though not officially or legally recognized. The evolution of TCP/IP created a de facto standard for that protocol, because it grew and became accepted, although it was not proposed as a standard until after its wide acceptance. The OSI (Open System Interconnection) reference model is a de jure standard.

The International Organization for Standardization (ISO) created the OSI model and released it in 1984 in order to provide a network model for vendors such that their products would interoperate on networks. The OSI reference model provides a hierarchical tool for understanding networking technology, as well as a basis for current and future network developments.

This model also takes into account the interconnectivity and interoperability challenges faced by the DARPA project engineers. The way that the OSI model answered these challenges was through a seven-layer protocol suite model, illustrated in Figure 1-1. By dividing the model into layers, the capability to interoperate and interconnect became manageable, since each layer was self-contained, not relying on the operating system or other factors. The layered approach benefited vendors, too, since they only needed to concentrate development efforts on the layers that their own product used, and could rely on the existing protocols at other layers. Not

FIGURE 1-1

OSI reference model

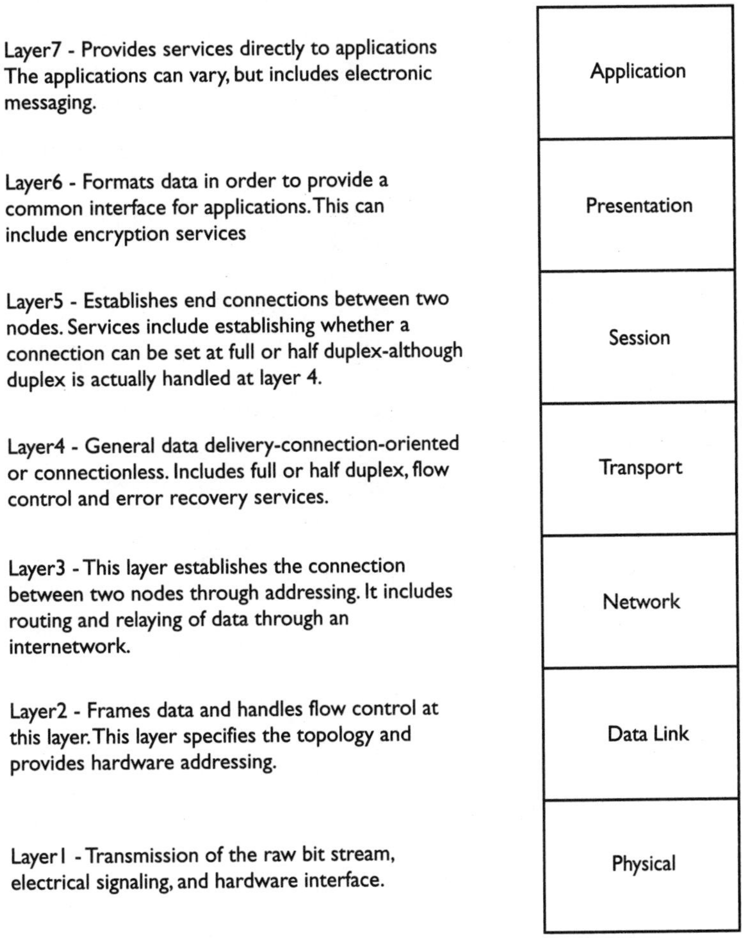

Description	Layer
Layer7 - Provides services directly to applications The applications can vary, but includes electronic messaging.	Application
Layer6 - Formats data in order to provide a common interface for applications. This can include encryption services	Presentation
Layer5 - Establishes end connections between two nodes. Services include establishing whether a connection can be set at full or half duplex-although duplex is actually handled at layer 4.	Session
Layer4 - General data delivery-connection-oriented or connectionless. Includes full or half duplex, flow control and error recovery services.	Transport
Layer3 - This layer establishes the connection between two nodes through addressing. It includes routing and relaying of data through an internetwork.	Network
Layer2 - Frames data and handles flow control at this layer. This layer specifies the topology and provides hardware addressing.	Data Link
Layer1 - Transmission of the raw bit stream, electrical signaling, and hardware interface.	Physical

only are development costs kept to a minimum, but marketability is increased, since the product works with other vendors' products.

The model describes how each layer communicates with a corresponding layer on the other node. Figure 1-2 illustrates how data works its way through a network. At the first node, the end user creates some data to be sent to the other node, such as an e-mail. At the application layer, an application header is added to the data. The presentation layer adds its own header to the data received from the application layer. Each layer adds its own header to the data received from the layer above. However, at lower layers, the data is broken up into smaller units and headers added to each of the units. For instance, the transport layer will have smaller datagrams, the network layer will have packets, and the data link layer will have frames. The physical layer handles the data in a raw bitstream. When this bitstream is received at the destination, the data is reassembled at each layer, and the headers of each layer discarded, until the e-mail is readable by the end user.

FIGURE 1-2 How the OSI model transports data

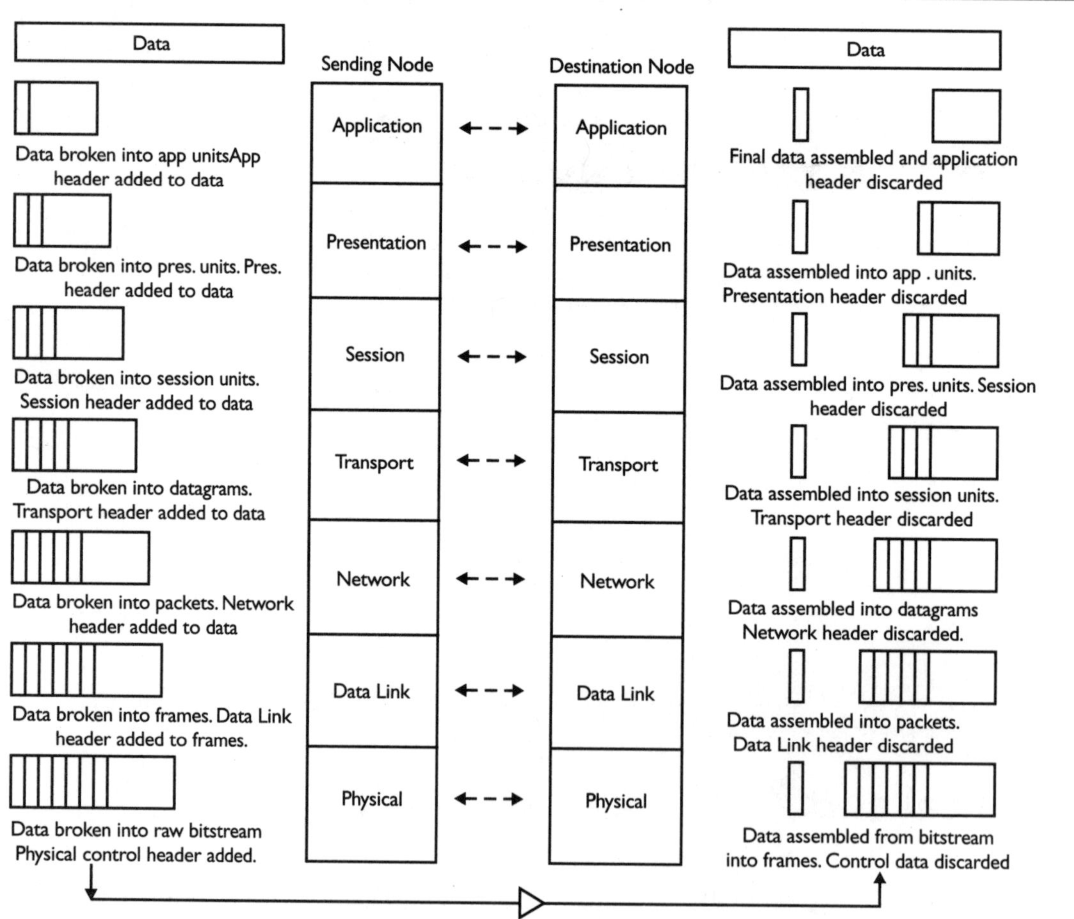

A common mnemonic device for remembering the layers (application, presentation, session, transport, network, data link, physical) in the right order is All People Seem To Need Data Processing.

Encapsulation

Encapsulation is the process of adding a header to the data, or *wrapping* the data. In order to send data out on a Token Ring network, the data must be wrapped with the Token Ring header before it is transmitted. The terms "wrapping" and "encapsulation" refer to both the header and the ending bits that are added to each bundle of data. Header bits are used to signify the beginning of a data bundle, and frequently include addressing and other features, depending on the protocol and layer. The ending bits are typically used for error checking. Header bits receive more attention, since they include most of the protocol feature implementation.

Encapsulation may occur at each layer in the OSI reference model. The entire packet from each layer is inserted into the data field of the next layer, and another header is added. Occasionally a layer splits the data unit (including previous layer header) into multiple, smaller data units, and each one of the smaller units is wrapped with a new header from the lower protocol layer. This process helps control data flow and addresses packet size limitations on the network. As the data moves down the model, it becomes smaller and more uniform in size and content.

When data is received, the corresponding layer at the receiving node reassembles the data field before passing it to the next layer. As the data moves back up the model at the destination, it is pieced back together like a puzzle.

CERTIFICATION OBJECTIVE 1.02

Physical and Data Link Layers

The physical layer, or layer 1, defines the actual mechanical specifications and electrical data bitstream. This includes the voltage level, the voltage changes, and the definition of which voltage level is a "1" and which is a

"0." The data rate of transmission, the maximum distances, and even physical connectors are all included in this level.

The data link layer, or layer 2, is also known as the link layer. It consists of two sublayers, the upper level being the Logical Link Control (LLC), and the lower level being the Media Access Control (MAC). Hardware addresses are actually MAC addresses in the data link layer. The physical address is placed here, since the physical layer handles only raw bitstream functions. The data is broken into small "frames" at this layer.

The physical and data link layers are usually implemented together in hardware/software combination solutions. Examples include hubs, switches and network adapters, and their applicable software drivers, as well as the media or cables used to connect the network nodes. The remaining layers are usually implemented in software only.

The IEEE (Institute for Electrical and Electronics Engineers) created several standards under the 802 series. Table 1-1 describes the 802 series of standards that are currently in existence or are still being developed.

TABLE 1-1

IEEE 802 Standards Series

Standard	Description
802.2	Defines LLC protocol that other 802 standards can use
802.3	Ethernet (CSMA/CD)
802.3u	Fast Ethernet 100BaseT
802.4	Token Bus (rarely used)
802.5	Token Ring
802.6	MANs (Metropolitan Area Network) using two fiber-optic buses in opposing directions
802.9	Isochronous Ethernet – channel sharing between one async channel and 96 dedicated channels providing 16 Mbps
802.11	Wireless LANs using CSMA/CA (Carrier Sense Multiple Access/Collision Avoidance)
802.12	100VG-AnyLAN

DIX and 802.3 Ethernet

Digital, Intel, and Xerox (collectively known as DIX) created Ethernet in the 1970s. This was used as the basis for the IEEE 802.3 standard released in 1980. DIX then updated their standard to match the IEEE 802.3 version. The term Ethernet is commonly used to refer to either one of these network standards.

However, Ethernet and IEEE 802.3 do have some differences. One difference is that 802.3 specifies the physical layer and the MAC portion of the data link layer, while DIX Ethernet specifies the entire physical and data link layers. 802.3 specifies different physical layers, but DIX Ethernet only specifies one. Table 1-2 compares the two standards.

Ethernet uses a carrier sense multiple access/collision detection (CSMA/CD) method. In the CSMA/CD network, nodes can access the network any time they have data to send. Before a node transmits data, it "listens" to see if the network is busy. If not, the node transmits data. If the network is in use, the node waits. Collisions occur if two nodes listen, hear nothing and then access the wire simultaneously. This ruins both transmissions, and both stations have to try a second time. There is a *backoff algorithm* that creates a random wait time for retransmissions so that a second collision will not occur. Figure 1-3 illustrates this process.

Ethernet, including 802.3, is a *broadcast* system. That means that all nodes see all data frames, whether or not that data is meant to be received

TABLE 1-2 Physical Layer Specifications for IEEE 802.3 and DIX Ethernet

	DIX	IEEE 802.3 Physical Standards					
	Ethernet	10BaseF	1Base5	10Broad36	10Base2	10Base5	10BaseT
Rate Mbps	10	10	1	10	10	10	10
Topology	Bus	Star	Star	Bus	Bus	Bus	Star
Media	50-ohm thick coaxial	Fiber-optic cable	Unshielded twisted-pair	75-ohm coaxial	50-ohm thin coaxial	50-ohm thick coaxial	Unshielded twisted-pair

FIGURE 1-3

Collisions on CSMA/CD network

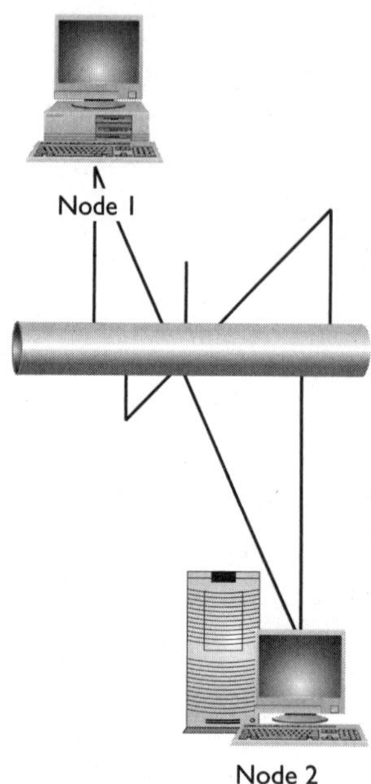

by that node. Each node examines the frame header addresses as the frames are received to determine if they are destined for that node. If not, the frames are forwarded on the network. If they are destined for the node, it passes them to the upper-level protocols for processing.

The IEEE 802.3 frame, shown in Figure 1-4, begins with a *preamble* of alternating ones and zeros that tells the receiving station that this is a new frame. The next byte is a start-of-frame delimiter (SOF) that ends with two consecutive one bits. The next part of the frame header is the destination and source address fields. An address consists of three bytes identifying the vendor, and a second three bytes that are specified by the vendor. After the source address, in IEEE 802.3 frames, there is a two-byte field that discloses the number of bytes of data contained within the frame. The data itself is next, at a minimum of 64 bytes (padded with extra bytes if it is too short), and finally the four-byte FCS field (Frame Check Sequence) ends the frame. The FCS field includes a cyclic redundancy check (CRC) value that is used to check for damage that may have happened to the data during transmission.

FIGURE 1-4

IEEE 802.3 frame format

Preamble	SOF	Destination address	Source address	Length Field	Data	FCS

802.5 Token Ring

Token Ring networks were originally a proprietary network specification created by IBM in the 1970s. Token Ring networks are nearly identical and compatible with the IEEE 802.5 specification developed later, which was based on IBM's Token Ring. The differences include:

- IEEE 802.5 does not specify a physical topology, but IBM's Token Ring specifies a star topology using a multi-station access unit.
- IEEE 802.5 does not specify a medium, but IBM's Token Ring specifies twisted-pair wiring.

The main concepts of Token Ring are described in its name. It is a token-passing network that connects nodes in a logical ring topology. Token passing (illustrated in Figure 1-5) uses a small, specially formatted frame, called a token, which is passed from node to node on the ring. When a node possesses the token, it is granted transmission rights. If there is nothing to transmit, the node sends the token on to the next node. When a node does have information to transmit, it flips one bit of the token and turns it into a start-of-frame field, then appends the data and forwards it on. Unless "early token release" is used, the node retains the token until the data frame travels around the ring back to the sender. The data follows the ring until it reaches the destination node, which copies the data. The data frame goes back to the sending station, where the originator can check whether the data transmission was successful.

There is also a method for *token-seizing*, (or *access priority*) in Token Ring, whereby priority can be assigned to stations so that they can use the network more frequently. A station with equal or higher priority than the priority value contained in a token can seize it for its use. In doing so, it raises the token's priority, and returns it to the original priority on the next pass.

FIGURE 1-5 Token passing

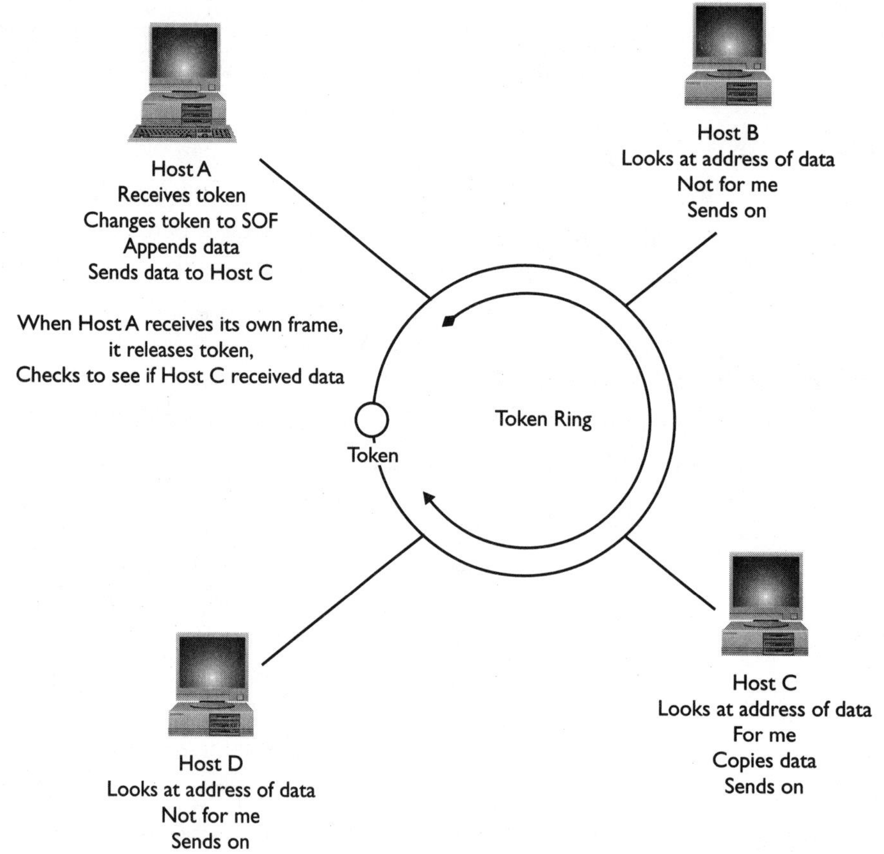

Beaconing is a Token Ring mechanism that detects network faults. If a station detects a failure in the network, it sends a beacon frame, which specifies the reporting station, its nearest active upstream neighbor (NAUN), and the failure area. Beaconing triggers *autoreconfiguration*, in which the network nodes attempt to reconfigure the network around the failed areas. A multistation access unit (MSAU) may "wrap" a port so that it is not part of the ring, bypassing all inactive or nonfunctional ports, but including all active, functioning ones.

There are two types of frames, a token and a data frame. A token (shown in Figure 1-6) is three bytes long. A data frame (shown in Figure 1-7) consists of the data sent by upper-layer protocols and the Token Ring header. There is a special data frame called a MAC frame, for commands that consist of Token Ring control information and header.

ANSI FDDI

In the mid 1980s, ANSI (American National Standards Institute) X3T9.5 standards committee created FDDI (Fiber Distributed Data Interface), which was developed to address the growing bandwidth needs in network systems. ANSI submitted FDDI to the International Organization for Standardization, which then created a compatible FDDI standard. The FDDI standard specifies the physical and MAC portion of the data link layers for a token-passing, dual-ring topology using fiber-optic media at 100 Mbps. Fiber has some advantages over copper wire:

- Immunity to electrical interference
- Higher throughput
- Immunity to traditional wiretap methods
- Capacity to be used for longer distances

The MAC layer specification defines the media access method, frame format, token passing method, MAC addressing, CRC (cyclic redundancy

FIGURE 1-6

Token Ring token format

Start delimiter	Access control	End delimiter
Alerts stations of a coming token	Contains priority and reservation fields. Also contains the token bit.	Notifies that this is the end of the frame

FIGURE 1-7

Token Ring data frame format

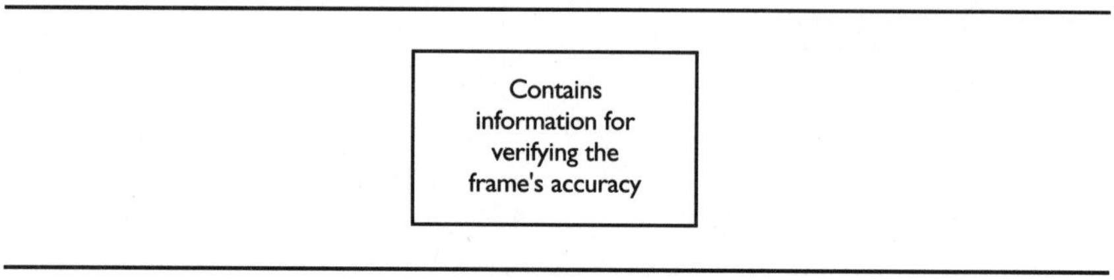

check), and error recovery. The physical layer specification defines the data framing, clocking requirements, and transmission media (bit error rates, optical components, fiber-optic connector, power levels). Also, FDDI provides for the station configuration, insertion, removal, fault recovery, ring configuration, and control.

In the dual ring configuration, traffic travels in one direction on one ring, and the other direction on the other ring. One ring is primary, and used for data transmission. The other is secondary, and used for backup. Class B stations attach to a single ring through a concentrator so that rebooting a station will not bring down the ring. Class B stations are known as SAS (single-attached stations). Class A stations attach to both rings, and are known as DAS (dual-attached stations). The dual ring provides fault tolerance, as shown in Figure 1-8. If a Class A station on the dual ring fails, it creates a ring failure. During that failure, stations on either side of the fault wrap their ports, restoring service through the backup ring. If there is more than one break in the ring, multiple separate rings can be the result.

FDDI supports both asynchronous and synchronous traffic. Synchronous is allocated a portion of the bandwidth for stations requiring continuous transmission; asynchronous is allocated the remainder. Stations using the asynchronous portion are assigned priority from a priority scheme of 8 levels, which are shown in Figure 1-9.

MAC Addresses

The data link layer consists of two sublayers: Logical Link Control (LLC) and Media Access Control (MAC). The MAC sublayer determines the address for the hardware at that layer. This address is network independent, such that wherever the hardware is "plugged in" to the internetwork, it would have the same MAC address, regardless of the network address. The vendor usually assigns the MAC address. In the Ethernet scheme, a series of

FIGURE 1-8

Dual ring fault tolerance

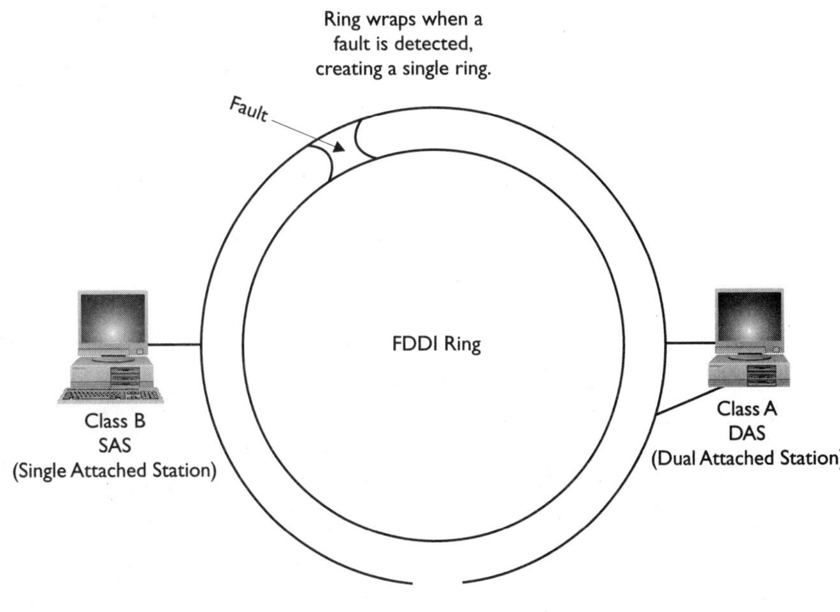

Ethernet MAC addresses are assigned to a vendor, who then assigns a different address to each interface produced. An Ethernet MAC address consists of 12 digits. The first six digits (the Organizationally Unique Identifier, or OUI) are the unique number assigned to the vendor by the IEEE, and the remaining six digits are the series. As a result, each network interface card will have a different MAC address on any given LAN or WAN.

Interfaces

The physical layer encompasses several different types of interfaces. These are either dictated by the protocol used on the segment, or by the proprietary specification of the vendor. Interfaces are used to connect data terminal

FIGURE 1-9

FDDI frame format

Preamble	Start delimiter	Frame control	Destination address	Source address	Data	End delimiter	Frame status

equipment (DTE) and data circuit-terminating equipment (DCE) devices. DTEs are network nodes such as routers and servers. DCEs are internetworking devices, such as packet switches, generally owned by the carrier, which provide clocking and switching.

RS-232

RS-232 is the EIA (Electronics Industries Alliance) serial port interface standard. In the RS-232 serial port, one pin is used to transmit data, another to receive data. The remaining pins are used to establish and maintain communication between two serial devices. There is both a 25-pin (DB-25) and a 9-pin (DB-9) version. The cable media must be configured so that each wire transmits or receives the type of data expected. RS-232 cables, which are rated to 19.2 Kbps, must be configured to properly connect DCE and DTE devices. Unique pinouts are required for cables that do not conform to the standard. The pinouts are described in Table 1-3.

V.35

ITU-T (International Telecommunication Union—Telecommunication Standardization Sector) created an entire V.*xx* series of standards. The V.35 standard is a physical layer protocol suitable for connections to a packet network at speeds up to 48 Kbps, and beyond, even to 4 Mbps. This standard specifies synchronous communication.

HSSI

Both the ISO and the ITU-T are currently reviewing HSSI (High Speed Serial Interface) for standardization. HSSI is a DTE/DCE interface that handles high-speed communication over WAN links. This is a physical layer specification of a point-to-point connection that runs at speeds up to 52 Mbps using shielded twisted-pair copper wire.

BRI Interfaces

BRI (Basic Rate Interface) is an ISDN (Integrated Services Digital Network) term for an ISDN connection consisting of two B channels at 64 Kbps and one D channel at 16 Kbps. A terminal adapter is a modem-like

TABLE 1-3 RS-232 Pinouts

9 Pin	25 Pin	Symbol	Signal Sent on That Pin	Input/Output Data
-	1		Protective ground	
3	2	TX	Transmit data	Output
2	3	RX	Receive data	Input
7	4	RTS	Request to send	Output
8	5	CTS	Clear to send	Input
6	6	DSR	Data set ready	Input
5	7		Signal Ground	
1	8	DCD	Data Carrier Detect	Input
-	9		Transmit Current Loop +	Output
-	11		Transmit Current Loop -	Output
-	18		Receive Current Loop +	Input
4	20	DTR	Data Terminal Ready	Output
9	22	RI	Ring Indicator	Input
-	23		Data Signal Rate Indicator	Input and Output
-	25		Receive Current Loop -	Input

device used to connect the DTE device to the ISDN circuit. The ITU-T's BRI standard specification for the physical layer includes data transmission for the B channels and signaling, framing control, and other overhead control information on the D channel.

Network Clock

Synchronizing network timing is handled at the physical layer of the OSI reference model. This clocking of the network bitstream can improve throughput, and is mandatory for WAN circuits. Specifications for clocking are included in the framing format and control mechanisms defined in interface standards.

FROM THE CLASSROOM

Setting Up a Lab Network

This is a long chapter, filled with dry information about abstract concepts. In the ICRC classes, this material used to take the better part of the first day. The students were always frustrated, because their primary motivation in coming to class in the first place was to get their hands on some actual routers! One of the things we used to do to help break up the tedium of non-stop lectures was to have the students help cable up the classroom network. In contrast to the course's focus on layer 3, with a little about layer 2, putting the equipment together into a network is purely a physical layer activity. I'd like to walk you through some of the considerations for setting up a classroom or a lab network, in case you need to set up one of your own someday.

The classroom network uses a combination of Ethernet and serial connections. The Ethernet connections are simple to set up, but there are still a few items to pay attention to. In the past, Cisco made no assumptions as to which Ethernet media the customer would use, so the interface provided on the older products is AUI only. This interface is useful for a 10Base5 network, but most customers use 10Base2 or 10BaseT, both of which require a transceiver to be attached to the AUI interface to convert the signal and make the physical connection to the network cable.

Newer Cisco products provide a dual-media interface for Ethernet, which you can recognize by the RJ-45 receptacle for a 10BaseT cable alongside an AUI interface. Cisco is not giving you two Ethernets for the price of one here; you can use one or the other, but not both simultaneously. The trick with this one is that the default media type for this interface is AUI, which is probably not the one you want! You will need to configure the router interface explicitly to use the RJ-45 connector. The command to use is MEDIA-TYPE 10BASET.

In most production networks, the serial interfaces would connect the router to a CSU/DSU, which would connect to a WAN service provider's network. The router would be a DTE device and would take a clock signal for that line from the provider's network clock. In the lab there's no provider to give us a clock signal, and there's no CSU/DSU. You will need to do two things to accommodate these differences in order to make the serial connections work in the lab: use back-to-back cable pairs, and configure a clock rate in the router.

Serial interfaces on most Cisco routers use a DB-60 high-density connector on the router end. The cables are called transition cables because the non-router end determines its electrical signaling. These might be

FROM THE CLASSROOM

EIA/TIA-232, V.35, X.21, or RS-449. In a production network, the cable you would buy to connect to your CSU/DSU would most likely be a male DTE V.35 cable. If we are making a connection between two routers in the lab, however, there won't be a CSU/DSU, so the male cable will need to connect to a female DCE cable of the same signaling type in a back-to-back arrangement.

Now we have a connection made, but the router needs to get clocking for those connections from somewhere, since we don't have a provider's network to take it from. In the lab, you need to configure one end—the DCE end only—of each serial connection with a clock rate, which will dictate the speed at which the connection will transfer data. Use the CLOCK RATE command for this. The maximum clock rate you can specify will depend on the cable you are using. The V.35 cable will allow a clock rate up to 4 Mbps, while the EIA/TIA-232 will allow only 128 Kbps. You don't need to configure a clock rate on the DTE end of the connection.

A last word about serial cables: Cisco cables list for $100 apiece, so if you are using serial connections in your lab, you will need a $200 cable pair for each one. You might think that you're getting a rugged product for that price, but you're not. There are two pitfalls here: folded pins and upside-down cable attachments. The DB-60 high-density connectors are extremely delicate and the pins will fold up inside very easily if you're careless, ruining the cable. Be sure to watch the orientation of your cables with respect to the router interface before you attach them! The 60 pins are arranged in a matrix with four identical rows of 15 pins each, and the metal sleeve of the D-connector is thin and pliable, so you can physically attach the cable to the router upside-down without noticing it. It won't work this way, of course, so you may be in for hours of futile troubleshooting before you discover the problem.

—By Pamela Forsyth, CCIE, CCSI, CNX

Wide Area Network Services

WAN services are networks in their own right, just without workstations connected to the link between the two networks. Figure 1-10 shows a WAN link. The purpose of a WAN connection is to be able to transmit

FIGURE 1-10

Two LANs connected by a WAN link

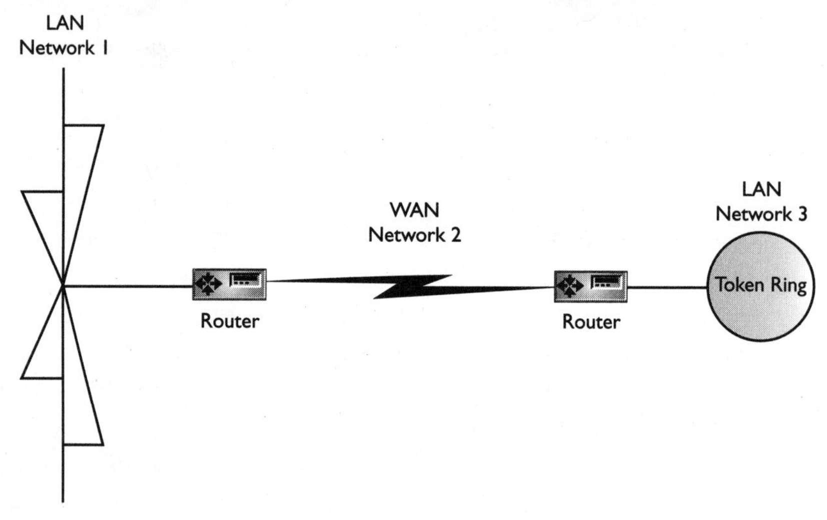

data between two distant networks as efficiently as possible. The more efficient the link, the more transparent the connection to the end users. WAN links are typically slower than LAN links. For example, a T-1 is 1.544 Mbps, while Ethernet 10BaseT is 10 Mbps.

Point to Point

SLIP (Serial Line Internet Protocol) is a legacy UNIX physical layer protocol for providing serial connections between two networks, or between a network and a remote node. Because of the universal nature of serial connection devices and interfaces, such as the RS-232 interface, SLIP was embraced.

PPP was designed to address the shortcomings of SLIP and the need for standard Internet encapsulation protocol. PPP (Point-to-Point Protocol) is the next generation of SLIP, but works at both the physical and the data link layers. PPP includes enhancements such as encryption, error control, security, dynamic IP addressing, multiple protocol support, and automatic connection negotiation. PPP will work over serial lines, ISDN, and high-speed WAN links. The PPP data frame is shown in Figure 1-11.

FIGURE 1-11

PPP data frame

Flag	Address	Control	Protocol	Data	Frame Check Sequence
01111110	11111111	00000011	2 bytes that identify the protocol	max 1500 bytes	2-or 4-byte field for error handling

In addition to a frame with data, there are other frames that PPP uses. An LCP (Link Control Protocol) frame is used to establish and configure the connection. An NCP (Network Control Protocol) frame is used to select and configure the network layer protocols. Explicit LCP frames are used to close the link.

Frame Relay

Frame Relay is a widely used packet-switched WAN protocol standardized by the ITU-T. Frame Relay relies on the physical and data link layer interface between DTE and DCE devices. Frame Relay networks are either public, and provided by carriers, or privately owned. The key benefit of Frame Relay is the capability to connect with multiple WAN sites through a single link. This makes Frame Relay much cheaper than point-to-point circuits for large WANs. Dedicated point-to-point circuits connect the customer into a nearby Frame Relay switch at the carrier. From there, the Frame Relay switches work like routers, forwarding packets through the carrier's network, based on addressing in the packet header.

Frame Relay is very similar to the X.25 protocol. It uses a virtual circuit—permanent (PVC) or switched (SVC)—between the source and destination, and uses statistical multiplexing for managing multiple data streams. Because of the reliability of the media, error correction is handled at higher protocol layers. There is a CRC to detect and discard corrupted data, but Frame Relay does not request retransmission. Instead Frame Relay relies on higher-level protocols for error correction.

SVCs are temporary links best used in networks with sporadic data transmission. An SVC session begins with a call setup that creates the virtual circuit. Then comes the data transfer, then an idle phase for a defined period, keeping the circuit open in case of more data. Finally, there is a call termination.

PVCs are permanently established links and are the most common implementation of Frame Relay. There are only two session operations, data transfer and idle. The carrier service configures the PVC, since it is routed through the carrier's internetwork. (See Figure 1-12.)

An important concept to know about Frame Relay is *Data Link Connection Identifier* (DLCI). The DLCI is a number used locally by a DTE and assigned by the Frame Relay provider. It refers to the connection between two DTEs in the Frame Relay network. Because it is a local identifier, each DTE may use a different number to identify the link.

In order to maximize throughput, flow control uses a congestion notification method. FECN (forward-explicit congestion notification) is a bit in the frame that is set to a "1" when the frame experiences congestion between source and destination. The DTE device sends this information to upper protocol layers in order to begin controlling the flow. BECN (backward-explicit congestion notification) is a bit that is set to "1" when an FECN frame has been received that experienced congestion between source and destination. FECN and BECN are one-bit fields that may be set to "0"

FIGURE 1-12

Carrier's Frame Relay network

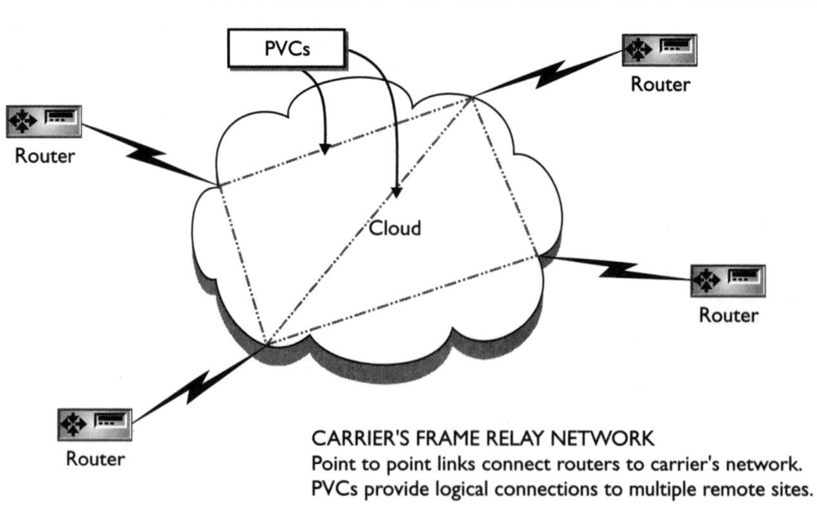

QUESTIONS AND ANSWERS

Shari is configuring the DLCI for a PVC between Portland and Phoenix. The provider gave her two numbers—12 and—14, and assigned them to the link. Shari arbitrarily uses 12 for Portland and 14 for Phoenix. When the link is completely configured, it does not work. Why?	The provider should have specified that the DLCI for Portland was 14 and that the DLCI for Phoenix was 12. The local identifier was wrong and the link did not come up.

as well, which means there is no congestion or that the congestion notification feature is not implemented by the switches in the network. The bits exist in the header at all times, no matter what their value. (See Figure 1-13.)

X.25

The ITU-T X.25 standard describes the physical, data link, and network layer protocols for a legacy packet-switching protocol. The physical layer protocol is X.21, which is roughly equivalent to the RS-232 serial interface. The data link layer protocol is LAPB (Link Access Protocol Balanced). The network layer specifies PLP (Packet Level Protocol).

Like Frame Relay, X.25 uses PVCs and SVCs, but its link speeds of 9.6 to 256 Kbps are slower. The data transfer rate is relatively slow compared to newer protocols, because X.25 was defined when media transmission quality was poor. As a result, the protocol specifies that each switching node must fully receive each packet and verify that there are no errors before sending it on to the next node. X.25 may utilize variable-sized packets. As a result of the hop-by-hop error checking and retransmission, and the variable packet size, X.25 is very slow. With the reliability of today's transmission lines, X.25 has a hard time competing with higher-performance protocols, like Frame Relay,

FIGURE 1-13

Frame Relay frame format

Flags	Address DLCI and Address information FECN, BECN, and Discard Eligibility bits	Data

that do not offer guaranteed delivery. Frame relay has no error recovery at all—errored packets are dropped without notification. Error checking is only done when the frame-relay frame gets to its final destination.

X.25 uses a point-to-point connection between DTE and DCE. Via a PAD (packet assembler/disassembler), the DTE connects to a carrier-provided DCE, which in turn connects to a packet-switching exchange (PSE or switch), and eventually reaches a destination DTE.

ISDN

Integrated Services Digital Network was standardized by the ITU-T. It was developed as a project to upgrade the Public Switched Telephone Network (PSTN) to a digital service. The physical specification for transmission medium is copper wire.

There are several components to ISDN, as illustrated in Figure 1-14. There is terminal equipment, network termination, and adapters of the following types.

- **TE1 – Terminal Equipment type 1** ISDN terminals
- **TE2 – Terminal Equipment type 2** pre-ISDN type terminals
- **NT1 – Network Termination type 1** equipment that connects the subscription 4 wires to the 2 wire local loop
- **NT2 – Network Termination type 2** equipment that performs protocol functions of the data link and network layers
- **TA – Terminal Adapter** used with a pre-ISDN terminal (TE2) to adapt it to an ISDN connection

When ordering ISDN, consumers usually have the choice between BR (Basic Rate) and PR (Primary Rate) and Hybrid. There are various digital channels that make up these two configurations. The available digital channels are:

- A analog telephone, 4 KHz
- B digital data, 64 Kbps
- C digital out-of-band, 8 or 16 Kbps

FIGURE 1-14 ISDN equipment connections

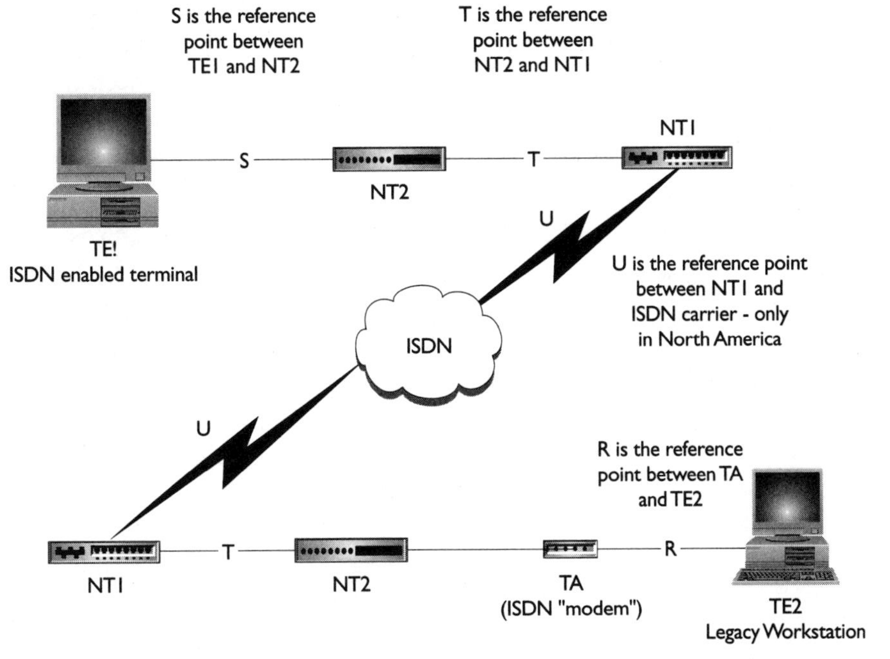

- D digital out-of-band, 16 or 64 Kbps with three sub-channels: s (signaling), t (telemetry), and p (packet data)
- E digital channel for internal ISDN signaling, 64 Kbps
- H digital channel at 384 Kbps, 1536 Kbps, or 1920 Kbps

BR consists of two B channels and one D channel, and with control information has an effective bit rate of 192 Kbps. PR consists of one D channel and 23 B channels, with a bandwidth of 1.544 Mbps. In Europe, PR has one D channel and 30 B channels. Hybrid is a single A channel and a single C channel.

Note that LAPD (link access procedure for the D channel) is the signalling protocol used to set up ISDN calls for ISDN BRI at the data link layer.

ATM

ATM (Asynchronous Transfer Mode) is a cell-switching protocol that uses a fixed 53-byte cell length and a cell relay method that reduces transmission delays. ATM can transmit voice, video, and data over variable-speed LAN and WAN links from DS-1 (1.544 Mbps) to as high as 622 Mbps. The key to ATM's high speed is within the fixed cell length. The fixed cell length enables routers to relay cells at the hardware level, using less processing power and increasing the data transmission.

The ITU-T developed ATM as the result of a broadband integrated services signal network study. It evolved further from the work of the ATM Forum founded by Cisco, Net/Adaptive, Northern Telecom, and Sprint. The technology used is VLSI (very large-scale integration), which segments data frames at high speeds into small, fixed units known as cells.

VLSI technology made possible the development of ASICs (application-specific integrated circuits) specifically to perform the segmentation and reassembly of data in hardware rather than in software. Along with the fixed cell size, this is what makes it possible to operate ATM circuits efficiently at such breathtaking speeds, now up to OC-48 (2 Gbps).

The cells relay through ATM switch devices that analyze the cell header and switch it to the correct output interface, in a switch-to-switch path until the cell reaches its final destination. The asynchronous method uses time slots that are available upon demand, rather than strict and wasteful time division multiplexing.

There are two header formats: UNI and NNI (Network Node Interface). UNI is the communication between end nodes and ATM switches. NNI is the communication between two ATM switches. The diagram in Figure 1-15 displays the two different header formats.

ATM uses its own reference model, parts of which are analogous to the OSI reference model. The ATM layer and the ATM adaptation layer are roughly equivalent to the data link layer, and the ATM physical layer is analogous to the OSI physical layer.

The ATM physical layer is responsible for the bitstream transmission. The ATM physical layer contains two sublayers: physical medium and transmission convergence. The physical medium transmits the bitstream and timing synchronization information. The physical media that are

FIGURE 1-15

UNI and NNI cell header formats

GFC - Generic flow control	VPI- Virtual path identifier	VCI- Virtual Channel Identifier	PT- Payload type	CLP- Congestion loss priority	HEC- Header error control

5-byte length UNI cell header

VPI- Virtual path identifier	VCI- Virtual Channel Identifier	PT- Payload type	CLP- Congestion loss priority	HEC- Header error control

5-byte length NNI cell header

Does not have GFC, instead the larger VPI field allows larger paths.

supported are SONET/SDH, DS-1, DS-3/E3, OC-3, OC-12, 155 Mbps UTP, 100 Mbps FDDI, and 155 Mbps Fiber Channel. The transmission convergence manages cell delineation and header error control data, and packages ATM cells into frames that work with the physical media.

The ATM layer establishes connections and relays cells using the cell header information. It is responsible for mapping network layer addresses to ATM addresses. The ATM adaptation layer (AAL) translates the larger data packets into cells.

ATM is similar to Frame Relay in its switching mechanisms. Instead of switching variable-length packets over PVCs and SVCs, ATM switches fixed-length cells through the internetwork. ATM devices connect directly to an ATM switch.

In order to deliver voice, video, and data in an appropriate fashion, ATM has implemented new features. One of these is called Quality of Service (QoS). Quality of Service allows an ATM device to prioritize data based on the content. Thus, delivery of a file transfer can take a backseat to a video transmission, since the bursty data transfer of the file will not affect the quality of the service. On the other hand, a video transmission that stopped in the middle of a screen would be considered problematic.

CERTIFICATION OBJECTIVE 1.03

Network Layer and Path Determination

The main services provided at the network layer are logical addressing of the node and network segments. As a result, the routing of data between the logical addresses is handled at the network layer. IP of the IP protocol suite is considered a network layer protocol. Data is broken into "packets" at this layer.

The network layer is where internetworking takes place. While the data link layer protocols have features that enable data to be passed from one node to another node on the same link, network layer protocols enable data to be passed from one network to another. This means that the network layer protocols must always contain addressing information that uniquely identifies networks within the internetwork.

Layer 3 Addresses

Networking itself is the capability to share data between two nodes. Being able to simply locate the nodes on the network is one of the most basic and important functions in networking. The network layer not only provides a unique node address, but also a unique network address. This enables the routing of data between networks.

Layer 3, or the network layer, is where addressing is most important. When applying the OSI reference model to the IP protocol suite, IP (Internet Protocol) would be at layer 3. The IP addressing scheme determines the network that a node is on and the logical node address on the network. The logical node address is often *the same* as the MAC address in other protocols, although it is not in IP. This is dealt with on the lower data link layer (layer 2). Note that in Novell IPX, for instance, the MAC address is used for the network-layer node address without modification.

A network layer address is also called a *logical address* or *software address.* Network layer addresses are hierarchical, and provide both the network and the node address. A router can easily separate the addresses to be sent on a particular interface by simply looking at the initial network portion of the address—the network address. When the packet reaches the destination network, the node address portion is used to locate the specific station.

Routed Protocols vs. Routing Protocols

Routed protocols are used by end nodes to encapsulate data into packets along with network-layer addressing information so it can be relayed through the internetwork. AppleTalk, IP, and IPX are all routed protocols. When a protocol does not support a network layer address, then it is a non-routed protocol.

Routers use routing protocols to build and maintain routing tables and to forward data packets along the best path toward their destination networks. Routing protocols enable routers to learn about the status of networks that are not directly connected to them, and to communicate to other routers about the networks they are aware of. This communication is carried out on a continuing basis so the information in the routing table is updated as changes occur in the internetwork.

The characteristics that distinguish one routing protocol from another include:

- the routed protocol for which it maintains information
- the way the routers communicate among each other
- how often this communication takes place
- the algorithm and metrics used to determine the best path
- how long it takes for news of a change to be communicated throughout the network

Examples of routing protocols include RTMP, OSPF, and RIP.

Routing Algorithms and Metrics

A routing algorithm is the calculation that the routing protocol uses to determine the best route to a destination network. The simpler the routing algorithm, the less processing power the router will use. This, in turn, keeps the overhead low on the router.

Metrics are values used to determine which route is preferable. Depending on the routing protocol, different factors determine a route's metric, including the number of hops, link speeds, delay, reliability, and load. The resulting metrics are stored with the routes in a routing table or a link-state database.

CERTIFICATION OBJECTIVE 1.04

Transport Layer

The transport layer provides data transport services, effectively shielding the upper layers from data transfer issues. Transport layer services are concerned with the reliability of the connection, establishing virtual circuits, error detection and recovery, and flow control. When the OSI model is applied to the IP protocol suite, TCP and UDP are both transport layer protocols.

Reliability

Transmission Control Protocol (TCP) is considered a *reliable, connection-oriented* protocol. User Datagram Protocol (UDP) is *unreliable* and *connectionless.* The difference between a reliable and unreliable protocol is the acknowledgment to the sender that data has been received. There is more overhead involved with a reliable protocol because of the acknowledgments. On the other hand, unreliable protocols do not guarantee delivery of data, and can be prone to more errors in delivery.

Connectionless, or unreliable, protocols are used quite often when reliability issues such as sequencing and error recovery are addressed at the application layer. The advantage is that because they have fewer features, the overhead is very low.

Windowing

When some transport protocols negotiate a reliable connection between two nodes on an internetwork, they also negotiate a moving target of the amount of data that can be transmitted at any one time. That moving target is called a *sliding window.* This process is called *Windowing.*

CERTIFICATION OBJECTIVE 1.05

Upper-Layer Protocols

The term upper-layer protocols refers to the session, presentation, and application layer protocols. The application layer provides basic services such as file transfer and network management to applications. It establishes the availability of destination nodes, and identifies the application synchronization between the nodes.

Presentation layer is aptly named, for this layer handles the formatting of data, or presentation of that data. Services in the presentation layer include data encryption. The presentation layer protocol can also negotiate the syntax of the data in order for translation to occur with the destination node.

As the name implies, the session layer establishes the session between two network nodes, maintains it, and terminates it as well. Services at this layer include class of service, data prioritization, and reporting errors for the upper two layers.

CERTIFICATION OBJECTIVE 1.06

Cisco Routers, Switches, and Hubs

Cisco IOS Software (Internetworking Operating System) is the software that runs on the Cisco products. This platform is integral to the interoperations of network devices in a Cisco internetwork. Cisco IOS includes security, access control, authentication, firewall, encryption, management services, and support for IBM connectivity, switching, voice and multimedia, and quality of service. The main purpose of IOS is to boot the Cisco hardware and begin the optimal transport of data across the internetwork.

Of the internetwork routers available from Cisco, the Gigabit Switched 12000 series routers are built to handle the fastest backbone traffic. Gigabit switched traffic is standard, where the backbones of these routers can handle up to 4, 8 or 12 cards (depending on which router selected) that are OC-3 to OC-48 compliant. The target network for a Gigabit Switched 12000 series router running Cisco IOS are Internet service providers, enterprise WAN backbones, and other high-throughput internetworks needing speeds of even 2.4 Gbps and up. It supports SONET, ATM, and DS-3/E-3 connections.

The platform for multiprotocol routers is the Cisco 7000 series routers, which run the Cisco IOS. The 7500 high-end series features Cisco Extended Bus (Cybus), which is connected to the external network through network interfaces connected to modular interface processors. The 7500 series supports any combination of the following.

- ATM
- Channelized T3
- FDDI
- Multichannel T1/E1
- HSSI
- Packet OC-3
- Synchronous serial
- Token Ring
- Ethernet
- Fast Ethernet

In order to avoid network service interruption, the 7500 series supports online software reconfiguration without rebooting, online insertion and removal of new interface processors without rebooting, a fast boot process, self-diagnostics, and dual power supply options for some of the versions.

Cisco offers several routers built to provide the price and performance needed in smaller, workgroup-oriented LANs and WANs. These routers include the 2500 series, the 3600 series, and the 4000 series. They support the most widely used protocols and physical media, from Ethernet and Token Ring to FDDI.

Switching services are becoming more popular due to the immediate speed improvements they can bring to a LAN. Switches can be connected to hubs or directly to workstations and servers. The algorithms used to determine the location of a hardware device effectively give each port a full throughput of 10 Mbps on Ethernet 10BaseT LANs.

Catalyst 1900/2820 switch is a flexible switch that can be integrated in anything from a small LAN to an enterprise WAN. It includes three switching modes: fastforward, fragmentfree, and store and forward. The fastforward mode begins forwarding a frame as soon as the MAC address is learned. Fragmentfree mode begins forwarding a frame as soon as it reaches 64 bytes, which is determined to be the threshold for fragment size. And store and forward receives the complete frame and checks it for errors before forwarding it. Fastforward is the default, as well as fastest mode. Store and forward is automatically used for packets travelling between 10 Mbps ports and 100 Mbps ports. The mode must be set for the switch if fastforward is not desired. The spanning tree protocol (IEEE 802.1d standard) is used for transparently reconfiguring the switch when the network topology changes.

Hubs are also available from Cisco in the FastHub Series. FastHubs are Ethernet hubs that can be used alone, stacked together in a LAN workgroup, or connected to Catalyst Switches to form VLANs (Virtual Local Area Network). Other Cisco products available include: Frame Relay PAD/routers, access routers for remote access users, ISDN routers, ATM switches, firewalls, and other network management hardware solutions.

CERTIFICATION OBJECTIVE 1.07

Configuring a Cisco Switch and Hub

For any type of switch or hub, the following instructions apply.

- Unpack the hardware and verify the contents matches the packing list.
- Stack or rack-mount (with the correct rubber feet or rack hardware) the switch in a location that is no more than 100 meters from any attached 10BaseT device, where the temperature is correct for the product, and which has sufficient airflow.
- When selecting cables, use straight-through cables for all ports *not* marked with an X. The X stands for crossover cables. Category 5 cables will work for all ports except for the 100BaseFX port, which requires fiber-optic media.
- Verify that the voltage of the power outlet is the same as the voltage indicated on the label, and connect the power.

There is a method to setting up a Cisco Catalyst 2820 switch. This method demonstrates out-of-band management. That is, it manages the switch from a terminal that is directly connected to a serial port on the switch. This method has the advantage of working regardless of whether network connectivity is available from the switch. The steps to setting up a Cisco Catalyst 2820 switch are:

1. Turn on the switch and watch POST (power on self-test) where all the port LEDs should turn Green and then Off.
2. Connect the devices to the hub using the correct cables.
3. Connect a VT-100 terminal or emulator to the EIA/TIA-232 (RS-232) port, using the settings for 9600 bps, 8 data bits, 1 stop bit, and no parity, and log in.
4. Press S to access the System Configuration menu, and change the Switching Mode by selecting S again. Then select the number for the

switching mode desired. This step is unnecessary if fastforward switching is desired.

5. Press X to exit to the main menu and then press N to access the Network Management menu, which is where the protocol configuration is.
6. Select I to access IP Configuration, then select I again to assign an IP address. When assigning an IP address any time after the first assignment, the switch must be reset for the address to take effect. Select S and G to assign the appropriate subnet mask and Default Gateway, respectively.
7. Select X to exit to the Main menu, select S again for the System, and select R to reset the switch and retain the assigned parameters.

Installing a FastHub 316C or FastHub 316T begins with the same unpacking and verification procedures as the switch installation. After unpacking and physically installing the hub, it can be further configured.

1. After plugging in the hub, and verifying POST, connect the devices to the RJ-45 ports.
2. Connect a node to the console port, and configure the terminal emulation program for 9600 baud, 8 data bits, 1 stop bit, and no parity.
3. At the management console, log in.
4. Select the IP Configuration menu. Set the IP address, subnet mask, default gateway, and DNS server. Disable RIP if another routing protocol is being used.
5. Exit to the Main menu and Exit the console.

CERTIFICATION SUMMARY

A model for internetworks had to answer the challenges of interoperability and interconnectivity. These challenges prompted the development of a layered protocol model, both as a standardized model and one that was accepted due to its popular use. TCP/IP developed as a four-layer popular model. The seven-layer OSI reference model was developed and standardized by the ISO. The seven layers of the OSI model are application, presentation, session, transport, network, data link, and physical. Data travels through the protocol layers at the source by being broken into smaller data units and having header information added for each layer. When the data is reassembled and passed to the upper protocols at the destination, the header is discarded for each layer that the data has passed through. This allows independence of layers from each other. The header addition for each protocol layer is called encapsulation.

The physical layer is responsible for the bitstream of data, and its transmission. The data link layer consists of two sublayers: Logical Link Control and Media Access Control. The MAC sublayer handles hardware addressing—MAC addresses. The LLC sublayer handles control information in the frames, which are the data units at the data link layer.

The IEEE (Institute for Electrical and Electronics Engineers) created an 802 series of standards for physical and data link layer protocols. These included the standards for Ethernet (802.3) and for Token Ring (802.5), among others. ANSI (American National Standards Institute) created FDDI, a physical and data link layer standard that uses optical fiber media.

Ethernet, originally created by DIX (Digital/Intel/Xerox) is a CSMA/CD protocol allowing all nodes access to the network. If a collision occurs, the protocol has a method of sensing the collision and retransmitting the data. Ethernet can use thick or thin coax or unshielded twisted-pair copper wire. The rate of data transmission is usually 10 Mbps, however, 1Base5 is 1 Mbps. The most common form of Ethernet is 10BaseT, but 100BaseT is gaining in popularity.

Token Ring is a token-passing ring topology that is wired in a star fashion. IBM initially developed Token Ring. The physical medium used is generally shielded or unshielded twisted-pair copper wire. In this protocol, any station that has data to send must wait until a token frame is received. When the token is received, that station may send the data. The receiving station copies the data and changes a bit on the header, then forwards that data on to the original sending node. When the sending node receives the frame, it releases the token and checks the header to see if the data was received at its destination. With Token Ring, there are no collisions, so data is only retransmitted if a frame is damaged.

FDDI (Fiber Distributed Data Interface) is a dual ring token-passing protocol, similar to Token Ring, based on fiber-optic media. This has high-capacity speed for 100 Mbps. The dual ring topology uses a similar token-passing mechanism to Token Ring, but includes the capacity for fault management by creating a single ring. FDDI can be installed without using hubs, and it uses the secondary fiber ring to recover from failures in the primary ring.

There are several physical interfaces used for connecting nodes to a network. The most prevalent of interfaces is the RS-232 serial interface. V.35 is a physical layer protocol. HSSI is a high-speed serial interface suitable for WAN connections. BRI interfaces are used to connect to an ISDN line.

WAN links include Point-to-Point Protocol, which is a standard IP protocol used to encapsulate data over IP, and can be used over serial connections. Frame Relay is a packet network standard. X.25 is a legacy packet network standard that is very slow as a result of its error checking at each packet switch in the data path. ISDN connects to the digital telephone network. ATM is a cell-switching protocol for high-speed LAN and WANs.

The network layer defines logical addresses for network nodes. Routed protocols support network and node addressing at this layer, enabling packets to be routed through the network. Routing protocols determine the path between two networks by using routing algorithms and metrics, and by advertising their routes.

The transport layer handles reliability of data transfer, and can negotiate a sliding window of data transmission in order to maximize throughput on a network.

The upper-layer protocols—application, presentation, and session—handle the data from the application, its format (such as encryption), and the session settings between the source and destination nodes.

TWO-MINUTE DRILL

- ❑ A potential CCNA must have the knowledge to install, configure, and operate simple-routed LAN, routed WAN, and switched LAN and LANE networks.
- ❑ Internetworking is the process and methodology applied to connecting multiple networks, regardless of their physical topologies and distance.
- ❑ Interconnectivity is the means of transporting information between the computers, inclusive of the physical media, the data packaging mechanism, and the routing between multiple network equipment pieces from the starting node until reaching the destination node.
- ❑ Interoperability is the methodology applied to make data understandable to computers that use proprietary or simply different computer operating systems and languages.
- ❑ The OSI reference model provides a hierarchical tool for understanding networking technology, as well as a basis for current and future network developments.
- ❑ The OSI model is a seven-layer protocol suite model.
- ❑ A common mnemonic device for remembering the layers (application, presentation, session, transport, network, data link, physical) in the right order is **A**ll **P**eople **S**eem **T**o **N**eed **D**ata **P**rocessing.
- ❑ Encapsulation is the process of adding a header to the data, or *wrapping* the data.
- ❑ The physical layer, or layer 1, defines the actual mechanical specifications and electrical data bitstream.
- ❑ The data link layer, or layer 2, is also known as the link layer. It consists of two sublayers, the upper level being the Logical Link Control (LLC), and the lower level being the Media Access Control (MAC).
- ❑ 802.3 specifies the physical layer and the MAC portion of the data link layer, while DIX Ethernet specifies the entire physical and

data link layers. 802.3 specifies different physical layers, but DIX Ethernet only specifies one.

- Token Ring networks are nearly identical and compatible with the IEEE 802.5 specification developed later, which was based on IBM's Token Ring.
- The FDDI standard specifies the physical and MAC portion of the data link layers for a token-passing, dual-ring topology using fiber-optic media at 100 Mbps.
- Interfaces are used to connect data terminal equipment (DTE) and data circuit-terminating equipment (DCE) devices.
- In the RS-232 serial port, one pin is used to transmit data, another to receive data.
- The V.35 standard is a physical layer protocol suitable for connections to a packet network at speeds up to 48 Kbps, and beyond, even to 4 Mbps.
- HSSI is a DTE/DCE interface that handles high-speed communication over WAN links.
- BRI (Basic Rate Interface) is an ISDN (Integrated Services Digital Network) term for an ISDN connection consisting of two B channels at 64 Kbps and one D channel at 16 Kbps.
- Synchronizing network timing is handled at the physical layer of the OSI reference model.
- The purpose of a WAN connection is to be able to transmit data between two distant networks as efficiently as possible.
- SLIP (Serial Line Internet Protocol) is a legacy UNIX physical layer protocol for providing serial connections between two networks, or between a network and a remote node.
- PPP includes enhancements such as encryption, error control, security, dynamic IP addressing, multiple protocol support, and automatic connection negotiation. PPP will work over serial lines, ISDN, and high-speed WAN links.

- Frame Relay is a widely used packet-switched WAN protocol standardized by the ITU-T. Frame Relay relies on the physical and data link layer interface between DTE and DCE devices.
- The ITU-T X.25 standard describes the physical, data link, and network layer protocols for a legacy packet-switching protocol.
- Integrated Services Digital Network was developed as a project to upgrade the Public Switched Telephone Network (PSTN) to a digital service.
- ATM (Asynchronous Transfer Mode) is a cell-switching protocol that uses a fixed 53-byte cell length and a cell relay method that reduces transmission delays.
- The main services provided at the network layer are logical addressing of the node and network segments.
- Layer 3, or the network layer, is where addressing is most important.
- Routed protocols are used by end nodes to encapsulate data into packets along with network-layer addressing information so it can be relayed through the internetwork.
- A routing algorithm is the calculation that the routing protocol uses to determine the best route to a destination network.
- The transport layer provides data transport services, effectively shielding the upper layers from data transfer issues.
- Transmission Control Protocol (TCP) is considered a *reliable*, *connection-oriented* protocol. User Datagram Protocol (UDP) is *unreliable* and *connectionless*.
- The term upper-layer protocols refers to the session, presentation, and application layer protocols.
- Cisco IOS Software (Internetworking Operating System) is the software that runs on the Cisco products. This platform is integral to the interoperations of network devices in a Cisco internetwork.

SELF TEST

The following questions will help you measure your understanding of the material presented in this chapter. Read all the choices carefully, as there may be more than one correct answer. Choose all correct answers for each question.

1. What were the two challenges of creating a network model? (Select two.)

   A. interconnectivity

   B. interaction

   C. internetworking

   D. interoperability

2. The Advanced Research Projects Agency created what network?

   A. Ethernet

   B. FDDI

   C. ARPANET

   D. Token Ring

3. What does OSI stand for?

   A. Organization for Standards Institute

   B. Organization for Internet Standards

   C. Open Standards Institute

   D. Open Systems Interconnection

4. What are the layers of the OSI reference model, in order?

   A. application, transport, network, physical

   B. application, presentation, session, network, transport, data link, physical

   C. application, presentation, session, transport, network, data link, physical

   D. application, session, transport, physical

5. What is the term for wrapping a data unit with a header and passing it to the next protocol?

   A. Windowing

   B. Encapsulation

   C. Wrapping

   D. Heading

6. Which of the following is not defined at the physical layer of the OSI reference model?

   A. hardware addresses

   B. bitstream transmission

   C. voltage levels

   D. physical interface

7. Which standards institute created the 802 series of physical/data link layer standards?

   A. ANSI

   B. DIX

   C. ITU-T

   D. IEEE

8. Who created Ethernet?

   A. ANSI

   B. DIX

   C. ITU-T

   D. IEEE

9. What is the function of CSMA/CD?

   A. It passes a token around a star topology

B. Nodes access the network and retransmit if they detect a collision

C. Nodes connect to a dual ring of fiber-optics and use a token-passing scheme

D. Nodes break the frames into tiny cells and forward them through a cell-switching network.

10. What is a backoff algorithm?

A. It is the fault tolerance calculation for FDDI

B. It is a routing calculation for determining the best route

C. It is the notification that a serious error has occurred on the network

D. It is the duration calculation to delay retransmission after a collision, before retransmitting in Ethernet.

11. IBM's Token Ring specification is nearly identical and compatible with IEEE's 802.5 specification.

A. True

B. False

12. What is beaconing?

A. It is the fault tolerance calculation for FDDI

B. It is a routing calculation for determining the best route

C. It is the notification that a serious error has occurred on the network

D. It is the duration calculation to delay retransmission after a collision, before retransmitting in Ethernet.

13. What two types of frames are found on a Token Ring network?

A. Token

B. Frame check sequence

C. Data

D. Address

14. The FDDI specification includes which layers of the OSI reference model?

A. Physical and network

B. Physical and transport

C. Physical and MAC sublayer of data link

D. Physical and data link

15. What is RS-232?

A. A standard serial port interface

B. A high-speed serial interface

C. An ISDN interface

D. An ATM switch

16. What is the maximum data transmission rate for HSSI?

A. 64 Kbps

B. 256 Kbps

C. 100 Mbps

D. 52 Mbps

17. What does the hierarchical network-layer address provide?

A. The hardware address

B. The node address and the hardware address

C. The network address and the node address

D. The network address mapped to the hardware address

18. What qualities match TCP?

A. connectionless, reliable

B. connection-oriented, reliable

C. connectionless, unreliable

D. connection-oriented, unreliable

19. What layer of the OSI reference model specifies data formats, such as encryption?

A. application

B. presentation

C. session

D. transport

E. network

F. data link

G. physical

20. What is out-of-band management?

A. It is the ability to manage a switch or hub from a networked workstation

B. It is the addition of a network management module to a hub

C. It is the fault tolerance feature of the dual ring FDDI creating a single ring

D. It is the ability to manage a device using a connection other than the network.

21. Interoperability means:

A. Transfer of data between systems

B. Ability to make data understandable by machines that use different operating systems, hardware or languages

C. Agreement between two equipment vendors for processing data

D. Ability of LAN to communicate with WAN

22. OSI is what kind of standard?

A. a standard created by major telecommunications service providers

B. a de facto standard

C. a de jure standard

D. a standard created by major equipment manufacturers

23. The layered approach of the OSI results in:

A. Increased development costs for a specific vendor product

B. Increased marketability for a specific vendor product

C. A hierarchical tool for network architecture

D. All of the above

E. B and C only

F. A and C only

24. Which of the following statements is true in general when an application at the source wishes to send data to an application at the destination address?

A. The lower layer at destination adds its own header information to the data it receives from the higher layer

B. The lower layer at source adds its own header information to the data it receives from the higher layer

C. The lower layer at destination strips header information from the data added by the higher layer

D. The higher layer at source strips header information added to the data by the lower layer

25. In the OSI model, encapsulation of the data may occur at:

A. Layer 7 of the source

B. Layer 1 of the destination

C. Layer 7 of the destination

D. All layers at source

E. Layer 1 of the source

26. The session layer functionality in the OSI model is usually implemented:

A. At user premises

B. In hardware

C. In software

D. In hardware and software

27. At the physical layer in the OSI model the data is broken into:

A. cells

B. fragments

C. bits

D. packets

28. Collision in a CSMA/CD network is said to occur when:

A. A node listens to the network and hears nothing

B. A node receives a message from the network

C. Two nodes hear nothing and then transmit data simultaneously

D. A node on the network has physical failure

29. A broadcast system means:

A. Only few nodes on the network see the data meant for these nodes

B. All nodes on the network see all the data frames

C. Network informs all the nodes of a network failure

D. None of the above

30. Which statements are true of a preamble in the IEEE 802.3 frame?

A. It is an indication that a node is receiving a new frame

B. It contains all zeros

C. It contains all ones

D. It contains alternating zeros and ones

E. A and B only

F. A and D only

G. A and C only

31. A Frame Check Sequence (FCS) in the IEEE 802.3 frame includes:

A. A receiving station address

B. A source station address

C. A Cyclic Redundancy Check (CRC) value

D. A sequence number of the frame

32. In a Token Ring network architecture, what does it mean when a node possesses a token?
    A. The node has the ability to transmit the data to the network
    B. The node has the right to pass the data to the network
    C. The node has the right to retain the token
    D. None of the above
33. In a Token Ring network architecture, if a node receives a token and has data to transmit, then:
    A. The node does nothing
    B. The node waits for data to be transmitted
    C. The node converts the token into a start-of-frame field
    D. None of the above
34. What is the main purpose of the dual ring architecture in Fiber Distributed Data Interface (FDDI)?
    A. To increase traffic on the network
    B. To allow bi-directional traffic on the network
    C. To provide fault tolerance
    D. To provide one path for traffic from selected nodes
35. Which statement is true of the Media Access Control (MAC) address?
    A. It is dependent on the hardware location.
    B. It is dependent on the network type
    C. It is assigned by a vendor
    D. It changes every time the hardware is plugged turned on and off
36. The Basic Rate Interface (BRI) in ISDN has:
    A. One B channel and one D channel
    B. 23 B channels and one D channel
    C. Two B channels and one D channel
    D. Two D channels and one B channel
37. Synchronization of network timing is done at which layer?
    A. Data link layer
    B. Transport layer
    C. Physical layer
    D. Session layer
38. What is a Network Control Protocol (NCP) frame in a Point-to-Point Protocol (PPP) used for?
    A. Establishing and configuring a connection
    B. Encryption of data
    C. Assigning a dynamic address
    D. Selecting and configuring the network layer protocol
39. In a Frame Relay network, which statement is true of Forward Explicit Congestion (FECN) when the network is congested?
    A. It is a bit that is set to "0"
    B. It is a bit that is set to "1"

C. It is sent by DTE to upper protocol layers
D. A and C only
E. B and C only

40. Data Link Connection Identifier (DLCI) in a Frame Relay network identifies what?
A. Data Terminal Equipment (DTE)
B. Data Circuit Termination Equipment (DCE)
C. A connection between two DTEs
D. All of the above

41. How does a Permanent Virtual Circuit (PVC) in a Frame Relay network differ from a Switched Virtual Circuit (SVC)?
A. It is a permanently established link
B. It terminates after the call has ended
C. It has a data transfer phase
D. It has an idle phase

42. The ITU X.25 Standard describes protocol for which layer or layers?
A. physical layer
B. session layer
C. transport layer
D. data link layer
E. network layer
F. A, B and C only
G. A, D and E only
H. A,C and D only

43. X.25 can handle data rates up to:
A. 1024 Kbps
B. 256 Kbps
C. 512 Kbps
D. 768 Kbps

44. Asynchronous Transfer Mode (ATM) is a:
A. Packet-switching technology
B. Frame-switching technology
C. Cell-switching technology
D. Circuit-switching technology

45. How many header formats are there in ATM terminology?
A. 5
B. 4
C. 3
D. 2
E. 1

46. Which of the following uses Internetwork Operating System (IOS)?
A. Bridges
B. DMS-100
C. 4ESS
D. Cisco routers
E. 5ESS

47. How many switching modes are included in Catalyst 1900/2820 switches?
A. 1
B. 2
C. 3
D. 4

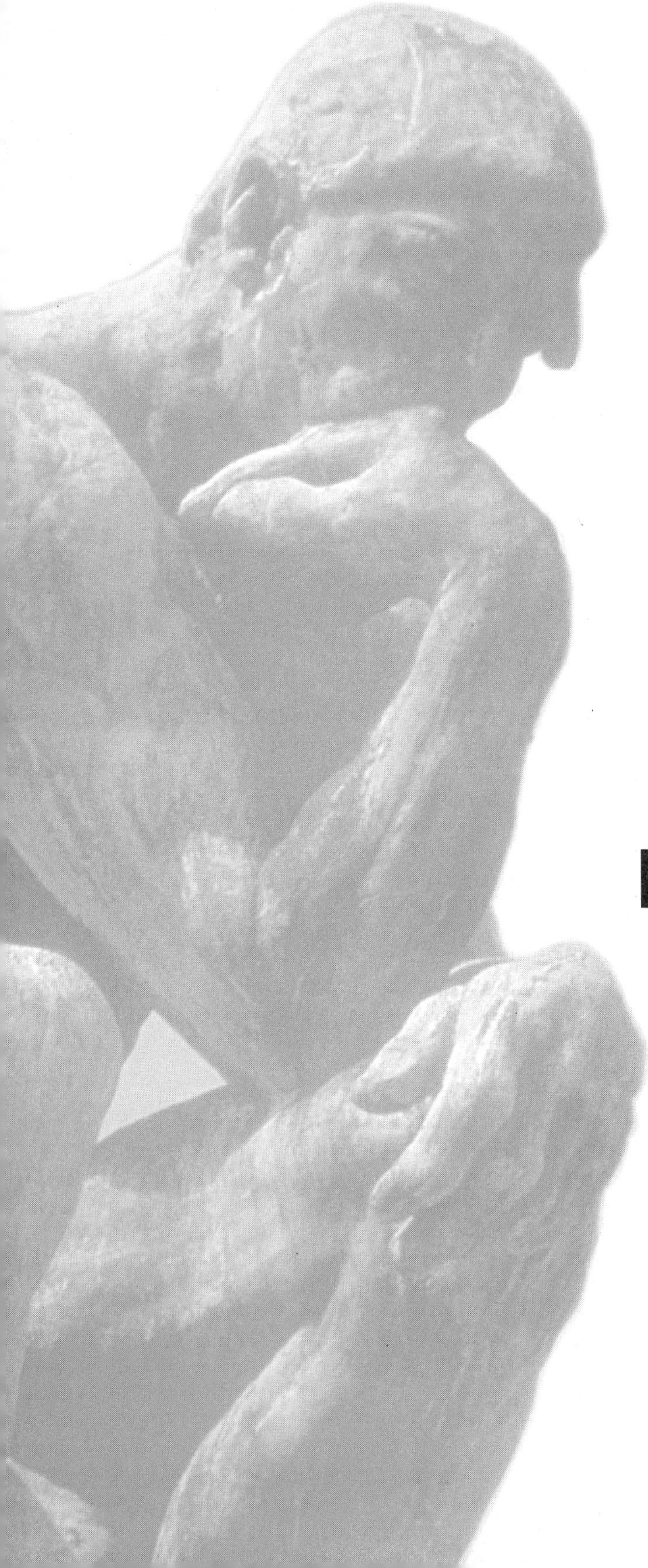

CCNA

CISCO CERTIFIED NETWORK ASSOCIATE

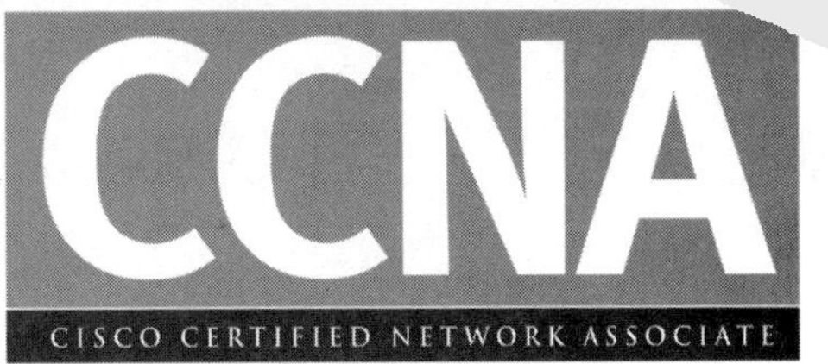

2

Getting Started with Cisco IOS Software

CERTIFICATION OBJECTIVES

2.01 User Interface

2.02 Router Basics

2.03 Initial Configuration

2.04 AutoInstalling Configuration Data

A router needs to be configured in order to operate within your network. Once it is configured, network operators often need to check the status of various router components. In this chapter you will learn about the configurable components of a router and how to use the features of the user interface to configure the router and to verify your configuration. You will also learn how to do some basic network testing using the Cisco IOS diagnostic capabilities, and how to gain remote access to other routers over the network. Finally, you will learn several techniques for manipulating configuration files.

CERTIFICATION OBJECTIVE 2.01

User Interface

The most common way to interact with the router is through the command-line interface provided by the Cisco IOS software. Every Cisco router has a console port that can be directly connected to a PC or terminal so that you can type commands at the keyboard and receive output on a terminal screen. The term "console" refers to this keyboard and screen that are directly attached to the router. The part of the Cisco IOS software that provides the user interface and interprets the commands you type is called the command executive, or EXEC.

This section will teach you how to log into the router, use the features provided by the user interface, and log out of the router again. It will also introduce the two primary modes of interacting with the router: user EXEC mode and privileged EXEC mode.

User and Privileged Modes

If you walk up to a router console that has been idle for some time, you will see a screen displaying the following lines:

```
east con0 is now available
Press RETURN to get started.
```

In order to begin working with the router from the console you will need to log in. If you press ENTER, you will be prompted for a password.

```
User Access Verification
Password:
Router>
```

You will not see the password characters appear on the console screen.

Once you have successfully entered the console password, you will see the prompt "Router>." The router is now waiting for you to type a command at the console keyboard. "Router" is the default hostname for all Cisco routers; the angled bracket following the hostname is a signal to you that you are in user EXEC mode (user mode). This is the lowest level of access to the router, and allows you to examine the status of most of the router's configurable components, see the contents of routing tables, and do basic non-disruptive network troubleshooting. You cannot change the router's configuration in user EXEC mode, nor can you view the contents of the router's configuration files. You should always use this mode for interacting with the router unless you actually need to change your router's configuration, or if you need to do disruptive testing on your network.

The highest level of access to the router is *privileged EXEC mode,* sometimes called enable mode, because the command you use to get into this mode is ENABLE. Here is what you would see at the router console as you enter privileged EXEC mode:

```
Router>enable
Password:
Router#
```

Notice how the prompt changes. You can confirm you are in privileged EXEC mode by the pound sign (#) after the router name. At this level you have full access to the router. In privileged EXEC mode, you have all the commands available for basic troubleshooting and status-checking that you had in user EXEC mode, plus commands that enable you to change the router's configuration, perform testing that could potentially disrupt network traffic, reboot the router, and view the configuration files.

To leave privileged EXEC mode and revert to user EXEC mode, use the command DISABLE.

```
Router#disable
Router>
```

Notice how the prompt changes back to the angled bracket. To log out of the router entirely and end your console session, use the command EXIT or LOGOUT. Once you are logged out of the router, the console screen will once again display the idle console message instructing you to "Press ENTER to get started."

The Command-Line Interface

Let's log back into our router again and learn how to use the context-sensitive Help feature. This is a feature that you will learn to depend on as you work with the command-line interface.

If you want to know all the commands available to you at any time, just enter a question mark (?) at the prompt. Here is a partial listing of commands available in user EXEC mode:

```
router>?
Exec commands:
 access-enable     Create a temporary Access-List entry
 clear             Reset functions
 connect           Open a terminal connection
 disable           Turn off privileged commands
 disconnect        Disconnect an existing network connection
 enable            Turn on privileged commands
 exit              Exit from the EXEC
 help              Description of the interactive help system
 lat               Open a lat connection
 lock              Lock the terminal
 login             Log in as a particular user
 logout            Exit from the EXEC
 mrinfo            Request neighbor and version information
                   from a multicast router
 mstat             Show statistics after multiple multicast
                   traceroutes
 mtrace            Trace reverse multicast path from
                   destination to source
```

```
 name-connection  Name an existing network connection
 pad              Open a X.29 PAD connection
 ping             Send echo messages
 ppp              Start IETF Point-to-Point Protocol (PPP)
 resume           Resume an active network connection
--More--
```

This display goes on for another screen or two. The "More" at the bottom of the display means that you may see the next screen of output by pressing the SPACEBAR, or see one additional line by pressing the ENTER key. Any other keypress will abort the display.

Now let's get into privileged EXEC mode and see how this display differs.

```
Router>enable
Password:
Router#?
Exec commands:
 access-enable    Create a temporary Access-List entry
 access-template  Create a temporary Access-List entry
 bfe              For manual emergency modes setting
 clear            Reset functions
 clock            Manage the system clock
 configure        Enter configuration mode
 connect          Open a terminal connection
 copy             Copy configuration or image data
 debug            Debugging functions (see also 'undebug')
 disable          Turn off privileged commands
 disconnect       Disconnect an existing network connection
 enable           Turn on privileged commands
 erase            Erase flash or configuration memory
 exit             Exit from the EXEC
 help             DEScription of the interactive help system
 lat              Open a lat connection
 lock             Lock the terminal
 login            Log in as a particular user
 logout           Exit from the EXEC
 mbranch          Trace multicast route down tree branch
 mrbranch         Trace reverse multicast route up tree
                  branch
 --More--
```

Many commands you will be using have many parts or *arguments*. The command executive uses a real-time interpreter to execute the commands you type at the console, and it checks the syntax of each one for correctness as you enter it. You can use this syntax checking, along with the context-sensitive Help feature, to learn what information the router expects you to type at any point in any command. Let's look at the example command, CLOCK SET.

```
Router#clk
Translating "clk"...domain server (255.255.255.255) % Name lookup aborted
```

The first thing to notice is that I am in privileged EXEC mode here. You can't set your router's clock from user EXEC mode. I made a mistake in typing the command. If the router sees a word it doesn't recognize as a command, it thinks you are specifying the name of an IP host you want to Telnet to over the network, and tries to resolve the hostname to an IP address. If you don't have a DNS server on your network, this process takes several seconds to time out. If you want to abort the name lookup, as I did here, use the keystrokes CTRL-SHIFT-6.

Now I want to find out which commands begin with "cl." I can do that by typing **cl?**. There is no space between the "l" and the question mark.

```
Router#cl?
clear  clock
```

Now I can use the question mark to find out the arguments I need to use for the CLOCK SET command. Watch the space between the last argument on the line and the question mark.

```
Router#clock ?
set  Set the time and date
Router#clock set ?
hh:mm:ss  Current Time
Router#clock set 17:50:00
% Incomplete command.
Router#clock set 17:50:00 ?
 <1-31>  Day of the month
 MONTH   Month of the year
Router#clock set 17:50:00 1
 % Incomplete command.
Router#clock set 17:50:00 1 ?
```

```
 MONTH  Month of the year
Router#clock set 17:50:00 1 August
 % Incomplete command.
Router#clock set 17:50:00 1 August ?
 <1993-2035>  Year
Router#clock set 17:50:00 1 August 1998
Router#
```

When I get the router prompt back again with no error message I know the command was correct in syntax.

Some of the commands you will type are very long. It is helpful to know some of the keystrokes that are available to you for moving around on the line you are working on. This feature is known as *enhanced editing.* If you are familiar with UNIX, you will recognize these keystrokes as the emacs editing keystrokes.

- CTRL-A go to the beginning of the line
- CTRL-E go to the end of the line
- ESC-B go back, to the beginning of the previous word
- ESC-F go forward, to the beginning of the next word
- CTRL-B go back one character
- CTRL-F go forward one character

If you are using a VT-100 terminal emulation, you may use the LEFT and RIGHT ARROW keys on your keyboard to move along the line. Use the DELETE and BACKSPACE keys to change characters on the line. Once you press the ENTER key, the command will take effect.

Enhanced editing also includes a feature that scrolls long lines to one side if they are longer than the terminal screen width. This is indicated by a $ next to the prompt, like so:

```
Router>$n extra long line to show how it scrolls under the router prompt
```

As soon as the line you are typing exceeds the width of the terminal screen, characters will appear to scroll under the router prompt. Use the CTRL-A keystroke to get back quickly to the beginning of the line.

If you don't want to use the enhanced editing feature, you may turn it off with the command TERMINAL NO EDITING. To enable it again, use the command TERMINAL EDITING.

The router keeps the last ten commands you entered during your console or terminal session in a special memory buffer called the command history. You may recall commands from the command history and re-use them or change them slightly to save yourself some typing. To see all the commands in the buffer, use the SHOW HISTORY command:

```
Router#show history
conf t
  show interfaces serial
  show interfaces
  show run
  clk
  clock set 17:50:00
  clock set 17:50:00 1
  clock set 17:50:00 1 August
  clock set 17:50:00 1 August 1999
  show history
Router#
```

Notice the commands are recalled exactly as they were typed, even if they were incomplete or erroneous.

You can recall the commands to the command line by moving backward and forward within the history buffer. CTRL-P recalls the previous command in the buffer, and CTRL-N recalls the next command in the buffer. If your terminal is using a VT-100 emulation you can use the UP and DOWN ARROW keys to move backward and forward within the buffer. Use the TERMINAL HISTORY SIZE command to change the size of the history buffer. For example, to increase the size of the buffer so it will store 100 lines instead of the default, enter the following:

```
Router#terminal history size 100
Router#
```

CERTIFICATION OBJECTIVE 2.02

Router Basics

A router is a computer, and has hardware elements that are similar to those of other computers. If you buy a PC from the local computer store, it will have:

- a processor (CPU)
- various sorts of memory, which it uses for storing information
- an operating system, which provides functionality
- various ports and interfaces to connect it to peripheral devices or to allow it to communicate with other computers

A router has these same elements. In this section we will learn about the configurable hardware elements of the router, how to configure them, and how to check their status.

Router Elements

Before we power up the router we need to understand some of its components. The hardware components of the router include memory, processor, lines, and interfaces.

The Cisco router uses the following types of memory:

- **Random-access memory (RAM)** Stores the running configuration, or active configuration file, routing and other tables and packet buffers. The Cisco IOS software executes from main memory.
- **Flash memory** Stores the operating system software image, or IOS image.

- **Nonvolatile RAM (NVRAM)** Special memory that does not lose its information when the router is powered off. Stores the system's startup configuration file and the virtual configuration register.
- **Read-only memory (ROM)** The image in ROM is the image the router first uses when it is powered up. This image is usually an older and smaller version of IOS without the features of a full IOS version.

The whole point of a router is to forward packets from one network to another, so it stands to reason that a router's interfaces will be of primary interest to us. Interfaces are those elements that physically connect the router to various types of networks. Some of the most common router interfaces are serial (which generally connect the router to wide-area links) and the LAN interfaces: Ethernet, Token Ring, and FDDI.

The final category of router component is the one that allows us to interact with the router. We have already learned about the console port, which connects the router to a local terminal. The router also has an auxiliary port, which is often used to connect the router to a modem for out-of-band management in case the network connections are down and the console is inaccessible.

Router Modes

The router's command executive has a hierarchy of modes that limit and organize the commands available to you, the user, as you configure the router. You have already learned the primary router modes, user EXEC mode and privileged EXEC mode, which can be used to check the router's operating status and troubleshoot your network. In order to configure the router, however, we need to understand the configuration modes and how to move among them.

You cannot change the router's configuration from user EXEC mode, so if you need to configure the router, you first must enter privileged EXEC mode.

Once you are in privileged EXEC mode, you may enter *global configuration mode.* This is the mode you would use to accomplish such tasks as naming your router, configuring a banner message for users logging into the router, and enabling various routed protocols. Any configuration command that affects the operation of the entire router would be entered in global configuration mode.

Enter global configuration mode by using the command CONFIGURE TERMINAL.

```
Router#configure terminal
Enter configuration commands, one per line. End with CNTL/Z.
Router(config)#hostname MyRouter
MyRouter(config)#
```

Notice how the prompt changes to remind you that you are in global configuration mode, instead of privileged EXEC mode.

To exit global configuration mode and get back to privileged EXEC mode, use the command EXIT or the keystroke CTRL-Z.

The commands take effect immediately when you press the ENTER key, and are placed in the running configuration in RAM, which is controlling operation of the router. You can see in the preceding display that as soon as the HOSTNAME command was entered, the router's prompt changed to reflect the new name.

Most users want to check their running configuration right away to see if the new command is reflected in it properly. If you want to do this, remember that you can't use any SHOW commands in global configuration mode, or in any other configuration mode for that matter. You must first exit back to privileged EXEC mode to use the SHOW commands.

Of course, you will want to configure the specific elements of your router. In order to do this you must first be in global configuration mode. All other configuration modes are entered from global configuration mode. Some of the more frequently used additional configuration modes available, with their special prompts, include:

- **Interface configuration mode** Router(config-if)#
- **Sub-interface configuration mode** Router(config-subif)#
- **Line configuration mode** Router(config-line)#
- **Router configuration mode** Router(config-router)#
- **IPX router configuration mode** Router(config-ipx-router)#

Table 2-1 shows the most commonly used router configuration modes and how to navigate the user interface from one to another.

Examine the Router Status

From time to time, you will be called upon to examine the status of your routers. Whether it is to see if a device is alive on the network, to verify the up/down status of an interface, or determine what is causing the router to go into a slowdown. The commands we use to view the status of router elements and processes are known collectively as SHOW commands.

You will need to know the basic SHOW commands that allow you to view the elements we have just discussed. One of the more commonly used

TABLE 2-1 Common Command Modes

Command Mode	Access Method	Router Prompt	Exit Method
User EXEC	Log in	Router>	Use the LOGOUT command
Privileged EXEC	From user EXEC mode; enter the ENABLE command	Router#	To exit to user EXEC mode, use the DISABLE, EXIT, or LOGOUT command
Global configuration	From the privileged EXEC mode, enter the CONFIGURE TERMINAL command	Router (config)#	To exit to the privileged EXEC mode, use the EXIT or END command. Or press CTRL-Z
Interface configuration	From the global configuration mode, enter the INTERFACE *type number* command, such as INTERFACE ETHERNET 0	Router (config-if)#	To exit to global configuration mode, use the EXIT command. To exit directly to the privileged EXEC mode press CTRL-Z

SHOW commands is the SHOW INTERFACE command. Here is an example of this command and its result:

```
Router1#show interface tokenRing 1
TokenRing1 is up, line protocol is up
 Hardware is TMS380, address is 0000.303a.c2cd (bia 0000.303a.c2cd)
 DEscription: Lab Backbone
 Internet address is 172.16.1.1/26
 MTU 4464 bytes, BW 16000 Kbit, DLY 630 usec, rely 255/255, load 1/255
 Encapsulation SNAP, loopback not set, keepalive set (10 sec)
 ARP type: SNAP, ARP Timeout 04:00:00
 Ring speed: 16 Mbps
 Single ring node, Source Route Transparent Bridge capable
 Source bridging enabled, srn 2699 bn 1 trn 2710 (ring group)
   proxy explorers disabled, spanning explorer enabled, NetBIOS cache disabled
 Group Address: 0x00000000, Functional Address: 0x0880011A
Ethernet Transit OUI: 0x000000
Last input 00:00:00, output 00:00:01, output hang never
Last clearing of "show interface" counters never
Queueing strategy: fifo
Output queue 0/40, 0 drops; input queue 0/75, 0 drops
5 minute input rate 42000 bits/sec, 11 packets/sec
5 minute output rate 1000 bits/sec, 1 packets/sec
9868965 packets input, 3658968237 bytes, 0 no buffer
Received 7911721 broadcasts, 0 runts, 0 giants, 0 throttles
0 input errors, 0 CRC, 0 frame, 0 overrun, 0 ignored, 0 abort
2157045 packets output, 366298970 bytes, 0 underruns
0 output errors, 0 collisions, 0 interface resets
0 output buffer failures, 0 output buffers swapped out
0 transitions
```

The first line of this command is the one most often consulted to determine the status of an interface. There are two parts to this line. The first describes the status of the physical layer components, the second of the data link layer. An interface that is "up, up" is one that is fully operational. "TokenRing1 is up" means that the interface hardware has detected appropriate electrical signaling, or "carrier detect." If there is no carrier signal, the interface will be down, and the line would read, "TokenRing1 is down, line protocol is down."

The second part of this line, "line protocol is up," means that the router is detecting keepalive messages on the ring. It is possible for a carrier signal to be present, but no keepalive messages. In this case the line would read, "TokenRing1 is up, line protocol is up."

If we wanted to turn off processing on this interface without physically connecting it to the network, we could put it in an *administratively down* status. If we had done this, the first line of output would read, "TokenRing1 is administratively down, line protocol is down."

Each type of physical interface, such as Ethernet or serial, has slightly different information in its SHOW INTERFACE display that is specific to that data-link technology.

Other SHOW commands that are useful include:

- **SHOW RUNNING-CONFIG** Displays the router configuration currently running in RAM
- **SHOW STARTUP-CONFIG** Displays the router configuration stored in NVRAM. This is the configuration the router will use when it is powered on, unless specifically configured otherwise.
- **SHOW FLASH** Displays the formatting and contents of Flash memory, including the filename of the IOS image in Flash
- **SHOW BUFFERS** Displays statistics for the buffer pools on the router
- **SHOW MEMORY** Shows statistics about the router's memory, including free pool statistics
- **SHOW PROCESSES CPU** Displays statistics about the active processes, or programs, running in the router
- **SHOW PROTOCOLS** Shows information about all the protocols configured in the router, and information about the network layer addresses configured on each of the interfaces.

- **SHOW STACKS** Displays information about the memory stack utilization of processes and interrupt routines, as well as the reason for the last system reboot
- **SHOW VERSION** Displays the configuration of the system hardware, the software version, the names and sources of configuration files, and the boot images

Cisco Discovery Protocol

Cisco Discovery Protocol (CDP) is one of the best methods of understanding your network topology. CDP is a Layer 2 media- and protocol-independent protocol that runs on all Cisco-manufactured equipment, including routers, switches, and access servers. The devices do not need to have any network layer protocols configured in order to use CDP, although if these addresses are configured, CDP will discover them. Each device configured for CDP sends out periodic messages to a MAC layer multicast address. These advertisements include information about the capabilities and software version of the advertising platform. This gives you an easy way to see other Cisco devices on your network, without having to figure out which devices are Cisco by the vendor code embedded in the Media Access Control (MAC) address. Contents of the CDP table can be viewed with the following commands:

```
ROUTER1#show cdp neighbor
Capability Codes: R - Router, T - Trans Bridge, B - Source Route Bridge
                  S - Switch, H - Host, I - IGMP, r - Repeater
Device ID        Local Intrfce     Holdtme    Capability  Platform  Port ID
ROUTER3            Tok 0            143            R B       RSP4      Tok 0/0/0
ROUTER2            Ser 1            170            R         4700      Ser 1
ROUTER2            Ser 0            170            R         4700      Ser 0
```

This command shows information about Cisco devices locally attached to this device. "Locally attached" indicates that a device is either on the same LAN segment, or connected via a serial interface. Device ID is the hostname of the advertising router. The "local Intrfce" column indicates the interface on the router whose console you are at, and the "Port ID" column indicates the attached interface on the remote router.

CDP multicasts are normally sent every 30 seconds. The default holdtime is 180 seconds. The holdtime figure indicates how long this entry will continue in the router's CDP table if no more advertisements are heard from this neighbor.

```
ROUTER1#show cdp neighbor detail
-------------------------
Device ID: Router4
Entry address(es):
  IP address: 10.1.0.1
  Novell address: 0.0000.b010.0000
  DECnet address: 10.300
Platform: cisco 2509,  Capabilities: Router
Interface: Serial1,  Port ID (outgoing port): Serial0
Holdtime : 169 sec
Version :
Cisco Internetwork Operating System Software
IOS (tm) 2500 Software (C2500-JS40-L), Version 11.2(2), RELEASE SOFTWARE (fc1)
Copyright (c) 1986-1996 by cisco Systems, Inc.
Compiled Wed 13-Nov-96 02:07 by ajchopra
```

This command takes the previous command one step farther. This command will show all network layer addresses of the advertising interface, as well as the IOS version. CDP is an excellent troubleshooting tool to determine neighboring devices that could be causing problems due to misconfigured addresses.

Remote Access to a Router

In a large network with many remote locations it is impossible for a network administrator to gain physical console access to a router each time he needs to check its status or to change its configuration. It makes good sense to use the network itself to provide remote access to the routers in the network whenever possible. This is known as *in-band* management. Most often, the application used for remote access over an IP network is Telnet.

Every Cisco router has the Telnet application included in the IOS. This enables the administrator to establish a Telnet session into the router from any other IP host with Telnet capability, or to Telnet from the router itself to another router or IP host. You can perform most of the same configuration and status-checking functions from a Telnet session that you can perform from the router console.

Telnet sessions to or from the router are also called *virtual terminal* sessions. The router contains five virtual terminal lines (VTY lines) to accept incoming Telnet sessions. A Telnet session may be carried through any of the router's physical interfaces, and attach to any of the router's VTY lines.

In order for a router to accept an incoming Telnet session, at least one of its VTY lines must be configured with a password.

To initiate a Telnet session with a router, you must know an IP address of one of the interfaces in the router, or a symbolic name that can be resolved to an IP address in the router. The network must also be capable of routing the IP packets to that address; that is, the network portion of the address must be known to the routers in the internetwork that are between the host you are initiating the Telnet session from, and the target router.

The user interface presented by the Telnet application is identical to the interface at the router console, and is navigated in the same way.

Once you have established a Telnet session you may terminate it by entering the EXIT or QUIT commands. Sometimes, however, you know you will want to go back to that session, but need to get back to the router you started from for a moment. If you want to suspend your session so you can go back to it within a short period of time, use the keystrokes CTRL-SHIFT-6-X. To get back to the suspended session, just press the ENTER key by itself on a line.

Basic Testing

The Cisco IOS software includes several commands that can be used to test basic connectivity in an IP network.

Ping is a tool that tests connectivity at the network layer only. It operates by sending a series of ICMP echo packets to the destination, and keeping track of the ICMP echo-replies that the destination sends back. You may use ping with its default characteristics (five 100-byte packets, two-second timeout) from user EXEC mode, but if you are in privileged EXEC mode, several other options become available to you. This is known as *extended ping*. Some of the other options available with extended ping include: varying the sizes of the packets, increasing the timeout value, sending more than five packets at one time, setting the "don't fragment" bit in the IP header, and even using ping for other protocols, such as IPX and AppleTalk.

Here is sample output of a default ping. 172.20.2.1 is the IP address of our destination host.

```
Router1# ping 172.20.2.1
Type ESCape sequence to abort.
Sending 5, 100-byte ICMP Echoes to 172.20.2.1, timeout is 2 seconds:
!!!!!
Success rate is 100 percent (5/5), round-trip min/avg/max = 1/15/64 ms
Router1#
```

The series of five exclamation points indicate the response packets received successfully by our router. A dot (period), instead of an exclamation point, indicates the request timed out, either because the ICMP echo request never reached its destination, or because the response was dropped or misrouted somewhere in the network.

Another command that tests network layer connectivity is the TRACEROUTE command. TRACEROUTE provides information about which path your traffic is taking through the internetwork, hop by hop, as well as how long each hop is taking. Here is an example of TRACEROUTE output:

```
Router1>trace 10.30.30.254
Type ESCape sequence to abort.
Tracing the route to 10.30.30.254
  1 10.2.0.2 12 msec 12 msec 12 msec
  2 10.1.0.1 16 msec 12 msec 8 msec
  3 10.3.0.1 60 msec 56 msec *
Router1>
```

Debug

Debug is a tool you can use to get detailed diagnostic information from your router about routing processes and messages the router is receiving, sending, or acting upon. The debug privileged EXEC commands can provide a wealth of information about the traffic being seen (or not seen) on an interface, error messages generated by nodes on the network, protocol-specific diagnostic packets, and other useful troubleshooting data.

Great care should be taken when using the DEBUG command. By issuing a DEBUG command, you are asking the router to not only process traffic as normal, but to report information to the console or VTY session. The amount of processing power consumed by the DEBUG command varies with the quantity of information written to the console screen, which can vary dramatically according to the size and traffic load of the network. Some DEBUG commands generate a single line of output per packet, and others generate multiple lines of output per packet. Some generate large amounts of output, and others generate only occasional output. A DEBUG command that produces a large quantity of output can be very processor intensive, and may occupy so many of the routers processor cycles that it can cause network interruptions or even cause the router's operating system to freeze or crash.

The DEBUG command is issued from privileged EXEC mode and always requires arguments. You should use the context-sensitive Help feature to discover what they are for your particular IOS version and feature set. Always be as specific about the debug output as you can in order to avoid overburdening your router. You want the minimum volume of debug output that will give you the information you are seeking.

If you are using a VTY or Telnet session to the router, you will not see any debug output unless you use the command TERMINAL MONITOR. By default, debug output will only appear on the console screen.

Always remember to use the NO DEBUG or UNDEBUG ALL command to disable the debug output as soon as you are finished. See the following example of a debug output for an IGRP routing update being broadcast on several interfaces:

```
Router# debug ip igrp events
IGRP: sending update to 255.255.255.255 via Ethernet0 (172.16.1.1)
IGRP: Update contains 104 interior, 0 system, and 0 exterior routes.
IGRP: Total routes in update: 104
IGRP: Update contains 62 interior, 42 system, and 0 exterior routes.
IGRP: Total routes in update: 104
IGRP: Update contains 0 interior, 57 system, and 0 exterior routes.
IGRP: Total routes in update: 57
IGRP: sending update to 255.255.255.255 via TokenRing1 (172.17.1.1)
IGRP: Update contains 1 interior, 3 system, and 0 exterior routes.
IGRP: Total routes in update: 4
IGRP: sending update to 255.255.255.255 via TokenRing1 (192.168.23.10)
IGRP: Update contains 0 interior, 0 system, and 0 exterior routes.
IGRP: Total routes in update: 0 - suppressing null update
```

So as you can see, DEBUG can be a very powerful tool to determine problems with your network. But keep in mind that you can cause serious network outages if you are not careful!

Routing Basics

Routers perform two basic functions: path determination and packet forwarding. The basic purpose of a router is to move information from one place to another. No matter what your protocol is—IP, IPX, AppleTalk, DECnet, or Vines—the purpose of the router does not change. It will perform the packet-forwarding function in the same way. When it receives a packet it will consult its routing table for that protocol to find the next-hop address that will get the packet toward its destination, and forward the packet out the interface toward that next hop.

A multiprotocol router maintains a separate routing table for each routed protocol. A routed protocol is a protocol that is used to carry user data, such as IPX or TCP/IP. A routing protocol is used only by the routers to tell each other what networks they know how to reach. A routing protocol is rarely used by host computers on a network. Routing protocols assist in the path-determination function by allowing the router to learn dynamically about the topology of the internetwork.

Path Determination

Routers use routing protocols to build and maintain routing tables and to forward data packets along the best path toward their destination networks. Routing protocols enable routers to learn about the status of networks that are not directly connected to them, and to communicate to other routers about the networks they are aware of. This communication is carried out on a continual basis, so the information in the routing table is updated as changes occur in the internetwork.

Routers that are neighbors on a link need to use the same routing protocol to communicate so that they can learn each other's routes and in turn, communicate them to other neighboring routers. More than one routing protocol can be operational within a single router, although this is a practice you should avoid in designing your network, because it requires extreme care in the configuration.

The characteristics that distinguish one routing protocol from another include:

- The routed protocol for which it maintains information
- The way the routers communicate among each other
- The frequency with which this communication takes place
- The algorithm and metrics used to determine the best path

There are two basic categories of routing protocols: distance vector and link-state.

Routers configured with a distance vector protocol use frequent broadcasts of their entire routing tables on all their interfaces in order to communicate with neighboring routers. The more routes in their routing tables, the more routes that are broadcast. This limits the size of network that can use a distance vector routing protocol efficiently. The *metric* (measure of preferability) of one link or path when compared to another, is usually *hop count*. The hop count increases by one each time a packet must transit a router.

Look at Figure 2-1 to see how distance vector protocols propagate routes through the network and build their routing tables. The routing tables contain: identifiers for the individual networks, an interface within the router through which the router learned about that network, and the number of hops away the network is. C stands for "directly connected."

Notice that it takes two updates for all the routers to contain the same networks in their routing tables. When this has happened, the network is said to have *converged*. The time it takes for convergence to occur after a change in network topology is called *convergence time*.

The advantage of distance vector protocols is their extreme simplicity. Hop count metrics are easy to administer, and the distance vector protocols usually come with very few configurable parameters for tuning purposes.

The disadvantage is that hop count metrics make every link look the same, whether it is a 622-Mbps Sonet ring or a 1.544-Mbps T1 line.

Consider Figure 2-2. If we are using a classic distance vector routing protocol to make our path determination for us, the lower path over the T1 link will look preferable, because it is only one hop. The upper path, even though the bandwidth is about 400 times as high, will not look as good, because it takes two hops to get from Router 1 to Router 2.

FIGURE 2-1 Routing table development in a distancevector environment

How routers learn each others' routes in a distance = vector network

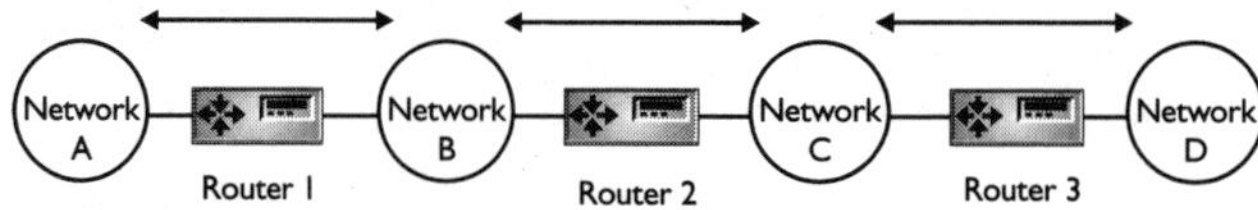

On power up, directly connected networks only are known, and the routing tables look like this:

A Int0 C	B Int0 C	C Int0 C
B Int1 C	C Int1 C	D Int1 C

After one update, networks one hop away are known, and the routing tables look like this:

A Int0 C	B Int0 C	C Int0 C
B Int1 C	C Int1 C	D Int1 C
C Int1 1	A Int0 1	B Int0 1
	D Int1 1	

After two updates, networks two hops away are known, and all routers know about the same routes. The network has converged:

A Int0 C	B Int0 C	C Int0 C
B Int1 C	C Int1 C	D Int1 C
C Int1 1	A Int0 1	B Int0 1
D Int1 2	D Int1 1	A Int0 2

FIGURE 2-2 Different metrics allow for different routing decisions

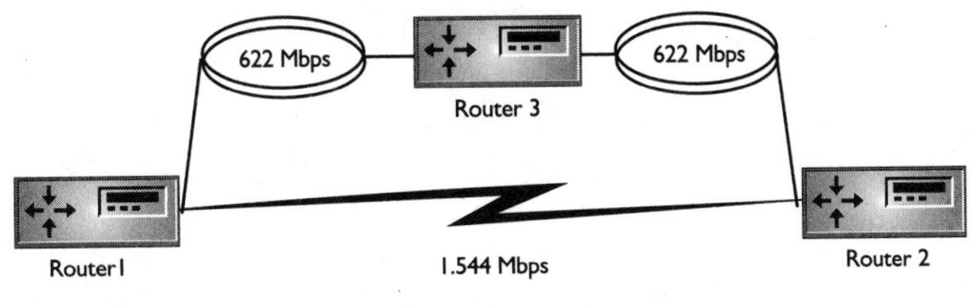

A link-state routing protocol can usually take bandwidth into account, because it uses a cost metric, which is inherently more sophisticated. Most cost metrics are based on factors such as bandwidth or delay. This enables the link-state protocol to make better routing decisions. It is also more efficient in terms of its bandwidth use for updates, because link-state protocols send out their updates only when a change occurs in the network.

Link-state protocols discover their neighboring routers by using a "hello" protocol, and keep track of the updates and hellos received from their neighbors. Link-state updates are usually acknowledged, so there is no need for sending out the same information again.

Convergence usually happens quickly in a link-state network, because updates are flooded immediately through the network, and are sourced by the router directly connected to the link that has changed. There is no need for each router to wait for a periodic update to transmit the new information to its neighbor.

Forwarding

This process is basically the same for all protocols. In most cases, a host device (PC or server) determines that it must send a packet to another host. Having acquired a gateway router's address by some means, the source host sends a packet addressed specifically to a router's physical MAC layer address, but with the protocol (network layer) address of the destination host.

On examining the packet's destination protocol address (as you recall, Layer 3) the router determines that it either knows or does not know how to forward the packet to the next hop. If the router does not know how to forward the packet, it will drop the packet. If the router knows how to forward the packet, it changes the destination physical address to that of the next hop, and transmits the packet.

The next hop may or may not be the ultimate destination host. If not, the next hop is usually another router, which executes the same switching decision process. As the packet moves through the internetwork, its physical address changes but its protocol address remains constant

Once a packet is routed to the destination, it must be placed on the LAN segment for which it was intended. The router will at that point repeat the same process as the host did before the packet was sent. The router will determine the destination host's MAC layer address. The router will then place that host's MAC address on the packet and forward it.

The key is that no matter what your routed protocol is, or what your routing protocol is, the routers each make independent forwarding decisions based on the routing information stored in their routing tables. The routers forward packets on a hop-by-hop basis, one step at a time.

CERTIFICATION OBJECTIVE 2.03

Initial Configuration

When you power up your router, it first needs to test its hardware, including memory and interfaces. The next step in the sequence is to find and load an IOS image—the operating system for the router. Finally, before the router can function properly in your network, it needs to find its configuration information and apply it.

If you are at the router console when it is powered on you should see something similar to the following:

```
System Bootstrap, Version 5.1(1) [daveu 1], RELEASE SOFTWARE (fc1)
Copyright (c) 1994 by cisco Systems, Inc.
C4500 processor with 32768 Kbytes of main memory
```

At this point the router has loaded the bootstrap program from ROM. Next, it will load its IOS image from Flash. It first verifies the file integrity, then decompresses the image as it loads into RAM. These processes are represented by "Rs" and "#s".

```
Booting yj11120n from flash memory RRRRRRRRRRRRRRRRRRRRRRRRRRRRRRRRRRRRRRR
RRRRRRRRRRRRRRRRRRRRRRRRRRRRRRRRRRRRRRRRRRRRRRRRRRRRRRRRRRRRRRRRRRRRRRRRRRRRRRRR
RRRRRRRRRRRRRRRRRRRRRRRRRRRRRRRRRRRRRRRRRRRRRRRRRRRRRRRRRRRRRRRRRRRRRRRRRRRRRRRR
RRRRRRRRRRRRRRRRRRRRRRRRRRRRRRRRRRRRRRRRRRRR
[OK - 1337256/3532618 bytes]
################################################################################
################################################################################
################################################################################
#########################################
F3: 1926336+46904+183152 at 0x12000
```

Next we see some copyright notices and other information about the software and its features.

```
Restricted Rights Legend
Use, duplication, or disclosure by the Government is
subject to restrictions as set forth in subparagraph
(c) of the Commercial Computer Software - Restricted
Rights clause at FAR sec. 52.227-19 and subparagraph
(c) (1) (ii) of the Rights in Technical Data and Computer
Software clause at DFARS sec. 252.227-7013.
cisco Systems, Inc.
170 West Tasman Drive
San Jose, California 94134-1706
Cisco Internetwork Operating System Software
IOS (tm) 4500 Software (C4500-AJ-M), Version 11.1(2)
Copyright (c) 1986-1996 by cisco Systems, Inc.
Compiled Mon 24-May-96 22:46 [mikehub 107]
cisco 4500 (R4K) processor (revision 0x00) with 32768K/4096K bytes of memory.
Processor ID 01242622
R4600 processor, Implementation 32, Revision 1.0
```

FROM THE CLASSROOM

A Perspective on Passwords

It is easy for students to be confused about how passwords are used in the Cisco routers, and what the implications are for setting or not setting them.

Your router needs at least four passwords set for minimal security: an enable password, a console password, an auxiliary line password, and a VTY password. Unless you have configured the router to refer to a separate authentication server for this function, passwords are stored in the router's configuration file. They can be encrypted or stored in clear text, depending on your security environment.

The primary password for router security is the enable password. This password controls access to privileged mode in your router, which allows the user to make configuration changes and do testing that could potentially disrupt network operations. By default, the enable password is not encrypted as it is stored in the configuration file.

You may have noticed during the section on the setup dialog that you are prompted for an "enable secret." The enable secret, if you have set one, overrides the enable password, and is always stored encrypted in the router's configuration. So if you have set an enable secret, the enable password will not be used unless your router boots from an old software version (possibly stored in ROM or on a network TFTP server) that does not recognize the enable secret. It is considered a bad idea to set the enable password the same as the enable secret. This eliminates the very security benefit the enable secret is designed to provide.

By default, the router requires that passwords be set on the VTY lines in order to use them for incoming Telnet sessions. If you don't set a password on your VTY lines and try to Telnet into the router, you will get an error message, "password required but none set." If you need those Telnet sessions for remote management, be sure to set a VTY password! If you are working in a lab environment and don't want to type in a password each time you Telnet to a router, remove the "login" command under the VTY line configuration. This will eliminate the requirement for this password.

The default router configuration does not require passwords on the auxiliary or console lines. If you want to require passwords on these lines, you must not only set a password on them but also configure a "login" command on them. Without the "login" command, the password prompt will not appear and your password will be ignored.

FROM THE CLASSROOM

In a lab or classroom environment you may choose not to set an enable password (or enable secret), but that isn't a good idea. If you don't set an enable password (or enable secret), the only connection from which you can get into privileged mode will be the console. That means that if you try to connect through the aux port or through a Telnet session, you won't have any access to privileged mode if you haven't set that enable password. There are situations in which you can be essentially locked out of the router without this password set—it has happened to me.

Cisco offers an encryption service for those passwords that normally would appear in clear text in the configuration file (not the enable secret). You can turn this on at the console by using the command, SERVICE PASSWORD-ENCRYPTION. Once you enter this command, each password you configure will be stored in encrypted form and cannot be recovered without a password-cracking program. This is useful if your configuration files are stored on a TFTP server; it will prevent a casual observer from determining your router passwords. It is not considered to be strong encryption, however, and will not discourage a determined hacker who wishes to break into your network.

Cisco uses the MD5 algorithm to encrypt the enable secret. There is no known way to reverse this algorithm. If you use the enable secret you will not be able to use the normal techniques for password recovery, which depend on viewing the password in clear text within the startup configuration file. You will need to reset the password, because there is no way to recover it.

—By Pamela Forsyth, CCIE, CCSI, CNX

```
G.703/E1 software, Version 1.0
Bridging software.
SuperLAT software (copyright 1990 by Meridian Technology Corp).
X.25 software, Version 2.0, NET2, BFE and GOSIP compliant.
TN3270 Emulation software (copyright 1994 by TGV Inc.).
```

Next, the router inventories and tests its interfaces. Because most of the Cisco routers come in a variety of hardware configurations, the software must be able to detect what particular interfaces are present in the router when it powers up.

```
2 Ethernet/IEEE 802.3 interfaces.
2 Token Ring/IEEE 802.5 interfaces.
4 ISDN Basic Rate interfaces.
2 Serial network interfaces.
128K bytes of non-volatile configuration memory.
8192K bytes of processor board System Flash (Read/Write)
4096K bytes of processor board Boot Flash (Read/Write)
Notice: NVRAM invalid, possibly due to write erase.
--- System Configuration Dialog ---
At any point you may enter a question mark '?' for help.
Refer to the 'Getting Started' Guide for additional help.
Use CTRL-C to abort configuration dialog at any prompt.
Default settings are in square brackets '[]'.
Would you like to enter the initial configuration dialog? [yes]:
```

If the router does not find a configuration file in NVRAM and is not configured to look for one on the network, it will begin the setup dialog. The nice thing is that this is menu driven; all you have to do is answer the questions. When you are asked, "Would you like to enter the initial configuration dialog?", if you answer **no** you will enter the normal operating mode. A **yes** answer will take you through the menu.

The setup dialog allows you to get your router running with a very basic configuration. It will allow you to name your router, set an enable password and enable secret, enable any of the network layer protocols and assign appropriate addresses to router interfaces, and enable dynamic routing protocols. You will want to check the configuration file produced by this process in order to refine the configuration.

Virtual Configuration Register Settings

Every Cisco router has a 16-bit configuration register, which is stored in a special memory location in NVRAM. This register controls a number of functions, some of which are listed below:

- Force the system into the bootstrap program

- Select a boot source and default boot filename
- Enable or disable the console Break function
- Set the console terminal baud rate
- Load operating software from ROM
- Enable booting from a TFTP server

The configuration register boot field is the portion of the configuration register that determines whether the router loads an IOS image, and if so, where to get this image from. The least significant four bits, bits 0 through 3, of the configuration register make up the boot field.

If the boot field value is 0x0 (all four bits set to zeros), the router will enter ROM monitor mode.

If the boot field value is 0x1 (binary 0001), the router will boot from the image in ROM.

If the boot field value is 0x2 through 0xF (binary 0010 through 1111) the router will follow the normal boot sequence, and will look for boot system commands in the configuration file in NVRAM.

Enter the SHOW VERSION EXEC command to display the configuration register value currently in effect, and the value that will be used at the next reload. The value will be displayed on the last line of the screen display as in the following example:

```
ROUTER1#show version
Cisco Internetwork Operating System Software
IOS (tm) 4500 Software (C4500-JS-M), Version 11.2(7a)P, SHARED PLATFORM, RELEASE
SOFTWARE (fc1)
Copyright (c) 1986-1997 by cisco Systems, Inc.
Compiled Wed 02-Jul-97 05:32 by ccai
Image text-base: 0x60008900, data-base: 0x60820000
ROM: System Bootstrap, Version 5.3(16) [richardd 16], RELEASE SOFTWARE (fc1)
BOOTFLASH: 4500 Software (C4500-BOOT-M), Version 11.1(7), RELEASE SOFTWARE (fc2)
ROUTER1 uptime is 12 weeks, 6 days, 10 hours, 30 minutes
System restarted by power-on at 01:09:36 Central Sun Apr 5 1998
System image file is "flash:c4500-js-mz.112-7a.P", booted via flash
```

```
Network configuration file is "pcmdiAAAa006h_162", booted via tftp from 172.16.1.1
cisco 4700 (R4K) processor (revision F) with 32768K/4096K bytes of memory.
Processor board ID 06755819
R4700 processor, Implementation 33, Revision 1.0 (512KB Level 2 Cache)
G.703/E1 software, Version 1.0.
Bridging software.
SuperLAT software copyright 1990 by Meridian Technology Corp).
X.25 software, Version 2.0, NET2, BFE and GOSIP compliant.
TN3270 Emulation software.
2 Token Ring/IEEE 802.5 interface(s)
4 Serial network interface(s)
128K bytes of non-volatile configuration memory.
8192K bytes of processor board System flash (Read/Write)
4096K bytes of processor board Boot flash (Read/Write)
Configuration register is 0x142 (will be 0x102 at next reload)
```

Startup Sequence — Boot System Commands

You can place special commands in the router's configuration file that will instruct it where to look for its IOS image. The router will scan these entries and try to execute them in sequence when it boots up. This provides you with several fallback options in case the router's flash memory becomes corrupted. These are called boot system commands.

Usually you will want the router to boot from flash memory. The boot system command for this is

```
Router1(config)# boot system flash
```

If you do not specify a filename, the router loads the first valid file it finds in flash memory.

In most cases you will want the router to find a backup IOS image on a TFTP server somewhere in your network if it cannot find and load an image from Flash memory. The command to designate this is:

```
Router1(config)# boot system tftp 172.16.1.150
```

You may wish to have more than one TFTP server on your network that stores your backup IOS images. You may have as many "boot system TFTP" commands as you like in your router configuration for redundancy.

```
Router1(config)# boot system rom
```

This command boots the router from ROM. This is a last resort, just to get the router running so you can diagnose the problem. The system image in ROM will not have as many features and capabilities as the full IOS version in Flash, so your router may not operate in a predictable way if it boots from ROM.

Be very careful of the order in which these commands are entered into the router. For best results you will need to enter THE BOOT SYSTEM FLASH prior to the BOOT SYSTEM ROM. If the ROM command is entered prior to the FLASH command; the router will reload IOS from ROM and not from Flash. That boot system ROM command is very useful to ensure that if the Flash image is corrupted in any way, the router will come back online—in a limited mode, but back online to allow you to download another IOS image.

Configuring to/from a TFTP Server

The router also has the capability to copy its configuration to and from a TFTP server. This gives the network administrator the ability to store configurations out to a server for configuration tracking, change auditing, or distress recovery. You will need to store your configuration on a TFTP server if it is larger than 32,000 bytes, which is the largest configuration that can fit into NVRAM. When you TFTP a configuration to the router, you can place it in Flash, NVRAM, or RAM memory. When you place the configuration into Flash, you will still need to place it into NVRAM or RAM in order for the router to be able to use it. The COPY TFTP commands can be done via either the console or a VTY session.

The commands for copying configuration files to and from TFTP servers are as follows:

- **COPY TFTP RUNNING-CONFIG** Configures the router directly from the TFTP server by copying into the configuration in RAM
- **COPY TFTP STARTUP-CONFIG** Overwrites the configuration file stored in NVRAM with the file from the TFTP server
- **COPY RUNNING-CONFIG TFTP** Makes a copy of the router's running configuration in RAM on the TFTP server
- **COPY STARTUP-CONFIG TFTP** Copies the configuration stored in NVRAM to the TFTP server

Before you try to TFTP your configuration, be sure to verify that you can reach your TFTP server. It's not going to do you much good to try and TFTP a file to or from server that is offline. The PING command is useful for verifying that your TFTP server can communicate with your router.

If the ping fails, verify that you have the correct IP address for the server and that the server is active (powered on), and repeat the PING command. Always remember to back up your work! Prior to downloading a new IOS or configuration file, copy the existing one in the router to the TFTP server. It is also a good idea to go to the TFTP server (or Telnet to it) and verify the exact filename as it exists on the server.

You may also change or upgrade your router's IOS image by copying a new file from a TFTP server, or back up your router's current image by copying it to a TFTP server. The following output shows the process of copying an IOS image from the router's Flash memory to a TFTP server.

```
Router1# copy flash tftp c4500-js-mz.111-17a.P
IP address of remote host [255.255.255.255]? 172.20.2.1
Name of file to copy []? c4500-js-mz.111-17a.P
writing c4500-js-mz.111-17a.P
!!!!!!!!!!!!!!!!!!!!!!!!!!!!!!!!!!!!!!!!!!!!!!!!!!!!
Router1#
```

You may also copy an IOS image from a TFTP server into the router's flash memory. This is accomplished by the command COPY TFTP FLASH.

```
Router1(config)#copy tftp flash
File name/status c4500-js-mz.111-17a.P
 [123816/2097152 bytes free/total
IP address or name of remote host [255.255.255.255]? 172.20.2.1
Name of file to copy ? c4500-js-mz.112-7a.P
Copy c4500-js-mz.112-7a.P from 172.20.2.1 into Flash address space ?
[confirm]<Return>
123752 bytes available for writing without erasure.
Erase Flash address space before writing? [confirm] <Return>
bank 0...zzzzzzzzzzzzzzzzvvvvvvvvvvvvvvvvveeeeeeeeeeeeeeee
bank 1...zzzzzzzzzzzzzzzzvvvvvvvvvvvvvvvvveeeeeeeeeeeeeeee
Loading from 172.20.2.1: !!!!!!!!!!!!!!!!!!!!!!!!!!!!!!!!!!!!!!!!!!!!!!!!!!!
!!!!!!!!!!!!!!!!!!!!!!!!!!!!!!!!!!!!!!!!!!!!!!!!!!!!!!!!!!!!!!!!!!!!!!!!!!!!!!!
!!!!!!!!!!!!!!!!!!!!!!!!!!!!!!!!!!!!!!!!!!!!!!!!!!!!!!!!!!!!!!!!!!!!!!!!!!!!!!!
!!!!!!!!!!!!!!!!!!!!!!!!!!!!!!!!!!!!!!!!!!!!!!!! [OK - 1337256/2097088 bytes]
Verify checksum...vvvvvvvvvvvvvvvvvvvvVerification successful:
 Length = 1337256, checksum = 0x5A1C
```

You are prompted for the filename of the image you want to copy. This name is case sensitive, so it pays to verify the exact name on the TFTP server. You will then be prompted for the IP address of the TFTP server. The router will verify the amount of free space in Flash memory, and will ask you if you want to erase the existing file in flash before copying the new one. Once Flash is erased, the router will load the new file from the TFTP server. Each exclamation point in the display signifies a block of the file successfully loaded. Finally the router will verify the integrity of the complete file.

Caution: do not make any typographical errors using the COPY TFTP FLASH command when you specify the filename of the system software image you are copying. If you type a filename that does not exist when using the COPY TFTP FLASH command, then tell the system to erase the current image, the router erases the existing image in Flash memory. If this happens, the router still has a working image in RAM, so your router will still function. If you think you have tried to load a nonexistent file, do not reboot the router! If you do, your router will not have a functional image in Flash memory. To recover from the accidental Flash memory erasure, execute the COPY TFTP FLASH command again to load the appropriate image into Flash memory.

CERTIFICATION OBJECTIVE 2.04

AutoInstalling Configuration Data

The AutoInstall process is designed to configure the router automatically after connection to your wide-area network (WAN). For AutoInstall to work properly, a Transmission Control Protocol/Internet Protocol (TCP/IP) host on your network must be running as a TFTP server, and preconfigured to provide the required configuration files. The TCP/IP host can exist anywhere on the network, as long as the following two conditions are maintained:

- The host must be on the remote side of the router's synchronous serial connection to the WAN.
- User Datagram Protocol (UDP) broadcasts to and from the router and the TCP/IP host must be enabled.

Your system administrator at the site where the TCP/IP host is located coordinates this functionality. You should not attempt to use AutoInstall unless the required files have been provided on the TCP/IP host. See the appropriate software configuration publications for information on how AutoInstall works.

Use the following procedure to prepare your router for the AutoInstall process:

1. Attach the appropriate synchronous serial cable to a synchronous serial interface on the router.
2. Turn on power to the router.

The router will load the operating system image from Flash memory. If the remote end of the WAN connection is connected and properly configured, the AutoInstall process will begin.

If the AutoInstall process completes successfully, you might want to write the configuration data to the router's NVRAM. Perform the following step to complete this task:

3. At the # prompt, enter the COPY RUNNING-CONFIG STARTUP-CONFIG command if you are running Cisco IOS Release 11.0 or later, or the WRITE MEMORY command if you are running a Cisco IOS release earlier than 11.0:

    Hostname# copy running-config startup-config

Taking this step saves the configuration settings that the AutoInstall process created in the router. If you fail to do this, your configuration will be lost the next time you reload the router.

CERTIFICATION SUMMARY

The Cisco router's user interface is a command-line interface. Router modes limit and organize the commands that are available to the user. The lowest level of access to the router is user EXEC mode, in which the user can verify router status and perform basic troubleshooting. The highest level of access is privileged EXEC mode, in which the user can change the router's configuration and perform extensive network testing and diagnostics. The command to enter privileged EXEC mode is ENABLE. Context-sensitive Help and advanced editing features facilitate configuration and verification tasks.

The router's configurable elements include memory (RAM, ROM, Flash, and NVRAM), interfaces for connecting to networks, and ports for user access and configuration. SHOW commands allow the user to verify the status or view the contents of these elements in an operational router.

Router modes allowing for configuration changes include global configuration mode, interface configuration mode, line configuration mode, and router configuration mode.

Cisco Discovery Protocol (CDP) allows Cisco devices to discover each other in the network regardless of whether they have network layer protocols configured. Telnet can be used to gain remote access to routers over the network. Ping and traceroute are useful to test network layer connectivity. Debug allows the user to get detailed information about almost every aspect of the router's operation, although it must be used with great care to prevent overburdening the router.

Dynamic routing protocols can be categorized as either distance vector or link-state. Distance vector routers broadcast their entire routing tables periodically to each other. Link-state routers keep track of their neighbors, and flood updates through the network only when changes occur. Convergence is a state in which all routers in the network have a consistent view of the network topology.

When a router first powers up, it tests its hardware, locates and loads an IOS image, and applies configuration information. The startup sequence is controlled by the lowest four bits in the configuration register—the boot field. The boot field is used in conjunction with boot system commands in the configuration file to tell the router where to find its configuration information and its IOS image.

If a router does not find a valid configuration file when it boots up, it will enter the setup dialog. The setup dialog can be used to create a basic configuration for your router.

In a WAN environment, a new router can get its configuration information automatically from a TFTP server on the network. This facilitates configuration of routers at remote sites.

TWO-MINUTE DRILL

- The most common way to interact with the router is through the command-line interface provided by the Cisco IOS software.
- In order to begin working with the router from the console you will need to log in.
- The highest level of access to the router is *privileged EXEC mode,* sometimes called enable mode, because the command you use to get into this mode is ENABLE.
- To leave privileged EXEC mode and revert to user EXEC mode, use the command DISABLE.

- ❑ To log out of the router entirely and end your console session, use the command EXIT or LOGOUT.
- ❑ If you want to know all the commands available to you at any time, just enter a question mark (?) at the prompt.
- ❑ Many commands you will be using have many parts or *arguments*.
- ❑ The hardware components of the router include memory, processor, lines, and interfaces.
- ❑ The whole point of a router is to forward packets from one network to another.
- ❑ Some of the most common router interfaces are serial (which generally connect the router to wide-area links) and the LAN interfaces: Ethernet, Token Ring, and FDDI.
- ❑ The router's command executive has a hierarchy of modes that limit and organize the commands available to you, the user, as you configure the router.
- ❑ Once you are in privileged EXEC mode, you may enter *global configuration mode.*
- ❑ The commands we use to view the status of router elements and processes are known collectively as SHOW commands.
- ❑ Each type of physical interface, such as Ethernet or serial, has slightly different information in its SHOW INTERFACE display that is specific to that data-link technology.
- ❑ Cisco Discovery Protocol (CDP) is one of the best methods of understanding your network topology. CDP is a Layer 2 media- and protocol-independent protocol that runs on all Cisco-manufactured equipment, including routers, switches, and access servers.
- ❑ In a large network with many remote locations it is impossible for a network administrator to gain physical console access to a router each time he needs to check its status or to change its configuration. This is known as *in-band* management.
- ❑ Every Cisco router has the Telnet application included in the IOS.
- ❑ In order for a router to accept an incoming Telnet session, at least one of its VTY lines must be configured with a password.

- The Cisco IOS software includes several commands that can be used to test basic connectivity in an IP network.
- *Ping* is a tool that tests connectivity at the network layer only.
- TRACEROUTE provides information about which path your traffic is taking through the internetwork, hop by hop, as well as how long each hop is taking.
- Debug is a tool you can use to get detailed diagnostic information from your router about routing processes and messages the router is receiving, sending, or acting upon.
- Routers perform two basic functions: path determination and packet forwarding.
- When you power up your router, it first needs to test its hardware, including memory and interfaces.
- Every Cisco router has a 16-bit configuration register, which is stored in a special memory location in NVRAM.
- You can place special commands in the router's configuration file that will instruct it where to look for its IOS image.
- The router also has the capability to copy its configuration to and from a TFTP server.
- The AutoInstall process is designed to configure the router automatically after connection to your wide-area network (WAN).

SELF TEST

The following Self Test questions will help you measure your understanding of the material presented in this chapter. Read all the choices carefully, as there may be more than one correct answer. Choose all correct answers for each question.

1. What command would you use to log out of the router and end your session? (Select two.)
   - A. TERMINATE
   - B. logout
   - C. exit
   - D. session end
2. If you type a command that the router doesn't recognize, what will the router do?
   - A. Display an error message
   - B. Try to resolve the command to an IP address
   - C. Try to execute the closest command it can find in its command set
   - D. Invalidate the configuration
3. You can confirm that you are in the privileged EXEC mode by which prompt?
   - A. Router>
   - B. Router(config)#
   - C. Router#
   - D. Router(config-if)#
4. A reload of the router is required to get the configuration changes to take place.
   - A. True
   - B. False
5. By default, how many commands are stored in the command history buffer?
   - A. 5
   - B. 10
   - C. 15
   - D. 20
6. The IOS image is normally stored in?
   - A. RAM
   - B. NVRAM
   - C. Shared
   - D. Flash
7. The startup configuration file is stored in NVRAM.
   - A. True
   - B. False
8. To determine the operational status of an interface, which command do you use?
   - A. DISPLAY INTERFACE STATUS
   - B. show interface
   - C. show status interface
   - D. display interface
9. The boot field consists of:
   - A. The lowest four bits of the configuration register
   - B. The same as the configuration register

C. The highest four bits of the configuration register
D. Bits 4 through 7 of the configuration register

10. A boot field value of 0x1 will cause the router to:

A. Boot from Flash
B. Look for boot system commands in the startup configuration
C. Look for an IOS image on a TFTP server
D. Boot from ROM

11. To view the configuration register settings, which command do you enter?

A. SHOW RUNNING-CONFIGURATION
B. show startup-configuration
C. show version
D. show controllers

12. What command is required to send Debug output to a VTY session?

A. SHOW DEBUG
B. show log
C. terminal monitor
D. debug all

13. Which keystroke would you use to recall the previous command in the command history buffer?

A. CTRL-N
B. CTRL-P
C. ESC-P
D. ESC-F

14. You must have an IP address assigned to an interface in order for CDP to operate.

A. True
B. False

15. What is the command to view the stored configuration in NVRAM?

A. SHOW RUNNING-CONFIG
B. show startup-config
C. show version
D. show NVRAM

16. When do configuration commands take effect?

A. When you reload the router
B. When they are saved in NVRAM
C. As soon as you press the ENTER key
D. When you enter the command ENABLE

17. What command is needed to see if an interface is up and operational?

A. SHOW CONTROLLERS
B. show running-config
C. show interface
D. show buffers

18. What is the best command to enter to determine which release of IOS the router is running?

A. SHOW FLASH
B. show running-config
C. show startup-config
D. show version

19. What is the command needed to copy the current operational configuration to a TFTP server?

    A. COPY RUNNING-CONFIG TFTP
    B. copy startup-config tftp
    C. copy tftp running-config
    D. copy tftp startup-config

20. What command would you use to see information about all the protocols enabled in the router?

    A. DISPLAY PROTOCOL INFORMATION
    B. display protocols
    C. show protocol route
    D. show protocols

21. What is the part of the IOS software that provides the user interface and interprets the commands you type?

    A. The virtual terminal
    B. The command executive
    C. The console port
    D. The configuration register

22. What command allows you to view the configuration in RAM?

    A. SHOW STARTUP-CONFIG
    B. show RAM-config
    C. show running-config
    D. show config

23. Which of the following represents access via a physical connection of a terminal to a router?

    A. Virtual terminal
    B. IOS
    C. Console
    D. All of the above

24. What command would you use to view the name of the filename in Flash memory?

    A. SHOW MEMORY ALL
    B. show flash
    C. show filename
    D. show flash partitions

25. What is the level of access to the router in which you are allowed to change the router's configuration?

    A. User EXEC mode
    B. High-level access mode
    C. Privileged EXEC mode
    D. Console mode

26. Changes to the router configuration are allowed from the user EXEC mode.

    A. True
    B. False

27. How can you confirm you are in privileged EXEC mode?

    A. By issuing the command CONFIRM MODE
    B. By viewing the output of the SHOW VERSION command
    C. By noting the router's prompt
    D. None of the above

28. After giving the command INTERFACE ETHERNET0 from global configuration mode, the router is most likely to respond with:

    A. router(config)#
    B. router#interface
    C. router(config-if)#
    D. router#(config-int)

29. To completely get out of the interface configuration mode and back to privileged EXEC mode, what should you use?

    A. CTRL-Z
    B. EXIT
    C. END CONFIG
    D. LOGOUT

30. The response to the command ROUTER# CONFIGURE ? will be:

    A. Connect, copy, configure
    B. Various paths from source to destination
    C. router(config)#
    D. A list of possible options from where the router can be configured

31. Which are the types of memory elements in a Cisco router?

    A. RAM, ROM, NVRAM, and Boot
    B. RAM, ROM, NVRAM, and Flash
    C. Config, RAM, ROM, NVRAM, and Flash
    D. Buffers, RAM, NVRAM, and Flash

32. How do you suspend a Telnet session?

    A. Use the command SUSPEND SESSION
    B. Use the keystrokes CTRL-ALT-6
    C. Use the keystrokes CTRL-SHIFT-6-X
    D. A Telnet session cannot be suspended. You must quit the session and initiate it again if you want to go back to it.

33. What is the characteristic of a link-state routing protocol that enables it to make better routing decisions?

    A. Its metrics take bandwidth into account
    B. It uses a hello protocol
    C. It broadcasts the contents of its routing table periodically to its neighbors
    D. None of the above.

34. What is the sequence of events that occurs when you power up your router?

    A. Find configuration file, load IOS image, test hardware
    B. Load IOS image, test hardware, find configuration file
    C. Test hardware, find configuration file, load IOS image
    D. Test hardware, load IOS image, find configuration file

35. The size of the configuration register is:

    A. 16 bits
    B. 12 bits
    C. 8 bits
    D. 4 bits

36. It is recommended that in order to obtain best results, BOOT SYSTEM FLASH command be entered after the BOOT SYSTEM ROM command.

    A. True

    B. False

37. The command routerx(config)#boot system tftp 189.12.3.172
will boot the router from:

    A. System image in Flash

    B. System image 189.12.3.172 from RAM

    C. System image 189.12.3.172 from TFTP

    D. System image from TFTP

38. A good connection is indicated by which of the following in an output display of the PING command?

    A. !!!!!

    B. .....

    C. xxxxx

    D. ******

39. If a mistake is made in specifying the file name in the COPY TFTP FLASH command, the router will still function because:

    A. It still has working image in ROM

    B. It still has working image in RAM

    C. It still has working image in Flash

    D. It still has working image in TFTP

40. The command COPY FLASH TFTP FILE2600 copies:

    A. Contents of file from Flash into file2600 of the TFTP server

    B. Contents of TFTP into file2600 in the Flash

    C. Contents of file2600 in the TFTP to file2600 in the Flash

    D. Contents of file2600 in the TFTP into Flash

41. What command can be used to see the router's neighbors from your local router if no network layer protocols are configured?

    A. SHOW CDP

    B. show cdp neighbor

    C. show neighbor

    D. show network

42. In order to show the neighbor's IOS version, what optional parameter can be used in the command SHOW CDP NEIGHBOR?

    A. VERSION

    B. IOS

    C. detail

    D. None of the above

43. In a Cisco router, configuration register information can be used to:

    A. Select a boot source and default file name

    B. Enable booting from a TFTP server

    C. Load operating software from ROM

    D. All of the above

3

IP Addressing

CERTIFICATION OBJECTIVES

- 3.01 Classes of IP Addresses
- 3.02 Subnetting and Subnet Masks
- 3.03 Subnet Planning
- 3.04 Complex Subnetting
- 3.05 Configuring IP Addresses with Cisco IOS

The specifications for the Internet Protocol (IP) were established by RFC 791 in 1982. Part of these specifications outlined a structure for IP addresses. This structure provides for a 32-bit logical address for each host and router interface. An IP address is expressed as four decimal values in the range of 0-255, separated by periods. These decimal values each represent 8 bits of the 32-bit address, known as an *octet*. This is called *dotted decimal* notation. An example of this would be 155.127.23.12.

The IP protocol is used for end-to-end routing of data across a network, which may mean that an IP packet must travel across multiple networks, and may cross several router interfaces to get to its destination. At the IP level, the destination IP address remains the same, but since each interface may have its own hardware address, the packet's destination hardware address changes as it crosses each interface on the way to the destination. The constant IP destination address forms the basis for routing the packet through the network to its final destination.

This chapter will cover the basics of IP addressing, including issues such as address structure and classes, and the role of subnet masks. It will also describe the process of segmenting a network into subnets through the use of subnet masks. Lastly, it will explain the command syntax used by Cisco IOS to configure IP addressing on a router.

When you have completed this chapter, you will be able to:

- Explain the use and implementation of IP address classes
- Explain subnetting and the use of subnet masks
- Describe the process of subnet planning
- Describe some complex subnetting techniques
- Describe IP address configuration and testing commands on a Cisco router

CERTIFICATION OBJECTIVE 3.01

Classes of IP Addresses

As originally defined, the IP addressing standard did not provide for address classes; these were later added to provide ease of administration. The implementation of address classes divided the address space into a limited number of very large networks (Class A), a much larger number of intermediate-sized networks (Class B), and a very large number of small networks (Class C). In addition, some special address classes were also defined, including Class D (used for multicasting), and Class E, which is generally referred to as the experimental or research class. Although there are exceptions to the rules expressed here, the focus of this chapter will be on *classful* IP addressing.

Structure of an IP Address

The 32-bit structure of an IP address is comprised of both a network address and a host address. The number of bits assigned to each of these components varies with the address class. The scheme employed in IP addressing is roughly analogous to the concept of a street address. Just as a house may be defined as being at 121 Main St., an IP address includes the network address (Main St.) as well as the host address (number 121). Our house address makes it possible for the mail to reach our house, and an IP address makes it possible to route data from a source host to its destination.

Figure 3-1 depicts the organization of network addresses using a network and host address.

The concept of *subnetting* extends the network portion of the address to allow a single network to be divided into a number of logical sections (subnets). Routers look at each of these subnets as distinct networks, and can

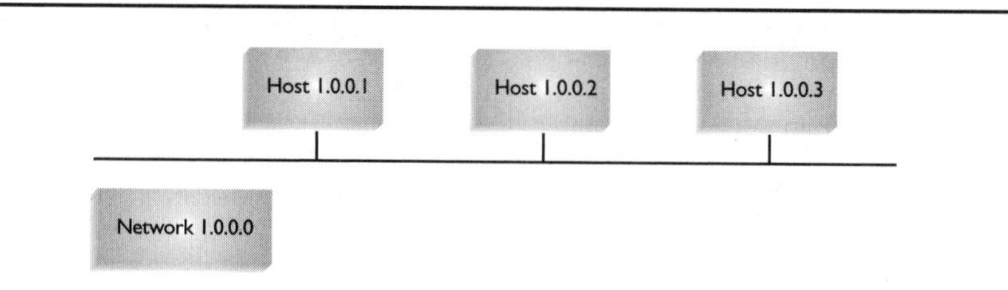

FIGURE 3-1 Network and host addresses

route among them. This helps in managing large networks, as well as isolating traffic between different portions of the network. This traffic isolation is possible because network hosts, by default, can only communicate with other hosts on the same network. In order to communicate with other networks, we need to use a router. A router is essentially a computer with multiple interfaces. Each interface is attached to a different network or subnet. Software within the router performs the function of relaying traffic between networks or subnets. To do this, it accepts packets via an interface with an address on the source network, and relays it through an interface attached to the destination network, as illustrated in Figure 3-2.

By using a router, only traffic that needs to traverse a network other than its local network will pass the router boundary. If the network is designed so that hosts routinely communicate within their own subnets, and only cross the router on an exception basis, the network can handle much more traffic than it could if it were not segmented.

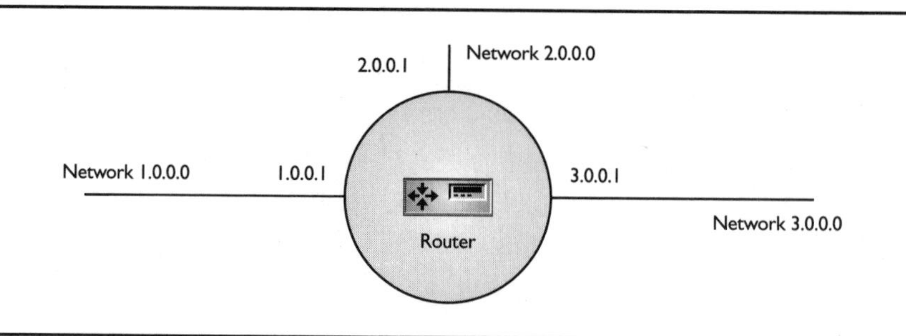

FIGURE 3-2 Router among networks showing router interface addresses

Special Cases: Loopback, Broadcast, and Network Addresses

Certain addresses in the IP address space have been reserved for special purposes, and are not normally allowed as host addresses. The rules for these reserved addresses are as follows:

- The network address portion of an IP address cannot be set to "all binary ones" or "all binary zeros"
- The subnet portion of an IP address cannot be set to "all binary ones" or "all binary zeros"
- The host address portion of an IP address cannot be set to "all binary ones" or "all binary zeros"
- The network 127.x.x.x cannot be used as a network address

Network Addresses

When all the bits in the host portion of an IP address are set to zero, it indicates the network, rather than a specific host on that network. These types of entries are often found in routing tables, since routers control traffic between networks, not individual hosts.

In a subnetted network, setting the host bits to zero would indicate the specific subnet. Also, the bits allocated for the subnet may not be all zeros, since this would refer to the network address of the parent network.

Lastly, the network bits cannot be all zeros, since zero is not an allowed network address, and is used to indicate an "unknown network or address."

Loopback Address

The network address 127.x.x.x has been designated as a local loopback address. The purpose of this address is to provide a test of the local host's network configuration. Using this address provides an internal loopback test of the protocol stack, as opposed to using the host's actual IP address, which would require a network connection.

Local Broadcast

When all the bits in an IP address are set to ones, the resulting address, 255.255.255.255, is used to send a broadcast message to all hosts on the local network. This configuration at the network layer is mirrored by a corresponding hardware address that is also all ones. Generally this hardware address will be seen as FFFFFFFFFFFF. Routers do not usually pass these types of broadcasts unless specifically configured to do so.

All-Hosts Broadcast

If we set all the host bits in an IP address to ones, this will be interpreted as a broadcast to all hosts on that network. This is also called a *directed broadcast*, and can be passed by a router if configured to do so. Sample all-host broadcast addresses would look like 132.100.255.255 or 200.200.150.255.

All-Subnets Broadcast

Another type of directed broadcast can be achieved by setting all the subnet address bits to ones. In this case, a broadcast would be propagated to all subnets within a network. All-subnets broadcasting is rarely implemented in routers.

Identifying Address Classes

The class of an IP address can be determined by looking at the first (most significant) octet in the address. The bit pattern associated with the highest-order bits determines the address class. The bit patterns also define the range of decimal values for the octet that are associated with each address class.

Class A

With a Class A address, eight bits are allotted to the network address, and 24 bits to host addresses. If the highest bit in the first octet is a zero (0), the address is a Class A address. This corresponds to possible octet values of 0-127. Of these, both zero and 127 have reserved functions, so the actual range is 1-126. There are only 126 possible networks that are Class A, since only eight bits are reserved for the network address, and the first bit must be a zero. However, with 24 bits available for host numbers, each network can have 16,777,213 hosts.

Class B

With a Class B address, 16 bits are allotted to the network address, and 16 bits to host addresses. A Class B address is characterized by a bit pattern of 10 at the beginning of the first octet. This corresponds to values from 128-191. Since the first two bits are pre-defined, there are actually 14 bits available for unique network addresses, so the possible combinations yield 16,383 networks, with each network accommodating 65,533 hosts.

Class C

Class C addresses allocate 24 bits to the network address, leaving 8 bits for host addresses. A Class C address will have a bit pattern of 110 leading the first octet, which corresponds to decimal values from 192-223. With a Class C address, only the last octet is used for host addresses, which limits each network to a maximum of 254 hosts per network. Since there are 21 bits available for unique network numbers (three bits are already preset to 110), there are 2,097,151 possible networks.

Class D

Class D addresses have a bit pattern that begins with 1110. This translates into octet values from 224-239. These addresses are not used for standard IP addresses. Instead, a Class D address refers to a group of hosts, who are registered as members of a *multicast group*. A multicast group is similar to an e-mail distribution list. Just as you can address a message to a group of individuals using a distribution list name, you can send data to a group of hosts by using a multicast address. Multicasting requires special routing configuration; it is not forwarded by default.

Class E

If the first four bits of the first octet are 1111, the address is a Class E address. These are addresses that start with 240-254. This class of address is not used for conventional IP addresses. This address class is sometimes referred to as the experimental or research class.

The bulk of our discussion will focus on address Classes A, B, and C, since these are the classes used for routine IP addressing. Table 3-1 summarizes the characteristics of address classes.

Importance of the Subnet Mask

An IP address cannot exist without an associated subnet mask. The subnet mask defines how many of the 32 bits that make up an IP address are used to define the network, or the network and associated subnets. The binary bits in the subnet mask form a filter that only passes that portion of the IP address that should be interpreted as the network address. The process by which this is done is called *bitwise ANDing*. Bitwise ANDing is a logical operation performed on each bit in the address, and the corresponding mask bit. The results of the AND operation are as follows:

1 and 1 = 1
1 and 0 = 0
0 and 0 = 0

So the only time this operation yields a 1 value is when both input values are a 1.

From the example shown in Table 3-2, we can see that an IP address of 189.200.191.239 with a subnet mask of 255.255.0.0 is interpreted as the address of a host on the 189.200.0.0 network, which has a host address of 191.239 on that network. To help you see the relationship of the bits and

TABLE 3-1

IP Address Ranges, Classes, and Bit Patterns

Address Class	Bit Pattern in the First Octet	Range of Addresses
Class A	0xxxxxxx	1-126
Class B	10xxxxxx	128-191
Class C	110xxxxx	192-223
Class D	1110xxxx	224-239
Class E	1111xxxx	240-254

the dotted decimal notation, the table shows the addresses and masks in both binary and decimal form. A quick way of doing these conversions is to use the Windows Calculator in scientific mode. It will translate between binary and decimal formats.

Each class of IP network has a *default subnet mask*, which defines how many bits of an IP address, for each address class, will represent the network address with no subnetting. These default masks are shown in Table 3-3.

Converting Between Binary and Decimal

In order to manage IP addresses, it is necessary to become intimately acquainted with the process of converting between binary and decimal equivalents. Just as the position of a digit in a decimal number indicates its value in powers of 10, the position of a bit in a binary number indicates its value in powers of 2, as described in Table 3-4. In other words, each bit value doubles as the bit position moves from right to left. This table only goes as far as eight bits (one octet). To extend this table, we would simply add bits to the left, with each new bit having a value double that of the previous bit.

Decimal to Binary Conversion

In order to convert a decimal number to its binary equivalent, the first step is to find the *highest-order* binary bit that will fit into the number. The highest-order bit means the bit position with the greatest decimal value. The decimal value of this bit is subtracted from the number, and

TABLE 3-2 How the Subnet Mask Determines the Network Address

	1st Octet	2nd Octet	3rd Octet	4th Octet
IP Address	10111101 (189)	11001000 (200)	10111111 (191)	11101111 (239)
AND (each bit)				
Subnet Mask	11111111 (255)	11111111 (255)	00000000 (0)	00000000 (0)
Result				
Network address	10111101 (189)	11001000 (200)	00000000	00000000

TABLE 3-3 Default Subnet Masks, Maximum Networks, and Hosts

Address Class	Default Subnet Mask	Network Bits	Networks	Host Bits	Hosts
Class A	255.0.0.0	8	126	24	16,777,206
Class B	255.255.0.0	16	16,383	16	65,533
Class C	255.255.255.0	24	2,097,151	8	254

then the highest-order bit that fits into this remainder is determined. This process is repeated until the remainder is zero. All intervening bit positions are set to zero.

As an example, let's convert the decimal 178 to binary.

1. Looking again at Table 3-4, we can see that the highest-order bit that will fit into 178 is the 128 (2^7). The next higher bit would be 256 (2^8), which will not fit into 178.
2. 178 – 128 = 50.
3. Looking again at the table, the highest bit that will fit into 50 is 32 (2^5).
4. 50 – 32 = 18.
5. The highest bit that will fit into 18 is 16 (2^4).
6. 18 – 16 = 2
7. This remainder fits exactly into the 2 (2^1), leaving a remainder of 0.

TABLE 3-4 Bits and Associated Decimal Values in an Octet

	Bit 7	Bit 6	Bit 5	Bit 4	Bit 3	Bit 2	Bit 1	Bit 0
Binary Bits	1	1	1	1	1	1	1	1
Power of 2	2^7	2^6	2^5	2^4	2^3	2^2	2^1	2^0
Decimal	128	64	32	16	8	4	2	1

TABLE 3-5 Converting 178 Decimal to 1011001 Binary

	Bit 7	Bit 6	Bit 5	Bit 4	Bit 3	Bit 2	Bit 1	Bit 0
Decimal	128	0	32	16	0	0	2	0
Binary Bits	1	0	1	1	0	0	1	0

This process we just went through is summarized in Table 3-5.

Binary to Decimal Conversion

To convert from binary to the decimal equivalent needed to express an IP address or a subnet mask, it is simply necessary to associate the decimal values with each bit expressed in a binary number, and then to add these decimal values together. This process is shown in Table 3-6, as we convert a binary number, 10011011, to its decimal equivalent.

TABLE 3-6 Converting 10011011 Binary to 155 Decimal

Bit Pattern	1	0	0	1	1	0	1	1	Decimal Values
	128								128
		0							0
			0						0
				16					16
					8				8
						0			0
							2		2
								1	1
								TOTAL	**155**

FROM THE CLASSROOM

Powers of 2—Some Numbers You Really Need to Know

The most confusing aspect of IP addressing for students to grasp is how to determine where the subnet boundaries lie when the mask does not coincide with an octet boundary. An IP address is a 32-bit number that we represent by using four decimal numbers, each representing eight bits of the 32. This is more convenient to write (who wants to write out 32 ones and zeros, anyhow?), and certainly keeps the decimal numbers we need to know to a minimum, but it can be difficult to see how the subnets and their host addresses are organized. In order to be fluent with this, you will need to spend a lot of time looking at binary numbers and powers of two. I hope I can give you a few ideas that will help you home in on the most important things to know.

The numbers you need to know by heart right now are the powers of 2 from 2^0 to 2^7, and just six others: 192, 224, 240, 248, 252, and 254. How did I get those six numbers? By adding powers of 2, starting at the most significant bit in the IP address octet. Let's work out the binary, and watch the pattern as it develops:

- 10000000 in binary equals 128 in decimal.
  This is the value of 2^7.
- 11000000 in binary equals 192 in decimal.
  This is the sum of the values of 2^7 and 2^6.
- 11100000 in binary equals 224 in decimal.
  This is the sum of the values of 2^7, 2^6, and 2^5.
- 11110000 in binary equals 240 in decimal.
  This is the sum of the values of 2^7, 2^6, 2^5, and 2^4.
- 11111000 in binary equals 248 in decimal.
  This is the sum of the values of 2^7, 2^6, 2^5, 2^4, and 2^3.
- 11111100 in binary equals 252 in decimal.
  This is the sum of the values of 2^7, 2^6, 2^5, 2^4, 2^3, and 2^2.
- 1111110 in binary equals 254 in decimal.
  This is the sum of the values of 2^7, 2^6, 2^5, 2^4, 2^3, 2^2, and 2^1.
- 11111111 in binary equals our friend 255, who needs no further explanation.

FROM THE CLASSROOM

These are the only numbers you will ever see in subnet masks, so if you know these you have the subnet masks licked.

Now we need to determine the actual boundaries of the subnets. If the masking is on the octet boundary, it's easy. So let's look at an example that isn't so straightforward.

Take the network 172.16.0.0 with a subnet mask of 255.255.252.0. What are the valid subnet numbers we can use, and the ranges of IP addresses within them?

If there's an octet where the mask is neither all zeros nor all ones, this is where you need to focus your attention. In this example, the third octet is of interest to us. Work out the binary for this mask: 252 is represented in binary by 11111100. In order to find the first valid subnet number we need to look at the least-significant bit that is a one in our subnet mask. The value of that bit position within the octet, in terms of powers of 2, is four. So our first valid subnet number is 172.16.4.0. To get the remaining subnet numbers, we just need to count up by fours: 172.16.8.0, 172.16.12.0, 172.16.16.0, 172.16.20.0, all the way up to 172.16.251.0, which is the last of the 63 valid subnet numbers in this example. If our mask happened to be 255.255.248.0 instead, our third octet mask would be 11111000 in binary, and we would start with 172.16.8.0 as our first subnet, and count up by eights instead of fours, because the value of the last bit position that is a one in the mask is eight.

The last thing to find out is the range of host addresses for each subnet. We won't use all zeros or all ones, because those are reserved for the network number and the directed broadcast. So our first host address for the first subnet is 172.16.4.1, and the last one is 172.16.7.254. Where did the 7 in that third octet come from? Remember, the two least significant bits in the third octet are part of the host number, so they need to be included in the counting. Host addresses for the next subnets would be 172.16.8.1 through 172.16.11.254, 172.16.12.1 through 172.16.15.254, and so on.

One last hint for learning about subnets: work out some other examples for yourself, and don't be afraid to write out the binary numbers if you need to!

—By Pamela Forsyth, CCIE, CCSI, CNX

CERTIFICATION OBJECTIVE 3.02

Subnetting and Subnet Masks

Up to this point, we have discussed the structure of an IP address, which contains both a network address and a host address. The portion of the IP address reserved for the network address is indicated by the subnet mask. We also discussed that, for each class of address, there is a default number of bits in the subnet mask. All bits not reserved for use as the network address can be used to indicate specific hosts on the network. We will now discuss how we can further segment a network into subnets by borrowing host address bits, and using them to represent a portion of our network.

Purpose of Subnetting

On a single network, the amount of traffic is proportional to the number of hosts, and the sum of the traffic generated by each host. As the network increases in size, this traffic may reach a level that overwhelms the capacity of the media, and network performance starts to suffer. In a wide-area network, reducing unnecessary traffic on the WAN links is also a major issue.

In looking at such problems, it is typical to discover that groups of hosts tend to communicate routinely with each other, and communicate less frequently outside their group. These groupings may be dictated by common usage patterns of network resources, or may be imposed by geographic distances that necessitate slow WAN links between LANs. By using subnets, we can segment the network, thus isolating the groups' traffic from each other. To communicate between these segments, a means must be provided to forward traffic from one segment to another.

One solution to this problem is to isolate the network segments using a bridge between them. A bridge will learn which addresses reside on each side of itself by looking at the MAC address, and will only forward packets that need to cross network segments. This is a quick and relatively inexpensive solution, but lacks flexibility. For example, a bridge would get confused if it found that it could reach a given address on either side of itself. This makes it generally impossible to build redundant pathways using bridges. Bridges also pass broadcasts.

A more robust solution is to use routers that direct traffic between networks, by using tables that associate network destinations with specific ports on the router. Each of these ports is connected to the source network, the destination network, or some intermediate network that leads to the ultimate destination. By using routers, we can define multiple pathways for data, enhancing the fault tolerance and performance of the network.

One solution to addressing in a routed network might be to simply give each network segment a different network address. This would work in an isolated network, but would not be desirable if the network were connected to the outside world. To connect to the Internet, we must have a unique network address, which must be assigned by a regulating agency. These network addresses are in great demand, and in scarce supply. We also increase the complexity of routing data from the public network to our internal networks if we don't have a common point of entry via a single network address.

To gain the economy and simplicity of a single network address, yet provide the capability to internally segment and route our network, we use subnetting. From the standpoint of external routers, our network would then appear as a single entity. Internally, however, we can still provide segmentation through subnets, and use internal routers to direct and isolate traffic between subnets. The following section will discuss the role of the subnet mask in defining subnets.

Adding Bits to the Default Subnet Mask

We have already learned that an IP address must be interpreted within the context of its subnet mask. The subnet mask defines the network address portion of the address. Each class of address has a default mask, which for Class A is eight bits, Class B is 16 bits, and Class C is 24 bits in length.

If we want to subnet a network, we add some number of bits to this default subnet mask, which reduces the number of bits used for the host address. The number of bits we add to the mask determines the number of subnets we can configure. Therefore, in a subnetted network, each address contains a network address, a subnet portion, and a host address.

The subnet bits are taken from the highest-order contiguous bits of the host address, and will start at an octet boundary, since the default masks always end on an octet boundary. As we add subnet bits, we count from the left to right, and convert to decimal using the values associated with their bit positions.

The number of subnets derived from each additional subnet bit is summarized in Table 3-7. Note that the smallest number of useful subnet bits is two, since we cannot use all ones or all zeros for our subnet ID. Also, the maximum number of bits must still leave at least two bits for the host address, due to a similar restriction on all zeros and all ones.

TABLE 3-7

Subnet Bits, Mask Formats, and Number of Subnets Provided

Bits Added to Default Mask	Decimal Value	Number of Subnets
1	128	0
2	192	2
3	224	6
4	240	14
5	248	30
6	252	62
7	254	126
8	255	254
9	255.128	510
10	255.192	1022
11	255.224	2046
12	255.240	4094
13	255.248	8190
14	255.252	16,382
15	255.254	32,766
16	255.255	65,534

CERTIFICATION OBJECTIVE 3.03

Subnet Planning

The process of subnet planning involves analyzing the traffic patterns on the network to determine which hosts should be grouped together in the same subnet. We also need to look at the total number of subnets that we will need, generally projecting some growth factor for a safety margin. We will also need to consider the class of network address we are working with, and the total number of hosts per subnet that we anticipate having to support.

Choosing a Subnet Mask

In choosing a subnet, the chief consideration is how many subnets we will need to support. The challenge, of course, is balancing the number of subnets with the maximum number of hosts per subnet. There are only 32 bits available for network, subnet and host portions of the address. If we choose a subnet mask that offers more subnets than we need, this will reduce the potential hosts we can support.

The other consideration in choosing the mask is to remember the restriction on subnet values that are all zeros, or all ones. This most often causes problems with a number like 31 subnets. While this is less than the 32 combinations we could achieve with five subnet bits, it would represent an illegal bit combination, since it would be all ones. We must therefore use six bits, which yields up to 62 available subnets.

For help in choosing an appropriate subnet mask based on the number of subnets, refer back to Table 3-7.

Impact on the Number of Hosts

Remember that the bits we use for subnetting are subtracted from the bits available to be assigned as host addresses. Each binary bit represents a power of 2, so each bit we take away will cut the potential hosts per subnet in half. Since the address class defines the maximum number of host bits, each class of address is impacted differently by subnetting.

Therefore, if given a network design with a certain number of subnets, proposed hosts per subnet, and a certain class of address, we may find that we have to use fewer subnets, support fewer hosts, or choose a different address class to meet our needs. For each class, the impact of subnetting on the number of hosts is outlined in Table 3-8.

Determining Address Ranges for Each Subnet

Once we have determined the appropriate subnet mask, the next challenge is to determine the address of each subnet, and the allowable range of host addresses on each subnet. The addresses for each of the subnets can be determined by looking at the lowest-order bit of the subnet mask. The value of this bit is the first subnet available. Since we cannot have a subnet ID whose bits are all zeros (this subnet address is reserved), setting all bits but this first one to zero results in the lowest subnet ID.

The interval range between the subnet IDs will also be equal to the value of the lowest subnet bit. This relates to the powers of 2 associated with the bits. If the lowest bit were a 16, the next bit value above it is a 32. Each time we increment the bits, the subnet value changes by the value of the lowest bit. This will continue up to the subnet value of all ones, which is not useable, since it is a broadcast address.

In Table 3-9, assume a network address of 135.120.0.0 with a subnet mask of 255.255.224.0.

Table 3-10 summarizes the process of determining subnet address values, and the interval between the subnets.

TABLE 3-8

Hosts per Subnet, Based on Mask and Address Class

Subnet Bits	Class A Hosts	Class B Hosts	Class C Hosts
0	16,777,212	65,531	254
2	4,194,303	16,382	62
3	2,097,147	8190	30
4	1,048,574	4094	14
5	524,286	2046	6
6	262,142	1022	2
7	131,070	510	N/A
8	65,533	254	N/A

TABLE 3-9

Determining Subnet Addresses

Subnet Bit Pattern	Subnet Value	Subnet Address	Comments
000	0	135.120.0.0	Not available
001	32	135.120.32.0	
010	64	135.120.64.0	
011	96	135.120.96.0	
100	128	135.120.128.0	
101	160	135.120.160.0	
110	192	135.120.192.0	
111	224	135.120.224.0	Not available

Once we have determined the addresses of each of the subnets, we can then determine the range of host addresses that are allowed within each subnet. The following example shows the guidelines used to determine the address range.

1. The first available host address is one bit higher than the subnet ID. In other words, if the subnet was 120.100.16.0, the first host address would be 120.100.16.1.
2. Assuming we are using four bits for subnetting, the next higher subnet address would be 120.100.32.0. If we subtract one bit from

TABLE 3-10

Determining Useable Subnet Addresses for a Given Mask

Subnet Bits	First Subnet	Interval Between Subnets	Number of Subnets
2	64	64	2
3	32	32	6
4	16	16	14
5	8	8	30
6	4	4	62
7	2	2	126
8	1	1	254

TABLE 3-11

Determining Address Ranges for Subnets

Function	Example	Guideline for Determining Value
First subnet address	120.100.16.0	Net.Work.Subnet.0
First host	120.100.16.1	Net.Work.Subnet.1
Last host	120.100.31.254	Next Subnet Address –2
Subnet broadcast	120.100.31.255	Next Subnet Address –1
Next subnet address	120.100.32.0	Net.Work.Subnet + Interval.0

this address, we obtain the broadcast address for the lower (16) subnet. This would be the address 120.100.31.255.

3. The highest available host address is one less than the broadcast address, or 120.100.31.254.

These guidelines are summarized in Table 3-11.

CERTIFICATION OBJECTIVE 3.04

Complex Subnetting

So far, we have confined our discussion of subnets to straightforward examples using classful IP addresses. This section will introduce more complex subnetting issues and practices. We will start off by considering subnet masks that cross octet boundaries, since these are frequently a source of confusion. We will also consider variable-length subnet masking (VLSM) as a means of gaining more flexibility in using subnet masks. Finally, we will consider a practice called supernetting, which could be described as subnetting in reverse, since we remove bits from the default subnet mask, rather than adding them.

Crossing Octet Boundaries with Subnet Bits

Whenever we use more than eight bits for subnets, we run into the issue of crossing octet boundaries. One challenge of dealing with these subnet masks is to keep straight the prohibitions concerning all ones and all zeros. To do this, we have to simultaneously be aware of the subnet bits as an isolated collection of bits, as well as remembering their bit positions, and associated values, in the 32-bit address.

When we cross octet boundaries with a subnet mask, the top eight bits, which consume an entire octet, will have an interval of 1 between subnets. This means any bit combination of 0–255 is permitted in this octet, as long as the additional subnet bits in the lower octet are not also all ones. At the same time, the bits in the lower octet will increment in values specified by the lowest significant bit in the lower octet. To see how this looks, review Table 3-12, which gives a sample of some of the subnet IDs associated with a Class A network (2.0.0.0) using 10 subnet bits (mask 255.255.192.0).

Variable-Length Subnet Masking

When we define a subnet mask, we have made the assumption that this single mask is going to be consistently used throughout our network. In many cases, this leads to a lot of wasted host addresses, since our subnets may vary widely in size. One prime example of this is where we have a subnet that connects two routers via their serial ports.

There are only two hosts on this subnet—one for each port—but we will have to allocate one entire subnet to these two interfaces. If we could take one of our subnets, and further divide it into a second level of subnetting, we could effectively "subnet the subnet" and retain our other subnets for more productive uses. This idea of "subnetting the subnet" forms the basis for VLSM.

TABLE 3-12

Samples of Subnet IDs Using 10 Subnet Bits

Subnet ID	Subnet Bit Values	Comments
2.0.64.0	0000 0000 01	First subnet ID
2.0.128.0	0000 0000 10	Next subnet
2.0.192.0	0000 0000 11	Lower octet bits all ones
2.1.0.0	0000 0001 00	Lower octet bits all zeros
2.255.0.0	1111 1111 00	Upper octet bits all ones
2.255.128.0	1111 1111 10	Last legal subnet

We have talked about an IP address having both a network address portion and a host address portion. With subnetting, we also have a portion of the address devoted to the subnet ID. Collectively, the masked bits representing the network and subnet IDs can be called the *prefix.* Routers can be generically said to route based on prefix. If there were a way to convey specific prefix information with an address, we could override the network-wide assumptions made on the basis of our single subnet mask. To accomplish this, we add explicit information on the prefix to each address reference. The format used to express this prefix (subnet mask) is called the *bitcount* format, which is added to the address using a trailing slash followed by a decimal number. For example, a reference to a Class B address would be represented as 135.120.25.20 /16. The "/16" defines 16 subnet bits, equating to the default mask, 255.255.0.0 (16 bits).

To use VLSM, we generally define a basic subnet mask that will be used to divide our first-level subnets, and then use a second-level mask to subdivide one or more of the primary subnets. VLSM is only recognized by newer routing protocols such as EIGRP or OSPF. When using VLSM, all subnet IDs, including the all-ones and all-zeros subnets, will be valid. Figure 3-3 illustrates the concept of VLSM.

Supernetting

In the introduction to this chapter, we referred to RFC 791 as the document that defined the standards for IP addressing. Part of this standard

FIGURE 3-3

Using variable-length subnet masks

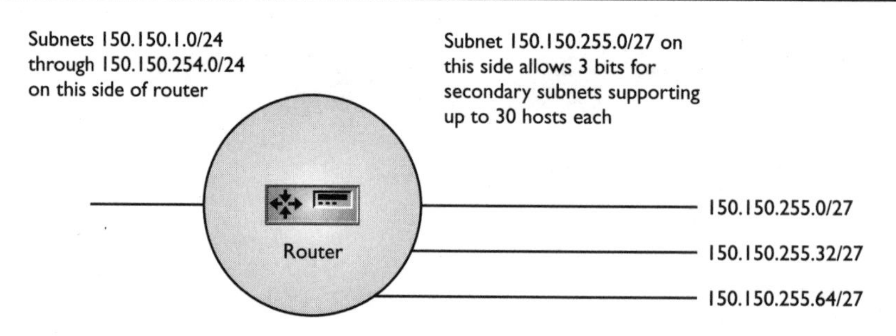

established the address classes and classful addressing. Implied in classful addressing is the assumption that we know what the default subnet mask is based on the first octet of the address. However, prior to RFC 791, an earlier RFC (760) had proposed an IP address format that was not class based. Address classes were considered a good idea in 1982, since the class assumptions eliminated having to send masking information with an IP address, but since we are now running out of registered IP addresses, the classes have become a serious problem.

The only available addresses that have not been assigned are the Class C addresses. Since a Class C network can only support 254 hosts, large organizations wishing to have a registered address may request multiple contiguous Class C addresses, and integrate them into a single entity using a process called supernetting. It is also sometimes referred to as classless interdomain routing (CIDR).

What supernetting does is to remove bits from the default mask, starting at the right-most bits and working to the left. To see how this works, let's look at an example.

Suppose we have been assigned the following Class C network addresses:

```
200.200.192.0
200.200.193.0
200.200.194.0
200.200.195.0
```

With the default mask of 255.255.255.0, these are separate networks. However, if we were to use a subnet mask of 255.255.192 instead, each of these networks would appear to be part of the 200.200.192.0 network, since all the masked bits are the same. The lower-order bit patterns in the third octet become part of the host address space.

Like VLSM, this technique involves a departure from the standard IP address classes. We have discussed these addressing options to provide a sample of the alternatives that have arisen in response to the limitations of classful addressing. When preparing to take the test, remember to focus on a thorough understanding of standard, class-based IP addressing.

FROM THE CLASSROOM

IP: The Next Generation

IP addressing is at a crossroads. The explosive growth of the Internet has caused a crisis with existing IP address formats. The only registered IP addresses that can be obtained right now are Class C addresses. As we have learned, these have severe limitations in terms of the maximum number of hosts supported, which has led to creative approaches such as supernetting.

The longer-term solution is to revamp the whole specification for IP addressing. The proposed solution is called IP version 6, or Ipv6 for short. The format for version 6 IP addresses will move from the present 32-bit address to an address format of 128 bits. This will be represented as 32 hexadecimal digits, expressed as shown in this example: A923.FF23.BA56.34F3.

Unfortunately, this address format is not compatible with existing IP addresses. Ipv6 will probably be implemented first with external IP addresses on the Internet, which would then be routed through gateways to internal networks that continue to use the existing 32-bit address format.

— *By John Pherson, MCSE, MCT, MCNE, CNI*

CERTIFICATION OBJECTIVE 3.05

Configuring IP Addresses with Cisco IOS

The focus of this section will be to take what we have learned about IP addressing and determine how to implement our IP addressing scheme on a Cisco router, using commands from the Cisco IOS command set. The syntax of the commands is shown in each section header, to help you remember them.

Setting IP Addresses and Parameters

The set of parameters we are about to discuss have to do with setting the IP address and subnet masks on the router interfaces, as well as global and per-line settings for how we will express our subnet mask.

ROUTER> TERMINAL IP NETMASK-FORMAT *{bitcount, decimal, or hex}*

This command is issued from the first-level prompt of the privileged or EXEC mode, which is designated by the # prompt. What it does is to define a global format we will use to view subnet masks during the current session. If we do not set this parameter, the default is to use the dotted decimal format.

Examples of the different formats are:

Bitcount: /24 (used for classless IP addressing)
Decimal: 255.255.255.0
Hexadecimal: 0xFFFFFF00

ROUTER(CONFIG-LINE)# IP NETMASK-FORMAT *{bitcount, decimal, or hex}*

This command does the same thing as the preceding command, only in this case we are defining the netmask format for a specific terminal line. To get to this command:

1. Enter the EXEC mode.
2. Issue the command ROUTER# CONFIGURE TERMINAL. This puts us at the prompt Router(config)#.
3. From here, type **line** {aux or console or vty 0 4} to get to the line you wish to configure.
4. You will then see the prompt Router(config-line)#, and can issue the command listed.

ROUTER(CONFIG-IF)# IP ADDRESS *address subnet-mask*

This command is also issued after you have selected an interface and entered the interface configuration mode shown by the Router(config-if)# prompt. This command assigns the IP address to a router interface, and both the address and subnet-mask portions must be specified. The format for the subnet-mask would have been assigned using the last command we discussed.

Host Name to Address Mappings

Host name to address mappings is a process that allows user-friendly names for network hosts, rather than having to specify them by their IP address. When we use these types of names, some method must be provided to convert from the names to the actual IP addresses. This would typically involve using a mapping file or table, and/or a server called a Domain Name Service (DNS) server.

When an address has been resolved from a host name, a router keeps that information in a local cache. This way it can avoid resubmitting the resolution request to the DNS server again later.

ROUTER(CONFIG)# IP HOST *hostname* [*tcp-port-number*] ADDRESS {*ip addresses*}

This command is issued from the global configuration prompt. It is used to add a mapping entry to the host cache used by the router for name-to-address resolution. It requires that you specify the name of the host, and also the IP address (or addresses) associated with that host. It also allows you to specify a TCP port number. If you don't use this parameter, the entry will default to TCP port 23, used for Telnet connections to that host.

ROUTER(CONFIG)#IP DOMAIN-NAME *domain name*

This command is used to specify the default domain name that will be added by the Cisco IOS to an incomplete or "unqualified" host name. A fully qualified domain name (FQDN) would be

```
server 1.abc.com
```

where server1 is the host in a domain called abc.com.

If we choose to refer to this server only as "server1," then IOS will append the default domain name to the host name for the purpose of submitting a name resolution request to a DNS server.

ROUTER(CONFIG)# IP NAME-SERVER {*name server ip addresses*}

This command is also issued from the global configuration prompt. It is used to specify the address (or addresses) of DNS servers that are available to the router for name-to-address mapping. Up to six name server addresses can be specified with a single command. If this parameter is not used, the router will use 255.255.255.255 (local broadcast address) to find the server.

ROUTER(CONFIG)# (NO) IP DOMAIN-LOOKUP

This command simply turns name resolution on and off. The default is on, with the name server address specified as a local broadcast.

ROUTER# SHOW HOSTS

To avoid "re-inventing the wheel," the router will request a name-to-address once, and then keep that information in a local cache. This will shorten the time required the next time the name needs to be resolved. This command will display the contents of this local cache, along with information about the source of the entry ("static" or "resolved by DNS," for example), and its status and age.

Using Ping

Ping (packet Internet groper) is a common utility used with IP to test connectivity between two IP hosts. It operates by sending a set of test packets using ICMP (Internet Control Message Protocol). These packets echo back to the source, showing whether the destination was reachable, and displaying some timing and timeout statistics.

Simple Ping

Simple ping is a command available in the USER mode on a Cisco router. It would use the following syntax:

```
Router> ping 131.199.130.3
```

The most common response symbols returned are:

!	successful echo
.	timed out waiting
U	destination unreachable
&	TTL exceeded

It will also summarize the results of sending five packets in a success rate percentage. If a ping is successful, it shows that the network protocol is working at least up to the network layer, and that two hosts can successfully connect up to that layer.

Extended Ping

Sometimes the defaults built into simple ping are insufficient to provide the testing desired. If this is the case, an extended PING command is provided in the EXEC command mode in IOS. This version of ping is interactive, and offers the capability to specify the number and size of test packets, the timeout value, and even data patterns, in response to various prompts. You can access this command by entering the EXEC mode, and typing **Router# ping** <CR>.

You will then be prompted for your settings. You can also access a help file for this command by typing **Router# ping** ? <CR>.

Using IP TRACE and Telnet

For those occasions when we need more than the PING command to test the operation of the network, there are a few other tools we can use. We may be interested not just in the fact that we can get packets from a source to destination host, but also in the route taken by the packets. We might also be interested in testing host connectivity at protocol layers higher than the network layer. For these tests, we can use IP TRACE for route information, and Telnet, a terminal emulation program that will validate connectivity at higher protocol levels.

Telnet

Telnet is not primarily a testing utility. The purpose of Telnet is to provide a means to emulate a terminal connection into a host system. However, since Telnet is an application that runs at the top of the protocol stack, it can be used to verify the proper functioning of all the intervening layers. Telnet can be used from the user mode in IOS by typing **Router>telnet** {IP address or hostname} or simply the name/address of the host.

IP TRACE

To issue this command, you may be in User mode or Exec mode (for extended TRACE). Type **Router> trace** {host name} **or** {IP address}.

In response, this utility will send out three test probes that will discover any routers on the path. It will list the IP address of each router, host name (if it can be resolved), and the return times for each of the three probes.

This list should conclude with the host name or address of the destination host originally specified.

CERTIFICATION SUMMARY

In this chapter we learned that an IP address is a 32-bit address, specified using dotted decimal notation (for example, 125.125.125.100). IP addresses are interpreted using a subnet mask, which defines which portion of the 32 bits represent the network address, and which represent a host number on that network.

IP address classes are assigned based on the value of the first octet of the IP address. These classes range from Class A through Class E. Only Classes A, B, and C are used for normal IP addressing. Each class of address has a default subnet mask, which defines the number of networks and the number of hosts per network for a given address class.

By adding bits to the right of the default subnet mask, we can segment a network into subnets. Subnetting uses bits that were originally reserved for host addresses, thus reducing the number of hosts possible in each subnet.

The following rule applies to the formation of network addresses, subnet IDs, and host numbers: The bit configuration cannot be all ones or all zeros. All zeros would indicate a network, not a specific address. All ones would represent broadcasts.

The addresses of subnets on a subnetted network are determined by taking the least significant bit in a subnet mask as the first subnet, and incrementing by the value of that bit. Host addresses on each subnet range from one above the subnet ID to two less than the value of the next higher subnet. One less than the next subnet ID would be a broadcast address for the lower subnet.

Cisco IOS provides commands that will configure the IP addresses of each router interface. Additional commands set the display format for the subnet mask. Several commands configure IP address-to-name translation for the router. Other commands are available for testing the IP configuration, including PING, TRACE, and Telnet.

TWO-MINUTE DRILL

- ❑ The IP protocol is used for end-to-end routing of data across a network, which may mean that an IP packet must travel across multiple networks, and may cross several router interfaces to get to its destination.
- ❑ The implementation of address classes divided the address space into a limited number of very large networks (Class A), a much larger number of intermediate-sized networks (Class B), and a very large number of small networks (Class C).
- ❑ The 32-bit structure of an IP address is comprised of both a network address and a host address.
- ❑ The concept of *subnetting* extends the network portion of the address to allow a single network to be divided into a number of logical sections (subnets).
- ❑ Certain addresses in the IP address space have been reserved for special purposes, and are not normally allowed as host addresses.
- ❑ When all the bits in the host portion of an IP address are set to zero, it indicates the network, rather than a specific host on that network.

- ❑ The network address 127.x.x.x has been designated as a local loopback address. The purpose of this address is to provide a test of the local host's network configuration.
- ❑ When all the bits in an IP address are set to ones, the resulting address, 255.255.255.255, is used to send a broadcast message to all hosts on the local network.
- ❑ If you set all the host bits in an IP address to ones, this will be interpreted as a broadcast to all hosts on that network. This is also called a *directed broadcast.*
- ❑ The class of an IP address can be determined by looking at the first (most significant) octet in the address.
- ❑ If the highest bit in the first octet is a zero (0), the address is a Class A address.
- ❑ A Class B address is characterized by a bit pattern of 10 at the beginning of the first octet.
- ❑ A Class C address will have a bit pattern of 110 leading the first octet, which corresponds to decimal values from 192-223.
- ❑ Class D addresses have a bit pattern that begins with 1110. A Class D address refers to a group of hosts, who are registered as members of a *multicast group*.
- ❑ If the first four bits of the first octet are 1111, the address is a Class E address.
- ❑ An IP address cannot exist without an associated subnet mask. The subnet mask defines how many of the 32 bits that make up an IP address are used to define the network, or the network and associated subnets.
- ❑ You can further segment a network into subnets by borrowing host address bits, and using them to represent a portion of our network.
- ❑ To gain the economy and simplicity of a single network address, yet provide the capability to internally segment and route our network, use subnetting.
- ❑ In a subnetted network, each address contains a network address, a subnet portion, and a host address.

- The process of subnet planning involves analyzing the traffic patterns on the network to determine which hosts should be grouped together in the same subnet.
- In choosing a subnet, the chief consideration is how many subnets you will need to support.
- Once you have determined the appropriate subnet mask, the next challenge is to determine the address of each subnet, and the allowable range of host addresses on each subnet.
- Whenever you use more than eight bits for subnets, you run into the issue of crossing octet boundaries.
- If you could take one of our subnets, and further divide it into a second level of subnetting, you could effectively "subnet the subnet" and retain our other subnets for more productive uses. This idea of "subnetting the subnet" forms the basis for VLSM.
- Supernetting removes bits from the default mask, starting at the right-most bits and working to the left.
- Host name-to-address mapping is a process that allows user-friendly names for network hosts, rather than having to specify them by their IP address.
- Ping (packet Internet groper) is a common utility used with IP to test connectivity between two IP hosts.
- You can use IP TRACE for route information, and Telnet, a terminal emulation program that will validate connectivity at higher protocol levels.

SELF TEST

The following questions will help you measure your understanding of the material presented in this chapter. Read all the choices carefully, as there may be more than one correct answer. Choose all correct answers for each question.

1. What is the network address for the address 96.2.3.16?

   A. 96.2.0.0

   B. 96.2.3.0

   C. 96.0.0.0

   D. Can't tell

2. What class of address is 190.233.27.13?

   A. Class A

   B. Class B

   C. Class C

   D. Class D

3. How many bits are in the default subnet mask for the address 219.25.23.56?

   A. 8

   B. 16

   C. 24

   D. 32

4. How many hosts are supported by a Class C network address, without subnetting?

   A. 254

   B. 65,000

   C. 255

   D. 16,000

5. What is the default mask for a Class B network?

   A. 255.0.0.0

   B. 255.255.255.0

   C. 255.255.0.0.

   D. 255.225.0.0

6. Approximately how many unique networks are possible with a Class B address?

   A. 254

   B. 16K

   C. 65K

   D. 2M

7. What is the decimal value of the binary number 11001011?

   A. 203

   B. 171

   C. 207

   D. 193

8. What is the binary value of the decimal number 219?

   A. 11101011

   B. 01011101

   C. 11101011

   D. 11011011

9. Subnet bits are added to________ to segment the network into subnets.

   A. The network address

B. The default subnet mask

C. The host address

D. The subnet ID

10. If eight bits were allocated to subnetting with a Class B address, how many subnets would be possible?

A. 62

B. 256

C. 254

D. 16K

11. Given the subnet mask 255.255.240 on a Class A address, how many bits are allocated to subnetting?

A. 4

B. 5

C. 9

D. 12

12. If the subnet mask for the network 150.25.0.0 is 255.255.224.0, which of these is a valid host address?

A. 150.25.0.27

B. 150.25.30.23

C. 150.25.40.24

D. 150.25.224.30

13. What is the first subnet ID for the network 25.0.0.0 with a subnet mask of 255.192.0.0?

A. 25.192.0.0

B. 25.64.0.0

C. 25.128.0.0

D. 25.192.64.0

14. What is the maximum number of subnet bits possible with a Class C address?

A. 6

B. 8

C. 14

D. 12

15. Given the address 220.195.227.12 with a subnet mask of 255.255. 224.0, what advanced subnetting technique is being used?

A. Subnetting across octets

B. VLSM

C. Supernetting

D. None

16. Given a subnet mask of 255.255.240, which of these addresses is not a valid host address?

A. 150.150.37.2

B. 150.150.16.2

C. 150.150.8.12

D. 150.150.49.15

17. How many hosts per subnet are possible with a Class B address, if five bits are added to the default mask for subnetting?

A. 510

B. 512

C. 1022

D. 2046

18. If you were issued a Class C address, and needed to divide the network into seven

subnets, with up to 15 hosts in each subnet, what subnet mask would you use?

A. 255.255.255.224

B. 255.255.224

C. 255.255.255.240

D. None of the above

19. What IOS command would you issue to set the IP address on a terminal line?

A. ROUTER(CONFIG-IF)# IP ADDRESS

B. ROUTER(CONFIG-LINE)#IP ADDRESS

C. Router(config)#ip address

D. None of the above

20. What IOS command would you use to define the subnet mask for an interface on the router?

A. ROUTER(CONFIG-IF)# IP ADDRESS

B. ROUTER# TERM IP-NETMASK FORMAT

C. Router(config-line)# ip netmask-format

D. Router(config)# ip subnetmask

21. What IOS command turns off name-to-address resolution?

A. ROUTER# NO IP DOMAIN-LOOKUP

B. ROUTER(CONFIG)# NO DOMAIN-LOOKUP

C. Router(config-if)# no ip domain-lookup

D. Router(config)# domain-lookup off

22. To view name-to-address mappings cached on the router, what IOS command would you issue?

A. ROUTER> SHOW HOSTS

B. ROUTER(CONFIG)# SHOW HOSTS

C. Router# ip name-server

D. Router(config)# ip name-server

23. If you received a !!!!! in response to a PING command, what would that indicate?

A. Destination unreachable

B. Successful echoes

C. Timeout

D. None of the above

24. Given an IP address of 125.3.54.56, without any subnetting, what is the network number?

A. 125.0.0.0

B. 125.3.0.0

C. 125.3.54.0

D. 125.3.54.32

25. The network 154.27.0.0 can support how many hosts, if not subnetted?

A. 254

B. 1024

C. 65,533

D. 16,777,206

26. Which of the following is a legitimate IP host address?

A. 1.255.255.2

B. 127.2.3.5

C. 225.23.200.9

D. 192.240.150.255

27. What is the significance of the address 3.255.255.255?

A. It is a host number

B. It is a local broadcast

C. It is a directed broadcast

D. It is an illegal address

28. How many bits are in the default subnet mask for a Class D network?

A. 8

B. 16

C. 24

D. None

29. A bit pattern of 1111 leading the first octet of an address would imply what class of network?

A. Class A

B. Class B

C. Class C

D. Class D

E. Class E

30. What is the binary equivalent of the decimal 234?

A. 11101010

B. 10111010

C. 10111110

D. 10101111

31. What is the decimal equivalent of 01011100?

A. 96

B. 92

C. 84

D. 154

32. The purpose of subnetting is to:

A. Segment and organize a single network at the network layer

B. Divide a network into several different domains

C. Allow bridging between network segments

D. Isolate groups of hosts so they can't communicate

33. Subnetting is achieved by the following actions:

A. Subtracting bits from the default subnet mask

B. Subtracting bits from the network address

C. Adding bits to the host address

D. Adding bits to the default subnet mask

34. If we add four bits to the default mask, what is the number of subnets we can define?

A. 16

B. 15

C. 14

D. 12

35. What is the maximum number of subnet bits we can add to a default mask?

    A. 8 bits
    B. 16 bits
    C. 30 bits
    D. Depends on address class

36. What is the subnet mask we would use with a Class B address that has three subnet bits added?

    A. 255.255.240.0
    B. 255.255.224.0
    C. 255.224.0.0
    D. 255.255.248.0

37. What would be the subnet mask if we added 12 subnet bits to a default Class A subnet mask?

    A. 255.255.255.240
    B. 255.255.240.0
    C. 255.240.0.0
    D. 255.225.224.0

38. Given a subnet mask of 255.255.255.0 with a Class B address, how many subnets are available?

    A. None
    B. 254
    C. 16K
    D. 65K

39. What happens to the number of hosts per subnet each time we add an additional subnet bit?

    A. Hosts are not affected
    B. Available hosts are decreased by two
    C. Hosts per subnet is approximately halved
    D. Hosts per subnet is doubled

40. In order to accommodate seven subnets, how many subnet bits are required?

    A. 3
    B. 4
    C. 6
    D. 7

41. If we included six subnet bits in the subnet mask for a Class C address, how many hosts would each network support?

    A. 254
    B. 30
    C. 4
    D. 2

42. What class of address would we have to use if we needed 2,000 subnets, with over 5,000 users each?

    A. Class A
    B. Class B
    C. Class C
    D. Class D

43. Given a subnet address of 140.125.8.0, with a subnet mask of 255.255.252.0, what is the subnet address of the next higher subnet?

    A. 140.125.16.0
    B. 140.125.17.0

C. 140.125.32.0

D. 140.125.12.0

44. Given a subnet address of 5.32.0.0 and a subnet mask of 255.224.0.0, what is the highest allowed host address on this subnet?

A. 5.32.255.254

B. 5.32.254.254

C. 5.63.255.254

D. 5.63.255.255

45. If we saw the following subnet addresses, what would be the subnet mask associated with these subnets?
140.120.4.0
140.120.8.0
140.120.12.0
140.120.16.0

A. 255.255.252.0

B. 255.252.0.0.

C. 255.255.248.0

D. 255.255.4.0.

46. Given the network 2.0.0.0 with a subnet mask of 255.255.224.0, which of these is not a valid subnet ID for this network?

A. 200.255.192.0

B. 200.0.224.0

C. 200.0.16.0

D. 200.254.192.0

47. What is the subnet mask for an address expressed as 175.25.0.0/24?

A. 255.255.0.0

B. 255.255.255.0

C. Depends on address class

D. 255.255.24.0

48. VLSM allows us to:

A. Use different subnet masks in different parts of the network

B. Divide a subnet into secondary subnets

C. Use classless IP addressing

D. Both A and B

49. What class of IP address is usually associated with supernetting?

A. Class A

B. Class B

C. Class C

D. Class D

50. Supernetting modifies the default subnet mask in what way?

A. Adds bits to the default subnet mask

B. Adds bits to the network address

C. Removes bits from the subnet ID

D. Removes bits from the default subnet mask

51. What is the appropriate prompt from which to enter the IP ADDRESS command?

A. Router>

B. Router#

C. Router(config-if)#

D. Router(config)#

52. Which of the following subnet mask formats do Cisco routers support?

    A. Dotted decimal
    B. Hexadecimal
    C. Bitcount
    D. All of the above

53. To configure a name-to-address mapping in the router mapping table, you would issue which of the following commands?

    A. ROUTER(CONFIG-IF)# IP HOST
    B. ROUTER(CONFIG-LINE)#IP NAME-SERVER
    C. ROUTER(CONFIG)#IP HOST
    D. Both A and C

54. When a PING command returns a series of periods, what does that indicate?

    A. Success
    B. Non-existent address
    C. Timeout
    D. Unreachable

55. Which of these commands could verify the operation of the protocol stack all the way to the Application layer?

    A. PING
    B. TRACE
    C. Extended ping
    D. Telnet

56. To perform an extended ping to address 1.1.1.1, you would issue which of the following commands?

    A. ROUTER> PING 1.1.1.1
    B. ROUTER# PING 1.1.1.1
    C. ROUTER(CONFIG)# PING
    D. ROUTER# PING

57. The length of an IP address is:

    A. 24 bits
    B. 16 bits
    C. 32 bits
    D. 48 bits

58. Which of the following classes is used for multicasting?

    A. Class A
    B. Class B
    C. Class E
    D. None of the above

59. Which of the following statements is true regarding IP host addresses?

    A. The host address part of an IP address can be set to "all binary ones" or to "all binary zeros."
    B. The subnet address part of an IP address can not be set to "all binary ones" or to "all binary zeros."
    C. The network address part of an IP address can be set to "all binary ones" or to "all binary zeros."

60. An IP address reserved for loopback test is:

    A. 164.0.0.0
    B. 130.0.0.0
    C. 200.0.0.0
    D. 127.0.0.0

61. An IP address used for local broadcasting (broadcasting to all hosts on the local network) is:

    A. 127.255.255.255
    B. 255.255.255.255
    C. 164.0.0.0
    D. 127.0.0.0

62. An IP address of 100.1.1.1 represents which class of network?

    A. Class B
    B. Class C
    C. Class A
    D. Class E

63. The Class D IP address pattern begins with:

    A. 1111
    B. 110
    C. 010
    D. 1110

64. The number 174 is represented in binary form by:

    A. 11001110
    B. 10101110
    C. 10101010
    D. 10110010

65. The subnet mask in conjunction with an IP address defines:

    A. A multicast address
    B. A host address
    C. The portion of the address that should be considered the network ID
    D. None of the above

66. The purpose of using subnets is:

    A. To divide a network into smaller subnetworks
    B. To improve network performance due to increased traffic
    C. To make the internetwork more manageable
    D. All of the above

67. The default subnet mask for Class B network is:

    A. 8 bits long
    B. 24 bits long
    C. 16 bits long
    D. 32 bits long

68. To add bits to a default subnet mask, the bits are taken from:

    A. The lowest-order contiguous bits of the host address
    B. The lowest-order contiguous bits of the host address
    C. The highest-order contiguous bits of the host address
    D. The highest-order contiguous bits of the host address

69. In planning subnets, the factors that need to be considered are:

    A. The number of subnets needed
    B. The number of hosts per subnet

C. The possible growth in number of subnets or hosts per subnet

D. All of the above

70. How many subnets for Class B are possible if six bits are added to the default mask?

A. 14

B. 30

C. 62

D. 510

71. The value 24 after / in the IP address 135.120.25.20/24 is called:

A. A robbed bit

B. A default bit

C. A prefix

D. A host bit

72. An IP address of 199.119.99.1/24 defines:

A. 24 subnet mask bits for Class A network

B. 24 subnet mask bits for Class B network

C. 24 subnet mask bits for Class C network

D. 24 subnet mask bits for Class E network

73. What IOS command would you use to define a global format to view the subnet mask during the "current session"?

A. ROUTER # IP ADDRESS

B. ROUTER # TERM DOMAIN-LOOKUP

C. ROUTER # SET FORMAT

D. ROUTER # TERM IP NETMASK-FORMAT

74. The router command ROUTER(CONFIG)# IP HOST {*hostname address*} is used for:

A. Viewing the route the packet has taken from source to destination

B. Viewing the host name and host address

C. Adding a static mapping of a host name to an address in the router's host cache

D. Showing source destination network's interfaces with other networks

75. The maximum number of name server addresses that can be specified using the ROUTER(CONFIG)# IP NAME-SERVER command is:

A. Four

B. Six

C. Five

D. Three

76. The following is a response to the ROUTER > PING 120.1.1.2 command:

.!!!!

Success rate is 80 percent (4/5), round trip min/avg/max = 28/75/112 ms

The success rate 80 percent in this response means:

A. Four out of five times, the response came back

B. Five packets were received at destination, and four were received at the source

C. Four times out of five, there was no response

D. Four packets out of a total of five packets reached the IP address 120.1.1.2

77. A user on a Washington DC network receives the following response after issuing a router command:

    Tracing the route to Honolulu
    1Tokyo(127.893.81.2) 800 ms 6 ms 4 ms
    2 Lisbon(141.925.64.7) 600 ms 8 ms 6 ms
    Honolulu(151.666.59.4) 400 ms 10 ms 8 ms
    Washington dc#

    This response was most likely obtained by issuing the command:

    A. ROUTER# TELNET 151.666.59.4)

    B. LISBON# SHOW IPROUTE

    C. WASHINGTONDC# SHOW IPROUTE

    D. WASHINGTONDC# TRACE HONOLULU

    E. HONOLULU# SHOW IP ROUTE

78. For an IP address of 165.3.34.35, netmask of 255.255.255.224, and a subnet ID of 165.3.34.32, the usable host address range is:

    A. From 165.3.34.34 to 165.3.34.64

    B. From 165.3.34.35 to 165.3.34.65

    C. From 165.3.34.33 to 165.3.34.62

    D. From 165.3.34.33 to 165.3.34.63

4

TCP/IP Protocol Suite

CERTIFICATION OBJECTIVES

4.01 Application Layer Services

4.02 Presentation and Session Layer Services

4.03 Detailed Protocol Structure

4.04 Network Layer

4.05 Operating System Commands

The TCP/IP protocol suite is not a static entity. Rather, it is a dynamically changing collection of internetworking protocols that continually push the state of the art in internetworking. Because of its academic origins, much of the significant development work in major universities is focused on TCP/IP. Researchers from around the world are continually developing and proposing extensions or enhancements to the TCP/IP protocol suite.

As a de facto standard, the TCP/IP protocol suite is not owned by any particular vendor, but is supported by everyone. For internetworks consisting of heterogeneous computer systems that need to communicate with each other, TCP/IP stands out as the common denominator across all types of platforms. The TCP/IP protocol suite has four major layers, which can roughly correspond to the seven layers of the OSI reference model. Figure 4-1 shows the general structure of the TCP/IP protocol suite as it

FIGURE 4-1

Four-layered TCP/IP model

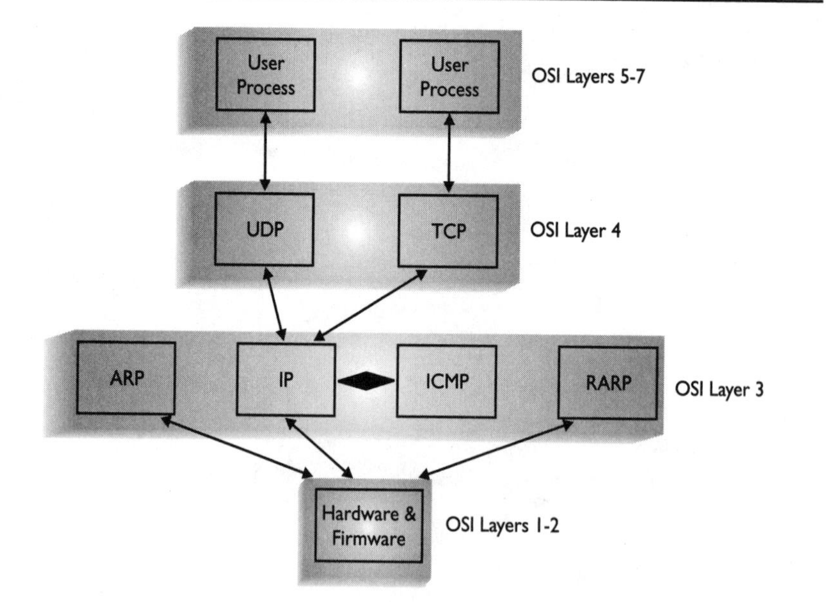

compares to the ISO/OSI Reference model. Explanations of each protocol component are presented in the following sections.

CERTIFICATION OBJECTIVE 4.01

Application Layer Services

The TCP/IP protocol suite includes several common application programs. Applications function at the OSI reference model layer 7, or layer 4 of the TCP/IP suite. It is important for anyone aiming for the CCIE certification to be familiar with the applications listed in Table 4-1 at the indicated level. Each application uses either UDP (unreliable) or TCP (reliable) as the transport mechanism.

TABLE 4-1 TCP/IP Services

TCP/IP Service	Transport Protocol and Port #	Function	Level of Familiarity Required for CCIE
Telnet	TCP 23	Remote terminal	Extremely
FTP	TCP 21 TCP 20	File transfer	Medium
TFTP	UDP 69	File transfer	Extremely
NFS		File services	None
SMTP	TCP 25	E-mail	Need to know transports and port # for firewalls
DNS	TCP 53	Name server	Need to know transports and port # for firewalls
HTTP	TCP 80	Hypertext www	Need to know transports and port # for firewalls
HTTPS	TCP 443	Encrypted Web traffic	Need to know transports and port # for firewalls

CERTIFICATION OBJECTIVE 4.02

Presentation and Session Layer Services

The TCP/IP protocol model does not have a formal presentation or session layer in general, although Sun Microsystems has offered eXternal Data Representation (XDR) as a presentation layer service along with their original Remote Procedure Call (RPC) design work. This RPC development work has been continued by the Open Software Foundation (OSF) as part of the Distributed Computing Environment (DCE) initiative.

Remote Procedure Calls

Remote procedure calls are a method for executing programs (here called "procedures") on other network nodes, such that they appear to be executing locally. Remote procedure calls (RPCs) do not fit in well with the OSI Reference Model. As a result, RPCs can only be identified as existing somewhere between the application and transport layer. An RPC can be viewed as a connectionless session. Part of the RPC function is to abstract the application layer from some of the networking details. In other words, one of the goals of RPC is transparency, in that they try to make remote calls look like local ones.

A common RPC implementation across heterogeneous computer platforms significantly enhances portability of applications between different systems. An example of a standard RPC mechanism is the Distributed Computing Environment (DCE) RPC. DEC, IBM, Hewlett-Packard, and Microsoft all conform to the DCE RPC model. The next generation of object-oriented middleware is being built on top of the DCE RPC model.

Sockets

Berkeley Sockets is a session layer Application Programming Interface (API). Sockets are built into the BSD UNIX operating system kernel.

Windows sockets (WinSock) runs on computer systems that use the Microsoft TCP/IP-32 stack. WinSock is a version of the popular BSD socket implementation. Sockets allow applications to share the TCP/IP connection to the network. WinSock is also a session layer API. The WinSock specification is not owned by Microsoft, and was created and developed through the cooperation of several software vendors. It was developed in both 16-bit and 32-bit versions. The 16-bit version was not included as part of Microsoft Windows 3.*x*. WinSock specifically addresses Internet connections. It is typically implemented as a DLL with additional programs, such as a dialer program, to initiate an Internet connection. However, WinSock does not provide the utilities, just the sockets API that the utilities access.

Transport Layer Interface

The transport layer interface (TLI) is a System V API that was introduced in Release 3.0 in 1986. The TLI is not a part of the UNIX kernel, and relies on library routines. TLI ensures that the transport layer will retain its independence from the session, presentation, and application layer services.

NetBIOS

The NetBIOS (Network Basic Input/Output System) encountered in Microsoft environments is not a protocol, but a session layer API. NetBIOS over TCP/IP is described in RFCs 1001/2, and can use either UDP or TCP as the underlying (routable) transport protocol.

Applications that are written to the NetBIOS API generally need more information than a DNS can provide in order to communicate with remote NetBIOS applications across a router. Microsoft has developed a proprietary NetBIOS name server, called the Windows Internet Name Server (WINS), which provides the capability to dynamically register NetBIOS computer names and provide NetBIOS name resolution across logical IP subnets (router hops).

A good understanding of NetBIOS is critical in any network that uses Microsoft LAN Manager or Windows NT as a network operating system. It should be noted that in the Microsoft model, NetBIOS, can bind to TCP/IP, IPX, or NetBEUI. Since NetBEUI does not have a network layer, it is not a routable protocol. NetBIOS, on the other hand, can be routed if WINS (or a static LMHOSTS file) is used, and if NetBIOS is bound to TCP/IP. Using NetBIOS over IPX is difficult to implement, since routers must be configured to forward IPX broadcasts to each of the internetwork segments. NetBIOS is not a strategic API for Microsoft. Their strategic direction is Network OLE and distributed objects, which are all built on top of the DCE RPC. In the meantime, NetBIOS will be around for a long while, so all one can really do is to migrate NetBIOS applications to use TCP/IP as the underlying transport, and away from NetBEUI (NetBIOS Extended User Interface), which forces bridging due to its inability to be routed.

CERTIFICATION OBJECTIVE 4.03

Detailed Protocol Structure

The TCP/IP protocol suite is a four-layer model. Even though it has four layers, it contains services that map to the entire seven layers of the OSI reference model. This is demonstrated by the incorporation of presentation- and session-type services such as TLI or RPCs. Where the OSI model has the upper layers (application, presentation, and session) separated, the TCP/IP model contains them in one layer. And where the OSI model has separated the physical hardware layer from the data link framing layer, the TCP/IP model lumps them together as well. Figure 4-2 illustrates the relationships among OSI reference model layer 1-7 entities, relative to the TCP/IP protocol model.

Transport Layer

The transport layer is the single-most important layer with respect to connectivity to other systems. Its function is to provide the reliable

FIGURE 4-2

The TCP/IP protocol model structure

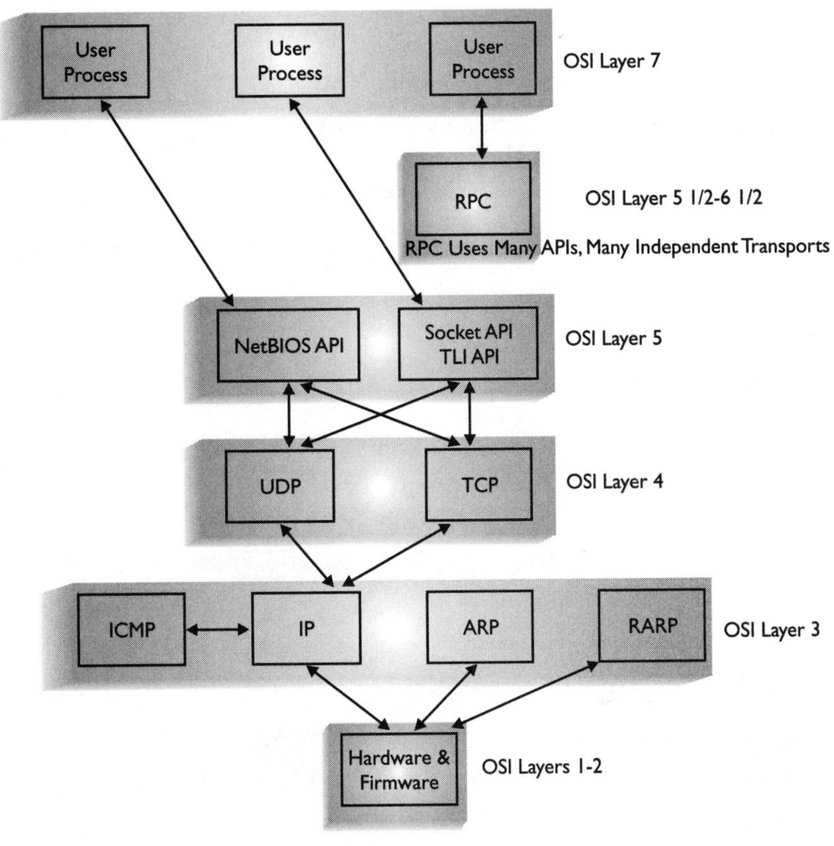

transport of data between two systems, regardless of the underlying networks in between. In the TCP/IP protocol suite, there are two transport layer protocols, Transmission Control Protocol (TCP) and User Datagram Protocol (UDP). Both are important and are used extensively by higher-layer applications.

Both TCP and UDP use the concepts of ports and sockets. Ports and sockets are important concepts when establishing or identifying a connection between two networked computer systems. The source and destination ports are used to identify the points where upper-layer source and destination processes access TCP services. A socket is an IP address plus a port.

- Sending socket = source IP address + source port number
- Receiving socket = destination IP address + destination port number

Knowledge of which port is used by a given TCP/IP application layer service is important when designing IP access filters. Table 4-2 illustrates some of the more common TCP/IP applications and their associated port numbers.

TCP

The Transmission Control Protocol is defined in RFC 793 and defines a reliable, connection-oriented full-duplex byte stream for a user process. It moves data in a continuous, unstructured byte stream. The TCP header, diagrammed in Figure 4-3, contains 11 fields plus a variable-length data field.

TABLE 4-2 Common TCP/IP Services and Transports

Service	Name	Protocol	Port
DNS	Domain Name Service	TCP, UDP	53
SMTP	Simple Mail Transport Protocol	TCP	25
FTP-Data	File Transfer Protocol — Data	TCP	20 and >1023
FTP	File Transfer Protocol	TCP	21
Telnet		TCP	23
NTP	Network Time Protocol	TCP, UDP	123
NNTP	Network News Transport Protocol	TCP	119
HTTP	Hypertext Transport Protocol	TCP	80
X-Windows		TCP	6000-6100

FIGURE 4-3

TCP header

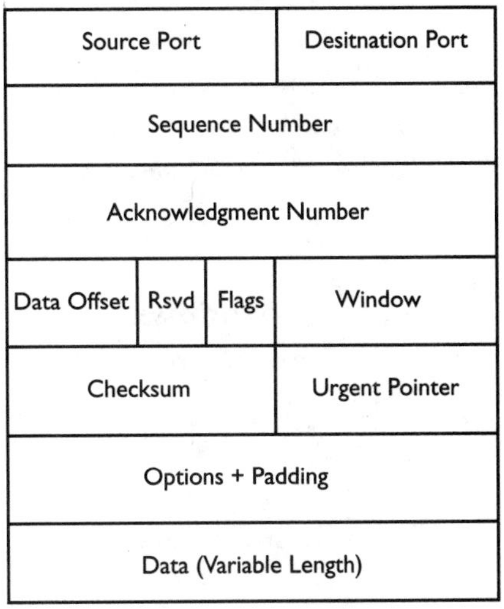

<table>
<tr><td colspan="3">Source Port</td><td>Desitnation Port</td></tr>
<tr><td colspan="4">Sequence Number</td></tr>
<tr><td colspan="4">Acknowledgment Number</td></tr>
<tr><td>Data Offset</td><td>Rsvd</td><td>Flags</td><td>Window</td></tr>
<tr><td colspan="3">Checksum</td><td>Urgent Pointer</td></tr>
<tr><td colspan="4">Options + Padding</td></tr>
<tr><td colspan="4">Data (Variable Length)</td></tr>
</table>

The TCP protocol provides the following major services:

- Reliable data transfer
- Connection-oriented virtual circuit
- Buffered transfer
- Resequencing
- Multiplexing
- Efficient, full-duplex transmission
- Flow control

Flow Control

TCP identifies each octet sent (remember that TCP is stream oriented) using a sequence number. The sequence number is used for purposes of acknowledgment, in the reordering of received octets, and also for the rejection of duplicates. Octets that may need to be retransmitted are contained in buffer space on the sending side until an ACK is received.

In TCP, efficient transmission over the network, and flow control between senders and receivers, is achieved by using a variable sliding window mechanism. It is important to understand a simple acknowledgment protocol before the reasoning behind sliding windows (and then variable sliding windows) becomes apparent. Figure 4-4 illustrates the basics of an acknowledgment protocol.

Sliding Windows

A mechanism is needed to make stream transmission efficient. The general approach is to use a *sliding window*. The idea is to make better use of the available network bandwidth by filling up the pipe at all times. The weakness with the simple positive acknowledgment protocol in the previous section is that there is often a significant amount of latency between

FIGURE 4-4

Sliding window messages

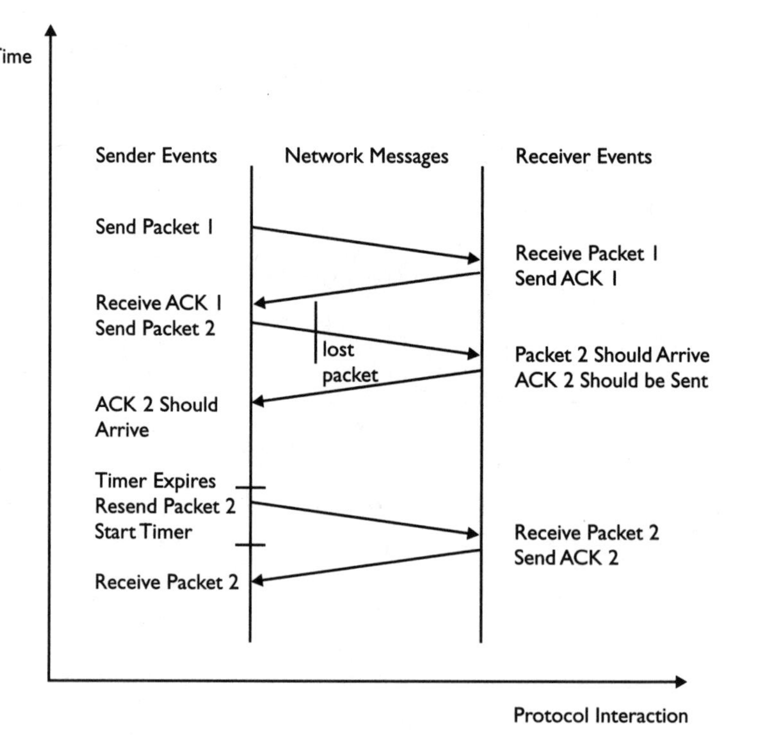

packets. Latency is the lag time between the initiation of the packet transfer and the completion of the packet transfer at the destination.

With sliding windows, several packets can be sent out at once. As acknowledgments come back, new packets are sent out. In this manner, more of the available bandwidth is used on an ongoing basis. A well-tuned sliding window protocol can keep the network completely saturated with packets and obtain substantially higher throughput.

It should be noted that TCP operates in full-duplex mode, so both the sender and receiver may be transferring data simultaneously over the same connection, one in each direction. The implication of this is that each end system maintains two windows per TCP connection, one for sending and the other for receiving. TCP uses a variable sliding window size as an enhancement to a fixed sliding window size. This "window advertisement" provides a dynamic method for TCP to tune itself between end systems, based on such things as availability of buffers.

It should be noted that variable sliding windows solve the end-to-end flow control problem, but have no concept of the intervening network. If an intermediate node such as a router becomes congested, there is no mechanism defined that can notify TCP. If a particular TCP implementation is reactive to timeouts and retransmits, this can severely exacerbate network congestion. Instead, most TCP implementations use congestion avoidance techniques. Congestion avoidance techniques are beyond the scope of the CCIE training. It should be noted, however, that congested gateways do send ICMP source quench messages to transmitting nodes requesting them to throttle back. This is discussed in the section on ICMP. ACKs (Acknowledgments) are embedded in return packets if there are packets queued to be sent. If there are no packets queued to be sent, an explicit ACK packet is sent.

UDP

UDP is a much simpler protocol than TCP, and is useful in situations where the reliability mechanisms of TCP are not necessary. UDP provides a connectionless, "unreliable" datagram service. The UDP header has only four fields: source port, destination port, length, and UDP checksum. The source and destination port fields serve the same functions as they do in the TCP header. The length field specifies the length of the UDP header and data, and the checksum field allows packet integrity checking. The UDP checksum is optional.

UDP Flooding

UDP flooding uses the IEEE 802.1d spanning-tree algorithm to forward packets in a controlled manner. Transparent bridging is enabled on each router interface for the sole purpose of building the spanning tree. The spanning tree prevents loops by stopping a broadcast from being forwarded out an interface on which the broadcast was received. The spanning tree also prevents packet duplication by placing certain interfaces in the blocked state (so that no packets are forwarded) and other interfaces in the forwarding state (so that packets that need to be forwarded are forwarded).

To enable UDP flooding, the router must be running software that supports transparent bridging, and bridging must be configured on each interface that is to participate in the flooding. If bridging is not configured for an interface, the interface will receive broadcasts, but the router will not forward those broadcasts and will not use that interface as a destination for sending broadcasts received on a different interface.

When configured for UDP flooding, the router uses the destination address specified by the IP broadcast-address command on the output interface to assign a destination address to a flooded UDP datagram. Thus, the destination address might change as the datagram propagates through the network. The source address, however, does not change.

IP Helper Addresses

The second approach that can be used to forward UDP broadcasts is the IP helper address. This is the default setting. In order to configure this, use the IP FORWARD-PROTOCOL UDP global configuration command. By default, the IP FORWARD-PROTOCOL UDP command enables forwarding for the following protocol services:

- TFTP
- DNS
- Time
- NetBIOS Name Server
- NetBIOS Datagram Server
- Boot Protocol
- TACACS

IP helper addresses are a form of static addressing. When using IP helper addresses, it is necessary to specify the IP helper address on every interface receiving broadcasts that need to be forwarded.

CERTIFICATION OBJECTIVE 4.04

Network Layer

The network layer deals primarily with addressing. The four main protocols in the TCP/IP protocol suite at this layer, which maps to OSI Reference Model Layer 3, are:

- **IP** Internet Protocol
- **ICMP** Internet Control Message Protocol
- **ARP** Address Resolution Protocol
- **RARP** Reverse Address Resolution Protocol
- **InARP** Inverse Address Resolution Protocol

IP is the protocol where network and node addresses are set. ICMP is a sub-protocol of IP, and handles the control messages at the network layer.

ARP, RARP, and InARP all resolve IP addresses in different ways, depending on what addressing resources the node is aware of.

Internet Protocol (IP)

The Internet Protocol is defined in RFC 791 and exists at the network layer of the OSI Reference Model. IP can be thought of as a delivery mechanism that moves packets from one host to another. Because it handles the delivery, it also supplies the addressing. IP provides three major functions:

- Connectionless, unreliable delivery service
- Packet fragmentation and reassembly
- Routing functions

Connectionless, Unreliable Delivery Service

The IP protocol is said to provide a connectionless, unreliable delivery service. What this means is that as a whole, the TCP/IP protocol has been designed to operate at different levels in a hierarchy. The term unreliable is used when describing IP because the IP protocol is a best-effort service, and does not guarantee delivery. Reliable delivery is handled at the transport layer by TCP. Connection-oriented activities are handled by TCP as well. The function of IP is to provide the delivery mechanism for getting packets to and from the transport layer protocols.

Packet Fragmentation and Reassembly

A further function of the IP protocol is to achieve efficiency by enforcing an upper limit to the datagram size, based on the maximum transmission unit (MTU). Since one of the major goals of network design is to hide the underlying network technology, IP chooses a convenient datagram size and then proceeds to divide larger datagrams into fragments. This process is called *fragmentation*, and usually occurs on a router somewhere between the source and destination end points of the datagram. Fragmentation is performed in a manner whereby the fragment is sized just right to fit into a single frame for shipment over the network. The fragments are then reassembled at the final destination.

Routing Functions

The IP protocol is best known for its routing functions. Please refer to Chapter 5 for a detailed discussion of IP routing.

Address Resolution Protocol (ARP)

Computers on the same physical network can communicate only if they know each other's physical MAC address. Local physical addresses are just that, local. There are many different physical networks, including Ethernet, Token Ring, and FDDI. As a way to abstract addressing and to provide routing capability, the IP protocol is used instead of local physical addresses. With IP, a unique IP address is bound to each and every unique MAC address. The IP address abstraction is necessary for several reasons.

- It makes addressing logically independent of the physical hardware
- It allows the use of multicast addresses to selected physical MAC addresses
- Administrators don't have to physically manage the MAC address of each NIC
- Replacing the NIC does not change the IP address, only the physical address
- It separates the routing function from the physical/data link layer
- Packets are routed based on destination network, not on destination host

The protocol used to map IP addresses to MAC addresses on broadcast networks is called the Address Resolution Protocol. ARP is a dynamic protocol that is easy to maintain, and has the added benefit of being efficient as well. ARP is a component of the physical (local) network delivery, and is not related to routing or internetworking per se. Figure 4-5 illustrates the ARP broadcast process.

Broadcasts are expensive, so each computer system on the network maintains a cache of all the IP address-to-MAC address mappings that it has learned. When sending to an IP address, a host will always check its ARP cache to see if it already knows the physical address it wants to send to. A host's ARP cache is good for a certain time period, and then times out.

Reverse Address Resolution Protocol (RARP)

The Reverse Address Resolution Protocol is used by systems that know their hardware MAC address but do not yet know their IP address. Examples include X-Windows Stations and diskless workstations. With RARP, a system broadcasts its hardware address. It is then up to a RARP server on the network to recognize that it has been configured with the requester's IP address. The server then contacts the originator directly and informs it of its IP address.

Inverse Address Resolution Protocol (InARP)

The Inverse ARP protocol is generally used in nonbroadcast networks such as Frame Relay. The goal is to dynamically associate a remote data-link connection identifier (DLCI) with an IP address. A router can dynamically determine a remote DLCI by querying the Frame Relay switch. Once it

FIGURE 4-5

ARP broadcast process

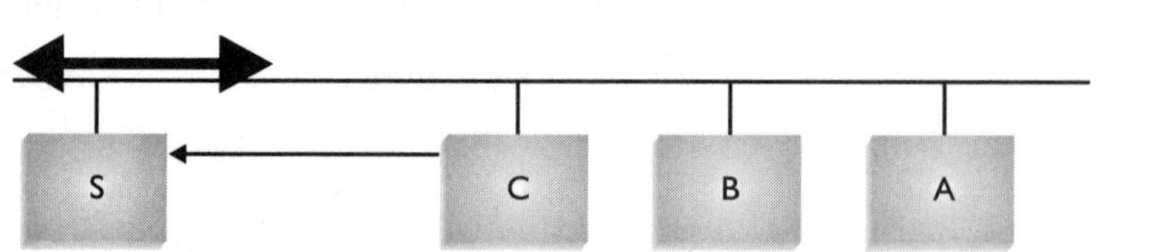

Host broadcasts an ARP request that contains the IP address of host C.
Host C responds with its IP and MAC address using an ARP reply.

knows the DLCI "hardware address," it is then possible to use InARP to obtain the IP address of the remote site.

Internet Control Message Protocol (ICMP)

The Internet Control Message Protocol is defined in RFC 792. ICMP messages are contained within IP datagrams. This ensures that the ICMP message will be able to find its way to the appropriate host within a group of subnets. Table 4-3 lists the ICMP message types.

ICMP Echo Reply (Ping)

The most frequently used ICMP message is popularly implemented in a program called *ping*. It provides feedback to the sender on the state of IP

TABLE 4-3

ICMP Message Types

Type Field	Message Type
0	Echo Reply
3	Destination Unreachable
4	Source Quench
5	Redirect
8	Echo Request
11	Time Exceeded for a Datagram
12	Parameter Problem on a Datagram
13	Timestamp Request
14	Timestamp Reply
15	Information Request
16	Information Reply
17	Address Mask Request
18	Address Mask Reply

connectivity and is often used as a debugging tool. Ping makes use of the ICMP ECHO REQUEST and ECHO REPLY parameters.

ICMP Redirects

The ICMP redirect message is sent by a gateway to the host, and instructs the host to use a different route when the router detects that its route is not as optimal as that of another router on the same network segment. If the gateway detects a better route for the IP datagram, it will send the host a redirect message with the address of the preferred gateway. TCP/IP will then send all traffic to this new IP address for another subnet.

ICMP Source Quench

IP provides a very basic form of flow control with the ICMP source quench message. The source quench message informs the originating host that the gateway or receiving host is being overrun and can't keep up with the traffic. The originating host then lowers the rate at which it sends datagrams to the receiving host, until it stops receiving "source quench" messages. After some time, the originating host may then gradually increase the rate at which it sends out datagrams.

CERTIFICATION OBJECTIVE 4.05

Operating System Commands

In order to access and use protocol services, the implementations of the TCP/IP protocol suite on various operating systems include protocol commands. Some of the most common commands included are FTP and PING. FTP is an extremely useful utility. It provides a way to transfer files from a remote node to the local workstation. PING is used to verify that a network node is accessible, by issuing an ICMP echo command to the address specified.

UNIX

One of the first operating systems to include TCP/IP, was BSD UNIX. The IP commands are integral to the UNIX operating system now. Even before the popularity of the Internet, TCP/IP was ported to other operating systems. But after Internet use became widespread, TCP/IP became fairly standard. Table 4-4 lists some UNIX commands that access TCP/IP protocol suite services. Note that some of these commands require switches in order to work properly. For example, ARP will reveal the ARP table by using the ARP –A command.

TABLE 4-4

UNIX TCP/IP Commands

Command	Usage
ARP	View the ARP table on the local computer to detect invalid entries.
HOSTNAME	Print the name of the current host. The HOSTNAME command can also be used to set the hostname on UNIX systems if logged in as root.
NETSTAT	Display protocol statistics and the state of current TCP/IP connections. The NETSTAT command is of particular use when determining the name of each physical interface that is configured on a given system.
IFCONFIG	Used to set the IP address, broadcast address, and netmask. May also be used to view the configuration of an interface determined from the NETSTAT –R command.
PING	The PING command is used to verify whether IP is configured correctly, and that a remote TCP/IP system can be reached.

FROM THE CLASSROOM

TFTP and Syslog

Anyone who works with Cisco routers will need to get comfortable with using TFTP and syslog servers. You will need to use TFTP to back up and possibly to load your configurations and software images, especially if you're not in an environment where you have a Cisco-specific management tool such as CiscoWorks. Fortunately, setting up these services is fairly easy, even if you're not a UNIX guru.

First of all, you need to find the software and set it up. All flavors of UNIX come with TFTP and syslog daemons, but if you're setting up a small lab and don't want to invest in a UNIX box, there are versions available for most Intel-based operating systems, including MS-DOS, Windows 95, and Windows NT. There's even a TFTP server application that runs as an NLM on a Novell NetWare server. Most of the large shareware sites on the Internet have several versions available for you to choose from. Make sure your TFTP server software will support multiple clients simultaneously, if this is a requirement for you. Not all of them do.

The main requirement for the TFTP server software is that there be a network (LAN) connection with a functioning IP stack on the box where you install it, and disk space available on the box with global read and write permissions. TFTP has no provision for authenticating clients, so if you are installing a TFTP server in a production network you will have some security concerns. UNIX versions of TFTP often require that a file be created on the server before it can be written to, and you will need to follow the file-naming conventions of whatever operating system the server software is running on.

The syslog server can be a great help to you if you are using the router's debug facility to troubleshoot a problem. Debug can be a dangerous thing for your router, because every character output from the router to the console screen requires a CPU interrupt, and some debug commands produce so much output they can use 100 percent of your router's CPU cycles, effectively shutting it down. It takes far less processing power for the router to put each debug message in a packet and forward it to a syslog server elsewhere on the network. This is a nicer way to look at debug output as well, because it is stored in a file that can be scrolled, output to a spreadsheet, and sorted, or manipulated in whatever way you like. And if you need to look at debug output from several routers at once, this is the only way to do it.

FROM THE CLASSROOM

Again, a search on the Internet can lead you to an inexpensive or free syslog application if you don't happen to have a UNIX box. Just be aware when you are configuring the router that by default the lowest level of console messages that will be forwarded to the syslog server is "informational." You will need to change that default on the router by using the global configuration command, LOGGING TRAP DEBUG. Don't forget to turn off the debug output to the console at the same time you enable logging to your syslog server.

—By Pamela Forsyth, CCIE, CCSI, CNX

32-bit Windows

TCP/IP commands were incorporated as part of 32-bit Microsoft operating systems, such as Windows NT, Windows 95, and Windows 98. Some of the utilities available are listed in Table 4-5.

The two commands IPCONFIG and WINIPCFG view the same type of IP settings information, and are similar to the UNIX IFCONFIG command used for viewing. However, IPCONFIG is a text-based command, while WINIPCFG has a graphical interface.

TABLE 4-5 Windows TCP/IP Commands

Command	Included in Windows NT	Included in Windows 95	Included in Windows 98
IPCONFIG /ALL	Yes	No	Yes
WINIPCFG	No	Yes	Yes
FTP	Yes	Yes	Yes
ARP	Yes	Yes	Yes
PING	Yes	Yes	Yes
TELNET	Yes	Yes	Yes

CERTIFICATION SUMMARY

Application layer services are user processes occurring at the OSI reference model layer 7, which correlates to the fourth layer of the TCP/IP protocol suite. CCIEs must be familiar with the usage, the transport protocol, and the port numbers for several TCP/IP applications, such as Telnet, TFTP, and FTP.

The OSI reference model presentation and session layer services correlate to the application layer of the TCP/IP model somewhat. However, there are some TCP/IP services that compare to the session and presentation layer functions. These include remote-procedure calls (RPCs), sockets, transport layer interface (TLI), and NetBIOS over TCP/IP.

RPCs are akin to a connectionless session. An RPC abstracts the application layer from the network layer so that remote calls act like local ones.

Sockets are a session layer software interface that allows a wide variety of applications to use and share an Internet connection. WinSock, a version of sockets implemented in Windows, is a dynamic link library (DLL) with some supporting programs, such as a dialer program that initiates the connection.

The transport layer interface (TLI) is a UNIX service that ensures that the transport layer retains its independence from the upper-layer protocols.

NetBIOS is a session layer API that can run over TCP or UDP transport protocols. NetBIOS is not a protocol, although NetBEUI is.

The TCP/IP protocol suite is a four-layer model, but it contains the same services that the OSI reference model yields.

The transport layer consists of two protocols: TCP and UDP. Upper-layer services use either one or the other, and are mapped to a port number in the protocol.

TCP (Transmission Control Protocol) is a connection-oriented, reliable transport. It uses a sliding window method of transporting data in order to control the flow of data. TCP manages the following: reliable data transfer, connection-oriented virtual circuit, buffered transfer, resequencing of data, multiplexing, full-duplex transmission, and flow control.

UDP (User Datagram Protocol) is a connectionless transport layer protocol in the TCP/IP protocol stack. UDP exchanges datagrams without acknowledgments or guaranteed delivery, which requires other protocols to handle error recovery and retransmission. UDP is defined in RFC 768.

The network layer handles addressing. The protocols in this layer are: ICMP, IP, ARP, InARP, and RARP. IP assigns the network and node address to the node. ICMP sends control messages using the IP address. ARP, InARP, and RARP all handle resolving the IP address of a node with the MAC address, depending on the information that the node already has.

There are a number of operating system commands that access TCP/IP functions. These commands include FTP, PING, and ARP. The commands enable the user to access the TCP/IP network connection and control various aspects of it.

TWO-MINUTE DRILL

- ❑ For internetworks consisting of heterogeneous computer systems that need to communicate with each other, TCP/IP stands out as the common denominator across all types of platforms.
- ❑ The TCP/IP protocol suite has four major layers, which can roughly correspond to the seven layers of the OSI reference model.
- ❑ Applications function at the OSI reference model layer 7, or layer 4 of the TCP/IP suite.
- ❑ The TCP/IP protocol model does not have a formal presentation or session layer in general.
- ❑ Remote procedure calls are a method for executing programs (here called "procedures") on other network nodes, such that they appear to be executing locally.
- ❑ Berkeley Sockets is a session layer Application Programming Interface (API).
- ❑ Windows sockets (WinSock) runs on computer systems that use the Microsoft TCP/IP-32 stack.

- ❑ TLI ensures that the transport layer will retain its independence from the session, presentation, and application layer services.
- ❑ The NetBIOS (Network Basic Input/Output System) encountered in Microsoft environments is not a protocol, but a session layer API.
- ❑ It should be noted that in the Microsoft model, NetBIOS, can bind to TCP/IP, IPX, or NetBEUI.
- ❑ The transport layer's function is to provide the reliable transport of data between two systems, regardless of the underlying networks in between.
- ❑ The Transmission Control Protocol is defined in RFC 793 and defines a reliable, connection-oriented full-duplex byte stream for a user process.
- ❑ In TCP, efficient transmission over the network, and flow control between senders and receivers, is achieved by using a variable sliding window mechanism.
- ❑ A well-tuned sliding window protocol can keep the network completely saturated with packets and obtain substantially higher throughput.
- ❑ UDP provides a connectionless, "unreliable" datagram service.
- ❑ UDP flooding uses the IEEE 802.1d spanning-tree algorithm to forward packets in a controlled manner.
- ❑ The second approach that can be used to forward UDP broadcasts is the IP helper address.
- ❑ The network layer deals primarily with addressing.
- ❑ IP can be thought of as a delivery mechanism that moves packets from one host to another.
- ❑ The protocol used to map IP addresses to MAC addresses on broadcast networks is called the Address Resolution Protocol (ARP).
- ❑ The Reverse Address Resolution Protocol is used by systems that know their hardware MAC address but do not yet know their IP address.

- ❑ The Inverse ARP protocol is generally used in nonbroadcast networks such as Frame Relay. The goal is to dynamically associate a remote data-link connection identifier (DLCI) with an IP address.
- ❑ ICMP messages are contained within IP datagrams. This ensures that the ICMP message will be able to find its way to the appropriate host within a group of subnets.
- ❑ Some of the most common protocol commands included are FTP and PING.
- ❑ One of the first operating systems to include TCP/IP was BSD UNIX.
- ❑ TCP/IP commands were incorporated as part of 32-bit Microsoft operating systems, such as Windows NT, Windows 95, and Windows 98.

SELF TEST

The following questions will help you measure your understanding of the material presented in this chapter. Read all the choices carefully, as there may be more than one correct answer. Choose all correct answers for each question.

1. Match the following application layer services to their corresponding transport layer protocol port:

A. SMTP	1. TCP/23
B. FTP	2. TCP/25
C. TFTP	3. TCP/80
D. Telnet	4. TCP/21
E. HTTP	5. UDP/69
F. DNS	6. TCP/53

2. Which OSI reference model layer does Telnet function at?

   A. Transport

   B. Network

   C. Session

   D. Application

3. How many layers does the TCP/IP protocol suite have, compared to the OSI reference model?

   A. TCP model has 4, OSI model has 6

   B. TCP model has 7, OSI model has 8

   C. TCP model has 4, OSI model has 7

   D. TCP model has 7, OSI model has 4

4. The TCP/IP protocol suite has a formal session layer that includes NetBIOS, RPCs, and TLI functions.

   A. True

   B. False

5. What is the function of RPCs?

   A. To move files from remote PCs to a local PC

   B. To make remote function calls transparent, so they appear to be local

   C. To initialize a program on a remote PC

   D. To send a procedure that is local to a remote node for processing elsewhere

6. What does RPC stand for?

   A. Remote personal computer

   B. Reserved-programming call

   C. Routed-procedure call

   D. Remote-procedure call

7. What OSI reference model layer do sockets function at?

   A. Application

   B. Presentation

   C. Session

   D. Transport

   E. Network

   F. Data link

   G. Physical

8. What function do sockets perform?
   - A. They make remote functions appear local, transparent to the user
   - B. They transfer files to and from remote nodes
   - C. They make the transport layer independent
   - D. They allow multiple applications to share the same connection to the network

9. What is WinSock?
   - A. A version of sockets for the Microsoft Windows platform
   - B. Sockets on BSD UNIX
   - C. A session layer API commonly considered to be its own protocol
   - D. A network layer service for Microsoft Windows

10. What does TLI do?
    - A. It makes remote functions appear local, transparent to the user
    - B. It transfers files to and from remote nodes
    - C. It makes the transport layer independent
    - D. It allows multiple applications to share the same connection to the network

11. What OSI layer does NetBIOS function at?
    - A. Application
    - B. Presentation
    - C. Session
    - D. Transport
    - E. Network
    - F. Data link
    - G. Physical

12. Which protocols can NetBIOS bind to? (Select all that are applicable.)
    - A. Appletalk
    - B. IPX
    - C. IP
    - D. NetBEUI

13. What layers do not exist in the TCP/IP model that are in the OSI model?
    - A. Application, presentation, and network
    - B. Presentation, session, and data link
    - C. Session, network, and physical
    - D. Presentation, data link, and physical

14. What is a socket in the transport layer?
    - A. The socket is an IP address plus a port
    - B. An API that makes the transport layer independent
    - C. An API that allows multiple applications to share a network connection
    - D. A function that makes remote procedures appear to be local

15. What is a port?
    - A. An API that makes the transport layer independent
    - B. An API that allows multiple applications to share a network connection
    - C. A function that makes remote procedures appear to be local

D. The point where upper-layer processes access transport layer services

16. Which of the following services uses a process called windowing?

    A. Reliable data transfer
    B. Connection-oriented virtual circuit
    C. Buffered transfer
    D. Resequencing
    E. Multiplexing
    F. Efficient, full-duplex transmission
    G. Flow control

17. What is UDP?

    A. An API that makes the transport layer independent
    B. A connectionless, unreliable transport protocol
    C. An API that allows multiple applications to share a network connection
    D. A function that makes remote procedures appear to be local

18. What is IP?

    A. It is the transport mechanism for upper layer services
    B. It is the session layer API for making the transport layer independent
    C. It is the network layer protocol that moves data from one node to another
    D. It is the physical layer protocol for Internet connections

19. What is ICMP?

    A. It is a network layer protocol that handles control messages
    B. It is a network layer protocol that resolves addresses
    C. It is a session layer API that makes remote procedures transparent to a user
    D. It is a transport layer function for unreliable transport

20. Ping sends an ICMP echo command to an IP address in order to determine whether a network connection exists to that node.

    A. True
    B. False

21. Which of the following best describes TCP/IP?

    A. A static protocol
    B. A proprietary protocol
    C. A collection of internetworking protocols

22. UDP and TCP represent mechanisms used by which layer of the TCP/IP?

    A. Data link layer
    B. Physical layer
    C. Presentation layer
    D. Transport layer

23. RPCs provide which of the following?

    A. Connection-oriented session
    B. Transparency to make remote calls look local

C. Portability of applications between heterogeneous systems

D. A and C only

E. B and C only

F. A, B, and C

24. Distributed Computing Environment (DCE) is an example of:

A. OSI model

B. RPC implementation

C. Extreme Data Representation

D. A and B

25. Which statement is true of WinSock?

A. It is a MAC application

B. It represents a graphical user interface

C. It represents a network layer

D. It provides the means for sharing an Internet connection between multiple IP protocol suite utilities

26. Which statement is true of TLI?

A. It is a layer in the OSI model

B. It is a layer in the TCP/IP model

C. It is a System V API

D. It is part of the UNIX Kernel

27. Which statement is true of Windows Name Server (WINS)?

A. It is a protocol

B. It provides capability for name resolution

C. It is a network layer

D. It is a proprietary name server

E. A, B, and D only

F. B and D only

28. ICMP, IP, ARP, and RARP of the IP protocol suite map to:

A. OSI layers 1 and 2

B. OSI layer 5

C. OSI layer 3

D. OSI layer 2

29. Which layer is most important in providing reliable data exchange between two systems?

A. Physical layer

B. Data link layer

C. Session layer

D. Transport layer

30. Which of the following does TCP provide?

A. Unreliable data stream

B. Connectionless virtual circuit

C. Flow control

D. Structured byte stream movement

31. Of the following, which field is not a part of the TCP header?

A. Subnet mask

B. Sequence number

C. Data offset

D. Destination port

32. What is the sequence number in a TCP header used for?

A. Acknowledgments

B. Reordering of the octets received

C. Rejecting duplicate octets

D. All of the above

33. Variable sliding windows provide an explicit mechanism for notifying TCP if an intermediate node (for example, a router) becomes congested.

A. True

B. False

34. Which of the following parameters is not a part of UDP header?

A. Source port

B. Urgent pointer

C. Checksum

D. Length

E. Destination port

35. When a router has been configured for UDP flooding, the source address might change, but the destination address will not change as the datagram propagates through the network.

A. True

B. False

36. The spanning-tree algorithm allows:

A. Forwarding of packets with no control

B. Forwarding of broadcasts to an interface which already has received the broadcast

C. Prevention of duplication of forwarding of packets

D. A and B only

37. IP helper addresses are a form of ________ addressing and require the command specification of ________ on every interface receiving broadcasts that need to be forwarded.

A. Static / IP header address

B. Dynamic / IP forward-protocol UDP

C. Dynamic / IP forward-protocol TCP

38. Which of the following protocols provide address resolution?

A. ICMP

B. RARP

C. IP

D. UDP

E. TCP

39. IP is described as an unreliable mechanism because it does not guarantee delivery.

A. True

B. False

40. What does fragmentation in TCP/IP represent?

A. Segmenting of datagrams into 53-byte packets for ATM applications

B. Division of larger datagrams into convenient size packets

   C. A process that occurs on a router
   D. A, B, and C
   E. A and C only
   F. B and C only

41. Which of the following statements is true of ARP?
   A. It makes a MAC address logically independent of the physical hardware
   B. It makes it necessary for the administrator to physically manage the MAC address of each NIC
   C. It integrates routing function with the physical and data link layers
   D. It routes packets based on destination host, not on destination network

42. A host's ARP cache is good forever once it has been created.
   A. True
   B. False

43. ARP is a broadcast protocol, and ARP caching is used because broadcasts are expensive.
   A. True
   B. False

44. Reverse Address Resolution Protocol (RARP) is termed "reverse" because:
   A. It is used by the system that knows its IP address but does not know its MAC address
   B. It is used by the system that knows its MAC address but does not know its IP address
   C. It is used by the system that knows the destination's IP address but does not know the destination's MAC address
   D. It is used by the system that knows the destination's MAC address but does not know the destination's IP address

45. Inverse Address Resolution Protocol (InARP) is generally used by:
   A. Broadcast networks
   B. Nonbroadcast networks
   C. Both broadcast and nonbroadcast networks

46. The PING command makes use of what ICMP parameter?
   A. Redirect
   B. Source quench
   C. Echo reply
   D. Destination unreachable

47. ICMP Redirect is sent by:
   A. A host to the gateway
   B. A gateway to the host
   C. A router to another router
   D. A router to a network

5

IP Routing Protocols

CERTIFICATION OBJECTIVES

5.01 Why Routing Protocols?

5.02 Static Routes and Dynamic Routes

5.03 Default Routes

5.04 Link State vs. Distance Vector

5.05 RIP

5.06 IGRP

5.07 OSPF

Imagine that continental United States has a single road that simply winds around to get to every place people need to go. Every car, every truck, every bicycle, every parade, and every pedestrian must use this single road. The traffic from millions of cars would be horrific—jams all over the place. Accidents would back traffic up from New York to Los Angeles. Obviously, that much traffic needs to be turned onto different roads to split it up into manageable portions. The roads still need to intersect, so that people can still reach whichever destination they need to reach. Multiple intersections can also provide redundant routes, so that huge traffic delays can be avoided. By sending traffic on different routes, a traffic jam makes less of an impact. Everything becomes more efficient and reliable.

In this same way, internetwork traffic needs to be split up to avoid network traffic jams. The process of directing internetwork traffic onto different networks is called *routing*.

CERTIFICATION OBJECTIVE 5.01

Why Routing Protocols?

Internetworks use routing to get data from one network to another. In order to keep data on the best path to its destination, some sort of map of the routes available on the network is needed. The mapping of the networks that the data travels to is handled by a routing protocol.

Local Area Networks (LANs) have an inherent performance limit, which is dependent upon size or complexity. Routers, and their routing protocols, can resolve some common bottlenecks and other conditions that degrade network efficiency. These limits include:

- Network physical segment size
- Number of hosts per segment
- Redundancy
- Amount of traffic
- Dissimilar network topologies

Depending on the type of network, whether Ethernet, Token Ring, or other protocol, the network segment size is limited. A new segment must be created to support nodes located beyond the distance limit set by the segment size—usually measured in cabling distance, or wireless limit. For instance, Ethernet segments using twisted-pair copper wiring are limited to a maximum physical distance from the node to the hub. When a new node is added beyond this limitation, and another segment is created, there must be some way of getting traffic from one segment to the other. This can be done by *bridging* or by *routing*, and more recently by *switching*. Bridging is the capability to connect two or more physical network segments such that the connection is transparent to the network. In bridging, broadcasts are sent to all nodes on the bridged segments, and all nodes are considered to be in the same logical network (subnet). Bridging occurs at the data link layer. Switching is a way to increase bandwidth (as well as limit the amount of traffic a node encounters) by providing a dedicated channel for each switched port. Switching occurs at the data link layer. In contrast to either of these network traffic-guiding methods, routing connects multiple logical networks such as Ethernet and Token Ring, into a single internetwork, with each separate logical network maintaining its logical network address. Routing occurs at the network layer, and includes the capability to separate the management of the segments on the internetwork.

The number of hosts allowed on each segment is limited on a network topology. This limit varies, depending on the type of network topology used. For example, an Ethernet segment using twisted-pair wiring is limited to the number of hosts, or nodes. Once the maximum number of hosts has been reached, another segment must be created, and the traffic to that segment must be bridged or routed.

Bridging can offer a single path for traffic between segments. However, when multiple transmission paths are needed, routing may be implemented to support those multiple paths. When redundancy is required for internetwork traffic, a routing protocol may be implemented with that option. Figure 5-1 illustrates redundancy with routing.

Congestion is the point where the amount of traffic exceeds the network capacity. Congestion in a network can be debilitating to its use. Bridging, switching, and routing can control the amount of traffic.

FIGURE 5-1

Redundant routes between two networks

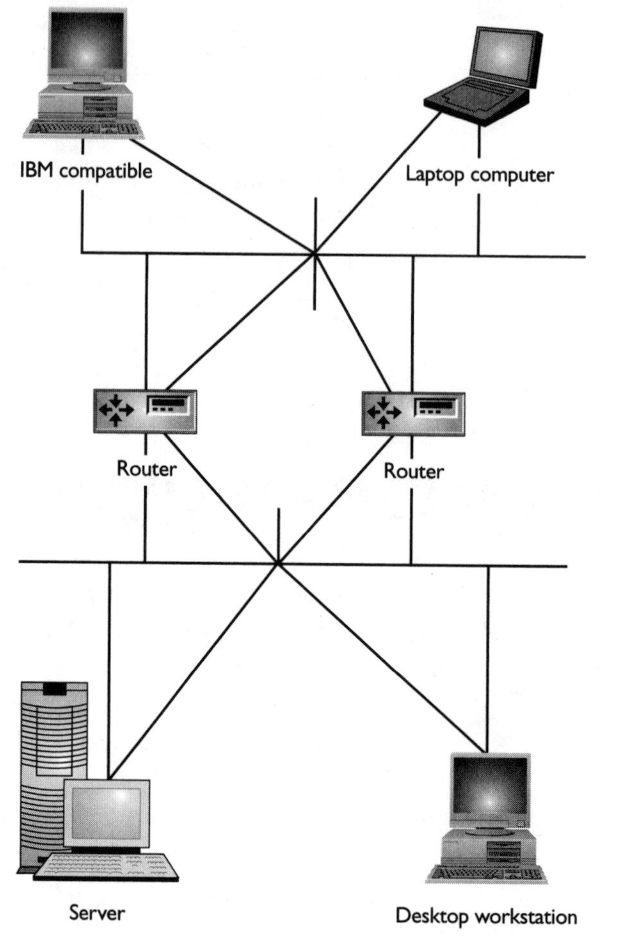

Some routing protocols can handle flow control, so that if a router is congested, another router sending internetwork traffic to it can be notified by the routing protocol to slow down the rate that data is being sent to the router. Routing protocols do this to ensure that minimal delay is encountered when routers become overloaded. Figure 5-2 illustrates the process of traffic control with routing.

FIGURE 5-2

Traffic controlled with routing

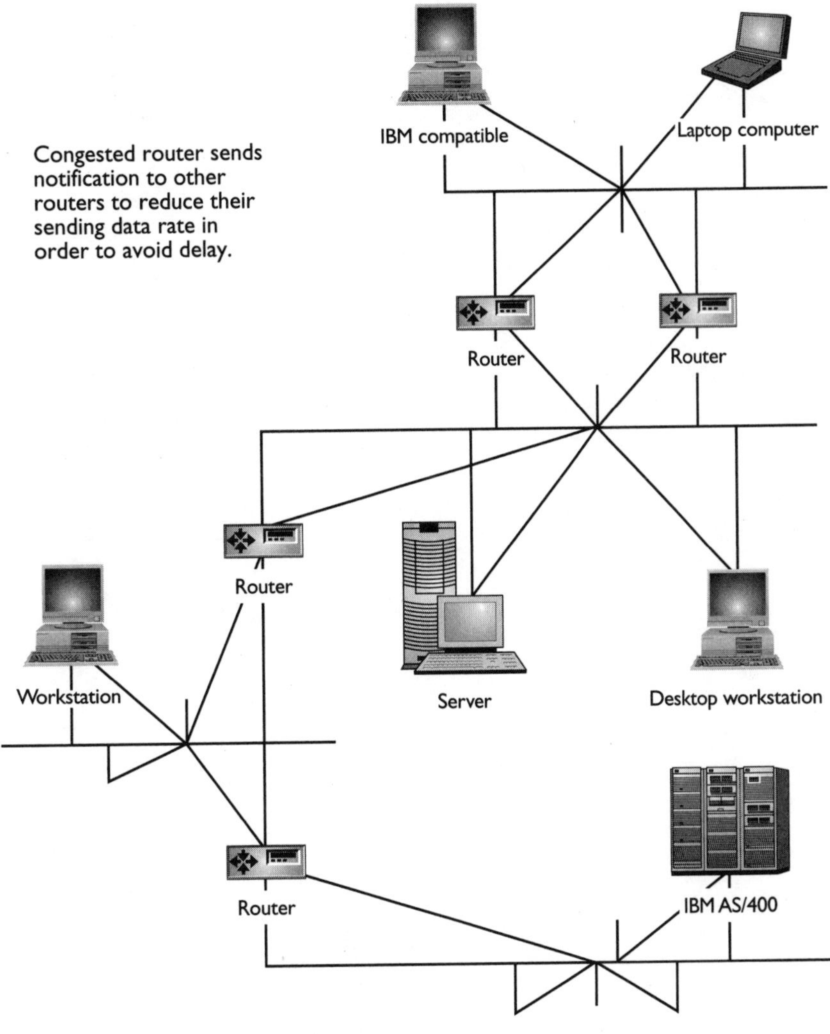

Dissimilar network topologies, such as FDDI, X.25, and ATM, cannot always be bridged or switched, because the nature of the physical media or physical layer protocol prevents it. In order to transmit internetwork traffic, dissimilar networks must be routed, as shown in Figure 5-3.

FIGURE 5-3

Dissimilar networks routed

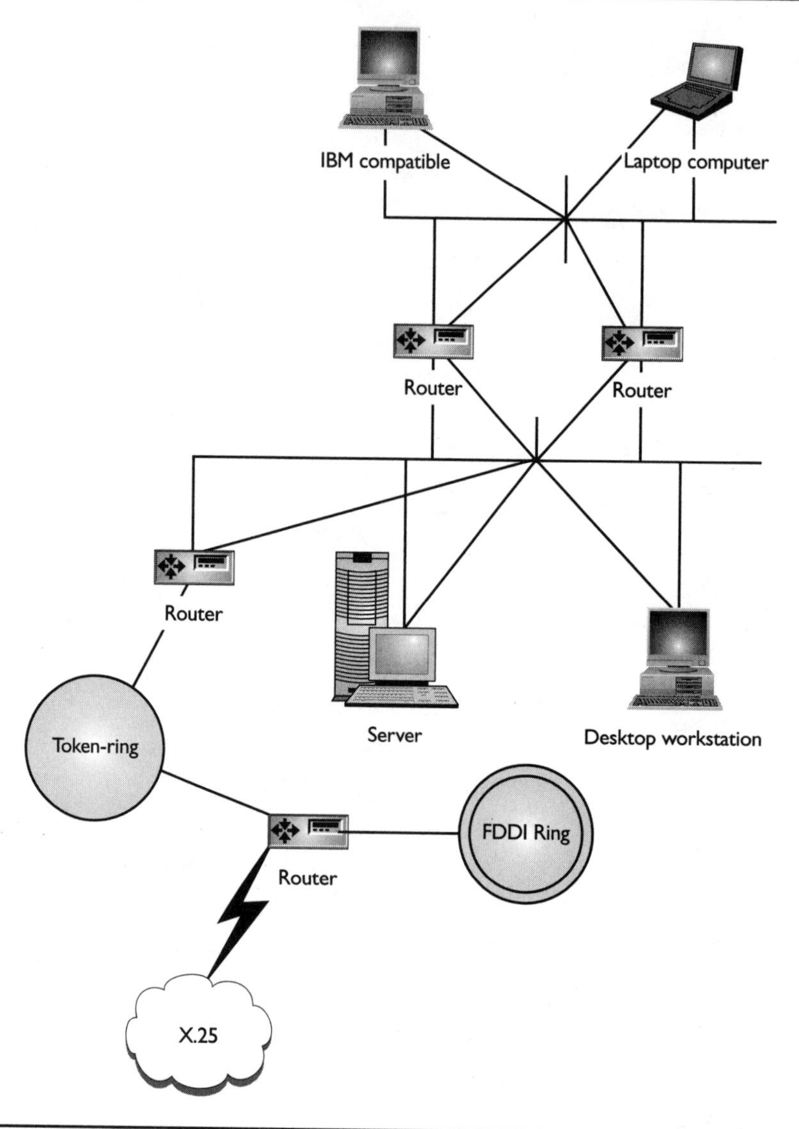

Theory

There are two basic mechanisms that make up routing:

- Determination of routes
- Transmission of data packets across the internetwork

These items will be discussed for each routing protocol. There are several different routing protocols, such as RIP or OSPF, and each determines the best routes in a different way. The data transmission itself is similar, if not identical across different routing protocols.

Algorithms for Route Determination

One of the terms to be aware of for route determination is *metric.* A metric is the value of a variable, such as the network delay, after the routing protocol algorithm has computed it. The purpose of the metric is to determine the best route for selection.

Routing protocols both create and maintain a *routing information table,* or *routing table.* This routing table is used in selecting the best route.

Depending on the type of routing protocol used, the routing table may contain different types of routing information about the path to a destination network. For example, in some routing protocols, the routing table may contain the destination network and the next *hop* associated with it. This information states that to get to the destination network, send the data through the interface connected to the "next hop." A *hop* is the next router that the data should hop to, or the router's interface that is connected to the network that the data should hop to. When determining the best route, the one with the least number of hops is selected.

There are algorithms providing an association of the destination with a metric, which is some value determining the distance or cost of the destination. This method allows the determination of the best route by the route with the optimal value. For example, when using a cost metric, the path with the least cost (the cheapest route) is considered optimal.

Another method of determining the routing table is to associate the destination with the path that needs to be taken to reach that destination. This is a simplistic, hops-based routing, without any metric determination based on any other factors, since some hops-based routing protocols can use other factors in determining the metric for a best route. It is a store-and-forward type of method, whereby the packet is stored in the router momentarily and then forwarded to the next path it needs to take at each router it encounters until it reaches the destination network. In Figure 5-4, an illustration of a simple two-router, three-segment network, the routing table would look something like this for Router A:

```
192.168.3.0 255.255.255.0 192.168.2.2
```

Router A does not need an associated route to the 192.168.1.0 or 192.168.2.0 networks, since they are directly connected to it, and the routing protocol will automatically create those routes for the directly-connected networks. The routing table typically includes the network, the subnet mask, and the next path, which in this case is the interface leading to that network.

Routing protocols also include a methodology for maintaining their routing tables. They exchange information such as a *routing update*. The routing update can consist of the router's entire routing table, or only the portion that has changed. These communications are essential for keeping the routing tables accurate, as well as allowing optimal routes to be chosen. Depending on the routing protocol used, a routing update can be sent on a periodic interval, or it can be triggered by a topology change. Figure 5-5 illustrates one example of an event triggering a routing update.

FIGURE 5-4

A simple three-segment network

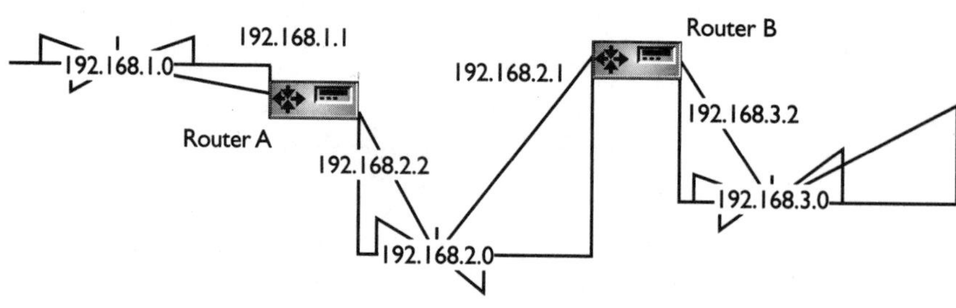

FIGURE 5-5

Routing updates

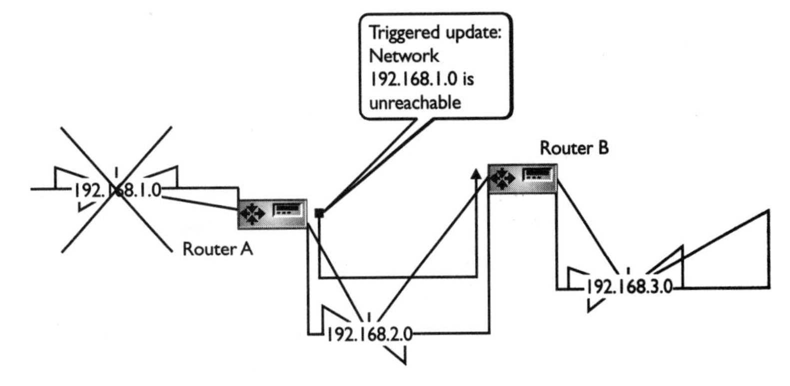

The algorithm for routing a data packet from one interface to another within the router is similar for most routing protocols. A node sends a packet to another node on a different network. It sends that packet using the network/node address of the destination node, which seems fairly straightforward. However, the node adds the MAC (Media Access Control) layer address of the *router* to the packet. The MAC layer address (also known as the hardware address) is part of the data link layer.

By virtue of that hardware address, the router receives the packet, and looks at the network/node address of the destination node. The router determines that it can or cannot forward the packet to the destination network. If it can, the router strips off its own MAC layer hardware address, and then puts the hardware address of the next hop onto the packet. If it cannot route the packet, the packet is either dropped or forwarded onto the default route.

If the next hop is not the ultimate destination node, it is almost always another router. That router can then perform the same operation on the packet by determining the next hop, stripping off the MAC layer address, adding the next hop's address, and forwarding the packet, and so on until the packet reaches the destination network/node. The one constant item is the network/node address. It does not change, whereas the hardware address changes at each hop.

There are three major objectives of a routing algorithm:

- Accuracy
- Low overhead
- Quick convergence

Accuracy is the capacity of the routing algorithm to determine the optimal route based on the metrics used. This means that the metrics of the routing algorithms are what determines the accuracy of the route selection.

Low overhead can be applied to both bandwidth and CPU usage. When referring to CPU usage, a routing protocol would need to be elementary in its computations. A router with limited or overused resources requires the simplest routing protocol. When referring to bandwidth usage, a routing protocol would require small communication messages, at the smallest of periodic intervals. This is essential for an efficient utilization of slow network links. A router should prove stable, as well as efficient, in order to maintain the low overhead criteria.

Convergence is the process of all routers synchronizing their routing information tables, or the time it takes for a single routing change to be reflected in all routers. The speedier the convergence process, the more accurate the routing tables, which leads to an efficient network. If there were never changes to an internetwork's topology, then convergence would not be an issue. However, multiple changes can be made on a network: additions of network segments, additions of routers, downed interfaces on a router, entire routers that are downed, bandwidth usage changes, network bandwidth changes for network links, increases or decreases in a router's CPU usage. All of these conditions can change how a routing protocol should select the optimal routes. A fast convergence also avoids a routing loop, which is discussed later in this chapter.

Some of the types of routing algorithms are:

- Static vs. dynamic
- Interior vs. exterior
- Distance vector vs. link state

Each of these types of algorithms determines an aspect of the routing protocol used. Each type has advantages that may make it more logical for a certain type of internetwork, depending on its size or complexity.

CERTIFICATION OBJECTIVE 5.02

Static Routes and Dynamic Routes

A router makes decisions about which network segment to send a packet on by consulting its routing information table. This table allows it to select just the next route step the packet needs to take, rather than selecting an entire path to the final destination. When the packet reaches another router, that next router will select the next segment to send the packet to.

Dynamic routing protocols include a method for dynamically configuring the routing information table. These are considered dynamic routes. Dynamic routes depend on which links are functioning. The path selection also is based on the criteria within the dynamic routing protocol. The main advantage to dynamic routing is that a route to a remote network can be automatically reconfigured if multiple routes exist and one has gone down due to a nonfunctioning router. This is an advantage to large internetworks. Dynamic routes are both scalable and adaptable.

A static route is a route that has been manually entered into the routing table. Figure 5-6 shows an example of a static route. There are many advantages to static routing.

- No need for a dynamic routing protocol, which reduces overhead on the routers
- Easily configured for small internetworks
- Control over the route selection

In Figure 5-6, each router would have static route configuration.

FIGURE 5-6

Static route

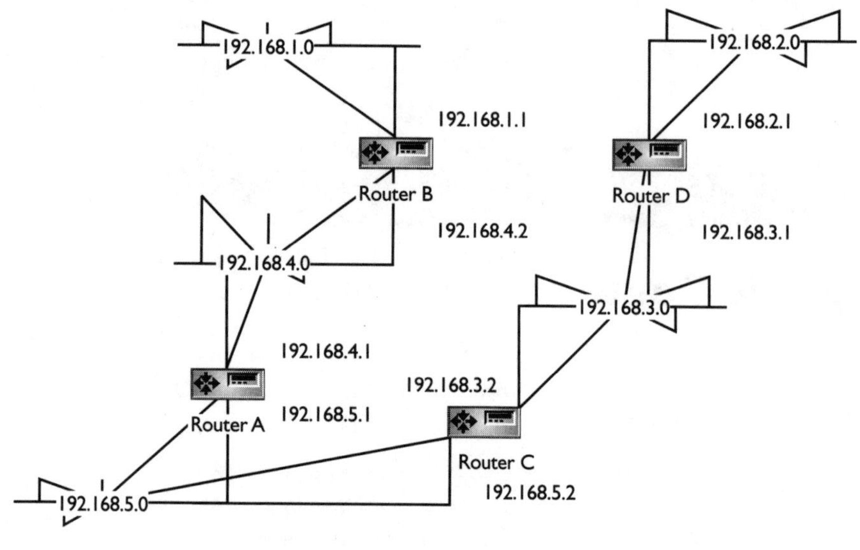

Router A's configuration is as follows:

```
hostname routera
!
interface ethernet 0
      ip address 192.168.4.1 255.255.255.0
!
interface ethernet 1
      ip address 192.168.5.1 255.255.255.0
!
ip route 192.168.1.0 255.255.255.0 192.168.4.2
ip route 192.168.2.0 255.255.255.0 192.168.5.2
ip route 192.168.3.0 255.255.255.0 192.168.5.2
```

Router B's configuration is as follows:

```
hostname routerb
!
interface ethernet 0
      ip address 192.168.1.1 255.255.255.0
!
```

```
interface ethernet 1
      ip address 192.168.4.2 255.255.255.0
!
ip route 192.168.2.0 255.255.255.0 192.168.4.1
ip route 192.168.3.0 255.255.255.0 192.168.4.1
ip route 192.168.5.0 255.255.255.0 192.168.4.1
```

Router C's configuration is as follows:

```
hostname routerc
!
interface ethernet 0
      ip address 192.168.3.2 255.255.255.0
!
interface ethernet 1
      ip address 192.168.5.2 255.255.255.0
!
ip route 192.168.1.0 255.255.255.0 192.168.5.1
ip route 192.168.2.0 255.255.255.0 192.168.3.1
ip route 192.168.4.0 255.255.255.0 192.168.5.1
```

Router D's configuration is as follows:

```
Hostname routerd
!
interface ethernet 0
      ip address 192.168.2.1 255.255.255.0
!
interface ethernet 1
      ip address 192.168.3.1 255.255.255.0
!
ip route 192.168.1.0 255.255.255.0 192.168.3.2
ip route 192.168.4.0 255.255.255.0 192.168.3.2
ip route 192.168.5.0 255.255.255.0 192.168.3.2
```

Note that when configuring a static route the IP ROUTE command is followed by the network that the route will be going to, the subnet mask, and finally the IP address of the next router's interface that data packets should use when addressed to that network.

Static routes are also important when the routing protocol used cannot determine the best route to the destination network. In order to remove a static route, the NO IP ROUTE global command is used.

So, a static routing "algorithm" is simply a definition of the routing table established by the network administrator in order to allow routing on the internetwork. The routing table never changes without a manual update by the administrator.

Static routing does not work well in an environment that encompasses frequent network changes. In a large and constantly changing internetwork, a static routing setup is simply not viable. However, in a small, self-contained internetwork environment with rare changes, static routing would work well.

The routing protocol algorithms described in this chapter (RIP, IGRP, EIGRP and OSPF) are all *dynamic.* They adjust to the changes that occur within the internetworking environment. The periodic updates that are sent throughout the internetwork are analyzed by the receiving routers to determine if there have been any internetwork topology changes. In the event that the internetwork topology has changed, the routers re-run their path selection algorithms and then update their routing tables with the selected routes.

A hybrid solution of dynamic and static routing can be used to increase the stability of an internetwork. In this solution, a static route is designated for the *default route* or a *router of last resort.* (The term *gateway of last resort* is also used.) Packets are forwarded to the default route if no routing entries match the destination address. This may not seem like the best solution, since a nonroutable packet would seem to be useless. However, in an internetwork that is connected to a larger internetwork, but which is self-contained and does not exchange routing information with that other internetwork, it works well. For example, note that in Figure 5-7, the internetwork knows all about the 192.168.1.0, 192.168.3.0, 192.168.4.0, and 192.168.5.0 networks. It is also aware of the network 202.12.37.0, which leads to the Internet. However, the network does not share routing information with the Internet without severely debilitating its routers due to the excessive overhead of all those routes. Nor is it going to be able to share information with other corporate networks, such as corporate customers to whom e-mail and files might be sent, who are also connected to the Internet, and who also do not share routing information with the Internet. In Figure 5-7, the hybrid solution works well for all packets that are

FIGURE 5-7

Default route

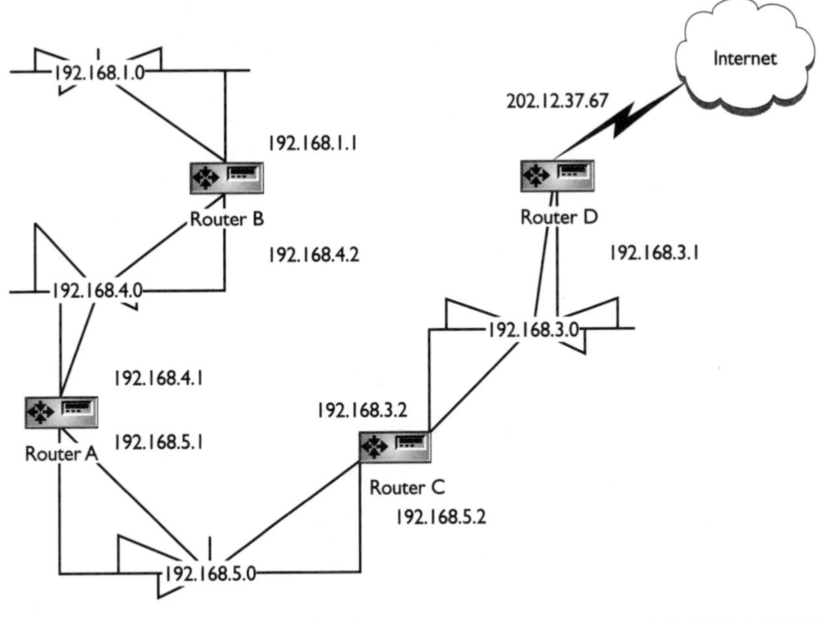

nonroutable—that is, are not sent to the 192.168.1.0, 192.168.3.0, 192.168.4.0, 192.168.5.0, and 202.12.37.0 networks. In this case, the *router of last resort* should be the Internet router connected to Router D, specifically its interface 202.12.37.67.

Some routing algorithms allow for a central control of the routing table. A central router would collect the routing information from all routers and then distribute their routing tables to them. The advantage to central control is that it frees up working routers from the route calculation overhead, and it keeps routing tables consistent. The disadvantage is that it has a single point of failure in the central control router.

Most routing protocols are distributed, and thus router fault tolerant. Each router maintains its own routing table. To synchronize the routing tables, or converge, some routing protocols allow for routers to periodically update each other about the status of their network links.

Some routing protocols allow for a network fault tolerance, since they support multiple "live" routes or redundant routes to the same destination

FROM THE CLASSROOM

Keeping Route Loops from Running You in Circles

Convergence time is important, because the routers in your network are making independent decisions about how to forward individual packets. If some routers have different information than their neighbors, as often happens in a network based on distance vector routing protocols, when a change in network topology occurs, packets can be forwarded from one router to another and back again until their Time to Live expires. A routing protocol with a faster convergence time will minimize the duration of these route-loop episodes, which usually correct themselves in a properly configured network.

If you have only a single routing protocol in use in your network, and your network topology is mainly hierarchical or star-shaped, rather than meshed, you should have no persistent problems with route loops. But if you use a combination of dynamic routing protocols, such as RIP and OSPF, or a combination of dynamic protocols and static routes, you will need to pay careful attention to your configurations. This will be especially true if your network includes many redundant paths, or if its topology is partially meshed.

The key to success here is to think about all your routers together as a system rather than as separately configured individuals. This can prevent loops that will never correct themselves. This is especially critical if you are making any changes to your static routes or to your dynamic protocol configurations. Be sure you understand what the impact on the entire system will be prior to making any changes.

—*By Pamela Forsyth, CCIE, CCSI, CNX*

network. In this case, a network segment can become unreachable by one router, but another route can be obtained to the network. Furthermore, some routing protocols allow for load balancing of network traffic across the multiple redundant routes to the single destination. Some protocols maintain a second-best, or *feasible successor*, entry for each route, so there is no interruption in traffic flow when the primary route fails.

An autonomous system (AS) is a group of networks, or small internetwork, within a larger internetwork. This is also known as an *area* or *domain.* The autonomous system setup is known as *hierarchical.* Newer routing protocols tend to be hierarchical, whereas older routing protocols support flat networks.

Hierarchical routing allows the limitation of routing information propagation throughout an entire internetwork. Instead, routing information is shared only by routers within the autonomous system. Only limited information needs to be shared by routers that are on the border of an autonomous system. Routes are freely exchanged among routers within an AS. By default, routes do not flow from one AS to another, and must be specifically configured to do so. This allows full control over how much detail is shared between autonomous systems.

CERTIFICATION OBJECTIVE 5.03

Default Routes

A default route is the one specified for data to follow if there is no explicit routing information for it to use in finding a direction. If a router has a connection to a small network segment, and a second connection to a large internetwork with multiple different IP subnets, then the interface connecting to the multiple different subnets would be the best interface to designate as the default route. So any packets received by the router that are not destined for the immediate network segments would be sent out the interface with the default route.

In Figure 5-8, both router B and router C can use a default route. In router B, the interface with the address 192.168.2.2 would be the default interface. In router C, the interface with the address 192.168.3.1 would be the default interface.

A default route is best used whenever a router cannot determine the routes to all other networks. One practice for designating default routers is to specify certain routers as *smart routers*. Smart routers contain the routing information for the entire internetwork. Then, designate a smart router as the default router for the other routers on the internetwork. A dynamic routing protocol can sometimes redistribute the default route, which is good when using the smart router internetwork configuration. Or the default router can be set manually on each individual router.

To specify a static default route, use the following command in global configuration mode on the router:

```
ip default-network {network-number }
```

That command looks like this for Router B in Figure 5-8:

```
ip default-network 192.168.4.0
```

This specifies that for all packets not destined for networks 192.168.1.0 and 192.168.4.0 should be sent through the network 192.168.4.0 in order to be forwarded across the internetwork to a final destination.

Here is a typical routing problem, such as you might encounter on the CCNA exam, or in the course of your work.

FIGURE 5-8

Default network example

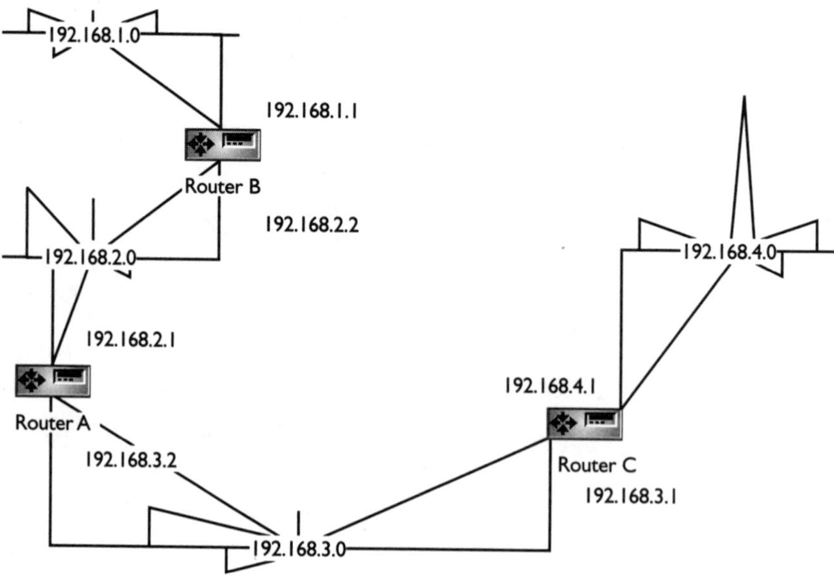

QUESTIONS AND ANSWERS

Gerald manages an internetwork consisting of three routers and four logical networks. He is using a static routing table. Gerald adds a connection to the Internet. If router A is connected to B, then to C, then to D, and then to the Internet, Gerald assumes that he can place a single default route on router D to send everything to the Internet. When the connection goes live, the people connected directly to networks on router D are able to use the Internet, but no one else can. What is the problem?	Because there are no default routes on Routers A, B, and C, the routers will drop the packets for which there are no existing routes. Then, the Internet cannot be reached. To correct the problem, a default route on C should send all packets to D, a default route on B should send all packets to C, and a default route on A should send all packets to B.

CERTIFICATION OBJECTIVE 5.04

Link State vs. Distance Vector

Dynamic routing protocols can be classified by the way they communicate with each other to determine the routing information table. The two types of dynamic routing are link state and distance vector.

Distance Vector Routing Protocols

Distance vector routing protocols are also called Bellman-Ford protocols. A distance vector protocol router periodically sends its neighboring routers two pieces of information:

- The distance in hops, the metric used, or numbers of networks it will take to get to the destination network
- What the next hop is, or which direction (vector) to take to get to the destination network

Distance vector routers periodically send their neighboring routers their entire routing table. The distance vector router builds its routing information table based on this information received from neighboring routers. Then the information is passed on to its neighbors. The result is that routing tables are built from second-hand information, as shown in Figure 5-9.

When a route becomes unavailable on the internetwork, the distance vector routers will learn of the change through either a route change or aging of the network link. A neighboring router to the downed link might send a "route change transmission" (or a "route unavailable") message throughout the internetwork. Aging is set for all routing information. When a route has become unavailable and the information is not sent to the network with the new information sent, the distance vector routing algorithm sets an aging timer on that route. When the route reaches the end of that aging timer, it is removed from the routing table. The aging timer differs according to which routing protocol is used.

Regardless of the type of routing algorithm used, the time it takes for all the routers on an internetwork to update all the changes in their routing tables is called *convergence*. Convergence in distance vector routing, therefore, consists of:

- Each router receiving the updated routing information
- Each router updating its routing information table
- Each router updating the metrics with its own information (for example, adding a hop)
- Each router broadcasting the new information to its neighbors

Distance vector routing is the oldest type of routing protocol algorithm. As stated, the nature of the algorithm is such that each router builds its routing tables on information received from other routers. This means that when the routers use second-hand information in their tables, they encounter at least one problem: the count to infinity problem.

The count to infinity problem is a routing loop that results from the way that distance vector routing protocols uses second-hand information when a router "goes down" or otherwise becomes unavailable to network traffic.

FIGURE 5-9

Distance vector router sending second-hand information

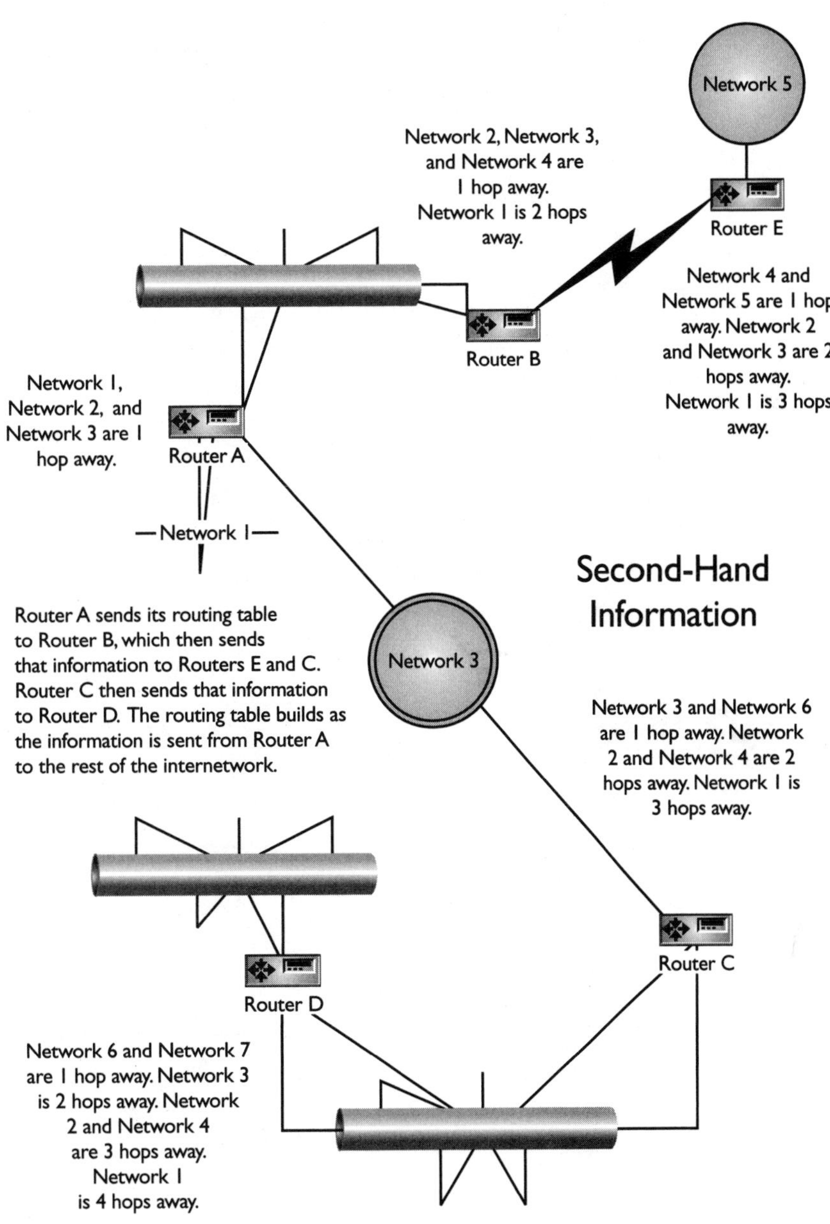

Convergence, or the process of updating routing tables on all routers in an autonomous system, is slow in a distance vector algorithm. This is due to the fact that all routing information in a router's table is sent at once. When all routers do this together, it simply takes a long time for every one to be updated and synchronized.

Figure 5-10 illustrates how a count to infinity problem occurs. Router A sends information about the network segment 192.168.1.0 to router B. Router B will tell Router C about the segment being two hops away, but can also tell Router A that the route exists two hops away. Router A would normally select the best route, which is the connected interface. However, should that segment go down, Router A would then tell Router B that the network segment was three hops away, assuming that router B would have an alternate route to the network. Router B would then advertise that the 192.168.1.0 segment was four hops away, and the hops would increase until they reached the maximum hops, or infinity, for that protocol. For example, if the maximum hops were 16, when the hops reached 16 for the router, it would then consider that route unreachable, remove it from its table and no longer advertise the route.

FIGURE 5-10

Count to infinity

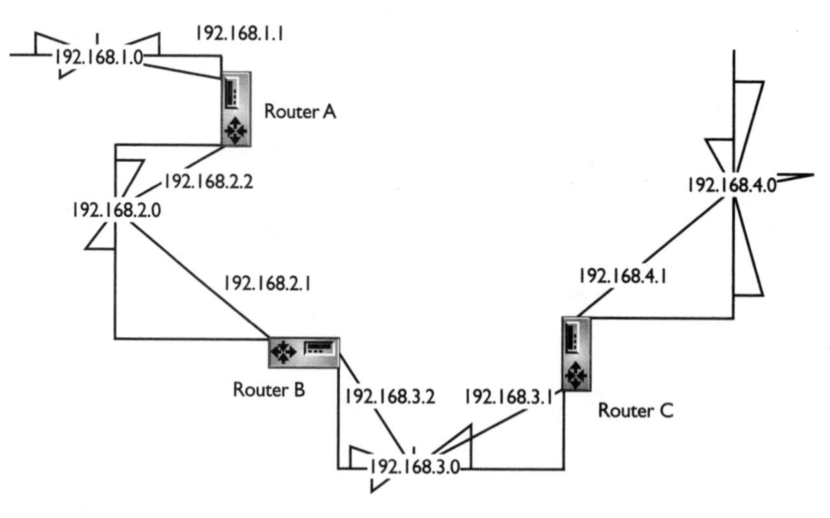

The count to infinity problem can cause an unstable network condition due to inaccurate routing that can last for several minutes. Some distance vector protocols have added some complexity to counteract this.

- Split horizon
- Poison reverse

Split horizon is when a router filters the updates it sends to its neighbors by omitting any references to networks learned from the interface to which it is sending updates. So in Figure 5-10, Router B would send the information about 192.168.1.0 to Router C, but not to Router A.

Poison reverse is a slightly modified version of split horizon. Instead of filtering the updates, it flags that route as unreachable, usually by increasing the hop count to the "infinity" level, when that route came from the interface that it was originally sent from. So, in our example, Router B would send the correct information that network 192.168.1.0 is 2 hops away to Router C. If infinity was defined as 16 hops, Router B would send the information that network 192.168.1.0 is 16 hops away to Router A.

Although split horizon and poison reverse can do much to stabilize a network, they still do not prevent more complex internetwork systems from encountering the count to infinity problem. Figure 5-11 illustrates how a count to infinity problem can still occur.

1. Router C will hear about network 192.168.1.0 from both Router A and Router D. It will select whichever route it hears from first. Assume that it selects Router A.
2. Router C will send an update to Router D that network 192.168.1.0 is available at three hops away, and send a "route unreachable" back to Router A.
3. Since Router D has a closer two-hop route through its other interface, it ignores this route and uses that interface.
4. If the interface on Router B to network 192.168.1.0 goes down, it will stop sending this route to both Router A and Router D. They will also stop sending the route to Router C.

5. However, Router D may receive information from Router C that the route is available three hops away, before Router C hears that the route is unavailable from the source Router A.
6. Instead of dropping the route, Router D updates Router B that it has another route available to the network 192.168.1.0, which Router B sends to Router A.
7. Then, when Router A tells Router C that its original route is not available, Router C will stop advertising that it has that route available to Router D.
8. But it will hear from Router A that another route is available to network 192.168.1.0 that is even further hops away.
9. The router will then tell Router D that this "new" further route is available.

FIGURE 5-11

Poison reverse and count to infinity

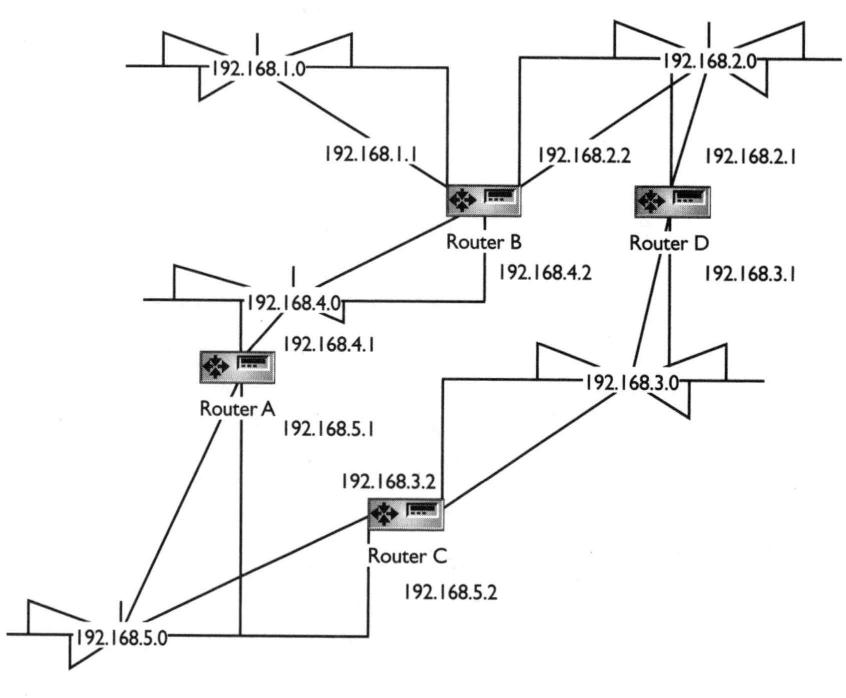

10. The routing loop continues until the "infinity" mark is reached.

To further counteract this behavior, a *holddown interval* was added to the distance vector routing protocol. In this method, when a router hears of a route that is no longer reachable, it starts a timer during which it ignores any information about that destination network. If the holddown interval is sufficiently long, it will prevent these problems. However, in large or complex internetworks, the holddown interval would have to be extremely long in duration in order to prevent the problems. For example, in a network with 100 routers, it is conceivable that an unreachable route might be advertised on a network for almost an hour before it is removed from the network.

To reduce this time, some distance vector routing protocols include *negative reachability* as information in their routing table updates. The route failure is usually updated in the format of having an unreachable hop count, or infinity. This propagates a route failure quickly and speeds convergence, or the delay between the time a route change has occurred and all routers being updated.

Flash updates (also know as triggered updates) are sent whenever a router's routing information table is changed in a way that affects its updates. If a router uses flash updates and negative reachability information, it can speed a failed route throughout a network in seconds. This greatly shortens convergence time.

Link-State Routing Protocols

The purpose of the link-state routing protocol is to map out the internetwork topology. Each link-state router provides information about the topology in its immediate vicinity. This includes:

- The segments (link) to which the router is attached
- The status (state) of the those links

The information is flooded across the network so that all routers receive first-hand information. Link-state routers do not broadcast all information included in their routing tables. Instead, the link-state routers will send information about routes that have changed. Link-state routers will send "hello" messages to their neighbors called a link-state packet (LSP) or link-state advertisement (LSA). The neighbors then copy the LSP to their routing tables and forward that information to the rest of the network. This process is called *flooding*. It results in the sending of first-hand information to the network, building an accurate map of updated routes for the network.

Link-state routing protocols use a method called *cost* rather than hops. Cost is assigned automatically or manually. Depending on the algorithm of the link-state protocol, cost can take into account the number of network segments that the packet will have to cross, the bandwidth of the links, the current load on the link, or even additional weighted amounts placed by the administrator.

1. When a link-state router comes upon a link-state internetwork, it sends a "hello" packet to learn about the neighbors.
2. The neighbors reply with the information about their connected links and the cost metrics associated with them.
3. The original router builds its routing table from this information.
4. Then, as part of the periodic update, the router sends a link-state packet to its neighbors. This LSP includes the links for that router and the associated costs.
5. Each neighbor copies the packet, and the LSP is forwarded on to the next neighbor. This process is called flooding.
6. Because the routers do not recalculate the routing database before flooding the LSP forward, the convergence time is reduced.

One of the major advantages to link-state routing protocols is the fact that a routing loop cannot form because of the way that link-state protocols build their routing information tables. The second advantage is that convergence is very quick in a link-state internetwork due to the updates being flooded to the internetwork immediately uon a change in the routing topology. These advantages, in turn, free up a router's resources, since there is little time spent in processing and bandwidth consumption of bad route information. Maintaining the link-state database for the router's area places a RAM burden on the router. Similarly, the Dijkstra algorithm has to be executed every time a route changes; this can places a huge CPU burden on all the routers. The Dijkstra algorithm is shortest path first, where iteration on path length determines the shortest path spanning tree. Table 5-1 compares the advantages of the two kinds of routing protocols.

Interior vs. Exterior Gateway Protocols

In a large internetwork, such as the Internet, smaller internetworks are divided into autonomous systems. Each AS is considered a self-managed internetwork. A large corporate network connected to the Internet is its own autonomous system, since other hosts on the Internet are not managed by it, and it does not share internal routing information with the Internet

TABLE 5-1

Link State vs. Distance Vector

	Distance Vector	Link State
Periodic updates	Entire routing table sent to neighboring routers	Link-state update packets of only the connected links are flooded to entire network
Routing table	Built on second-hand information	Built on first-hand information
Size of updates	Large	Small
Overhead	More bandwidth consumption for routing table being sent, although limited to local router links for each router	More difficult computations taking up more CPU usage
Convergence	Slow	Fast
Routing loops	More prone, uses split-horizon, poison reverse, and timers to avoid	Less prone. Creates a consistent network map
Routing metric	Hops	Cost

routers. By the same token, no other systems on the Internet manage that corporate network either, nor do they share their routing information with the corporation's autonomous system. One key benefit of an AS is the filtering of granular routes. Instead, only summary routes are exchanged. This minimizes the number of routing updates from flapping routes.

Certain routing protocols were developed for managing systems within an autonomous system. They are called Interior Gateway Protocols (IGP). Interior Gateway Protocols are also known as intra-domain, since they work within the domain, but not between domains. These protocols recognize that the routers they deal with are part of their system and freely exchange routing information with them.

Certain routing protocols were also developed for connecting autonomous systems in a larger internetwork. They are called Exterior Gateway Protocols (EGP). Exterior Gateway Protocols are known as inter-domain, since they work between domains. These protocols recognize that they are on the edge of their system, and only exchange the minimum of information necessary to maintain the capability to route information.

FIGURE 5-12

Autonomous systems

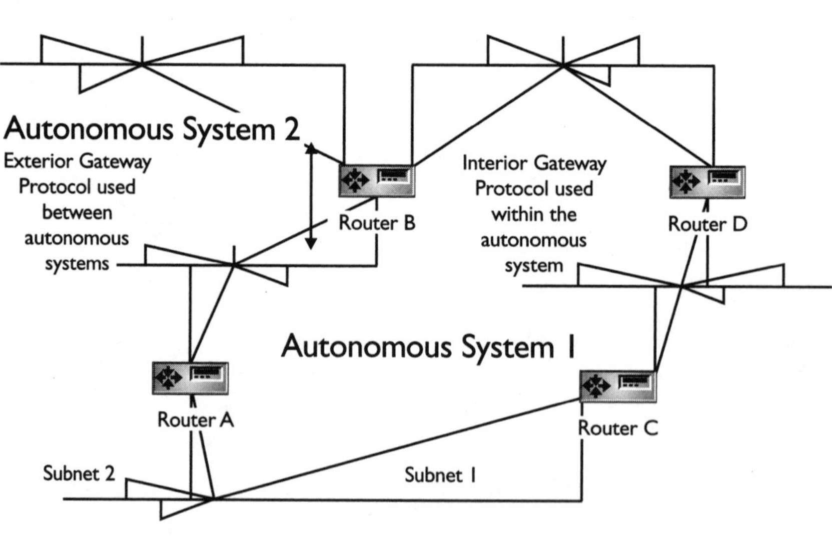

This adds a security level to the autonomous system. Figure 5-12 illustrates an IGP and an EGP.

CERTIFICATION OBJECTIVE 5.05

RIP

Routing Information Protocol (RIP) is a distance vector protocol for use intra-domain (on the interior of a gateway). There are actually two versions of RIP in the TCP/IP protocol suite. Version 1 is the original. Version 2 is the updated version. Version 2 is used almost exclusively because of its enhanced capabilities.

The original RIP was designed for the Xerox PARC Universal Protocol (PUP) in 1980 and subsequently used in XNS (Xerox Network Service protocol suite). In 1982, BSD (Berkeley Standard Distribution) UNIX implemented RIP in routed protocols. RIP was finally defined in 1988 in RFC 1058. Other implementations of RIP exist in other protocol suites, such as Novell's IPX-based RIP, but they will not be discussed in this chapter.

RIP was designed for small networks. It has a limitation of 16 hops, which severely limits the size and design of a network. Routes are chosen based on the hop count, not on the bandwidth or availability of a link. This means that a network with a hop count of two would be selected over a network with a hop count of three, even if the latter network had much more available bandwidth. In Figure 5-13, Router D would select the 56-Kbps link before selecting the route through Router C, and subsequently Router A, in order to reach network 192.168.1.0 through Router B. So RIP can present a large problem when requiring flexibility in route selection criteria.

RIP version 2 includes the following enhancements:

- Authentication

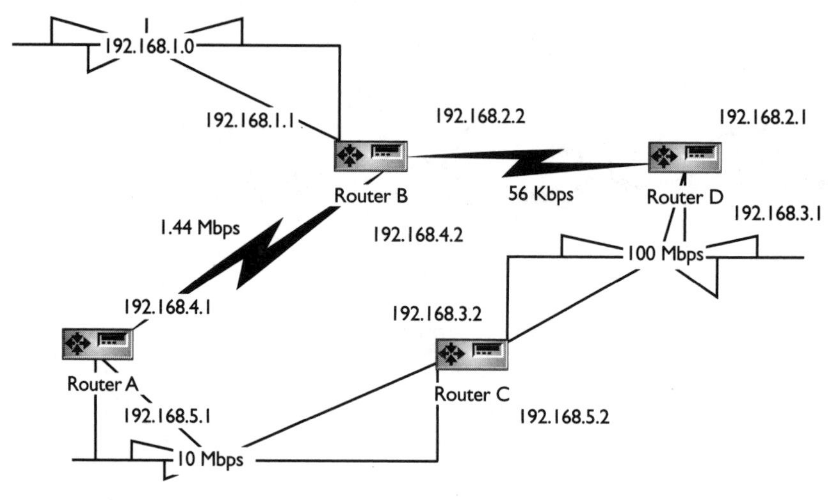

FIGURE 5-13

RIP network selection

- Automatic route summarization
- Variable-length subnet masking (VLSM)

For a router with three interfaces that will be using RIP, basic RIP configuration would be as follows.

```
Router rip
 Network 192.168.1.0
 Network 192.168.2.0
 Network 192.168.3.0
```

The first statement identifies the routing protocol and enables RIP. The next three statements associate the router's directly attached interfaces with RIP. These are the only two required statement sets for RIP to be configured on a router. The remaining RIP configuration statements are optional.

In order to enable RIP routing updates to be sent to nonbroadcast networks, the router must be configured to add those routers to its neighbor's list. The statement neighbor 192.168.2.4 identifies a router with that address to be a neighbor from a nonbroadcast network. The neighbor command is NEIGHBOR *{IP address}*.

Sometimes, there is a need to increase the routing metrics for routes learned from RIP, either for incoming or outgoing route updates. The way to do this is with an offset-list command. The offset-list command is OFFSET-LIST *{name or access list number}* {in|out} *{offset amount}*.

RIP uses a 30-second update timer for when it sends updates to neighboring routers. There are other timers used in managing how RIP works. To adjust the various timers used, there is a single command to use: TIMERS BASIC *{update | invalid | holddown | flush}*. The timers are:

- **Update** the number of seconds between updates
- **Invalid** the number of seconds after which a route is declared invalid
- **Holddown** the holddown interval of seconds on all interfaces for a route that was declared unreachable by one interface, before new updates will be accepted for that network
- **Flush** the number of seconds before a route is removed from the routing information table.

In order to specify a version of RIP, the command VERSION 1|2 can be used. The default configuration is that the router receives RIP version 1 and version 2 updates, but will only send version 2 updates. The VERSION command allows restriction to receive and send only one version of RIP. To override the behavior for a specific interface, the IP RIP SEND VERSION 1|2 command and the IP RIP RECEIVE VERSION 1|2 command can be used.

When using RIP version 2, RIP authentication can be used. The key-chain parameter determines the set of keys that can be used for that interface. The key-chain must be configured for authentication to work on the interface. The command to use is IP RIP AUTHENTICATION KEY-CHAIN *{name of chain}*. The interface can use either MD5 or plain text authentication using the command IP RIP AUTHENTICATION MODE *{text|MD5}*.

To disable the automatic route summarization of RIP version 2, use the command NO AUTO-SUMMARY.

The router automatically validates the source of incoming RIP updates. For invalid source addresses, the update gets discarded. This behavior might not be desirable, and to disable it, use the command NO VALIDATE-UPDATE-SOURCE.

RIP can use the split-horizon mechanism to reduce routing loops. The split-horizon behavior might not be desirable for nonbroadcast networks. To enable split-horizon, use IP SPLIT-HORIZON. To disable split horizon, use NO IP SPLIT-HORIZON. The split-horizon command is interface-level, not router.

When a fast router sends updates to a slower router, there might be a need for a delay in the RIP updates. The default behavior is that there is no delay. To enable a delay of 8 – 50 milliseconds, use the OUTPUT-DELAY *{#of milliseconds}* command.

```
Router rip
 Network 192.168.1.0
 Network 192.168.2.0
 Network 192.168.3.0
!
 neighbor 192.168.2.4
!
 offset-list ethernet 0 in 2
!
 timers basic update 60
!
 version 2
!
 ip rip authentication key-chain chain1
 ip rip authentication mode md5
!
 no auto-summary
!
 no validate-update-source
!
!
 output-delay 40

interface ethernet 0
      ip address 192.168.2.1 255.255.255.0
!
ip split-horizon
```

CERTIFICATION OBJECTIVE 5.06

IGRP

IGRP stands for Interior Gateway Routing Protocol. It is a dynamic distance vector routing protocol created by Cisco. IGRP is used in an autonomous system and includes the capability to advertise interior routes, exterior routes, and system routes, as illustrated in Figure 5-14.

- **Interior routes** routes between subnets in the network attached to a router's interface
- **Exterior routes** routes to networks outside the autonomous system
- **System routes** routes within the autonomous system

FIGURE 5-14

Interior, exterior, and system routes

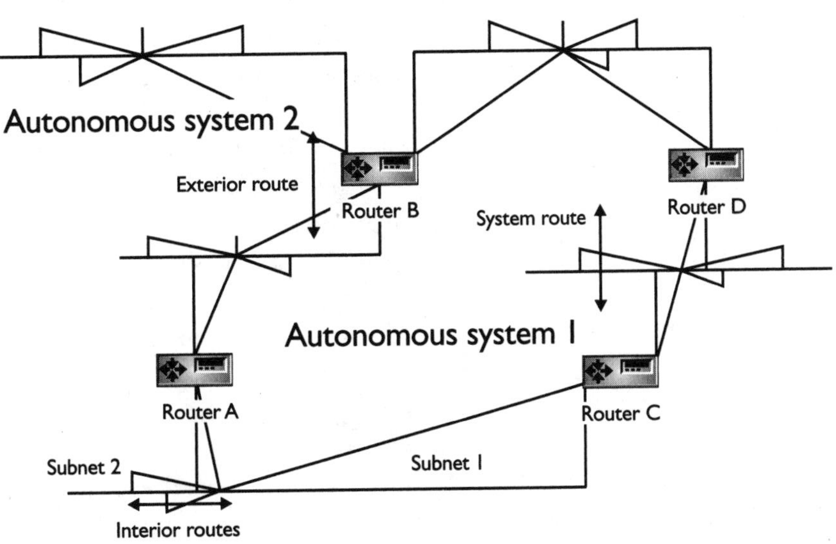

IGRP also includes a concept for the gateway of last resort, which is the route chosen from the exterior routes to be used when there is no other route known for a destination network. Each router can use a different gateway of last resort. When connecting to the Internet, the Internet-connected interface would be a good gateway of last resort choice.

IGRP updates are broadcast every 90 seconds. After a route is missed for three update periods, the route is considered unreachable. After seven update periods, the route is removed from the routing information table. In addition to the periodic updates, IGRP uses flash updates that advise of route changes and poison reverse updates of routes that are unreachable. This is to expedite convergence. Poison reverse is used with the holddown interval, in order to prevent routing loops.

IGRP is an Interior Gateway Protocol using distance vector algorithm. It was designed by Cisco in the mid-1980s for use in complex or large networks. In order to be used on large networks, IGRP has some significant differences from RIP. The first is that the IGRP uses a combination of metrics to determine the best route selection. This includes the bandwidth, the internetwork delay, load, and reliability as factors in determining that optimal path selection. The administrator is given the ability to set the metrics weighting factors to control how routes are selected. If the administrator does not set a weighting factor, then the default weightings are used to calculate the routes.

IGRP also allows multiple redundant paths to a destination network. Multiple paths are automatically failed over from a primary path to an alternate path if the primary path becomes unavailable.

Just like RIP, IGRP uses split-horizon, poison reverse, and holddown intervals to reduce the occurrence of routing loops. Also, flash updates are sent when a route is determined to be unavailable, in order to speed convergence.

There are a few tasks for configuring IGRP on a router. The minimum commands for configuring IGRP are ROUTER IGRP *{autonomous-system}* and NETWORK *{network number}*, which enable IGRP and associate a network with the IGRP protocol, respectively. If no network is associated with IGRP, then it will not be advertised.

IGRP can be configured further. In order to increase the metrics for routes learned via IGRP, an offset list can be set, just as it was for RIP using the OFFSET-LIST { *access list number|name* } { in|out } { *offset #* }.

Like RIP, IGRP is a broadcast protocol. In order to send IGRP routing updates to nonbroadcast networks, use the NEIGHBOR {*ip address*} command.

IGRP allows *unequal-cost load balancing*, which enables network traffic to be distributed across up to four unequal-cost routes to the same destination network. The *path variance* (the difference in advantage of the primary and alternate paths) is used to determine whether a path is *feasible*—that is, it can be included in the routing table by virtue of the closeness of the next router in the path to the destination network. If that metric is within the specified variance, the path is included. The variance is by default set to 1, enabling an equal-cost load balancing. To allow unequal-cost load balancing, use the VARIANCE *{number multiplier}* command. To distribute network traffic proportionately to the ratio of the path costs, or to select a minimum-cost route, use the TRAFFIC-SHARE {*balanced* | *min*} command.

The timers command for RIP is identical for that of IGRP. The timers that can be adjusted are:

- **Update** the number of seconds between updates
- **Invalid** the number of seconds after which a route is declared invalid
- **Holddown** The holddown interval of seconds on all interfaces for a route that was declared unreachable by one interface before new updates will be accepted for that network
- **Flush** the number of seconds before a route is removed from the routing information table

The command for timers is TIMERS BASIC {*update* | *invalid* | *holddown* | *flush*} {*#of seconds*}.

To disable the holddown period, use the command NO METRIC HOLDDOWN. This can be configured to shorten convergence time in

IGRP. Note that all holddown configurations must be identical on all routers within an autonomous system.

IGRP has a maximum hop count of 255 hops. The default configuration for a router is 100 hops. To change this, use the command METRIC MAXIMUM-HOPS *{number of hops}*.

To turn off the feature that validates the source IP address for incoming route updates, use the command NO VALIDATE-UPDATE-SOURCE.

To enable or disable the split-horizon algorithm, especially for nonbroadcast networks like Frame Relay or SMDS, use the commands IP SPLIT-HORIZON and NO IP SPLIT-HORIZON.

```
Router igrp 1
 Network 192.168.1.0
!
 offset-list ethernet 0 out 8
!
 neighbor 192.168.8.11
!
 variance 3
!
 traffic-share balanced
!
 timers basic flush 60
!
 no metric holddown
!
 metric maximum-hops 60
!
 no validate-update-source
!
interface ethernet 0
ip address 192.168.1.8
no ip split-horizon
!
```

EIGRP

Enhanced Interior Gateway Routing Protocol is an updated version of IGRP. EIGRP uses the same distance vector algorithm and distance information as IGRP. It has enhanced convergence properties, and effectively, the same efficiency. The convergence technology is known as Diffusing Update Algorithm (DUAL). DUAL guarantees that there will be no routing loops, and allows all the routers involved in a routing change to synchronize simultaneously. Routers that are not affected by the routing change do not need to synchronize.

EIGRP includes the following features:

- Automatic redistribution of IGRP routes into EIGRP interfaces, and EIGRP routes into IGRP interfaces, when EIGRP and IGRP use the same AS on the same router
- Maximum hops of 224
- Partial updates are sent when the state of a destination network changes, instead of the entire routing information table, resulting in less bandwidth and CPU usage
- Variable-length subnet masks to increase the available IP addresses, or distribute them more appropriately
- Neighbor discovery through a hello system used to identify neighboring routers

The neighbor discovery system is the process that routers use to identify neighboring routers dynamically, and to determine when those routes become unreachable. Small, low-overhead hello packets are used to discover the neighboring routers, and maintain the functioning status of neighbors through the continued receipt of hello packets.

Some EIGRP packets use reliable, acknowledged transport protocols, while others, such as the hello packets, do not. EIGRP gains in reliability as well as bandwidth usage with this scheme.

DUAL has a decision process for route computations. This DUAL finite-state machine uses the distance information (metric) and selects routes to be added to the routing information table based on the feasible successors. A successor is defined as a neighboring router used for packet forwarding with a least-cost path to a destination, and guaranteed not to be a part of a routing loop.

EIGRP, like OSPF, requires an autonomous system number statement in its router configuration. When using multiple processes in EIGRP, the routers in different ASs do not exchange information. The following is a common router configuration for EIGRP:

```
router eigrp 1
 network 192.168.1.0
 network 192.168.2.0
 network 192.168.3.0
```

CERTIFICATION OBJECTIVE 5.07

OSPF

OSPF stands for Open Shortest Path First. It is a link-state protocol for the TCP/IP protocol suite. OSPF uses a concept known as *adjacency*. OSPF routers are considered adjacent when they have synchronized link-state databases (the link-state version of a routing information table).

Route aggregation is also something that OSPF can do. Route aggregation is the capability to limit the number of entries in the link-state database through the use of a different subnet mask, making multiple routes appear to be a single route entry. For the example networks of 192.168.1.0 through 192.168.254.0, the route aggregate would be 192.168.0.0 with a subnet mask of 255.255.0.0, appearing to be the equivalent of a single Class B IP addressed network, while actually consisting of 254 Class C networks. The reduction in traffic overhead by using route aggregation can be huge when used in large, complex internetworks.

OSPF introduces *areas* (similar to autonomous systems) as a level of hierarchy not used in many other protocols. An area is a contiguous portion of the internetwork that does not share its internal routing information with other areas. This adds a level of scalability for larger networks, since not every destination subnet will require an entry in the routing table of every router. Routers that have all interfaces connected to a single area are called *internal routers.* Routers that are connected only to the backbone are *backbone routers.* Routers on the edge of multiple areas, which have interfaces connected to more than one area, are called *area border routers.* An *autonomous system border router* (ASBR) connects OSPF to another IGP or EGP. In configuring areas, use the following criteria:

- Each area must be contiguous
- Each area must border, or connect to, area 0 directly
- Each network (and by virtue of connection, each router interface) must connect to a single area
- OSPF link-state advertisements will only propagate throughout a single area, but not further

The OSPF version 2 supported by Cisco is described in RFC 1583. The following features are supported:

- Stub areas, which are connected to a single area through one router, which means that the network can be moved without significant reconfiguration
- Route redistribution, when a route is learned from any IP routing protocol, allowing routes to be used regardless of how they are connected
- Authentication, which uses either plain text or MD5 authentication, to control which neighboring routers will be allowed to gain access to this OSPF router in order to exchange routing information
- NSSA (Not So Stubby Areas) as described in RFC 1587
- OSPF over demand circuit as described in RFC 1793

When configuring OSPF, keep in mind that OSPF area IDs can be represented as ordinal numbers, or in dotted-decimal equivalent (for example, 0.0.0.0 is the same as area 0). In order to configure OSPF, the minimum commands needed are to enable OSPF and associate the interface with a defined area. These commands are ROUTER OSPF { *autonomous system*} and NETWORK {*address*} {*mask*} AREA {*area-id*}.

The following are some basic OSPF configuration commands. To configure the OSPF costs, use the command IP OSPF COST {*cost*}. To change the number of seconds between link-state advertisement retransmissions, use the command IP OSPF RETRANSMIT-INTERVAL *{seconds}*. To specify the number of seconds it should take to transmit a link-state advertisement, use the command IP OSPF TRANSMIT-DELAY *{seconds}*. To set the priority in order to select the designated router for an OSPF network, use IP OSPF PRIORITY *{number}*. To specify the number of seconds between hello packets, use the command IP OSPF HELLO-INTERVAL *{seconds}*. To state the number of seconds that a certain router's hello packets must be missing before the neighboring routers declare that it is down, use the command IP OSPF DEAD-INTERVAL *{seconds}*. To assign a password to be used by neighboring routers for OSPF simple password authentication, use IP OSPF AUTHENTICATION-KEY *{key}*. To enable OSPF MD5 authentication, use IP OSPF MESSAGE-DIGEST-KEY *{keyid}* MD5 *{key}*.

```
router ospf 1
 network 192.168.1.0 0.0.0.255 area 1
 network 0.0.0.0 255.255.255.255 area 0
!
 ip ospf cost 10
 ip ospf retransmit-interval 40
 ip ospf transmit-delay 20
 ip ospf priority 4
 ip ospf hello-interval 90
 ip ospf dead-interval 90
```

CERTIFICATION SUMMARY

Routing is used to segment congested networks, increase the number of nodes allowed on the network, filter, and manage traffic. Routing protocols are used to maintain the routes available to the network.

Metrics are used to determine the distance or cost of the destination networks from the initiating router. A metric is the value of a route variable, as computed by the routing protocol. A routing information table is maintained by the routing protocol to aid in selecting the best path to a destination network.

Routing algorithms include the capability to manage routes in a routing information table by manually updating it. These are static routes. Most routing protocols offer a dynamic method for determining routes and maintaining routing tables.

A default route is a static route that is used for any packets that are nonroutable (for which a route to their destination network address does not exist). This allows any packet with a destination address not existing in a router's routing information table to still be handled and forwarded.

Distance vector protocols are older routing algorithm protocols that select routes based on the least hop count. Hops are the number of routers that must be transversed before the destination network is reached. Distance vector protocol routers send their entire routing information table to their neighboring routers. This information is copied to that neighbor's table and then recomputed with a new hop count before being forwarded on to other neighbors. This means that distance vector routing tables are based on second-hand information. Distance vector protocols have low CPU overhead because of the simplicity of the routing table recomputation and route selection algorithms. Distance vector routing protocols easily fall prey to routing loops, but usually include split-horizon, poison reverse, or holddown intervals to counteract them.

Link-state protocols were created to be more scalable to large networks. They use a cost metric for route selection, and store the routing information in link-state databases. When a link-state router comes up on a network, it sends hello packets to its neighbors. The neighbors reply with the information about their connected links and the costs associated with them. The original router builds its link-state database from the neighbor's information. Periodically, a link-state router sends a link-state advertisement to its neighbors, including the links for that router and the associated costs. Each neighbor copies the packet, and the LSA is forwarded on to the next neighbor, through a process called flooding. Because the routers do not recalculate the routing database before flooding the LSA forward, the convergence time is reduced.

Routing Information Protocol has version 1 and version 2. Version 2 is more common. RIP is an older, distance vector protocol. It is also an Interior Gateway Protocol, with a maximum hop count of 16. Updates occur every 30 seconds. At each update period, a router sends its entire routing table to its neighbors. The neighbors recalculate routes based on any changes included in the updates. RIP uses split-horizon, poison reverse, and holddown intervals to avoid routing loops.

Interior Gateway Routing Protocol is a distance vector protocol, as well as an Interior Gateway Protocol, with a maximum hop count of 224. IGRP was created by Cisco, and has an enhanced version available: EIGRP. Instead of relying on periodic updates, IGRP uses flash updates whenever a change occurs on the network. This process speeds up convergence.

TWO-MINUTE DRILL

- ❑ Internetworks use routing to get data from one network to another.
- ❑ Bridging is the capability to connect two or more physical network segments such that the connection is transparent to the network.
- ❑ Switching is a way to increase bandwidth (as well as limit the amount of traffic a node encounters) by providing a dedicated channel for each switched port. Switching occurs at the data link layer.
- ❑ Routing occurs at the network layer, and includes the capability to separate the management of the segments on the internetwork.
- ❑ There are two basic mechanisms that make up routing:
  - ❑ Determination of routes
  - ❑ Transmission of data packets across the internetwork
- ❑ One of the terms to be aware of for route determination is *metric*. A metric is the value of a variable, such as the network delay, after the routing protocol algorithm has computed it.
- ❑ Routing protocols both create and maintain a *routing information table*, or *routing table*.
- ❑ The *routing update* can consist of the router's entire routing table, or only the portion that has changed.

- There are three major objectives of a routing algorithm:
  - Accuracy
  - Low overhead
  - Quick convergence
- *Convergence* is the process of all routers synchronizing their routing information tables, or the time it takes for a single routing change to be reflected in all routers.
- Some of the types of routing algorithms are:
  - Static vs. dynamic
  - Interior vs. exterior
  - Distance vector vs. link state
- Dynamic routing protocols include a method for dynamically configuring the routing information table.
- A static route is a route that has been manually entered into the routing table.
- Hierarchical routing allows the limitation of routing information propagation throughout an entire internetwork.
- A default route is the one specified for data to follow if there is no explicit routing information for it to use in finding a direction.
- The two types of dynamic routing are link state and distance vector.
- A distance vector protocol router periodically sends its neighboring routers two pieces of information.
- *Flash updates* (also know as triggered updates) are sent whenever a router's routing information table is changed in a way that affects its updates.
- The purpose of the link-state routing protocol is to map out the internetwork topology.
- Interior Gateway Protocols are also known as intra-domain, since they work within the domain, but not between domains. These protocols recognize that the routers they deal with are part of their system and freely exchange routing information with them.

- Exterior Gateway Protocols are known as inter-domain, since they work between domains. These protocols recognize that they are on the edge of their system, and only exchange the minimum of information necessary to maintain the capability to route information.
- Routing Information Protocol (RIP) is a distance vector protocol for use intra-domain (on the interior of a gateway).
- IGRP is used in an autonomous system and includes the capability to advertise interior routes, exterior routes, and system routes.
- EIGRP uses the same distance vector algorithm and distance information as IGRP. It has enhanced convergence properties, and effectively, the same efficiency.
- OSPF stands for Open Shortest Path First. It is a link-state protocol for the TCP/IP protocol suite. OSPF uses a concept known as *adjacency*.

SELF TEST

The following questions will help you measure your understanding of the material presented in this chapter. Read all the choices carefully, as there may be more than one correct answer. Choose all correct answers for each question.

1. Company A has recently merged with Company B, which exists in the same building and is physically close enough for all the computers to belong on the same network segment. Company A uses an ATM backbone and Fast Ethernet for all nodes. Company B has a Token Ring environment on shielded twisted-pair wiring. Why will Company A and Company B select a router for their newly merged network?
   A. Network segment size has reached the maximum
   B. Network addresses are not sufficient for a merged network
   C. Traffic must be segmented to prevent an expected bandwidth overload
   D. A router is the usual way to connect dissimilar network types
2. What are the two basic mechanisms that make up a routing protocol?
   A. Route selection
   B. Flooding
   C. Autonomous Systems
   D. Data Transmission
3. What is a routing table used for?
   A. It is the physical support for the router to sit on
   B. It contains a list of all the timers used to prevent routing loops
   C. It is used to select the best route
   D. It manages the periodic update algorithm
4. What types of information can be found in different types of routing protocol routing tables? (Select 3.)
   A. The destination network associated with the next hop
   B. The destination network associated with the cost metric
   C. The destination network associated with the subnet mask
   D. The destination network associated with the next path or interface to use
5. What is a routing update used for?
   A. Routing updates notify neighboring routers with a hello
   B. Routing updates redistribute routes learned from other routing protocols
   C. Routing updates maintain the routing table
   D. Routing updates increase the network addresses available by changing the subnet masks
6. When a node on one network sends a packet to a node on another segment that is three hops away, what addresses are

included in the initial addressing of that packet? (Select 2.)

A. The network address of the router
B. The MAC layer address of the router
C. The network address of the destination node
D. The MAC layer address of the destination node

7. What are three objectives for a routing protocol?

A. Accuracy
B. Quick holddowns
C. Rapid convergence
D. Low overhead

8. Define convergence.

A. Convergence is the updates that are triggered by network changes
B. Convergence is the process of sending hello packets
C. Convergence is two routers merging their routing tables into one
D. Convergence is the synchronizing of all routing tables on the internetwork, or simply the synchronization of a single route change across all routers.

9. Why are dynamic routing protocols considered dynamic?

A. Because each route is dynamically selected for each packet with a destination network not attached to the router
B. Because new routes are dynamically recomputed whenever there is a change in the internetwork topology
C. Because convergence happens faster
D. Because all the routes remain the same no matter what changes happen on the network

10. What is a static route?

A. A static route is one that has been manually entered into the routing table and is not updated by a routing protocol
B. A static route is one that is recomputed whenever a change is made on the internetwork
C. A static route is one that is redistributed when it has been learned by another routing protocol
D. A static route is one that comes already configured in the router from the manufacturer

11. What type of network is best when using static routes?

A. A large network with hundreds of routers and networks
B. A complex internetwork that changes often
C. An autonomous system with multiple connections to other autonomous systems
D. A small network with few routers and infrequent changes

12. What is an autonomous system?

    A. An area
    B. A domain
    C. A contiguous set of routers defined within a larger internetwork that do not share routing information with the external internetwork
    D. All of the above
    E. None of the above

13. What is a default route?

    A. A type of static route
    B. A destination for any nonroutable packet
    C. Gateway of last resort
    D. All of the above
    E. None of the above

14. What type of information does a distance vector router build its routing table with?

    A. Hello packets
    B. Second-hand information
    C. LSPs
    D. First-hand information

15. What is the count to infinity problem?

    A. A routing loop that results from the way distance vector protocols use second-hand information
    B. The inability of routers to process more than 16 hops
    C. The excessive CPU overhead presented by distance vector algorithms
    D. The result of using both RIP and IGRP on the same internetwork

16. What is poison reverse?

    A. A change to the default update period timer
    B. A routing loop that occurs when using second-hand information to update route tables
    C. A router virus
    D. A version of split-horizon that sends back a "route unreachable" update to the router that the route was learned from, in order to avoid routing loops

17. What is RIP?

    A. RIP is an older distance vector Interior Gateway Protocol with a 30-second update timer and maximum of 15 hops (where "infinity" is 16 hops)
    B. RIP is a new link-state protocol created by Cisco
    C. RIP is a proprietary protocol created by Cisco that has two versions; only version 2 is used currently
    D. RIP is a distance vector Interior Gateway Protocol with a 224 maximum network diameter (maximum 224 hops)

18. What is IGRP?

    A. IGRP is an older distance vector Interior Gateway Protocol with a 30-second update timer and a maximum of 15 hops (where "infinity" is 16 hops)
    B. IGRP is a new link-state protocol created by Cisco

C. IGRP is a proprietary protocol created by Cisco that has two versions; only version 2 is used currently

D. IGRP is a distance vector and Interior Gateway Protocol with a 224 maximum network diameter (maximum 224 hops)

19. What is the purpose of a flash update in IGRP?

A. A flash update is a standard 90-second update

B. After three flash updates, a route is considered unreachable

C. A flash update is sent immediately upon a change in the network topology, in order to speed convergence

D. After seven flash updates, a route is removed from the routing table

20. How can the administrator change how IGRP selects routes?

A. The administrator can set update timers

B. The administrator can enable or disable split horizon

C. The administrator can set up load balancing across redundant routes

D. The administrator can adjust the metric weights used for determining the route selection

21. The way to get traffic from one segment of the network to another segment is:

A. Bridging

B. Routing

C. Switching

D. All of the above

22. Routing occurs at which layer?

A. Physical layer

B. Data link layer

C. Network layer

D. Transport layer

23. In general, the best route selected by a router is one with:

A. Least cost

B. Shortest distance

C. Lowest metric value

D. None of the above

24. A routing table typically includes which of the following?

A. Destination network address

B. The total number of networks

C. The number of nodes in each network

D. The total number of routers in a network

25. When a router receives a packet, it accepts or rejects a packet by examining what?

A. The MAC address of the source of the packet

B. The address of the source network/node number

C. The address of the destination network/node

D. The MAC address of the next router

26. Low overhead of a routing algorithm is normally associated with:
    A. Optimal route
    B. CPU usage
    C. Accuracy
    D. Convergence

27. Convergence is not an issue if:
    A. Routers are added to the network
    B. Some of the network interfaces are down
    C. CPU/bandwidth usage of the routers changes
    D. An invariant network topology is selected for the network architecture

28. An Internet Protocol (IP) router selects:
    A. An entire path from source to destination
    B. The next route step
    C. The two adjacent routers to itself
    D. All of the above

29. IP ROUTE configuration command for a static route includes which of the following parameters?
    A. Subnetwork number of the destination network
    B. Subnet mask of the source network
    C. IP address of the interface of the router which the packet should use
    D. MAC address of the next router on the path

30. Given the following portion of the network:

    Network A →Router X →Router Y → Network B
    Interface: Interface: 86.0.0.0
    X0 Y0
    35.3.3.4

    and assuming a network mask of 255.0.0.0 for both A and B networks, which one of the following represents a correct command to configure Router X to send data from Network A to Network B?
    A. #IP ROUTE 85.0.0.0 255.0.0.0 35.3.3.3
    B. #ip route 86.0.0.0 255.0.0.0 35.3.3.4
    C. #ip route 86.0.0.0 255.0.0.0 35.3.3.3
    D. #ip route 85.0.0.0 255.0.0.0 35.3.3.4

31. A static routing table can be changed at any time without manual intervention.
    A. True
    B. False

32. In a hybrid solution of static and dynamic routing, the nonroutable packets are sent to:
    A. The next router
    B. The central router
    C. The gateway of last resort
    D. The source router where the packets originated

33. How is fault tolerance on a routing algorithm achieved?
    A. By providing a central control router
    B. By a distributed routing protocol
    C. By load balancing of the traffic
    D. All of the above
34. The configuration command IP DEFAULT for a default static router requires which of the following parameters?
    A. Network mask
    B. Router interface number
    C. Subnet ID
    D. Network number
35. In a distance vector routing protocol, aging is set for:
    A. Only the next available router
    B. All routing information
    C. Only the unavailable routers
    D. Only the routers in the lowest metric route
36. In a distance vector algorithm, the holddown interval for large or complex networks:
    A. Cannot be used
    B. Would need to have a much larger value
    C. Is equal to negative reachability parameter
    D. Would need to have a smaller value to reach convergence
37. What do link-state protocols use as a metric?
    A. Hops
    B. Cost
    C. CPU usage
    D. Network operational time
38. Flooding in link-state protocol means what?
    A. A router sending all routing information to its neighbors
    B. A router broadcasting all information to all routers in the network
    C. The neighbors of a link-state router receiving a link-state packet, copying it, and then forwarding it to the rest of the network
    D. A router sending information about the routers that have changed
39. Which statement is true of Interior Gateway Protocols?
    A. They apply to Internet domains
    B. They apply to autonomous systems within the network
    C. They apply to external networks
    D. They allow systems in the Internet to manage areas in the network where IGP is implemented
40. Exterior Gateway Protocols are known as:
    A. Inter-domain
    B. Areas
    C. Domains
    D. Intra-domain

41. Routing Information Protocol (RIP) can have a maximum of:

A. 24 hops

B. 16 hops

C. 12 hops

D. 8 hops

42. How many commands are required to configure a router for RIP?

A. Four

B. Three

C. Two

D. One

43. RIP authentication command can be used with which version of RIP?

A. RIP version 1

B. RIP version 2

C. RIP version 1 and RIP version 2

D. None of the above

44. In the Interior Gateway Routing Protocol, a route is removed from the routing table after:

A. Three update periods

B. 60 seconds

C. Five update periods

D. Seven update periods

E. 90 seconds

45. Which of the following is used to calculate metric in Interior Gateway Routing Protocol?

A. Internetwork delay

B. Bandwidth

C. Load

D. Reliability

E. All of the above

46. What is the maximum allowable number of hops in Enhanced Interior Routing Gateway Protocol?

A. 64

B. 224

C. 128

D. 232

E. 256

47. Enhanced Interior Routing Gateway Protocol uses which of the following?

A. Link-state vector

B. Diffusion Update Algorithm

C. Distance vector

D. A and B only

E. B and C only

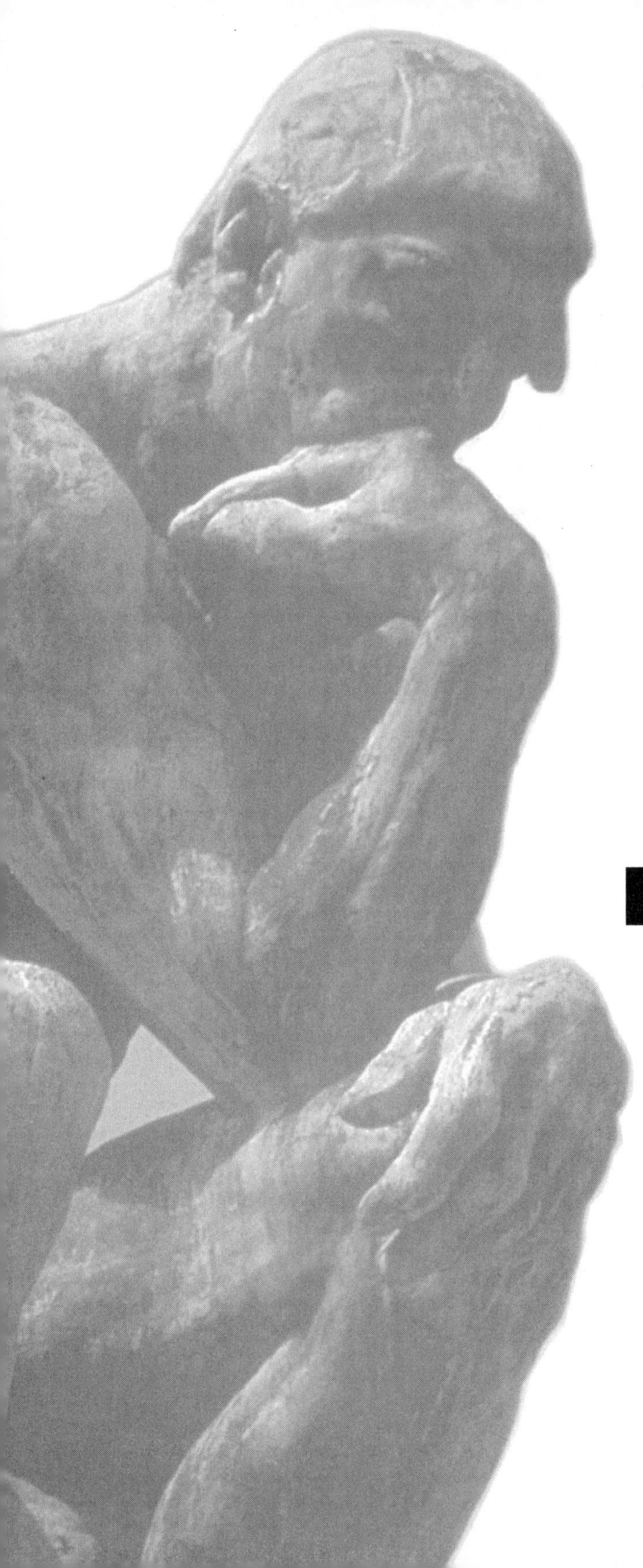

CCNA
CISCO CERTIFIED NETWORK ASSOCIATE

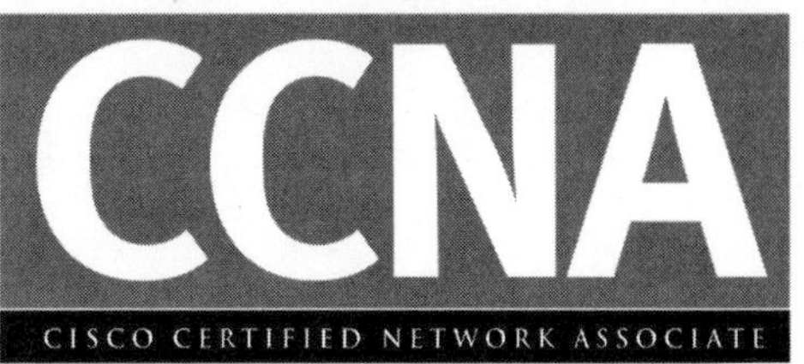

6
IP Configuration

CERTIFICATION OBJECTIVES

6.01 IP Configuration Commands
6.02 Configuring Static Routes
6.03 Configuring Default Routes
6.04 Configuring RIP Routing
6.05 Configuring IGRP Routing
6.06 IP Host Tables
6.07 DNS and DHCP Configuration
6.08 Secondary Addressing

TCP/IP is the most prevalent network protocol in use today. Virtually any LAN you will manage or even build has some facet revolving around IP, if not entirely based on it. Whether or not you have the luxury of starting from scratch on your network is irrelevant. This chapter will explain the configuration of IP, from an interface level to interconnectivity between routers. For the interface, it will detail assigning IP addresses and configuring DNS lookups, DHCP, and host tables. For interconnectivity, it will outline the basic configuration of RIP and IGRP routing, and explain how to set up static and default routes.

CERTIFICATION OBJECTIVE 6.01

IP Configuration Commands

Configuration of IP takes place on a per-interface basis. To set the primary IP address and subnet mask to an interface, enter its configuration mode and type the command:

```
Ip address ip-address mask
```

Note it is possible to add more IP addresses to interfaces, but this will be covered in the last section of this chapter.

There are some circumstances in which you might want to enable IP across an interface without having to assign an explicit IP address. This functionality is available exclusively on Cisco routers and is called IP unnumbered. It is used on point-to-point links where the same subnet mask is being used on both sides of the connection. It works by allowing communication to occur across the connection via the Ethernet interfaces, with the benefit of not having to allocate an entire subnet for the link. IP unnumbered is configured on a per-interface basis. The following is an excerpt from the configuration of a router running with an unnumbered interface:

```
interface ethernet0
  ip address 10.10.10.45 255.255.255.0
```

```
!
interface serial1
  ip unnumbered ethernet 0
```

CERTIFICATION OBJECTIVE 6.02

Configuring Static Routes

Routes between network segments sometimes have to be added manually. There are several advantages that static routes have over dynamic routes. One advantage is that there is less overhead for the router, since it doesn't have to perform calculations on the fly and send out router updates. Another advantage of using static routes is that the paths between two destinations are always known, and this helps reduce the number of places where faults can lie.

Of course, with advantages there are always going to be disadvantages. One of the obvious drawbacks to static routing is its lack of scalability. From the looks of the example in Figure 6-1, it would appear that static routing is pretty easy to implement. This is true when you are only talking about a handful of network segments. Imagine, though, if you had 50 network segments inter-connected with about 25 routers! The overhead involved to enter all of those routes would be tremendous.

If a router learns a route to a network from more than one source, it uses a ranking called *administrative distance* to determine which one to place in its IP routing table. All routes, whether dynamic or static, are assigned an administrative distance. The route with the lowest value will be used. The default administrative distances for some of the more common routing methods are listed in Table 6-1.

Routes are added with the IP ROUTE command. This is done as a global configuration, since routes are not dependent on an interface.

To understand how static routes are implemented, look at the example in Figure 6-1. The configuration for each router is listed following the example.

TABLE 6-1

Default Administrative Distances

Method	Administrative Distance
Directly Connected	0
Static	1
EIGRP	90
IGRP	100
OSPF	110
RIP	120

FIGURE 6-1

Static routes

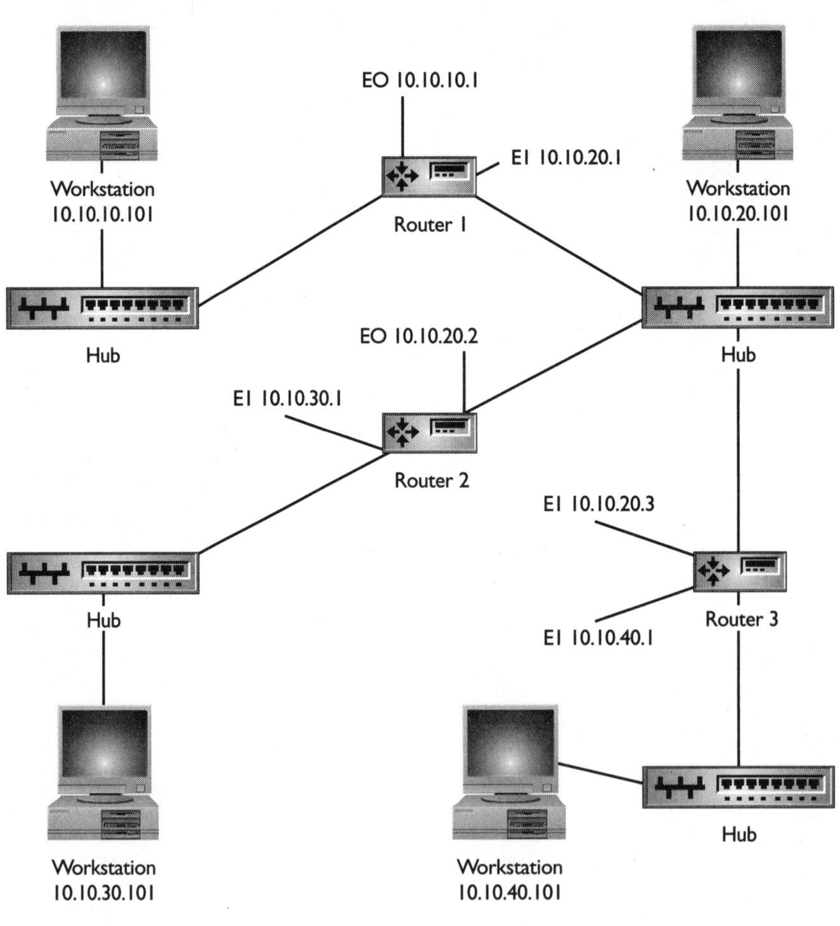

Router 1

```
Router1#wr t
Building configuration…
Current configuration:
!
Version 11.1
!
hostname router1
!
enable secret 5 $1$F4Sds42cRfAK204jKLIFNO$Mpruh.
Enable password mayo
!
interface ethernet0
  ip address 10.10.10.1 255.255.255.0
!
interface ethernet1
  ip address 10.10.20.1 255.255.255.0
!
ip route 10.10.30.0 255.255.255.0 10.10.20.2
ip route 10.10.40.0 255.255.255.0 10.10.20.3
!
line con 0
line aux 0
  transport input all
line vty 0 4
  password vbm
  login
!
end
```

Router 2

```
Router2#wr t
Building configuration…
Current configuration:
!
Version 11.1
!
hostname router2
!
enable secret 5 $1$F4Sds42cRfAK204jKLIFNO$Mpruh.
Enable password mayo
!
interface ethernet0
  ip address 10.10.20.2 255.255.255.0
```

```
!
interface ethernet1
  ip address 10.10.30.1 255.255.255.0
!
ip route 10.10.10.0 255.255.255.0 10.10.20.1
ip route 10.10.40.0 255.255.255.0 10.10.20.3
!
line con 0
line aux 0
  transport input all
line vty 0 4
  password vbm
  login
!
end
```

Router 3

```
Router3#wr t
Building configuration…
Current configuration:
!
Version 11.1
hostname router3
!
enable secret 5 $1$F4Sds42cRfAK204jKLIFNO$Mpruh.
Enable password mayo
!
interface ethernet0
  ip address 10.10.20.3 255.255.255.0
!
interface ethernet1
  ip address 10.10.40.1 255.255.255.0
!
ip route 10.10.10.0 255.255.255.0 10.10.20.1
ip route 10.10.30.0 255.255.255.0 10.10.20.2
!
line con 0
line aux 0
  transport input all
line vty 0 4
  password vbm
  login
!
end
```

CERTIFICATION OBJECTIVE 6.03

Configuring Default Routes

As I'm sure you can imagine, in large networks and internetworks every router cannot know the exact route to every other router. This is where the default route is useful. The default route specifies where to send non-local packets. The router assumes that it can send the packet to the default router, and that router will know what to do with it. This feature is only used when IP routing is disabled. It is typically only used in "stub" networks, where there is only a single link to the rest of the internetwork. If the next router doesn't know the necessary route, it sends the packet to its own default route, and this process continues on until the destination network is reached. Configuration of the default route is performed with the following command:

```
Ip default route ip address
```

You can view the address of the current default route by entering:

```
show ip route
```

CERTIFICATION OBJECTIVE 6.04

Configuring RIP Routing

The enabling of RIP is performed at the global level, but a lot of the configuration can be performed on a per-interface basis. You can enable or disable RIP by entering the following command.

```
[no] router rip
```

All timing issues regarding how often RIP updates are performed and how long before they are either stored or removed from tables can be configured with the TIMERS BASIC command, shown here:

```
timers basic update invalid holddown flush [sleeptime]
```

RIP updates are sent, by default, every 30 seconds. This number can be changed through the UPDATE argument. When no update is received from a route after a specified amount of time, the route is declared invalid. This amount of time, in seconds, is set with the INVALID argument. This number is typically three times the period set for the sending of RIP updates. Now when the route becomes invalid, it enters a holddown period, which is the next argument to configure. During the holddown period the router will not allow information regarding other paths to be added. When it is in the holddown period the route acts like it is inaccessible, but it will still be used for forwarding packets. This is also specified in seconds. The final setting, FLUSH, specifies the amount of time that must expire before it flushes the route from its routing table. This is also specified in seconds and must be, at minimum, equal to the summation of INVALID and HOLDDOWN. The last setting is for IGRP use only and will be discussed in the next section of this chapter.

CERTIFICATION OBJECTIVE 6.05

Configuring IGRP Routing

The basic configuration of IGRP is a pretty straightforward process. First, you need to assign an *autonomous system number* to the IGRP process. The autonomous system number allows other routers that use the same number to exchange route information. This is followed by telling the router which directly connected networks it should advertise its initial IGRP packet on. Look at the diagram listed in Figure 6-2, and at each router's configuration.

Router 1

```
Router1#wr t
Building configuration…
Current configuration:
!
Version 11.1
hostname router1
!
```

FIGURE 6-2

IGRP routing

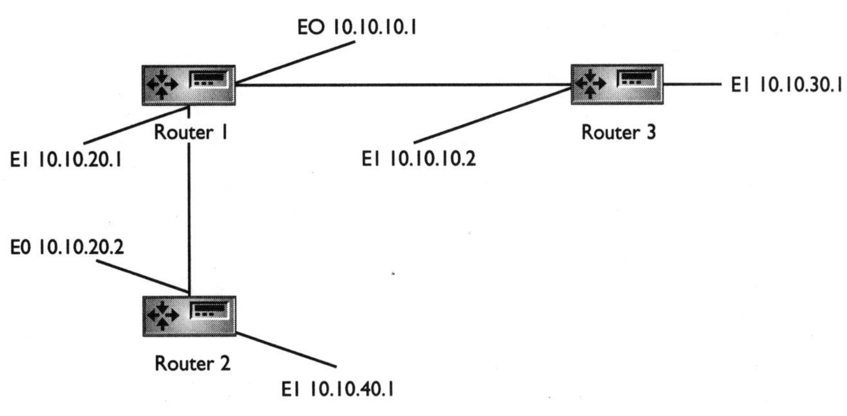


```
enable secret 5 $1$F4Sds42cRfAK204jKLIFNO$Mpruh.
Enable password mayo
!
interface ethernet0
  ip address 10.10.10.1 255.255.255.0
!
interface ethernet1
  ip address 10.10.20.1 255.255.255.0
!
router igrp 7
  network 10.0.0.0
!
line con 0
line aux 0
  transport input all
line vty 0 4
  password vbm
  login
!
end
```

Router 2

```
Router2#wr t
Building configuration…
Current configuration:
!
Version 11.1
```

```
hostname router2
!
enable secret 5 $1$F4Sds42cRfAK204jKLIFNO$Mpruh.
Enable password mayo
!
interface ethernet0
  ip address 10.10.20.2 255.255.255.0
!
interface ethernet1
  ip address 10.10.40.1 255.255.255.0
!
router igrp 7
  network 10.0.0.0
!
line con 0
line aux 0
  transport input all
line vty 0 4
  password vbm
  login
!
end
```

Router 3

```
Router3#wr t
Building configuration…
Current configuration:
!
Version 11.1
hostname router3
!
enable secret 5 $1$F4Sds42cRfAK204jKLIFNO$Mpruh.
Enable password mayo
!
interface ethernet0
  ip address 10.10.10.2 255.255.255.0
!
interface ethernet1
  ip address 10.10.30.1 255.255.255.0
!
router igrp 7
  network 10.0.0.0
!
line con 0
line aux 0
```

```
  transport input all
line vty 0 4
  password vbm
  login
!
end
```

FROM THE CLASSROOM

Changing Traffic Flow with IGRP

The fact that IGRP uses a cost metric to make routing decisions gives us an opportunity to manipulate those decisions in a way that is not possible with RIP. We can't change the number of hops an interface is worth, and we can't change the IGRP cost directly, but there is an interface parameter we can play with—bandwidth—that figures into the algorithm for calculating the cost of a path.

Many students are surprised to find out that changing the bandwidth parameter on an interface has nothing to do with the actual speed of data transmission over that link. The router has no way to measure the actual speed of the serial link, so this parameter has a default value, which is equivalent to a T1 bandwidth. If your network's serial links are all identical in terms of bandwidth, this won't be a problem for you. On the other hand, if you have a variety of links with varying bandwidths, you will probably want to make this value reflect the actual bandwidths of those links in order for IGRP to give you optimal routing. The interface configuration command to do this is BANDWIDTH, which takes one argument, an integer representing thousandths of bits per second. You should see the effect in the output of the SHOW INTERFACE SERIAL command.

If you don't care about optimal routing, or if for some reason (such as monetary cost) you just need to make traffic flow another way, you can make the bandwidth appear to be very low on the less desirable links and very high on the most desirable links, in order to fool the IGRP routing protocol. Again, changing the bandwidth parameter has absolutely no effect on actual speed of transmission. In a production network you would be getting your clocking from the provider's network. In a lab situation, the DCE end of the link would be configured with the CLOCK RATE command.

—By Pamela Forsyth, CCIE, CCSI, CNX

CERTIFICATION OBJECTIVE 6.06

IP Host Tables

As I'm sure you're aware from using the Internet, IP addresses typically have host names mapped to them. If you wish to access a site, you can enter the name associated with that particular location instead of having to remember a string of numbers. It is much easier to remember mylocation.com rather than 10.20.14.83.

Cisco routers keep a table of host name-to-address mappings in their host cache. Entries can be added and removed with the IP HOST command. When issuing this command you can optionally assign a TCP port number to use when establishing a connection. The default is the Telnet port 23. You can then bind multiple IP addresses to the host name, up to a maximum of eight, as shown here:

```
ip host name [tcp-port-number] address1 [address2-address8]
[no] ip host name address1
```

CERTIFICATION OBJECTIVE 6.07

DNS and DHCP Configuration

The capability to dynamically look up host name-to-address mappings is a feature of Domain Name Service (DNS). This is used for connectivity with devices in networks where you don't control the name assignments. Dynamic Host Configuration Protocol (DHCP) is used for the dynamic distribution of IP addresses to client machines. Cisco routers have the capability to forward DHCP requests across different subnets. The following sections will outline each of these features.

DNS Configuration

DNS capability is enabled by default in the Cisco IOS, but if it is disabled it can be re-enabled with the following command.

```
Ip domain-lookup
```

To enable DNS lookups, you should tell the router where the name servers that it is to use for lookups are located. If you do not specify them, a broadcast DNS request will be made by the router. The advantage to manually specifying them is to cut down on the broadcast requests being transmitted. You have the ability to add up to six with the command:

```
Ip name-server server1 {server 2…server 6}
```

Where server1, server 2, and so on, are IP addresses of the servers, not the host names.

You can also specify the default domain that the IOS will use to complete the domain name requests. What this does is allow IOS to add requests that are not fully qualified domain names in domains you frequently access. I say "domains" (plural) because you have the ability to make multiple listings. By stating the default, the domain name you specify is appended to the host name before being added to the host table in the cache.

To specify a single domain, enter the following:

```
Ip domain-name name
```

To specify a list of default domains to use, enter the following:

```
Ip domain-list name
```

Cisco also supplies a way to use the DNS to discover International Organization for Standardization Connectionless Network Service (ISO CLNS) addresses. This feature is used when your router has both IP and ISO CLNS enabled and you want to use an ISO CLNS network service access point (NSAP) address. DNS has the capability to query these by default. This option is configured globally.

```
[no] ip domain-lookup nsap
```

Forwarding DHCP Requests

By default Cisco routers (or any router for that matter) will not forward broadcast-based traffic. One type of broadcast traffic is User Datagram Protocol (UDP) packets. If you wish to forward UDP-type traffic, you need to add the host address in an IP helper-address statement. A helper-address statement will forward selected protocols received on that interface to the specified host address. When you invoke the IP HELPER-ADDRESS statement, UDP packets from the certain ports will be forwarded by default, as described in Table 6-2.

If you wish to select other protocols to forward, you can use the IP FORWARD-PROTOCOL command. DHCP uses UDP for its transport, and uses the BOOTP protocol for its operation. DHCP information is encapsulated within BOOTP datagrams. The following example lists the configuration found in Figure 6-3. Even though BOOTP packets are forwarded by default after invoking the HELPER-ADDRESS command, I chose to specify the BOOTP ports anyway, to show an example of implementing the IP FORWARD command.

TABLE 6-2

Protocol and Port Numbers

Protocol	Familiar Name	Port
Trivial File Transfer Protocol	TFTP	69
Domain Name Service	DNS	53
Time Service	-	37
NetBIOS Name Server	-	137
NetBIOS Datagram Server	-	138
Boot Protocol (Client and Server)	BOOTP	67 and 68
TACACS	TACACS	49

FIGURE 6-3

DHCP

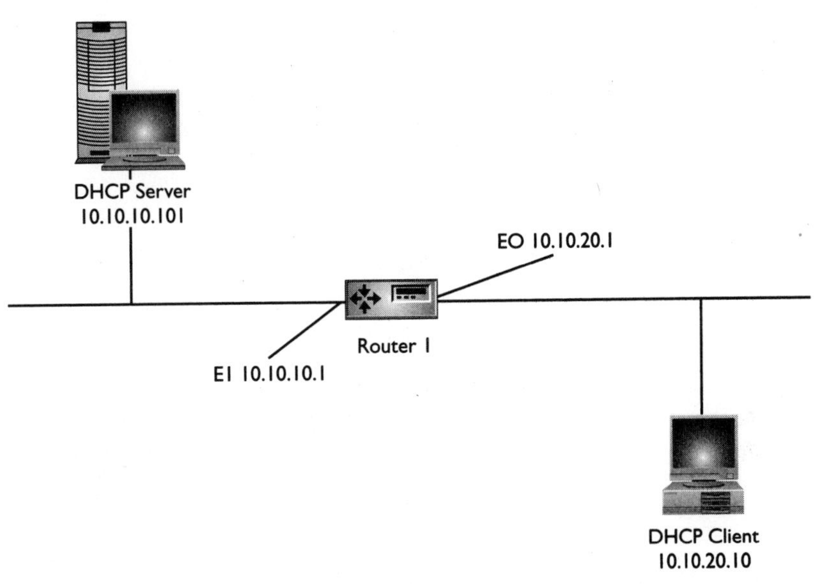

Router 1

```
Router1#wr t
Building configuration…
Current configuration:
!
Version 11.1
hostname router1
!
enable secret 5 $1$F4Sds42cRfAK204jKLIFNO$Mpruh.
Enable password mayo
!
interface ethernet0
  ip address 10.10.10.1 255.255.255.0
!
interface ethernet1
  ip address 10.10.20.1 255.255.255.0
  ip helper-address 10.10.10.101
!
ip forward-protocol udp 67
ip forward-protocol udp 68
!
```

```
line con 0
line aux 0
  transport input all
line vty 0 4
  password vbm
  login
!
end
```

There are a couple of things to note about the IP HELPER-ADDRESS command. The command is placed on the interface where it will hear the client's broadcast request. When the broadcast is forwarded, it is changed by the router to the address specified in the IP HELPER-ADDRESS command. If that address is a host address, the request will be forwarded as a unicast. If it is a directed broadcast address, it will be forwarded as a directed broadcast.

Another thing to notice in the preceding example is that the forwarding of UDP is performed at a global level. Also, if you have a situation where you want to prevent a protocol from being forwarded from only one interface, you will have to build an access list and apply it to the interface. Configuration of access lists will be covered later in this book.

CERTIFICATION OBJECTIVE 6.08

Secondary Addressing

Along with the normal IP addressing you are familiar with, the Cisco IOS also supports adding multiple secondary addresses to single interfaces. To understand the benefit of this, imagine this scenario: Let's say we are implementing a Class C addressing scheme, where there are 254 host IDs available. Our company expands, and we are now to the point where we need to accommodate 350 users, and they all need their own IP addresses. To avoid adding more hardware, we can assign a secondary IP address on the outgoing router to allow two logical subnets across the same physical interface. We can now split the 350 users across the two subnets, at no additional cost.

If you decide to implement secondary addressing on a router, you should remember that all other routers that attach to the same physical subnet as the one that has the secondary address will also need a secondary address on that same subnet. The reason for this is as follows. Look at the example shown in Figure 6-4. We have two users who are on different logical subnets, but are connected to the same physical interface. We are implementing a secondary address only on Router A. With the situation that is listed, both User 1 and User 2 will be able to reach Server A, since Router A knows of both subnets on E1. However, if both users wish to connect to Server B, only User 1 will be able to reach it. This is because Router B has no idea about the 10.10.20.0 network that it should have access to on E0.

To apply a secondary address, you use the same syntax as assigning a primary address to an interface, except you end it with the SECONDARY argument, as shown here:

```
Ip address ip-address mask secondary
```

Here are some sample IP configuration problems such as you might encounter on the CCNA exam, or in your work.

FIGURE 6-4

Secondary addressing I

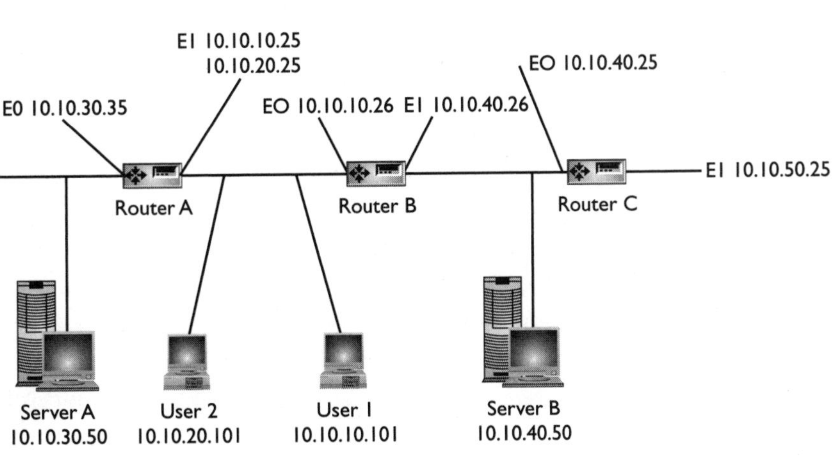

QUESTIONS AND ANSWERS	
I entered a static route that I want to use as a last resort. We are using OSPF, but currently my route takes precedence over OSPF entries. How do I change the configuration?	Change the administrative distance for your static route to any number above 110, which is OSPF's default.
I am running RIP across a 64-kbps WAN link. The updates are taking up too much bandwidth. What should I do?	Change the update period to a slower amount than the default 30 seconds.
How do I get my workstations to receive their IP addresses via DHCP on a different subnet than the DHCP server?	On the router that connects the two network segments, enter an IP helper address and point it to the DHCP server.
We are using Internet-assigned IPs and are running low on the ones left in our range. We are adding another remote site, and we can't afford to waste an entire subnet. What should we do?	Use IP unnumbered on the two ends of the point-to-point link.
We just added 26 more users on a segment to bring the total to 262 hosts. Am I going to have to add another router to accommodate the new people?	No. Use a secondary IP address on the interfaces connecting each end of the segment.

CERTIFICATION SUMMARY

Implementing static routes is advantageous in small networks and in situations where you need to cut down on the amount of processing being performed by the router. Dynamic routing is more suited for larger networks that require something more scalable and that don't require as much overhead. Routers may learn routes from a variety of sources: their directly connected interfaces, static routes configured by an administrator, or from many dynamic IP routing protocols. If the router learns routes to a network from more than one source, it will use the one with the smallest administrative distance.

RIP is the easiest dynamic routing protocol to implement. Its updates are sent out by default every 30 seconds, but this is configurable with the TIMERS BASIC command. IGRP is a more efficient routing protocol that uses autonomous system numbers to distinguish which routers are to communicate with which others.

Dynamic lookup of host name-to-address mappings can be performed with DNS. DNS is enabled by default on Cisco routers, and you can specify up to six name servers to use. Cisco also supports relaying DHCP requests across subnets. DHCP is a UDP-type packet that is encapsulated within BOOTP. You can enable this functionality with the IP HELPER–ADDRESS command.

TWO-MINUTE DRILL

- ❑ Configuration of IP takes place on a per-interface basis.
- ❑ There are some circumstances in which you might want to enable IP across an interface without having to assign an explicit IP address. This functionality is available exclusively on Cisco routers and is called IP unnumbered.
- ❑ Two advantages that static routes have over dynamic routes are
  - ❑ There is less overhead for the router, since it doesn't have to perform calculations on the fly and send out router updates.
  - ❑ The paths between two destinations are always known, and this helps reduce the number of places where faults can lie.
- ❑ The default route specifies where to send non-local packets. The router assumes that it can send the packet to the default router, and that router will know what to do with it. This feature is only used when IP routing is disabled.
- ❑ The enabling of RIP is performed at the global level, but a lot of the configuration can be performed on a per-interface basis.
- ❑ The basic configuration of IGRP is a pretty straightforward process. First, you need to assign an *autonomous system number* to the IGRP process. The autonomous system number allows other routers that use the same number to exchange route information. This is followed by telling the router which directly connected networks it should advertise its initial IGRP packet on.

- ❑ Cisco routers keep a table of host name-to-address mappings in their host cache.
- ❑ The capability to dynamically look up host name-to-address mappings is a feature of Domain Name Service (DNS).
- ❑ Dynamic Host Configuration Protocol (DHCP) is used for the dynamic distribution of IP addresses to client machines. Cisco routers have the capability to forward DHCP requests across different subnets.
- ❑ DNS capability is enabled by default in the Cisco IOS.
- ❑ By default Cisco routers (or any router for that matter) will not forward broadcast-based traffic.
- ❑ Along with the normal IP addressing you are familiar with, the Cisco IOS also supports adding multiple secondary addresses to single interfaces.

SELF TEST

The following Self Test questions will help you measure your understanding of the material presented in this chapter. Read all the choices carefully, as there may be more than one correct answer. Choose all correct answers for each question.

1. What is the administrative distance for directly connected routes?

   A. 0

   B. 1

   C. 100

   D. 120

2. How many IP addresses can be bound to each host name using the IP HOST command?

   A. 1

   B. 2

   C. 8

   D. 255

3. Which command do you use to view the currently configured default route?

   A. SHOW IP CONFIG

   B. show default gateway

   C. show ip route

   D. show default network

4. Which routing protocol uses autonomous system numbers?

   A. RIP

   B. IGRP

   C. OFLP

   D. OSPF

5. How many DNS servers can be added to a router's configuration?

   A. One

   B. Two

   C. Four

   D. Six

6. When configuring IGRP, what is the minimum amount for the FLUSH argument in the TIMERS BASIC command?

   A. 30 seconds

   B. Three times the period set for sending RIP updates

   C. The summation of INVALID and HOLDDOWN

   D. UPDATE minus SLEEPTIME

7. Which of the following is not true regarding IP unnumbered?

   A. Major drawback is the loss of an IP subnet

   B. IP unnumbered is only available on Cisco routers

   C. Can be used to communicate across serial interface through Ethernet interface

   D. Used on point-to-point links

8. Identify the proper syntax for assigning a secondary IP address to an interface.
   A. IP SECONDARY ADDRESS 10.10.10.10 255.0.0.0
   B. IP 10.10.10.10 255.255.0.0 secondary
   C. IP address secondary 10.10.10.10 255.255.255.0
   D. IP address 10.10.10.10 255.255.255.0 secondary
9. Which of the following are advantages to static routing?
   A. Less overhead on router
   B. Paths are created on the fly
   C. Reduction in places where faults can lie
   D. Scalable
10. What does the IP DOMAIN-NAME command do?
   A. Names the domain that the Cisco router belongs to
   B. Names domains the router cannot find directly
   C. Appends a domain to unqualified requests
   D. Broadcasts domain name across subnets
11. By default, what happens to broadcast UDP packets that come across Cisco routers?
   A. They are denied
   B. They are converted into broadcast-based packets
   C. They are routed to all IP interfaces
   D. They are sent to UDP queues
12. What are the default ports for BOOTP traffic?
   A. 23 and 24
   B. 67 and 68
   C. 138–141
   D. 9 and 10
13. Which syntax for setting the default gateway is correct?
   A. IP DEFAULT-GATEWAY 10.10.10.100
   B. IP 10.10.10.100 default-gateway
   C. Default-gateway 10.10.10.100 255.255.255.0
   D. IP default-gateway 10.10.10.100 255.255.255.0
14. Which is true regarding secondary addressing?
   A. Secondary addressing must exist on the same subnet as the primary
   B. Secondary addressing can only be applied to serial interfaces
   C. A maximum of three address can be assigned per interface
   D. All attached routers need a secondary address on same subnet
15. Which of the following statements about administrative distance are true?
   A. It is used when two routing protocols advertise the same route

B. All routes have an administrative distance

C. The lowest value always wins

D. Static routes have an administrative distance of 1

16. Which of the following acronyms is not accurate?

    A. DNS—Dynamic Naming Service

    B. UDP—User Datagram Protocol

    C. DHCP—Dynamic Host Configuration Protocol

    D. TFTP—Trivial File Transfer Protocol

17. Where can DHCP information be found?

    A. Encapsulated within UDP packets

    B. Encapsulated within the TCP part of TCP/IP

    C. Encapsulated within BOOTP packets

    D. Encapsulated within DNS traffic

18. Which of the following is performed at a global level?

    A. Forwarding of UDP

    B. DNS lookup

    C. Adding routes

    D. Enabling RIP

19. Where are the host name-to-address mappings stored?

    A. Address cache

    B. Host cache

    C. Static RAM

    D. IP Config table

20. If you add more users than there are available host addresses on a given subnet, which of the following principles can you apply to remedy the situation?

    A. IGRP

    B. Shared IP

    C. Secondary addressing

    D. IP unnumbered

21. An IP UNNUMBERED command does which of the following?

    A. It allows use of different subnet masks on two ports on each side of the link

    B. It is used in a point-to-multipoint configuration

    C. It allows the same netmask number to be used on each side of the link

    D. It makes an effective use of IP addresses

22. In static routing, the route to a destination network:

    A. Is not known prior to configuration

    B. Remains permanently in the routing table

    C. Is determined in real time

    D. Is known prior to configuration

23. If two routing protocols recommend the same route to a router, the router will:

    A. Select either of the two routes at random, with no preference for one over the other

B. Select the route that has a lower administrative distance value

C. Select the route that has a higher administrative distance value

D. Place both the routes in the routing table

24. What is the command used to remove static routes from the routing tables?

A. SHOW IP ROUTE

B. show ip redirect

C. change ip route

D. no ip route

25. What is the default time interval at which RIP updates are sent?

A. 30 seconds

B. 15 seconds

C. 60 seconds

D. 90 seconds

26. In the TIMERS BASIC command, the parameter to specify the time after which the route is to be taken out from the routing table is:

A. SLEEPTIME

B. holddown

C. invalid

D. flush

27. In an IGRP command TIMERS BASIC 15 45 0 60, the number 45 represents:

A. holddown time

B. update time

C. invalid time

D. flush time

28. In an IGRP command ROUTER IGRP 7, the number 7 is:

A. An autonomous system number

B. A gateway number

C. A port number

D. A terminal number

29. In the command IP MYNETWORK 132.2.2.2, what port number is used in establishing a connection?

A. 21

B. 23

C. 25

D. 69

30. In Cisco routers the DNS lookup capability must be enabled.

A. True

B. False

31. In order to forward broadcast traffic for certain UDP requests, which of the following commands should be used?

A. IP HELPER-ADDRESS

B. ip address

C. ip forward-protocol

D. interface

E. A and C only

F. B and C only

32. What is the purpose of secondary addressing?

    A. To increase the number of hosts on the same network by increasing the IP address capacity
    B. To increase the number of subnets
    C. To limit hardware cost
    D. A and B only
    E. B and C only
    F. A and C only

33. If we implement a secondary address on router X, and we need all other routers to be able to route traffic to its attached hosts, all other routers attached to the same physical subnet as router X will also need a secondary address on the same subnet.

    A. True
    B. False

34. The secondary address configuration can be achieved by applying the identical set of commands that are used for configuring the primary address.

    A. True
    B. False

35. IP unnumbered is configured:

    A. Globally for all interfaces
    B. On each interface as needed
    C. On serial interfaces only
    D. On Ethernet only

36. Match the protocol on the left with administrative distances on the right.

A. Static	1. 120
B. OSPF	2. 100
C. RIP	3. 1
D. IGRP	4. 110

7

Configuring Novell IPX

CERTIFICATION OBJECTIVES

- 7.01 IPX Protocol Stack
- 7.02 IPX Datagram
- 7.03 IPX Encapsulation Types
- 7.04 SAP and RIP
- 7.05 IPX Configuration

The Internetwork Packet Exchange (IPX) protocol is the native networking protocol for Novell NetWare. It was designed by Novell based on Xerox Network System (XNS) protocols. While not particularly well suited to very large internetworks (especially those utilizing slow wide-area links), IPX is still a very popular protocol.

This chapter will familiarize you with the structure, purpose, and operation of IPX and the related protocols making up the IPX protocol stack. It will then show how to configure IPX using Cisco IOS.

CERTIFICATION OBJECTIVE 7.01

IPX Protocol Stack

IPX provides the basis for the stack of protocols designed by Novell to support NetWare. IPX provides only a connectionless, unreliable datagram service. The transmitting station sends packets, but has no way of knowing whether they are received at the destination. Error detection and recovery is left to other protocol layers. To add some reliability, and to provide more services than IPX can provide, a number of other protocols needed to be defined. Figure 7-1 shows how these protocols relate to IPX, and also how they relate to the various layers of the OSI model. (This mapping to the OSI model isn't precise, and is open to interpretation.)

The protocols shown in Figure 7-1 are described briefly here. Some of particular interest will be examined in more detail later in the chapter.

- **RIP** Routing Information Protocol is used to propagate routing information between IPX routers, and also by clients to locate paths to remote networks.
- **SPX** Sequenced Packet Exchange adds fields to the IPX header to allow it to provide reliable sequenced delivery. SPX is a connection-oriented protocol.
- **NCP** NetWare Core Protocol is used by NetWare clients to access the services provided by NetWare servers. Among other things, it is used to manage connections and to access files and printers.

FIGURE 7-1

The IPX stack and its relationship to the OSI network model

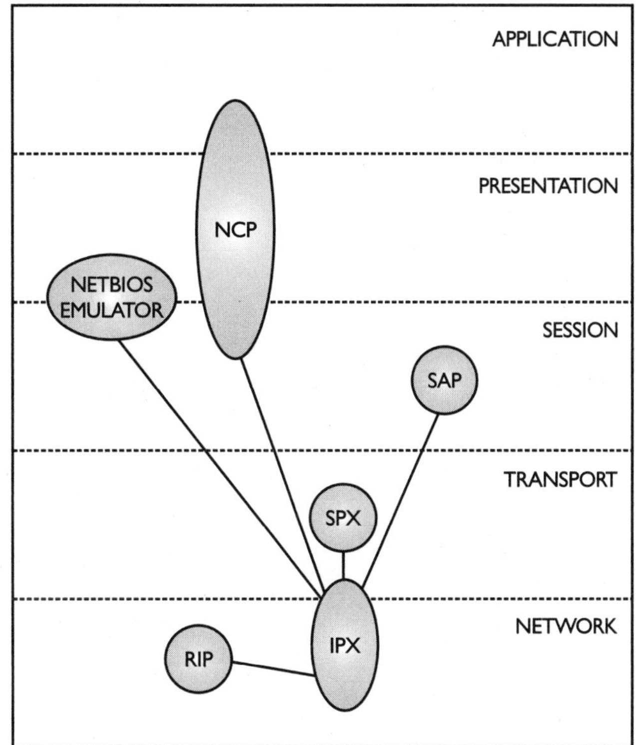

- **SAP** Service Advertising Protocol is used by servers to advertise their available services on the network. Routers and NetWare servers collect these advertisements into internal databases. Client machines can send SAP requests to locate specific servers.
- **NetBIOS Emulation** allows NetBIOS applications to run over IPX.

There are also a number of small protocols such as the Watchdog, Serialization, and Diagnostics packets defined by Novell. To the network these appear as IPX packets and are not treated any differently.

CERTIFICATION OBJECTIVE 7.02

IPX Datagram

An IPX datagram consists of a 30-byte header followed by the user data. The IPX header contains these fields:

Field	Description
Checksum (2 bytes)	Normally set to 0xFFFF and not used. Detection of transmission errors is left to the MAC (Media Access Control) level checksum.
Length (2 bytes)	Shows the length of the packet, including the IPX header and the following data.
Transport Control (1 byte)	Initialized to zero when the packet is generated, and is incremented every time the packet crosses a router. If the value reaches 16, the packet is discarded. This places a 16-hop limit on the diameter of an IPX internetwork.
Packet Type (1 byte)	Identifies the protocol of the packet. Common values are: 0 or 4: IPX 5: SPX 17: NCP
Destination Address (12 bytes)	Contains a full IPX internetwork address, complete with socket number.
Source Address (12 bytes)	Also contains a full IPX internetwork address, complete with socket number.

IPX Addressing

Each IPX network is given a 32-bit network number. These numbers are generated by network administrators and must be unique throughout the IPX internetwork. Network numbers are normally written in hexadecimal form, with any leading zeros being omitted. The network 00001200 would be written as 1200. The network numbered zero (00000000, or just "0") is reserved. When a packet is addressed to network 0, it is taken as being addressed to the current network (the same IPX network as the transmitter).

Each IPX-capable device has a 48-bit node address. The node address is normally copied directly from the MAC (hardware) address of the network card, so doesn't have to be manually assigned. The node address is written in hexadecimal form. To make reading easier, there is normally a period (.) inserted between every four digits. 0000.8012.5abc is a valid IPX node address. The address ffff.ffff.ffff is reserved as the broadcast address. A packet addressed to the broadcast address will be received by all IPX devices on the destination network.

A network address together with a node address forms an IPX internetwork address, which is sufficient to locate a single node on an IPX internetwork.

A network device may have multiple processes communicating over IPX simultaneously. To allow the IPX stack to identify which process an incoming packet is destined for, each process is associated with a socket number. A socket is a 16-bit number. Some socket numbers are reserved by Novell for specific purposes; others are available for use dynamically by an IPX client.

By specifying a network number, node address, and socket number together, you can identify an individual process running on a single IPX node. Figure 7-2 shows an example of a fully specified IPX internetwork address, with socket number.

IPX Routing

Network cards and their low-level drivers only have knowledge of MAC-level addresses, and protocols. MAC addresses are 48-bit addresses encoded into the network card on manufacture. MAC protocols only allow communications between devices on the same physical network segment. To pass packets between network segments, we need:

- A protocol that supports multiple networks, and includes network addressing information in the packet header. In our case, this is IPX.
- A device that has ports connected to more than one network, and understands the addressing and packet formats of the internetwork protocol in use. This is a router.

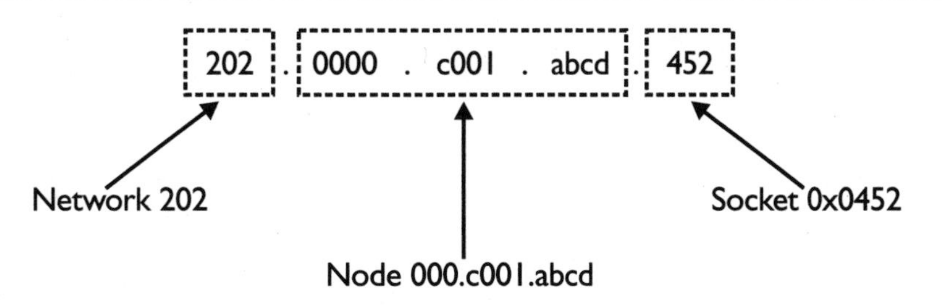

FIGURE 7-2

IPX addressing (written format)

When an IPX node wishes to send a packet to a remote network, it must locate an IPX router that knows of a route to the network. When it finds the router, it forwards the packet to the router for delivery. The router receives the packet and retransmits it along the next hop towards its destination. Eventually the packet is delivered to its destination node. A packet may pass through multiple routers on its path between source and destination devices.

Internal Networks

NetWare file servers have an internal virtual IPX network. This network is purely logical and exists only inside the server. It is given a network address just like a "real" physical network, but there are no LAN cards or MAC addresses associated with it. The server is always node 0000.0000.0001 on its internal network.

The internal network exists to simplify addressing. A device with multiple interfaces has a separate IPX internetwork address for each interface. In each case, the address is made up of the network number for the IPX network on that interface, together with the node address, which is the MAC address for the interface. By creating an internal network, the device can use its internal network address in all communications rather than having to use a different address depending on which interface it is communicating with.

The internal network behaves exactly like a "real" network. For a packet to get from the external (physical) network onto the internal network, there must be an IPX router between the two. Because of this, NetWare file servers are by definition IPX routers. They participate in the routing on the network exactly like other routers. Figure 7-3 shows a network with two routers. This figure also shows the internal network in the server.

The address Server1 uses in all communications is 3.0000.0000.0001. Packets flowing from PC1 to Server1 follow this path:

1. Transmitted by PC1 to Router1 over Network 1
2. To Router2 over Network 4
3. To Server1 over Network 2
4. Routed by Server1 to Internal Network 3 and delivered to the server process

FIGURE 7-3 IPX network showing two routers and a server internal network

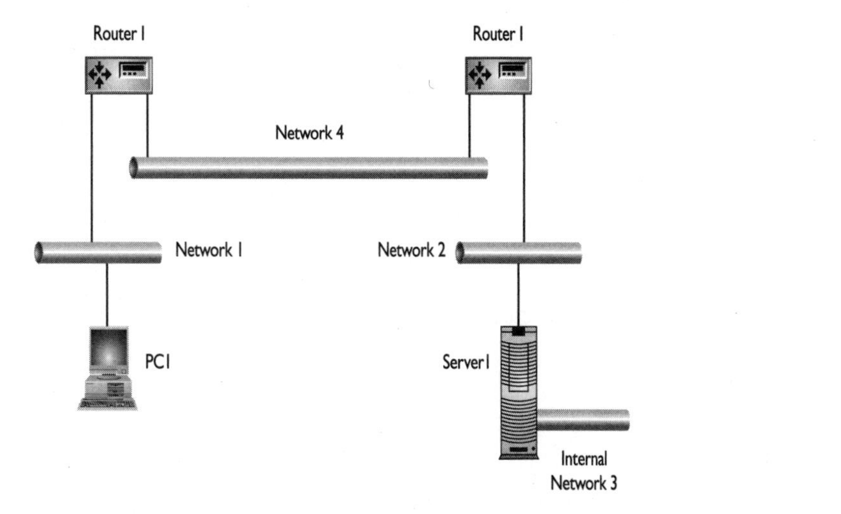

CERTIFICATION OBJECTIVE 7.03

IPX Encapsulation Types

Before an IPX packet can be transmitted onto a network, it must be placed inside a MAC frame. A MAC frame is a Layer 2 frame that is dependent on the media type in use on a network. As the IPX packet travels through the network, each router that receives the packet will strip off the received MAC header and extract the IPX packet. When the packet is to be retransmitted, a new MAC frame, in a format suitable for transmission across the next hop, is generated for the packet. Figure 7-4 shows how an IPX packet is encapsulated in the Data field of a MAC frame.

As is common in networking, over the years there have been multiple differing MAC frame types developed. On an Ethernet LAN, there are four types supported. These are Ethernet_II, Ethernet_802.2, Ethernet_802.3, and Ethernet_SNAP. For two devices to be able to communicate directly (without a router) they must be using the same frame type.

Novell and Cisco use different terminology in this area. What Novell refers to as a frame type, Cisco calls an encapsulation. The Cisco IOS configuration commands also use different names for the Novell frame types discussed.

FIGURE 7-4

Encapsulation of an IPX packet in a MAC frame

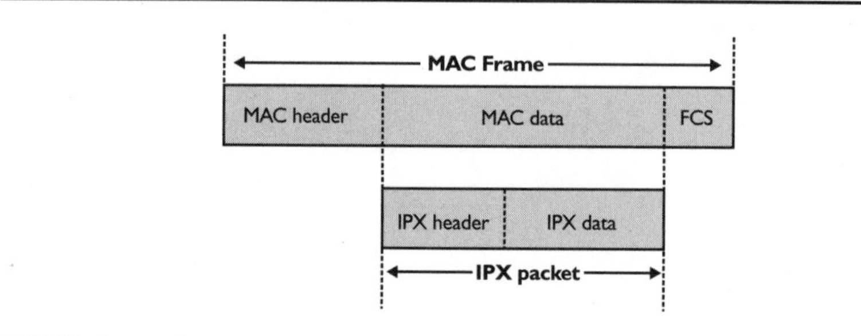

Table 7-1 associates the Novell frame type terminology with the applicable Cisco IOS encapsulation name.

These are the encapsulations commonly used on IPX Ethernet interfaces. There are other encapsulations supported by IOS on various media that aren't discussed here.

TABLE 7-1

Novell Frame Types and Their Cisco IOS Equivalents

Novell Frame Type	Cisco IOS Encapsulation Name
Ethernet_II	arpa
Ethernet_802.2	SAP
Ethernet_802.3	novell-ether
Ethernet_SNAP	SNAP

Ethernet_II

Ethernet_II was released around 1982. The frame format is as follows:

Destination Address (6 bytes)	A 48-bit MAC address.
Source Address (6 bytes)	A 48-bit MAC address.
Type (2 bytes)	Specifies which higher-level protocol is contained in the packet. For IPX this field contains 0x8137 (hexadecimal).

Data (46 – 1500 bytes)	The IPX packet is inserted into this portion of the packet.
Frame Check Sequence (4 bytes)	The frame check sequence (FCS) is a cyclic redundancy check (CRC) calculated on all fields from the Destination Address on. It is used to detect corrupted packets on the network.

Ethernet_802.3

The Ethernet_802.3 frame is also called "802.3 raw" in some documentation. This is the default encapsulation for NetWare versions up to (and including) 3.11.

The format of the Ethernet_802.3 frame is:

Destination Address (6 bytes)	A 48-bit MAC address.
Source Address (6 bytes)	A 48-bit MAC address.
Length (2 bytes)	The number of bytes in the Data field of the packet.
Data (46 – 1500 bytes)	The IPX packet is inserted into this portion of the packet. If the packet is below the minimum size for a legal packet, extra bytes are added to the *Padding* field to expand the packet out to the minimum size.
Frame Check Sequence (4 bytes)	The frame check sequence is a cyclic redundancy check calculated on all fields from the Destination Address on. It is used to detect corrupted packets on the network.

Ethernet_802.2

The Ethernet_802.2 frame type uses the same base frame format as Ethernet_802.3, but includes the LLC (802.2) information as well. This is the default encapsulation for NetWare 3.12 and 4.*x*.

Most of the fields are identical to the Ethernet_802.3 frame type. The additional three fields are described in the following list.

Destination Address (6 bytes)	A 48-bit MAC address.
Source Address (6 bytes)	A 48-bit MAC address.
Length (2 bytes)	The number of bytes in the Data field of the packet.
DSAP (1 byte)	The Destination Service Access Point specifies which protocol is being carried. For IPX this field contains the number 0xE0.
SSAP (1 byte)	The Source Service Access Point also specifies which protocol is being carried. For IPX this field contains the number 0xE0.
Control (1 byte)	The Control byte always contains the number 0x03 when used by IPX. This specifies an unnumbered information frame.
Data (43 – 1497 bytes)	The IPX packet is inserted into this portion of the packet.
Frame Check Sequence (4 bytes)	The frame check sequence is a cyclic redundancy check calculated on all fields from the Destination Address on. It is used to detect corrupted packets on the network.

Ethernet_SNAP

The Ethernet_II frame uses a two-byte number to specify which upper-level protocol is contained within the frame. In the Ethernet_802.2 frame, there is only one byte available (the SSAP/DSAP fields). To allow protocols to continue to use the Ethernet_II packet type numbers, the Subnetwork Access Protocol (SNAP) was devised. This protocol uses the number 0xAA for the DSAP and SSAP fields. It then uses other fields to specify the protocol, including the original two-byte protocol number.

In the format for the Ethernet_SNAP, the fields up to the control byte are identical to the Ethernet_802.2 frame type.

Field	Description
Destination Address (6 bytes)	A 48-bit MAC address.
Source Address (6 bytes)	A 48-bit MAC address.
Length (2 bytes)	The number of bytes in the Data field of the packet.
DSAP (1 byte)	Contains the number 0xAA.
SSAP (1 byte)	Contains the number 0xAA.
Control (1 byte)	The Control byte always contains the number 0x03 when used by IPX. This specifies an unnumbered information frame.
Organization Code (3 bytes)	The Organization Code for IPX packets contains all zero bytes.
Ethernet Type (2 bytes)	The same Novell Ethernet type number is used as in the Ethernet_II frame (0x8137).
Data (38 – 1492 bytes)	The IPX packet is inserted into this portion of the packet.

Routing with Multiple Frame Types

Multiple frame types can be in use on one physical network segment. Doing this effectively splits the network into logically separate networks. Devices on the network can only communicate directly with other devices that use the same frame type. The only way for users of different frame types to communicate is through a router.

Using multiple frame types complicates the administration of network numbers, as each frame type in use on a network requires its own network number. It is useful to reserve one digit of the IPX network number to specify the frame type. You then only need to generate a single base IPX network number for each network, and modify it in a standard way to generate the IPX network number for each frame type in use.

As an example, you could decide to use the last digit of the IPX network number to specify the frame type. A "1" could represent Ethernet_II, "2" could be Ethernet_802.2, "3" Ethernet_802.3, and "4" Ethernet_SNAP.

Applying this scheme to two IPX networks with base numbers of 400 and 500 would give IPX network numbers for the four frame types as described in Table 7-2.

Using a standard like this makes it easier to remember which numbers to configure for which frame types, and also makes it easier to spot mistakes.

Figure 7-5 shows a single network containing a server, a workstation, and a router. The server is using the Ethernet_802.3 frame type, and is configured so that this network is IPX network number 503. The router is configured to use both Ethernet_SNAP and Ethernet_802.3 frame types on the same physical port. To do this, it must use a different IPX network number for each frame type. In this case it is using Network 503 for the Ethernet_802.3 Frame Type, and Network 504 for the Ethernet_SNAP frame type. The PC is using Ethernet_SNAP. At initialization it discovers it is on Network 504.

Although PC1 and Server1 are physically connected to the same network, they cannot communicate directly because they are using different frame types. When PC1 looks up the address of Server1, and finds that the server is located on Network 503, it must find a path to this network. The router can provide the path, as it has interfaces on both Networks 503 and Network 504. The fact that both these interfaces are the same physical port doesn't make any difference to the operation of the protocol.

All traffic between PC1 and Server1 must flow through the router. Obviously this isn't very efficient, and normally this situation would be

TABLE 7-2

Multiple Frame Types on Two Networks

Network	Frame Type	IPX Network
400	Ethernet_II	401
400	Ethernet_802.2	402
400	Ethernet_802.3	403
400	Ethernet_SNAP	404
500	Ethernet_II	501
500	Ethernet_802.2	502
500	Ethernet_802.3	503
500	Ethernet_SNAP	504

FIGURE 7-5

Use of multiple frame types on a single network

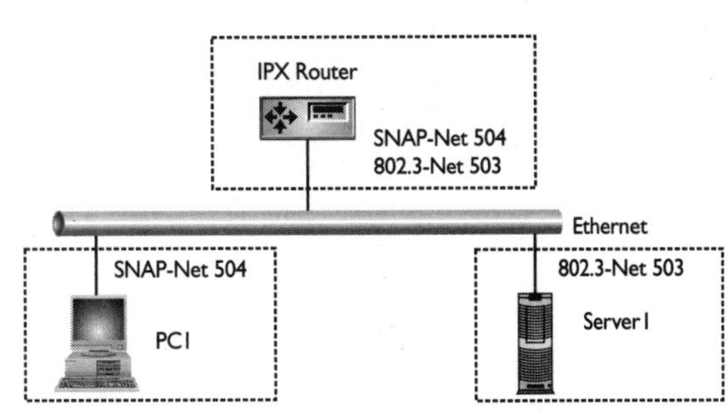

avoided by ensuring that devices on the same physical segment are using the same frame type.

Remember that running multiple frame types on the same physical network effectively divides the network into multiple, separate IPX networks.

FROM THE CLASSROOM

Four Encapsulations on an Ethernet: a Recipe for Networking Disaster

One of the questions that comes up frequently in the classroom is, "Can you have more than one encapsulation simultaneously on an Ethernet interface?" The answer is yes. The bigger question is, can you afford to do it?

Early on in my networking career I encountered a campus network environment where various organizations were tied together over a campus-wide fiber backbone. The backbone and the routers were maintained by one organization, and the others had no control over how the routers were configured. Most of the servers were Novell NetWare of one flavor or another, and there were well over 300 of them.

The group I was working with had its own 10-Mbps Ethernet "backbone" separated from the fiber backbone by a Cisco router. Hanging off this local Ethernet backbone were 16 NetWare 3.1*x* file servers, each with two LAN connections, which acted as routers for IPX traffic from the local backbone onto another Ethernet, where the 60 or so users for that server were located.

FROM THE CLASSROOM

The network was installed in the very early 1990s, when the frame type of choice for clients was Ethernet_802.3 (novell-ether encapsulation, in Cisco terms), so many of the PCs were using it quite happily. They had started to upgrade hardware and software, though, so the newer PCs were using Ethernet_802.2 (SAP encapsulation on the Cisco router, not to be confused with Service Advertising Protocol), which became the default starting with NetWare 3.12. Presently, they wanted to add IP connectivity to their network, which required the PCs to add Ethernet_II (arpa encapsulation, for us Cisco folks) to the frame type soup. Then, there were a few of the networks with Macintosh users, so the servers needed Ethernet_SNAP (SNAP encapsulation). That made as many as four encapsulations on a single Ethernet, each constituting a different logical IPX network. Hold that thought while we look at RIPs and SAPs.

The Cisco router was picking up all the RIP and SAP traffic for those 300 servers and building its internal IPX routing table and SAP table, just as every good IPX router should, and broadcasting them every 60 seconds onto the local Ethernet backbone. Each NetWare server on the local backbone was picking up the RIP and SAP broadcasts from the router, and building its own internal IPX routing table and SAP table, then broadcasting those entries out onto the local Ethernet, the one with the users. 300 servers doesn't sound like so many, does it? Well, each Novell server typically advertises between four and ten services, and these were no exception; the SAP tables on our servers contained over 2,500 entries. The IPX routing tables contained over 1,400 entries. When those broadcasts came across the backbone, the servers' CPU utilization went up to 100 percent and stayed there for several seconds while they processed all that information. This happened every 60 seconds.

Remember the four encapsulations? When it came time for the servers to broadcast the RIP and SAP information out onto the local Ethernet, it now had to do it once for each encapsulation. Why? Because each encapsulation is a separate logical network, even though it is sharing the same physical wire. The RIP broadcasts weren't so bad; 1,400 entries could fit into 28 RIP packets, so even with four encapsulations there were just over 100 packets each minute that were wasting bandwidth and CPU cycles in the users' PCs; but the SAPs are another story. Only seven SAP entries can fit in a packet, so it took 358 packets to accommodate the full table, and with four encapsulations that's 1,432 packets taking up bandwidth and CPU cycles on PCs that couldn't use the information anyway. Novell clients don't listen to periodic SAP broadcasts.

FROM THE CLASSROOM

To be fair to Novell, newer versions of NetWare have some sophisticated features built in for filtering RIP and SAP traffic that existed only in the Cisco router software when I encountered this network of horrors. The moral of the story is that back then, we could have used some help from our router administrators. IPX is still out there, and you can still find networks like this, especially where the network was put in by the lowest bidder! So pay close attention when we look at SAP filtering in Chapter 9.

—By Pamela Forsyth, CCIE, CCSI, CNX

CERTIFICATION OBJECTIVE 7.04

SAP and RIP

The last few examples have spoken about the workstation finding a route to a remote network and looking up the address for a server, but haven't described how these processes work. This section will fill in the missing pieces.

To provide information on the topology of the network, and the services available on it, IPX servers, routers, and clients use two protocols: Service Advertising Protocol (SAP), and Routing Information Protocol (RIP). Both these protocols use IPX broadcasts to propagate information around the network.

SAP

SAP allows servers to advertise the services they provide on the network. There are three types of SAP packets defined: periodic updates, service queries, and service responses. SAP packets can be identified by a value of 0x452 in the source or destination socket number.

Periodic SAP Updates

When a server has a service to advertise, it sends a SAP broadcast listing the service's name, type, and IPX internetwork address (including the socket number that this service is listening on). IPX routers listen for these broadcasts and add the advertised services to an internal database. Routers periodically broadcast these databases onto all their directly attached networks, so that the advertisements propagate across the network. By default these broadcasts are sent every 60 seconds.

Get Nearest Server Queries

When a NetWare client is initializing, it needs to locate a server to connect to. To do this it sends a SAP Get Nearest Server (GNS) query. This query is a broadcast, and all routers and servers that know of at least one suitable server respond. The response includes the full IPX internetwork address and the socket number for the client to use in connecting with the server. Once the client is connected to a NetWare server, it can query the server directly using NCP requests to obtain the same information. (The SAP Get Nearest Server requests are also known as Nearest Service queries.)

Note that because the GNS request is a broadcast, it doesn't travel off the network on which it was generated. This means that the client will only get responses from servers and routers connected to the same IPX network as the client. To make it possible to locate servers on other networks, IPX routers respond to GNS requests on behalf of remote servers.

The SAP query fits into the Data field of the IPX packet, and holds only two fields:

Field	Description
Packet Type (2 bytes)	Can be "3" for a Nearest Service query, or "1" for a general service query.
Service Type (2 bytes)	Contains the number of the service type requested (0x0004 for a NetWare server, or 0x0047 for a print server). These numbers are allocated by Novell.

SAP Response

The SAP response is also contained in the Data portion of an IPX packet. Each response packet can contain up to seven records. The format of the SAP response is:

Field	Description
Packet Type (2 bytes)	Contains "4" for a Nearest Service response, or "2" for a general service response.
Service Type (2 bytes)	One of the same Novell-allocated numbers.
Server Name (48 bytes)	The textual name of the server.
Server Address (12 bytes)	Contains the full IPX internetwork address and socket number of the server.
Intermediate Networks (2 bytes)	Gives the distance in network hops to the network.
... Repeated ...	The fields from Service Type to Intermediate Networks (inclusive) are repeated for each entry.

SAP Split Horizon

When sending SAP updates and responses, a router advertises onto each IPX network to which it is directly connected all services it knows about, except for services it learned about from updates received on this same network. Put another way, a router will not re-advertise a service back onto the network it learned it from. This function is called split horizon, and is used with RIP and other routing protocols, as well as with SAP. Its purpose is to avoid retransmitting information onto networks where it is already known.

SAP packets can be a source of worry on large internetworks, especially where slow wide-area links are in use. When there are a large number of servers on the network, the bandwidth used by SAP packets can be a significant part of the available bandwidth. The problem is worse when using multiple frame types on each network segment, as the updates are transmitted separately over each frame type.

RIP

While SAP advertises and distributes service information, RIP is used to propagate IPX routing information. IPX routers send RIP broadcasts to advertise the IPX networks to which they know routes. In the broadcasts, each router advertises networks it is directly connected to, as well as networks it has learned from other routers. To avoid routing loops, a router will never advertise a learned route back onto the network that it learned the route from. This is the same split-horizon principle mentioned in the preceding section.

RIP is a distance vector protocol, which means that it bases its choice of the best route to a given destination on the distance to the destination via the route. The parameters it uses to measure the distance are hop count (the number of routers a packet must cross to reach the network) and time ticks (the number of 1/18-second intervals a packet will take to reach the network). The operation of IPX RIP is similar to the RIP protocol used with TCP/IP.

The flow of routing information is shown in Figure 7-6, where two routers and three networks are interconnected.

The arrows represent the periodic RIP updates being transmitted by each router. The associated numbers show which network numbers are being advertised on each interface. Although both routers will hold a RIP database containing Networks 1, 2, and 4, the routers only advertise routes that didn't originate from the target network. Because Router1 receives the

FIGURE 7-6

RIP routing flow

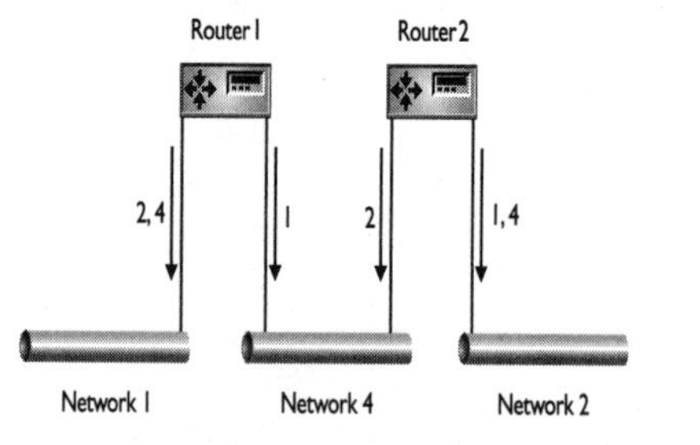

updates for Network 2 from Network 4, it doesn't retransmit the Network 2 updates onto Network 4, only onto Network 1. This is the same split-horizon functionality as was described under SAP.

RIP packets are transmitted in the Data field of a standard IPX packet. The IPX socket number used is 0x0453.

IPX routers using RIP broadcast their routing tables every 60 seconds. They also transmit when initializing to request RIP information from other routers, and when their routing table changes. If being "downed" cleanly, a router will send packets advising all other IPX routers that it can no longer provide routes to the networks it has been advertising. Other routers can then purge the routes from their tables.

Workstations and other end devices send RIP request packets whenever they need to locate a route to a remote IPX network.

The packet format for RIP requests and responses are identical, although some fields are only valid in responses.

Field	Description
Packet Type (2 bytes)	The Packet Type for a request packet is 0x0001; for a response it is 0x0002.
Network Number (4 bytes)	The Network Number field holds the IPX network number being searched for (in requests), or advertised (in responses).
Hops Away (2 bytes)	Hops Away is a count of the number of routers a packet has to cross to get to this network. This field is valid only in response packets. In request packets, it should contain the value 0xFFFF.
Time Ticks (2 bytes)	Time Ticks measures the time to reach the remote network. Approximately 18.2 ticks make up one second. This field is valid only in response packets. In request packets, it should contain the value 0xFFFF.
... Repeated ...	A single IPX packet can hold up to 49 RIP entries. For each entry, all the fields from Network Address to Time Ticks (inclusive) are repeated.

As with SAP, RIP transmissions can be a problem on large networks, especially where there are multiple encapsulations in use. The RIP information is broadcast separately onto each locally attached IPX network.

With multiple encapsulations, each encapsulation in use is configured as a separate IPX network, and so receives its own copy of any updates.

There is one limiting factor on how far a route will be advertised. A hop count of 16 specifies that a network is unreachable. If a router receives a RIP advertisement for a network that is 16 hops away, it discards the route.

SAP and RIP Operation Example

As an example of how SAP and RIP work together on a network, consider the case of a NetWare client workstation booting up. It needs to find a server to connect to, and then find a route to the server. Remember that even if the workstation and server are on the same network, the address the server advertises is its internal network address, so the workstation still needs to find a route to the internal network.

In the network shown in Figure 7-7, there is a workstation (PC1) connected to IPX Network 1, and the file server's internal network number is 3.

FIGURE 7-7

Sample IPX network

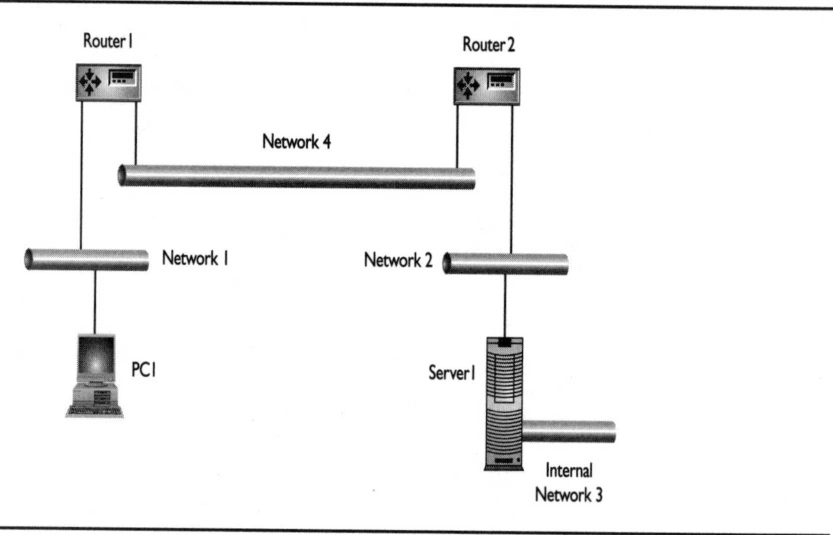

PC1 sends a GNS request looking for a server of the type 0x0004 (NetWare file server). The request will look like this:

```
Packet Type = 0x0003
Service Type = 0x0004
```

Router1 has received SAP updates from Router2, advertising Server1 with a Service Type of 4, so Router1 sends a SAP reply to PC1 containing this information:

```
Packet Type = 0x0004
Service Type = 0x0004
Server Name = 'SERVER1'
Server Address = 3.0000.0000.0001:451 (NCP)
Intermediate Networks = 0x0003
```

PC1 now has the IPX address for Server1, so it needs to find a route to Network 3. PC1 sends a RIP request:

```
Packet Type = 0x0001
Network Address = 3
Hops Away = 0xFFFF
Time (ticks) = 0xFFFF
```

Router1 has received RIP updates from Router2, advertising Network 3 as a reachable network, so Router1 responds with a RIP Response packet:

```
Packet Type = 0x0002
Network Address = 3
Hops Away = 0x0003
Time (ticks) = 0x0001
```

The workstation now builds a connection packet and addresses it to the IPX destination address received in the SAP response: 3.0000.0000.0001:451. It places a packet inside a MAC frame of the appropriate type and sends this MAC frame addressed to the MAC address of Router1's interface on Network 1.

When the server needs to respond to the workstation, it must locate a route to the workstation's network. It uses its internal routing table to locate this route.

CERTIFICATION OBJECTIVE 7.05

IPX Configuration

Now that we have been over the operation of IPX, we get down to actually configuring it using Cisco IOS.

Preparation

Before you start to configure IPX, you need to either obtain or generate a plan for the network. You need to know which encapsulations and IPX network numbers to use. If it is a new installation in an isolated network, you can pick your own numbers. But if it is an established network, or one that will have connections to other IPX networks, you will need to have numbers allocated by the responsible administrator.

If the network has existing routers, you will also need to know what routing protocols are in use, and the associated parameters. In particular you'll need to know any of the settings that have been changed from the defaults, so that you can set the new router(s) to match. Having mismatched routing parameters in a network leads to unreliable routing.

For our purposes we will re-use our sample network from Figure 7-7. We will develop a configuration file for Router1 in that diagram. Assume that the left-hand interface on Router1 in the figure is Ethernet 0, and the right-hand interface is Ethernet 1. We'll also assume that all networks are using *arpa* encapsulation. The configuration details for Router 1 are:

Interface	Network	Encapsulation
Ethernet 0	1	arpa
Ethernet 1	4	arpa

Enabling IPX and Configuring the Interfaces

Once you have the required configuration details, you can begin to configure the router.

The first step is to enable IPX routing using the IOS command IPX ROUTING. This command is issued in the global configuration mode.

Now that you have IPX enabled, you can configure the router interfaces. You need to assign the network number, and optionally the encapsulation, to each interface as you enable it. If you don't specify the encapsulation, a default is used. For Ethernet, this default is novell-ether. This is not what we want, so we will have to specify the encapsulation. This configuration sample configures Router1 as per our requirements.

```
cisco(config)#ipx routing
cisco(config)#interface ethernet 0
cisco(config-if)#ipx network 1 encapsulation arpa
cisco(config)#interface ethernet 1
cisco(config-if)#ipx network 4 encapsulation arpa
```

The router will start transmitting RIP updates on an interface as soon as the interface has a network number assigned.

If you need to use multiple encapsulations on each physical interface, you need to use either subinterfaces or secondary networks.

```
cisco(config)#ipx routing
cisco(config)#interface ethernet 0.1
cisco(config-subif)#ipx network 101 encapsulation arpa
cisco(config)#interface ethernet 0.2
cisco(config-subif)#ipx network 102 encapsulation snap
```

This script has defined two subinterfaces, Ethernet 0.1 and 0.2. Subinterface Ethernet 0.1 is using IPX network 101 with Ethernet_II encapsulation. Subinterface Ethernet 0.2 is using IPX network 102 with Ethernet_SNAP encapsulation.

The syntax for configuring multiple encapsulations using primary and secondary networks is:

```
cisco(config)#interface ethernet 1
cisco(config-if)#ipx network 201 encapsulation novell-ether
cisco(config-if)#ipx network 202 encapsulation sap secondary
```

If you attempt to configure an IPX network number that is already in use on another interface, or you attempt to use the same encapsulation type on more than one subinterface of the same physical interface, IOS will issue an error message and ignore the change.

IOS forwards packets along the least-cost path to a destination. If there are multiple paths available of equal cost, it will by default only keep one in the routing table, and discard the others. All traffic to the network is then forwarded along this one path. By using the IPX MAXIMUM-PATHS <*number*> command, you can configure IOS to hold up to a maximum of <*number*> equal-cost paths to each destination network. If multiple paths to a destination do exist, traffic will be shared among the paths in a round-robin fashion. IPX MAXIMUM PATHS is a global configuration command.

Confirming Operation

Once the router has been up and running for a couple of minutes, its internal SAP and RIP databases should have had enough time to discover any other SAP or RIP devices on the network. There are a number of IOS commands available to check the configuration and operation of IPX.

The SHOW IPX INTERFACE command allows you to check the configuration of the interface. It shows the configured network numbers, encapsulation types, and operational status of the interface. If the interface is not specified, all IPX interfaces are listed. The lines of most interest from the output of this command are as follows:

```
cisco#show ipx interface ethernet 0
Ethernet0 is up, line protocol is up
IPX address is 1.00e0.b064.2892, ARPA [up] line-up, RIPPQ: 0, SAPPQ: 0
Delay of this IPX network, in ticks is 1 throughput 0 link delay 0
....
RIP packets received 0, RIP packets sent 5
SAP packets received 0, SAP packets sent 1
```

The full output can contain a lot more detail than required. To provide a concise listing of each interface, and its IPX configuration, you can use the IPX INTERFACE BRIEF variant of this command.

```
cisco#show ipx interface brief
Interface          IPX Network Encapsulation Status                IPX State
Ethernet0          1           ARPA          up                    [up]
Ethernet1          4           ARPA          up                    [up]
Serial0            unassigned  not config'd  administratively down n/a
Serial1            unassigned  not config'd  administratively down n/a
```

Once you know that the interfaces are configured correctly, you can use the SHOW IPX TRAFFIC command to look at the amount of activity on the network. This command shows the number of packets sent and received. Of most interest at the moment will be the SAP and RIP counters, which will allow you to see whether the router is successfully receiving IPX traffic from the network.

```
cisco#show ipx traffic
System Traffic for 0.0000.0000.0001 System-Name: cisco
Rcvd:  42 total, 55 format errors, 0 checksum errors, 0 bad hop count,
       2 packets pitched, 40 local destination, 0 multicast
Bcast: 35 received, 74 sent
Sent:  74 generated, 0 forwarded
       0 encapsulation failed, 0 no route
SAP:   4 SAP requests, 0 SAP replies, 2 servers
       18 SAP advertisements received, 20 sent
       0 SAP flash updates sent, 0 SAP format errors
RIP:   4 RIP requests, 0 RIP replies, 9 routes
       14 RIP advertisements received, 18 sent
       16 RIP flash updates sent, 0 RIP format errors
Echo:  Rcvd 0 requests, 0 replies
Sent 0 requests, 0 replies
      0 unknown: 0 no socket, 0 filtered, 0 no helper
      0 SAPs throttled, freed NDB len 0
Watchdog: 0 packets received, 0 replies spoofed
Queue lengths:
IPX input: 0, SAP 0, RIP 0, GNS 0
SAP throttling length: 0/(no limit), 0 nets pending lost route reply
Delayed process creation: 0
```

The SHOW IPX SERVERS command shows the SAP database in the router. You should be able to see any local servers you have running in the list. Each entry appears on a line by itself.

```
Type Name            Net      Address     Port       Route Hops Itf
P 4 SERVER1       C0A80201.0000.0000.0001:0451     2/01    1  Et1.1
```

In this example, there is a file server (type 4) called SERVER1 at IPX address C0A80201.0000.0000.0001, listening on socket 0x451. You should recognize this IPX address as the internal network address of a file server (due to the node address). The P at the start of the line shows that this is a periodic entry—it was learned from the network via a periodic SAP broadcast.

The SHOW IPX ROUTE command will display the IPX routing table.

```
C         501 (ARPA),           Et1.1
R         201 [02/01] via       501.0260.8c6b.a7a3,     8s, Et1.1
```

The first line shows a directly connected network (C) number 501. It is located on interface Ethernet 1.1. The bottom line shows network 201, which has been learned from RIP (R), and is reachable via the router at 501.0260.8c6b.a7a3.

If you don't see the services and routes you expect, check the encapsulations and network numbers you have configured for the interfaces. If you have any NetWare servers running on the network, they may show error messages to the effect that, "Router at aaaaaaaaaaaa claims IPX Network XXXXXXXX should be YYYYYYYY". If you see this, it means that at least one router on the network is configured with the wrong IPX network number/encapsulation combination. If you have just configured a new router, that's probably the one!

If RIP or SAP updates aren't working as you expect, you may have to look deeper into the operation of these protocols. This is possible through two debug commands, DEBUG IPX ROUTING ACTIVITY and DEBUG IPX SAP ACTIVITY.

The DEBUG IPX ROUTING ACTIVITY command allows you to see the routing updates as they are being sent and received. In the example below, the first two IPXRIP: lines show an update being broadcast by the router onto its interface, Ethernet 1. The third IPXRIP: line shows an update being received from router 504.0260.8c6b.a7a3, and the lines following show the contents of the received update. The first of these lines shows a route to network number C0A80201, which is one router hop away. The other is for network 201, which is also one hop away.

```
cisco#debug ipx routing activity
IPX routing debugging is on
cisco#terminal monitor
cisco#
IPXRIP: positing full update to 504.ffff.ffff.ffff via Ethernet1 (broadcast)
IPXRIP: sending update to 504.ffff.ffff.ffff via Ethernet1
IPXRIP: update from 504.0260.8c6b.a7a3
C0A80201 in 1 hops, delay 2
201 in 1 hops, delay 2
```

Finally, to allow monitoring of the operation of the SAP protocol, you can use the DEBUG IPX SAP ACTIVITY command:

```
cisco#debug ipx sap activity
IPX service debugging is on
cisco#terminal monitor
cisco#
IPXSAP: at 00095450:
I SAP Response type 0x2 len 96 src:504.0260.8c6b.a7a3
dest:504.ffff.ffff.ffff(452)
type 0x4, "DAVENW", C0A80201.0000.0000.0001(451), 1 hops
IPXSAP: at 00094520:
I SAP Response type 0x2 len 96 src:504.0260.8c6b.a7a3
dest:504.ffff.ffff.ffff(452)
type 0x640, "DAD", 202.0000.1b32.9e17(E885), 2 hops
```

This example shows a SAP update being received from router 504.0260.8c6b.a7a3, containing advertisements for two servers. DAVENW is a server of type 4 at address C0A80201.0000.0000.0001, listening on socket 0x452. DAD, is a server type 0x640 with an address of 202.0000.1b32.9e17, listening on socket 0xE885.

Some common problems or questions you may come across are:

QUESTIONS AND ANSWERS	
When I plug my new router into the network, all the NetWare servers start beeping...	This is normally caused by a mismatch in network numbers. Check that the network numbers you have configured match the server's configurations.
The router is not listing my servers when I use the SHOW IPX SERVERS command...	Check that the server is using the same frame type as the router interface on the network. If they're not using the same frame types, they won't be able to see each other.
When I use the SHOW IPX ROUTE command, I can't see any remote networks...	Remember that it can take a minute or so for the routes to show up.
How do I configure the clients with their IPX address?	The client addressing with IPX is pretty much automatic. You normally configure the router and servers with the correct network address and encapsulation, and as long as you have the correct encapsulation configured on the clients, they will detect their network number. Of course, the node address is automatically generated from the MAC address in the LAN card.

Routing Protocols

RIP is the default routing protocol when IPX routing is enabled. There are other protocols available that can be configured to make more effective use of bandwidth, and allow larger networks to be built than with RIP alone.

NetWare Link Services Protocol (NLSP) is a link-state protocol similar to the OSPF protocol used with TCP/IP. Each NLSP router builds up a database recording the states of links between routers in the network. This database gives a view of the network topology and allows calculation of the best routes to any given destination. Routing tables aren't broadcast as with RIP, but changes in the state of links are advertised as they occur.

Enhanced Interior Gateway Routing Protocol (EIGRP) is a distance vector protocol, but has been designed to cause less overhead on the network than RIP. Like NSLP, updates are only sent when something changes.

It is also possible to designate static routes. These are routes that aren't learned or calculated using a routing protocol, but are manually entered into the router's configuration. The syntax to do this is:

IPX ROUTE *network destination* [FLOATING-STATIC]

This is a global configuration command in which *network* specifies the target network for this route. It can be in three forms.

- A single network number.
- A network number with a mask.
- The word "default," which means that this route is used if there are no other known routes for a network.

Destination specifies where to send the packet. It can be the IPX address of another router, or an interface name for serial interfaces.

Appending FLOATING-STATIC marks the entry as floating, which means that it can be overridden if a dynamic route is learned covering the same network.

CERTIFICATION SUMMARY

This chapter has shown the IPX protocol stack, with an overview of the main protocols. It has explained the IPX *network.node.node.node:socket* addressing, how routers provide paths to allow packets to travel between different networks, and how RIP is used to pass routing updates around the network. The operation of the various SAP packet types was also discussed.

Remember that every IPX network number in the internetwork must be unique, and that when using multiple encapsulation types on the same interface (with subinterfaces or primary/secondary networks), a unique network number must be configured for each one.

The most useful commands for monitoring the network and confirming its operation are the SHOW IPX TRAFFIC, SHOW IPX INTERFACE, DEBUG IPX ROUTING ACTIVITY, and DEBUG IPX SAP ACTIVITY commands.

TWO-MINUTE DRILL

- The Internetwork Packet Exchange (IPX) protocol is the native networking protocol for Novell NetWare.
- IPX provides the basis for the stack of protocols designed by Novell to support NetWare.
- An IPX datagram consists of a 30-byte header followed by the user data.
- Each IPX network is given a 32-bit network number. These numbers are generated by network administrators and must be unique throughout the IPX internetwork.
- When an IPX node wishes to send a packet to a remote network, it must locate an IPX router that knows of a route to the network.
- NetWare file servers have an internal virtual IPX network.
- Before an IPX packet can be transmitted onto a network, it must be placed inside a MAC frame.
- What Novell refers to as a frame type, Cisco calls an encapsulation.
- The Cisco IOS configuration commands also use different names for the Novell frame types.
- The Ethernet_802.3 frame is also called "802.3 raw" in some documentation. This is the default encapsulation for NetWare versions up to (and including) 3.11.
- The Ethernet_802.2 frame type uses the same base frame format as Ethernet_802.3, but includes the LLC (802.2) information as well. This is the default encapsulation for NetWare 3.12 and 4.*x*.
- To allow protocols to continue to use the Ethernet_II packet type numbers, the Subnetwork Access Protocol (SNAP) was devised.
- Multiple frame types can be in use on one physical network segment.
- To provide information on the topology of the network, and the services available on it, IPX servers, routers, and clients use two protocols: Service Advertising Protocol (SAP), and Routing

Information Protocol (RIP). Both these protocols use IPX broadcasts to propagate information around the network.

- SAP allows servers to advertise the services they provide on the network.
- There are three types of SAP packets defined: periodic updates, service queries, and service responses.
- While SAP advertises and distributes service information, RIP is used to propagate IPX routing information.
- RIP is a distance vector protocol, which means that it bases its choice of the best route to a given destination on the distance to the destination via the route.
- Before you start to configure IPX, you need to either obtain or generate a plan for the network.
- The first step in configuration is to enable IPX routing using the IOS command IPX ROUTING.
- Once you have IPX enabled, you can configure the router interfaces.
- The SHOW IPX INTERFACE command allows you to check the configuration of the interface.
- Once you know that the interfaces are configured correctly, you can use the SHOW IPX TRAFFIC command to look at the amount of activity on the network.
- The SHOW IPX SERVERS command shows the SAP database in the router.
- The SHOW IPX ROUTE command will display the IPX routing table.
- The DEBUG IPX ROUTING ACTIVITY command allows you to see the routing updates as they are being sent and received.
- RIP is the default routing protocol when IPX routing is enabled.
- NetWare Link Services Protocol (NLSP) is a link-state protocol similar to the OSPF protocol used with TCP/IP.
- Enhanced Interior Gateway Routing Protocol (EIGRP) is a distance vector protocol, but has been designed to cause less overhead on the network than RIP.

SELF TEST

The Self Test questions will help you measure your understanding of the material presented in this chapter. Read all the choices carefully, as there may be more than one correct answer. Choose all correct answers for each question.

1. The service provided by IPX is:
   A. Guaranteed delivery
   B. Datagram
   C. Connection-oriented
   D. Sequenced
2. The Transport Control field in the IPX header holds what information?
   A. The age of the packet
   B. Protocol type
   C. Router hop count
   D. Level of service required
3. What is the length of an IPX network number?
   A. 16 bits
   B. Variable
   C. 48 bits
   D. 32 bits
4. In the IPX address 0102.0000.8045.1700, what is the node address?
   A. 1700
   B. 0102.0000.8045
   C. 0102.0000
   D. 0000.8045.1700
5. What can you say about this address: 47.0000.0000.0001?
   A. It is the address of a NetWare print server
   B. It is an internal network address
   C. The included socket number is 0001
   D. Nothing
6. The Checksum field in the IPX header is normally set to:
   A. A checksum of the entire IPX packet
   B. A checksum of the IPX header fields only
   C. 0xFFFF
   D. 0
7. If an IPX node is configured to use the Ethernet_802.2 encapsulation, which other machines can it communicate with directly (without going through a router) on the same network?
   A. Machines running any encapsulation
   B. Machines running either Ethernet_802.2 or Ethernet_802.3
   C. Machines running Ethernet_II
   D. Machines running Ethernet_802.2
8. To run multiple encapsulations on a single physical interface, a router has to:
   A. Use a different network number for each encapsulation
   B. Use subinterfaces, not secondary networks

C. Enable NLSP routing

D. Use an access list

9. Which protocol does a workstation use to locate a server providing a particular type of service?

A. RIP

B. NCP

C. SAP

D. EIGRP

10. Periodic SAP updates are sent by:

A. Routers and servers

B. NetWare servers only

C. Workstations and routers

D. Workstations only

11. The RIP protocol is used by:

A. Routers only

B. Servers only

C. Workstations, servers, and routers

D. Print servers

12. Which command which must be given first to enable IPX?

A. CISCO(CONFIG)#ENABLE IPX ROUTING

B. cisco>ipx routing

C. cisco(config-if)#ipx routing on

D. cisco(config)#ipx routing

13. Which of the following allow you to use multiple IPX networks on a single physical interface?

A. Secondary networks

B. Dynamic frame types

C. Subinterfaces

D. None. This is not supported.

14. Which IOS command allows you to view the router's internal SAP database?

A. SHOW SERVERS

B. show ipx servers

C. servers

D. ipx servers

15. Which of the following kinds of information do you need to collect before you can configure IPX using IOS?

A. The number of NetWare servers on the network

B. The encapsulations in use

C. IPX network numbers

D. The IPX address of another router

16. What does this command do: CISCO(CONFIG-IF)#IPX NETWORK 3

A. Nothing. It is incomplete.

B. Sets up a static route to Network 3

C. Configures IPX Network 3 on this interface with the default frame type

D. Nothing. The router is in the wrong configuration mode.

17. What does this IOS command do? IPX ROUTE 4 5.0000.8004.4563 FLOATING-STATIC

A. Configures 4 static routes

B. Configures static SAP entries for servers of type 4

C. Configures a static route to network 4

D. Says that to get to network 5, you must go via network 4

18. In the command IPX ROUTE 4 5.0000.8004.4563 FLOATING-STATIC, what does the FLOATING-STATIC keyword on the end mean?

A. Set all static routes to floating.

B. Allow this route to be overridden by a route received dynamically.

C. Apply this route to all network numbers from 1 to 4.

D. Lock this route so that it cannot be changed.

19. The IPX MAXIMUM-PATHS command does what?

A. Allows IOS to share traffic to a given network over multiple paths

B. Allows a slow link to be used as a backup for a faster one

C. Sets the maximum number of router hops a packet can travel

D. Sets the maximum number of interfaces IPX can be configured on

20. Which command is used to show a concise list of the configured IPX interfaces?

A. SHOW CONFIG

B. show ipx interface

C. show ipx interface brief

D. show interface

21. If two devices are plugged into the same physical network, but are using different encapsulations, what is required before they can communicate?

A. A cross-over cable

B. A repeater

C. A router configured for the appropriate encapsulations

D. Nothing. They can communicate directly.

22. When does a workstation normally send a GNS request?

A. When trying to communicate with another workstation

B. When trying to locate the nearest router

C. When it needs to send a SAP update

D. When trying to locate a server at initialization

23. How many router hops does a GNS request travel?

A. 16

B. None

C. 4

D. Unlimited

24. In a SAP update packet, what does the Server Address field contain?

A. The network the server is on

B. The server's node number

C. The socket number the server is listening on

D. All of the above

25. Which of the following protocols is used by servers to advertise their services to the clients?

    A. Routing Information Protocol (RIP)
    B. Sequenced Packet Exchange (SPX)
    C. Network Core Protocol (NCP)
    D. Service Advertising Protocol (SAP)

26. On an Ethernet LAN how many IPX encapsulation types are supported?

    A. 4
    B. 3
    C. 2
    D. 1

27. The frame check sequence checks with which fields in an Ethernet_802.3 frame?

    A. The Source Address and Destination Address
    B. The packet data
    C. Everything from the Destination Address on
    D. Source Service Access Point (SSAP)

28. Which of the following fields is not common to both Ethernet_802.3 and Ethernet_802.2 frames?

    A. Source Address
    B. Length
    C. DSAP
    D. Data

29. In SAP packets, the numbers in the Service Type field are assigned by:

    A. The system administrator
    B. The end user
    C. Novell
    D. Server

30. SAP requests, responses, or broadcasts can be recognized by which value of source or destination socket number?

    A. 0x0452
    B. 0xE0
    C. 0x03
    D. 0x0453

31. In RIP Packets, the Hops Away and Time Ticks fields are valid both for request and response packets.

    A. True
    B. False

32. Up to how many RIP entries can a single IPX packet hold?

    A. 44
    B. 47
    C. 49
    D. 51

33. In RIP, which number of hop counts indicates that a network is unreachable?

    A. 12
    B. 16
    C. 8
    D. 20

34. Match a Novell term on the left with an IOS term on the right.

A. Ethernet_SNAP	1. SAP
B. Ethernet_802.2	2. SNAP
C. Ethernet_II	3. novell-ether
D. Ethernet_802.3	4. arpa

35. If a user attempts to set the same encapsulation type on more than one subinterface on the same physical interface, what will the IOS do?

    A. Assign default values for encapsulation types
    B. Issue a warning but allow the change
    C. Issue an error message and ignore the change
    D. Allow the change

36. Which of the following is a default routing protocol when IPX routing is enabled?

    A. RIP
    B. NLSP
    C. EIGRP
    D. CDP

37. When there are multiple paths available at the same cost, then by default IOS:

    A. Will keep all paths in the routing table
    B. Will keep only one path in the routing table
    C. Will keep all paths in the table and route the traffic in a round-robin manner
    D. B and C

38. What is the purpose of the split-horizon function?

    A. To divide the network traffic in two for faster throughput
    B. To avoid sending redundant data back out the interface it was received on
    C. So that each person only has to manage half the routers on a network
    D. To set traffic priority levels

39. By default, RIP routers broadcast periodic updates every:

    A. 30 seconds
    B. 60 seconds
    C. 5 minutes
    D. 10 minutes

40. When would a workstation send a RIP request?

    A. On initialization, to locate a server
    B. Whenever it needs to find a route to a remote network it doesn't have a route for
    C. To connect to a NetWare server
    D. Every 60 seconds

41. If an interface was configured like this:
    CISCO(CONFIG)#INTERFACE ETHERNET 1
    CISCO(CONFIG-IF)#IPX NETWORK 201 ENCAPSULATION NOVELL-ETHER
    CISCO(CONFIG-IF)#IPX NETWORK 202 ENCAPSULATION SAP SECONDARY
    How many copies of each SAP update would be sent out the physical interface?

    A. 1
    B. 2
    C. 3
    D. 4

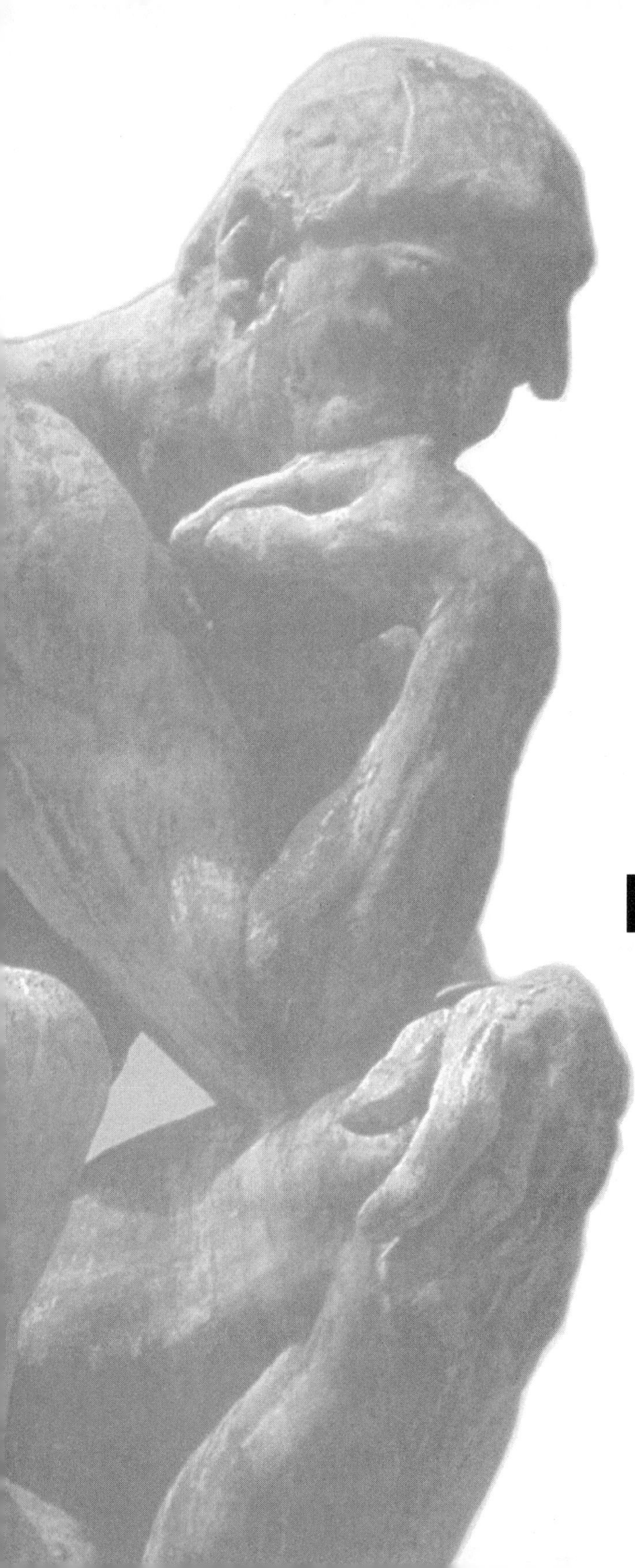

CCNA

CISCO CERTIFIED NETWORK ASSOCIATE

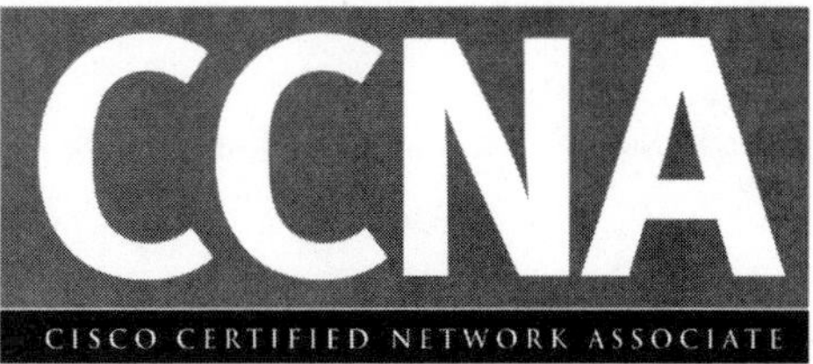

8

AppleTalk Configuration

CERTIFICATION OBJECTIVES

8.01 AppleTalk Protocol Stack

8.02 AppleTalk Services

8.03 AppleTalk Addressing

8.04 AppleTalk Zones

8.05 AppleTalk Routing

8.06 AppleTalk Discovery Mode

8.07 AppleTalk Configuration

AppleTalk (AT) is the name given to the suite of network protocols created by Apple Computer, Inc. (Apple) for use on their Macintosh line of personal computers. The various protocols in the protocol stack are used to provide communications services for file servers, printers, electronic mail, and other network applications. Table 8-1 identifies the protocols that make up the AT protocol suite. It also shows how the protocols relate to each other and to the OSI model. Cisco routers and switches support the AppleTalk protocol stack. Using Cisco networking equipment, an AppleTalk network can span the entire globe providing global file, print, and application services to Macintosh computer users. Cisco has maintained a strong commitment to the AppleTalk protocol suite even in the face of a shrinking AppleTalk user community. In the late 1980s and early 1990s Macintosh desktop and laptop computers were standard fare in many Cisco offices. The relationship between Apple and Cisco is evident in Cisco's strong IOS support for the AT protocols, including the newly added support for inbound access control lists (IOS version 11.3). Cisco currently provides a host of advanced routing features to support the protocols created by its Silicon Valley neighbor. Although AppleTalk is given limited treatment in the latest Cisco courseware, AppleTalk is still fair examination material for most certification tests.

In this chapter we shall discuss the aspects of AppleTalk that will prepare you for Cisco certification tests. We will start by introducing the AppleTalk protocol stack, which will be followed by a brief discussion of AppleTalk services. The next sections will explain the AppleTalk addressing scheme, AppleTalk zones, AppleTalk routing, and AppleTalk discovery mode. The

TABLE 8-1

AppleTalk Protocol Stack

Layer	OSI Name	AppleTalk Protocols
7/6	Application/Presentation	AppleTalk Filing Protocol (AFP)
5	Session	ASP, ZIP, ADSP
4	Transport	RTMP, AEP, ATP, NBP
3	Network	Datagram Delivery Protocol (DDP)
2/1	Data link/Physical	EtherTalk, TokenTalk, FDDITalk, LocalTalk

last section of the chapter will discuss and illustrate how to configure your router to route AppleTalk traffic and apply access control mechanisms to AppleTalk data in your network.

CERTIFICATION OBJECTIVE 8.01

AppleTalk Protocol Stack

The AppleTalk protocol stack was created by Apple engineers to provide a communications infrastructure for resource sharing and client-server information exchange. It was designed to be a user-friendly network implementation that would hide the complexities of network operations from the user. Apple did not want to burden the user with mundane chores such as address assignment, for which AppleTalk uses an automatic address assignment procedure. The ease-of-use design goal is also evident in the Routing Table Maintenance Protocol and Name Binding Protocols that maintain AppleTalk network tables without user intervention. In this section, the various parts of the AppleTalk protocol stack will be examined to see how they work together and how they correlate to the seven-layer OSI model.

Physical and Data-Link Layers

The AppleTalk protocol suite has a number of data link and physical layer protocol options. The most popular physical and data link protocols are Ethernet/EtherTalk, Token Ring/TokenTalk, Fiber Distributed Data Interface (FDDI)/FDDITalk and LocalTalk. EtherTalk, TokenTalk, and FDDITalk are Apple Computer's implementation of Ethernet, Token Ring, and FDDI, respectively. LocalTalk is a 230-kbps physical/data link networking protocol that is standard on all Apple Macintosh computers and most Apple printers designed to operate with Macintosh computers.

The physical and data link layers of the AppleTalk protocol suite provide media access control and encoding services to the Datagram Delivery Protocol (DDP). DDP relies on the lower-layer protocols to provide the highway over which AppleTalk datagrams (also known as packets) can be transmitted from one node to another. They also specify the mechanical and electrical characteristics of the cables and connectors used to carry AppleTalk traffic. Table 8-2 summarizes the AppleTalk physical and data link types, along with the bandwidth and type of cabling usually associated with each data link type.

Network Layer

The network layer protocol used in the AppleTalk protocol stack is called the Datagram Delivery Protocol. DDP provides the same connectionless service that the Internet Protocol (IP) provides in the TCP/IP protocol stack. The DDP header contains, among other things, the source and destination AppleTalk address for each packet. The presence of the source and destination AppleTalk address in the DDP header makes the AppleTalk traffic routable. Without DDP addresses, AppleTalk data would have to be bridged or encapsulated like the Local Area Transport (LAT), SNA, and NETBIOS

TABLE 8-2

AppleTalk Data Link Types

Data Link Type	Speed	Cable Type
EtherTalk	10 and 100 Mbps	Copper unshielded twisted-pair, coaxial Thinnet and Thicknet, fiber
LocalTalk	230 kbps	Copper unshielded twisted-pair
TokenTalk	4 or 16 Mbps	IBM Type 1 shielded twisted-pair (unshielded can be used on some implementations)
FddiTalk	100 Mbps	Fiber optic

protocols. Therefore, DDP operates as the delivery vehicle for all upper-layer AppleTalk protocols. These upper-layer protocols provide routing table maintenance, zone processing, name resolution, and other services.

Upper-Layer Protocols

The AppleTalk protocol stack uses several upper-layer protocols, as shown in Table 8-1. The upper-layer protocols discussed in this section are the Zone Information Protocol (ZIP), Routing Table Maintenance Protocol (RTMP), and Name Binding Protocol (NBP). The Zone Information Protocol is used to manage AppleTalk zone processing. In AppleTalk, zones are used to combine individual network resources into logical workgroups. Each of these zones is given a unique zone name (for example, Accounting zone). Typically, all network resources commonly used by a given department are assigned to the same zone. Therefore, when a member of a workgroup wants to select a network resource such as a printer, she will select her workgroup and a list of available printers in her workgroup will appear in the Chooser application. Printers assigned to other zones will not be on the list. Since the Chooser application would otherwise send network resource requests to all devices of the type selected, using zones to control such requests reduces network overhead. When used properly, ZIP causes Chooser resource requests to be sent only to the currently selected zone. Otherwise, such requests would propagate across the network. ZIP works in cooperation with the NBP and RTMP to allow access to network resources. NBP and RTMP and are discussed in more detail later in this chapter.

The AppleTalk protocol responsible for creating and maintaining the AppleTalk routing tables is the Routing Table Maintenance Protocol. As a distance vector routing protocol, RTMP causes a router's routing table to be broadcast to its neighbors on a periodic basis. The frequency of the routing table updates, in the case of RTMP, is every ten seconds. Cisco routers also support the optional Apple Update-Based Routing Protocol (AURP) and Enhanced Interior Gateway Routing Protocol (EIGRP) for creating and maintaining AppleTalk routing tables; however, these two routing protocols are most frequently used on wide-area network links between routers.

FROM THE CLASSROOM

Why Study AppleTalk?

One of the most difficult protocols to convince students to learn about is AppleTalk. "Get rid of it. I'll never see it," they insist. But there still are some pretty big networks out there running AppleTalk, and they need your help. Where do you find them? In the academic and research worlds, in the graphic and musical arts, in publishing, and in the education communities. Businesses that wanted instant productivity for their workers used to choose Macintosh computers over Intel-based PCs because they were so easy to use and administer. Cisco Systems used Apple computers to run its business until only a few years ago. It was big news in mid-1998 when Motorola announced that it would no longer use the Macintosh for its internal staff, but would switch to PCs instead. Remember who made the processor for the Apple computers: Motorola.

Think about what dynamic addressing means to the AppleTalk network administrator. All he needs to do if he wants to move that user and his PC is pick up the computer and take it (or ship it) to its new location, and plug it into the network. The computer learns its cable range from the local router, and tries out the node address it had before. If no other computer is using it, the user is ready to go. If he wants to print, all he has to do is open Chooser, and he is presented with a dynamically updated list of all the printers available to him. It's great from the user's perspective, and it's easy to manage those moves, adds, and changes.

In order to implement that ease of use, there has to be a lot of complexity in the protocols. Pamela's Rule is: The easier a network system is for the end user, the harder it is for the network administrator to manage its protocols. AppleTalk protocols are both complex and difficult to manage in a large network. Like IPX, the other major protocol that originated in a LAN environment, AppleTalk relies extensively on broadcasts and multicasts for communication among network devices, and devices in an AppleTalk network communicate more often than in any other kind of network.

Think about that dynamically updated list of printers the user sees in his Chooser. The list is dynamically updated because of Name Binding Protocol responses coming back to the computer every few seconds from all the printers in his zone, for as long as the Chooser remains open. What if the user decides to

FROM THE CLASSROOM

print to a zone that's across a 56-Kbps serial link, and the zone has 500 printers, and the user leaves his Chooser open while he goes into a two-hour meeting?

The Apple world is evolving toward TCP/IP as its protocol of choice, but in the meantime there are still plenty of networks where you can apply the tools provided in the Cisco IOS for managing AppleTalk traffic.

—By Pamela Forsyth, CCIE, CCSI, CNX

CERTIFICATION OBJECTIVE 8.02

AppleTalk Services

The AppleTalk protocol suite uses special protocols to provide services to applications running on host devices. File delivery, print spooling, and name resolution services are the most important services provided by the AppleTalk protocol suite. File delivery service is provided via the AppleTalk Filing Protocol (AFP). AFP is used to find and manipulate files sent to and received from AppleTalk host devices using the AppleShare file sharing software. Since most user-created files must eventually be printed, Apple created a protocol to enable that function. The AppleTalk Printer Access Protocol (PAP) is used to spool print jobs to printers, and otherwise manage the AppleTalk printing process. Printing services are accessed through the Chooser menu, and are managed by the specific printer driver and the background printer manager.

In the Apple networking paradigm, users are not expected to deal with addresses. Instead, each device of a given type in an AppleTalk network has a unique name. The user interface uses these names to allow users to select network resources. These names are in turn associated with addresses by the Name Binding Protocol. NBP provides this service to all applications and protocols requiring access to network resources. The function of NBP is analogous to that of the Domain Name System (DNS) protocols in the TCP/IP protocol stack. The difference is that NBP is a deeply integrated and indispensable part of AppleTalk, whereas DNS is just an added convenience in TCP/IP networks.

The AppleTalk Data Stream Protocol (ADSP), AppleTalk Transaction Protocol (ATP) and AppleTalk Session Protocol are often chosen for application-to-application data exchange. ADSP is often preferred, because it implements a reliable bi-directional data stream over DDP. As mentioned earlier in this chapter, DDP carries the AppleTalk addresses described more fully in the next section.

CERTIFICATION OBJECTIVE 8.03

AppleTalk Addressing

All routable protocols require an addressing system. This addressing system is used by Cisco routers to determine which outgoing interface should be used to forward each incoming packet. As seen in earlier chapters, the term "packet" is used to describe a string of ones and zeros, which have been organized into fields. The most important fields in a packet header are the source and destination address fields. The source address field contains the address of the computer that sent the packet, and the destination address field contains the address of the computer to which the packet is to be delivered. The source and destination addresses used at this layer (the network layer) are not like the Media Access Control (MAC) addresses discussed in Chapter 1. Those so-called addresses used at the data link layer are actually "names" which are burned into ROM chips on network interfaces. By contrast, a network-layer address must be configured on each network interface. Layer-3 addresses are not "burned-in" and can be changed as needed. Burned-in MAC addresses cannot be changed. However, the most important difference between MAC addresses and network layer addresses is illustrated by the following example.

I have a friend named Juan. Juan is originally from Puerto Rico, but he now lives in North Carolina. If I want to send mail to Juan, I send the letter to his address in North Carolina. When Juan travels to Puerto Rico for a visit, I must change the address to which my letters are sent. If I want Juan to get my letters while he is in Puerto Rico, I must use his Puerto Rico address. However, when I address the letter, I must still include the name Juan on the envelope.

Notice that Juan's name did not change when he went to Puerto Rico, but his address did change. This illustrates the difference between an address and a name, as used in computing. Juan's address had to change because his location changed. This is in contrast with Juan's name, which did not change even though he went to Puerto Rico. MAC addresses are like names. They stay with a device wherever the device goes. Network layer addresses, however, contain a location component to them. Therefore, when a computer is moved from one network to another, the address of the computer must be changed as well.

AppleTalk addresses have two components. The first component is called the network number and the second component is called the node number. The network number identifies the network segment to which the computer is attached. Routers make these network number assignments. The network portion of the AppleTalk address can be compared to a street name. Every house on Willshire Drive has Willshire Drive as part of its address. Similarly, every computer on a given network must have the same network number. Furthermore, just as every house on Willshire Drive has its own individual house number, each computer on a given network segment must have its own unique node number. Figure 8-1 illustrates the relationship between the two parts of an AppleTalk network layer address.

Figure 8-1 illustrates what has come to be known as AppleTalk Phase 1 addressing. Current versions of the Cisco IOS supports AppleTalk Phase 2 addressing, also known as extended addressing. Using extended AppleTalk addressing, a network segment is not assigned just one network number. Instead, a range of network numbers identifies each network segment. Figure 8-2 shows the relationship between network segments and cable ranges.

FIGURE 8-1

AppleTalk Phase I addressing

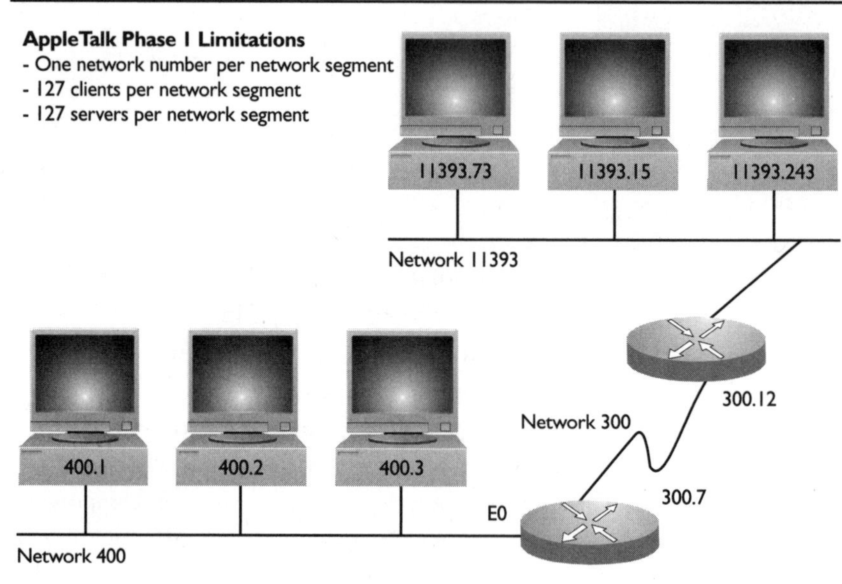

Notice that in Figure 8-2 not every computer on the network segment has the same network number. Also notice that all of the computers have network numbers within the range 400–499. The range 400–499 is known as the cable range of the network segment. If this cable range is configured on router interface Ethernet 0, the router knows to route any AppleTalk packets with destination network numbers within the range 400–499 to the Ethernet 0 interface. The router will also advertise this cable range to other routers in the network using Routing Table Maintenance Protocol or AppleTalk Update-Based Routing Protocol.

Address Structure

All network addresses must have a structure that allows the different parts of an address to be identified. In AppleTalk, addresses are written in *network node* format, as seen in Figure 8-2. In binary, the AppleTalk addresses are 24 bits long, and are formatted such that the high-order 16 bits represent the network part of the address, and the low-order eight bits comprise the node portion of the address. When written in network node notation, the network and node numbers are converted into their decimal equivalents.

FIGURE 8-2

AppleTalk Phase 2 addressing

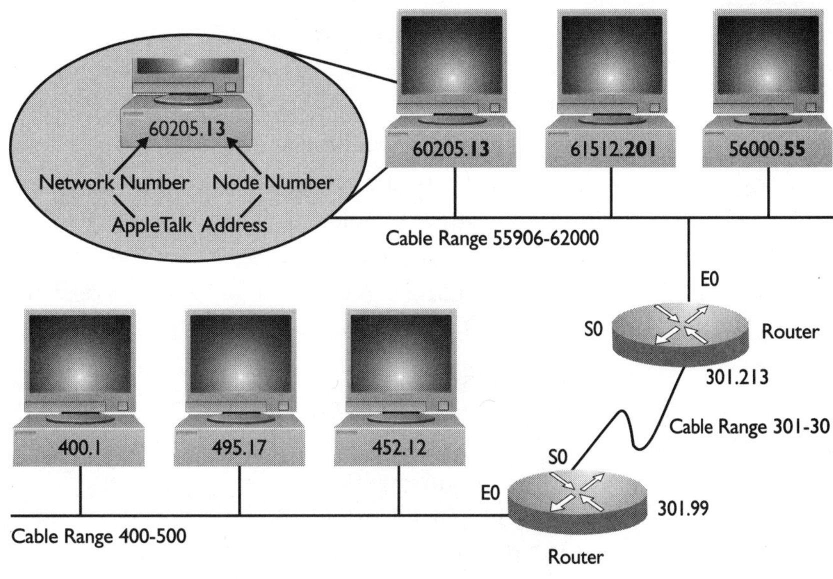

Therefore, all AppleTalk network numbers must be less than 65,536, because the network portion of an AppleTalk address has 16 bits. Similarly, all AppleTalk node numbers must be less than 256, because of the eight-bit length of the node portion of an AppleTalk address. It is also important to note that zero and 255 are special node numbers. Zero is not allowed as a node number in AppleTalk networks, and 255 is the broadcast node number for AppleTalk networks. As a result, each network number can support a maximum of 254 nodes. Extending that concept to a cable range implies that $n \times 254$ = MAX, where n is the number of network numbers in the cable range and MAX is the maximum number of addressable hosts on a cable range.

Address Assignment

AppleTalk address assignment is dynamic for Macintosh clients, and semi-automatic for routers. First, let's see how routers get their addresses. When a router is configured to run the AppleTalk protocol suite, one of the required commands is the APPLETALK CABLE-RANGE command. The

APPLETALK CABLE-RANGE command is used to assign a cable-range to a network link. The network number assigned to each network segment must be unique. Network numbers cannot be reused, and nor can the assigned ranges overlap. You cannot assign network segment A the cable range 300–400, and then assign segment B a cable range of 400–500. If your router would accept such a configuration, network 400 would belong to two different cable ranges. To solve this problem, network segment A should be assigned a cable range of 300–399, and segment B should be assigned a cable range of 400–499. There is no requirement that consecutive cable ranges be used. Therefore, we could assign segment B a cable range of 7000–7049 instead of 400–499. Now that we understand how to assign network numbers, let's see how they are used to form a complete address.

Any number within a network segment's cable range can be used as the network portion of the AT address for a node on that link. Notice in Figure 8-2 that the cable range for the upper E0 interface is 55906–62000. If you examine the network portion of all the nodes on the E0 segment, you will notice that all of the cable ranges fit within the assigned range. But how did the nodes get these addresses? Since address assignment is automatic in AppleTalk, each node uses a built-in algorithm to obtain a complete AT address. First, the node will send a broadcast query to any AT routers on the link to find out what the cable range is for the network link to which it is attached. Once the router responds with the appropriate cable range, the node will choose a network number within the cable range to use as its network number. It then starts picking node numbers to pair with the previously chosen network number. But before using the newly selected network and node numbers, the node will query the network link to see if any other device is already using the combination of network and node number it has just selected. If another device on the network is already using the address in question, the host will try additional network and node combinations until an unused address is found. Routers use the same procedure for obtaining the AppleTalk addresses for their AppleTalk interfaces, unless the network and node number are statically configured on the end of the CABLE-RANGE command.

CERTIFICATION OBJECTIVE 8.04

AppleTalk Zones

An AppleTalk zone is a subset of an AppleTalk internetwork. Each zone usually contains related network resources. Since all network nodes must belong to a zone, the zone mechanism in AppleTalk allows related nodes to be grouped together in what one might call a workgroup. The fascinating thing about zones is that members of a zone can be located anywhere in the AppleTalk internetwork, regardless of the geographical proximity of the zone members. This is very similar to the concept of virtual LANs that perform a similar function in many Ethernet switches, such as the Cisco Catalyst 5000. The Zone Information Protocol is responsible for maintaining a table of information that includes zone names and associated network numbers. If zones are not used, all NBP requests are sent throughout the entire AppleTalk internetwork, creating unnecessary overhead traffic. Figure 8-3 contains a sample configuration of a cable range assigned to its primary AppleTalk zone.

Figure 8-4, by contrast, shows a configuration with a cable range assigned to two zones. In this configuration, Twilight will be seen as the primary AppleTalk zone for both routers, and Ozone will be seen as an "additional" zone.

Assigning the same cable range to multiple zones is permitted with the Cisco operating system, and it is also permissible to have more than one router attached to a network link. However, it is important to note that any two or more routers attached to the same network link must agree on both the cable range and the zone name(s) assigned to the network link. Failure to keep this aspect of the configurations synchronized will result in a configuration error. The configurations in Figure 8-4 are considered synchronized, because the cable range and zone names for the Ethernet interfaces are identical on both routers.

The power of the zone concept can be illustrated by the following example. General Engines is a multinational corporation with its headquarters in Detroit, Michigan. The company's operations are divided

FIGURE 8-3

Single AppleTalk zone assignment

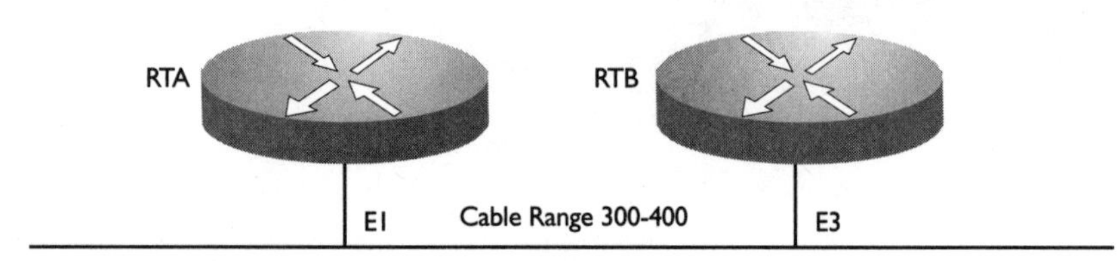

Twilight Zone

```
RTA
appletalk routing
interface e0
appletalk cable range 300-400
appletalk zone Twilight
```

```
RTB
appletalk routing
interface e3
appletalk cable range 300-400
appletalk zone Twilight
```

Note: Zone names are case sensitive! If zone names are misconfigured, the network will not synchronize. It may take several minutes for an improperly configured network to synchronize itself after correction is made.

into three regions of the world, and each region has its own vice president. General Engines' global AppleTalk network supports its worldwide manufacturing operations. A special Executive zone has been created in this network to contain all of the network resources that are used by the top company executives and their staffs. The routers that support the Detroit, Paris, and Johannesburg offices each have their Ethernet 0 interfaces assigned to the Executive zone. This allows the executive resources to be installed on the Ethernet 0 network segments of each router. When an executive in Detroit requests file services from the Executive zone, NBP will return a list of all the Detroit, Paris, and Johannesburg executive file servers. Similarly, the Engineering and Accounting departments have their own zones, which contain their network resources. The Zone Information Protocol makes functional grouping of network resources possible without respect to the geographical locations involved. ZIP updates are exchanged among the routers in the internetwork, and non-router network nodes obtain zone information from the routers via the AppleTalk GETZONELIST command.

FIGURE 8-4

Multiple zone assignment

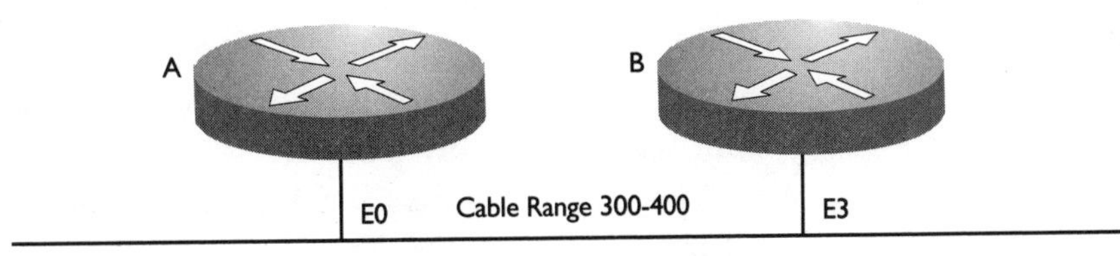

RT outer A
appletalk routing
interface e0
appletalk cable range 300-400
appletalk zone Twilight
appletalk zone Ozone

RT outer B
appletalk routing
interface e3
appletalk cable range 300-400
appletalk zone Twilight
appletalk zone Ozone

CERTIFICATION OBJECTIVE 8.05

AppleTalk Routing

Cisco currently supports three routing protocols for maintaining AppleTalk routing tables. The default routing protocol on Cisco routers is the Routing Table Maintenance Protocol. The Apple Update-Based Routing Protocol and Enhanced Interior Gateway Routing Protocol are also supported in the Cisco IOS, but they are primarily used on WAN links between routers. AppleTalk routing tables contain information about the cable ranges assigned to each link in the internetwork, and which path is the best path to each network, as identified by its cable range. The metric used to calculate which path is best is called the hop count metric. Hop count is the number of additional routers through which a packet leaving a router interface must travel to reach the destination cable range.

Since RTMP is a distance vector routing protocol, it exchanges routing updates with neighboring routers on a periodic basis. The AppleTalk designers chose to set the default frequency for AppleTalk RTMP updates at ten seconds. This means that every ten seconds, an RTMP update will be broadcast from every router interface configured to support AppleTalk. As a result, operating an AppleTalk network with RTMP produces a large amount of overhead traffic on the internetwork. These routing updates can cause congestion on low-speed links with large routing tables, because routing updates must compete with user data for access to the available bandwidth on each network link.

RTMP updates are issued from every RTMP capable router every ten seconds. The content of the update represents each router's view of the network topology as represented by the cable ranges. Each update consists of a set of data structures called *tuples*, which contain a cable range and a hop count value. The hop count associated with a cable range indicates the number of additional routers through which a packet must travel to reach that cable range. You should find the RTMP behavior described here similar that of other distance vector routing protocols, like RIP, described in Chapter 5. RTMP also shares the 15-hop maximum that is found in RIP version 1.

To view an AppleTalk routing table on a Cisco router, the SHOW APPLETALK ROUTE command is used. This command will display the current AppleTalk routing table regardless of which routing protocol is used to create and maintain the routing table. Likewise, the SHOW APPLETALK GLOBALS command can be used to display how many RTMP updates have been sent from, and received by, this router. A sample RTMP routing table is shown and described in the section called "Verifying and Monitoring AppleTalk Configurations," later in this chapter.

RTMP, like other distance vector routing protocols, employs the split-horizon concept to help prevent routing loops and reduce the size of the routing tables. Unfortunately, the Cisco operating system does not permit the split-horizon feature to be deactivated, as can be done with IP routing protocols. As a result, an AppleTalk network that is not fully meshed (as is frequently seen in Frame Relay networks), may not be able to communicate with all of the other Frame Relay routers. You can use subinterfaces to resolve this problem, by assigning one subinterface per Frame Relay virtual circuit.

CERTIFICATION OBJECTIVE 8.06

AppleTalk Discovery Mode

Cisco routers support a feature called AppleTalk discovery (AD) mode. A router interface in AD mode (known as a non-seed router) will query the routers already configured on a network segment (known as seed routers) to find its cable range and zone name automatically. AD only works on Ethernet, Token Ring, and FDDI interfaces, and there are two ways to put a router interface into AD mode. The first method is to use the command CABLE-RANGE 0-0. 0-0 is a special cable range that signals the IOS to use AD mode on a given interface. The second method of placing an interface into AD mode involves using a standard cable range command followed by the command APPLETALK DISCOVERY. Tables 8-3 and 8-4 illustrate the two AppleTalk discovery methods. As these tables show, configuration files that use AD mode are modified once the discovery process has learned the cable range and zone name. Table 8-3 shows the pre-AD configuration files, and Table 8-4 shows the post-AD configuration files. In order for AD to work correctly, the seed routers must already be in place and operating before the AD processes are started on the non-seed routers.

TABLE 8-3

AppleTalk Discovery Mode Commands Before Discovery

Command	Explanation
APPLETALK ROUTING	Starts AppleTalk routing process
INTERFACE E0	Switches to interface configuration mode for interface Ethernet 0
APPLETALK CABLE-RANGE 0-0 or APPLETALK DISCOVERY	Puts interface Ethernet 0 into AppleTalk discovery mode

TABLE 8-4

AppleTalk Discovery Mode Commands After Discovery

Command	Explanation
APPLETALK ROUTING	Starts AppleTalk routing process
INTERFACE E0	Switches to interface configuration mode for interface Ethernet 0
APPLETALK CABLE-RANGE 200-299	Cable range discovered by AD process
APPLETALK ZONE ETHERZONE	Primary zone name discovered by AD process
APPLETALK ZONE APPLEZONE	Secondary zone name discovered by AD process

CERTIFICATION OBJECTIVE 8.07

AppleTalk Configuration

This section consists of three parts. The first part identifies the commands required to make a Cisco router process (route) AppleTalk packets. In the second part, we will examine the commands required to implement AppleTalk access control lists (ACLs), and we end the chapter by describing some of the AppleTalk "show" commands.

Required AppleTalk Commands

The first command required to start routing AppleTalk traffic on a Cisco router is the APPLETALK ROUTING global configuration command. This must be followed by the APPLETALK CABLE-RANGE and APPLETALK ZONE interface configuration commands. The purpose of each command is listed in Table 8-5. For a basic AppleTalk configuration, no other commands are required. However, the router does have many other commands for tailoring the AppleTalk configuration to meet more advanced requirements. Some of these advanced commands are discussed later in this section.

TABLE 8-5

Basic AppleTalk Configuration Commands

Command	Configuration Mode	Purpose
APPLETALK ROUTING	Global	Start the AppleTalk routing process
APPLETALK CABLE-RANGE 300-399	Interface	Assign cable range to the link attached to the interface
APPLETALK ZONE TWILIGHT	Interface	Assign zone name to the link attached to an interface
APPLETALK PROTOCOL RTMP	Interface	Starts the RTMP routing protocol. (This command is not normally required. The operating system will automatically start the RTMP routing protocol on all interfaces with proper cable range and zone name assignments. It is only required when the routing protocol desired is on a given interface that is not RTMP.)

Cable ranges are usually configured on each router interface according to a plan created by the network administrator, network manager, or network designer. It is also important to remember that the router will not accept any AppleTalk interface configuration commands until AppleTalk routing is enabled with the APPLETALK ROUTING global configuration command. Figure 8-5 shows a basic AppleTalk network with cable ranges properly assigned.

Each link in a network must have a unique cable range, and cable ranges must not overlap. Figure 8-6 shows an improperly configured network with duplicate and overlapping cable ranges. Even if your enterprise network spans the globe, the cable ranges must still be unique for each network link in the entire enterprise.

To expand the configuration to include access control lists, some additional commands are required. These commands are the subject of the next section.

FIGURE 8-5

AppleTalk network with cable ranges properly assigned

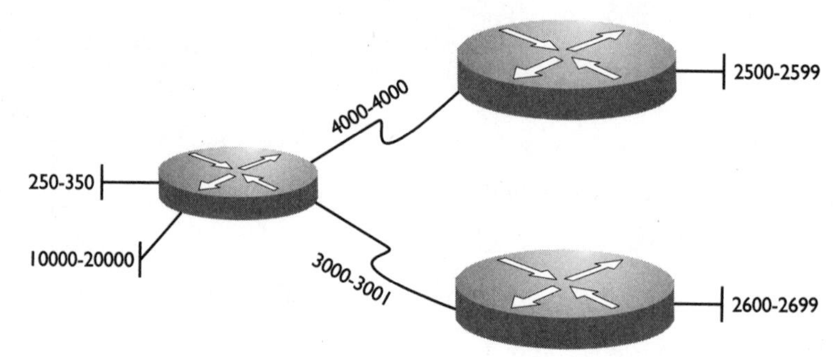

The final required command in a bare AppleTalk routing configuration is the APPLETALK ZONE command. The purpose of this command is to assign one or more zone names to the network link connected to an interface. Network resources residing in a particular zone can be logically grouped together. Such grouping controls the spread of broadcasts associated with the Chooser application.

AppleTalk Filtering

Cisco routers can filter AppleTalk packets, routing table updates, ZIP replies, ZIP updates, and NBP entities. All AT filtering is accomplished with access control lists. AppleTalk access lists must be numbered between 600 and 699. Named access lists and inbound packet filtering ACLs are not currently supported in the IOS for AT. The best way to explain the use of

FIGURE 8-6

Improper AppleTalk cable range assignments

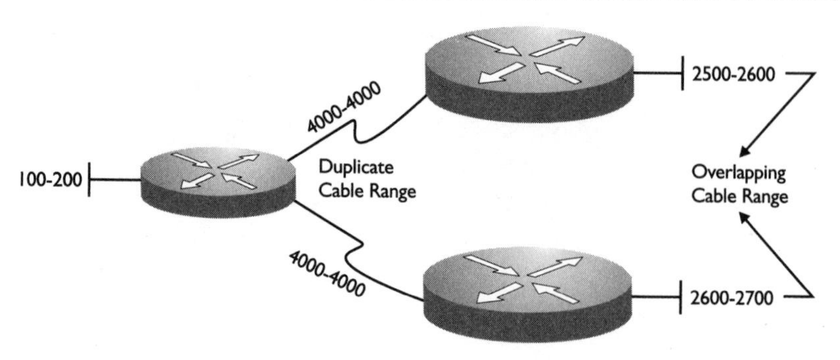

AppleTalk ACLs is to work through some examples. Let's begin by considering the network shown in Figure 8-7. The Staff zone is connected to the Ethernet 0 (E0) interface of RTA, and the Student zone is connected to the E1 interface of the same router. The objective of our first filter will be to deny packets originating on cable range 200–299 access to the Staff network (located in the Staff zone). To do this we will employ one AppleTalk packet filtering ACL. Since such ACLs are only supported in the outbound direction, we must apply the filter on the E0 interface. Table 8-6 shows how the ACCESS LIST command will accomplish our objective. Notice that the ACCESS LIST command is a global configuration mode command, but it is not sufficient on its own. The APPLETALK ACCESS-GROUP command is required to activate the access list on the interface.

Now let us use an ACL to deny hosts in the Student zone access to the Staff zone. In the preceding example, the existence of the Staff zone would be known, because the GETZONELIST command issued by the Student

FIGURE 8-7 Protecting network resources in the Staff zone

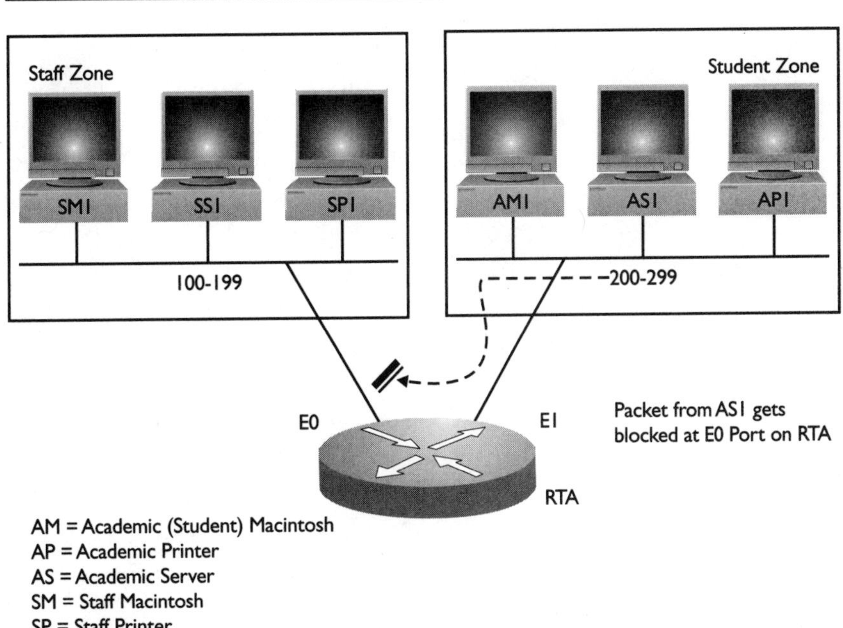

TABLE 8-6

Basic AppleTalk Access List Configuration

Command	Explanation
ACCESS-LIST 600 DENY CABLE-RANGE 200-299	First line of access list 600. Denies any packets with source network number between 200 and 299
ACCESS-LIST 600 PERMIT OTHER-ACCESS	Allows packets from all other cable ranges
INTERFACE E0	Switches to interface configuration mode for interface Ethernet 0
APPLETALK CABLE-RANGE 100-199	Assigns cable range for Ethernet 0
APPLETALK ZONE STAFF	Assigns Ethernet 0 to the zone called Staff
APPLETALK ACCESS-GROUP 600	Applies access list 600 to interface Ethernet 0 in the outbound direction (all AppleTalk access lists are outbound unless otherwise specified. Inbound AppleTalk access lists are supported in Cisco IOS version 11.3)

Macintosh computer would have returned the names of all the zones in the network. In this example, a computer in the Student zone will not even know the Staff zone exists, because the content of the zone list returned to the computers in the Student zone will be filtered to exclude the Staff zone. All other zones in the network will be listed normally. Table 8-7 shows the configuration required for a GETZONELIST filter. In the previous example, attempts to access services in the Staff cable range fail with an error message. In this example, there will be no attempts to reach the forbidden resources, because as far as the Student zone is concerned, the Staff zone does not exist. The computers in the Staff zone do have access to the resources in the whole network (including those in the Student zone). In other words, using the GETZONELIST filter allows us to create one-way access filters. These types of filters are very useful in situations where the administrator or staff needs access to a public zone, but the public zone should not have access to the administrative resources, where sensitive information is kept.

TABLE 8-7

AppleTalk GETZONELIST Filter Configuration

Command	Explanation
AppleTalk routing	Starts the AppleTalk routing process
Access-list 600 deny zone Staff	First line of Access list 600. It denies (filters) the zone called Staff.
Access-list 600 permit additional-zones	Second line of Access list 600. It permits all other zones to pass through the filter.
Interface e0	Switches to interface configuration mode for interface Ethernet 0
APPLETALK CABLE-RANGE 100-199	Assigns cable range for Ethernet 0
AppleTalk zone Staff	Assigns Ethernet 0 to the zone called Staff
Interface e1	Switches to interface configuration mode for interface Ethernet 1
APPLETALK CABLE-RANGE 200-299	Assigns cable range for Ethernet 1
AppleTalk zone Student	Assigns Ethernet 1 to the zone called Student
AppleTalk GETZONELIST-filter 600	Applies access list 600 to interface Ethernet 0 as a GETZONELIST filter. When a client on E0 (a student client) queries the router for the AppleTalk zone list, the router will not include the zone Staff on the list, because access list 600 denies the zone called Staff.

The access lists for AppleTalk illustrate the power of the operating system. There are many more options available to control and tailor the AppleTalk environment. One such enhancement is filtering the content of RTMP updates to include only those cable ranges you wish to advertise. Another feature is the capability to prevent a router from learning about a zone with the ZIP-REPLY-FILTER command. With so many options available, it is important to be able to manage the options and determine the current state of the router's configuration. The next section describes the most important commands for managing and monitoring AppleTalk configurations.

Verifying and Monitoring AppleTalk Configurations

The three most important commands for monitoring AppleTalk configurations on a Cisco router are SHOW APPLETALK INTERFACE, SHOW APPLETALK ROUTE, and SHOW APPLETALK ZONE. These commands are used to check that AppleTalk is running, to check the AppleTalk routing table, and to check the AppleTalk zone table, respectively.

SHOW APPLETALK INTERFACE

The SHOW APPLETALK INTERFACE command is one of the most useful AppleTalk show commands, because it will tell you whether you have improperly configured an interface, or whether the operating system has not yet processed the changes. This is important in AppleTalk configurations, because many AppleTalk configuration changes can take several minutes to reflect in the other show commands. Usually this is due to AppleTalk's verification process. As shown is the output below, this command will tell the operator when AppleTalk verification has completed.

```
RTB#sh appletalk interface e0
Ethernet0 is up, line protocol is up
  AppleTalk port disabled, Verifying port net information
  AppleTalk cable range is 300-399
  AppleTalk address is 395.192, Valid
  AppleTalk primary zone is "EtherZone"
  AppleTalk additional zones: "AppleZone"
  AppleTalk address gleaning is disabled
  AppleTalk route cache is disabled, port initializing
```

The message "AppleTalk port disabled" in the preceding example, indicates that the Ethernet 0 interface is not yet active for processing AppleTalk packets, even though the cable ranges, address, and zone names have been found. The interface is attempting to verify the information to make sure that there is no configuration conflict with an existing router. Once the verification process has completed successfully, the router will issue the following console message. If screen logging is enabled, the message will be visible on the console.

%AT-6-CONFIGOK: Ethernet0: AppleTalk interface enabled; verified by 395.192

A follow up SHOW APPLETALK INTERFACE command reveals that the port is now ready to process AppleTalk packets, because the "AppleTalk port disabled" line is absent.

```
Ethernet0 is up, line protocol is up
  AppleTalk cable range is 300-399
  AppleTalk address is 395.192, Valid
  AppleTalk primary zone is "EtherZone"
  AppleTalk additional zones: "AppleZone"
  AppleTalk address gleaning is disabled
  AppleTalk route cache is enabled
```

The SHOW APPLETALK INTERFACE command is the most important show command for managing AppleTalk configurations, but the SHOW APPLETALK ROUTE command is also useful, especially when troubleshooting.

SHOW APPLETALK ROUTE

The SHOW APPLETALK ROUTE command displays the AppleTalk routing table. A sample routing table would be:

```
RTA#show appletalk route
Codes: R - RTMP derived, E - EIGRP derived,
       C - connected, A - AURP
       S - static, P - proxy
3 routes in internet
```

The first zone listed for each entry is its default (primary) zone.

```
R Net 100-199 [1/G] via 200.54, 7 sec, Serial0, zone EtherZone2
              Additional zones: 'AppleZone'
C Net 200-200 directly connected, Serial0, zone WanZone
              Additional zones: 'AppleZone
C Net 300-399 directly connected, Ethernet0, zone EtherZone
             Additional zones: 'AppleZone'
```

There are three networks (cable ranges) shown in the listing above. Moving through the information on the first network entry from left to right reveals a great deal of information about cable range 100–199. The "R" in front of the first entry indicates that the 100–199 cable range was learned through RTMP. This line also tells us that the advertised network is one hop away, the route is considered good (hence the "G"), and the neighbor router that advertised the 100–199 cable range has an AppleTalk address of 200.54. This router received its last update about cable range 100 –199 seven seconds ago through the Serial0 interface. We also see that cable range 100–199 belongs to EtherZone2 and AppleZone. EtherZone2 is the primary zone for the cable range, and AppleZone is a secondary or "additional" zone. As we will see next, the zone information is duplicated in the SHOW APPLETALK ZONE command. (If cable range 100–199 had been learned via EIGRP or AURP, the routing table entry would begin with an "E" or "A" respectively, instead of the "R" shown above.)

SHOW APPLETALK ZONE

The SHOW APPLETALK ZONE command displays the cable range-to-zone associations for the entire internetwork. This sample AppleTalk zone table indicates that there are currently three properly configured AppleTalk zones in the network.

```
RTB#Show appletalk zone
Name                                Network(s)
EtherZone                           300 - 399
AppleZone                           200 - 200 300 - 399
WanZone                             200 - 200
```

EtherZone and WanZone only cover one cable range each. AppleZone, however, covers both cable range 200–200 and cable range 300–399. Put another way, cable range 300–399 has been assigned to zone EtherZone and to zone AppleZone. Cable range 200–200 has been assigned to zone WanZone and to zone AppleZone.

In this section, we have introduced the three most important "show" commands associated with the AppleTalk protocol. The first was the SHOW APPLETALK INTERFACE command. Its purpose is to identify the AppleTalk address and zone name configurations for each interface, and to indicate whether AppleTalk processing is enabled. The second command discussed in this section is the SHOW APPLETALK ROUTE command. The purpose of the SHOW APPLETALK ROUTE command is to identify the presence of other network links not directly connected to the current router. The SHOW APPLETALK ROUTE command lists each network connection by cable-range and also identifies both "primary" and "additional" zone assignments. Finally, the SHOW APPLETALK ZONE command shows the ZIP table for the AppleTalk internetwork. Like the SHOW APPLETALK ROUTE command, it also reveals the zone name-to-cable range associations. However, the SHOW APPLETALK ZONE command output is indexed by zone name instead of cable range. Careful use of these three commands will enable a network manager to successfully monitor AppleTalk configurations.

CERTIFICATION SUMMARY

In this chapter we have explored the most important aspects of the AppleTalk protocol for Cisco routers. The AppleTalk protocol stack and AppleTalk Services sections gave us an overview of the protocols used in AppleTalk. The AppleTalk Addressing and AppleTalk Configuration sections showed us how to configure routers to process AppleTalk traffic, and introduced two types of AppleTalk access lists. The "show" commands at the end of the chapter indicated how to verify proper operation of the AppleTalk configuration on a router. Mastery of these topics will provide the knowledge required to score well on the AppleTalk questions in the Cisco Certified Network Associate examination.

✓ TWO-MINUTE DRILL

- ❑ Cisco routers and switches support the AppleTalk protocol stack.
- ❑ The AppleTalk protocol stack was created by Apple engineers to provide a communications infrastructure for resource sharing and client-server information exchange.
- ❑ The most popular physical and data link protocols are Ethernet/EtherTalk, Token Ring/TokenTalk, Fiber Distributed Data Interface (FDDI)/FDDITalk, and LocalTalk.
- ❑ EtherTalk, TokenTalk, and FDDITalk are Apple Computer's implementation of Ethernet, Token Ring, and FDDI, respectively.
- ❑ The physical and data link layers of the AppleTalk protocol suite provide media access control and encoding services to the Datagram Delivery Protocol (DDP).
- ❑ DDP provides the same connectionless service that the Internet Protocol (IP) provides in the TCP/IP protocol stack.
- ❑ The upper-layer protocols are the Zone Information Protocol (ZIP), Routing Table Maintenance Protocol (RTMP), and Name Binding Protocol (NBP).
- ❑ File delivery, print spooling, and name resolution services are the most important services provided by the AppleTalk protocol suite.
- ❑ All routable protocols require an addressing system. This addressing system is used by Cisco routers to determine which outgoing interface should be used to forward each incoming packet.
- ❑ The source address field contains the address of the computer that sent the packet, and the destination address field contains the address of the computer to which the packet is to be delivered.
- ❑ All network addresses must have a structure that allows the different parts of an address to be identified. In AppleTalk, addresses are written in *network node* format.

- ❑ AppleTalk address assignment is dynamic for Macintosh clients, and semi-automatic for routers.
- ❑ An AppleTalk zone is a subset of an AppleTalk internetwork. Each zone usually contains related network resources.
- ❑ Assigning the same cable range to multiple zones is permitted with the Cisco operating system, and it is also permissible to have more than one router attached to a network link.
- ❑ Cisco currently supports three routing protocols for maintaining AppleTalk routing tables.
- ❑ The default routing protocol on Cisco routers is the Routing Table Maintenance Protocol.
- ❑ The Apple Update-Based Routing Protocol and Enhanced Interior Gateway Routing Protocol are also supported in the Cisco IOS, but they are primarily used on WAN links between routers.
- ❑ Cisco routers support a feature called AppleTalk discovery (AD) mode.
- ❑ The first command required to start routing AppleTalk traffic on a Cisco router is the APPLETALK ROUTING global configuration command. This must be followed by the APPLETALK CABLE-RANGE and APPLETALK ZONE interface configuration commands.
- ❑ Cisco routers can filter AppleTalk packets, routing table updates, ZIP replies, ZIP updates, and NBP entities.
- ❑ The three most important commands for monitoring AppleTalk configurations on a Cisco router are SHOW APPLETALK INTERFACE, SHOW APPLETALK ROUTE, and SHOW APPLETALK ZONE.

SELF TEST

The following questions will help you measure your understanding of the material presented in this chapter. Read all the choices carefully, as there may be more than one correct answer. Choose all correct answers for each question.

1. How long is an AppleTalk address (in bits)?

   A. 16 bits

   B. 32 bits

   C. 24 bits

   D. 8 bits

2. What are the two parts of an AppleTalk address?

   A. Network and node

   B. Source and destination

   C. Logical and physical

   D. Standard and extended

3. Which of the following is standard on almost all Macintosh computers?

   A. EtherTalk

   B. TokenTalk

   C. FDDITalk

   D. LocalTalk

4. How many bits of an AppleTalk address are reserved for the node number?

   A. 8 bits

   B. 16 bits

   C. 24 bits

   D. 32 bits

5. Network resources used by a particular group or department are grouped into what AppleTalk structure?

   A. Workgroup

   B. Zone

   C. Cable Range

   D. Virtual LAN

6. What is the name of the AppleTalk layer-3 protocol?

   A. Datagram Post Office Protocol

   B. Datagram Delivery Protocol

   C. AppleTalk Transport Protocol

   D. Zone Information Protocol

7. Which statement is true?

   A. Two ZIPs can be assigned to an interface

   B. Two cable ranges can be assigned to an interface

   C. Two AppleTalk RTMPs can be assigned to an interface

   D. Two zone names can be assigned to an interface

8. What command sets the range of network numbers associated with an AppleTalk network?

   A. APPLETALK ZONE NAME

   B. APPLETALK CABLE-RANGE

C. APPLETALK CABLE RANGE

D. appletalk network-range

9. Which of these protocols cannot be used for maintaining AppleTalk routing tables?

A. RTMP

B. AURP

C. EIGRP

D. IGRP

10. How often does RTMP send out routing table updates?

A. Every 10 seconds

B. Every 20 seconds

C. Whenever a topology change occurs

D. Every 30 seconds

11. Which of the following commands is not necessary for a basic AppleTalk configuration?

A. APPLETALK PROTOCOL RTMP

B. APPLETALK CABLE-RANGE 1234-4321

C. APPLETALK ZONE OZONE

D. APPLETALK ROUTING

12. What is the range of numbers used for AppleTalk access control filters?

A. 100–299

B. 500–699

C. 600–700

D. 600–699

13. Which command displays the RTMP metrics?

A. SHOW RTMP

B. show appletalk zone

C. show appletalk metrics

D. SHOW APPLETALK ROUTE

14. If router A and router B are directly connected via their Serial 0 interfaces, which command would be most useful on router A for hiding zone President Zone (on the E0 interface) from router B?

A. APPLETALK ACCESS-GROUP 600

B. appletalk zone-filter 600

C. appletalk GETZONELIST-filter 600

D. appletalk zip-reply-filter 600

15. If client M is connected to router A via Ethernet 0, which command would be the most useful for hiding zone SerialZone (located elsewhere in the network) from client M?

A. APPLETALK ACCESS-GROUP 600

B. appletalk zone-filter 600

C. appletalk GETZONELIST-filter 600

D. appletalk zip-reply-filter 600

16. Which command assigns a zone name to an interface?

A. APPLETALK ZIP-NAME

B. appletalk zone

C. appletalk zip-reply-filter

D. appletalk GETZONELIST-filter

17. Which command causes a router to automatically obtain its AppleTalk

configuration information by querying other routers already on the network?

A. APPLETALK AUTO-CONFIG

B. appletalk discovery

C. appletalk discovery-mode enable

D. appletalk cable–range auto

18. Which of the following sets of commands are all interface configuration commands?

A. APPLETALK ROUTING, APPLETALK ZIP-REPLY-FILTER, APPLETALK CABLE-RANGE

B. appletalk zip-reply-filter, appletalk zone, APPLETALK CABLE-RANGE

C. appletalk GETZONELIST filter, appletalk access-list, APPLETALK CABLE-RANGE

D. appletalk access-list, appletalk zone, APPLETALK CABLE-RANGE

19. Which command causes a network and node number to be assigned to a router interface?

A. APPLETALK CABLE-RANGE

B. APPLETALK ADDRESS-ENABLE

C. APPLETALK NODE-ENABLE

D. appletalk address auto-config

20. Which of the following commands are required in a router configuration that routes AppleTalk traffic?

A. APPLETALK ADDRESS 301.64

B. appletalk processing enable

C. appletalk range

D. appletalk routing

21. Match the OSI Layer on the left with the corresponding AppleTalk protocols on the right.

A. Data link/ physical	1. AFP
B. TRANSPORT	2. ASP
C. APPLICATIO N	3. RTMP
D. SESSION	4. ETHERTALK

22. Which Data-link type supports speeds of up to 100 Mbps?

A. LocalTalk

B. FDDITalk

C. TokenTalk

D. All of the above

23. Name Binding Protocol (NBP) is a protocol for:

A. The application layer

B. The session layer

C. The transport layer

D. The physical layer

24. Which statement is true of zoning?

A. It reduces the number of devices (hardware)

B. It reduces the number of nodes on the network

C. It causes client requests to propagate through the entire network

D. It reduces overhead

25. Which statement is true of RTMP?

A. It uses the shortest path algorithm
B. It uses distance vector protocol
C. It is a link-state protocol
D. It is a minimum metric algorithm

26. Name Binding Protocol is used for what purpose?

A. To convert addresses into names
B. To create unique names for devices
C. To associate names with addresses
D. To create unique addresses

27. Which of the following protocols is most often preferred because of the capability of bi-directional data stream support over DDP?

A. ADSP
B. ATP
C. ASP
D. AFP

28. Whereas MAC addresses may change from location to location, the network addresses will remain the same from location to location.

A. True
B. False

29. Network number assignments are made by:

A. Network queue
B. Client
C. Server
D. Router

30. The major characteristic of an Extended AppleTalk addressing scheme is:

A. That a single network number is assigned to a single segment
B. That a single segment can be associated with a range of network numbers
C. That a single network number can be assigned multiple zones
D. B and C only
E. All of the above

31. Which is a true statement about a cable range?

A. It is a range of addresses assigned to a device
B. It is associated with a network segment
C. It is associated with an interface on the router
D. All of the above
E. B and C only

32. All AppleTalk network numbers must be:

A. Greater than 65,536
B. Greater than 255
C. Less than 65,536
D. Less than 255

33. What is the broadcast node number in AppleTalk?

A. 255
B. 0
C. 256
D. None of the above

34. For a cable range of 450–454, what is the maximum number of hosts?

A. 762

B. 2286

C. 1016

D. 1270

35. Which of the following is not true of cable ranges?

A. They are assigned with the APPLETALK CABLE-RANGE command.

B. They are ranges of network numbers assigned to a segment.

C. They cannot overlap with a previously assigned cable range.

D. None of the above

36. A network segment X is given a cable range of 200–300. What is the acceptable value of cable range for segment Y?

A. 250–350

B. 6301–6400

C. 300–400

D. All of the above

37. A segment has a cable range of 700–750. When a node wants to get an address, it may pick up any network number in the range that is not currently in use.

A. True

B. False

38. Which command would be most appropriate for finding out whether the network has verified a cable range assignment for E0?

A. SHOW APPLETALK ADDRESS

B. SHOW APPLETALK ROUTE

C. Show appletalk interface

D. Show appletalk zone

39. What cable range is used to indicate to IOS to use AppleTalk discovery mode on a given interface?

A. 1–1

B. 0–0

C. 255–255

D. 254–254

40. For AppleTalk discovery to work properly:

A. A router must have cable range assigned to it

B. The seed routers must be in place

C. The seed routers must be non-operational

D. All of the above

41. For a basic AppleTalk configuration, how many commands are necessary?

A. One

B. Two

C. Three

D. Four

42. For activation of an access list, which of the following commands is required?

A. ACCESS-GROUP

B. zone

C. cable-range

D. interface

43. The default direction for access list for IOS versions earlier than 11.3 is:

A. Outbound

B. Inbound

C. Inbound and outbound (bi-directional)

D. None of the above

44. Which of the following commands is used for monitoring Apple Talk configuration?

A. APPLETALK CABLE-RANGE

B. appletalk GETZONELIST

C. SHOW APPLETALK ZONE

D. access list

45. The following is displayed in response to the SHOW APPLETALK ROUTE command:

R Net 300-399[3/G] via 400.97, 10 sec, Serial0, zone EtherZone2

In this display, R is:

A. A router name

B. RIP

C. RTMP

D. All of the above

46. The following is displayed in response to the SHOW APPLETALK ROUTE command:

R Net 300-399[3/G] via 400.97, 10 sec, Serial0, zone EtherZone2

In this display, 10 sec is:

A. The time it takes for a packet to travel from source to destination

B. The time elapsed since the last RTMP update for cable range 300–399 was received

C. The holddown time for cable range 300–399

D. The time interval indicating how long the packet will be held by the router

47. The following is displayed in response to the SHOW APPLETALK ROUTE command:

R Net 300-399[3/G] via 400.97, 10 sec, Serial0, zone EtherZone2

In this display, 400.97 is:

A. The destination address of a packet going to network 300–399

B. The source address of a packet coming from network 300–399

C. The address of the router that advertised the cable range

D. None of the above

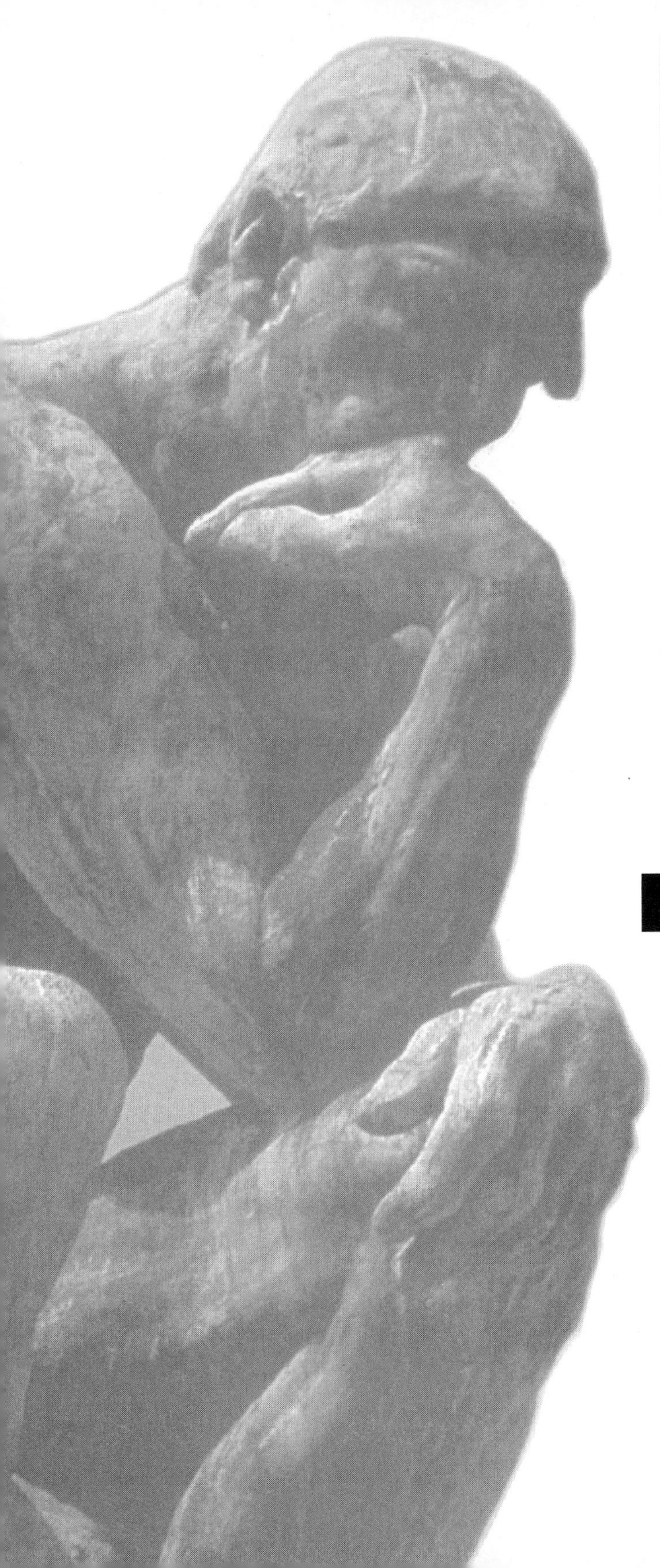

CCNA
CISCO CERTIFIED NETWORK ASSOCIATE

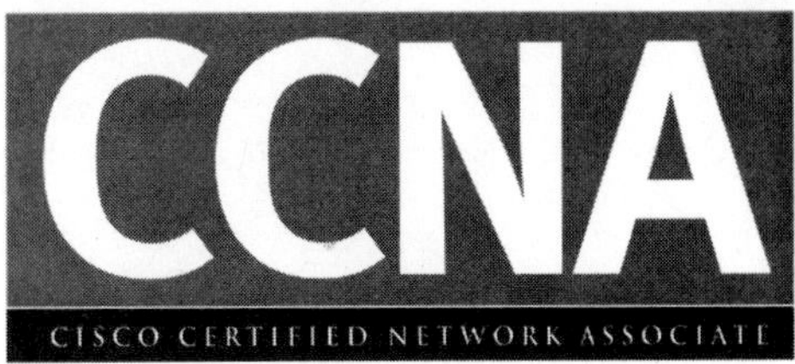

9

Basic Traffic Management with Access Lists

CERTIFICATION OBJECTIVES

9.01 Standard IP Access Lists

9.02 Extended IP Access Lists

9.03 Named Access Lists

9.04 Standard IPX Access Lists

9.05 IPX SAP Filters

9.06 AppleTalk Access Lists

Packet filtering is used to control the flow of data across a network. By implementing it, you can limit network traffic and restrict network access to certain users or devices. Packet filtering is performed on Cisco routers through the use of access lists. Access lists can be used to control the transmission of packets across an interface, to restrict traffic across virtual terminal lines, or to restrict routing updates. You enter rules to permit or deny packets within each access list, and the access lists are identified by a number. All statements within a single list must have the same number. The number used is up to you, but it has to fall within the ranges listed in Table 9-1, depending on what service you are applying the access list to. The protocols marked with an asterisk (*) are the ones that are discussed in this chapter, and will be covered on the test.

This chapter explains how to create access lists and how to apply them to interfaces and services.

TABLE 9-1

Number Ranges for Access Lists

Protocol	Range
IP*	1–99
Extended IP*	100–199
Ethernet type code	200–299
DECnet	300–399
XNS	400–499
Extended XNS	500–599
AppleTalk*	600–699
Ethernet address	700–799
IPX*	800–899
Extended IPX	900–999
IPX SAP*	1000–1099

CERTIFICATION OBJECTIVE 9.01

Standard IP Access Lists

An IP access list is a collection of permit and deny rules that are applied to IP addresses. The router processes each access list statement in sequence against each packet. If the router reaches the end of the list and has found no match for the packet, the packet will be discarded. (This is known as implicit DENY ANY.) Therefore, it is important that each access list contain at least one PERMIT statement. And because the first match is the one followed, it is critical to pay attention to the order.

Cisco IOS Release 11.1 introduced significant changes in the syntax and implementation of access lists. It does, however, provide backward compatibility, and if you upgrade from a release prior to 11.1, it will convert your access lists to the new format automatically.

There are three basic types of IP access lists: standard, extended, and dynamic extended. Standard access lists use source addressing for applying rules. This provides very basic forms of filtering. Extended access lists use both source and destination addresses for filtering, and even allow filtering by protocol type. This allows a more granular method of controlling data flow. Finally, dynamic extended access lists grant access to destinations on a per-user basis, through an authentication process.

The router uses a *wildcard mask* (sometimes known as an inverse mask) along with the source or destination IP address, to identify a range of addresses to match. Just as a subnet mask tells the router which bits of the IP address belong to the network number and which belong to the host address, the wildcard mask tells the router how many bits of the IP address it needs to examine in order to make a matching determination. This address mask pair allows us to specify a range of IP addresses with just two 32-bit numbers. This is very handy, because if you didn't have a mask available, you'd have to put in an individual access list statement for each IP host address you wanted to match, causing a lot of extra typing for you and a lot of extra processing for your router! So an address mask pair is a beautiful thing.

You already know that in a subnet mask, a mask bit set to 1 means that the corresponding bit in the IP address belongs to the network part of the address. Conversely, the wildcard mask bit set to 1 in an access list means the corresponding bit in the IP address will match either a 1 or a 0. Sometimes you will see these 1 bits referred to as "don't-care" bits, because the router doesn't care about them as it tries to make a match. Mask bits set to 0 identify corresponding bits in the IP address that the router must match exactly.

Here are some sample address mask pairs as they might appear in an access list, so you can see how this concept works:

```
124.220.7.0  0.0.0.255
```

The last octet of the mask is all ones, so the router will allow any value for these bits. It will try to match the first three octets exactly. This pair identifies all the IP addresses between 124.220.7.0 and 124.220.7.255 as matches for this pair.

```
193.62.0.0  0.255.255
```

The last two octets of this mask are all ones, so the router will allow any value in the corresponding bits. That is, the last two octets of the IP address we are matching could be anything, as long as the first two octets are 193.62 exactly. This address mask pair matches every IP address between 193.62.0.0 and 193.62.255.255.

```
172.16.16.0  0.0.7.255
```

Not all masks have the boundary between "match-exactly" bits and "don't-care" bits on the boundary between two octets. This sometimes makes it tough to figure out what matches and what doesn't. It always helps to work out the binary on these, and if you do enough of them you will get very good at remembering the powers of two! Let's look at the breakdown, in binary, of just the third octet of the last example.

Address bits: `16 = 00010000`

Mask bits: `7 = 00000111`

You can see that if we don't care about corresponding bits in the address where the mask bits are "ones," then this pair of numbers describes a range of eight possible numbers, 16 through 23. You can prove this by counting up from 16 through 24, in binary, as follows:

```
=   00010000
=   00010001
=   00010010
=   00010011
=   00010100
=   00010101
=   00010110
=   00010111
=   00011000
```

Notice that when we get to 24, the 2^3 bit in the address changes from a 0 to a 1. The 2^3 bit does not fall under the mask, so it is not within the range we are describing with this pair.

Looking at the entire address mask pair, you can see that the full range of IP addresses described is 172.16.16.0 through 172.16.23.255.

The matching process for an access list statement actually has three steps. In packet filtering, we are examining an IP packet header for its IP addresses in order to make a match. Let's say our access list statement contains the address mask pair 172.16.0.0 0.0.255.255. A packet comes in with source IP address of 172.16.10.22. The router does the following:

1. Performs a "logical OR" against the address and mask in the access list statement. This means that any bit with a 1 in either the address

or the mask will be a 1 in the result. The result of this operation is 172.16.255.255.

2. Performs a "logical OR" against the IP address in the packet header and the mask in the access list statement. The result is 172.16.255.255.
3. Subtracts the two results. If the two results are identical, the result of the subtraction is exactly zero, and we have a match, as we have in this example. If the result of the subtraction is not zero, there is no match and we go on and repeat these steps for the address mask pair in the next statement.

There are two keywords that can be used to save us some typing with the IP access list address mask pairs. The first is "any," which can be used in place of the address mask pair 0.0.0.0 255.255.255.255. As you can see from the address mask pair, this combination allows any combination of address bits to match. The other keyword is "host," which can be used in extended access lists only, to replace the 0.0.0.0 mask. In a standard access list, omitting the 0.0.0.0 mask is the same as specifying it. If you omit the mask, the address will be considered a host address.

All access lists are defined in global configuration mode. The basic format for adding a standard access list is as follows:

ACCESS-LIST *access-list-number* {DENY|PERMIT}
{SOURCE[*source-wildcard*]|ANY}

The ACCESS-LIST-NUMBER is a number within a specific range that signifies which list the command you are entering is to join. You then stipulate whether the entry permits or denies traffic from the specified address. SOURCE is just as it sounds, dictating the source IP address the access list rule applies to. If you add a subnet address you can change the source address from a specific host to a range of IP addresses. The SOURCE-WILDCARD basically identifies which bits in the address field are matched. If you add the argument ANY at the end, you are implying the addresses 0.0.0.0 with a subnet mask of 255.255.255.255, which of course matches any address. Here is an example of a standard IP access list that might be found in a network such as that depicted in Figure 9-1:

```
ACCESS-LIST 1 PERMIT 10.10.10.101
ACCESS-LIST 1 DENY 10.10.10.0 0.0.0.255
```

Now this alone will not totally accomplish what we want to do. Access list configuration is a two-step process, and it can be done in any order. You not only establish the access list you want to use, but you must also specifically apply it to each interface you want to use it on. One thing to remember is that if you apply the list to an interface before you define the

FIGURE 9-1 Packet filtering with standard IP access lists

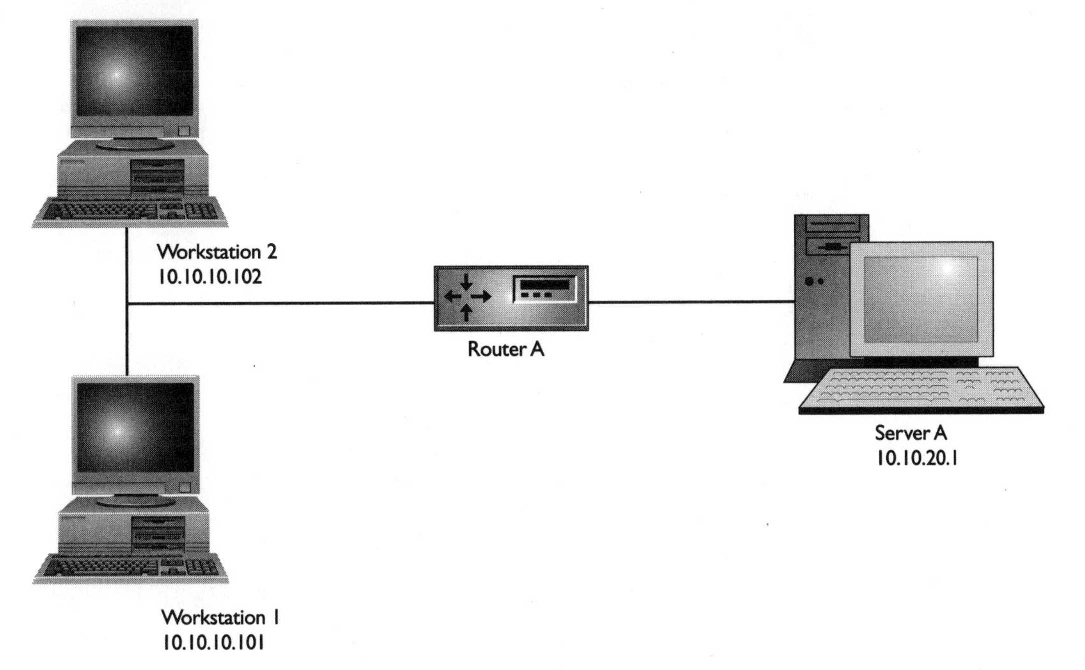

statements, or if you negate an existing list that has been applied, you will have an undefined list.

We have two choices if we want to apply the list above as a packet filter. We could apply it as an inbound filter on Router A's interface to network 10.10.10.0, or as an outbound filter on Router A's interface to network 10.10.20.0. Outbound filters are less processor intensive for the router, so let's apply it outbound.

Get into interface configuration mode for the appropriate interface and use the command IP ACCESS-GROUP 1 OUT to put this interface into the group that uses access list 101 for packet filtering. A single access list can be used on many different interfaces in the same router if that's appropriate for your network—there's no need to define an identical list for each interface that needs it. Notice the argument OUT at the end of the command. OUT is the default, and it means that the packets will be filtered on their way outbound from the router. Because out is the default, you are allowed to leave it off the command altogether. So IP ACCESS-GROUP 101 would mean exactly the same thing.

If we wanted to use an inbound packet filter on the interface to network 10.10.10.0, we could use the command IP ACCESS-GROUP 101 IN.

From this example we see that because of the explicit acceptance of Workstation 1, it is allowed to pass to Server A. The second server, however, falls under the next statement, where any system on the 10.10.10.0 network is denied. At first it would seem that Workstation 1 would fall under this rule also. This would be the case if the DENY statement were listed first. Remember, in IP access lists, the order of listing is very important.

Another interesting feature of IP access lists is the implicit DENY statement at the end. I mentioned this briefly earlier, and what it means is that you have to explicitly permit traffic, otherwise it is automatically denied. With this knowledge, we see from the example in Figure 9-1 that the last line is actually not needed; it has already been inferred. Remember that this is not the case with the absence of access lists. If you don't apply any access lists to an interface, or if you attempt to apply an access list that has not been defined, it will pass all traffic by default.

After an access list is created, any additions to that list number are placed at the end. Unfortunately, what this means is that you can't selectively add or remove items. The only removing that can be done is to remove the entire access list, which can obviously be a nuisance if you have extensive lists. To save time, you can cut and paste the list to a text document for editing.

Once you have created your access list, you then need to associate it to an interface. The syntax for performing this is IP ACCESS-GROUP *ACCESS-LIST-NUMBER* {IN|OUT}. The command is entered when in the configuration mode of the interface you want to apply it to.

Most of the arguments are self-explanatory. The ACCESS-LIST-NUMBER is the previously created access list number you want to apply. The IN|OUT options specify whether this rule applies inbound or outbound. If you wish for the access list to apply in both directions, two statements need to be added, one for in and one for out. You can apply only one access list per protocol per interface per direction.

You can also set up access lists to restrict traffic on virtual terminal lines. This is accomplished with the ACCESS-CLASS command:

```
ACCESS-CLASS ACCESS-LIST-NUMBER {IN | OUT}
```

The following example of this shows that only those hosts in the 10.10.10.0 subnet are allowed to establish a connection with the router's terminal port.

```
CONFIG TERMINAL

ACCESS-LIST 1 PERMIT 10.10.10.0 0.0.0.255

ACCESS-CLASS 1 IN
```

FROM THE CLASSROOM

Approaching Access Lists

Remember the implicit DENY ANY!

How many times have I waved my arms about like a crazy person, shouted, pleaded with the class to think about what they are denying by implication, only to see them turn to the lab and create a list that denies Telnet traffic. Then all the dynamically learned routes disappear from their routing tables, and they complain they can't ping the routers on the other side of the network any more. "Look at the traffic you're denying," I say. "Now tell me what you're permitting." If the list has only one statement, and that statement is denying traffic, as soon as you apply that list as a traffic filter you are effectively shutting down the interface for that protocol. The reason is the implicit DENY ANY. Your access list must contain at least one PERMIT statement. Otherwise you might just as well save your router some processor cycles and not configure the protocol on that interface in the first place.

When you're planning an access list there are two different ways you can approach it. If you know exactly what traffic you want to permit, and can describe that traffic in only a few statements, you can permit that traffic explicitly and deny everything else. Conversely, if you can describe what you want to deny with only a few statements, you might want to explicitly deny that traffic and end the list with a PERMIT ANY. Neither method is more correct than any other, but the list with fewer statements will use fewer CPU cycles in your router.

Speaking of performance, you will want to have a look at your list after it has been in place for a few days to see if it needs tuning. Remember that the router stops processing the list with the first statement that matches a packet. That means that you will get better performance if the bulk of your traffic matches statements near the top of the list. Your router will keep track of how many packets match against each statement in the list, and you can often use this information to rearrange the statements so the ones with the most matches are at, or near, the top. Be careful, though, to keep more specific statements higher in the list than more general ones pertaining to the same networks or subnets.

Be careful when you create access lists on routers in a production network. If you have applied your list as a traffic filter on an interface before you start to configure the list statements, remember that the implicit DENY ANY takes effect as soon as you enter the first

FROM THE CLASSROOM

statement into the router's configuration. It's a better idea to get the statements configured, check them several times for sanity, then apply the list on the interface.

You can use the same list on any number of interfaces. If your router has 20 different interfaces, all of which require the same restrictions, re-use the same list as a traffic filter on all those interfaces.

And here's a pitch for documentation. In the place where you keep the documentation for your network, document each list, statement by statement, telling exactly what each statement is intended to do. This exercise serves two purposes. If you can describe your list in this way, it is an indication that you have thought it through carefully. And, since most of us have enough to remember already, it will save your sanity some day by preventing your having to figure out why you are denying traffic from this particular network.

And remember the implicit DENY ANY!

—By Pamela Forsyth, CCIE, CCSI, CNX

CERTIFICATION OBJECTIVE 9.02

Extended IP Access Lists

Extended IP access lists allow you to control traffic at a more granular level. Extended IP uses both the source and destination address when it tries to match up packets to your list, and you can optionally use protocol type information for even finer control.

A lot of the rules you learned from standard IP are the same in Extended IP. A few of them are as follows:

- You cannot selectively add or remove from a list. Whenever you add an entry, it is placed at the bottom.

- The access list itself does not do anything. You must apply it to an interface for it to be used.
- At the end of the list, by default, there is an implicit DENY ALL statement.

The syntax for adding and removing access lists is as follows:

{NO} ACCESS-LIST *access-list-number* {DENY | PERMIT} *protocol source source-wildcard destination destination-wildcard*

Let's break this command down. You first enter the ACCESS-LIST command, then the number of the list, followed by whether you want to permit or deny the specified traffic. You then need to specify what type of protocol you are going to be using, such as TCP, UDP, ICMP, or IP. You then tell the router the specific source and destination, or give it a wildcard such as ANY.

Here is an example of how you might use an extended IP access list. Figure 9-2 shows a network where we want to limit certain kinds of IP traffic.

FIGURE 9-2

Restricting IP traffic in a small network

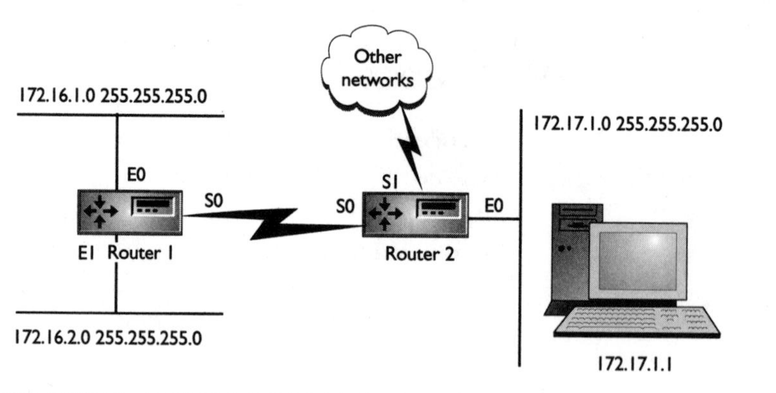

The network manager configures Router 2 with the following access list:

```
ACCESS-LIST 102 PERMIT TCP 172.16.1.0 0.0.0.255 HOST 172.17.1.1
EQ TELNET

ACCESS-LIST 102 PERMIT TCP 172.16.2.0 0.0.0.255 HOST 172.17.1.1
EQ FTP

ACCESS-LIST 102 PERMIT ICMP 172.16.0.0 0.0.255.255 ANY

ACCESS-LIST 102 DENY   IP ANY ANY
```

He applies this access list as a traffic filter outbound on Ethernet 0 using the IP ACCESS-GROUP command:

```
INTERFACE ETHERNET 0

IP ACCESS-GROUP 102 OUT
```

This list is extremely restrictive. The only traffic permitted on 172.17.1.0 is Telnet traffic from network 172.16.1.0, FTP traffic from network 172.16.2.0 destined for the host 172.17.1.1, and ICMP traffic to any destination. All other traffic is denied explicitly. If the DENY IP ANY ANY line had not been configured, the list would operate in the same way, as any traffic that is not explicitly permitted is denied by implication. Notice the keywords for the IP protocols, and for the TCP applications Telnet and FTP.

Notice that with the list applied as a filter on Router 2's Ethernet 0 interface, hosts on networks 172.16.1.0 and 172.16.2.0 can still access other networks through Router 1's serial 1 interface. Consider the different effect if the same list were configured on Router 1 and applied using the IP ACCESS-GROUP 102 OUT command on Router 1's serial 0 interface. With this new configuration in place, hosts on networks 172.16.1.0 and 172.16.2.0 are only allowed to send ICMP traffic (ping, most likely) to other networks, as well as the previous allowances for Telnet and FTP traffic to host 172.17.1.1.

CERTIFICATION OBJECTIVE 9.03

Named Access Lists

With the advent of IOS release 11.2, you can also use Named access lists. Since it is new in version 11.2, it is not backward compatible with older releases. With Named lists you can identify IP access lists, whether standard or extended, with an alphanumeric name instead of a number. This allows you to exceed the previous limit of 99 for standard and 100 for extended. You should not, however, assume that all access lists that use a number can also use a name. If you choose to use this method the mode and command syntax is a little different.

To use this type of access list, you first enter a command that puts you in a mode to enter named access lists: IP ACCESS-LIST STANDARD *name* or IP ACCESS-LIST EXTENDED *name.*

You then enter your commands as follows: {DENY | PERMIT} *protocol source source-wildcard destination destination-wildcard.*

The same rules apply as did with regular standard and extended lists. The syntax example above is for an extended named list and would be changed to match the syntax of standard, if that is what you were using.

You then exit the access list configuration mode by simply typing in Exit. One final thing to note is that, as of now, only packet and route filters can use a named list.

Verifying IP Access Lists

Once you have configured your IP access lists you will want to see if they are configured correctly. You can verify your IP access lists with the SHOW ACCESS-LISTS command and the SHOW IP INTERFACES command.

SHOW ACCESS-LISTS provides a display of all access lists configured in the router, including IP, IPX, and AppleTalk. Here is some sample output for the SHOW ACCESS-LISTS command, showing IP standard and extended access lists configured in this router.

```
Router1#show access-lists
IPX access list 800
    deny C011
    permit FFFFFFFF
IPX access list 900
    permit any
    permit any any all AA11.00cf.b200.0000 0000.00ff.ffff all
    permit any BB22 all AA11
IPX SAP access list 1009
    deny FFFFFFFF 0 parallel
    permit FFFFFFFF
Standard IP access list 40
    deny   12.1.0.0, wildcard bits 0.0.255.255
    permit any
Standard IP access list list1
    deny   13.0.0.0, wildcard bits 0.255.255.255
    permit 172.16.0.0, wildcard bits 0.0.255.255
Extended IP access list 130
    permit ospf any any (452 matches)
    permit icmp any any echo (63 matches)
    permit icmp any any echo-reply (10 matches)
    permit tcp any any eq ftp
    permit tcp any any eq telnet (958 matches)
Extended IP access list list2
    permit ospf any any (12 matches)
    permit ip 136.25.16.0 0.0.7.255 any
    permit tcp host 10.1.0.1 any
Extended IP access list list3
    permit ospf any any
    deny   tcp any any eq telnet
    permit ip any any
Router1#
```

We can see that SHOW ACCESS-LISTS displays the configuration details for all sorts of access lists in the router, not just IP access lists. We could have specified an access list number on the command line to see an individual list in isolation from all others.

We can see the configurations of various IP access lists. List 40 is a standard IP access list, denying any packets from subnet 12.1.0.0, and permitting all others. List 130 is an Extended IP access list. We can see the various protocol keywords permitting any OSPF packets, any ping packets, any FTP packets, and any Telnet packets.

What is being denied here in list 130? Every other IP packet! Remember the implicit DENY ANY. This is an IP extended access list, not just TCP or ICMP. The DENY ANY applies to all of IP.

Notice the notations in parentheses, indicating matches for each line. The router keeps track of the number of times packets have come across the interface matching each of the IP access list statements. Here's what we can see from the output for IP access list 130:

- 452 OSPF packets have been received on this interface since we applied this access list against the interface
- 63 responses to pings (responses to a neighboring router's pings, since this list was applied as an input packet filter)
- 10 pings originated in this router
- 958 Telnet packets have come into this interface

We can also see three named IP access lists, list2 and list3. List1 is a standard IP access list. List2 has been applied, and has some matches. List3 has been defined in the router configuration, and has not been applied to any interface, so it is not being used for packet filtering. There are no matches against list3.

SHOW IP INTERFACES provides information on IP-specific aspects of your interface configuration. In this context, it is used specifically to see what packet filters are applied on the interface. It does not show the contents of the list, only the list number. You need to use SHOW ACCESS-LIST <NUMBER> to see the filtering rules for the list. Packet filters are indicated in the lines "Inbound access list is" and "Outgoing access-list is." Here we see that we have applied list 130, an IP extended access list, as a packet filter inbound on interface serial 1.

```
Router1#show ip interface serial 1
Serial1 is up, line protocol is up
  Internet address is 10.1.0.2/16
  Broadcast address is 255.255.255.255
  Address determined by non-volatile memory
  MTU is 1500 bytes
  Helper address is not set
  Directed broadcast forwarding is enabled
```

```
Multicast reserved groups joined: 224.0.0.5 224.0.0.6
Outgoing access list is not set
Inbound  access list is 130
Proxy ARP is enabled
Security level is default
Split horizon is enabled
ICMP redirects are always sent
ICMP unreachables are always sent
ICMP mask replies are never sent
IP fast switching is enabled
IP fast switching on the same interface is enabled
IP multicast fast switching is enabled
Router Discovery is disabled
IP output packet accounting is disabled
IP access violation accounting is disabled
TCP/IP header compression is disabled
Probe proxy name replies are disabled
Gateway Discovery is disabled
Policy routing is disabled
Network address translation is disabled
```

CERTIFICATION OBJECTIVE 9.04

Standard IPX Access Lists

IPX access lists permit or deny traffic across interfaces based on either specified network nodes or messages sent using particular protocols and services. Just as in IP access lists, the order of rules applied in the access list is critical. The first matching entry, whether it is a Permit or a Deny, is followed. And, also as with IP lists, if you do not explicitly enter a Permit Everything at the end, an implicit DENY ALL is made. There are two caveats to IPX access lists. First, while you can filter at the boundary of NLSP, RIP, and SAP, you cannot filter within an NLSP area. Second, IPX standard access lists are different from IP in that they filter on both source and destination.

You can break down IPX access list types into five main categories, as described in Table 9-2.

TABLE 9-2

IP Access List Types

Type	Traffic Is Restricted Based on . . .	Access List Number Range
Standard access lists	Source and destination network and node address	800–899
Extended access lists	Complete source and destination address (network, node, socket, and protocol)	900–999
SAP access lists	SAP type, service name, and network/node address of service	1000–1099
NLSP Route	Network areas	1200–1299
NetBIOS access lists	"Host" filter on names, "bytes" filter on numbers	Name

We will be concerning ourselves with standard access lists in this section and SAP's version of access lists, better known as *filters*, in the next.

Standard access lists permit or deny traffic based on the source network number. You can also restrict by optionally specifying a destination address, and even by applying address masks on both. The access list number for Standard IPX can be anything between 800 and 899.

ACCESS-LIST *access-list-number* {DENY|PERMIT}
SOURCE-NETWORK[OPTIONS]

The SOURCE-NETWORK variable is the eight-digit hexadecimal address, ranging from 1 to FFFFFFFD, of the network where the packet originated. You can also use 0 for the local network and –1 to specify all networks. Notice how I said it had to be an eight-digit hex number, yet I listed 1 as a valid entry. This is because leading zeros do not need to be stated => 1 equals 00000001.

Look at the example in Figure 9-3. Let's say we want to stop the users on Network AA from using the services on Network BB, but we want the users

FIGURE 9-3 Standard IPX access lists used as packet filters

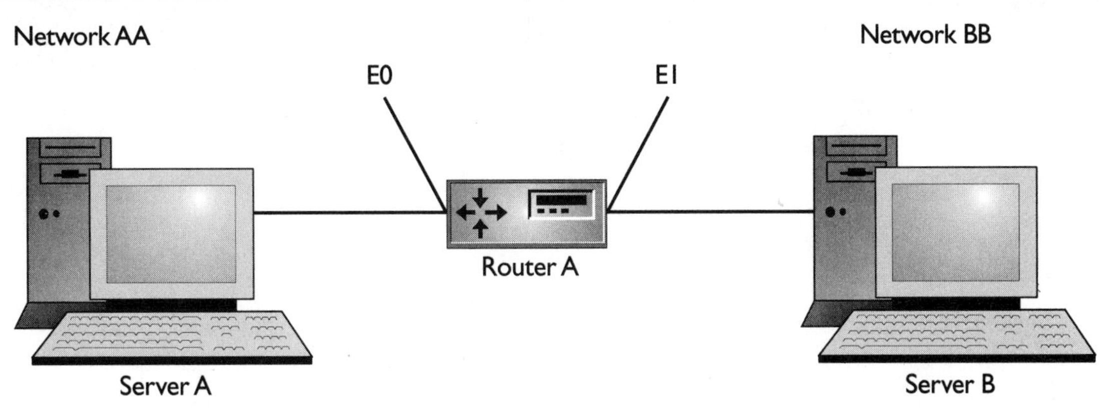

on BB to be able to use the services on AA. If we apply an access list as a packet filter outbound on Ethernet 1, we can block the packets from Network AA. We do not, however, need an access list on Ethernet 0, since the lack of an access list implies PERMIT ALL. If we filter with a standard access list using only a network number, we would also filter out the response packets coming from servers on Network AA to the users on BB. In order to filter packets requesting services, and not filter responses coming back to users, we will need to know the node address of the server's services. Let's see how this would work:

```
ACCESS-LIST 850 DENY AA BB.072C.FA34.0075
ACCESS-LIST 850 PERMIT –1
```

We apply this list using the IPX ACCESS-GROUP command as a packet filter on Ethernet 1.

The effect of this list is that all packets from Network AA destined for Server B will be blocked when they are forwarded to Router A's Ethernet 1 interface. The response packets coming back from Server A to the users on Network BB will be permitted by the last statement. PERMIT –1 is the same in the IPX world as PERMIT ANY is in the world of IP.

CERTIFICATION OBJECTIVE 9.05

IPX SAP Filters

All servers on a NetWare-type network can dynamically advertise their services and addresses using the Service Advertising Protocol (SAP). The other components on a network—besides the rest of the servers—such as routers, keep a complete list of the services available across the network. These service advertisements synchronize the list of available services.

Each SAP service is identified by a hexadecimal number. Several common examples are File Server–4, Printer Server–7, and Remote Bridge-Server (router)–24. A Cisco router does not forward each broadcast it receives. Rather, it will advertise the entire SAP table at scheduled intervals, with the default being every 60 seconds. Cisco routers do act like NetWare servers though, in that they listen to the SAP broadcasts from other servers and routers to build their internal SAP tables.

Since broadcast-type traffic across WANS is to be avoided as much as possible, SAP needs to be filtered. Filtering can be done for both inbound and outbound traffic. To help make this functionality more scalable, the Cisco IOS allows you to specify which services are added to the SAP table. This is accomplished with the command IPX INPUT-SAP-FILTER {*access-list-number* | *name* }. An example of this is found in Figure 9-4.

If we want to configure a SAP filter for Router 1 that would filter Server A's advertisements, but allow advertisements from the other servers on the segment, we would enter the following commands, in global configuration mode:

```
ACCESS-LIST 1001 DENY 1A01.0000.0000.0001

ACCESS-LIST 1001 PERMIT –1
```

The first statement denies all services originating from IPX address 1a01.0000.0000.0001. In a real Novell network, the node address 0000.0000.0001 always refers to the internal IPX network number of a NetWare server, and this is the address for all of the server's services.

FIGURE 9-4 SAP filtering in an IPX network

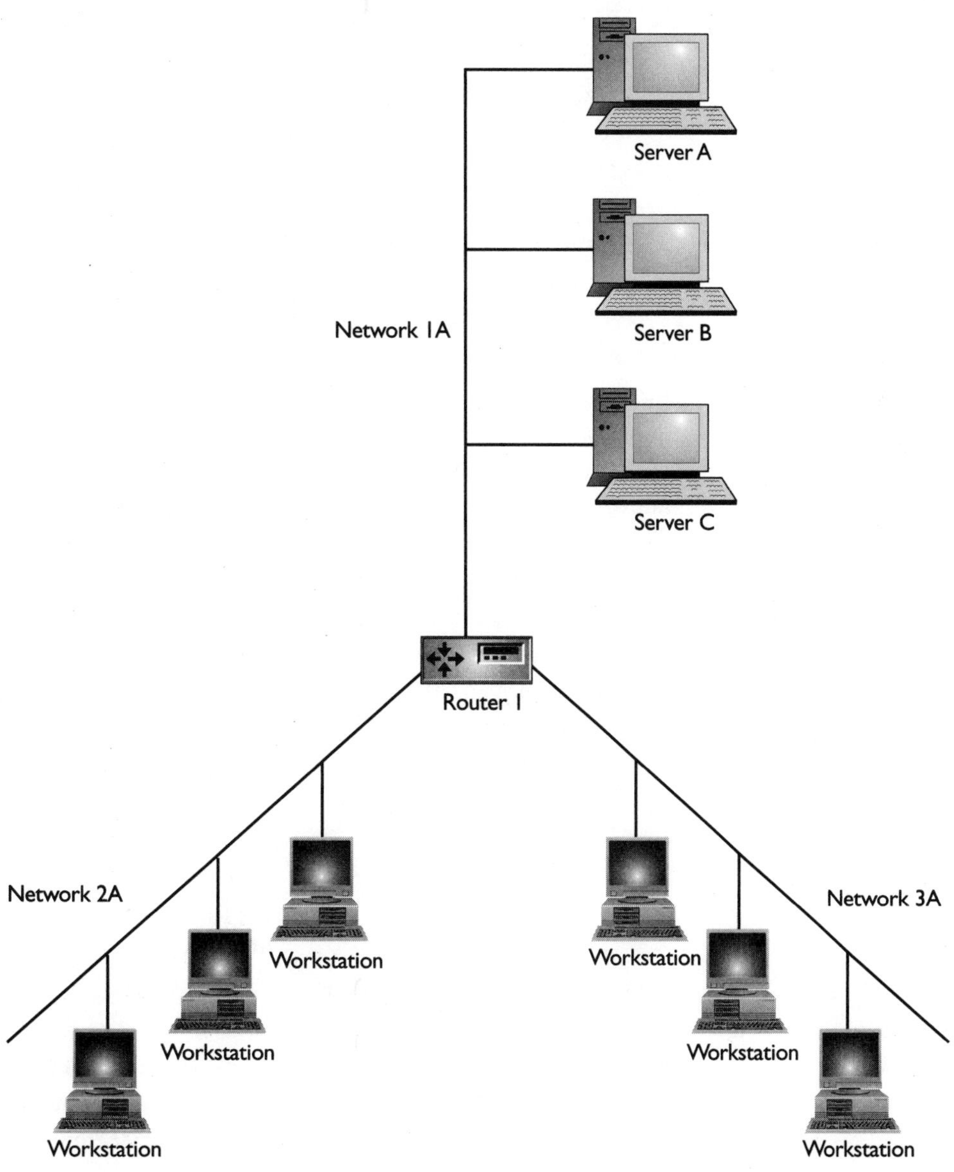

So the effect of this statement is to deny all services from the server whose internal IPX network number is 1a01. The second statement permits all other services. The –1 is the way to specify "all networks" in an IPX access list.

We can use this access list in one of two ways. If we don't want Server A's service entries accepted into Router1's SAP table at all, we can apply the list as an input SAP filter using the command IPX INPUT-SAP-FILTER 1001 in interface configuration mode for Ethernet 0.

The number 1001, of course, refers to the list number of access list 1001. This command will cause Router 1 to examine all SAP packets it receives on its Ethernet 0 interface, and filter out only the entries whose service addresses specify 1a01.0000.0000.0001. Note that the router is examining the individual entries inside the SAP packet to find this address, not the source address in the SAP packet's IPX header.

The second way to use this list is as an output SAP filter. Suppose we wanted the services from Network 1a01 to be advertised on Network 2a but not on Network 3a. If we used an input SAP filter on Ethernet 0, we would block the advertisements altogether. But if we put an output SAP filter on Ethernet 1, we can cause the router to filter out the SAP entries with service addresses of 1a01.0000.0000.0001 as it constructs the SAP packets it will broadcast on that interface. The command we need to configure an output sap filter is IPX OUTPUT-SAP-FILTER 1001. This command, like the INPUT-SAP-FILTER, is an interface configuration command.

There are two other options available for filtering in the SAP access list. We can filter by service type and also by service name. If we wanted to filter Server A's services by name, we could construct a statement like ACCESS-LIST 1001 DENY –1 0 SERVERA.

Again, "–1" means any network, "0" means all service types. Even though we are specifying ANY and ALL, these arguments are necessary to preserve the syntax of the statement. SERVERA, of course, is the string that the router will match when examining SAP entries for filtering. These strings are case sensitive, so always check the output of SHOW IPX SERVERS to see exactly how you need to configure this string.

Suppose we wanted to filter only file services, type 4, from Server A. There are two ways to do it. The first is to specify the internal IPX network number with service type 4: ACCESS-LIST 1001 DENY 1A01 4.

1A01 is the IPX internal network number for Server A, the network address of its services. We didn't really need the node address; if we are referring to the internal IPX network number, the node will always be 0000.0000.0001, and there are no other nodes on that network, so we could leave it out. "4" represents type 4 services. So only Server A's file services will be denied.

We could also use the string SERVERA to filter type 4 services from Server A: ACCESS-LIST 1001 DENY –1 4 SERVERA.

We are specifying any network (–1), but instead of all services, this time we specify type 4, along with the character string SERVERA. Don't forget: all access lists have an implicit DENY ANY at the end, so if you don't permit some services in another statement in this list, all SAPs will be filtered out.

Another part of IPX SAP is a Get Nearest Server (GNS) request. A GNS packet is sent out by Novell clients to request a non-server-specific service. The closest NetWare server that offers the requested service responds with another SAP. The GNS response designates a server's resources as available to the client, which will then log on to the server. Once the client has attached to the server, it can access the server's service directly; no further GNS is needed. If a GNS request is received by a Cisco router, it has the capability to respond with the first server in its SAP table. This should only occur if there are known local servers, since they should actually be the first ones to respond. You can create a GNS filter with the command IPX OUTPUT-GNS-FILTER *access-list-number.*

As was just stated, the local servers should be the first to respond. If this does not occur on your Novell IPX network, you can configure a GNS delay. The delay is measured in milliseconds, with the default being 0 (No Delay): IPX GNS-RESPONSE-DELAY *milliseconds.*

If you wish to view the list of IPX servers on your network that have been discovered through SAP you would issue the command SHOW IPX

SERVERS {UNSORTED} | {SORTED [NAME | NET | TYPE]} {REGEXP NAME}. By default, the output displayed will be listed numerically by SAP service type.

You can change this default with the optional UNSORTED and SORTED arguments listed above. UNSORTED does just as it says; it displays the IPX servers without any form of sorting. SORTED allows you to sort by server name (NAME), by network number (NET), or by the default SAP service type (TYPE). The REGEXP NAME allows you to display only IPX servers that match the name or expression you list.

Here is a sample output of SHOW IPX SERVERS:

```
east#show ipx servers
Codes: S - Static, P - Periodic, E - EIGRP, N - NLSP, H - Holddown, + =
       detail
10 Total IPX Servers

Table ordering is based on routing and server info

    Type Name                       Net      Address     Port      Route Hops Itf
S      4 EAST-D04              B00D.0000.0000.0001:0451    conn    2  Lo13
S      4 EAST-F04              B00F.0000.0000.0001:0451    conn    2  Lo15
P      4 DABNEY            BBBB0002.0000.0000.0001:0451    2/01    1  Et0.2
P      4 DESTINY           AAAA0001.0000.0000.0001:0451    2/01    1  Et0.2
N      4 WEST-D04              C00D.0000.0000.0001:0451   82/02    4  Se0
N      4 WEST-F04              C00F.0000.0000.0001:0451   82/02    4  Se0
P     47 PRINTSRV          BBBB0002.0000.0000.0001:8060    2/01    2  Et0.2
P    107 DABNEY            BBBB0002.0000.0000.0001:8104    2/01    2  Et0.2
P    26B UNIVERSE_1________ AAAA0001.0000.0000.0001:0005    2/01    1  Et0.2
P    278 UNIVERSE_1________ AAAA0001.0000.0000.0001:4006    2/01    1  Et0.2
```

Servers are displayed in numeric order by service type. Type 4 is file service, which is required for login (known as "general service" in Novell terms). These are the servers that will be used in GNS responses by the router.

The "net.address" columns are where you would look if you wanted to construct a SAP filter for these services based on their address. Notice that the addresses are all 0000.0000.0001. This is because services are advertised with an address of the internal IPX network number of the server, not the physical address of the NIC on the wire. This internal IPX network number is the one you must filter on for your SAP filters to operate properly. You can see which services are located on which physical server by matching up their internal IPX network numbers.

Verifying IPX Access List Configuration

SHOW IPX INTERFACES allows you to view all the various types of filters that can be set for IPX packets, routes, routers, SAPs, and NetBIOS packets. The Cisco IOS is rich in commands that help you to manage IPX traffic on your network, and all these parameters are configurable.

```
east#show ipx interface ethernet 0.2
Ethernet0.2 is up, line protocol is up
  IPX address is D.0000.0c47.6643, NOVELL-ETHER [up]
  Delay of this IPX network, in ticks is 1 throughput 0 link delay 0
  IPXWAN processing not enabled on this interface.
  IPX SAP update interval is 1 minute(s)
  IPX type 20 propagation packet forwarding is disabled
  Incoming access list is 800
  Outgoing access list is not set
  IPX helper access list is not set
  SAP GNS processing disabled, delay 500 ms, output filter list is 1000
  SAP Input filter list is not set
  SAP Output filter list is 1013
  SAP Router filter list is not set
  Input filter list is not set
  Output filter list is not set
  Router filter list is not set
  Netbios Input host access list is not set
  Netbios Input bytes access list is not set
  Netbios Output host access list is not set
  Netbios Output bytes access list is not set
  Updates each 60 seconds, aging multiples RIP: 3 SAP: 3
  SAP interpacket delay is 55 ms, maximum size is 480 bytes
  RIP interpacket delay is 55 ms, maximum size is 432 bytes
  IPX accounting is disabled
  IPX fast switching is configured (enabled)
  RIP packets received 294, RIP packets sent 152
  SAP packets received 295, SAP packets sent 150
```

Notice the lines in boldface. "Incoming access list is 800" indicates a packet filter applied inbound to the router with the IPX ACCESS-GROUP 800 IN command. "SAP Output filter list is 1013" indicates that access list 1013 has been applied as an output SAP filter with the IPX OUTPUT-SAP-FILTER 1013 command.

SHOW ACCESS-LISTS will show all access lists, not just IP or IPX. In the following example, we have both IPX and IP access lists configured in the router. If you want to view a specific IPX access list in isolation, use the list number as an argument for the command.

```
Router1#sh access-lists
IPX access list 800
    deny C011
    permit FFFFFFFF
IPX access list 900
    permit any
    permit any any all AA11.00cf.b200.0000 0000.00ff.ffff all
    permit any BB22 all AA11
IPX SAP access list 1000
    deny B00F 47
    permit FFFFFFFF
IPX SAP access list 1009
    deny FFFFFFFF 0 parallel
    permit FFFFFFFF
IPX SAP access list 1013
    deny C000.0000.0000.0000 F.ffff.ffff.ffff
    deny FFFFFFFF 47 E*
    permit FFFFFFFF
Standard IP access list 40
    deny   12.1.0.0, wildcard bits 0.0.255.255
    permit any
```

CERTIFICATION OBJECTIVE 9.06

AppleTalk Access Lists

Access lists are basically implemented in one of three ways. The most common way is to use them to control the packets that are transmitted across an interface. You can also use them to specify the interesting traffic that will launch a dial-on-demand (DDR) connection, or to control routing updates. Access lists for AppleTalk networks are basically like IP and IPX lists. You specify any number between 600 and 699 for referencing the access list, and you can include any number of access list commands under it.

To set up an access list, you enter the following command when in configuration mode: ACCESS-LIST *access-list-number* {DENY | PERMIT} *options.*

The *access-list-number* is a number from 600 to 699, which is used to reference the list you are adding to or creating. PERMIT and DENY either allow or disallow the type of traffic specified.

AppleTalk access lists can be broken down into two basic types: AppleTalk-style and IP-style. AppleTalk-style access lists are based on AppleTalk zones and NBP named entities. NBP stands for Name Binding Protocol, and it is what maps network names to AppleTalk addresses. It basically allows you to control network access at the network entity level. You can use these mapped names to permit or deny NBP packets from a specific NBP entity, or even from all NBP entities within a given area. The name given to an NBP entity is also known as an NBP *tuple.*

An AppleTalk zone is basically a logical group of networks, and every AppleTalk network's architecture is based on one of two Phases. Phase 1 networks were originally made for workgroups, and are limited to having only one zone. Phase 2 networks have many enhancements over Phase 1, including being designed with routing capabilities for larger networks. Phase 2 networks can have up to 255 zones. When you specify a zone, it is just like you individually specified every network number that is contained in that zone. One of the advantages of using AppleTalk style is that you don't have to reconfigure each router whenever you add new network segments. This is because you defined access on logical entities, which has no regard for topology. This luxury is not the case when dealing with IP style.

To create an access list based upon zones, you would enter the following command in the configuration mode: ACCESS-LIST *access-list-number* {PERMIT | DENY} ZONE *zonename.*

The *zonename* argument can include special characters from the Apple Macintosh set. If you want to use a special character, you enter a colon followed by the two corresponding hexadecimal characters. If your zonename's first character is a space, enter :20 to signify it.

You can define an access list for a specific NBP entity, such as a particular application, for a class of NBP entities like all printers, or for NBP entities that belong to a specific zone. To establish an access list for NBP named entity, use the following syntax while in configuration mode: ACCESS-LIST *access-list-number* {PERMIT | DENY} NBP *seq* *{type|object|zone* }STRING.

The *seq* argument references the sequence number, which allows you to associate two or three portions of an NBP name. Even if you aren't going to associate portions to the name, you are still required to enter a sequence number here. This allows you to deny or permit packets down to the entity level. The sequence number can also allow you to keep track of the number of NBP entries you have made in your access list. STRING identifies the type, object, or zone of the entity named. The same two allowances for Macintosh characters and for having the lead character be a space apply here. You can do either with the same solutions listed earlier. Here is an example of forwarding all packets except those coming from the zone sales or from servers of type AFPServer:

```
ACCESS-LIST 601 DENY NBP 1 ZONE SALES

ACCESS-LIST 601 DENY NBP 1 TYPE AFPSERVER

ACCESS-LIST 601 PERMIT OTHER-NBPS

ACCESS-LIST 601 PERMIT OTHER-ACCESS
```

One difference between AppleTalk and IP or IPX access lists is in regard to the order of listings. In IP and IPX, a packet will go through the applied access list until it finds its first matching rule, and it will be acted upon accordingly. In AppleTalk, the ordering of your rules is unimportant. As a result, you cannot overlap entries with other entries in a single list. Below is a simple example of overlapping. In the case where you overlap rules, the latter one will overwrite and remove the previous listing.

```
ACCESS-LIST 601 PERMIT NETWORK 10
ACCESS-LIST 601 DENY NETWORK 10
```

If this example were entered in a router, a SHOW RUN command would only list the statements as ACCESS-LIST 601 DENY NETWORK 10.

If you have a multiple-zone network, and you wish to deny access only to a few, you can explicitly define the ones to deny and apply the PERMIT OTHER-ACCESS at the end. If you wanted to permit access to all zones expect for Sales and Accounting, you could enter the following configuration:

```
ACCESS-LIST 601 DENY ZONE SALES
ACCESS-LIST 601 DENY ZONE ACCOUNTING
ACCESS-LIST 601 PERMIT ADDITIONAL-ZONES
```

IP-style access lists are based on network numbers. This controls the disposition of networks that overlap, are contained within, or exactly match a network number range. If you use this type, it will prevent you from assigning conflicting network numbers by restricting the network numbers and zones a department can advertise to only those which are authorized. As stated earlier, there is one big disadvantage to these. It ignores the logical mappings created by AppleTalk zones, thereby making it less scalable. If you add or alter the topology of your network, you have to reconfigure your routers to accommodate the changes.

You can configure IP-style access lists for both networks and cable ranges. To define an access list for a non-extended single network, enter the following command in configuration mode: ACCESS-LIST *access-list-number* {PERMIT | DENY} NETWORK *network*.

For example, if you have two networks, and you want to deny packets from Network 1 but permit packets from Network 2, you would enter the following access list:

ACCESS-LIST 601 DENY NETWORK 1

ACCESS-LIST 601 PERMIT NETWORK 2

If you want to set up an access list for a cable range in an extended network, you would enter the following command in configuration mode: ACCESS-LIST *access-list-number* {PERMIT I DENY} CABLE-RANGE *cable-range.*

For example, if you wanted to forward all packets from cable range 200–250, but deny packets from cable range 300–350, you would enter the following:

ACCESS-LIST 601 PERMIT CABLE-RANGE 200-250

ACCESS-LIST 601 DENY CABLE-RANGE 300-350

Cisco IOS provides the functionality to define an AppleTalk access list for an extended or a non-extended network that is completely contained within a specific cable-range:

ACCESS-LIST6 *access-list-number* {PERMIT | DENY} WITHIN *cable-range*

The following example allows access to any network or cable range that is completely included in the range of 200-250:

ACCESS-LIST 601 PERMIT WITHIN 200-250

You can change WITHIN to INCLUDES to allow more flexibility for overlapping networks—in the following example, for any network that overlaps any part of networks 200-250.

ACCESS-LIST 601 PERMIT INCLUDES 200-250

You can also permit or deny access for either extended or non-extended networks that overlap across a cable range or a range of network numbers:

ACCESS-LIST *access-list-number* {PERMIT | DENY} INCLUDES *cable-range*

QUESTIONS AND ANSWERS	
I added an IP access list entry to a new server, but nobody can reach it.	Make sure you add the explicit allowances at the beginning. (The first available match is applied.)
I added the following line to my router, but it doesn't seem to be working: ACCESS-LIST 550 DENY NBP I ZONE SALES	The range for AppleTalk access lists is 600–699. You need to change the 550 to something within this range.
Which method of AppleTalk access lists should I implement: IP or AppleTalk style? I need the most scalable method.	AppleTalk would probably be a better method. You don't have to reconfigure the routers every time you add or change network segments.
Servers on one network segment cannot see the servers on the other, but the opposite works. Where should I investigate?	Check your SAP filters that are bound to the interface next to the side that can view the others.
When using a protocol analyzer, I see a lot of requests for remote servers being transmitted across my 64 kbps link. How can I reduce this?	Use an output GNS filter to keep the router from providing those remote servers in response to GNS requests.

CERTIFICATION SUMMARY

In an IP access list, a source or destination address is tested against each item in the list. The first match found is the one that is used to determine whether the packet is permitted or disregarded. Because the first match is the one followed, it is critical to pay attention to the order. When you establish an IP list, if no applicable rule is found, it is implicitly denied. The correct syntax for permitting or denying packets across interfaces is as follows:

ACCESS-LIST *access-list-number* {DENY | PERMIT}
{SOURCE[*source-wildcard*]|ANY}

IPX access lists permit or deny traffic based on either specified network nodes or messages sent using particular protocols and services. Just as in IP access lists, the order of rules applied in the access list is critical. The first matching entry, whether it is a PERMIT or a DENY, is followed. And also like IP lists, if you do not explicitly enter a PERMIT EVERYTHING at the end, an implicit DENY ALL is made. The syntax for a basic IPX access list is as follows:

ACCESS-LIST *access-list-number* {DENY | PERMIT}
SOURCE-NETWORK[OPTIONS]

All servers on a NetWare-type network can dynamically advertise their services and addresses using the Service Advertisement Protocol (SAP). The other components on a network besides the remainder servers, such as routers, keep a complete list of the services available across the network. These service advertisements synchronize the list of available services. You can deny SAP-type traffic with the command ACCESS-LIST 1001 DENY 1A01.0000.0000.0001.

AppleTalk access lists can be broken down into two basic types: AppleTalk-style and IP-style. AppleTalk-style access lists are based on AppleTalk zones and NBP named entities. NBP is what maps network names to AppleTalk addresses. It allows you to control network access at the network entity level. You can use these mapped names to permit or deny NBP packets from a specific NBP entity, or from all NBP entities within a given area. An NBP entity is also known as an NBP tuple. The correct syntax for establishing an AppleTalk access list is:

ACCESS-LIST *access-list-number* {DENY | PERMIT} *options*

TWO-MINUTE DRILL

- ❑ Packet filtering is performed on Cisco routers through the use of access lists. Access lists can be used to control the transmission of packets across an interface, to restrict traffic across virtual terminal lines, or to restrict routing updates.
- ❑ An IP access list is a collection of permit and deny rules that are applied to IP addresses.
- ❑ Cisco IOS Release 11.1 introduced significant changes in the syntax and implementation of access lists.
- ❑ There are three basic types of IP access lists: standard, extended, and dynamic extended.

- The basic format for adding a standard access list is:

  ACCESS-LIST *access-list-number* {DENY|PERMIT} {SOURCE[*source-wildcard*]|ANY}
- Extended IP uses both the source and destination address when it tries to match up packets to your list, and you can optionally use protocol type information for even finer control.
- The syntax for adding and removing access lists is:

  {NO} ACCESS-LIST *access-list-number* {DENY | PERMIT} *protocol source source-wildcard destination destination-wildcard*
- With Named lists you can identify IP access lists, whether standard or extended, with an alphanumeric name instead of a number.
- You can verify your IP access lists with the SHOW ACCESS-LISTS command and the SHOW IP INTERFACES command.
- IPX access lists permit or deny traffic across interfaces based on either specified network nodes or messages sent using particular protocols and services.
- All servers on a NetWare-type network can dynamically advertise their services and addresses using the Service Advertising Protocol (SAP).
- SHOW IPX INTERFACES allows you to view all the various types of filters that can be set for IPX packets, routes, routers, SAPs, and NetBIOS packets.
- SHOW ACCESS-LISTS will show all access lists, not just IP or IPX.
- Access lists for AppleTalk networks are basically like IP and IPX lists.
- AppleTalk access lists can be broken down into two basic types: AppleTalk-style and IP-style.

SELF TEST

The following questions will help you measure your understanding of the material presented in this chapter. Read all the choices carefully, as there may be more than one correct answer. Choose all correct answers for each question.

1. Match which of these protocols go with which access list range.

   A. Novell SAP 1. 800–899
   B. AppleTalk 2. 1000–1099
   C. Novell 3. 1–99
   D. IP 4. 600–699

2. What happens to access lists previously created if the IOS is upgraded from version 10.1 to 11.1?

   A. They are dropped since they are no longer applicable
   B. Access lists didn't exist prior to version 9.1
   C. They will be converted to the new format
   D. They will be left alone since IOS 11.1 provides backward compatibility

3. In what ways are access lists typically implemented on AppleTalk networks?

   A. To control packets transmitted across an interface
   B. To specify interesting traffic to launch a DDR connection
   C. To restrict SAP broadcasts
   D. To advertise available servers

4. What do NetWare servers do to advertise their services and addresses to other servers?

   A. Broadcast NetBIOS packets
   B. Register with an SAP server
   C. Broadcast SAP packets
   D. Register with a NetBIOS server

5. In the event of no matching rule being found in an IP access list, what happens to the transmission packet at the end?

   A. It is dropped
   B. It is allowed to pass
   C. A broadcast is sent out notifying the sending host
   D. A Packet Return (PR) is issued to the sending host

6. For which of the following reasons are IP-style AppleTalk access lists implemented?

   A. For controlling the disposition of networks that overlap a network number range
   B. For controlling the disposition of networks that are contained within a network number range
   C. For controlling the disposition of networks that no longer exist within a network number range
   D. For controlling the disposition of networks that exactly match a network number range

7. Which of the following statements are true regarding IP access lists?
   A. After an access list is created, any additions to that list are placed at the end
   B. You can't selectively add or remove items
   C. You need to explicitly associate the access list to whatever it is you are intending to use it for, such as an interface
   D. There is an implicit DENY statement at the end
8. On what basis do IPX access lists permit or deny traffic?
   A. Specified network nodes
   B. Messages sent using a particular ICMP
   C. Messages sent using a particular protocol
   D. Messages sent using a particular service
9. How often does a Cisco router broadcast perodic SAP advertisements?
   A. As soon as it receives the complete packet
   B. Every 30 seconds
   C. Every 60 seconds
   D. Every 300 seconds (5 minutes)
10. What is GNS?
   A. An ICMP connectivity error packet
   B. Generic NetWare Service (Allows a Cisco router to appear as a NetWare server)
   C. AppleTalk's default network routing algorithm
   D. A packet sent out to request specific services from servers
11. Which of the following are valid types of IPX access lists?
   A. SAP
   B. NetBIOS
   C. ICMP
   D. Extended
12. What are the two basic styles of AppleTalk lists?
   A. AppleTalk style
   B. Macintosh style
   C. NBP style
   D. IP style
13. Which of the following are true statements regarding Phase 1 and Phase 2 AppleTalk networks?
   A. Phase 1 networks are more efficient at WAN communication
   B. Phase 2 networks can have up to 255 zones
   C. Phase 1 networks can have only 1 zone
   D. Phase 2 networks introduced routing
14. How should you arrange your entries in AppleTalk access lists?
   A. The order doesn't matter
   B. From the most specific to the most general

C. From the most general to the most specific
D. Zones first, followed by systems

15. What will happen to packets that cross an interface where no access list has been defined?

A. They will be discarded
B. They will be allowed to pass through
C. They will be queued up
D. They will be returned to the sending host

16. Which of the following examples follow the correct syntax for adding special Macintosh characters in zone names?

A. /B2
B. –B2
C. [B2]
D. :B2

17. Which of these are valid types of IP access lists?

A. Dynamic
B. Dynamic Extended
C. Extended
D. Standard

18. Which of the following examples uses the correct syntax to define an AppleTalk access list for an extended or a non-extended network that is completely contained within a specific cable-range?

A. ACCESS-LIST 599 PERMIT WITHIN 100-150
B. access-list permit 225-240 within 699
C. access-list permit 225-240 within 599
D. access-list 699 permit within 100-150

19. Which of the following statements regarding SAP broadcasts is correct?

A. SAP-type broadcasts do not work well across WANs
B. Each SAP service is identified by an eight-digit binary number
C. Because of sequencing issues, the times between SAP table updates cannot be changed
D. SAP stands for Secondary Addressing Protocol

20. Consider the following access list:

ACCESS-LIST 50 DENY 136.120.3.1

ACCESS-LIST 50 DENY 143.22.1.0 0.0.0.255

Which statement represents the most complete description of the results of applying this list as a packet filter?

A. It will deny all traffic destined for any host on network 136.120.3.0
B. It will deny all traffic destined for network 143.22.1.0
C. It will deny all traffic from the host at 136.120.3.1
D. It will deny all IP traffic

21. Which command would be used to configure a packet filter for IP traffic?

A. ROUTER(CONFIG-IF)#IP ACCESS-LIST 100
B. Router(config-if)#ip access-group 42
C. Router(config)#access-group 102
D. Router(config-if)#access-group 75
E. Router(config-if)#ip output-packet-filter 112

22. Which command would be used to configure an inbound packet filter for TCP traffic?

A. ROUTER(CONFIG-IF)#TCP PACKET-FILTER 101
B. Router(config-if)#ip packet-filter 101 in
C. Router(config-if)#ip access-group 99 in
D. Router(config-if)#ip access-group 100 in
E. Router(config-if)#ip access-group 100

23. The address mask pair 172.16.64.0 0.0.3.255 specifies which range of IP addresses?

A. 172.16.64.255 through 172.16.67.255
B. 172.16.67.0 through 172.16.70.255
C. 172.16.64.0 through 172.16.67.255
D. 172.16.63.0 through 172.16.64.255

24. The following statement appears in an IP extended access list:
ACCESS-LIST 125 PERMIT IP ANY HOST 136.25.2.128
What does this line permit?

A. Any IP traffic from host 136.25.2.128
B. IP traffic to any host on network 136.25.2.128
C. IP traffic from any address to the host at 136.25.2.128
D. The statement is invalid because there is no mask

25. The following access list, containing only one line, is applied as a packet filter on an interface.

ACCESS-LIST 100 PERMIT TCP 145.22.3.0 0.0.0.255 ANY EQ TELNET

What is the best description of the traffic that is denied by the implicit DENY ALL?

A. All IP traffic
B. All Telnet traffic
C. All TCP traffic
D. All TCP traffic except Telnet

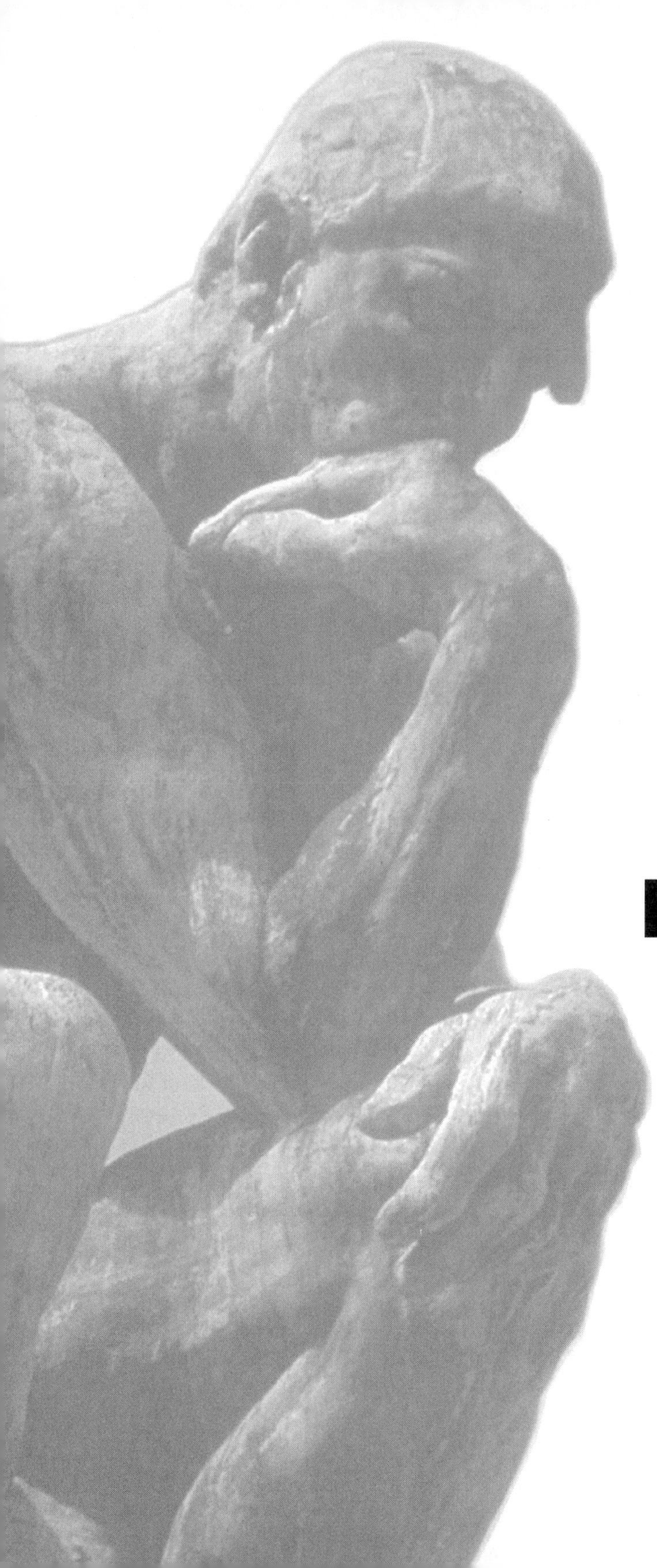

CCNA

CISCO CERTIFIED NETWORK ASSOCIATE

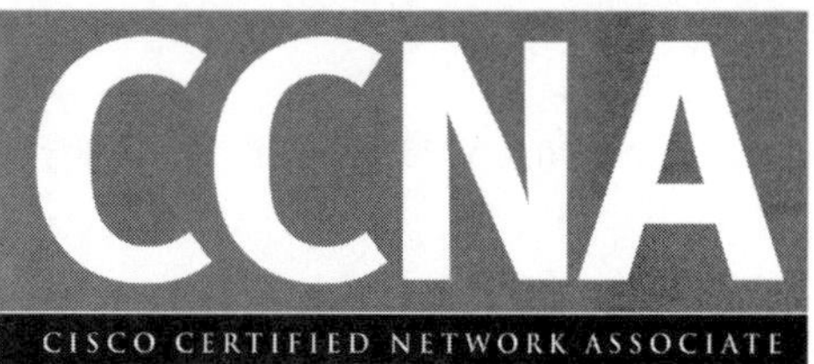

10

Wide Area Networking

CERTIFICATION OBJECTIVES

10.01 Configuring ISDN

10.02 Configuring X.25

10.03 Configuring Frame Relay

10.04 Configuring ATM

10.05 Configuring PPP and Multilink PPP

These days, almost any business of significant size needs, or already has, some form of a WAN in its infrastructure. Unfortunately, because of many companies' poor preparation and limited knowledge of the subject, many such WANs are not functioning to their potential. This chapter's goals are to outline the specifics of the WAN technologies currently available, and how to configure each one.

CERTIFICATION OBJECTIVE 10.01

Configuring ISDN

Today's current analog modem connections for Internet connectivity have two major drawbacks. First, whenever a line is used for data transmissions, a voice line is taken up. This can obviously be a serious problem when a small business might only have one line! Second, current technology only allows a throughput of 56 Kbps, and this is possible only if the quality of both the connections and the phone system is nearly perfect. The solution to this problem has been around for several years, but is only now becoming popular: ISDN. ISDN is the digital equivalent to the analog phone line. The phone companies developed it in an effort to deliver not only voice but also high-speed data at a reasonable price, and across the already installed copper wires.

ISDN lines are composed of multiple 64Kb bearer channels (B channels) and one data channel of either 16Kb or 64Kb (D channel). The purpose of each might sound reversed, but the bearer channels are what transmit the data or carry the voice signals, and the data channel is what is used for call signaling. ISDN is ordered as either Basic Rate Interface (BRI) or Primary Rate Interface (PRI). It is comprised of two B channels along with one 16Kb D channel, enabling a possible throughput of 128Kb.

BRI is typically configured as a type of dial-on-demand routing (DDR). A DDR link looks the same to IP, or to any other network protocol for that matter—as a serial link that is only there when in use. Configuration of IP on a DDR is pretty straightforward, but it can be fairly complex to determine how to specify the mapping of IP addresses to phone numbers, and when and how to connect or disconnect the links.

Configuring ISDN BRI

In order for a call to be placed across an ISDN network, there needs to be network-wide configuration information. ISDN uses directory numbers and service profile identifiers (SPIDs). The directory number is simply a telephone number you will use when you call. The SPID is a number the telephone company uses to identify the equipment on your ISDN connection. Another thing you need to know is the switch type used by your ISDN provider. In the United States, the switch type is most likely either an AT&T 5ess or 4ess, or a Northern Telecom DMS-100. A diagram of a basic ISDN network is shown in Figure 10-1.

Let's look at the configuration of the sample found in Figure 10-1.

```
Hostname router1
Isdn switch-type basic-dms 100
!
interface BRI0
ip address 10.10.10.1 255.255.255.0
isdn spid1 1234567890 5551234
encapsulation ppp
ppp authentication chap
dialer-group 1
dialer idle-timeout 300
dialer map ip 10.10.10.2 name Router2 speed 56 broadcast 2465551212
dialer hold-queue 5
dialer load-threshold 100
```

Following the host name of the router is the global command specifying the type of switch used on the phone company's end. Then, after entering the configuration of the interface, which is BRI 0 on Router 1, you set the IP address (if applicable) and the SPID and directory numbers assigned to you by the phone company. The two lines referencing PPP will be discussed later in the chapter.

The last five lines all deal with the dialer's settings. The DIALER-GROUP command adds the interface to the group listed, stating it will

FIGURE 10-1

An ISDN network

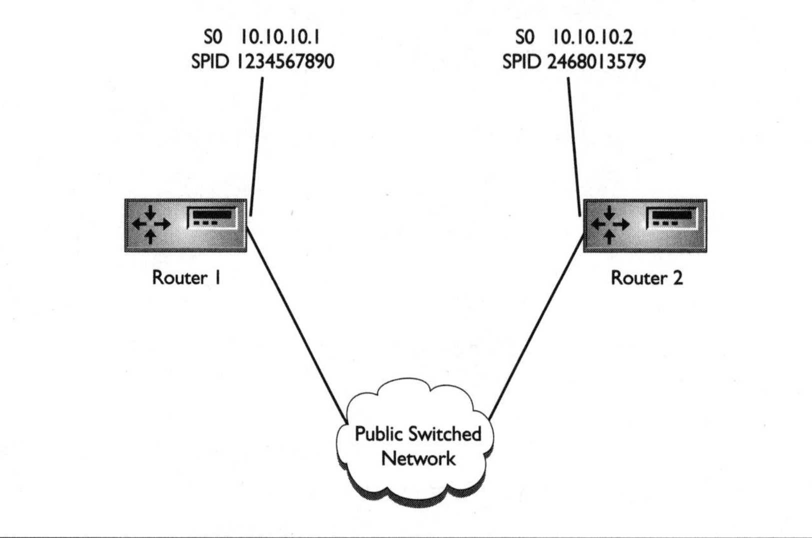

respond to *interesting* packets. Interesting traffic is traffic that, when routed to the interface that has been placed in the dialer-group, will cause the interface to dial the remote router and make a connection. Traffic routed to the interface that does not match the dialer-list will be dropped if the circuit is down, and will not cause the circuit to be activated. When the period of time defined by the DIALER IDLE-TIMEOUT has elapsed without interesting traffic (there might be other traffic on the line once it is up that is not interesting), the dialer will terminate the connection.

The idle-timeout references, in seconds, how long of a period the system will wait where there is no activity before disconnecting. The next line actually does the mapping of the IP address of the remote router to its number. The HOLD-QUEUE specifies the number of interesting packets the router will hold in its queue while a connection is being established. The DIALER LOAD-THRESHOLD configures the bandwidth maximum load before another dial-on-demand call is placed. While this particular line has no real significance in this scenario (since we only have one dial-up setting), I wanted to show you an example, since you will encounter it in most multi-modem configurations.

Configuring ISDN PRI

Implementation of ISDN PRI loses the benefit of using existing copper. It is delivered via a T-1 circuit and is comprised of 23 B channels and one 64Kb D channel. One thing to note is that when a T-1 is used for any type of channelized service, 8 kbps is lost to the channelization process. Since a T-1 provides 1.544 Mbps, its bandwidth is reduced to 1.536 Mbps.

A common implementation of ISDN PRI would be to provide 23 ports for a company's remote workers to dial in. ISDN PRI has two features that combine to make using it an attractive remote-access (RAS) solution. One is that an ISDN line uses separate phone numbers for each channel, just as the analog lines in your house each have their own number. The other is that an ISDN PRI interface can be terminated into a RJ-45 connector, which can be directly connected to a Cisco access router or an ISDN PRI interface on a 7000. What this means is that you can introduce a great RAS solution to your company without having to mess with multiple lines, cables, and modems.

CERTIFICATION OBJECTIVE 10.02

Configuring X.25

X.25 is similar to Frame Relay (which will be discussed in the next section) in that it is a packet-switched technology that typically operates as permanent virtual circuit (PVC). Since data on a packet-switched network is capable of following any available circuit path, it is almost always drawn as clouds in graphical representations like the one in Figure 10-2. Being configured as a PVC means that all data entering the cloud at point A is automatically forwarded to point B.

X.25 was introduced at a time when wide-area network links, traveling through the public switched network, were primarily analog lines producing errors and poor transmissions. X.25 sought to remedy this through built-in error correction and flow control. The trade-off for this reliability is performance. With all the acknowledgments, buffering, and retransmission that happens within X.25, latency becomes an issue. In the grander scheme

FIGURE 10-2

Basic X.25 configuration

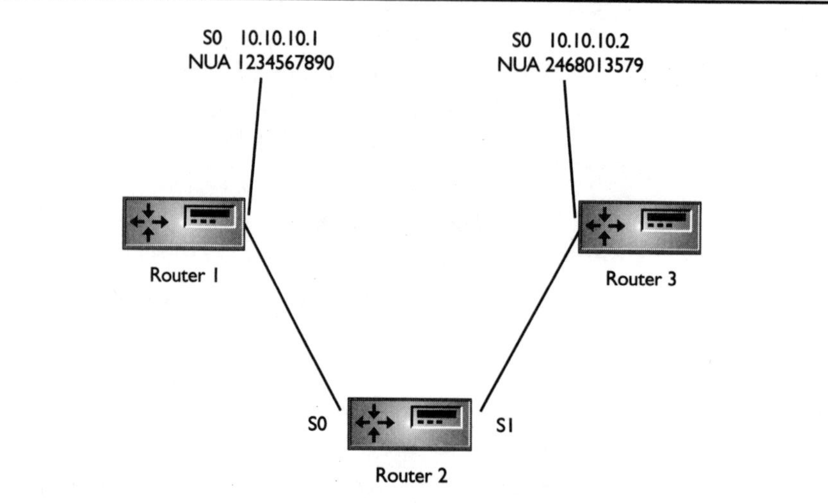

of things, for protocols that provide their own error detection and correction, such as TCP, it is a poor performer.

X.25 encompasses the first three layers of the OSI model. On each end of an X.25 connection, along the physical layer of the OSI model, is a data terminal equipment (DTE) device and a data circuit-terminating equipment (DCE) device. ATM connections occur between these devices on logical circuits. Circuits exist as one of two types: SVC or PVC. SVCs (switched virtual circuits) are a lot like telephone calls—a connection is established, data is transferred, and then the connection is terminated. Each DTE on an X.25 network is given a unique address, which can be used much like a telephone number. PVCs (permanent virtual circuits) are closer to a leased line idea, in that their connection is always present. No call needs to take place, since the connection is already established.

To establish an SVC connection, the calling DTE sends a Call Request packet, which includes the address of the remote DTE to be contacted. The Call Request packet contains both the sender and the destination DTE addresses, along with some other configurable information. At this point, the called DTE can use this information to decide whether or not it wants to accept the call. If it decides to accept it, a Call Accepted packet is sent. If it decides not to accept it, a Clear Request packet is sent.

Once the DTE that placed the call receives the Call Accepted packet, the virtual circuit is established and data transmissions begin to occur. At any point in the communication process, either DTE can terminate the call by issuing a Clear Request packet to the other DTE. It then responds with a Clear Confirmation packet, and the call is ended. The destination for each packet sent is identified by means of the logical channel identifier (LCI) or logical channel number (LCN). This allows the PSN to route each packet to its intended DTE. (This is a lot like DLCI numbers you will read about in the Frame Relay section of this chapter.) LCNs only have significance locally, so many of the same number can be found throughout a given X.25 network.

Devices throughout an X.25 network have a unique address assigned to them, which are known as network user addresses (NUAs). These addresses conform to the X.121 recommendation for public data networks. This specification stipulates that 14 digits be assigned, with 12 being mandatory and 2 being optional. The first four digits are known as the Data Network Identification Code (DNIC). Out of these four digits, the first three signify the country and the fourth specifies the network within the country. The next eight digits are the national number, and the last two are the optional ones I mentioned. They are used for sub-addresses, and are assignable by the network user.

X.25 relies on the underlying strengths of the layer-2 HDLC LAPB protocol to transmit data across an X.25 network. HDLC LAPB is a very efficient protocol. A minimum amount of overhead is required to perform flow control, synchronization, and error recovery. If the connection is configured as full duplex, where data is flowing in both directions, the data frames themselves carry all the information required to provide data integrity.

X.25 makes use of something called frame windows. A frame window is used to send multiple frames before receiving confirmation that the first frame has been received. This means that data can continue to flow, unlike the other protocols where there may be latency because of the sending and receiving of integrity confirmation-type packets.

An X.25 packet makes up the data field of an LAPB frame. Additional flow control and windowing are provided for each logical channel at the X.25 level.

Maximum packet sizes vary from 64 bytes to 4096 bytes, with 128 bytes being the default on most networks. Both maximum packet size and packet-level windowing may be negotiated between DTEs on call setup.

I recently read an article where somebody accurately described X.25 as a data pump. What this means is that there has to be some higher-level protocol that is able to make sense of the bits. There are standards for allowing certain applications to make use of X.25. Among them is IBM's QLLC protocol, which defines how SNA traffic can be carried over X.25 networks. Another is the asynchronous X.25 PAD.

Configuration of X.25 is pretty straightforward. Here is a sample configuration for Router 1 from Figure 10-2.

```
X25 routing
!
Interface ethernet0
Ip address 10.10.10.1 255.255.255.0
!
Interface serial0
No ip address
Encapsulation x25 dce
Clockrate 19200
!
X25 route 2468013579 interface serial0
```

Most commands listed above should be understandable to you now. The first command establishes the routing based on the NUA of the router. The next four commands specify the IP address, or lack thereof, for each interface on the router. The ENCAPSULATION command ends in DCE, thereby configuring the serial port to be a X.25 DCE device. The CLOCKRATE command lets you specify to the router the rate at which the data is going to be transferring. The last command tells the router to send all traffic destined for the listed NUA out through serial 0.

If you want to view the status of your X.25 connections, you can use the SHOW X25 command, followed by one of the arguments listed in Table 10-1 (for example, SHOW X.25 MAP). You should try each of these to view the output and see how it can help you in the troubleshooting process.

TABLE 10-1

Show X.25 Arguments

Argument	Definition
MAP	Displays X.25 address maps
ROUTE	Displays the X.25 routing table
VC	Lists information about active SVCs and PVCs
REMOTE-RED	Displays one-to-one mapping of local and remote IP addresses

CERTIFICATION OBJECTIVE 10.03

Configuring Frame Relay

Frame Relay is not a certain type of interface, rather it is an encapsulation method that operates at layer 2 and runs on top of nearly any serial interface. Frame Relay is a packet-switching technology that multiplexes multiple logical data streams onto one physical link. These data streams are called virtual circuits, and each is identified by something known as a data-link connection identifier. The acronym for this is DLCI, which is pronounced dell-see. This DLCI number is not used as a network-wide unique descriptive destination, like a MAC address is on a typical layer-2 protocol. It only has significance locally, and can change on each physical link. The number is used to identify which pipe leads to which specific layer-3 protocol address, such as IP. In the example in Figure 10-3, DLCI 4 leads to the IP address of serial 0 at the location of Router 2.

In a Frame Relay cloud, other locations could, and most likely do, use the same DLCI numbers, since they are only locally significant. This really puts a limit on its functionality, and it has in fact been antiquated by use of Local Management Interface (LMI) extensions. LMI provides Frame Relay with many new features, with one of the most important being the use of inverse ARP to automatically determine the protocol address of the device on the remote end of a DLCI. You can just accept this as being a good

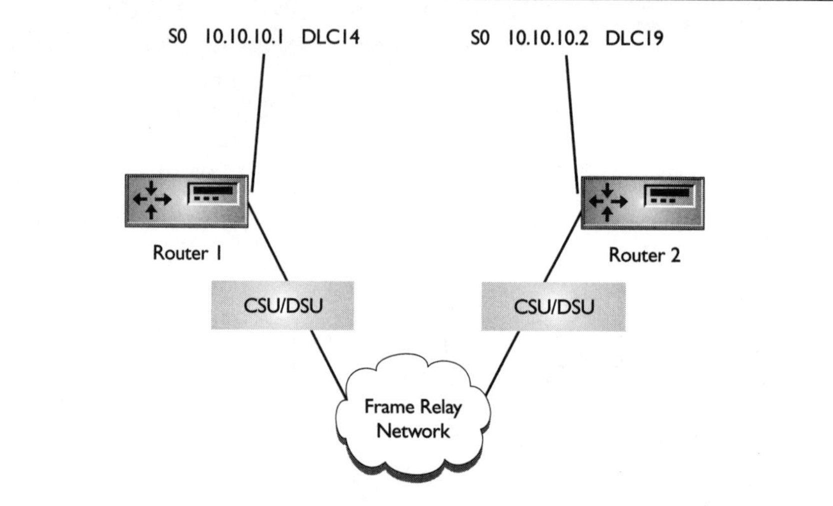

FIGURE 10-3 A Frame Relay network

thing for now, and later in this section we will see how much this helps us in configurations! LMI also adds flow control functionality to Frame Relay, as well as the capability to multicast.

Virtual circuits are statistically multiplexed, meaning bandwidth is dynamically assigned as needed per circuit. This technique is the opposite of another type of switching technology called time-division multiplexing (TDM), where each and every channel is allocated a fixed amount of bandwidth over a given time. The disadvantage to TDM is that each channel is given its specified bandwidth, whether it takes advantage of it or not. Let's look at the following example to understand not only the rationale but also the implementation of dynamic allocation.

If a company requires a leased line between two locations, the amount of bandwidth they need will fluctuate constantly throughout the day. If they purchase an amount close to the average, there will be occasions when they max out their line and network traffic slows to a crawl. Yet they don't want to spend the extra money every month for bandwidth they rarely use. However, if multiple companies are in this situation and they share a line that provides more than adequate bandwidth for each of their averages collectively, the odds that all the companies involved will all require their maximum bandwidth simultaneously is statistically improbable. So bandwidth is dynamically assigned to each company where needed. This results in greater efficiency of bandwidth allocation collectively, which itself produces a reduction of costs to and from the phone company.

Many people are concerned when first presented with this option, thinking they might not get the bandwidth required just for normal, day-to-day operations. To prevent this from happening, Frame Relay provides something called the committed information rate (CIR). What this does is guarantee the customer a fixed amount of throughput based upon what they deem acceptable. In other words, the customers set the minimum they require, and even though their line is shared, their available bandwidth will never drop below that amount.

Virtual Circuits

There are two types of virtual circuits that Frame Relay can create. This is exactly like what you learned in the X.25 section, but for clarity, we will re-explain it. The first type of circuit is a permanent virtual circuit (PVC) and the second is a switched virtual circuit (SVC). A PVC is manually created by an administrator with a source and destination, and operates very much like a leased line. As its name implies, it is a permanent connection and remains until it is manually removed. An SVC on the other hand, is dynamically created by software through a call setup procedure. This is similar to the process by which two people operate a telephone. When communication is required, a call is placed, and it is disconnected when the transmission has ended.

Since these circuits are multiplexed on each link, Frame Relay can operate in either a point-to-point or a multipoint mode. Point-to-point operation is just like that of a leased line. Communication exists across a single virtual circuit between two interfaces at two destinations. In multipoint mode, an interface can communicate with one of multiple destinations across one of multiple circuits. While an interface has the capability to communicate with each remote location, each communication is performed as an independent, point-to-point session. In other words, a broadcast packet cannot be sent without recreating it onto each individual circuit.

Error Correction

Frame Relay also has error correction built into it, but not nearly to the extent that X.25 has. Similar to the cyclic redundancy check (CRC) in an Ethernet network, Frame Relay uses a Frame Check Sequence (FCS) and it is appended to the end of each frame passed. When a station receives a frame, it computes a new FCS on the data portion and compares it to the FCS that was in the frame. If they are different, it drops the packet without notifying the sending station. While this may sound bad, it is in fact a good thing. Because of this technique, Frame Relay is faster at transferring data than X.25, because no time is lost in the overhead of having to process error checking or having to re-send information. Instead, Frame Relay relies on the next layer that is communicating over it to handle error recovery, since most level-3 protocols do. If the protocol that is running over Frame Relay is connection oriented, such as the TCP half of TCP/IP, there are no problems, since it will handle it's own error recovery and flow control. But if the protocol is connectionless, like that of UDP, the application that is implementing it must be specifically coded for self-recovery.

Logical Interfaces

Frame Relay, like ATM, allows multiple logical network interfaces to be bound to each physical interface. Each of these logical interfaces can have its own IP address, subnet mask, and entry in the routing tables, and each will have a different subnetwork ID associated with it. Each of these logical interfaces can run on one or even multiple virtual circuits, but each virtual circuit typically only has one logical interface associated with it. To assign subnetwork IDs to each interface, Cisco IOS uses what are called sub-interfaces. Sub-interfaces allow you to split up each of your physical interfaces into multiple logical ports. The naming convention used for these ports is simply the name of the interface being addressed, then a period, followed by the number of the sub-interface. From Router 3 in the Frame Relay example in Figure 10-4, serial 0.2 is the second sub-interface on serial 1.

FIGURE 10-4

Frame Relay allows multiple logical network interfaces on each physical interface

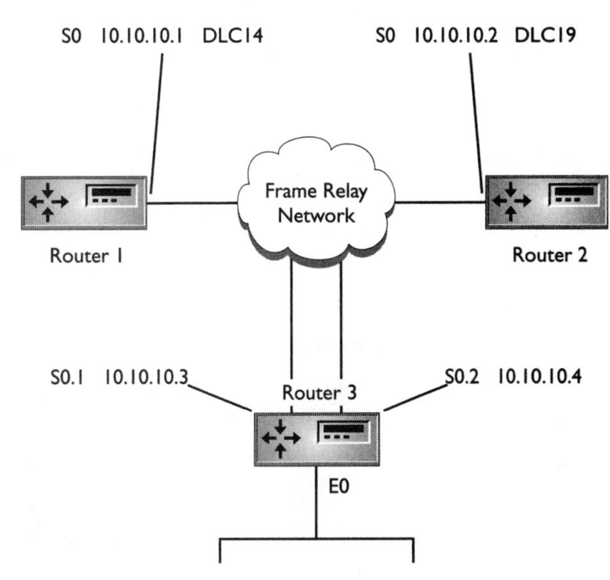

Configuring Frame Relay on a Cisco Router

Configuring Frame Relay on a Cisco router includes the mapping of IP addresses to DLCIs and telling the router which virtual circuits are connected. The way this is done is the same whether it is operating in point-to-point or in multipoint mode. The only difference is, whatever you do to a point-to-point interface has to be repeated for each logical circuit on a multipoint. Point-to-point and multipoint connections operate in either explicit or implicit mode. In explicit mode, a map of the remote IP address to the DLCI is made manually. In implicit mode, an assumption is made that the router on the other end of the circuit matches the IP address it wants to send the packet to. You will probably recognize this concept as being similar to IP unnumbered, and in fact point-to-point Frame Relay can be configured in this way! To configure Router 3 in Figure 10-4 for explicit mode, you would enter the following:

```
interface serial0
encapsulation Frame Relay {ietf}
```

```
interface serial 0.1 point-to-point
IP address 10.10.10.3 255.255.255.0
Frame Relay map 10.10.10.1 7 broadcast
```

The first command configures the interface for Frame Relay encapsulation. The IETF at the end optionally changes the encapsulation method from Cisco's own method to comply with the IETF standard. This is used in situations where the router at the other end is a non-Cisco product. The INTERFACE command creates a point-to-point sub-interface and the next line maps an IP address to it. The last line is where the explicit configuration is made. It states that at the end of the DLCI 7 pipe is the destination IP address of 10.10.10.1. The BROADCAST argument tells the router that broadcasts such as router updates should be sent across this PVC. Of course, to be able to send router updates both ways, Router 1 would have to be configured to also allow broadcast messages.

The next example assumes an implicit configuration is desired, and now we get to see the great LMI added feature of reverse ARP that we promised earlier!

```
interface serial0
encapsulation Frame Relay {ietf}
Frame Relay lmi-type ansi
interface serial0.1 point-to-point
IP address 10.10.10.3 255.255.255.0
Frame Relay interface-dlci 7 broadcast
```

A lot of this looks the same, but the FRAME RELAY LMI-TYPE is new. This command enables LMI extensions, and specifies which of these three standards it is to implement: ansi, q933a, or the default of Cisco. The FRAME RELAY command in the last line associates DLCI 7 to the sub-interface, but why is the IP address of the remote interface not listed?

By simply telling the router of the DLCIs in use, the router will use inverse ARP to build a table of the IP address of the (sub-)interface at the end of the PVC, matched with each respective DLCI. The use of INVERSE-ARP rather than explicit configuration would obviously save time and simplify the setup and management if you had multiple sites and each site had multiple PVCs.

FROM THE CLASSROOM

Addresses and Connection Identifiers

At this point in the ICRC course it would be time to do a Frame Relay lab exercise so you could apply what you have learned about this popular WAN service. This is also where I would learn how well or how badly I had gotten the key points across (or who was playing solitaire while I was explaining about DLCIs). The thing that causes the most trouble for students in configuring Frame Relay is understanding the DLCI and what it actually represents.

As the name implies, the Data-Link Connection Identifier is a number used to identify a particular permanent virtual circuit (PVC) connection to a Frame Relay switch. It is not an address. The DLCI is often said to be "locally significant" between the switch and the router. What that means to you when you configure your router for Frame Relay service is that you don't need to worry about the DLCI at the other end of the PVC. It may be the same, or it may be different; it doesn't matter. The most common mistake students make in the Frame Relay lab is to try to figure out what the DLCI is at the destination and try to put the remote DLCI into their local router configuration. A look at what happens inside the Frame Relay "cloud" might be helpful in understanding why that won't work.

The Frame Relay service provider will give you an access line (a T-1, for example) that connects your site to a switch providing an access point into the provider's "cloud." You may have several destinations (let's say Denver, Chicago, and Atlanta) to be reached via the same access line. This capability is what has made Frame Relay such a popular service. The provider will configure a PVC through his network to each of these locations. The provider will assign a different DLCI for each PVC. If you have configured your router correctly, the DLCI for the PVC to Atlanta will be placed inside the frame header for all the traffic destined for Atlanta as it leaves your router. Likewise, the DLCIs for Chicago and Denver will be placed inside the frame headers encapsulating the traffic destined for those locations. Traffic leaving your router for each of three destinations is sharing the same interface and access line, and the only way the provider's switch can sort out one destination's traffic from another's is by inspecting the DLCI in the frame header. The DLCI tells the provider's switch which PVC to use for that traffic. The switch your router is connected to doesn't know about DLCIs anywhere else in the network. If you try to configure the remote DLCI on your local router, the switch

FROM THE CLASSROOM

wouldn't know what to do with that traffic, because it only knows about its locally configured DLCIs.

Once the traffic gets inside the cloud it may get a totally different identifier, or it may even be converted to ATM cells. In any case, the DLCI it had when it entered the first switch is no longer being used because WAN switches have their own conventions for identifying PVCs. When the traffic gets to the destination switch, though, it will be converted back to Frame Relay (if necessary) for transmission to the destination router, and it will be given a DLCI that identifies the same PVC, but this time between the destination router and its access switch. Even though this DLCI identifies the same PVC, the DLCI may be a different number at this destination end of the circuit.

Just to confuse the issue a little more, some providers now offer a feature called *global addressing* for their Frame Relay service. Don't be fooled by this terminology. With global addressing, the provider will establish consistent DLCIs for your organization across his network for each of your PVC destinations. For example, let's say you have PVCs between Houston and Atlanta, between Chicago and Atlanta, and between Denver and Atlanta. The DLCIs at Houston, Chicago and Denver that identify PVCs with an Atlanta destination will all use exactly the same number. This makes it appear that the DLCI has become an address, because every router in your network with a PVC to Atlanta will use the same DLCI number to refer to that PVC. The DLCIs are still locally significant, and the switches and routers still use them in the same way when you have global addressing. The only difference is in the way the numbers have been assigned.

—*By Pamela Forsyth, CCIE, CCSI, CNX*

CERTIFICATION OBJECTIVE 10.04

Configuring ATM

At first glance ATM seems very close to Frame Relay. Using switching and multiplexing technologies, virtual circuits, and dynamic bandwidth allocation, it is obvious that ATM was at least based on the foundations of Frame Relay. Where Frame Relay ends as an excellent WAN technology, ATM continues to the LAN. ATM blurs the lines between LAN and WAN technologies, creating for the first time a viable all-in-one solution.

One key difference between ATM and Frame Relay is the guarantee of delivery. Earlier we discussed how Frame Relay was a layer-2 technology that relied on the encapsulated layer-3 protocol for error-recovery. ATM differs in that, depending on the transmission, it has the capability to provide a guaranteed delivery at a specific rate.

ATM's packet sizes are created at a fixed length, instead of varying like Frame Relay and X.25. As shown in Figure 10-5, the ATM cell is 53 bytes long and is referred to as a cell. A five-byte header contains the address information and other fields of information used to route the cell through the network. After the header comes a 48-byte information field called a payload. Because of this fixed length, ATM can predict and control the number of packets, to control bandwidth utilization.

Having a cell of a fixed length also means that buffers can be designed at a set length, thereby allowing hardware switching. Using switching technology in hardware rather than in software tables helps minimize latency for time-critical data such as video and sound.

One of the reasons ATM is so fast is a result of its use of virtual channels and virtual paths to route traffic through the network. By implementing virtual channel connections (VCC), the routes to be used by the ATM routing device are determined before data is even transferred. Using this method, the transfer of data does not require complex routing decisions to be made in real time through software-based routing tables. Routing decisions are made in the hardware, thereby minimizing latency in data transfer.

As I just explained, the VCC is an identification for the path that data will travel over. To be more specific the VCC is an index determined by the combination of a one-byte virtual path identifier (VPI) and a two-byte virtual channel identifier (VCI). The VPI can be thought of as a larger group that contains either multiple VCIs or just one single VCI. In the vast majority of the cases, the VPI will be equal to 0, which is its default. The

FIGURE 10-5

The ATM cell

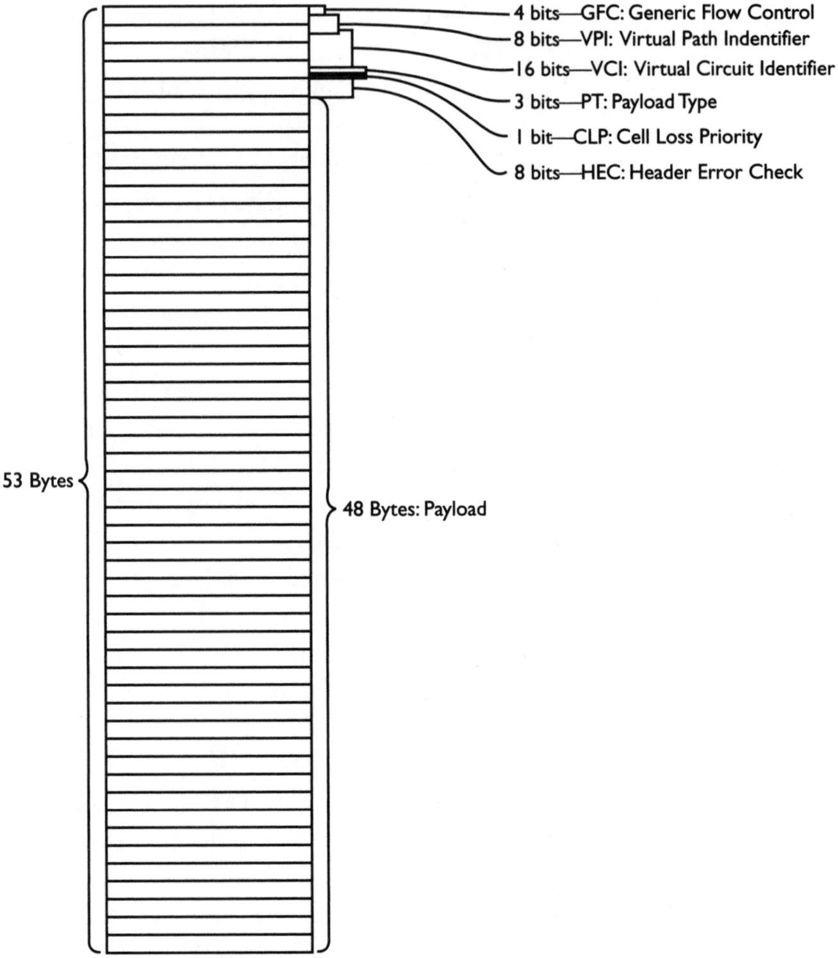

4 bits—GFC: Generic Flow Control
8 bits—VPI: Virtual Path Indentifier
16 bits—VCI: Virtual Circuit Identifier
3 bits—PT: Payload Type
1 bit—CLP: Cell Loss Priority
8 bits—HEC: Header Error Check
53 Bytes
48 Bytes: Payload

FIGURE 10-6

Virtual path identifiers contain virtual channel identifiers

VCI 78
VCI 37
VCI 91
VPI 0
VCI 23
VCI 37
VCI 42
VCI 41
VPI 1
VCI 44

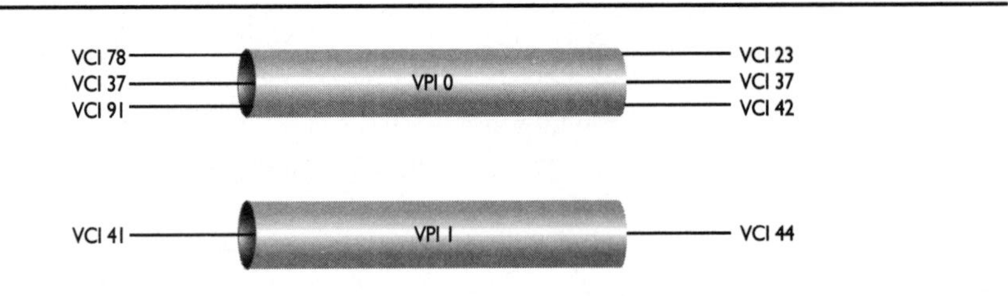

VCI identifies the individual circuit within the larger VPI. Figure 10-6 gives a visual representation of how the VPI and VCI could relate between two switches.

The VPI and VCI numbers in ATM are similar to the DLCI number found in Frame Relay, in that they only have relevance locally. In this case "locally" refers to a segment, which can be either between a host and a switch, or between two switches. Even though two switches might recognize the VCC by different numbers, it is still the same circuit.

Also just like in Frame Relay, virtual circuits can be categorized into two groups: permanent virtual circuits and switched virtual circuits. A permanent virtual circuit is a connection between end points that is not dynamically established or removed. If you'll recall, PVC connections are manually implemented and manually released. Implementation in an ATM network is typically found at the WAN level. A switched virtual circuit is a connection that is dynamically established and released. It is most often found at the LAN level, all the way to the desktop.

ATM is often referred to as a shared-media LAN. The one characteristic of shared-media LANs that is fairly obvious is that with each user you add, less is available for everybody else. Hosts must contend for access to the transmission medium, since in a shared-media LAN, the network is available to only one user at a time.

ATM LANs can operate over several different types of media. Using a special piece of hardware, ATM can run at 155 Mbps over Category 5 twisted pair. And while this is the most widely adapted configuration to the desktop, ATM also has the capability to run at 25 Mbps over two pairs of Category 3 or 4 cable. Finally, for higher ATM speeds and distances of more than 100 meters, fiber-optic cable is required. Over fiber, ATM can run up to 622 Mbps.

Implementation of ATM can occur by one of two methods. The first method applies specifically to the routing of IP over ATM. The Internet Engineering Task Force (IETF) has adopted this support and defined a Request For Comment (RFC) 1577 on *Classical IP and ARP over ATM.* Cisco supports RFC 1577 in the Cisco 4000, 7000, and 7500 router families.

The second method for data transfer across an ATM network is through something called LANE technology. LANE is a layer-2 bridging protocol that takes an ATM network, which is connection-oriented, and modifies it to look and behave like a shared connectionless Ethernet or Token Ring LAN segment. Since it acts as a layer-2 service, LANE can handle not only routable protocols such as TCP/IP and IPX, but also non-routable protocols such as NetBIOS and SNA.

Now that you have a pretty good background on ATM, here is a sample configuration:

```
Interface atm1
Ip address 10.10.10.1 255.255.255.0
Atm pvc 1 0 32 aal5mux ip
Atm pvc 2 0 45 aal5mux ip
Map-group samplegroup
!
Map-list samplegroup
Ip 10.10.10.5 atm-vc 1
Ip 10.10.10.6 atm-vc 2 broadcast
```

Each of the ATM PVC statements creates PVCs on the interface. The first number is the VCD, the second is the VPI, and the third is the VCI. One thing to note is that either the VPI or the VCI can be 0, but not both. The last argument lists the adaptation layer and encapsulation type. When aal5mux is chosen, the following statement must specify DecNET, IP, Novell, Vines, or XNS as the protocol being used.

The MAP-GROUP command assigns a map-list to the interface. The MAP-LIST command defines an arbitrary name to the subsequent group that will be defined. The list is defined with the IP statements, specifying the IP address to map to each VCD. If you will recall, ATM does not directly do broadcasts, but it can pseudo-broadcast by replicating each broadcast packet across each VC that is set up to receive them, with the broadcast argument at the end.

CERTIFICATION OBJECTIVE 10.05

Configuring PPP and Multilink PPP

The Point-to-Point Protocol (PPP) is described in RFCs 1661 and 1332. What PPP does is encapsulate network layer protocol information over point-to-point links. PPP can be configured on the following types of physical interfaces.

- ISDN
- Asynchronous serial
- Synchronous serial
- HSSI

Since PPP encapsulation is bound to physical interfaces, PPP can also be set up on calls placed by the dialer interfaces that use the physical interfaces. The current implementation of PPP supports:

- Authentication using CHAP or PAP
- The binding of multiple protocols over one link
- Dynamic address assignment
- Both synchronous and asynchronous communication

We will look at each of these in detail later in this section. We will not address PPP encapsulation across synchronous connections directly, since the configuration of PPP itself is the same. You should be able to tell which parts only apply to async connections.

PPP Configurations

The first step in establishing a PPP connection is the authentication process. Authentication using Password Authentication Protocol (PAP) is a step better than nothing, but is in no way a secure method. In a PAP negotiation, the remote router attempting to connect to the local router or access server is required to send an authentication request. If the username and password specified are correct, the Cisco IOS software sends an authentication acknowledgment.

The way Challenge Handshake Authentication Protocol (CHAP) works is, when a remote device such as a router wishes to make a connection with a local device, the local router or access server sends a CHAP packet to the remote device. What this CHAP packet does is request or "challenge" the remote device to respond. The challenge packet consists of an ID, a random number, and the host name of the local router. The required response contains an encrypted version of the ID, a one-way encrypted password, the random number, and either the host name of the remote device or the name of the user on the remote device.

After the local device receives the response, it verifies the secret by performing the same one-way encryption on its password and compares the results. If they match, it then looks up the remote device's host name or username. Since the password is transmitted by this encrypted method, it is never sent in clear text. These CHAP transactions only occur when the link is first established. The local router or access server does not initiate a request for a password for the duration of the call. The following listing outlines the beginning steps to establishing a PPP connection.

```
Interface serial0
Encapsulation PPP
PPP authentication {CHAP | PAP} {if-needed}
```

The majority of this first part is pretty self-explanatory. You first enter which interface you are binding the information to, which in this case is serial 0. You then specify to encapsulate PPP, followed by the authentication method. The IF-NEEDED argument is used in TACACS and XTACACS configurations, whereby PPP or CHAP authentication is not performed if the user has already provided authentication. It would then be followed with the name of a list of TACACS authentication methods to use. The lists are created with the AAA AUTHENTICATION PPP command. One thing to note is that the if-needed option is only available on asynchronous interfaces.

The next step in configuring PPP is defining which network protocol(s) to encapsulate. Generally you have the choice of IPCP and IPXCP. As you can probably guess from their names, IPCP is for IP traffic and IPXCP is for IPX traffic. It is possible, however, to provide support for both simultaneously across the same session. Each layer-3 protocol negotiates the specifics for its own communication independently. This process is the same as with the other WAN technologies we've already discussed. For instance, in an IP environment you can go with either IP classless or static assigned addresses. IP addresses can also be assigned dynamically in the PPP authentication process.

As you probably already know, either hardware or software can be used to control the flow for asynchronous communications. Hardware flow relies on pin signaling like the data set ready (DSR) or the data terminal ready (DTR) pins. Software flow control uses specific characters sent during the transmission to signal starts and stops. The problem with this is that there is always the chance that a string to be transmitted across could be the same as that of a flow control command. This is where asynchronous control character maps (ACCMs) come into play. An ACCM tells the port to ignore specified control characters within the data stream. In order for an asynchronous port to know to ignore XON/XOFF (the software control), the hexadecimal number A0000 must be passed. If, however, the router at the other end of the connection does not support ACCM negotiation, the port will be forced to use FFFFFFFF. If this is your situation, you can easily set the ACCM manually with the following command:

```
Ppp accm match 000a0000
```

Another configuration issue to address is the DTE rate. The DTE rate is the speed at which a router sends information to the modem. The modem, in turn, must decompress the data it receives before it can be sent to the router. If the amount of decompressed data is larger than the DTE rate, then data will bottleneck and slow down. For example, let's say we set the DTE to 38400.

```
Line 1
Rxpseed 38400
Txspeed 38400
```

Now, if our connecting modems are capable of establishing 28.8 connections, data will flow to the modem at 38400, but the modem will not allow more than 28.8 to flow across the line. This is where compression comes in. Using compression schemes such as V.42bis, throughput can be increased by a factor of four.

In order to control the amount of buffered packets held before the router starts dropping them, Cisco IOS has the HOLD-QUEUE command. The following commands increase the amount to 100 for both incoming and outgoing.

```
Hold-queue 100 in
Hold-queue 100 out
```

PPP also supports link quality monitoring (LQM). LQM will do just as it says. It monitors the quality of the link, and if the quality drops below a pre-configured percentage, the router shuts down the link. LQM is enabled for both the incoming and outgoing directions. The quality is calculated by comparing the total number of bytes sent with the total number of bytes received by each device each direction. When LQM is enabled link quality reports (LQRs) are sent every keepalive period, and in fact are sent instead of the normal keepalives. To setup LQM, you enter the command PPP QUALITY *percentage*, where *percentage* is a number from 1 to 100 that quality should not drop below.

One thing you need to decide on is whether or not to use the Cisco IOS compression. Compression reduces the size of a PPP frame via lossless data compression. The compression algorithm typically used is the RAND predictor algorithm, which uses a compression dictionary to predict the next character in the frame. In the Cisco 7000 series only, another compression alternative is available: hardware and distributed compression. Whether or not this it is available in your 7000 depends on the interface processor and compression service adapter hardware installed in the router.

It is Cisco's recommendation that you disable software compression if the router CPU load exceeds 65 percent. To view the CPU load, use the command SHOW PROCESS CPU in EXEC mode.

Also, if the majority of your traffic is already compressed files, do not use compression. Compression is enabled with the PPP predictor command:

```
PPP predictor {compress | stac}
```

Another form of compression is TCP header compression, also known as Van Jacobsen header compression. You will almost always use this form of compression in asynchronous modes. Obviously, TCP headers aren't a large percentage of the packets sent, but in asynchronous communication, every little bit of bandwidth savings helps.

```
Ip tcp header-compression on
```

Configuring Multilink PPP

Multilink Point-to-Point Protocol (PPP), according to RFC 1717, provides the following functionality:

- Load balancing over multiple WAN links
- Packet fragmentation with proper sequencing in the resassembly
- Load calculations on both inbound and outbound traffic

We will be addressing Cisco's conformation to the packet fragmentation and sequencing division of this standard. What Multilink PPP (MLP) does is allow packets to be fragmented and sent at the same time over multiple point-to-point links to the same destination. The multiple links needed are established in response to a dialer load threshold that is defined. The load can be calculated on either the inbound or outbound traffic needed between the sites. In other words, Multilink PPP provides the capability of splitting and recombining packets to a single destination across one logical pipe. This concept is similar to the combing of VCIs to form VPIs in ATM networks. Multilink PPP is able to provide bandwidth on demand and reduce latency across your WAN.

Multilink PPP can work over single or multiple interfaces of the following types:

- Asynchronous serial interfaces
- Basic Rate Interfaces (BRIs)
- Primary Rate Interfaces (PRIs)

Each interface must be configured to support both dial-on-demand routing (DDR) and PPP encapsulation. A sample configuration of the multilink portion of a PPP connection is as follows:

```
Interface dialer 100
No ip address
Encapsulation ppp
Dialer in-band
Dialer load-threshold load [inbound | outbound | either]
Ppp multilink
```

The first command assigns a number from 0 to 255 to the dialer rotary group. I've chosen not to use an IP address here, but this option is available if your situation requires it. The next two statements enable PPP encapsulation and the DDR functionality for the interface. The DIALER LOAD-THRESHOLD command sets the maximum threshold before another call is placed. This number is between 1 and 255, and is required. The last argument is optional, with the EITHER argument meaning that the calculated load is the maximum of the inbound and the outbound load. Finally, the last command enables the multilink functionality.

QUESTIONS AND ANSWERS

I need an all-in-one solution for my new LAN/WAN. Cost isn't really an issue.	ATM would be an excellent solution, since it can travel over fiber and twisted pair.
My company needs a new inexpensive solution for Internet connectivity. We have found that we need more bandwidth than an ISDN BRI interface can provide.	Try implementing Multilink PPP over two or more ISDN lines.
The average bandwidth required by my company has increased over the past six months. We have a shared T-1 line, and don't have the extra money to get our own dedicated.	Contact your ISP and have your committed information rate (CIR) increased to a little above your average.
We want to run classical IP over ATM. Which Cisco router would be best for a medium-sized business?	Classical IP is based on RFC 1577 and is supported in the 4000, 7000, and 7500 families. Depending on your budget, any of the three would be an excellent choice.
I need a secure method of connection and authentication for my point-to-point site. I am worried about somebody "listening" in on the line and getting access passwords. What should I use?	Use PPP encapsulation across the line with CHAP authentication. CHAP is much more secure than PAP, since passwords are never sent.
We are using software-based flow control, but we are having problems receiving the data correctly. What should we look at for possible problems?	Some of your data might contain the strings that are used for signaling a DSR or a DTR. Either implementation of hardware flow control or ACCMs would be a good place to start.

CERTIFICATION SUMMARY

ISDN is the digital equivalent to the analog phone line. It is comprised of multiple 64Kb bearer (B) channels and one data (D) channel that is either 16Kb or 64Kb in length. ISDN is ordered as either Basic Rate Interface (BRI) or Primary Rate Interface (PRI). ISDN BRI is typically configured as dial-on-demand routing (DDR) and ISDN PRI is typically used for RAS, since it can provide 23 ports for dial-in.

X.25 is a packet-switched technology that operates as permanent virtual circuit. X.25 has built-in error correction and flow control, thereby providing a guaranteed delivery. X.25 relies on the layer-2 protocol HDLC LAPB to transmit the data across the network. It compensates for latency in the network by using windowing techniques.

Frame Relay is an encapsulation method that operates at layer 2 on top of practically any serial interface. Frame Relay is a packet-switching technology that multiplexes multiple logical data streams onto one physical link. It uses DLCI numbers as a local reference for which pipe leads to which remote IP address. For ease of configuration, LMI extensions provide inverse ARP to automatically determine the protocol address of the remote device.

ATM is a lot like Frame Relay except that it doesn't provide the guaranteed delivery. ATM's packets are 53 bytes in length, and are routed through something called virtual channel connections (VCC). ATM can operate at 622 Mbps over fiber, 155 Mbps over Category 5, and 25 Mbps over two pairs of Category 3 or 4 cable.

PPP encapsulates network layer protocol over point-to-point links. Authentication can be performed with either CHAP or PAP. CHAP authentication is based on a random number and a password, thereby making it the more secure method. PPP also supports link quality monitoring (LQM) to monitor the quality of the link. Multilink PPP allows packets to be fragmented across multiple connections, and reassembles them into the proper sequence at the remote end.

TWO-MINUTE DRILL

- ISDN is the digital equivalent to the analog phone line. The phone companies developed it in an effort to deliver not only voice but also high-speed data at a reasonable price, and across the already installed copper wires.
- ISDN is ordered as either Basic Rate Interface (BRI) or Primary Rate Interface (PRI).
- BRI is typically configured as a type of dial-on-demand routing (DDR). A DDR link looks the same to IP, or to any other network protocol for that matter—as a serial link that is only there when in use.
- Implementation of ISDN PRI loses the benefit of using existing copper. It is delivered via a T-1 circuit and is comprised of 23 B channels and one 64Kb D channel. ISDN uses directory numbers and service profile identifiers (SPIDs).
- X.25 is similar to Frame Relay in that it is a packet-switched technology that typically operates as permanent virtual circuit (PVC).
- X.25 encompasses the first three layers of the OSI model. On each end of an X.25 connection, along the physical layer of the OSI model, is a data terminal equipment (DTE) device and a data circuit-terminating equipment (DCE) device.
- Circuits exist as one of two types: SVC or PVC.
- SVCs (switched virtual circuits) are a lot like telephone calls—a connection is established, data is transferred, and then the connection is terminated.
- PVCs (permanent virtual circuits) are closer to a leased line idea, in that their connection is always present.
- If you want to view the status of your X.25 connections, you can use the SHOW X25 command.
- Frame Relay is not a certain type of interface, rather it is an encapsulation method that operates at layer 2 and runs on top of nearly any serial interface.

- LMI provides Frame Relay with many new features, with one of the most important being the use of inverse ARP to automatically determine the protocol address of the device on the remote end of a DLCI.
- Configuring Frame Relay on a Cisco router includes the mapping of IP addresses to DLCIs and telling the router which virtual circuits are connected.
- ATM blurs the lines between LAN and WAN technologies, creating for the first time a viable all-in-one solution.
- One key difference between ATM and Frame Relay is the guarantee of delivery.
- One of the reasons ATM is so fast is a result of its use of virtual channels and virtual paths to route traffic through the network.
- The VPI and VCI numbers in ATM are similar to the DLCI number found in Frame Relay, in that they only have relevance locally.
- ATM LANs can operate over several different types of media.
- PPP encapsulates network layer protocol information over point-to-point links.
- The first step in establishing a PPP connection is the authentication process. Authentication using Password Authentication Protocol (PAP) is a step better than nothing, but is in no way a secure method.
- Multilink Point-to-Point Protocol (PPP), according to RFC 1717, provides the following functionality:
  - Load balancing over multiple WAN links
  - Packet fragmentation with proper sequencing in the resassembly
  - Load calculations on both inbound and outbound traffic

SELF TEST

The following questions will help you measure your understanding of the material presented in this chapter. Read all the choices carefully, as there may be more than one correct answer. Choose all correct answers for each question.

1. What does DDR stand for?
   A. Dial-up direct request
   B. Direct dial relocation number
   C. Dial-on-demand request
   D. Dial-on-demand routing
2. Which of the following is required to configure an ISDN BRI interface?
   A. SPID
   B. LUN
   C. PVC number
   D. DLCI
3. Which of the following statements regarding ISDN PRI is true?
   A. ISDN PRI runs on existing copper
   B. ISDN PRI can basically run at the same speed as a T-1
   C. Because ISDN PRI uses SVCs and PVCs, it makes it an excellent solution to the desktop
   D. It is comprised of two B channels and 23 D channels
4. Which layer(s) of the OSI model does X.25 cover?
   A. 1 and 2
   B. 1, 2, and 3
   C. 2 and 3
   D. 2, 3, and 4
5. Which of these is not a characteristic of PVCs?
   A. They must each be set up manually
   B. They are similar to a leased line
   C. The connections can be established very quickly when the bandwidth is needed
   D. They require a DTE and a DCE to operate
6. A X.25 connection deals with which of the following technology pieces?
   A. LCN
   B. LCI
   C. NUA
   D. All of the above
7. What is contained within an LAPB frame?
   A. LUN information
   B. X.25 packet
   C. Flow control and error-recovery information
   D. QLLC packet for frame window configuration
8. What does the following command accomplish?
   X25 ROUTE 2468013579 INTERFACE SERIAL0

A. Routes all information from 2468013579 through serial 0
B. Denies traffic bound for 2468013579 from passing through serial 0
C. Adds a manual route statement to send IP datagrams through serial 0
D. Routes all information destined for 2468013579 through serial 0

9. Which of the following arguments for the SHOW X.25 command displays a one-to-one mapping of the local and remote IP addresses?

A. MAP
B. ROUTE
C. VC
D. REMOTE-RED

10. Which of the following technologies are associated with Frame Relay?

A. TDM
B. LMI
C. Inverse ARP
D. CIR

11. How would you reference sub-interface 1 on Serial 0 with the Cisco IOS?

A. Serial0.1
B. Serial 0 sub 1
C. Serial.0.sub.1
D. Serial.0.0

12. What is the purpose of Inverse ARP?

A. Autodiscovers DLCI numbers
B. Automatically configures PVCs
C. Gets all connected routers' MAC addresses
D. Builds a table of the IP address

13. Which statement about ATM packets is false?

A. It is 56 bytes long
B. Contains a 5-byte header
C. The information field is 48 bytes long
D. Because of its fixed length, it can control bandwidth utilization.

14. Which of these statements regarding VCI and VPI are true?

A. VPI identifies a larger group than VCI
B. VCI is a unit
C. Both VPI and VCI only have significance locally
D. A VCC contains BOTH VPI and VCI

15. What is the correct speed for ATM?

A. 155 Mbps
B. 25 Mbps
C. 622 Mbps
D. None of the above

16. Which of the following is a good, accurate description of LANE?

A. Layer-3 routing protocol
B. Layer-2 bridging protocol
C. Layer-3 bridging protocol
D. Layer-2 routing protocol

17. Which command maps a list of IP addresses to an ATM interface?

   A. MAP-LIST
   B. Map-ID
   C. Map-Group
   D. Map-IPList

18. Which of the following are supported by PPP?

   A. CHAP/PAP
   B. Binding of multiple protocols over one link
   C. Dynamic address assignment
   D. Synchronous communication

19. Which syntax listed below is correct if you want to authenticate with CHAP?

   A. PPP authentication CHAP
   B. PPP authentication CHAP/PAP
   C. Authentication CHAP
   D. Authentication CHAP/PAP

20. Of what benefit is Multilink PPP?

   A. Provides load balancing
   B. Re-assembles fragmented packets
   C. Combines multiple successive SLIP connections and appears as one connection
   D. Provides load calculations on both inbound and outbound traffic

21. Basic Rate Interface in ISDN has:

   A. One B channel and one D channel
   B. 23 B channels and one D channel
   C. Two B channels and one D channel
   D. Two D channels and one B channel

22. In the U.S., an ISDN service provider may use:

   A. 5ESS switch
   B. 4ESS switch
   C. MS-100 switch
   D. All of the above

23. Primary Rate Interface in ISDN has:

   A. One B channels and two D channels
   B. Two B channels and one D channel
   C. One B channel and 23 D channels
   D. 23 B channels and one D channel

24. Which statement is true of X.25?

   A. It is a cell-based technology
   B. It is a packet-based technology
   C. It supports only PVC

25. One of the parameters required for establishing an ISDN connection is:

   A. SAPI (Service Access Port Identifier)
   B. DN (directory number)
   C. SVC number
   D. CKTID (CircuitID)

26. Which statement is true of the logical channel number (LCN) in X.25?

   A. It is unique throughout the X.25 network

B. It has local significance only

C. It identifies a physical link to DTE

D. It is used by DTE

27. Maximum packet size in X.25 packet can be:

    A. 64 bytes

    B. 128 bytes

    C. 4096 bytes

    D. 2048 bytes

28. In a Frame Relay network, the DLCI:

    A. Identifies a pipe which leads to a layer-2 protocol address

    B. Identifies a pipe which leads to a layer-3 protocol address

    C. Is a network-wide identifier

    D. May not change on each physical link

29. Local Management Interface (LMI) in Frame Relay provides:

    A. The same functionality as DLCI alone

    B. Less functionality than DLCI alone

    C. Greater functionality than DLCI alone

    D. None of the above

30. In Frame Relay, which one of the following allows a station to accept or reject a frame?

    A. Frame Number

    B. DLCI

    C. LMI

    D. Frame Check Sequence (FCS)

31. The optional argument that can be supplied at the end of ENCAPSULATION command in configuring a Frame Relay service is:

    A. IETF

    B. MAP

    C. INT

    D. ROUTE

32. In the configuration command FRAME RELAY MAP IP 15.20.21.2 5 BROADCAST, number 5 represents:

    A. Destination node

    B. Source node

    C. DLCI pipe

    D. LCN

33. How many allowable standards can the LMI type in a command support?

    A. one

    B. three

    C. five

    D. four

34. ATM guarantees which of the following that Frame Relay does not?

    A. Multicasting

    B. Delivery

    C. Error checking

    D. Flow control

35. ATM does direct broadcast.

    A. True

    B. False

36. The length of a header in an ATM cell is:

    A. Three bytes
    B. Five bytes

37. For speeds of 622 Mbps or higher, the physical medium in ATM technology is generally:

    A. Category 5 cable
    B. Four bytes
    C. Two bytes
    D. Category 3 cable
    E. Optical fiber
    F. All of the above

38. LANE can handle only non-routable protocols.

    A. True
    B. False

39. In ATM, which of the following statements is false?

    A. VPI can be non-zero
    B. Both VPI and VCI can be non-zero
    C. VCI can be non-zero
    D. VPI and VCI both can be zero

40. The configuration command ROUTER(CONFIG-LINE)#RXSPEED 38400 sets:

    A. Transmit DTE rate
    B. Transmit DCE rate
    C. Receive DTE rate
    D. Transmit DTE rate

41. Which of the following commands is used to set up link quality monitoring (LQM) in PPP?

    A. HOLD-QUEUE
    B. PPP QUALITY
    C. SHOW PROCESS CPU
    D. PPP PREDICTOR

42. What does a committed information rate (CIR) mean?

    A. A user is allowed to transmit data only at a fixed rate
    B. A user is guaranteed that a transmission rate will not fall below a certain threshold value
    C. A maximum rate at which a user can transmit data
    D. A fixed cost to the customer for transmission of data

43. In Challenge Handshake Authentication Protocol (CHAP):

    A. The challenge packet contains an encrypted password
    B. The challenge is sent from the remote device to the central control router
    C. The challenge is sent from the central control router to the remote device
    D. The possibility of intrusion by an outsider is greater than in the Password Authentication Protocol (PAP)

44. Which of the following tells the port in an asynchronous communication in PPP to ignore specified control characters in the data stream?

    A. DSR

    B. DTR

    C. XOFF

    D. ACCM

45. In the command HOLD-QUEUE 100, the number 100 means:

    A. 100 incoming packets will be held in queue before the interface starts dropping packets

    B. 100 outgoing packets will be held in queue before the interface starts dropping packets

    C. 100 incoming and 100 outgoing packets will be held in queue before the interface starts dropping packets

    D. None of the above

11

Virtual Local Area Networking (VLAN)

CERTIFICATION OBJECTIVES

11.01 Switching and VLANs

11.02 Spanning-Tree Protocol and VLANs

11.03 Default VLAN Configuration

11.04 Configuring a VLAN Across a Domain

11.05 Grouping Switch Ports to VLANs

Imagine you are sitting at your desk and the Chief Information Officer (CIO) startles you with the latest article in the trade magazines on network design. "I just read this great article about how VLANs provide flexibility, improve performance, and reduce management costs! How can we implement VLANs in our network?" the CIO asks. Suddenly, the CIO is gone, leaving you with the task of integrating VLANs into your existing network.

You've probably heard the term VLAN and wondered, what are they and how can I use them? The term VLAN is short for virtual local-area network and is most commonly associated with switches. Using VLANs in your network design can help you solve business and technical needs, but they should be used with discretion. Creating too many VLANs in your network design can cause an administrative nightmare. If your organization is going to invest in a Layer 2 switch that supports VLANs, take advantage of the switching technology. Layer 2 switches provide wire-speed forwarding of frames, and do not incur the latency that traditional software-based routers do. If you are going to build a switched network, try to switch using Layer 2 as much as possible, and route using Layer 3 when necessary. There are many new products appearing in the networking market that provide Layer 3 routing of frames at Layer 2 speeds, but they are beyond the scope of this chapter.

It is important to fully understand your business and technical requirements when deciding how to use VLANs. Remember that each VLAN you create essentially creates a Layer 3 network that must be routed, so unless your traffic is purely workgroup-based, you will always need a routing function in your network. The rapid growth of e-mail, intranets, and the Internet led to the rapid growth of *server farms.* Server farms can contain shared file, application, and database servers, usually grouped in a dedicated VLAN or VLANs, and require users to communicate across VLAN boundaries using a router. As a reminder, try to keep your design as simple and flexible as possible. Start simple first, then implement a more complex design if requirements can't be met with the existing design. Use VLANs to make your life easier, not more difficult.

In this chapter, we will review the benefits of VLANs and their close ties to switching. The configurations we use are based on the Cisco Catalyst 5500 platform.

CERTIFICATION OBJECTIVE 11.01

Switching and VLANs

The original switches did not provide the capability to create VLANs, since they were used simply to forward frames rapidly between devices. The market for switches grew quickly when shared media hubs could not keep pace with the growing demand for increased bandwidth due to client-server applications providing a graphical user interface (GUI).

The key difference between a switch and hub is how they handle frames. A hub receives frames on a port, then copies and transmits (repeats) the frame to all of its other ports. In this way, it is repeating the signal, basically extending the length of the network segment to all attached stations. A hub repeats all frames to all ports except the port the frame was received on: *unicast* frames (destined for a particular MAC address), *broadcast* frames, (destined for all MAC addresses on the local segment), and *multicast* frames (destined for a subset of devices on the segment). This does not scale well for larger numbers of users, since each workstation and server attached to the hub must examine each frame to determine whether it is addressed to its Layer 2 MAC address. The larger the network, the greater the number of frames the network interface card (NIC) must process, wasting valuable CPU cycles. Hubs are cheaper than switches, and they are sufficient for small workgroups and transmissions that are short and bursty in nature.

A frame switch handles frames intelligently—the switch reads the source MAC address of inbound frames and saves this information in its switching table. This table contains the MAC address and its associated port. The switch builds this table in volatile memory so it knows which MAC addresses are on each of its ports. The Catalyst switch learns these addresses by examining each frame as it is read into memory, adding new addresses to the switching table if not previously stored. In Cisco switches, this table is referred to as the CAM (content-addressable memory) table. This table is constantly updated and rebuilt every time the switch is powered on, and you can adjust the refresh timers higher or lower depending on your needs. Figure 11-1 shows the CAM table from a Catalyst 5000.

FIGURE 11-1

Cisco CAM table

```
Cat5500> show cam dynamic
VLAN  Destination MAC     Destination Ports or VCs
----  -----------------   ------------------------
1     00-60-2f-9d-a9-00   3/1
1     00-b0-2f-9d-b1-00   3/5
1     00-60-2f-86-ad-00   5/12
1     00-c0-0c-0a-bd-4b   4/10
Cat5500>
```

In this example, the VLAN column refers to the VLAN number the destination port belongs to. The Destination MAC column refers to the MAC address learned from the port. Remember that multiple MAC addresses can be associated with the same port, so verify the number of MAC addresses your switch can support. The Destination Ports column describes which port the MAC address was learned from.

Next, the switch examines the destination MAC address of outbound frames and immediately looks in the switching table. If the switch finds the matching address, it copies the frame only to that port. If it does not find the address, it copies the frame to all ports. Unicast frames are sent only to the necessary port(s), while multicast and broadcast frames are repeated to all ports.

Switching was introduced as a "new" technology that increased bandwidth and improved performance, but essentially, switches are high-density bridges with additional features. Switching is a term most commonly used to describe Layer 2 network devices that forward Ethernet and Token Ring frames based on the destination Media Access Control (MAC) address.

The two most common methods vendors use to forward traffic through switches are *cut-through* and *store and forward.*

Cut-through switches generally achieve lower port-to-port latency than store and forward because in this mode, the switch can begin forwarding a frame to its intended port(s) without waiting until it has received the complete incoming frame. The switch only has to read enough of the frame to identify the source and destination MAC addresses located near the beginning of Token Ring and Ethernet frames. Most cut-through switches start forwarding once the first 30 to 40 bytes of the frame header have been received.

Store and forward switches receive the entire frame before it is switched. This method incurs more latency but has more advantages. The capability to filter and manage and control traffic is a major benefit of this approach. In addition, runts and damaged frames are not propagated, since they are not valid frames. Switches must have memory buffers to read in and store the frames before making their switching decision, which increases the cost of the switch.

As switching technology improved and the market embraced switching as the new craze, VLANs began to appear. The easiest way to understand Virtual LANs is to compare them to physical LANs. A physical LAN can be a group of end stations, bounded by a router or routers, which share a common physical connection. A VLAN is a logical collection of end stations on the same Layer 2 (and Layer 3) segment, which communicate directly without a router. Traditionally, users in separate physical locations would need to communicate to other segments using a router. Switches with VLAN capabilities were initially implemented in the core of large campus networks, and for smaller workgroup networks. Initially, switching was deployed as needed, but it is now common to implement switching and VLANs to the desktop.

Each end station on a VLAN (and only those end stations) process broadcast traffic sent by other VLAN members. For example, workstations A, B, and C are connected to VLAN 1. VLAN 1 contains three Catalyst 5500 switches. Each switch is located on a different floor and connected via fiber, communicating via a trunking protocol. Workstation A is connected to switch A, workstation B is connected to switch B and workstation C is connected to switch C. If workstation A sends a broadcast frame, workstations B and C will receive the message, even though they are physically connected to different switches. Workstation D is connected to switch A, but defined to VLAN 2. When D sends a broadcast, workstation

A does not see the traffic, because even though they are on the same physical switch, they are not in the same virtual LAN, and the switch will not forward the traffic to A. Remember that VLANs operate at Layer 2, so communication among VLANs requires a Layer 3 routing decision. In addition, workstations B and C do not see broadcasts from D.

Virtual LANs (VLANs) offer the following primary benefits:

- Broadcast control
- Functional workgroups
- Enhanced security

Broadcast Control

Unlike traditional LANs bounded by a router/bridge interface, a VLAN can be viewed as a broadcast domain with logically configured boundaries. VLANs offer more freedom than traditional LANs. Previous designs were based on the physical limitations of hub-based networks; basically, the physical boundaries of a LAN segment were limited to the effective distance an electrical signal could travel from a hub port. Extending LAN segments beyond these effective distances required the use of a repeater, a device that strengthens and re-sends the signal. VLANs permit broadcast domains that are independent of physical location, the LAN media, the MAC type, and the transmission rates. Members can be located wherever they need to be rather than being forced to move to a specific location to connect to the LAN. VLANs increase network performance by containing broadcasts to a smaller and more manageable logical broadcast domain. In traditional switched environments that don't support VLANs, all broadcast packets go to each and every individual port. Using VLANs, all broadcasts are confined to a specific broadcast domain.

Functional Workgroups

The most fundamental benefit of VLAN technology is the capability to create workgroups based on function rather than on physical location or media. Traditionally, network administrators grouped users under the same functional department by physically moving users, their desktop, and servers into a common environment such as a shared LAN segment. All team members had to be physically connected to the same media to take advantage of the localized higher-speed server connection. VLANs allow administrators to create, group, and regroup LAN segments logically and instantaneously, without changing physical infrastructure and taking users and servers down. The ability to easily add, move, and change users to the network is a key benefit of VLANs.

Enhanced Security

VLANs also offer the added benefit of security. Users in a defined group are prevented from accessing another group's data, because each VLAN is a closed, logically defined group. Imagine a company in which the Accounting department, working on confidential financial statements, is spread across all three floors of a building. The Engineering and Marketing departments are spread across all three floors as well. Using VLANs, the Engineering and Marketing workgroups can be located on all three floors as members of two different VLANs, and the Accounting department can be members of a third VLAN that spans all three floors. Now the network traffic generated by Accounting will only be accessible to employees of that department, and the Engineering and Marketing teams will not be able to access Accounting's confidential data. Obviously, there are several other requirements to ensure complete security, but VLANs can be part of an overall network security strategy. Figure 11-2 illustrates how functional VLANs can span traditional physical boundaries.

Since VLANs are defined within the device, they can be quickly and easily modified at any time to add, delete, move, or change users as required.

VLANs can be assigned by:

- Port (most common)
- MAC address (very rare)
- User ID (very rare)
- Network address (rare due to growth of DHCP)

FIGURE 11-2 VLANs crossing physical boundaries

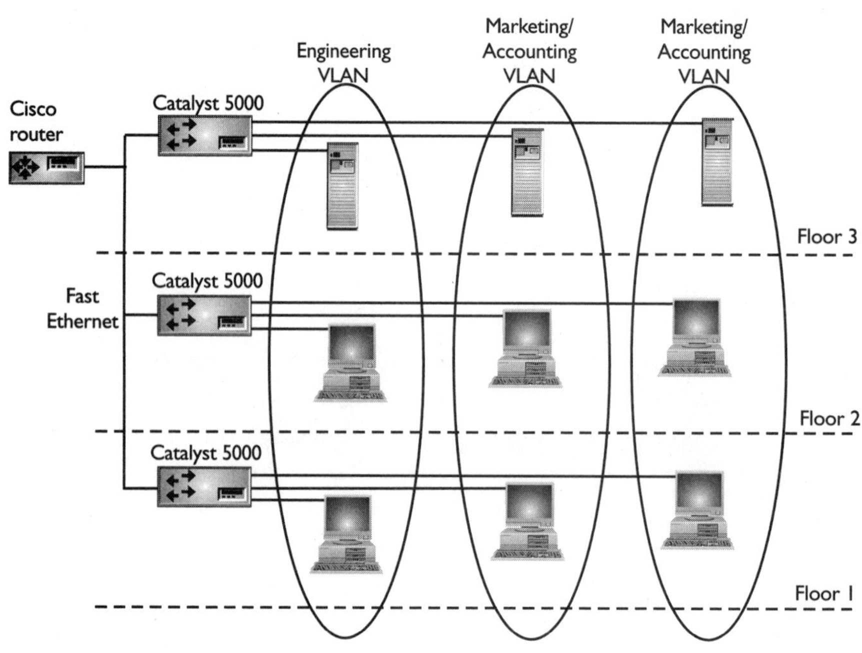

Port-based VLANs allow the assignment of switch ports to VLANs. Ports can be assigned individually, by groups, by entire row, and even across switches communicating via a trunking protocol. This is the simplest and most common method of VLAN assignment. It is common to implement port-based VLANs when assigning TCP/IP addresses to workstations using Dynamic Host Configuration Protocol (DHCP).

MAC address-based VLANs allow the user to participate in the same VLAN, even when the user moves from one location to another. This method requires the administrator to identify each workstation's MAC address and then configure this information into the switch. This method can be complex to troubleshoot if a user changes MAC addresses. Changes to any desktop require communication to the network administrator, which can be an administrative burden.

Network address-based VLANs allow the user to participate in the same VLAN, even when the user moves from one location to another. This method moves the VLAN associated with the workstation's Layer 3 address to each switch the user is connected to. This method can be useful in situations where security is important, and access is controlled to resources via access lists on routers. Thus, a user in the "secure" VLAN, can move to another building and still communicate to the same devices, because the Layer 3 address remains the same. Network address-based VLANs can be complex to troubleshoot.

CERTIFICATION OBJECTIVE 11.02

Spanning-Tree Protocol and VLANs

The Spanning-Tree Protocol allows redundant physical links in bridged networks, yet only one physical link forwards frames. The protocol places redundant physical connections to the same network segment in blocking mode. When there is a change in the topology to these links, the Spanning-Tree Protocol re-calculates which link will forward frames, and blocks the rest. There are two major methods of bridging, transparent and source-route. Spanning-Tree Protocol is used in transparent bridging environments to ensure a loop-free path to every network segment participating in the calculation, while also providing redundancy in the event of failure.

Transparent bridging is used primarily in Ethernet environments. It places the burden of determining the path from the source to the destination device on the bridges. Ethernet frames do not contain a Routing Information Field (RIF) like Token Ring frames, so devices simply send frames and assume that they will reach their destination. The process a bridge uses to forward frames is similar to the way Layer 2 switches operate. A transparent bridge examines the incoming frame and learns the destination MAC address. The bridge looks for this address in its bridging table; if it finds a match, it forwards the address out the corresponding port. If the MAC address is not found, it copies and forwards the frame out all connected ports except the port from which it came.

Source-route bridging is used in Token Ring environments. It places the responsibility of locating the destination device on the sending station. Token Ring devices send out a test frame to determine if the device is on the local ring. If no answer is received to the test frame, the device sends an explorer frame in the form of a broadcast. The broadcast is forwarded across the network by other bridges, with each bridge adding the ring number and bridge number it's connected to, until the frame reaches its final destination. The combination of ring and bridge numbers is contained in the RIF field. The destination device responds to the explorer frame, and the source device eventually receives the response frame. Communication now begins with each station using the RIF value appended to each frame. Source-route bridges forward frames based on this RIF and do not build a bridging table of MAC addresses and ports, since the end devices provide the source-to-destination information in the RIF.

For our discussion, we will examine the problems associated with loops and transparent bridging, since they are most prevalent today. Imagine two network segments, segment A and segment B with one workstation on each: workstation A and workstation B, respectively. Two transparent bridges are connected to both segment A and segment B, creating a loop in the network. Workstation A sends a broadcast frame for workstation B, and both bridges read the frame from their segment A interfaces and forward it out their segment B interfaces. Both bridges associate the address of workstation A with their segment A interfaces in their bridging table. The Ethernet frame shows the source address as workstation A and the destination address as a broadcast. After the bridges forward the frames to segment B, the frame still contains the same source and destination address, since bridges operate at Layer 2 and do not change the source address when forwarding frames. The frame is received by both bridges on their segment B interfaces, and the bridges correctly forward the broadcast frame back to segment A, since bridges forward broadcasts out all other ports. In addition, the bridges update their tables to associate the address of workstation A with their segment B interfaces. The bridges will continue to forward these broadcast frames over and over. This obviously will degrade performance on the network, since every device will have to process the frame over and over, wasting each device's CPU time, and consuming network bandwidth. This topology is illustrated in Figure 11-3.

This is a major reason the Spanning-Tree Protocol was developed—to eliminate loops in the network. The Spanning-Tree Protocol ensures this loop-free path by placing one of the bridge ports in "blocking mode," preventing the forwarding of packets. Note that the interface could be enabled in the event an active port in the network goes down. When there is a change in the topology of the network, the bridges re-calcuate the spanning tree by sending out Bridge Protocol Data Units (BPDUs). BPDUs

FIGURE 11-3

Redundant topology with loops

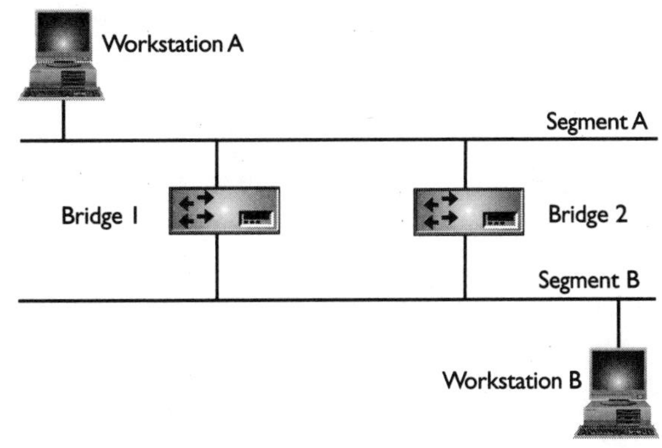

are exchanged between devices in a transparent bridging environment to determine which ports need to be placed in blocking mode.

Now that we understand the basics of spanning tree, how do they pertain to switches? Switches function identically to bridges, so each switch participates in the spanning-tree process unless it is disabled. You should use extreme caution if you choose to disable spanning tree on your switch, since it can cause serious problems. Switches ensure a loop-free topology by executing the spanning-tree algorithm (STA). The spanning-tree algorithm will enforce a loop-free topology for each VLAN configured on your switch. Thus, connecting any network devices other than servers and workstations could cause a loop in your network if the spanning-tree process is disabled. The major problem created by loops in the network is a broadcast storm. This network state is created when switches or bridges continue to forward broadcast frames out each port they are connected to; other switches and bridges connected to the same networks creating a loop will continue to forward the same broadcast frames back to the forwarding switch or bridge. This problem severely degrades network performance, since the network devices are constantly busy copying the broadcast frames to all of their other ports.

CERTIFICATION OBJECTIVE 11.03

Default VLAN Configuration

The Catalyst switch has several VLANs defined by default. VLAN 1 is defined, and all active ports are grouped in this VLAN. If you want to add more VLANs, you will need to create them using the SET VLAN command. VLAN 1 will appear using the name DEFAULT in any SHOW VLAN commands. In addition, VLANs 1002 – 1005 for FDDI and Token Ring are defined. You do not need to worry about removing these VLANs, since they are part of the default configuration. An example of the default configuration appears in Figure 11-4.

FIGURE 11-4 Showing VLANs on a Catalyst 5500

```
Cat5500> (enable) show vlan

VLAN Name                             Status    Mod/Ports, Vlans

----------------------------------------------------------------

1    default                          active    1/1-2

                                                3/1-24

                                                4/1-24

1002 fddi-default                     active

1003 token-ring-default               active

1004 fddinet-default                  active

1005 trnet-default                    active

VLAN Type  SAID       MTU   Parent RingNo BrdgNo Stp  BrdgMode Trans1 Trans2

---------------------------------------------------------------------

1    enet  100001     1500  -      -      -      -    -        0      0

1002 fddi  101002     1500  -      0x0    -      -    -        0      0

1003 trcrf 101003     1500  0      0x0    -      -    -        0      0

1004 fdnet 101004     1500  -      -      0x0    -             0      0

1005 trbrf 101005     1500  -      -      0x0    -             0      0

VLAN AREHops STEHops Backup CRF

---- ------- ------- ----------

1003 7       7       off

Cat5500> (enable)
```

CERTIFICATION OBJECTIVE 11.04

Configuring a VLAN Across a Domain

Any solid network design includes gathering the user requirements to determine the most efficient, simple, and logical use of network resources. Before creating VLANs on your switches, you should spend time creating a logical design of your network. Useful questions to ask include:

- How many users will be in each VLAN?
- Do VLANs need to span physical boundaries?
- How much control should be maintained over creation of new VLANs?

In order to exchange VLAN information between switches in your network, you will need to create trunk ports on your switches. A trunk port is any port or group of ports used to send VLAN information to other network devices connected and running a trunking protocol. A trunking protocol is the "language" that switches use to exchange VLAN information. Examples of trunking protocols include ISL and IEEE 802.1Q. Note that regular switch ports do not advertise VLAN information, but any ports can be configured to trunk VLAN information. You must activate trunking on the desired ports, as it is disabled by default. Trunk ports are ports dedicated solely to sending this VLAN information by a trunking protocol. Cisco switches commonly use the Inter-Switch Link (ISL) trunking protocol to provide the capability to communicate this information.

In order to automatically exchange VLAN information across trunk ports, you will need to configure Cisco's VLAN Trunk Protocol (VTP), which allows switches to send VLAN information in the form of advertisements to neighboring devices. The information transmitted includes the domain, the revision number, active VLANs, and other information. You will configure servers and optionally, clients. The advantage of using VTP is that you can control the adding, deleting, or changing of VLANs in your switch design. The disadvantage is unnecessary traffic sent over trunk ports to devices that may not need that information. Cisco switches provide the capability to limit the VLAN information sent across trunk ports using the pruning option. Using VTP, you can ensure that any changes to your VLAN design are propagated to all switches running VTP in the same domain. VTP sends VLAN information via trunk ports to a multicast address, but not over regular switch (non-trunk) ports.

The other option is to configure the switch for transparent mode, and manually configure each VLAN on every switch that will contain devices participating in that VLAN. This is an important decision in your network design. If your network will contain many switches, containing many VLANs spanning across multiple switches, VTP probably makes sense. If your network design will remain fairly static, and VLANs will not be added or changed from the initial design, transparent mode may work better. VTP is required to use Cisco's network management software, VLAN Director, to manage your switches. If administrative control is a concern, VTP can provide the solution. You have the option of setting a password on the VTP domain to control the changing of VLAN information in your network. In addition, by leaving the VTP server default option active on your core switches, you can control the update process. After configuring your VTP server switches, the rest of the switches in your network can be configured as clients, which can only receive VLAN information.

EXERCISE 11-1

Configuring VTP

1. Log in to the switch using the console port. If the switch is configured with an IP address and default route, you can Telnet.
2. Enter enable mode.
3. Define the VTP domain by typing **set vtp domain *name***.
4. Enable pruning (optional) by typing **set vtp pruning enable**.
5. Set a password (optional) by typing **set vtp password *password***.
6. Create the VLAN by typing **set vlan 2**.

Verify that you have configured VTP by using the SHOW VTP STATISTICS command, shown in Figure 11-5.

FIGURE 11-5 Showing VTP statistics on a Catalyst 5500

```
Cat5500> (enable) show vtp statistics
VTP statistics:
summary advts received          0
subset  advts received          0
request advts received          0
summary advts transmitted       3457
subset  advts transmitted       13
request advts transmitted       0
No of config revision errors    0
No of config digest errors      0


VTP pruning statistics:

Trunk     Join Transmitted  Join Received  Summary advts received from
                                           non-pruning-capable device
--------  ---------------  -------------  ---------------------------
 1/1-2    0                 0              0
Cat5500> (enable)
```

The output from the SHOW VTP DOMAIN command is shown in Figure 11-6. The Domain Name value is the name provided when you use the SET VTP DOMAIN <*name*> command. The local mode specifies server, client, or transparent mode. Servers can update VLAN information in a VTP domain; clients only receive VLAN information. The Vlan-Count field identifies the number of VLANs configured on this switch.

FIGURE 11-6 Showing VTP configuration on a Catalyst 5500

```
Cat5500> (enable) show vtp domain
Domain Name                      Domain Index VTP Version Local Mode  Password
-------------------------------- ------------ ----------- ----------- 
----------
Cisco                            1            2           server      -


Vlan-count Max-vlan-storage Config Revision Notifications
---------- ---------------- --------------- -------------
6          1023             4               disabled


Last Updater    V2 Mode  Pruning  PruneEligible on Vlans
--------------- -------- -------- -------------------------
172.16.21.252   disabled disabled 2-1000
Cat5500> (enable)
```

Another option when configuring VLANs is to use a friendly name when adding VLANs to your network. In practice, it's simpler to use numbers, and document that information on your switches. It may be easier for your users to refer to VLAN 1 as the Marketing VLAN, or refer to VLAN 2 as the Sales VLAN. If your organization decides to invest in Cisco's Route Switch Module (RSM), you will probably want to stick with the numbering scheme for your VLANs. The RSM is basically a full-featured Cisco router that resides in Catalyst 5*x*00 series switches. The RSM does not have any external interface ports, because it contains an interface to the backplane of the Catalyst switch. Interfaces are configured as VLANs on the RSM, and correlate exactly to the VLANs defined on your Catalyst switches. For administrative purposes, it's easier to refer to numbers, so if users have issues on VLAN 2, you will easily remember which router interface to check when troubleshooting. If you decide to use friendly names for your VLANs, however, the Catalyst switch will support them.

EXERCISE 11-2

Configuring a VLAN with Names

1. Log in to the switch using the console port. If the switch is configured with an IP address and default route, you can Telnet.
2. Enter enable mode.
3. Enable VTP version 2 by typing **set vtp v2 enable**.
4. Define the VTP domain by typing **set vtp domain *name***.
5. Place the switch in server mode by typing **set vtp mode server**.
6. Enable pruning (optional) by typing **set vtp pruning enable**.
7. Set a password (optional) by typing **set vtp password *password***.
8. Create the VLAN by typing **set vlan 2 name *vlan_name* state active**.

If you want to name your VLAN, be sure to include the NAME parameter and the VLAN name in step 8.

CERTIFICATION OBJECTIVE 11.05

Grouping Switch Ports to VLANs

The next step is to assign ports to your VLAN. This option provides the flexibility to efficiently assign switch ports to the necessary VLAN, without wasting ports. Let's say you have a Catalyst 5500 with ten 24-port cards, for a total of 240 ports. Now, let's assume you have 60 users in VLAN 1 and you expect they will grow to 150. You also have 40 users in VLAN 2 and expect them to grow to 80. You could define exactly 60 ports to VLAN 1 and 40 ports to VLAN 2, or you can assign the extra ports to support their expected growth.

In practice, it's probably easier to define the additional ports for each VLAN and group them by physical card, to minimize the administrative burden. For example, assign your ports to VLAN 1 sequentially from card 3, port 1 through card 3, port 24. Repeat the assignment of VLAN 1 for cards 4, 5, 6, 7, and 8 to give you a total of 144 ports in VLAN 1. Now assign card 9, port 1 through card 9, port 24. Repeat for cards 10, 11, and 12 to give you a total of 96 ports in VLAN 2. Figure 11-7 illustrates the two VLANs and their associated ports.

The assignment of ports to sequential cards will keep the cost of day-to-day user administration lower. Which is easier to understand—two VLANs assigned sequentially across a switch, or mixed between cards? For example, it would seem confusing if VLAN 1 was assigned to cards 3 – 6 and VLAN 2 is assigned to cards 7 – 8. Then VLAN 1 adds 24 more users to card 9. Now the importance of your network documentation just became greater. What if you are out sick and a relatively inexperienced person tries to add more users to VLAN 2, but plugs them into a card using VLAN 1? Remember to keep it simple.

FIGURE 11-7

VLAN assignments

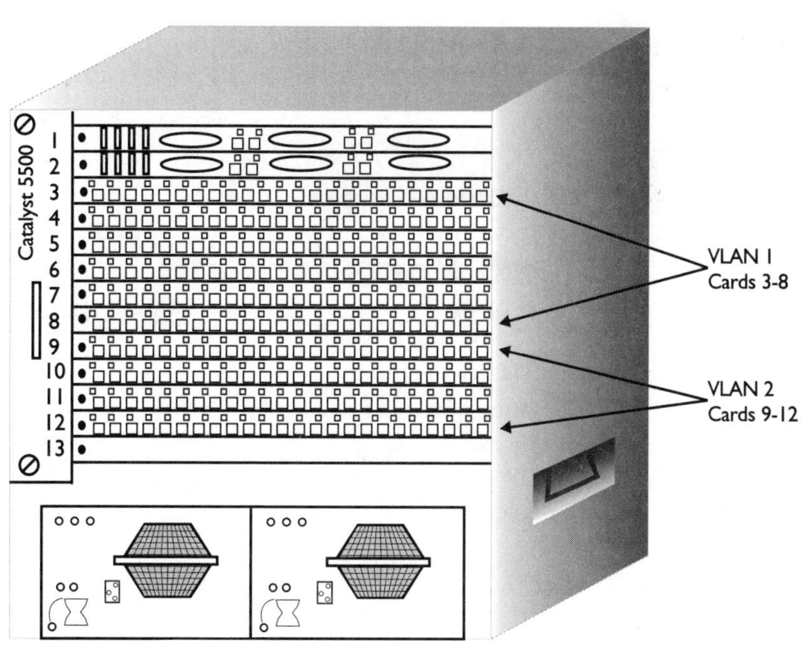

It's important to note the different options available for grouping switch ports based on the type of line card module. The Catalyst 5000 24 Port 10/100 Dedicated Switch Module lets you configure each port to be in a separate VLAN, if needed. The Catalyst 5000 24 Port 100 Mb Group Switching Module contains three switch ports across the 24 user ports. Ports 1 – 8 are tied to switch port #1, Ports 9 – 16 are tied to switch port #2, and Ports 17 – 24 are tied to switch port #3. Thus, you could define a maximum of three different VLANs on the group-switching module. Reserve time to read the configuration guide included with your hardware to understand which VLAN grouping features your card supports.

For our configuration example, we will configure a 24 Port 10/100 Dedicated Switch Module. You should have already configured your VLAN from Exercise 11-2, but it is not required. In the next exercise, there are ten line cards in slots 3 – 12, and VLANs 1 and 2 have already been defined. Remember that you are free to assign ports in the manner best for your organization—assigning them sequentially is only a suggestion to simplify administration.

EXERCISE 11-3

Grouping Switch Ports to VLANs

1. Log in to the switch using the console port. If the switch is configured with an IP address and default route, you can Telnet.
2. Enter enable mode.
3. Assign your ports for VLAN 1 by typing **set vlan 1 3/1-24, 4/1-24, 5/1-24**
4. Assign your ports for VLAN 2 by typing **set vlan 2 6/1-24, 7/1-24**

Verify that you have configured your switch ports correctly using the commands in Figures 11-8 and 11-9.

After configuring your switch ports to VLANs, you should consider enabling the portfast option on your switch ports to reduce the chance for day-to-day connectivity problems. Remember that switches participate in the spanning-tree process; each switch port must ensure that its connection

FIGURE 11-8 Showing port status on a Catalyst 5500

```
Cat5500> (enable) show port status
Port  Name              Status     Vlan       Level  Duplex Speed Type
----- ------------ ---------- ---------- ------ ------ ----- ------------
 1/1  SUP II PRIMARY     connected  trunk      normal   full  100 100BaseFX
 1/2  SUP II PRIMARY     connected  trunk      normal   full   100 100BaseFX
 3/1                     connected  1          normal a-half a-100
10/100BaseTX
 3/2                     connected  1          normal a-full a-100
10/100BaseTX
 3/3                     connected  1          normal a-full a-100
10/100BaseTX
 3/4                     connected  1          normal a-full a-100
10/100BaseTX
 3/5                     notconnect 1          normal   auto  auto
10/100BaseTX
 3/6                     notconnect 1          normal   auto  auto
10/100BaseTX
 3/7                     notconnect 1          normal   auto  auto
10/100BaseTX
 3/8                     notconnect 1          normal   auto  auto
10/100BaseTX
 3/9                     notconnect 1          normal   auto  auto
10/100BaseTX
 3/10                    notconnect 1          normal   auto  auto
10/100BaseTX
Cat5500> (enable)
```

FIGURE 11-9 Showing VLAN assignments on a Catalyst 5500

```
Cat5500> (enable) show vlan
VLAN Name                             Status    Mod/Ports, Vlans
---- -------------------------------- --------- --------------------------
1    default                          active    1/1-2
                                                3/1-24
                                                4/1-24
                                                5/1-24
2    VLAN0002                         active    6/1-14
                                                7/1-24
1002 fddi-default                     active
1003 token-ring-default               active
1004 fddinet-default                  active
1005 trnet-default                    active


VLAN Type  SAID       MTU   Parent RingNo BrdgNo Stp  BrdgMode Trans1 Trans
---- ----- ---------- ----- ------ ------ ------ ---- -------- ------ -----
1    enet  100001     1500  -      -      -      -    -        0      0
2    enet  100002     1500  -      -      -      -    -        0      0
Cat5500> (enable)
```

Note: VLAN 1 is named "default" VLAN on Cisco switches

does not create a loop in the network. For example, imagine that a user accidentally plugs a crossover cable into a switch port on VLAN 1 and connects the other end to another switch port on VLAN 1. A loop has been created in the network, which must be eliminated. STA will take care of this, and during this process, both ports will progress through various stages during the calculation. There are five major states a switch port can exist in:

1. **Blocking** is the default state for all ports, and frames are not forwarded by the port in this state. After the switch is powered on, all ports are in this state.
2. **Listening** is the state following the blocking state. The switch port is still not forwarding frames at this point, but is participating in the spanning-tree process to determine whether to continue toward the forwarding state.
3. **Learning** is the state following the listening state. The switch port is still not forwarding frames at this point, but is preparing to move to the forwarding state. The switch port is analyzing frames to learn the connected MAC addresses.
4. **Forwarding** is the state following the learning state. The switch port is now forwarding frames, and continues to participate in the spanning-tree process. This is the state connected devices require for normal operation.
5. **Disabled** is the state following the listening state. The switch port is not forwarding.

When a device is first connected to a switch port, the port goes from the blocking to the listening and learning states before it starts forwarding frames, assuming the spanning-tree process does not identify a redundant path. Figure 11-10 illustrates these stages and potential paths.

Fortunately, Cisco provides the capability to bypass this process when a device connects to the switch. The *portfast* option will place the port in the forwarding state, and bypass the listening and learning states. By default, portfast is disabled on all ports. A workstation or server that connects to a port with portfast disabled may initially behave as if it is not connected to the network. After the port changes to the forwarding state (after some

FIGURE 11-10

Port states

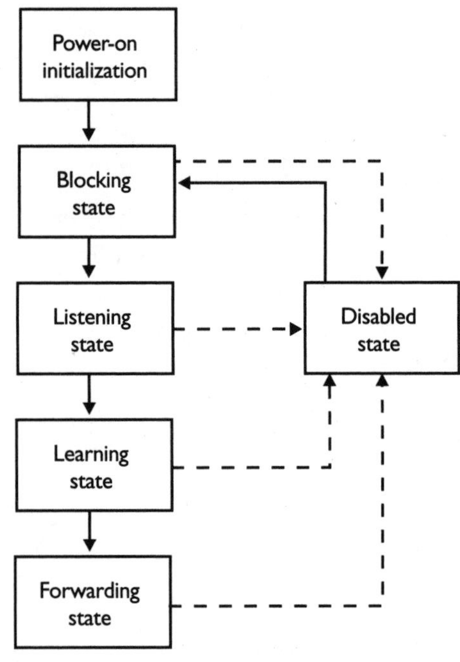

period of time) the device will function normally. When portfast is disabled, workstations or servers may not be able to ping, acquire a DHCP address consistently, or log into a Novell Directory Services tree or NetWare server. The devices behave this way because the switch port is not forwarding these frames for the ping, DHCP request, and NDS login. You can avoid this problem by enabling the portfast option across all ports that you know will be used for workstations and servers. Use this command with caution, as it can cause loops in your network.

EXERCISE 11-4

Enabling Portfast

1. Log in to the switch using the console port. If the switch is configured with an IP address and default route, you can Telnet.
2. Enter enable mode.

3. Enable portfast for VLAN 1 by typing **set spantree portfast 3/1-24 enable**.
4. You will be shown the warning in Figure 11-11.

Verify that you have configured portfast correctly using Figure 11-12. The Fast-Start column will either contain the value Enabled or Disabled. Enabled signifies that fast-start is enabled and the port will forward frames as soon as a device is connected and powered on. The number signifies the card number in the switch. You can also type the same command with no number to see the portfast information for all ports.

Trunks are used to exchange VLAN information between switches, providing the capability to build VLANs that span physical boundaries. The concept of trunking is similar to routing protocols used by routers to build a network topology. Switches use trunking protocols used to determine which port to send frames if a VLAN spans physical boundaries. By using trunking protocols, the same VLAN can be defined on each switch located

FIGURE 11-11

Enabling Portfast on a Catalyst 5500

```
Cat5500> (enable) set spantree portfast 3/1-24 enable


Warning: Spantree port fast start should only be enabled
on ports connected to a single host.  Connecting hubs,
concentrators, switches, bridges, etc. to a fast start
port can cause temporary spanning tree loops.  Use with
caution.


Spantree port 3/1-24 fast start enabled.

Cat5500> (enable)
```

on each floor of a 12-story building. Catalyst switches support several different trunking methods:

- **Inter-Switch Link (ISL)** Fast Ethernet (100 Mbps), Gigabit Ethernet (1000 Mbps)
- **IEEE 802.1Q** Fast Ethernet (100 Mbps), Gigabit Ethernet (1000 Mbps)
- **IEEE 802.10** Fiber/Copper Distributed Data Interface (FDDI)/(CDDI) (100 Mbps)
- **LAN Emulation** ATM (155 Mbps OC-3 and 622 Mbps OC-12)

It's always a good idea to review the release notes for new versions of switch code, since they are adding new features and functionality. This helps ensure that your switch will support the features you need to successfully implement your network design.

FIGURE 11-12 Verifying portfast on a Catalyst 5500

```
Cat5500> (enable) show port span 3

Port      Vlan  Port-State     Cost   Priority  Fast-Start  Group Method
--------  ----  -------------  -----  --------  ----------  ------------
 3/1      1     not-connected    100        32  enabled
 3/2      1     not-connected    100        32  enabled
 3/3      1     not-connected    100        32  enabled
 3/4      1     not-connected    100        32  enabled
 3/5      1     not-connected    100        32  enabled
Cat5500> (enable)
```

Next, we will briefly discuss the ISL and IEEE 802.1Q trunking protocols and learn the commands to configure ISL. The IEEE 802.10 and LAN Emulation trunking methods are beyond the scope of this chapter.

Configure ISL Trunking

ISL is a trunking protocol developed by Cisco exclusively for their products. It allows trunking between switches, and transports Ethernet, FDDI, or Token Ring frames between switches. Cisco routers running ISL can understand and route between VLANs without requiring a physical router interface port for each VLAN. Using ISL, one Fast Ethernet router port can route between two VLANs on a switch.

EXERCISE 11-5

Configuring ISL

1. Determine which ports you will trunk over.
2. Log in to the switch using the console port, or Telnet.
3. Enter enable mode.
4. Configure the port as ISL trunk by typing **set trunk *mod_num/port_num* on**.
5. Remove VLANs from trunk (optional) by typing **clear trunk *mod_num/port_num vlan_num***.
6. Add VLANs to trunk (optional) by typing **set trunk *mod_num/port_num vlan_num***.

Verify that you have configured your trunk ports correctly using the commands in Figure 11-13.

IEEE 802.1Q Trunking

IEEE 802.1Q is an industry-standard trunking protocol developed for inter-operability. It allows the exchange of VLAN information between network devices of different manufacturers. For example, a Cisco switch

FIGURE 11-13 Verifying trunking on a Catalyst 5500

```
Cat5500> (enable) show trunk
Port      Mode         Encapsulation  Status       Native vlan
--------  -----------  -------------  ------------ -----------
 1/1      auto         isl            trunking     1

Port      Vlans allowed on trunk
--------  ---------------------------------------------------------------------
 1/1      1-1005

Port      Vlans allowed and active in management domain
--------  ---------------------------------------------------------------------
 1/1      1,4-5,1003,1005

Port      Vlans in spanning tree forwarding state and not pruned
--------  ---------------------------------------------------------------------
 1/1      1005
Cat5500> (enable)
```

running IEEE 802.1Q can communicate with another vendor's switch running IEEE 802.1Q. The IEEE 802.1Q feature is available on the Catalyst series using switch code 4.1 and later. Please reference the configuration guides for the configuration commands.

Troubleshooting VLANs

Implementing VLANs requires additional tools to identify and resolve connectivity issues. There are several techniques to quickly identify and resolve connectivity problems using Catalyst switches. The following three problems and suggested solutions should help to reinforce the material we have covered in this chapter.

PROBLEM: A workstation on VLAN 1 can't communicate with another workstation on VLAN 1. The workstations are connected to the same switch.

Suggestion #1: Check the port speed and duplex of the workstation in question. Cisco switches provide the auto-negotiate feature for speed and duplex of switch ports. Depending on the network interface card and software drivers, you can experience connectivity problems. In practice, it is very common to manually set the port speed and duplex.

Example: Use the command SET PORT SPEED 3/1 10 to set the speed to 10 Mbps, as shown in Figure 11-14.

Use the command SET PORT DUPLEX 3/1 HALF to set the duplex to half, as shown in Figure 11-15.

Use the command SHOW PORT STATUS 3/1 to verify the changes, as shown in Figure 11-16.

Suggestion #2: Check the VLAN assignment of the ports in question. Remember that devices connected to switch ports in different VLANs will not be able to communicate without traversing a router.

Example: Use the command SHOW PORT 4/1 to verify the VLAN assignment.

PROBLEM: A workstation on VLAN 1 can't communicate with another workstation on VLAN 1. The workstations are connected to different switches.

FIGURE 11-14

Setting port speed on a Catalyst 5500

```
Cat5500> (enable) set port speed 3/1 10
Port(s) 3/1 speed set to 10Mbps.
Cat5500> (enable)
```

FIGURE 11-15

Setting port duplex on a Catalyst 5500

```
Cat5500> (enable) set port duplex 3/1 half
Port(s) 3/1 set to half-duplex.
Cat5500> (enable)
```

Suggestion #1: Check the VLAN assignment of the ports in question. Remember that devices connected to switch ports in different VLANs will not be able to communicate.
Example: Use the command SHOW PORT MOD_NUM/PORT_NUM to verify the VLAN assignment. Repeat this step on both switches for the correct port numbers. Verify that the workstations are connected and are members of VLAN 1, as shown in Figure 11-17.
Suggestion #2: Verify that trunking is enabled and functioning properly between the switches.
Example: Use the command SHOW TRUNK to verify that trunking is enabled, as shown in Figure 11-18. Check the Port, Mode, Encapsulation and Status fields.
PROBLEM: A workstation can't communicate with any servers or other workstations, and you are not sure which port the user is connected to, since your patch cables are not labeled.
Suggestion: Identify the MAC address of the workstation using whatever utility is available, and check the CAM table on the switch for this address.

FIGURE 11-16 Verifying port speed and duplex on a Catalyst 5500

```
Cat5500> (enable) show port status 3/1
Port  Name               Status     Vlan       Level  Duplex Speed Type
----- ------------------ ---------- ---------- ------ ------ ----- ------------
 3/1                     connected  1          normal   half    10 10/100BaseTX
Cat5500> (enable)
```

FIGURE 11-17 Verifying VLAN port assignment on a Catalyst 5500

```
Cat5500> (enable) sh port 5/1

Port  Name               Status     Vlan       Level  Duplex Speed Type

----- ------------------ ---------- ---------- ------ ------ ----- ------------

 5/1  Workstation A      connected  1          normal   full   100 10/100BaseTX


Port   Security  Secure-Src-Addr    Last-Src-Addr      Shutdown  Trap

-----  --------  -----------------  -----------------  --------  --------

 5/1   disabled                                        No        disabled


Port     Broadcast-Limit Broadcast-Drop

-------- --------------- --------------

 5/1                   -              0


Port  Align-Err  FCS-Err    Xmit-Err   Rcv-Err    UnderSize

----- ---------- ---------- ---------- ---------- ---------

 5/1           0          0          0          0         0


Port  Single-Col Multi-Coll Late-Coll  Excess-Col Carri-Sen Runts     Giants

----- ---------- ---------- ---------- ---------- --------- --------- ---------

 5/1           0          0          0          0         0         0         0

Last-Time-Cleared

--------------------------

Wed Jul 15 1998, 20:04:06

Cat5500> (enable)
```

FIGURE 11-18 Verifying trunking on a Catalyst 5500

```
Cat5500> (enable) show trunk
Port      Mode         Encapsulation  Status       Native vlan
--------  -----------  -------------  ------------  -----------
 1/1      on           isl            trunking      1
 1/2      on           isl            trunking      1

Port      Vlans allowed on trunk
--------  ----------------------------------------------------------------------
 1/1      1-1005
 1/2      1-1005

Port      Vlans allowed and active in management domain
--------  ----------------------------------------------------------------------
 1/1      1-12
 1/2      1-12

Port      Vlans in spanning tree forwarding state and not pruned
--------  ----------------------------------------------------------------------
 1/1      1-12
 1/2      1-12
Cat5500> (enable)
```

FIGURE 11-19 Locate a MAC address on a Catalyst 5500

```
Cat5500> (enable) show cam 00-90-f2-79-f8-00
* = Static Entry. + = Permanent Entry. # = System Entry. R = Router Entry.

VLAN  Dest MAC/Route Des  Destination Ports or VCs / [Protocol Type]
----  ------------------  ----------------------------------------------------
1     00-10-f3-96-e7-01   7/14 [ALL]
Total Matching CAM Entries Displayed = 1
Cat5500> (enable)
```

Example: Use the command SHOW CAM <*mac_address*> to identify the port the workstation is connected to, as shown in Figure 11-19. Use the command SHOW PORT MOD_NUM/PORT_NUM to verify the VLAN assignment. For example, you would type **show cam 00-80-C7-BB-2A-4D** to display which port the workstation containing this MAC address is connected to. Verify the VLAN, Dest MAC/Route Destination, and Destination Ports fields. Use the destination port value to continue troubleshooting with the SHOW PORT command.

CERTIFICATION SUMMARY

VLANs provide flexibility when designing and implementing switched network infrastructures. They are closely tied to switching, and provide valuable features such as increased security, the capability to create workgroups based on functional needs, and broadcast control. The early switches simply provided increased performance over traditional hubs; the next generation of switches offered the capability to create VLANs to further increase performance and segment your network.

VLANs are part of any comprehensive network design, but you should understand your user requirements and traffic flows before implementing.

FROM THE CLASSROOM

A Tour of the Cisco IOS Documentation

Once you've finished this book you'll probably want more information on individual router or switch commands, so you'll need to consult the Cisco IOS documentation.

Like all other software developers, Cisco has incorporated ever more features into the IOS over the years, until it has become difficult to find the information you need in the documentation. That's why I like to give the students in my classes an overview of how the documentation is organized.

The IOS documentation comes in several formats. You can buy the documentation for IOS 11.3 in paper form from Cisco Systems for $760. Older versions are only a little less costly. Be sure to reserve about four feet of shelf space for it in your library. You can buy individual configuration guides or command references from Cisco, if your interest in the software is limited to one or two protocol suites or technologies. Cisco Press has recently started publishing these documentation volumes for the general public, so you can get them in bookstores now, as well.

If you buy a Cisco router or switch, attend a Cisco training course, or work for a company that has a partnership with Cisco, you will have access to the documentation for all Cisco products, including all versions of IOS back to version 8.2, on CD-ROM. If you don't have the documentation CD, don't despair; anyone who can get to the Internet with a Web browser can visit the Cisco Web site and view all of the same documentation. Follow the links from the *Service and Support* page at www.cisco.com.

Once you pick the IOS version you want to consult, you'll want to look at the section called *Configuration Guides and Command References.* The documentation is organized into topics, and each topic has both a configuration guide and a command reference. When I have the paper documentation, I use the two parts side by side. The configuration guide gives you an overview of the topic, and step-by-step instructions on how to configure the router to support individual features, along with the commands you would use and the functions they perform. In the back of each section of each configuration guide you will find examples of actual router configurations. You will need to consult the command reference for the details on each command, any parameters or options you can use with it, and any warnings that pertain to it.

The topics you'll want to consult to reinforce the knowledge you've gained in this book will be "Configuration Fundamentals," "Wide Area Networking," and "Switching Services." The "Network Protocols" topics are divided

FROM THE CLASSROOM

into three categories. Network Protocols I has everything about configuring TCP/IP-related features, and Network Protocols II contains information on Novell IPX and AppleTalk.

Happy studying, and good luck in your certification efforts!

—By Pamela Forsyth, CCIE, CCSI, CNX

Weigh the benefits of additional VLANs from a performance and administration perspective: Will additional VLANs improve performance in your network, or will they place an increased load on your routers? How will you manage these new VLANs on a day-to-day basis? Will more VLANs be easier or more complex to maintain and administer?

The Spanning-Tree Protocol was developed to eliminate redundant loops in networks, and is used in switched networks. The lack of active physical loops in your network will still provide redundancy, but you must understand the convergence time after a failure in your network. After a trunk fails, spanning tree will place your redundant port in active mode after it has ensured that there are no other loops in your topology.

Cisco switches provide VLAN 1 by default and all active ports are assigned to that VLAN. In addition, other default VLANs already defined are FDDI and Token Ring. If your network is comprised of multiple switches, you have two options for trunking this information between the switches in your network. VLAN Trunk Protocol (VTP), developed by Cisco, provides the capability to add, delete, and change VLANs from a central point of administration. You can create a VTP server switch, with all other switches being clients; or they can all be servers, capable of updating VLAN information in your network. The other option is to place your switches in transparent mode and manually configure VLANs across each switch as they are needed. Reserve time in your design process to consider the requirements for user adds, moves, and changes, as these will impact your needs for VLAN changes across your switches. If your users will move between floors and buildings, and their VLANs must follow, you should probably consider VTP. If your users will not move, or you implement a centralized server farm, transparent mode may be best. When resources are centralized on VLANs in the data center, and you use DHCP for IP addressing of workstations, a user's VLAN location does not matter. Adds, moves, and changes are simple and are not VLAN dependent.

After you have created your VLANs, you will want to assign them to switch ports across your Catalysts. The different ways to assign ports to VLANs depends on the line cards you order for your chassis. In our examples, we configured the 24 Port 10/100 module, since each port can be configured to a separate VLAN. By default, all ports on this card are assigned to VLAN 1 when the module is installed in the chassis.

VLAN trunks are required to exchange VLAN information between switches. There are several different methods for trunking, including ISL, IEEE 802.1Q, IEEE 802.10, and LAN Emulation. ISL is a protocol developed by Cisco to exchange VLAN information between routers and switches.

VLANs allow you to design a flexible network that can easily support changing user requirements. It is important to weigh the costs of many VLANs from a support perspective. They are a part of detailed design and can provide many benefits to you and your users. Cisco switches provide the capability to add, change, and delete VLANs, as well as assign them quickly and easily.

TWO-MINUTE DRILL

- The term VLAN is short for virtual local-area network and is most commonly associated with switches.
- *Server farms* can contain shared file, application, and database servers, usually grouped in a dedicated VLAN (or VLANs), and require users to communicate across VLAN boundaries using a router.
- A hub receives frames on a port, then copies and transmits (repeats) the frame to all of its other ports.

- A frame switch handles frames intelligently—the switch reads the source MAC address of inbound frames and saves this information in its switching table.
- The two most common methods vendors use to forward traffic through switches are *cut-through* and *store and forward.*
- Virtual LANs (VLANs) offer the following primary benefits:
  - Broadcast control
  - Functional workgroups
  - Enhanced security
- Unlike traditional LANs bounded by a router/bridge interface, a VLAN can be viewed as a broadcast domain with logically configured boundaries.
- The most fundamental benefit of VLAN technology is the capability to create workgroups based on function rather than on physical location or media.
- VLANs also offer the added benefit of security. Users in a defined group are prevented from accessing another group's data, because each VLAN is a closed, logically defined group.
- VLAN's can be assigned by:
  - Port (most common)
  - MAC address (very rare)
  - User ID (very rare)
  - Network address (rare due to growth of DHCP)
- The Spanning-Tree Protocol allows redundant physical links in bridged networks, yet only one physical link forwards frames.
- Transparent bridging is used primarily in Ethernet environments. It places the burden of determining the path from the source to the destination device on the bridges.
- Source-route bridging is used in Token Ring environments. It places the responsibility of locating the destination device on the sending station.
- The Catalyst switch has several VLANs defined by default.

- Before creating VLANs on your switches, you should spend time creating a logical design of your network.
- In order to automatically exchange VLAN information across trunk ports, you will need to configure Cisco's VLAN Trunk Protocol (VTP), which allows switches to send VLAN information in the form of advertisements to neighboring devices.
- Assigning ports to your VLAN provides the flexibility to efficiently assign switch ports to the necessary VLAN, without wasting ports.
- Trunks are used to exchange VLAN information between switches, providing the capability to build VLANs that span physical boundaries.
- ISL is a trunking protocol developed by Cisco exclusively for their products. It allows trunking between switches, and transports Ethernet, FDDI, or Token Ring frames between switches.
- IEEE 802.1Q is an industry-standard trunking protocol developed for inter-operability. It allows the exchange of VLAN information between network devices of different manufacturers.
- There are several techniques to quickly identify and resolve connectivity problems using Catalyst switches.

SELF TEST

The Self Test questions will help you measure your understanding of the material presented in this chapter. Read all the choices carefully, as there may be more than one correct answer. Choose all correct answers for each question.

1. Which trunking protocol was developed by Cisco?
   A. LAN Emulation
   B. Inter-Switch Link (ISL)
   C. IEEE 802.10
   D. IEEE 802.1Q
2. VLANs operate at which layer of the OSI model?
   A. Layer 8
   B. Layer 2
   C. Layer 3
   D. Layer 5
3. What are the two modes on a Catalyst switch for VLAN creation and updates?
   A. Transparent and VTP
   B. Transparent and translational
   C. Translational and source-route
   D. Forwarding and blocking
4. Identify two common trunking protocols.
   A. PNNI and OSPF
   B. IEEE 802.3 and IEEE 802.5
   C. IEEE 802.1D and LAN Emulation
   D. ISL and IEEE 802.1Q
5. Identify the protocol used to avoid loops in switches and VLANs.
   A. Spanning-Tree Protocol (STP)
   B. VLAN Trunk Protocol (VTP)
   C. Private Network-to-Network Interface (PNNI)
   D. Border Gateway Protocol (BGP)
6. Identify two advantages that VLANs provide.
   A. Broadcast control
   B. Increased security
   C. Eliminates need for routers
   D. Decreased performance
7. What is the most common method of VLAN assignment?
   A. IP address
   B. MAC address
   C. Port
   D. Workstation type
8. Identify the option that allows you to control the VLANs that are advertised over trunk ports using VTP.
   A. Trimming
   B. Pruning
   C. Blocking
   D. Shunning
9. Identify the port state that a port will enter before forwarding frames.

A. Blocking

B. Forwarding

C. Disabled

D. Learning

10. What is the switch code needed to implement industry-standard IEEE 802.1Q trunking?

A. 2.3

B. 3.2

C. 4.1

D. 1.5

11. The term VLAN is most commonly associated with:

A. Routers

B. Hubs

C. Switches

D. Bridges

12. Implementation of VLAN creates a network that must be routed. This network belongs to:

A. Layer 4

B. Layer 3

C. Layer 2

D. Layer 1

13. Client-server applications providing graphical user interface created a need for:

A. Increased bandwidth

B. More switches

C. Increased number of operations support systems

D. None of the above

14. A hub directs all frames to:

A. All ports

B. Only to the port on which the frame was received

C. Only to a subset of ports in a multicast system

D. All ports except the port on which the frame was received

15. A unicast frame is destined for:

A. All ports

B. Only one MAC address

C. All MAC addresses

D. A subset of MAC addresses

16. Content Addressable Memory (CAM) is:

A. A Cisco product

B. A routing table

C. Updated every time the switch is turned on

D. All of the above

17. If a switch does not find an address that matches the destination address, what does the switch do?

A. Copies the frame to default ports assigned for "no-match" scenario

B. Copies the frame to all ports meant for broadcasting

C. Copies the frame to all ports

D. Copies the frame to all ports meant for multicasting

18. Switching is a term most commonly used to describe:

    A. Layer 2 devices
    B. Layer 1 devices
    C. Layer 3 devices
    D. Layer 4 devices

19. Which type of switching method allows the switch to forward traffic without receiving the entire frame?

    A. store and forward
    B. cut-through
    C. circuit switching
    D. packet switching

20. What is the main reason a switch using the store and forward method is costlier than a switch using the cut-through method?

    A. The added capability to control traffic
    B. The capability to propagate damaged frames
    C. The capability to switch the entire frame
    D. The need for buffer space

21. Which is the best description of VLAN?

    A. A group of end stations sharing a common physical connection
    B. A group of end stations sharing a common logical connection
    C. A group of end stations at the same location
    D. A group of end stations on the same LAN segment

22. Consider the following scenario:
    VLAN 1: Stations A, B, and C
    Station A connected to switch A
    Station B connected to switch B
    Station C connected to switch C
    VLAN 2: Stations D and E
    Station D connected to switch A
    Station E connected to switch C
    A broadcast message sent by Station B will be received by

    A. Stations A and D
    B. Stations C and E
    C. Stations A, B, and C
    D. Stations C, D, and E

23. Broadcast domain is dependent upon

    A. Physical location
    B. LAN media
    C. Transmission rates
    D. None of the above

24. The major benefit of VLAN is that it allows creation of workgroups based on:

    A. Functions
    B. Physical location
    C. Switching technology
    D. Transmission media

25. In the source-route bridging method, the path is specified by:

    A. The next router on the path
    B. A source station

C. A source router
D. A network broadcast

26. The spanning-tree algorithm is used in:
    A. Source-route bridging
    B. Cut-through switching
    C. Transparent bridging
    D. Store and forward switching

27. Transparent bridging is primarily used in what environment?
    A. Token Ring
    B. FDDI
    C. Ethernet
    D. All of the above

28. A Routing Information Field (RIF) is applicable in Token Ring environments.
    A. True
    B. False

29. A Routing Information Field may contain:
    A. Ring number
    B. Bridge number
    C. Port number
    D. A and B only
    E. B and C only

30. The design of transparent bridging network may result in:
    A. Loops
    B. Broadcast frames not being received by some stations
    C. Forwarding frames over and over

31. When might a Bridge Protocol Data Unit have to be used?
    A. In a changing network topology
    B. In a static network topology
    C. To indicate which ports are to be opened for traffic
    D. All of the above

32. Which of the following is not a default VLAN number for FDDI or Token Ring?
    A. 1002
    B. 1003
    C. 1004
    D. 1

33. In configuring a VLAN Trunk Protocol (VTP), which of the following commands is optional?
    A. SET VTP DOMAIN NAME
    B. set vtp mode server
    C. set vtp password
    D. set vtp enable

34. For Catalyst switches, which of the following commands is used to obtain a summary of advertisements transmitted?
    A. SHOW VTP DOMAIN
    B. show vtp statistics
    C. show port status
    D. show router status

35. The assignments of ports to VLANS must be done in a sequential way.

A. True

B. False

36. Which of the following commands will result in assigning ports 1 – 24 on card 6 to VLAN 1, and ports 7 – 12 on card 9 to VLAN 2?

A. SET VLAN 1 6

B. set vlan1 6/1-24 , set vlan 9

C. SET VLAN 1 6 9

D. set vlan 1 6/1-24, set vlan 2 9/7-12

37. How many major states can a port have?

A. Five

B. Four

C. Three

D. Two

38. What does the portfast option in Cisco allow?

A. Bypassing the blocking state

B. Bypassing the listening state

C. Bypassing the forwarding state

D. Bypassing the disabled state

39. In the default configuration, the portfast settings will allow:

A. Ping

B. Acquiring a DHCP address consistently

C. Enabling portfast

D. Logging into Novell Directory Server(NDS)

A

Self Test Answers

Chapter 1 Answers

1. What were the two challenges of creating a network model? (Select two.)

   A. interconnectivity

   B. interaction

   C. internetworking

   D. interoperability
   A, D. Interconnectivity and interoperability were the challenges of creating a networking model.

2. The Advanced Research Projects Agency created what network?

   A. Ethernet

   B. FDDI

   C. ARPANET

   D. Token Ring
   C. ARPANET was created by the DARPA project.

3. What does OSI stand for?

   A. Organization for Standards Institute

   B. Organization for Internet Standards

   C. Open Standards Institute

   D. Open Systems Interconnection
   D. OSI stands for Open Systems Interconnection

4. What are the layers of the OSI reference model, in order?

   A. application, transport, network, physical

   B. application, presentation, session, network, transport, data link, physical

   C. application, presentation, session, transport, network, data link, physical

   D. application, session, transport, physical
   C. The layers of the OSI reference model—application, presentation, session, transport, network, data link, and physical—can easily be remembered with the mnemonic device: All People Seem To Need Data Processing.

5. What is the term for wrapping a data unit with a header and passing it to the next protocol?

   A. Windowing

   B. Encapsulation

   C. Wrapping

   D. Heading
   B. The term for wrapping a data unit with a header is encapsulation.

6. Which of the following is not defined at the physical layer of the OSI reference model?

   A. hardware addresses

   B. bitstream transmission

   C. voltage levels

   D. physical interface
   A. Hardware addresses are defined at the MAC portion of the data link layer.

7. Which standards institute created the 802 series of physical/data link layer standards?

   A. ANSI

B. DIX

C. ITU-T

D. IEEE

D. The IEEE (Institute of Electrical and Electronics Engineers) created the 802 standard series.

8. Who created Ethernet?

A. ANSI

B. DIX

C. ITU-T

D. IEEE

B. DIX (Digital, Intel, and Xerox) co-created Ethernet.

9. What is the function of CSMA/CD?

A. It passes a token around a star topology.

B. Nodes access the network and retransmit if they detect a collision.

C. Nodes connect to a dual ring of fiber-optics and use a token-passing scheme.

D. Nodes break the frames into tiny cells and forward them through a cell-switching network.

B. The function of CSMA/CD is to detect collisions. Nodes access the network. If they detect a collision, they retransmit the data.

10. What is a backoff algorithm?

A. It is the fault tolerance calculation for FDDI.

B. It is a routing calculation for determining the best route.

C. It is the notification that a serious error has occurred on the network.

D. It is the duration calculation to delay retransmission after a collision, before retransmitting in Ethernet.

D. A backoff algorithm is used to prevent two nodes from retransmitting simultaneously and creating an endless number of collisions by delaying the retransmission for a variable length of time on each node.

11. IBM's Token Ring specification is nearly identical and compatible with IEEE's 802.5 specification.

A. True

B. False

A. The two specifications are nearly identical, since 802.5 was based on IBM's Token Ring specificiation.

12. What is beaconing?

A. It is the fault tolerance calculation for FDDI.

B. It is a routing calculation for determining the best route.

C. It is the notification that a serious error has occurred on the network.

D. It is the duration calculation to delay retransmission after a collision, before retransmitting in Ethernet.

C. Beaconing is a Token Ring mechanism for notifying other stations that a serious error has occurred on the network.

13. What two types of frames are found on a Token Ring network?

    A. Token

    B. Frame check sequence

    C. Data

    D. Address

    A, C. There is a token frame and a data frame used on a Token Ring network.

14. The FDDI specification includes which layers of the OSI reference model?

    A. Physical and network

    B. Physical and transport

    C. Physical and MAC sublayer of data link

    D. Physical and data link

    C. FDDI specifies protocols at both the MAC sublayer and the physical layer of the OSI reference model.

15. What is RS-232?

    A. A standard serial port interface

    B. A high-speed serial interface

    C. An ISDN interface

    D. An ATM switch

    A. RS-232 is an extremely common serial port interface.

16. What is the maximum data transmission rate for HSSI?

    A. 64 Kbps

    B. 256 Kbps

    C. 100 Mbps

    D. 52 Mbps

    D. The maximum data transmission rate for HSSI is 52 Mbps.

17. What does the hierarchical network layer address provide?

    A. The hardware address

    B. The node address and the hardware address

    C. The network address and the node address

    D. The network address mapped to the hardware address

    C. A hierarchical network layer address provides the address of the network as well as the individual node.

18. What qualities match TCP?

    A. Connectionless, reliable

    B. Connection-oriented, reliable

    C. Connectionless, unreliable

    D. Connection-oriented, unreliable

    B. TCP is a connection-oriented, reliable transport-layer protocol.

19. What layer of the OSI reference model specifies data formats, such as encryption?

    A. Application

    B. Presentation

    C. Session

    D. Transport

    E. Network

F. data link

G. physical

B. The presentation layer of the OSI reference model is concerned with data formats and syntax.

20. What is out-of-band management?

A. It is the ability to manage a switch or hub from a networked workstation.

B. It is the addition of a network management module to a hub.

C. It is the fault tolerance feature of the dual ring FDDI creating a single ring.

D. It is the ability to manage a device using a connection other than the network.

D. Out-of-band management is network fault tolerant, because it can manage a switch or hub even when network services are interrupted.

21. Interoperability means:

A. Transfer of data between systems

B. Ability to make data understandable by machines that use different operating systems, hardware, or languages.

C. Agreement between two equipment vendors for processing data

D. Ability of LAN to communicate with WAN

B. Interoperability involves making sure that the data can be understood by equipment manufactured by different vendors that use different operating systems, hardware, or languages.

22. OSI is what kind of standard?

A. A standard created by major telecommunications service providers

B. A de facto standard

C. A de jure standard

D. A standard created by major equipment manufacturers

C. OSI is a de jure standard. De jure implies a standard accepted as legal by a certain organization—in this case, a standards body called International Organization for Standardization (ISO).

23. The layered approach of the OSI results in:

A. Increased development costs for a specific vendor product

B. Increased marketability for a specific vendor product

C. A hierarchical tool for network architecture

D. All of the above

E. B & C only

F. A & C only

E. Use of a layered approach such as the one described by the OSI seven-layer model will result in reduced cost, and ultimately increases marketability of a product.

24. Which of the following statements is true in general when an application at the source wishes to send data to an application at the destination address?
    - A. The lower layer at destination adds its own header information to the data it receives from the higher layer.
    - B. The lower layer at source adds its own header information to the data it receives from the higher layer.
    - C. The lower layer at destination strips header information from the data added by the higher layer.
    - D. The higher layer at source strips header information added to the data by the lower layer.

    B. At the source, each lower layer adds its own header information to the data it receives from the layer above it. At the destination, this process is reversed until the data is delivered to the application.

25. In the OSI model, encapsulation of the data may occur at:
    - A. Layer 7 of the source
    - B. Layer 1 of the destination
    - C. Layer 7 of the destination
    - D. All layers at the source
    - E. Layer 1 of the source

    D. Encapsulation in the OSI model occurs at all layers of the source.

26. The session layer functionality in the OSI model is usually implemented:
    - A. At user premises
    - B. In hardware
    - C. In software
    - D. In hardware and software

    C. The session layer is usually implemented in the software. The physical and data link layers are usually implemented in hardware and software. The remaining layers are usually implemented in the software.

27. At the physical layer in the OSI model the data is broken into:
    - A. cells
    - B. fragments
    - C. bits
    - D. packets

    C. Bits. At the physical layer in the OSI model, the data is broken into smaller frames.

28. Collision in a CSMA/CD network is said to occur when:
    - A. A node listens to the network and hears nothing
    - B. A node receives a message from the network
    - C. Two nodes hear nothing and then transmit data simultaneously
    - D. A node on the network has physical failure

    C. Collision occurs only when nodes attempt to send the data simultaneously.

29. A broadcast system means:

    A. Only few nodes on the network see the data meant for these nodes

    B. All nodes on the network see all the data frames

    C. The network informs all the nodes of a network failure

    D. None of the above

    B. In a broadcast system all the nodes see all data frames, whether or not that data is meant to be received by that node.

30. Which statements are true of a preamble in the IEEE 802.3 frame?

    A. It is an indication that a node is receiving a new frame

    B. It contains all zeroes

    C. It contains all ones

    D. It contains alternating zeros and ones

    E. A and B only

    F. A and D only

    G. A and C only

    F. The preamble is an indication of the start of a new frame. It contains alternating zeroes and ones.

31. A Frame Check Sequence (FCS) in the IEEE 802.3 frame includes:

    A. A receiving station address

    B. A source station address

    C. A Cyclic Redundancy Check (CRC) value

    D. A sequence number of the frame

    C. The FCS includes a CRC value.

32. In a Token Ring network architecture, what does it mean when a node possesses a token?

    A. The node has the ability to transmit the data to the network

    B. The node has the right to pass the data to the network

    C. The node has the right to retain the token

    D. None of the above

    B. When a node receives the token, if the node has data to transmit, it flips a bit in the token and transmits the data. If the node has no data to transmit, it sends the token to the next node.

33. In a Token Ring network architecture, if a node receives a token and has data to transmit, then:

    A. The node does nothing

    B. The node waits for data to be transmitted

    C. The node converts the token into a start-of-frame field

    D. None of the above

    C. When a node receives the token, if the node has data to transmit, it flips a bit in the token and transmits the data. If the node has no data to transmit, it sends the token to the next node.

34. What is the main purpose of the dual ring architecture in Fiber Distributed Data Interface (FDDI)?

A. To increase traffic on the network

B. To allow bi-directional traffic on the network

C. To provide fault tolerance

D. To provide one path for traffic from selected nodes

C. Dual ring architecture mainly provides fault tolerance. If a station on the dual ring fails (or if a break occurs in one of the rings), the dual ring is "wrapped" so that traffic doubles back the route it came from.

35. Which statement is true of the Media Access Control (MAC) address?

A. It is dependent on the hardware location

B. It is dependent on the network type

C. It is assigned by a vendor

D. It changes every time the hardware is turned on and off

C. The MAC address is network independent, such that wherever the hardware is plugged into the network, it would have the same MAC address.

36. The Basic Rate Interface (BRI) in ISDN has:

A. One B channel and one D channel

B. 23 B channels and one D channel

C. Two B channels and one D channel

D. Two D channels and one B channel

C. The BRI consists of two B channels at 64 Kbps and one D channel at 16 Kbps.

37. Synchronization of network timing is done at which layer?

A. Data link layer

B. Transport layer

C. Physical layer

D. Session layer

C. Synchronization of network timing is done at the physical layer and involves an electrical signal generally provided by the carrier network.

38. What is a Network Control Protocol (NCP) frame in a Point-to-Point Protocol (PPP) used for?

A. Establishing and configuring a connection

B. Encryption of data

C. Assigning a dynamic address

D. Selecting and configuring the network layer protocol

D. A Network Control Protocol frame in a Point-to-Point Protocol is used for selecting and configuring the network layer protocol. A Link Control Protocol (LCP) is used to establish and configure a connection.

39. In a Frame Relay network, which statement is true of Forward Explicit Congestion (FECN) when the network is congested?

A. It is a bit that is set to "0"
B. It is a bit that is set to "1"
C. It is sent by DTE to upper protocol layers
D. A and C only
E. B and C only
E. Both FECN and Backward Explicit Congestion (BECN) contain a bit that is set to "1" and is sent by DTE to upper protocol layers to notify of traffic congestion between source and destination.

40. Data Link Connection Identifier (DLCI) in a Frame Relay network identifies what?

A. Data Terminal Equipment (DTE)
B. Data Circuit Termination Equipment (DCE)
C. A connection between two DTEs
D. All of the above
C. Data Link Connection Identifier in a Frame Relay network identifies a connection between two DTEs.

41. How does a Permanent Virtual Circuit (PVC) in a Frame Relay network differ from a Switched Virtual Circuit (SVC)?

A. It is a permanently established link
B. It terminates after the call has ended
C. It has a data transfer phase
D. It has an idle phase
A. PVC is a permanently established link. SVC terminates after the call has ended. Both SVC and PVC have a data transfer phase and an idle phase.

42. The ITU X.25 Standard describes protocol for which layer or layers?

A. physical layer
B. session layer
C. transport layer
D. data link layer
E. network layer
F. A, B, and C only
G. A, D, and E only
H. A, C, and D only
G. The ITU X.25 Standard applies to the physical, data link, and network layers' protocols.

43. X.25 can handle data rates up to:

A. 1024 Kbps
B. 256 Kbps
C. 512 Kbps
D. 768 Kbps
B. The data rate range for X.25 is from 9.6 Kbps to 256 Kbps.

44. Asynchronous Transfer Mode (ATM) is a:

A. Packet-switching technology
B. Frame-switching technology
C. Cell-switching technology
D. Circuit-switching technology
C. ATM is a cell-switching technology that can be used to transport data in a variety of different formats, including voice, video, and bursty LAN data.

45. How many header formats are there in ATM terminology?

 A. 5
 B. 4
 C. 3
 D. 2
 E. 1

 D. The two header formats in ATM terminology are: User Network Interface (UNI) and Network Node Interface (NNI).

46. Which of the following uses the Internetwork Operating System (IOS)?

 A. Bridges
 B. DMS-100
 C. 4ESS
 D. Cisco routers
 E. 5ESS

 D. Cisco routers use IOS for configuring the routers.

47. How many switching modes are included in Catalyst 1900/2820 switches?

 A. 1
 B. 2
 C. 3
 D. 4

 C. The three switching modes included in Catalyst 1900/2820 switches are: fastforward, fragmentfree, and store and forward.

Chapter 2 Answers

1. What command would you use to log out of the router and end your session? (Select two.)

 A. TERMINATE
 B. logout
 C. exit
 D. session end

 B, C. You would use either LOGOUT or EXIT to log out of the router and end your session. The others are not valid IOS commands.

2. If you type a command that the router doesn't recognize, what will the router do?

 A. Display an error message
 B. Try to resolve the command to an IP address
 C. Try to execute the closest command it can find in its command set
 D. Invalidate the configuration

 B. The router will try to resolve the incorrect command to an IP address, thinking it is a hostname, so it can establish a Telnet session with it.

3. You can confirm that you are in the privileged EXEC mode by which prompt?

 A. Router>
 B. Router(config)#
 C. Router#

D. Router(config-if)#
C. The prompt Router# confirms that you are in the privileged EXEC mode. The privileged EXEC mode allows you to go into the configuration mode, and then to the interface configuration mode. The first mode you access is user EXEC mode.

4. A reload of the router is required to get the configuration changes to take place.

   A. True

   B. False
   B. False. Cisco routers do not require a reload to get configuration changes to take effect. The changes are dynamic, and take effect immediately when you press the ENTER key.

5. By default, how many commands are stored in the command history buffer?

   A. 5

   B. 10

   C. 15

   D. 20
   B. The command history buffer will allow you to paste in your last 10 commands. This can be changed with the command HISTORY SIZE X.

6. The IOS image is normally stored in?

   A. RAM

   B. NVRAM

   C. Shared

   D. Flash
   D. The IOS image is usually stored in Flash and booted from Flash. RAM stores routing tables and the running configuration. NVRAM is for the startup configuration.

7. The startup configuration file is stored in NVRAM.

   A. True

   B. False
   A. True. The startup configuration file is stored in NVRAM. NVRAM is memory that retains its contents after the router is powered off.

8. To determine the operational status of an interface, which command do you use?

   A. DISPLAY INTERFACE STATUS

   B. show interface

   C. show status interface

   D. display interface
   B. To determine the operational status of an interface, use the SHOW INTERFACE command. The other commands are invalid.

9. The boot field consists of:

   A. The lowest four bits of the configuration register

   B. The same as the configuration register

   C. The highest four bits of the configuration register

   D. Bits 4 through 7 of the configuration register
   A. The boot field is the lowest four bits of the configuration register.

10. A boot field value of 0x1 will cause the router to:
    A. Boot from Flash
    B. Look for boot system commands in the startup configuration
    C. Look for an IOS image on a TFTP server
    D. Boot from ROM
    D. The boot field set to 0x1 will cause the router to boot from ROM.
11. To view the configuration register settings, which command do you enter?
    A. SHOW RUNNING-CONFIGURATION
    B. show startup-configuration
    C. show version
    D. show controllers
    C. The configuration register setting is at the last line of the SHOW VERSION command. This command also shows router up time and IOS version.
12. What command is required to send Debug output to a VTY session?
    A. SHOW DEBUG
    B. show log
    C. terminal monitor
    D. debug all
    C. TERMINAL MONITOR sends Debug output to the VTY session. By default the VTY sessions do not log any errors message, like the console sessions do.
13. Which keystroke would you use to recall the previous command in the command history buffer?
    A. CTRL-N
    B. CTRL-P
    C. ESC-P
    D. ESC-F
    B. The CTRL-P keystroke recalls the previous command in the command history buffer. If your terminal emulator allows it, you may also use the UP ARROW key.
14. You must have an IP address assigned to an interface in order for CDP to operate.
    A. True
    B. False
    B. False. CDP will multicast to a functional MAC address. There is no need to have any network layer address assigned to the interface to get the CDP messages to go out.
15. What is the command to view the stored configuration in NVRAM?
    A. SHOW RUNNING-CONFIG
    B. show startup-config
    C. show version
    D. show NVRAM
    B. The SHOW STARTUP-CONFIG will show the configuration stored in NVRAM. The SHOW RUNNING-CONFIG will show the configuration currently running.

16. When do configuration commands take effect?

    A. When you reload the router
    B. When they are saved in NVRAM
    C. As soon as you press the ENTER key
    D. When you enter the command ENABLE.

    C. The commands you enter take effect immediately, as soon as you press the ENTER key.

17. What command is needed to see if an interface is up and operational?

    A. SHOW CONTROLLERS
    B. show running-config
    C. show interface
    D. show buffers

    C. SHOW INTERFACE will tell you if the interface is adminstratively down, or down because of a failure, or up and operational.

18. What is the best command to enter to determine which release of IOS the router is running?

    A. SHOW FLASH
    B. show running-config
    C. show startup-config
    D. show version

    D. SHOW VERSION will display the current IOS release. A SHOW FLASH will show what file is stored in Flash, and usually the filename will include the version number. Under most circumstances the two should match, but if the router booted from ROM or TFTP, it will not be using the Flash IOS.

19. What is the command needed to copy the current operational configuration to a TFTP server?

    A. COPY RUNNING-CONFIG TFTP
    B. copy startup-config tftp
    C. copy tftp running-config
    D. copy tftp startup-config

    A. The COPY RUNNING-CONFIG TFTP tells the router to copy from the configuration in RAM to the TFTP server identified. The other commands are valid commands, but have other effects.

20. What command would you use to see information about all the protocols enabled in the router?

    A. DISPLAY PROTOCOL INFORMATION
    B. display protocols
    C. show protocol route
    D. show protocols

    D. SHOW PROTOCOLS displays information about all the protocols enabled in the router. The other choices are not valid IOS commands.

21. What is the part of the IOS software that provides the user interface and interprets the commands you type?

    A. The virtual terminal
    B. The command executive

C. The console port

D. The configuration register
B. The command executive is the part of the IOS software that provides the user interface and interprets the commands you type. A virtual terminal is another way of referring to a Telnet session. The console port is a hardware interface for attaching a terminal to the router. The configuration register is a memory location in NVRAM that controls the router's operation as it boots up.

22. What command allows you to view the configuration in RAM?

A. SHOW STARTUP-CONFIG

B. show RAM-config

C. show running-config

D. show config
C. SHOW RUNNING-CONFIG allows you to view the configuration in RAM. SHOW STARTUP-CONFIG allows you to see the configuration file stored in NVRAM. SHOW CONFIG is an older (pre-IOS 10.3) command that allows you to see the configuration in NVRAM. Answer B is not a valid command.

23. Which of the following represents access via a physical connection of a terminal to a router?

A. Virtual terminal

B. IOS

C. Console

D. All of the above
C. The console represents a physical connection to a router. The virtual terminal has the same look and feel as the console port, but it does not represent a physical connection.

24. What command would you use to view the name of the filename in Flash memory?

A. SHOW MEMORY ALL

B. show flash

C. show filename

D. show flash partitions
B. You would use SHOW FLASH to view the name of the filename in Flash memory.

25. What is the level of access to the router in which you are allowed to change the router's configuration?

A. User EXEC mode

B. High-level access mode

C. Privileged EXEC mode

D. Console mode
C. You are allowed to change the router's configuration in privileged EXEC mode. You cannot change configurations from user EXEC mode. There is no such thing as high-level access mode or console mode.

26. Changes to the router configuration are allowed from the user EXEC mode.

A. True

B. False
B. False. Changes to the router configuration are not allowed from the user EXEC mode.

27. How can you confirm you are in privileged EXEC mode?

A. By issuing the command CONFIRM MODE

B. By viewing the output of the SHOW VERSION command

C. By noting the router's prompt

D. None of the above
C. The router's prompt will end with a pound sign (#) in privileged EXEC mode.

28. After giving the command INTERFACE ETHERNET0 from global configuration mode, the router is most likely to respond with:

A. router(config)#

B. router#interface

C. router(config-if)#

D. router#(config-int)
C. After the command INTERFACE ETHERNET0 from global configuration mode, the router is most likely to respond with router(config-if)#.

29. To completely get out of the interface configuration mode and back to privileged EXEC mode, what should you use?

A. CTRL-Z

B. EXIT

C. END CONFIG

D. LOGOUT
A. CTRL-Z will get the user completely out of the configuration mode. EXIT takes the user back one step. LOGOUT terminates your session.

30. The response to the command ROUTER# CONFIGURE ? will be:

A. Connect, copy, configure

B. Various paths from source to destination

C. router(config)#

D. A list of possible options from where the router can be configured
D. The response to the command ROUTER# CONFIGURE ? will be a list of possible options from where the router can be configured. The "?" results in a list of arguments being displayed.

31. Which are the types of memory elements in a Cisco router?

A. RAM, ROM, NVRAM, and Boot

B. RAM, ROM, NVRAM, and Flash

C. Config, RAM, ROM, NVRAM, and Flash

D. Buffers, RAM, NVRAM, and Flash
B. The memory types are RAM, ROM, Flash Memory, and NVRAM.

32. How do you suspend a Telnet session?

A. Use the command SUSPEND SESSION

B. Use the keystrokes CTRL-ALT-6

C. Use the keystrokes CTRL-SHIFT-6 X

D. A Telnet session cannot be suspended. You must quit the session and initiate it again if you want to go back to it.

C. To suspend a Telnet session, use the keystrokes CTRL-SHIFT-6 X. Choices A and B are invalid commands or keystrokes.

33. What is the characteristic of a link-state routing protocol that enables it to make better routing decisions?

A. Its metrics take bandwidth into account

B. It uses a hello protocol

C. It broadcasts the contents of its routing table periodically to its neighbors

D. None of the above

A. The characteristic of a link-state routing protocol that enables it to make better routing decisions is that its metrics take bandwidth into account. Answer C is characteristic of a distance vector routing protocol.

34. What is the sequence of events that occurs when you power up your router?

A. Find configuration file, load IOS image, test hardware

B. Load IOS image, test hardware, find configuration file

C. Test hardware, find configuration file, load IOS image

D. Test hardware, load IOS image, find configuration file

D. The router first tests its hardware, then attempts to locate and load an IOS image, and finally locates and applies its specific configuration information.

35. The size of the configuration register is:

A. 16 bits

B. 12 bits

C. 8 bits

D. 4 bits

A. The configuration register has 16 bits.

36. It is recommended that in order to obtain the best results, the BOOT SYSTEM FLASH command should be entered after the BOOT SYSTEM ROM command.

A. True

B. False

B. False. If the ROM command is entered prior to the FLASH command, the router will reload IOS from ROM and not from Flash.

37. The command routerx(config)#boot system tftp 189.12.3.172 will boot the router from:

A. System image in Flash

B. System image 189.12.3.172 from RAM

C. System image 189.12.3.172 from TFTP

D. System image from TFTP
C. That command will boot the router from system image 189.12.3.172 from TFTP. Answer D is not complete.

38. A good connection is indicated by which of the following in an output display of the PING command?

A. !!!!!
B. .....
C. xxxxx
D. ******
A. A series of exclamation points (!!!!!) indicates a good connection. A series of dots (.....) indicates that the pings timed out. The symbols in answers C and D do not exist.

39. If a mistake is made in specifying the file name in the COPY TFTP FLASH command, the router will still function because:

A. It still has a working image in ROM.
B. It still has a working image in RAM.
C. It still has a working image in Flash.
D. It still has a working image in TFTP.
B. If a mistake is made in specifying the file name in the COPY TFTP FLASH command, the router will still function because it still has a working image in RAM. Answers C and D are incorrect, because the purpose of the command is to copy a new image from TFTP server into Flash.

40. The command COPY FLASH TFTP FILE2600 copies:

A. Contents of file from Flash into file2600 of the TFTP server
B. Contents of TFTP into file2600 in the Flash
C. Contents of file2600 in the TFTP to file2600 in the Flash
D. Contents of file2600 in the TFTP into Flash
A. Contents of Flash memory will be copied to file2660, which is in the TFTP server.

41. What command can be used to see the router's neighbors from your local router if no network layer protocols are configured?

A. SHOW CDP
B. show cdp neighbor
C. show neighbor
D. show network
B. SHOW CDP NEIGHBOR can be used to see the router's neighbors from your local router if no network layer protocols are configured. Answers A and C are incomplete. Answer D is not a valid option.

42. In order to show the neighbor's IOS version, what optional parameter can be used in the command SHOW CDP NEIGHBOR?

A. VERSION
B. IOS

C. detail

D. None of the above

C. The command SHOW CDP NEIGHBOR DETAIL will show the IOS version.

43. In a Cisco router, configuration register information can be used to:

A. Select a boot source and default file name

B. Enable booting from a TFTP server

C. Load operating software from ROM

D. All of the above

D. Configuration register information can be used to select a boot source and default filename, enable booting from a TFTP server, and load operating software from ROM.

Chapter 3 Answers

1. What is the network address for the address 96.2.3.16?

A. 96.2.0.0

B. 96.2.3.0

C. 96.0.0.0

D. Can't tell

C. This is a Class A network address. The default netmask is eight bits, which defines the network.

2. What class of address is 190.233.27.13?

A. Class A

B. Class B

C. Class C

D. Class D

B. Class B addresses range from 128-191 in the first octet.

3. How many bits are in the default subnet mask for the address 219.25.23.56?

A. 8

B. 16

C. 24

D. 32

C. This is a Class C address, which has a default mask of 24 bits.

4. How many hosts are supported by a Class C network address, without subnetting?

A. 254

B. 65,000

C. 255

D. 16,000

A. There are 8 bits (256 addresses) available for hosts in a Class C network, but host numbers 0 and 255 are not allowed.

5. What is the default mask for a Class B network?

A. 255.0.0.0

B. 255.255.255.0

C. 255.255.0.0.

D. 255.225.0.0

D. A Class B network uses 16 bits to represent the network address. Answer C was added to demonstrate a common typographical error in assigning a subnet mask.

6. Approximately how many unique networks are possible with a Class B address?

   A. 254

   B. 16K

   C. 65K

   D. 2M

   B. A Class B address allocates 16 bits (65K) for the network address, but the address class predetermines three of these bits. In other words, 128 through 191 are the only possible values for the first octet.

7. What is the decimal value of the binary number 11001011?

   A. 203

   B. 171

   C. 207

   D. 193

   A. The decimal value of the binary number 11001011 is 128+64+8+2+1=203

8. What is the binary value of the decimal number 219?

   A. 11101011

   B. 01011101

   C. 11101011

   D. 11011011

   D. The binary value of the decimal number 219 is 219-128-64-16-8-2-1 = 0

9. Subnet bits are added to________ to segment the network into subnets.

   A. The network address

   B. The default subnet mask

   C. The host address

   D. The subnet ID

   B. We add bits to the default mask to create subnets, which reduces the number of available host addresses available on each subnet. The network address for the parent network will remain the same, while each subnet address will include an extended network address identifying the subnet, and zeros in the host portion.

10. If eight bits were allocated to subnetting with a Class B address, how many subnets would be possible?

    A. 62

    B. 256

    C. 254

    D. 16K

    C. Eight bits provide for 256 bit combinations, but the all-zeros and all-ones combinations are not valid, leaving only 254.

11. Given the subnet mask 255.255.240 on a Class A address, how many bits are allocated to subnetting?

    A. 4

    B. 5

    C. 9

    D. 12

    D. Because the default mask for a Class A address is 255.0.0.0, this subnet mask has added the entire second octet plus four additional bits for subnetting.

12. If the subnet mask for the network 150.25.0.0 is 255.255.224.0, which of these is a valid host address?

    A. 150.25.0.27

    B. 150.25.30.23

    C. 150.25.40.24

    D. 150.25.224.30

    C. This address is within the address range for the first subnet, which is 150.25.32.0. In both answer A and answer B, the subnet bits are all zeros, which is not valid. In answer D, the subnet bits are all ones, which is not valid for a host address.

13. What is the first subnet ID for the network 25.0.0.0 with a subnet mask of 255.192.0.0?

    A. 25.192.0.0

    B. 25.64.0.0

    C. 25.128.0.0

    D. 25.192.64.0

    B. The value of the first subnet is equal to the lowest-order bit of the subnet mask. Answer C would be the second subnet. Answer A is an all-ones combination.

14. What is the maximum number of subnet bits possible with a Class C address?

    A. 6

    B. 8

    C. 14

    D. 12

    A. Since there are only eight bits in the host portion of a Class C address, we must leave at least two bits for hosts, which would only provide two legal bit combinations, 01 and 10 for host addresses.

15. Given the address 220.195.227.12 with a subnet mask of 255.255. 224.0, what advanced subnetting technique is being used?

    A. Subnetting across octets

    B. VLSM

    C. Supernetting

    D. None

    C. The address given is a Class C address, which should have a default mask of 255.255.255.0. The fact that the given mask is less than this indicates that bits have been taken away. This technique for combining multiple Class C networks into one entity is called supernetting.

16. Given a subnet mask of 255.255.240, which of these addresses is not a valid host address?

    A. 150.150.37.2

    B. 150.150.16.2

    C. 150.150.8.12

    D. 150.150.49.15

    C. The addresses given are Class B, which means the subnet mask includes four bits for subnetting. The lowest-order bit is 16, which means the first legal subnet is 150.150.16.0.

17. How many hosts per subnet are possible with a Class B address, if five bits are added to the default mask for subnetting?

    A. 510

    B. 512

    C. 1022

    D. 2046

    D. A Class B address would have 16 bits available for host addresses if it were not subnetted. Taking five bits away for subnetting leaves 11 bits for host addresses. This would leave host addresses of 0 – 2047. However, all zeros and all ones are not permitted, so the address range becomes 1 – 2046.

18. If you were issued a Class C address, and needed to divide the network into seven subnets, with up to 15 hosts in each subnet, what subnet mask would you use?

    A. 255.255.255.224

    B. 255.255.224

    C. 255.255.255.240

    D. None of the above

    D. This is an impossible situation. To achieve seven subnets we would need to use four subnet bits. This is because even though three bits would give us eight possible subnet addresses, all zeros and all ones are not permitted. If we use four bits for subnetting, this only leaves four bits for host addresses, which will only accommodate 14 hosts for subnets.

19. What IOS command would you issue to set the IP address on a terminal line?

    A. ROUTER(CONFIG-IF)# IP ADDRESS

    B. ROUTER(CONFIG-LINE)#IP ADDRESS

    C. Router(config)#ip address

    D. None of the above

    D. This is a trick question, in that we do not assign IP addresses to terminal lines. The terminal lines include the console, auxiliary port, and virtual terminal lines 0 – 4, which are used to configure the router. IP addresses are assigned to the interfaces on the router.

20. What IOS command would you use to define the subnet mask for an interface on the router?

    A. ROUTER(CONFIG-IF)# IP ADDRESS

    B. ROUTER# TERM IP-NETMASK FORMAT

    C. Router(config-line)# ip netmask-format

    D. Router(config)# ip subnetmask

    A. You would use the command ROUTER(CONFIG-IF)# IP ADDRESS to define the subnet mask for an interface on the router. The subnet mask for an interface is assigned as part of assigning the IP address. Answers B and C refer to setting the format for viewing subnet masks. Answer D is not a legitimate command.

21. What IOS command turns off name-to-address resolution?

    A. ROUTER# NO IP DOMAIN-LOOKUP

    B. ROUTER(CONFIG)# NO DOMAIN-LOOKUP

    C. Router(config-if)# no ip domain-lookup

    D. Router(config)# domain-lookup off
    B. To turn off name-to-address resolution, the NO DOMAIN-LOOKUP command is issued from the global command prompt.

22. To view name-to-address mappings cached on the router, what IOS command would you issue?

    A. ROUTER> SHOW HOSTS

    B. ROUTER(CONFIG)# SHOW HOSTS

    C. Router# ip name-server

    D. Router(config)# ip name-server
    A. The SHOW HOSTS command can be issued from the User mode. The IP NAME-SERVER command is used to define the addresses of DNS servers for name lookup, and is issued from the global configuration prompt.

23. If you received a !!!!! in response to a PING command, what would that indicate?

    A. Destination Unreachable

    B. Successful echoes

    C. Timeout

    D. None of the above
    B. The five exclamation points indicate that each of five ICMP echo packets were returned before the timeout interval expired.

24. Given an IP address of 125.3.54.56, without any subnetting, what is the network number?

    A. 125.0.0.0

    B. 125.3.0.0

    C. 125.3.54.0

    D. 125.3.54.32
    A. The network number is 125.0.0.0. Since the address is a Class A address, the default mask is eight bits, so the network number consists of the first octet, and is represented as shown.

25. The network 154.27.0.0 can support how many hosts, if not subnetted?

    A. 254

    B. 1024

    C. 65,533

    D. 16,777,206
    C. The network 154.27.0.0 can support 65,533 hosts, if not subnetted. The address shown is a Class B address, which allows 16 bits for the host address. These sixteen bits allow 65,533 hosts per network.

26. Which of the following is a legitimate IP host address?

A. 1.255.255.2
B. 127.2.3.5
C. 225.23.200.9
D. 192.240.150.255
A. 1.255.255.2 is the only legitimate IP host address. Answer B uses the 127 network, which is reserved for loopback testing. Answer C is a Class D address, which is used for multicasting. Answer D is a broadcast address.

27. What is the significance of the address 3.255.255.255?

A. It is a host number
B. It is a local broadcast
C. It is a directed broadcast
D. It is an illegal address
C. The significance of the address 3.255.255.255 is that it is a directed broadcast to network 3.0.0.0. A host number cannot have all ones. A local broadcast would have all ones (for example, 255.255.255.255). While this is not a legal host address, it is perfectly valid as a broadcast address.

28. How many bits are in the default subnet mask for a Class D network?

A. 8
B. 16
C. 24
D. None
D. A Class D network is used for multicasting, not for normal IP network/host addressing, so it doesn't have a default subnet mask.

29. A bit pattern of 1111 leading the first octet of an address would imply what class of network?

A. Class A
B. Class B
C. Class C
D. Class D
E. Class E
E. The leading bit pattern 1111 is associated with Class E addresses, which range from 240-254 in the first octet.

30. What is the binary equivalent of the decimal 234?

A. 11101010
B. 10111010
C. 10111110
D. 10101111
A. The binary equivalent of the decimal 234 is 11101010. 234 uses the 128, 64, 32, 8, and 2 binary bits.

31. What is the decimal equivalent of 01011100?

A. 96
B. 92
C. 84
D. 154
B. The decimal equivalent of 01011100 is 92. The bits are set for 64, 16, 8, and 4.

32. The purpose of subnetting is to:

    A. Segment and organize a single network at the network layer
    B. Divide a network into several different domains
    C. Allow bridging between network segments
    D. Isolate groups of hosts so they can't communicate

    A. The purposes of subnetting are to segment and organize a single network at the network layer. This is the best answer. A subnet does not create separate domains. It provides a way to route between network segments, not bridge between them. It does provide isolation between groups of hosts, but is not implemented to prevent them from communicating.

33. Subnetting is achieved by the following actions:

    A. Subtracting bits from the default subnet mask
    B. Subtracting bits from the network address
    C. Adding bits to the host address
    D. Adding bits to the default subnet mask

    D. Subnetting adds bits to the default mask. This has no effect on the network address, but does reduce the bits available for the host address.

34. If we add four bits to the default mask, what is the number of subnets we can define?

    A. 16
    B. 15
    C. 14
    D. 12

    C. Four bits would allow a range of 0 – 15. However, a subnet cannot contain all ones or all zeros (the first and last subnets are reserved), which limits the range from 1 – 14.

35. What is the maximum number of subnet bits we can add to a default mask?

    A. 8 bits
    B. 16 bits
    C. 30 bits
    D. Depends on address class

    D. The number of total host bits available to borrow depends on the address class. We must insure that we leave at least two host bits, so we can have a host address that is not all ones or zeros.

36. What is the subnet mask we would use with a Class B address that has three subnet bits added?

    A. 255.255.240.0
    B. 255.255.224.0
    C. 255.224.0.0
    D. 255.255.248.0

    B. The default subnet mask for a Class B is 255.255.0.0. To this we add three bits, with a decimal value of 128+64+32 = 224.

37. What would be the subnet mask if we added 12 subnet bits to a default Class A subnet mask?

    A. 255.255.255.240

    B. 255.255.240.0

    C. 255.240.0.0

    D. 255.225.224.0

    B. A default mask for a Class A address would be 255.0.0.0. Adding 12 bits means that we take the entire second octet (255) and four bits of the third octet (240).

38. Given a subnet mask of 255.255.255.0 with a Class B address, how many subnets are available?

    A. None

    B. 254

    C. 16K

    D. 65K

    B. The default mask for a Class B address is 255.255.0.0. The given mask shows that we have added eight bits for subnetting. This will allow us 0 – 255 subnets, with 0 (all-zeros) and 255 (all ones) disallowed.

39. What happens to the number of hosts per subnet each time we add an additional subnet bit?

    A. Hosts are not affected

    B. Available hosts are decreased by two

    C. Hosts per subnet is approximately halved

    D. Hosts per subnet is doubled

    C. Each time we take a bit from the host portion of the IP address for use in subnetting, we cut the available number of hosts roughly in half. For example, eight host bits gives us 254 hosts (256-2). Reducing this to seven host bits would result in 126 valid hosts (128-2). In each case we are excluding the all-zeros and all-ones bit combinations.

40. In order to accommodate seven subnets, how many subnet bits are required?

    A. 3

    B. 4

    C. 6

    D. 7

    B. Although three bits will yield eight bit combinations, two of them—the all-zeros and all-ones combinations—are not valid. Therefore we must include four bits, which will provide up to 14 subnets.

41. If we included six subnet bits in the subnet mask for a Class C address, how many hosts would each network support?

    A. 254

    B. 30

    C. 4

    D. 2

    D. If we included six subnet bits in the subnet mask for a Class C address, each network would support two hosts. With only two bits left for host addresses, the only legal bit patterns are 01 and 10, which provides for two hosts.

42. What class of address would we have to use if we needed 2,000 subnets, with over 5,000 users each?

A. Class A

B. Class B

C. Class C

D. Class D

A. Referring to Table 3-7, We see that it would require 11 subnet bits to accommodate 2,000 subnets. This immediately eliminates a Class C, which can only provide six subnet bits maximum. For a Class B address, using 11 subnet bits would only leave five bits for host addresses, which would allow only 30 hosts per subnet. Class A addresses with 11 subnet bits have 13 bits left for host addresses. This would permit 8,190 hosts per subnet.

43. Given a subnet address of 140.125.8.0, with a subnet mask of 255.255.252.0, what is the subnet address of the next higher subnet?

A. 140.125.16.0

B. 140.125.17.0

C. 140.125.32.0

D. 140.125.12.0

D. The subnet mask shows that the lowest bit of the subnet mask is a 4. This means that the first subnet will be 4, and they will increment by 4. The given subnet address is the second in the series, and the third will be 140.125.12.0.

44. Given a subnet address of 5.32.0.0 and a subnet mask of 255.224.0.0, what is the highest allowed host address on this subnet?

A. 5.32.255.254

B. 5.32.254.254

C. 5.63.255.254

D. 5.63.255.255

C. The mask shows that we are using three subnet bits, with the lowest value being 32. The interval between subnets is 32, so the next higher subnet would be 5.64.0.0. Subtracting 1 from this value leaves 5.63.255.255, the "32" subnet's broadcast address. One less than this is the highest host address for the subnet, 5.63.255.254.

45. If we saw the following subnet addresses, what would be the subnet mask associated with these subnets?
140.120.4.0
140.120.8.0
140.120.12.0
140.120.16.0

A. 255.255.252.0

B. 255.252.0.0.

C. 255.255.248.0

D. 255.255.4.0.

A. The pattern of subnet addresses reveals that the interval is 4 and the lowest subnet has a value of 4. In order to use contiguous high-order bits in our subnet mask, this would mean that we have six bits reserved for subnetting. Since we are dealing with a Class B address, we add these six bits to the default subnet mask of 255.255.0.0.

46. Given the network 2.0.0.0 with a subnet mask of 255.255.224.0, which of these is not a valid subnet ID for this network?

    A. 200.255.192.0

    B. 200.0.224.0

    C. 200.0.16.0

    D. 200.254.192.0

    C. The invalid subnet ID is 200.0.16.0. This represents an ID where all the subnet bits are zero.

47. What is the subnet mask for an address expressed as 175.25.0.0/24?

    A. 255.255.0.0

    B. 255.255.255.0

    C. Depends on address class

    D. 255.255.24.0

    B. The /24 tells us that there are 24 bits in the address prefix, which equates to 255.255.255.0.

48. VLSM allows us to:

    A. Use different subnet masks in different parts of the network

    B. Divide a subnet into secondary subnets

    C. Use classless IP addressing

    D. Both A and B

    D. VLSM allows us to use different subnet masks in different parts of the network and to divide a subnet into secondary subnets. Answer C is not correct, because we can use classless addressing without implementing VLSM.

49. What class of IP address is usually associated with supernetting?

    A. Class A

    B. Class B

    C. Class C

    D. Class D

    C. Supernetting is often used to combine several Class C networks.

50. Supernetting modifies the default subnet mask in what way?

    A. Adds bits to the default subnet mask

    B. Adds bits to the network address

    C. Removes bits from the subnet ID

    D. Removes bits from the default subnet mask

    D. Supernetting removes some of the rightmost bits of the default subnet mask, which summarizes several contiguous Class C networks into a single network entity.

51. What is the appropriate prompt from which to enter the IP ADDRESS command?

    A. Router>

    B. Router#

C. Router(config-if)#

D. Router(config)#
C. The IP ADDRESS command applies to a specific router interface, and would be entered after selecting the interface to be configured.

52. Which of the following subnet mask formats do Cisco routers support?

A. Dotted-decimal

B. Hexadecimal

C. Bitcount

D. All the above
D. All the formats listed are supported by Cisco, and can be selected using the IP NETMASK-FORMAT commands.

53. To configure a name-to-address mapping in the router mapping table, you would issue which of the following commands?

A. ROUTER(CONFIG-IF)# IP HOST

B. ROUTER(CONFIG-LINE)#IP NAME-SERVER

C. Router(config)#ip host

D. Both A and C
D. Both A and C are correct. These commands will be accepted from any level of configuration prompt, although they are global commands.

54. When a PING command returns a series of periods, what does that indicate?

A. Success

B. Non-existent address

C. Timeout

D. Unreachable
C. The period (.) indicates that the echo packet did not return within the specified timeout interval. This interval is configurable using the extended PING command.

55. Which of these commands could verify the operation of the protocol stack all the way to the Application layer?

A. PING

B. TRACE

C. Extended ping

D. TELNET
D. Telnet is the only command that would test all layers of the protocol. PING, in both versions, tests only up to the network layer. TRACE also operates at the network layer to reveal the routing path between two hosts.

56. To perform an extended ping to address 1.1.1.1, you would issue which of the following commands?

A. ROUTER> PING 1.1.1.1

B. Router# ping 1.1.1.1

C. Router(config)# ping

D. Router# ping
D. Extended ping requires Privileged mode, and also requires that no command-line options be entered (because it prompts for each option).

57. The length of an IP address is:

A. 24 bits

B. 16 bits

C. 32 bits

D. 48 bits

C. The IP address is a 32-bit (4 octets) logical address.

58. Which of the following classes is used for multicasting?

A. Class A

B. Class B

C. Class E

D. None of the above

D. Class D is used for multicasting purposes.

59. Which of the following statements is true regarding IP host addresses?

A. The host address part of an IP address can be set to "all binary ones" or to "all binary zeros."

B. The subnet address part of an IP address cannot be set to "all binary ones" or to "all binary zeros."

C. The network address part of an IP address can be set to "all binary ones" or to "all binary zeros."

B. For a valid host address, neither network address part, subnet address part, nor host address part can be set to "all binary ones" or "all binary zeros."

60. An IP address reserved for loopback test is:

A. 164.0.0.0

B. 130.0.0.0

C. 200.0.0.0

D. 127.0.0.0

D. 127.0.0.0 is reserved for assigning local loopback addresses and therefore, can not used as a network address.

61. An IP address used for local broadcasting (broadcasting to all hosts on the local network) is:

A. 127.255.255.255

B. 255.255.255.255

C. 164.0.0.0

D. 127.0.0.0

B. An IP address used for local broadcasting is 255.255.255.255. When all the bits in an IP address are set to ones, the resulting address is 255.255.255.255, which is used to send broadcast messages to all hosts on the network.

62. An IP address of 100.1.1.1 represents which class of network?

A. Class B

B. Class C

C. Class A

D. Class E

C. The Class A network address can take values from 1 – 126.

63. The Class D IP address pattern begins with:

A. 1111

B. 110

C. 010

D. 1110

D. The Class D addresses have bit pattern which begins with 1110. This allows values from 224 – 239 to be assigned for the purpose of multicasting.

64. The number 174 is represented in binary form by:

A. 11001110

B. 10101110

C. 10101010

D. 10110010

B. 10101110 = { 2^7 + 2^5 + 2^3 + 2^2 + 2^1 }={ 128 + 32 + 8 + 4 + 2 }= 174

65. The subnet mask in conjunction with an IP address defines:

A. A multicast address

B. A host address

C. The portion of the address that should be considered the network ID

D. None of the above

C. The subnet mask filters those bits that will be considered network address bits. The remaining bits not filtered form the host address portion.

66. The purpose of using subnets is:

A. To divide a network into smaller subnetworks

B. To improve network performance due to increased traffic

C. To make the internetwork more manageable

D. All of the above

D. The purposes of using subnets are: to divide a network into smaller subnetworks; to improve network performance due to increased traffic; and to make the internetwork more manageable.

67. The default subnet mask for Class B network is:

A. 8 bits long.

B. 24 bits long.

C. 16 bits long.

D. 32 bits long.

C. The default subnet mask for Class B is 255.255.0.0, which is 16 bits long.

68. To add bits to a default subnet mask, the bits are taken from:

A. The lowest-order contiguous bits of the network address

B. The lowest-order contiguous bits of the host address

C. The highest-order contiguous bits of the host address

D. The highest-order contiguous bits of the network address

C. Subnet bits are taken from the highest-order contiguous bits of the host address.

69. In planning subnets, the factors that need to be considered are:

A. The number of subnets needed

B. The number of hosts per subnet

C. The possible growth in number of subnets or hosts per subnet

D. All of the above
D. The number of subnets needed, the number of hosts per subnet, and the possible growth in number of subnets or hosts per subnet are all factors that must be considered when planning subnets.

70. How many subnets for Class B are possible if six bits are added to the default mask?

A. 14

B. 30

C. 62

D. 510
C. Six bits could create 64 bit combinations, but the first and last subnet addresses are not available.

71. The value 24 after / in the IP address 135.120.25.20/24 is called:

A. A robbed bit

B. A default bit

C. A prefix

D. A host bit
C. The prefix defines the subnet bits for the network. In this case /24 means the subnet bits are 24.

72. An IP address of 199.119.99.1/24 defines:

A. 24 subnet mask bits for Class A network

B. 24 subnet mask bits for Class B network

C. 24 subnet mask bits for Class C network

D. 24 subnet mask bits for Class E network
C. An IP address of 199.119.99.1/24 defines 24 subnet mask bits for Class C network. Class C address range is 192 – 223.

73. What IOS command would you use to define a global format to view the subnet mask during the "current session"?

A. ROUTER # IP ADDRESS

B. ROUTER # TERM DOMAIN-LOOKUP

C. Router # set format

D. Router # term ip netmask-format
D. The IOS command you would use to define a global format to view the subnet mask during the "current session" is ROUTER # TERM IP NETMASK-FORMAT. Note: Answer C is not a valid router command.

74. The router command ROUTER(CONFIG)# IP HOST {*hostname address*} is used for:

A. Viewing the route the packet has taken from source to destination

B. Viewing the host name and host address

C. Adding a static mapping of a host name to an address in the router's host cache

D. Showing source destination network's interfaces with other networks

C. The command ROUTER(CONFIG)# IP HOST {*hostname address*} adds a static entry to the router's host cache, where it is used for resolving the host name to an address. It requires the user to specify the name of the host and also the IP address associated with the host.

75. The maximum number of name server addresses that can be specified using the ROUTER(CONFIG)# IP NAME-SERVER command is:

A. Four

B. Six

C. Five

D. Three

B. Up to six name server addresses can be specified using the ROUTER(CONFIG)# IP NAME-SERVER command.

76. The following is a response to the ROUTER > PING 120.1.1.2 command:

.!!!!

Success rate is 80 percent (4/5), round trip min/avg/max = 28/75/112 ms

The 80 percent success rate in this response means:

A. Four out of five times, the response came back

B. Five packets were received at destination, and four were received at the source

C. Four times out of five, there was no response

D. Four packets out of a total of five packets reached the IP address 120.1.1.2

A. Success rate indicates the percentage of packets originating at the source that are successfully echoed by the destination. Destination may receive every packet, but you will receive a timeout if the reply does not come back.

77. A user on a Washington, DC network receives the following response after issuing a router command:

Tracing the route to Honolulu
1Tokyo(127.893.81.2) 800 ms 6 ms 4 ms
2 Lisbon(141.925.64.7) 600 ms 8 ms 6 ms
Honolulu(151.666.59.4) 400 ms 10 ms 8 ms
Washington dc#

This response was most likely obtained by issuing the command:

A. ROUTER# TELNET 151.666.59.4)

B. Lisbon# show iproute

C. washingtondc# show iproute

D. washingtondc# trace honolulu

E. honolulu# show ip route

D. This response was most likely obtained by issuing the command WASHINGTONDC# TRACE HONOLULU. The response tells that it is tracing the route to Honolulu. Also note that the last line of response is washingtondc#

78. For an IP address of 165.3.34.35, netmask of 255.255.255.224, and a subnet ID of 165.3.34.32, the usable host address range is:

A. From 165.3.34.34 to 165.3.34.64

B. From 165.3.34.35 to 165.3.34.65

C. From 165.3.34.33 to 165.3.34.62

D. From 165.3.34.33 to 165.3.34.63

C. The usable host address range is from 165.3.34.33 to 165.3.34.62. The netmask tells us that three bits are taken from the host address for subnet mask. This leaves five bits for host addresses, which is {2^5} 32 possible addresses for the host. However, we cannot use all zeros or all ones. Therefore, there are 30 possible hosts. The address 165.3.32.32 is already assigned to the subnet. Therefore, the starting address for the host is 165.3.34.33. The address 165.3.34.63 is used for broadcasting.

Chapter 4 Answers

1. Match the following application layer services to their corresponding transport layer protocol port.

A. SMTP 1. TCP/23

B. FTP 2. TCP/25

C. TFTP 3. TCP/80

D. Telnet 4. TCP/21

E. HTTP 5. UDP/69

F. DNS 6. TCP/53

A-2, B-4, C-5, D-1, E-3, F-6

2. Which OSI reference model layer does Telnet function at?

A. Transport

B. Network

C. Session

D. Application

D. Telnet is an application layer service.

3. How many layers does the TCP/IP protocol suite have, compared to the OSI reference model?

A. TCP model has 4, OSI model has 6

B. TCP model has 7, OSI model has 8

C. TCP model has 4, OSI model has 7

D. TCP model has 7, OSI model has 4

C. The TCP/IP protocol suite has four layers, while the OSI reference model has seven.

4. The TCP/IP protocol suite has a formal session layer that includes NetBIOS, RPCs, and TLI functions.

A. True

B. False

B. False. The TCP/IP protocol suite does not have a formal session layer.

5. What is the function of RPCs?

A. To move files from remote PCs to a local PC

B. To make remote function calls transparent, so they appear to be local
C. To initialize a program on a remote PC
D. To send a procedure that is local to a remote node for processing elsewhere
B. The function of RPCs is to transparently access remote procedures, making them appear local.

6. What does RPC stand for?
A. Remote personal computer
B. Reserved-programming call
C. Routed-procedure call
D. Remote-procedure call
D. RPC is the acronym for remote-procedure call.

7. What OSI reference model layer do sockets function at?
A. Application
B. Presentation
C. Session
D. Transport
E. Network
F. Data link
G. Physical
C. Sockets function at the session layer.

8. What function do sockets perform?
A. They make remote functions appear local, transparent to the user
B. They transfer files to and from remote nodes
C. They make the transport layer independent
D. They allow multiple applications to share the same connection to the network
D. Sockets allow multiple applications to use the same TCP/IP connection.

9. What is WinSock?
A. A version of sockets for the Microsoft Windows platform
B. Sockets on BSD UNIX
C. A session layer API commonly considered to be its own protocol
D. A network layer service for Microsoft Windows
A. WinSock is a Microsoft Windows version of sockets.

10. What does TLI do?
A. It makes remote functions appear local, transparent to the user
B. It transfers files to and from remote nodes
C. It makes the transport layer independent
D. It allows multiple applications to share the same connection to the network
C. The transport layer interface makes the transport layer independent from upper-layer services.

11. What OSI layer does NetBIOS function at?
A. Application
B. Presentation
C. Session
D. Transport
E. Network

F. Data link

G. Physical
C. NetBIOS functions at the OSI model session layer.

12. Which protocols can NetBIOS bind to? (Choose all that apply.)

A. Appletalk

B. IPX

C. IP

D. NetBEUI
B, C, D. NetBIOS can run over IPX, IP, and NetBEUI.

13. What layers do not exist in the TCP/IP model that are in the OSI model?

A. Application, presentation, and network

B. Presentation, session, and data link

C. Session, network, and physical

D. Presentation, data link, and physical
B. There are no formal presentation, session, or data link layers in the TCP/IP model.

14. What is a socket in the transport layer?

A. An IP address plus a port

B. An API that makes the transport layer independent

C. An API that allows multiple applications to share a network connection

D. A function that makes remote procedures appear to be local
A. A socket is an IP address plus a port

15. What is a port?

A. An API that makes the transport layer independent

B. An API that allows multiple applications to share a network connection

C. A function that makes remote procedures appear to be local

D. The point where upper-layer processes access transport layer services
D. A port is where upper-layer processes access the transport layer.

16. Which of the following services uses a process called windowing?

A. Reliable data transfer

B. Connection-oriented virtual circuit

C. Buffered transfer

D. Resequencing

E. Multiplexing

F. Efficient, full-duplex transmission

G. Flow control
G. Windowing is a form of flow control.

17. What is UDP?

A. An API that makes the transport layer independent

B. A connectionless, unreliable transport protocol

C. An API that allows multiple applications to share a network connection

D. A function that makes remote procedures appear to be local
B. UDP is a connectionless, unreliable transport protocol.

18. What is IP?

A. It is the transport mechanism for upper layer services
B. It is the session layer API for making the transport layer independent
C. It is the network layer protocol that moves data from one node to another
D. It is the physical layer protocol for Internet connections
C. IP (Internet Protocol) is the network layer protocol that moves data from one node to another.

19. What is ICMP?

A. It is a network layer protocol that handles control messages
B. It is a network layer protocol that resolves addresses
C. It is a session layer API that makes remote procedures transparent to a user
D. It is a transport layer function for unreliable transport
A. ICMP handles control messages at the network layer.

20. Ping sends an ICMP echo command to an IP address in order to determine whether a network connection exists to that node.

A. True
B. False
A. True. Ping sends an ICMP echo command to an IP address, and from the response, verifies that the address is reachable from the local host.

21. Which of the following best describes TCP/IP?

A. A static protocol
B. A proprietary protocol
C. A collection of internetworking protocols
C. TCP/IP is a dynamically changing collection of internetworking protocols.

22. UDP and TCP represent mechanisms used by which layer of the TCP/IP?

A. Data link layer
B. Physical layer
C. Presentation layer
D. Transport layer
D. TCP and UDP represent transport mechanism in the TCP/IP protocol structure.

23. RPCs provide which of the following?

A. Connection-oriented session
B. Transparency to make remote calls look local
C. Portability of applications between heterogeneous systems
D. A and C only
E. B and C only

F. A, B, and C
E. RPCs provide transparency to make remote calls look local, and portability of applications between heterogeneous systems. RPC is a connectionless session.

24. Distributed Computing Environment (DCE) is an example of:

A. OSI model
B. RPC implementation
C. Extreme Data Representation
D. A and B
B. DCE is an implementation of RPC.

25. Which statement is true of WinSock?

A. It is a MAC application
B. It represents a graphical user interface
C. It represents a network layer
D. It provides the means for sharing an Internet connection between multiple IP protocol suite utilities
D. WinSock represents a session layer API allowing multiple applications to share an Internet connection. It is not a GUI.

26. Which statement is true of TLI?

A. It is a layer in the OSI model
B. It is a layer in the TCP/IP model
C. It is a System V API
D. It is part of the UNIX Kernel
C. TLI represents a System V Application Programming Interface.

27. Which statement is true of Windows Name Server (WINS)?

A. It is a protocol
B. It provides capability for name resolution
C. It is a network layer
D. It is a proprietary name server
E. A, B, and D only
F. B and D only
F. WINS is a Microsoft proprietary NetBIOS name server that provides capability for name resolution.

28. ICMP, IP, ARP, and RARP of the IP protocol suite map to:

A. OSI layers 1 and 2
B. OSI layer 5
C. OSI layer 3
D. OSI layer 2
C. ICMP, IP, ARP, and RARP all map to OSI layer 3.

29. Which layer is most important in providing reliable data exchange between two systems?

A. Physical layer
B. Data link layer
C. Session layer
D. Transport layer
D. The transport layer is the single most important layer in assuring reliable data transfer regardless of the underlying networks in between the TCP/IP protocol suite.

30. Which of the following does TCP provide?

A. Unreliable data stream

B. Connectionless virtual circuit

C. Flow control

D. Structured byte stream movement

C. TCP provides a connection-oriented virtual circuit with reliable byte stream, where the byte stream is both continuous and unstructured.

31. Of the following, which field is not a part of the TCP header?

A. Subnet mask

B. Sequence number

C. Data offset

D. Destination port

A. The subnet mask is not a part of the TCP header.

32. What is the sequence number in a TCP header used for?

A. Acknowledgments

B. Reordering of the octets received

C. Rejecting duplicate octets

D. All of the above

D. The sequence number in a TCP header is used for acknowledgments, for reordering of the octets received, and for rejecting duplicate octets.

33. Variable sliding windows provide an explicit mechanism for notifying TCP if an intermediate node (for example, a router) becomes congested.

A. True

B. False

B. False.

34. Which of the following parameters is not a part of UDP header?

A. Source port

B. Urgent pointer

C. Checksum

D. Length

E. Destination port

B. The urgent pointer is not a part of the UDP header. The UDP header has only four parameters: source port, destination port, length, and UDP checksum.

35. When a router has been configured for UDP flooding, the source address might change, but the destination address will not change as the datagram propagates through the network.

A. True

B. False

B. False. The destination address might change, but the source address does not change.

36. The spanning-tree algorithm allows:

A. Forwarding of packets with no control

B. Forwarding of broadcasts to an interface which already has received the broadcast

C. Prevention of duplication of forwarding of packets

D. A and B only
C. Spanning tree forwards packets in a controlled manner.

37. IP helper addresses are a form of ________ addressing and require the command specification of ________ on every interface receiving broadcasts that need to be forwarded.

A. Static / IP header address
B. Dynamic / IP forward-protocol UDP
C. Dynamic / IP forward-protocol TCP
A. IP helper addresses are a form of static addressing and require specification of IP header address on every interface receiving broadcasts that need to be forwarded.

38. Which of the following protocols provide address resolution?

A. ICMP
B. RARP
C. IP
D. UDP
E. TCP
B. RARP is a Reverse Address Resolution Protocol.

39. IP is described as an unreliable mechanism because it does not guarantee delivery.

A. True
B. False
A. True. IP is described as an unreliable mechanism because it does not guarantee delivery.

40. What does fragmentation in TCP/IP represent?

A. Segmenting of datagrams into 53-byte packets for ATM applications
B. Division of larger datagrams into convenient size packets
C. A process that occurs on a router
D. A, B, and C
E. A and C only
F. B and C only
F. Fragmentation is a process that occurs on a router somewhere between the source and destination. This process segments the datagram into a convenient size to fit into a single frame for transport over the network.

41. Which of the following statements is true of ARP?

A. It makes a MAC address logically independent of the physical hardware
B. It makes it necessary for the administrator to physically manage the MAC address of each NIC
C. It integrates routing function with the physical and data link layers
D. It routes packets based on destination host, not on destination network
A. With ARP, an administrator does not have to physically manage the MAC address of each NIC. ARP separates routing function from the physical and data link layers. ARP routes packets based on destination network, and not destination host.

42. A host's ARP cache is good forever once it has been created.

    A. True

    B. False
    B. False. The host's ARP cache is good only for a certain time period, and then it times out.

43. ARP is a broadcast protocol, and ARP caching is used because broadcasts are expensive.

    A. True

    B. False
    A. True. ARP is a broadcast protocol, and ARP caching is used because broadcasts are expensive.

44. Reverse Address Resolution Protocol (RARP) is termed "reverse" because:

    A. It is used by the system that knows its IP address but does not know its MAC address

    B. It is used by the system that knows its MAC address but does not know its IP address

    C. It is used by the system that knows the destination's IP address but does not know the destination's MAC address

    D. It is used by the system that knows the destination's MAC address but does not know the destination's IP address
    B. RARP is used by a system to resolve its IP address.

45. Inverse Address Resolution Protocol (InARP) is generally used by:

    A. Broadcast networks

    B. Nonbroadcast networks

    C. Both broadcast and nonbroadcast networks
    B. Inverse Address Resolution Protocol (InARP) is generally used by nonbroadcast networks such as Frame Relay.

46. The PING command makes use of what ICMP parameter?

    A. Redirect

    B. Source quench

    C. Echo reply

    D. Destination unreachable
    C. The PING command makes use of the echo request and echo reply parameter.

47. ICMP Redirect is sent by:

    A. A host to the gateway

    B. A gateway to the host

    C. A router to another router

    D. A router to a network
    B. ICMP Redirect is sent by a gateway to the host. It instructs the host to use a different route when the router detects that its route is not as optimal as that of another router.

Chapter 5 Answers

1. Company A has recently merged with Company B, which exists in the same building and is physically close enough for all the computers to belong on the same network segment. Company A uses an ATM backbone and Fast Ethernet for all nodes. Company B has a Token Ring environment on shielded twisted-pair wiring. Why will Company A and Company B select a router for their newly merged network?
   A. Network segment size has reached the maximum
   B. Network addresses are not sufficient for a merged network
   C. Traffic must be segmented to prevent an expected bandwidth overload
   D. A router is the usual way to connect dissimilar network types
   D. A router is used when connecting dissimilar network types.

2. What are the two basic mechanisms that make up a routing protocol?
   A. Route selection
   B. Flooding
   C. Autonomous Systems
   D. Data Transmission
   A, D. The two mechanisms that make up a routing protocol are selecting the best route and transmitting the data.

3. What is a routing table used for?
   A. It is the physical support for the router to sit on
   B. It contains a list of all the timers used to prevent routing loops
   C. It is used to select the best route
   D. It manages the periodic update algorithm
   C. The routing table is used for selecting the best route.

4. What types of information can be found in different types of routing protocol routing tables? (Select 3.)
   A. The destination network associated with the next hop
   B. The destination network associated with the cost metric
   C. The destination network associated with the subnet mask
   D. The destination network associated with the next path or interface to use
   A, B, D. The routing information table contains the destination network address and the associated value, which provides the route selection criteria: hop, cost metric, or next path.

5. What is a routing update used for?
   A. Routing updates notify neighboring routers with a hello
   B. Routing updates redistribute routes learned from other routing protocols

C. Routing updates maintain the routing table

D. Routing updates increase the network addresses available by changing the subnet masks

C. Routing updates are the method used to maintain the routing table.

6. When a node on one network sends a packet to a node on another segment that is three hops away, what addresses are included in the initial addressing of that packet? (Select 2.)

A. The network address of the router

B. The MAC layer address of the router

C. The network address of the destination node

D. The MAC layer address of the destination node

B, C. The initial packet sends the packet with the network address of the destination node, and the MAC layer, (hardware address of the router).

7. What are three objectives for a routing protocol?

A. Accuracy

B. Quick holddowns

C. Rapid convergence

D. Low overhead

A, C, D. Three objectives for a routing protocol are: accuracy, rapid convergence, and low overhead.

8. Define convergence.

A. Convergence is the updates that are triggered by network changes

B. Convergence is the process of sending hello packets

C. Convergence is two routers merging their routing tables into one

D. Convergence is the synchronizing of all routing tables on the internetwork, or simply the synchronization of a single route change across all routers.

D. Convergence happens when all router's routing information tables synchronize.

9. Why are dynamic routing protocols considered dynamic?

A. Because each route is dynamically selected for each packet with a destination network not attached to the router

B. Because new routes are dynamically recomputed whenever there is a change in the internetwork topology

C. Because convergence happens faster

D. Because all the routes remain the same no matter what changes happen on the network

B. Dynamic routing protocols are dynamic because routes are recomputed whenever a change occurs in the internetwork topology.

10. What is a static route?

A. A static route is one that has been manually entered into the routing table and is not updated by a routing protocol

B. A static route is one that is recomputed whenever a change is made on the internetwork

C. A static route is one that is redistributed when it has been learned by another routing protocol

D. A static route is one that comes already configured in the router from the manufacturer

A. A static route is manually entered into the routing table and never updated by a routing protocol.

11. What type of network is best when using static routes?

A. A large network with hundreds of routers and networks

B. A complex internetwork that changes often

C. An autonomous system with multiple connections to other autonomous systems

D. A small network with few routers and infrequent changes

D. Only small networks with few routers and infrequent changes are appropriate for static routes, because static routing depends on the administrator to update each router whenever a change is made on the internetwork.

12. What is an autonomous system?

A. An area

B. A domain

C. A contiguous set of routers defined within a larger internetwork that do not share routing information with the external internetwork

D. All of the above

E. None of the above

D. An autonomous system is also known as an area or a domain. It is a contiguous set of routers defined within a larger internetwork; though they share routing information with each other, they do not propagate that information outside the area.

13. What is a default route?

A. A type of static route

B. A destination for any nonroutable packet

C. Gateway of last resort

D. All of the above

E. None of the above

D. A default route is normally a type of static route that can be known as the gateway of last resort, where all nonroutable packets are forwarded to for further handling.

14. What type of information does a distance vector router build its routing table with?

A. Hello packets

B. Second-hand information

C. LSPs

D. First-hand information
B. Because distance vector routers copy their neighbor's routing tables, update them, and forward them on, they use second-hand information.

15. What is the count to infinity problem?

A. A routing loop that results from the way distance vector protocols use second-hand information

B. The inability of routers to process more than 16 hops

C. The excessive CPU overhead presented by distance vector algorithms

D. The result of using both RIP and IGRP on the same internetwork
A. The count to infinity problem is a routing loop resulting from second-hand information.

16. What is poison reverse?

A. A change to the default update period timer

B. A routing loop that occurs when using second-hand information to update route tables

C. A router virus

D. A version of split-horizon that sends back a "route unreachable" update to the router that the route was learned from, in order to avoid routing loops
D. Poison reverse is a version of split-horizon that sends back a "route unreachable" update to the router from which it learned of that route, in order to avoid routing loops.

17. What is RIP?

A. RIP is an older distance vector Interior Gateway Protocol with a 30-second update timer and maximum of 15 hops (where "infinity" is 16 hops)

B. RIP is a new link-state protocol created by Cisco

C. RIP is a proprietary protocol created by Cisco that has two versions; only version 2 is used currently

D. RIP is a distance vector Interior Gateway Protocol with a 224 maximum network diameter (maximum 224 hops)
A. RIP is an older distance vector protocol and Interior Gateway Protocol, with 30-second update period and maximum of 15 hops.

18. What is IGRP?

A. IGRP is an older distance vector Interior Gateway Protocol with a 30-second update timer and maximum of 15 hops (where "infinity" is 16 hops)

B. IGRP is a new link-state protocol created by Cisco

C. IGRP is a proprietary protocol created by Cisco that has two versions; only version 2 is used currently

D. IGRP is a distance vector and Interior Gateway Protocol with a 224 maximum network diameter (maximum 224 hops)
D. IGRP is a distance vector and Interior Gateway Protocol with a 224

maximum network diameter (maximum 224 hops).

19. What is the purpose of a flash update in IGRP?

    A. A flash update is a standard 90-second update

    B. After three flash updates, a route is considered unreachable

    C. A flash update is sent immediately upon a change in the network topology, in order to speed convergence

    D. After seven flash updates, a route is removed from the routing table

    C. Flash updates are used to speed convergence.

20. How can the administrator change how IGRP selects routes?

    A. The administrator can set update timers

    B. The administrator can enable or disable split horizon

    C. The administrator can set up load balancing across redundant routes

    D. The administrator can adjust the metric weights used for determining the route selection

    D. The administrator can adjust the metric weights used for route selection.

21. The way to get traffic from one segment of the network to another segment is:

    A. Bridging

    B. Routing

    C. Switching

    D. All of the above

    D. Bridging, routing, and switching are used to move traffic from one segment to another.

22. Routing occurs at which layer?

    A. Physical layer

    B. Data link layer

    C. Network layer

    D. Transport layer

    C. Routing takes place at the network layer.

23. In general, the best route selected by a router is one with:

    A. Least cost

    B. Shortest distance

    C. Lowest metric value

    D. None of the above

    C. Metric is used to select the best route. Cost and distance are used by some routing algorithms as metric in determining the best route.

24. A routing table typically includes which of the following?

    A. Destination network address

    B. The total number of networks

    C. The number of nodes in each network

    D. The total number of routers in a network

    A. A router normally has information on the network address of the destination node on the path.

25. When a router receives a packet, it accepts or rejects a packet by examining what?
    A. The MAC address of the source of the packet
    B. The address of the source network/node number
    C. The address of the destination network/node
    D. The MAC address of the next router
    C. Upon receiving a packet, the router examines the address of the destination node. If it cannot send the packet to the destination address, it either drops the packet or forwards it to a default router.
26. Low overhead of a routing algorithm is normally associated with:
    A. Optimal route
    B. CPU usage
    C. Accuracy
    D. Convergence
    B. The overhead is normally associated with bandwidth and CPU usage. Accuracy is associated with optimal route.
27. Convergence is not an issue if:
    A. Routers are added to the network
    B. Some of the network interfaces are down
    C. CPU/bandwidth usage of the routers changes
    D. An invariant network topology is selected for the network architecture
    D. Convergence is not an issue if an invariant network topology is selected for the network architecture. Answers A, B, and C all indicate a changing network, which would require monitoring of convergence.
28. An Internet Protocol (IP) router selects:
    A. An entire path from source to destination
    B. The next route step
    C. The two adjacent routers to itself
    D. All of the above
    B. An IP routing tables allows it to select the next route step the packet needs to take.
29. The IP ROUTE configuration command for a static route includes which of the following parameters?
    A. Subnetwork number of the destination network
    B. Subnet mask of the source network
    C. IP address of the interface of the router which the packet should use
    D. MAC address of the next router on the path
    C. The IP ROUTE command includes the IP address of the interface of the router that the packet should use. It also includes the network number that the route will be going to, and the subnet mask of that network.
30. Given the following portion of the network:

Network A → Router X → Router Y →
Network B
Interface: Interface: 86.0.0.0
X0 Y0
35.3.3.4
and assuming a network mask of 255.0.0.0 for both A and B networks, which one of the following represents a correct command to configure Router X to send data from Network A to Network B?

A. #IP ROUTE 85.0.0.0 255.0.0.0 35.3.3.3

B. #ip route 86.0.0.0 255.0.0.0 35.3.3.4

C. #ip route 86.0.0.0 255.0.0.0 35.3.3.3

D. #ip route 85.0.0.0 255.0.0.0 35.3.3.4

B. The correct command is #IP ROUTE 86.0.0.0 255.0.0.0 35.3.3.4. Answer A tries to route traffic to Network A through interface on Router X. Answer C tries to route traffic to Network B through interface on Router X. Answer D tries to route traffic to Network A through interface on Router Y.

31. A static routing table can be changed at any time without manual intervention.

A. True

B. False

B. False. To change a static table, an intervention by an authorized person is required.

32. In a hybrid solution of static and dynamic routing, the nonroutable packets are sent to:

A. The next router

B. The central router

C. The gateway of last resort

D. The source router where the packets originated

C. In hybrid network, the nonroutable packets are routed to a static router designated a router of last resort.

33. How is fault tolerance on a routing algorithm achieved?

A. By providing a central control router

B. By a distributed routing protocol

C. By load balancing of the traffic

D. All of the above

B. Distributed routing protocol provides fault tolerance in case of failures.

34. The configuration command IP DEFAULT for a default static router requires which of the following parameters?

A. Network mask

B. Router interface number

C. Subnet ID

D. Network number

D. The IP DEFAULT command requires a network number.

35. In a distance vector routing protocol, aging is set for:

A. Only the next available router

B. All routing information

C. Only the unavailable routers

D. Only the routers in the lowest metric route

B. Aging in a distance vector routing algorithm is set for all routing information.

36. In a distance vector algorithm, the holddown interval for large or complex networks:

A. Cannot be used

B. Would need to have a much larger value

C. Is equal to negative reachability parameter

D. Would need to have a smaller value to reach convergence

B. For larger or complex networks, if the holddown period is made sufficiently large, then problems associated with the network stability could be minimized, though not eliminated in all cases.

37. What do link-state protocols use as a metric?

A. Hops

B. Cost

C. CPU usage

D. Network operational time

B. As a metric, link-state protocols use cost, and not hops.

38. Flooding in link-state protocol means what?

A. A router sending all routing information to its neighbors

B. A router broadcasting all information to all routers in the network

C. The neighbors of a link-state router receiving a link-state packet, copying it, and then forwarding it to the rest of the network

D. A router sending information about the routers that have changed

C. Flooding in link-state protocol means that the neighbors of a link-state router receive a link-state packet, copy it, and then forward it to the rest of the network.

39. Which statement is true of Interior Gateway Protocols?

A. They apply to Internet domains

B. They apply to autonomous systems within the network

C. They apply to external networks

D. They allow systems in the Internet to manage areas in the network where IGP is implemented

B. IGPs apply to autonomous systems within the network.

40. Exterior Gateway Protocols are known as:

A. Inter-domain

B. Areas

C. Domains

D. Intra-domain

A. Exterior Gateway Protocols are known as inter-domain, because they work between domains.

41. Routing Information Protocol (RIP) can have a maximum of:

    A. 24 hops
    B. 16 hops
    C. 12 hops
    D. 8 hops

    B. RIP has a limitation of 16 hops.

42. How many commands are required to configure a router for RIP?

    A. Four
    B. Three
    C. Two
    D. One

    C. The RIP configuration requires one command to enable RIP, and a second to activate an interface for RIP.

43. RIP authentication command can be used with which version of RIP?

    A. RIP version 1
    B. RIP version 2
    C. RIP version 1 and RIP version 2
    D. None of the above

    B. RIP authentication command can be used only with RIP version 2.

44. In the Interior Gateway Routing Protocol, a route is removed from the routing table after:

    A. Three update periods
    B. 60 seconds
    C. Five update periods
    D. Seven update periods
    E. 90 seconds

    D. A route is removed from the routing table after seven update periods. In IGRP, updates are broadcast every 90 seconds. After three update periods where a route is missed, the route is considered unreachable. After seven periods, the route is removed.

45. Which of the following is used to calculate metric in Interior Gateway Routing Protocol?

    A. Internetwork delay
    B. Bandwidth
    C. Load
    D. Reliability
    E. All of the above

    E. In IGRP, internetwork delay, load, bandwidth, and reliability are used to calculate metric value.

46. What is the maximum allowable number of hops in Enhanced Interior Routing Gateway Protocol?

    A. 64
    B. 224
    C. 128
    D. 232
    E. 256

    B. The maximum number of hops used in EIGRP is 224.

47. Enhanced Interior Routing Gateway Protocol uses which of the following?

    A. Link-state vector

B. Diffusion Update Algorithm
C. Distance vector
D. A and B only
E. B and C only
E. EIGRP uses the distance vector with DUAL, which enhances the convergence properties.

Chapter 6 Answers

1. What is the administrative distance for directly connected routes?

A. 0
B. 1
C. 100
D. 120
A. Directly connected routes have an administrative distance of 0.

2. How many IP addresses can be bound to each host name using the IP HOST command?

A. 1
B. 2
C. 8
D. 255
C. Each host address can have a maximum of eight IP addresses.

3. Which command do you use to view the currently configured default route?

A. SHOW IP CONFIG
B. show default gateway
C. show ip route
D. show default network
C. SHOW IP ROUTE is the command for viewing the current default route.

4. Which routing protocol uses autonomous system numbers?

A. RIP
B. IGRP
C. OFLP
D. OSPF
B. IGRP uses autonomous system numbers to identify separate IGRP processes.

5. How many DNS servers can be added to a router's configuration?

A. One
B. Two
C. Four
D. Six
D. You can add six DNS servers with the IP NAME-SERVER command.

6. When configuring IGRP, what is the minimum amount for the FLUSH argument in the TIMERS BASIC command?

A. 30 seconds
B. Three times the period set for sending RIP updates
C. The summation of INVALID and HOLDDOWN
D. UPDATE minus SLEEPTIME
C. FLUSH must be the summation of

INVALID and HOLDDOWN at minimum.

7. Which of the following is not true regarding IP unnumbered?

   A. Major drawback is the loss of an IP subnet

   B. IP unnumbered is only available on Cisco routers

   C. Can be used to communicate across serial interface through Ethernet interface

   D. Used on point-to-point links

   A. The advantage of IP unnumbered is that it prevents the loss of an entire subnet by not requiring the assignment of IPs to the two routers' serial interfaces.

8. Identify the proper syntax for assigning a secondary IP address to an interface.

   A. IP SECONDARY ADDRESS 10.10.10.10 255.0.0.0

   B. IP 10.10.10.10 255.255.0.0 secondary

   C. IP address secondary 10.10.10.10 255.255.255.0

   D. IP address 10.10.10.10 255.255.255.0 secondary

   D. The correct syntax is IP ADDRESS *ip-address mask* SECONDARY, therefore IP ADDRESS 10.10.10.10 255.255.255.0 SECONDARY would be correct.

9. Which of the following are advantages to static routing?

   A. Less overhead on router

   B. Paths are created on the fly

   C. Reduction in places where faults can lie

   D. Scalable

   A, C. The advantages to static routing are that it creates less overhead on routers, and reduces the number of places where faults can lie. There are more actions that take place in dynamic routing, so more needs to be investigated to find problems.

10. What does the IP DOMAIN-NAME command do?

    A. Names the domain that the Cisco router belongs to

    B. Names domains the router cannot find directly

    C. Appends a domain to unqualified requests

    D. Broadcasts domain name across subnets

    C. The IP DOMAIN-NAME command will append the domain listed to unqualified domain requests in order to try to find a fully qualified host name.

11. By default, what happens to broadcast UDP packets that come across Cisco routers?

    A. They are denied

    B. They are converted into broadcast-based packets

    C. They are routed to all IP interfaces

D. They are sent to UDP queues
A. By default, all broadcast UDP packets are denied.

12. What are the default ports for BOOTP traffic?

A. 23 and 24
B. 67 and 68
C. 138 – 141
D. 9 and 10
B. The default ports for BOOTP traffic are 67 and 68.

13. Which syntax for setting the default gateway is correct?

A. IP DEFAULT-GATEWAY 10.10.10.100
B. IP 10.10.10.100 default-gateway
C. Default-gateway 10.10.10.100 255.255.255.0
D. IP default-gateway 10.10.10.100 255.255.255.0
A. The correct syntax is IP DEFAULT-GATEWAY IP-ADDRESS, therefore IP DEFAULT-GATEWAY 10.10.10.100 would be correct.

14. Which is true regarding secondary addressing?

A. Secondary addressing must exist on the same subnet as the primary
B. Secondary addressing can only be applied to serial interfaces
C. A maximum of three address can be assigned per interface
D. All attached routers need a secondary address on the same subnet.
D. All directly attached routers need a secondary address on the same subnet as the referenced router.

15. Which of the following statements about administrative distance are true?

A. It is used when two routing protocols advertise the same route
B. All routes have an administrative distance
C. The lowest value always wins
D. Static routes have an administrative distance of 1
A, B, C, D. All these statements are correct. When two routing protocols advertise the same route, the administrative distance is used. All routing protocols have a default value, and the route with the lowest value will win and be added to the cache. Static routes have an administrative distance of 1, while directly connected routes have an administrative distance of 0.

16. Which of the following acronyms is not accurate?

A. DNS — Dynamic Naming Service
B. UDP — User Datagram Protocol
C. DHCP — Dynamic Host Configuration Protocol
D. TFTP — Trivial File Transfer Protocol
A. DNS stands for Domain Name Service.

17. Where can DHCP information be found?

    A. Encapsulated within UDP packets

    B. Encapsulated within the TCP part of TCP/IP

    C. Encapsulated within BOOTP packets

    D. Encapsulated within DNS traffic
    C. DHCP information is contained in the data portion of BOOTP packets

18. Which of the following is performed at a global level?

    A. Forwarding of UDP

    B. DNS lookup

    C. Adding routes

    D. Enabling RIP
    A, B, C, D. The forwarding of UDP packets, DNS lookup, adding routes, and enabling RIP are all done at the global level.

19. Where are the host name-to-address mappings stored?

    A. Address cache

    B. Host cache

    C. Static RAM

    D. IP Config table
    B. The table of host name-to-address mappings is stored in the host cache.

20. If you add more users than there are available host addresses on a given subnet, which of the following principles can you apply to remedy the situation?

    A. IGRP

    B. Shared IP

    C. Secondary addressing

    D. IP unnumbered
    C. Secondary addressing is what you use to assign multiple IP addresses to single interfaces. Adding a second IP address to a NIC enables you to add another subnet to the physical segment, thereby increasing your number of available hosts.

21. An IP UNNUMBERED command does which of the following?

    A. It allows use of different subnet masks on two ports on each side of the link

    B. It is used in a point-to-multipoint configuration

    C. It allows the same netmask number to be used on each side of the link

    D. It makes an effective use of IP addresses
    C, D. The IP UNNUMBERED command allows the same netmask to be used on either side of the link, thus minimizing the waste of IP addresses. It also uses your available IP addresses effectively, since it prevents you from wasting an entire subnet across the link.

22. In static routing, the route to a destination network:

    A. Is not known prior to configuration

    B. Remains permanently in the routing table

    C. Is determined in real time

    D. Is known prior to configuration
    D. In static routing, the path between two destinations is known prior to configuring a router.

23. If two routing protocols recommend the same route to a router, the router will:

A. Select either of the two routes at random, with no preference for one over the other

B. Select the route that has a lower administrative distance value

C. Select the route that has a higher administrative distance value

D. Place both the routes in the routing table

B. The router will select a route associated with the protocol that has the lower administrative distance value.

24. What is the command used to remove static routes from the routing tables?

A. SHOW IP ROUTE

B. show ip redirect

C. change ip route

D. no ip route

D. The NO IP ROUTE command removes static routes from the routing tables.

25. What is the default time interval at which RIP updates are sent?

A. 30 seconds

B. 15 seconds

C. 60 seconds

D. 90 seconds

A. RIP updates are sent every 30 seconds unless specified otherwise.

26. In the TIMERS BASIC command, the parameter to specify the time after which the route is to be taken out from the routing table is:

A. SLEEPTIME

B. holddown

C. invalid

D. flush

D. FLUSH tells the router to take the entry out of the routing table after a certain time.

27. In an IGRP command TIMERS BASIC 15 45 0 60, the number 45 represents:

A. holddown time

B. update time

C. invalid time

D. flush time

C. The number 45 represents the invalid time. The invalid time represents time at which the route becomes invalid and is typically set at three times the value of the update parameter (15 sec in this case is the update parameter).

28. In an IGRP command ROUTER IGRP 7, the number 7 is:

A. An autonomous system number

B. A gateway number

C. A port number

D. A terminal number

A. The number 7 is an autonomous system number.

29. In the command IP MYNETWORK 132.2.2.2, what port number is used in establishing a connection?

A. 21

B. 23

C. 25

D. 69

B. When no port is specified, a default port number of 23 is used for Telnet.

30. In Cisco routers the DNS lookup capability must be enabled.

A. True

B. False

B. In Cisco routers the DNS capability is enabled by default. If it has been disabled, then an enable command is needed.

31. In order to forward broadcast traffic for certain UDP requests, which of the following commands should be used?

A. IP HELPER-ADDRESS

B. ip address

C. ip forward-protocol

D. interface

E. A and C only

F. B and C only

E. The IP HELPER command identifies the network where the broadcasts are to be directed, and the IP FORWARD command tells the router that it needs to forward the packets sent by UDP.

32. What is the purpose of secondary addressing?

A. To increase the number of hosts on the same network by increasing the IP address capacity

B. To increase the number of subnets

C. To limit hardware cost

D. A and B only

E. B and C only

F. A and C only

F. Secondary addresses are used to add hosts on a network without adding additional hardware.

33. If we implement a secondary address on router X, and we need all other routers to be able to route traffic to its attached hosts, all other routers attached to the same physical subnet as router X will also need a secondary address on the same subnet.

A. True

B. False

A. True. All other routers attached to the same physical subnet as router X will also need a secondary address on the same subnet.

34. The secondary address configuration can be achieved by applying the identical set of commands that are used for configuring the primary address.

A. True

B. False

B. False. For configuring secondary addresses, a secondary parameter is required at the end of the command.

35. IP unnumbered is configured:
    A. Globally for all interfaces
    B. On each interface as needed
    C. On serial interfaces only
    D. On Ethernet only
    B. IP unnumbered is configured on one interface at a time.
36. Match the protocol on the left with administrative distances on the right.
    A. Static 1. 120
    B. OSPF 2. 100
    C. RIP 3. 1
    D. IGRP 4. 110
    A-3, B-4, C-1, D-2 See Table 6-1 for information on administrative distances.

Chapter 7 Answers

1. The service provided by IPX is:
    A. Guaranteed delivery
    B. Datagram
    C. Connection-oriented
    D. Sequenced
    B. IPX only provides an unreliable, connectionless datagram service.
2. The Transport Control field in the IPX header holds what information?
    A. The age of the packet
    B. Protocol type
    C. Router hop count
    D. Level of service required
    C. The Transport Control field in the IPX header holds router hop count information. The Transport Control field is initialized to zero when the packet is generated, and incremented each time it travels through a router.
3. What is the length of an IPX network number?
    A. 16 bits
    B. Variable
    C. 48 bits
    D. 32 bits
    D. The Network Number is a fixed-length 32-bit number, although it is normally written with leading zeroes omitted.
4. In the IPX address 0102.0000.8045.1700, what is the node address?
    A. 1700
    B. 0102.0000.8045
    C. 0102.0000
    D. 0000.8045.1700
    D. The node address is 0000.8045.1700. An IPX address is always written with the network number first, followed by the node address. A socket number is sometimes appended.
5. What can you say about this address: 47.0000.0000.0001?
    A. It is the address of a NetWare print server

B. It is an internal network address

C. The included socket number is 0001

D. Nothing
B. It is an internal network address. Servers are always node 0000.0000.0001 on their internal network.

6. The Checksum field in the IPX header is normally set to:

A. A checksum of the entire IPX packet

B. A checksum of the IPX header fields only

C. 0xFFFF

D. 0
C. The Checksum field in the IPX header is not used by default. It is set to 0xFFFF when the packet is generated.

7. If an IPX node is configured to use the Ethernet_802.2 encapsulation, which other machines can it communicate with directly (without going through a router) on the same network?

A. Machines running any encapsulation

B. Machines running either Ethernet_802.2 or Ethernet_802.3

C. Machines running Ethernet_II

D. Machines running Ethernet_802.2
D. To communicate directly, nodes must be running the same frame type.

8. To run multiple encapsulations on a single physical interface, a router has to:

A. Use a different network number for each encapsulation

B. Use subinterfaces, not secondary networks

C. Enable NLSP routing

D. Use an access list
A. Each encapsulation in use on an interface forms its own IPX network, and so must be given its own network number. Each network number must still be unique across the IPX internetwork.

9. Which protocol does a workstation use to locate a server providing a particular type of service?

A. RIP

B. NCP

C. SAP

D. EIGRP
C. A workstation uses Service Advertising Protocol (SAP) to locate a server providing a particular type of service.

10. Periodic SAP updates are sent by:

A. Routers and servers

B. NetWare servers only

C. Workstations and routers

D. Workstations only
A. Periodic SAP updates are sent by routers and servers. All servers advertise their available services using broadcasts. Routers record these advertisements and re-broadcast them as part of their own SAP databases. Workstations only broadcast GNS queries, and never transmit updates.

11. The RIP protocol is used by:
    A. Routers only
    B. Servers only
    C. Workstations, servers, and routers
    D. Print servers
    A. Workstations, servers, and routers all use RIP to locate routes to remote networks.

12. Which command which must be given first to enable IPX?
    A. CISCO(CONFIG)#ENABLE IPX ROUTING
    B. cisco>ipx routing
    C. cisco(config-if)#ipx routing on
    D. cisco(config)#ipx routing
    D. The command IPX ROUTING must be given first to enable IPX. Although answer B has the correct command, the router is in the wrong mode to accept it.

13. Which of the following allow you to use multiple IPX networks on a single physical interface?
    A. Secondary networks
    B. Dynamic frame types
    C. Subinterfaces
    D. None. This is not supported.
    A, C. Both secondary networks and subinterfaces allow you to have multiple IPX networks on one physical interface. Each separate network on the interface must run over a different encapsulation, though.

14. Which IOS command allows you to view the router's internal SAP database?
    A. SHOW SERVERS
    B. show ipx servers
    C. servers
    D. ipx servers
    B. The command SHOW IPX SERVERS allows you to view the router's internal SAP database. This will display the contents of the SAP table.

15. Which of the following kinds of information do you need to collect before you can configure IPX using IOS?
    A. The number of NetWare servers on the network
    B. The encapsulations in use
    C. IPX network numbers
    D. The IPX address of another router
    B, C. The encapsulations in use and the IPX network numbers are both required if problems are to be avoided in the install.

16. What does this command do: CISCO(CONFIG-IF)#IPX NETWORK 3
    A. Nothing. It is incomplete.
    B. Sets up a static route to Network 3
    C. Configures IPX Network 3 on this interface with the default frame type
    D. Nothing. The router is in the wrong configuration mode.

C. The encapsulation hasn't been specified, so the default for the media type on this interface will be used.

17. What does this IOS command do? IPX ROUTE 4 5.0000.8004.4563 FLOATING-STATIC

A. Configures 4 static routes

B. Configures static SAP entries for servers of type 4

C. Configures a static route to network 4

D. Says that to get to network 5, you must go via network 4

C. Configures a static route to network 4. 5.0000.8004.4563 is the router that is the next hop to network 4.

18. In the command IPX ROUTE 4 5.0000.8004.4563 FLOATING-STATIC, what does the FLOATING-STATIC keyword on the end mean?

A. Set all static routes to floating

B. Allow this route to be overridden by a route received dynamically

C. Apply this route to all network numbers from 1 to 4

D. Lock this route so that it cannot be changed

B. The FLOATING-STATIC keyword on the end means that if a route advertised by RIP or another routing protocol was received for network 4, it would take precedence over the static route. Without this, incoming dynamic routes for this network will be ignored.

19. The IPX MAXIMUM-PATHS command does what?

A. Allows IOS to share traffic to a given network over multiple paths

B. Allows a slow link to be used as a backup for a faster one

C. Sets the maximum number of router hops a packet can travel

D. Sets the maximum number of interfaces IPX can be configured on

A. The IPX MAXIMUM-PATHS command allows multiple paths to a given network. The paths must have an equal cost. By default, IOS only uses one path to each destination network.

20. Which command is used to show a concise list of the configured IPX interfaces?

A. SHOW CONFIG

B. show ipx interface

C. show ipx interface brief

D. show interface

C. The command SHOW IPX INTERFACE BRIEF shows a concise list of the configured IPX interfaces. Although answer B does show a list, it is not concise!

21. If two devices are plugged into the same physical network, but are using different encapsulations, what is required before they can communicate?

A. A cross-over cable

B. A repeater

C. A router configured for the appropriate encapsulations

D. Nothing. They can communicate directly.
C. If they aren't running the same encapsulations, a router is the only device that will allow them to connect.

22. When does a workstation normally send a GNS request?

A. When trying to communicate with another workstation

B. When trying to locate the nearest router

C. When it needs to send a SAP update

D. When trying to locate a server at initialization
D. When the workstation first comes up, it needs to find a NetWare server to connect to. Once connected, it can use the server's database to locate services.

23. How many router hops does a GNS request travel?

A. 16

B. None

C. 4

D. Unlimited
B. The GNS request is a broadcast. By default, routers block these broadcasts, so they are only seen on their local network.

24. In a SAP update packet, what does the Server Address field contain?

A. The network the server is on

B. The server's node number

C. The socket number the server is listening on

D. All of the above
D. The SAP update contains the full internetwork address, with the socket number for the server

25. Which of the following protocols is used by servers to advertise their services to the clients?

A. Routing Information Protocol (RIP)

B. Sequenced Packet Exchange (SPX)

C. Network Core Protocol (NCP)

D. Service Advertising Protocol (SAP)
D. SAP announcements are broadcast by servers to advertise their services.

26. On an Ethernet LAN how many IPX encapsulation types are supported?

A. 4

B. 3

C. 2

D. 1
A. The four types of IPX encapsulation supported on an Ethernet LAN are: Ethernet_II, Ethernet_802.2, Ethernet_802.3, and Ethernet_SNAP.

27. The frame check sequence checks with which fields in an Ethernet_802.3 frame?

A. The Source Address and Destination Address

B. The packet data

C. Everything from the Destination Address on

D. The source Service Access Point (SSAP)

C. The FCS is used to detect corrupted packets, and checks all the IPX packet fields.

28. Which of the following fields is not common to both Ethernet_802.3 and Ethernet_802.2 frames?

A. Source Address

B. Length

C. DSAP

D. Data

C. The DSAP field is in the Ethernet_802.2 frame and not in the Ethernet_802.3 frame.

29. In SAP packets, the numbers in the Service Type field are assigned by:

A. The system administrator

B. The end user

C. Novell

D. The server

C. The Service Type field contains a number assigned buy Novell.

30. SAP requests, responses, or broadcasts can be recognized by which value of source or destination socket number?

A. 0x0452

B. 0xE0

C. 0x03

D. 0x0453

A. SAP requests, responses, or broadcasts can be recognized by a source or destination socket number of 0x0452. 0xE0 is used by Ethernet_802.2 frames in the DSAP and SSAP fields. 0x03 is the value of the Control byte in an Ethernet_802.2 frame. 0x0453 is used as a socket number in RIP frame.

31. In RIP Packets, the Hops Away and Time Ticks fields are valid both for request and response packets.

A. True

B. False

B. False. In RIP requests, both of these fields contain the value 0xFFFF. In response packets, they contain valid values.

32. Up to how many RIP entries can a single IPX packet can hold?

A. 44

B. 47

C. 49

D. 51

C. A single IPX packet can hold up to 49 RIP entries.

33. In RIP, which number of hop counts indicates that a network is unreachable?

A. 12

B. 16

C. 8

D. 20
B. In RIP a hop count of 16 specifies that a network is unreachable.

34. Match a Novell term on the left with an IOS term on the right.

A. Ethernet_SNAP	1. SAP
B. Ethernet_802.2	2. SNAP
C. Ethernet_II	3. novell-ether
D. Ethernet_802.3	4. arpa

A-2, B-1, C-4, D-3. These equivalents are described in Table 7-1.

35. If a user attempts to set the same encapsulation type on more than one subinterface on the same physical interface, what will the IOS do?

A. Assign default values for encapsulation types
B. Issue a warning but allow the change
C. Issue an error message and ignore the change
D. Allow the change
C. If a user attempts to set the same encapsulation type on more than one subinterface on the same physical interface, then the IOS will issue an error message and ignore the change.

36. Which of the following is a default routing protocol when IPX routing is enabled?

A. RIP
B. NLSP
C. EIGRP
D. CDP
A. RIP is the default routing protocol when IPX is enabled.

37. When there are multiple paths available at the same cost, then by default IOS:

A. Will keep all paths in the routing table
B. Will keep only one path in the routing table
C. Will keep all paths in the table and route the traffic in a round-robin manner
D. B and C
B. By default IOS only uses the best known path to each network, and sends all traffic down this path.

38. What is the purpose of the split-horizon function?

A. To divide the network traffic in two for faster throughput
B. To avoid sending redundant data back out the interface it was received on
C. So that each person only has to manage half the routers on a network
D. To set traffic priority levels
B. The purpose of the split-horizon function is to avoid redundancy. By not advertising SAP entries back onto the segment they were originally received from, the amount of traffic is reduced on the segment, and confusing loops are avoided.

39. By default, RIP routers broadcast periodic updates every:

A. 30 Seconds
B. 60 Seconds
C. 5 Minutes
D. 10 Minutes
B. By default periodic RIP updates are sent every 60 seconds.

40. When would a workstation send a RIP request?

A. On initialization, to locate a server
B. Whenever it needs to find a route to a remote network it doesn't have a route for
C. To connect to a NetWare server
D. Every 60 seconds
B. Workstations use RIP to locate routes to remote networks.

41. If an interface was configured like this:
CISCO(CONFIG)#INTERFACE ETHERNET 1
CISCO(CONFIG-IF)#IPX NETWORK 201 ENCAPSULATION NOVELL-ETHER
CISCO(CONFIG-IF)#IPX NETWORK 202 ENCAPSULATION SAP SECONDARY
How many copies of each SAP update would be sent out the physical interface?

A. 1
B. 2
C. 3
D. 4
B. There would be two copies of each SAP update sent—one to network 201 on the novell-ether encapsulation, and one to network 202 on the SAP encapsulation.

Chapter 8 Answers

1. How long is an AppleTalk address (in bits)?

A. 16 bits
B. 32 bits
C. 24 bits
D. 8 bits
C. An AppleTalk address is 24 bits long. It contains a 16-bit network number and an eight-bit node number.

2. What are the two parts of an AppleTalk address?

A. Network and node
B. Source and destination
C. Logical and physical
D. Standard and extended
A. The two parts of an AppleTalk address are the 16-bit network number and the eight-bit node number.

3. Which of the following is standard on almost all Macintosh computers?

A. EtherTalk
B. TokenTalk
C. FDDITalk
D. LocalTalk
D. LocalTalk is standard on almost

all Macintosh models. Most AppleTalk printers have a LocalTalk interface as well.

4. How many bits of an AppleTalk address are reserved for the node number?

   A. 8 bits

   B. 16 bits

   C. 24 bits

   D. 32 bits

   A. The node part of an AppleTalk address is eight bits. The network part of the address is 16 bits. Together, they make up a 24-bit AppleTalk address.

5. Network resources used by a particular group or department are grouped into what AppleTalk structure?

   A. Workgroup

   B. Zone

   C. Cable Range

   D. Virtual LAN

   B. Network resources used by a particular group or department are grouped into a zone. Functional groupings are made via the AppleTalk Zone concept. Workgroup and Virtual LAN are generic terms, not AppleTalk structures. Cable ranges are used to assign a range of network numbers to a network link.

6. What is the name of the AppleTalk layer-3 protocol?

   A. Datagram Post Office Protocol

   B. Datagram Delivery Protocol

   C. AppleTalk Transport Protocol

   D. Zone Information Protocol

   B. AppleTalk uses the Datagram Delivery Protocol to provide connectionless datagram delivery service to the upper-layer protocols.

7. Which statement is true?

   A. Two ZIPs can be assigned to an interface

   B. Two cable ranges can be assigned to an interface

   C. Two AppleTalk RTMPs can be assigned to an interface

   D. Two zone names can be assigned to an interface

   D. Multiple zones can be assigned to an interface. ZIP and RTMP are protocols. They are not "assigned" to an interface. Two cable ranges can not be assigned to an interface. Cable range assignments must be unique.

8. What command sets the range of network numbers associated with an AppleTalk network?

   A. APPLETALK ZONE NAME

   B. APPLETALK CABLE-RANGE

   C. APPLETALK CABLE RANGE

   D. appletalk network-range

   B. The APPLETALK CABLE-RANGE command assigns a range of network numbers to be used on a given network interface. The

ZONE NAME command (answer A) assigns zones to an interface. Answer C is close, but it is missing the hyphen between cable and range.

9. Which of these protocols cannot be used for maintaining AppleTalk routing tables?

   A. RTMP
   B. AURP
   C. EIGRP
   D. IGRP

   E. IGRP handles IP traffic only. All the other routing protocols can be used to help maintain AppleTalk routing tables.

10. How often does RTMP send out routing table updates?

    A. Every 10 seconds
    B. Every 20 seconds
    C. Whenever a topology change occurs
    D. Every 30 seconds

    A. RTMP broadcasts its routing table to its neighbors every 10 seconds.

11. Which of the following commands is not necessary for a basic AppleTalk configuration?

    A. APPLETALK PROTOCOL RTMP
    B. APPLETALK CABLE-RANGE 1234-4321
    C. APPLETALK ZONE OZONE
    D. APPLETALK ROUTING

    A. APPLETALK PROTOCOL RTMP is not necessary in a basic AppleTalk configuration. RTMP is automatically started on an interface as soon as the cable range and zone name have been properly assigned.

12. What is the range of numbers used for AppleTalk access control filters?

    A. 100 – 299
    B. 500 – 699
    C. 600 – 700
    D. 600 – 699

    D. The access list numbers used for AppleTalk filtering are 600 – 699.

13. Which command displays the RTMP metrics?

    A. SHOW RTMP
    B. show appletalk zone
    C. show appletalk metrics
    D. SHOW APPLETALK ROUTE

    D. The command SHOW APPLETALK ROUTE displays all known cable ranges and the hop count (metric) required to reach each network identified by cable range.

14. If router A and router B are directly connected via their Serial 0 interfaces, which command would be most useful on router A for hiding zone President Zone (on the E0 interface) from router B?

    A. APPLETALK ACCESS-GROUP 600
    B. appletalk zone-filter 600
    C. appletalk GETZONELIST-filter 600

D. appletalk zip-reply-filter 600
D. Clients use the GETZONELIST command to obtain the list of zones from the router. Routers exchange zone information via ZIP, not the ATP-based GETZONELIST command. The zip-reply-filter is the mechanism that filters ZIP among routers; therefore answer D is best.

15. If client M is connected to router A via Ethernet 0, which command would be the most useful for hiding zone SerialZone (located elsewhere in the network) from client M?

    A. APPLETALK ACCESS-GROUP 600

    B. appletalk zone-filter 600

    C. appletalk GETZONELIST-filter 600

    D. appletalk zip-reply-filter 600
    C. Since clients use the GETZONELIST command to obtain zone lists from routers, filtering this list with a GETZONELIST-FILTER would prevent client M from learning about the existence of SerialZone. The ZIP-REPLY FILTER will only filter ZIP. The GETZONELIST command is implemented via ATP, so using a ZIP-REPLY FILTER would be ineffective.

16. Which command assigns a zone name to an interface?

    A. APPLETALK ZIP-NAME

    B. appletalk zone

    C. appletalk zip-reply-filter

    D. appletalk GETZONELIST-filter
    B. The command APPLETALK ZONE is used to assign zone names to interfaces. The syntax is APPLETALK ZONE MYZONE. It is an interface-level command.

17. Which command causes a router to automatically obtain its AppleTalk configuration information by querying other routers already on the network?

    A. APPLETALK AUTO-CONFIG

    B. appletalk discovery

    C. appletalk discovery-mode enable

    D. appletalk cable–range auto
    B. APPLETALK DISCOVERY activates the auto discovery process in Cisco routers.

18. Which of the following sets of commands are all interface configuration commands?

    A. APPLETALK ROUTING, APPLETALK ZIP-REPLY-FILTER, APPLETALK CABLE-RANGE

    B. appletalk zip-reply-filter, appletalk zone, APPLETALK CABLE-RANGE

    C. appletalk GETZONELIST filter, appletalk access-list, APPLETALK CABLE-RANGE

    D. appletalk access-list, appletalk zone, APPLETALK CABLE-RANGE
    B. These commands are all interface configuration commands. Answer A is wrong because APPLETALK ROUTING is a global configuration command. Answers C and D are wrong

because APPLETALK ACCESS-LIST is not a command at all.

19. Which command causes a network and node number to be assigned to a router interface?

    A. APPLETALK CABLE-RANGE

    B. APPLETALK ADDRESS-ENABLE

    C. APPLETALK NODE-ENABLE

    D. appletalk address auto-config
    A. The APPLETALK CABLE-RANGE command assigns the cable range to the interface, but it also causes the automatic node address assignment to occur. The results of the node assignment can be seen with a SHOW RUN command, which will display the APPLETALK CABLE-RANGE command with the automatically assigned node number immediately following the cable range. The other commands listed are not valid.

20. Which of the following commands is required in a router configuration that routes AppleTalk traffic?

    A. APPLETALK ADDRESS 301.64

    B. appletalk processing enable

    C. appletalk range

    D. appletalk routing
    D. APPLETALK ROUTING is a global configuration command that is required to cause the router to route AppleTalk packets. Without the APPLETALK ROUTING command, a router could bridge AppleTalk traffic (if properly configured), but routing would not occur.

21. Match the OSI layer on the left with the corresponding AppleTalk protocols on the right.

A. Data link/Physical	1. AFP
B. Transport	2. ASP
C. Application	3. RTMP
D. Session	4. EtherTalk

    A-4, B-3, C-1, D-2

22. Which Data link type supports speeds of up to 100 Mbps?

    A. LocalTalk

    B. FDDITalk

    C. TokenTalk

    D. All of the above
    B. FDDITalk supports 100 Mbps. TokenTalk supports 4 or 16 Mbps. LocalTalk supports 230 Kbps.

23. Name Binding Protocol (NBP) is a protocol for:

    A. The application layer

    B. The session layer

    C. The transport layer

    D. The physical layer
    C. NBP is a transport layer protocol.

24. Which statement is true of zoning?

    A. It reduces the number of devices (hardware)

    B. It reduces the number of nodes on the network

C. It causes client requests to propagate through the entire network

D. It reduces overhead

D. Zoning reduces overhead by allowing requests to be directed towards devices in a specified zone. The purpose of zoning is to prevent propagation of requests through the entire network.

25. Which statement is true of RTMP?

A. It uses the shortest path algorithm

B. It uses distance vector protocol

C. It is a link-state protocol

D. It is a minimum metric algorithm

B. RTMP is responsible for maintaining the routing table and does so by using a distance vector routing protocol.

26. Name Binding Protocol is used for what purpose?

A. To convert addresses into names

B. To create unique names for devices

C. To associate names with addresses

D. To create unique addresses

C. One of the major functions of the NBP is to map names to addresses and to provide this service to applications.

27. Which of the following protocols is most often preferred because of the capability of bi-directional data stream support over DDP?

A. ADSP

B. ATP

C. ASP

D. AFP

A. ADSP is the preferred protocol for data exchange between applications.

28. Whereas MAC addresses may change from location to location, the network addresses will remain the same from location to location.

A. True

B. False

B. False. MAC addresses do not change from location to location. Network addresses can be different in different locations.

29. Network number assignments are made by:

A. Network queue

B. Client

C. Server

D. Router

D. Routers make the network number assignments. Network numbers identify the segment associated with a client device.

30. The major characteristic of an Extended AppleTalk addressing scheme is:

A. That a single network number is assigned to a single segment

B. That a single segment can be associated with a range of network numbers

C. That a single network number can be assigned multiple zones

D. B and C only

E. All of the above
D. Extended AppleTalk addressing allows multiple network numbers to be assigned to a segment. Thus, in this addressing scheme up to 65,535 networks can be associated with a segment. In a non-extended addressing scheme, the network is assigned only one network ID and one zone name.

31. Which is a true statement about a cable range?

A. It is a range of addresses assigned to a device
B. It is associated with a network segment
C. It is associated with an interface on the router
D. All of the above
E. B and C only
E. In a strict sense the answer is B—a cable range is associated with a network segment. However, the router interface is used to route traffic to appropriate network. Therefore answer C is also valid.

32. All AppleTalk network numbers must be:

A. Greater than 65,536
B. Greater than 255
C. Less than 65,536
D. Less than 255
C. All AppleTalk network numbers must be less than 65,536. The network address is 16 bits long. This means a limit of 65,536.

33. What is the broadcast node number in AppleTalk?

A. 255
B. 0
C. 256
D. None of the above
A. 255 is used as broadcast node number.

34. For a cable range of 450 – 454, what is the maximum number of hosts?

A. 762
B. 2286
C. 1016
D. 1270
D. For a cable range of 450 – 454, the maximum number of hosts is 1270. The number of hosts equals the number of network numbers times 254. 5 X 254 = 1270.

35. Which of the following is not true of cable ranges?

A. They are assigned with the APPLETALK CABLE-RANGE command
B. They are ranges of network numbers assigned to a segment
C. They cannot overlap with a previously assigned cable range
D. None of the above
D. Cable ranges are assigned with the APPLETALK CABLE-RANGE command; they are ranges of network numbers assigned to a segment; and

they cannot overlap with a previously assigned cable range.

36. A network segment X is given a cable range of 200 – 300. What is the acceptable value of cable range for segment Y?

A. 250 – 350

B. 6301 – 6400

C. 300 – 400

D. All of the above

B. Among these choices, 6301 – 6400 is the only acceptable value of cable range for segment Y. Answers A and C are overlapping with 200 – 300 and therefore cannot be used.

37. A segment has a cable range of 700 – 750. When a node wants to get an address, it may pick up any network number in the range that is not currently in use.

A. True

B. False

A. True. The node may pick any network number within the range.

38. Which command would be most appropriate for finding out whether the network has verified a cable range assignment for E0?

A. SHOW APPLETALK ADDRESS

B. SHOW APPLETALK ROUTE

C. Show appletalk interface

D. Show appletalk zone

C. SHOW APPLETALK INTERFACE tells the status of an interface and indicates whether the interface configuration has been verified.

39. What cable range is used to indicate to IOS to use AppleTalk discovery mode on a given interface?

A. 1 – 1

B. 0 – 0

C. 255 – 255

D. 254 – 254

B. The 0 – 0 cable range is used to indicate to IOS that AD should be used.

40. For AppleTalk discovery to work properly:

A. A router must have cable range assigned to it

B. The seed routers must be in place

C. The seed routers must be non-operational

D. All of the above

B. For AppleTalk discovery to work properly, seed routers must be in place and operational before the AppleTalk discovery is applied to non-seed routers.

41. For a basic AppleTalk configuration, how many commands are necessary?

A. One

B. Two

C. Three

D. Four

C. The three necessary commands are APPLETALK ROUTING,

APPLETALK CABLE-RANGE, and APPLETALK INTERFACE.

42. For activation of an access list, which of the following commands is required?

    A. ACCESS-GROUP

    B. zone

    C. cable-range

    D. interface

    A. The ACCESS-GROUP command and the ACCESS-LIST command are required to activate an access list on the interface.

43. The default direction for access list for IOS versions earlier than 11.3 is:

    A. Outbound

    B. Inbound

    C. Inbound and outbound (bi-directional)

    D. None of the above

    A. For IOS versions earlier than 11.3, the default is outbound. IOS version 11.3 supports inbound direction.

44. Which of the following commands is used for monitoring AppleTalk configuration?

    A. APPLETALK CABLE-RANGE

    B. appletalk GETZONELIST

    C. SHOW APPLETALK ZONE

    D. access list

    C. The commands used to monitor AppleTalk configurations are SHOW APPLETALK INTERFACE, SHOW APPLETALK ROUTE and SHOW APPLETALK ZONE.

45. The following is displayed in response to the SHOW APPLETALK ROUTE command:
    R Net 300-399[3/G] via 400.97, 10 sec, Serial0, zone EtherZone2
    In this display, R is:

    A. A router name

    B. RIP

    C. RTMP

    D. All of the above

    C. R indicates that the cable range 300 – 399 was learned via RTMP.

46. The following is displayed in response to the SHOW APPLETALK ROUTE command:
    R Net 300-399[3/G] via 400.97, 10 sec, Serial0, zone EtherZone2
    In this display, 10 sec is:

    A. The time it takes for a packet to travel from source to destination

    B. The time elapsed since the last RTMP update for cable range 300 – 399 was received

    C. The holddown time for cable range 300 – 399

    D. The time interval indicating how long the packet will be held by the router

    B. 10 seconds is the elapsed time since the last RTMP update that included an entry for cable range 300 – 399. When RTMP is operating properly, this number should never be more than 10 seconds, because the RTMP update interval is 10 seconds.

47. The following is displayed in response to the SHOW APPLETALK ROUTE command:
R Net 300-399[3/G] via 400.97, 10 sec, Serial0, zone EtherZone2
In this display, 400.97 is:
    A. The destination address of a packet going to network 300 – 399
    B. The source address of a packet coming from network 300 – 399
    C. The address of the router that advertised the cable range
    D. None of the above
    C. 400.97 is the AppleTalk address of the router that advertised the cable range.

Chapter 9 Answers

1. Match which of these protocols go with which access list range.

A. Novell SAP	1) 800 – 899
B. AppleTalk	2) 1000 – 1099
C. Novell	3) 1 – 99
D. IP	4) 600 – 699

A-2, B-4, C-1, D-3. Novell SAP uses 1000 – 1099; AppleTalk uses 600 – 699; Novell uses 800 – 899; IP uses 1 – 99.

2. What happens to access lists previously created if the IOS is upgraded from version 10.1 to 11.1?
    A. They are dropped since they are no longer applicable
    B. Access lists didn't exist prior to version 9.1
    C. They will be converted to the new format
    D. They will be left alone since IOS 11.1 provides backward compatibility
    C. They will be converted to the new format. Even though 11.1 does provide backward compatibility, it is only for the allowance of converting prior version's access lists.

3. In what ways are access lists typically implemented on AppleTalk networks?
    A. To control packets transmitted across an interface
    B. To specify interesting traffic to launch a DDR connection
    C. To restrict SAP broadcasts
    D. To advertise available servers
    A, B. Access lists in AppleTalk networks are used in one of two ways. First, to control packets transmitted across an interface. Second, to specify interesting traffic that will launch a DDR connection.

4. What do NetWare servers do to advertise their services and addresses to other servers?
    A. Broadcast NetBIOS packets
    B. Register with an SAP server
    C. Broadcast SAP packets

D. Register with a NetBIOS server

C. NetWare servers advertise their services and addresses to other servers by broadcasting SAP packets.

5. In the event of no matching rule being found in an IP access list, what happens to the transmission packet at the end?

A. It is dropped

B. It is allowed to pass

C. A broadcast is sent out notifying the sending host

D. A Packet Return (PR) is issued to the sending host

A. It is dropped. If no matching rule is found in an access list, it is implicitly denied.

6. For which of the following reasons are IP-style AppleTalk access lists implemented?

A. For controlling the disposition of networks that overlap a network number range

B. For controlling the disposition of networks that are contained within a network number range

C. For controlling the disposition of networks that no longer exist within a network number range

D. For controlling the disposition of networks that exactly match a network number range

A, B, D. IP-style access lists are based on network numbers and are used for controlling the disposition of networks that overlap, are contained within, or exactly match a network number range.

7. Which of the following statements are true regarding IP access lists?

A. After an access list is created, any additions to that list are placed at the end

B. You can't selectively add or remove items

C. You need to explicitly associate the access list to whatever it is you are intending to use it for, such as an interface

D. There is an implicit DENY statement at the end

A, B, C, D. All are correct statements regarding IP access lists.

8. On what basis do IPX access lists permit or deny traffic?

A. Specified network nodes

B. Messages sent using a particular ICMP

C. Messages sent using a particular protocol

D. Messages sent using a particular service

A, C, D. Packets are permitted or denied based on specified network nodes or messages sent using a particular service or protocol.

9. How often does a Cisco router forward SAP broadcasts?

A. As soon as it receives the complete packet

B. Every 30 seconds

C. Every 60 seconds

D. Every 300 seconds (5 minutes)
B. Cisco routers broadcast periodic SAP advertisements every 30 seconds. Cisco routers forward packets every 60 seconds by default.

10. What is GNS?

A. An ICMP connectivity error packet

B. Generic NetWare Service (allows a Cisco router to appear as a NetWare server)

C. AppleTalk's default network routing algorithm

D. A packet sent out to request specific services from servers
D. A GNS is a Get Nearest Server request. A GNS packet is sent out by Novell clients to request a nonserver-specific service.

11. Which of the following are valid types of IPX access lists?

A. SAP

B. NetBIOS

C. ICMP

D. Extended
A, B, D. SAP, NetBIOS, and Extended are three of the four types of IPX access lists. ICMP is a protocol option for IP extended access lists.

12. What are the two basic styles of AppleTalk lists?

A. AppleTalk style

B. Macintosh style

C. NBP style

D. IP style
A, D. AppleTalk and IP are the two styles of access lists.

13. Which of the following are true statements regarding Phase 1 and Phase 2 AppleTalk networks?

A. Phase 1 networks are more efficient at WAN communication.

B. Phase 2 networks can have up to 255 zones.

C. Phase 1 networks can have only 1 zone.

D. Phase 2 networks introduced routing.
B, C, D. Phase 2 networks are routable and can have up to 255 zones, while Phase 1 networks are limited to one.

14. How should you arrange your entries in AppleTalk access lists?

A. The order doesn't matter

B. From the most specific to the most general

C. From the most general to the most specific

D. Zones first, followed by systems
A. It doesn't matter how you arrange your entries in AppleTalk access lists. The order is unimportant because overlapping entries are not allowed. The router automatically puts

PERMIT OTHER-NBPS, PERMIT OTHER-ACCESS, and PERMIT ADDITIONAL-ZONES at the end of the list.

15. What will happen to packets that cross an interface where no access list has been defined?

    A. They will be discarded
    B. They will be allowed to pass through
    C. They will be queued up
    D. They will be returned to the sending host
    B. If you don't apply any access lists to an interface, or if you attempt to apply an access list that has not been defined, it will pass all traffic by default.

16. Which of the following examples follow the correct syntax for adding special Macintosh characters in zone names?

    A. /B2
    B. –B2
    C. [B2]
    D. :B2
    D. :B2. If you want to use a special character, you enter a colon followed by the two corresponding hexadecimal characters.

17. Which of these are valid types of IP access lists?

    A. Dynamic
    B. Dynamic extended
    C. Extended
    D. Standard
    B, C, D. There are three basic types of IP access lists: standard, extended, and dynamic extended

18. Which of the following examples uses the correct syntax to define an AppleTalk access list for an extended or a non-extended network that is completely contained within a specific cable-range?

    A. ACCESS-LIST 599 PERMIT WITHIN 100-150
    B. access-list permit 225-240 within 699
    C. access-list permit 225-240 within 599
    D. access-list 699 permit within 100-150
    D. The correct syntax is as follows, remembering that AppleTalk's range is 600 – 699: ACCESS-LIST *access-list-number* {PERMIT | DENY} WITHIN *cable-range.*

19. Which of the following statements regarding SAP broadcasts is correct?

    A. SAP-type broadcasts do not work well across WANs
    B. Each SAP service is identified by an eight-digit binary number
    C. Because of sequencing issues, the times between SAP table updates cannot be changed
    D. SAP stands for Secondary Addressing Protocol
    A. SAP broadcasts do not work well across WANs.

20. Consider the following access list:
ACCESS-LIST 50 DENY 136.120.3.1
ACCESS-LIST 50 DENY 143.22.1.0
0.0.0.255
Which statement represents the most complete description of the results of applying this list as a packet filter?
    A. It will deny all traffic destined for any host on network 136.120.3.0.
    B. It will deny all traffic destined for network 143.22.1.0.
    C. It will deny all traffic from the host at 136.120.3.1.
    D. It will deny all IP traffic.
    D. The access list number, 50, falls within the range for standard IP access lists, which filter on source address only, not destination address, so answers A and B cannot be correct. Because there is an implicit DENY ANY at the end of each access list, all traffic not explicitly permitted is denied. Because we have not explicitly permitted any traffic, all traffic will be denied.

21. Which command would be used to configure a packet filter for IP traffic?
    A. ROUTER(CONFIG-IF)#IP ACCESS-LIST 100
    B. ROUTER(CONFIG-IF)#IP ACCESS-GROUP 42
    C. ROUTER(CONFIG)#ACCESS-GROUP 102
    D. ROUTER(CONFIG-IF)#ACCESS-GROUP 75
    E. ROUTER(CONFIG-IF)#IP OUTPUT-PACKET-FILTER 112
    B. The IP ACCESS-GROUP command is an interface configuration command. The other commands are invalid.

22. Which command would be used to configure an inbound packet filter for TCP traffic?
    A. ROUTER(CONFIG-IF)#TCP PACKET-FILTER 101
    B. ROUTER(CONFIG-IF)#IP PACKET-FILTER 101 IN
    C. ROUTER(CONFIG-IF)#IP ACCESS-GROUP 99 IN
    D. ROUTER(CONFIG-IF)#IP ACCESS-GROUP 100 IN
    E. ROUTER(CONFIG-IF)#IP ACCESS-GROUP 100
    D. A packet filter to filter TCP traffic would be applied using the IP ACCESS-GROUP command, using an IP extended access list. There is no such command as TCP PACKET-FILTER or IP PACKET-FILTER. Answer C is incorrect because list 99 would be a standard IP access list, which cannot specifically filter TCP traffic. Answer E is incorrect because the keyword IN needs to be specified. The default direction is outbound.

23. The address mask pair 172.16.64.0 0.0.3.255 specifies which range of IP addresses?
    A. 172.16.64.255 through 172.16.67.255
    B. 172.16.67.0 through 172.16.70.255
    C. 172.16.64.0 through 172.16.67.255
    D. 172.16.63.0 through 172.16.64.255
    C. The range begins at 172.16.64.0 and includes all IP addresses through172.16.67.255. All bits in the address corresponding to "0" bits in the wildcard mask will always be the same throughout the range, while all bits in the address corresponding to "1" bits in the mask may be any value.

24. The following statement appears in an IP extended access list:
    ACCESS-LIST 125 PERMIT IP ANY HOST 136.25.2.128
    What does this line permit?
    A. Any IP traffic from host 136.25.2.128
    B. IP traffic to any host on network 136.25.2.128
    C. IP traffic from any address to the host at 136.25.2.128
    D. The statement is invalid because there is no mask.
    C. The ANY argument represents "any source network." The HOST keyword replaces the mask 0.0.0.0 for the destination IP address 136.25.2.128.

25. The following access list, containing only one line, is applied as a packet filter on an interface:
    ACCESS-LIST 100 PERMIT TCP 145.22.3.0 0.0.0.255 ANY EQ TELNET
    What is the best description of the traffic that is denied by the implicit DENY ALL?
    A. All IP traffic
    B. All Telnet traffic
    C. All TCP traffic
    D. All TCP traffic except Telnet
    A. Even though the statement explicitly refers to TCP and Telnet traffic, the implicit DENY ALL applies to all IP traffic.

Chapter 10 Answers

1. What does DDR stand for?
    A. Dial-up direct request
    B. Direct dial relocation number
    C. Dial-on-demand request
    D. Dial-on-demand routing
    D. DDR stands for dial-on-demand routing.

2. Which of the following is required to configure an ISDN BRI interface?
    A. SPID
    B. LUN
    C. PVC number
    D. DLCI
    A. The service profile identifier (SPID) is a required number supplied by the phone company.

3. Which of the following statements regarding ISDN PRI is true?

A. ISDN PRI runs on existing copper

B. ISDN PRI can basically run at the same speed as a T1

C. Because ISDN PRI uses SVCs and PVCs, it makes it an excellent solution to the desktop

D. It is comprised of two B channels and 23 D channels

B. ISDN PRI can provide speeds up to 1.536 Mbps, which is roughly the speed of a T1.

4. Which layer(s) of the OSI model does X.25 cover?

A. 1 and 2

B. 1, 2, and 3

C. 2 and 3

D. 2, 3, and 4

B. X.25 encompasses the first three layers of the OSI model.

5. Which of these is not a characteristic of PVCs?

A. They must each be set up manually.

B. They are similar to a leased line.

C. The connections can be established very quickly when the bandwidth is needed.

D. They require a DTE and a DCE to operate.

C. PVC connections are permanent and take time to set up.

6. A X.25 connection deals with which of the following technology pieces?

A. LCN

B. LCI

C. NUA

D. All of the above

D. A X.25 connection has both an LCN (which is also known as an LCI) and a NUA.

7. What is contained within an LAPB frame?

A. LUN information

B. X.25 packet

C. Flow control and error-recovery information

D. QLLC packet for frame window configuration

B. An X.25 packet makes up the data field of an HDLC frame.

8. What does the following command accomplish?
X25 ROUTE 2468013579 INTERFACE SERIAL0

A. Routes all information from 2468013579 through serial 0

B. Denies traffic bound for 2468013579 from passing through serial 0

C. Adds a manual route statement to send IP datagrams through serial 0

D. Routes all information destined for 2468013579 through serial 0

C. This command tells the router to send all traffic destined for the listed NUA out through the specified serial interface.

9. Which of the following arguments for the SHOW X.25 command displays a one-to-one mapping of the local and remote IP addresses?

A. MAP

B. ROUTE

C. VC

D. REMOTE-RED
D. REMOTE-RED displays one-to-one mappings.

10. Which of the following technologies are associated with Frame Relay?

A. TDM

B. LMI

C. Inverse ARP

D. CIR
B,C, D. are all correct. LMI is the Local Management Interface extension, which adds functionality to Frame Relay such as Inverse ARP. CIR is the committed information rate, and is the guaranteed rate the end user will receive out of a shared T1.

11. How would you reference sub-interface 1 on Serial 0 with the Cisco IOS?

A. Serial0.1

B. Serial 0 sub 1

C. Serial.0.sub.1

D. Serial.0.0
A. The naming convention used for these ports is simply the name of the interface being addressed, then a period, followed by the number of the sub-interface.

12. What is the purpose of Inverse ARP?

A. Autodiscovers DLCI numbers

B. Automatically configures PVCs

C. Gets all connected routers' MAC addresses

D. Builds a table of the IP address
D. Inverse ARP builds a table of the IP address of the (sub)interfaces at the end of the PVC, matched with each respective DLCI.

13. Which statement about ATM packets is false?

A. It is 56 bytes long

B. Contains a 5-byte header

C. The information field is 48 bytes long

D. Because of its fixed length, it can control bandwidth utilization.
A. An ATM packet is 53 bytes in length.

14. Which of these statements regarding VCI and VPI are true?

A. VPI identifies a larger group than VCI.

B. VCI is a unit.

C. Both VPI and VCI only have significance locally.

D. A VCC contains BOTH VPI and VCI.
A, B, C, D. All four answers are true statements regarding VCIs and VPIs.

15. What is the correct speed for ATM?

A. 155 Mbps

B. 25 Mbps

C. 622 Mbps

D. None of the above
A,B,C. All three are valid speeds and are dependent on the type of hardware they are travelling over.

16. Which of the following is a good, accurate description of LANE?

A. Layer-3 routing protocol

B. Layer-2 bridging protocol

C. Layer-3 bridging protocol

D. Layer-2 routing protocol
B. LANE is a layer-2 bridging protocol.

17. Which command maps a list of IP addresses to an ATM interface?

A. MAP-LIST

B. MAP-ID

C. MAP-GROUP

D. MAP-IPLIST
C. MAP GROUP assigns a map-list to an interface.

18. Which of the following are supported by PPP?

A. CHAP/PAP

B. Binding of multiple protocols over one link

C. Dynamic address assignment

D. Synchronous communication
A, B, C, D. All of the items listed are supported by PPP.

19. Which syntax listed below is correct if you want to authenticate with CHAP?

A. PPP authentication CHAP

B. PPP authentication CHAP/PAP

C. Authentication CHAP

D. Authentication CHAP/PAP
A. The correct syntax to authenticate with CHAP is PPP authentication CHAP.

20. Of what benefit is Multilink PPP?

A. Provides load balancing

B. Re-assembles fragmented packets

C. Combines multiple successive SLIP connections and appears as one connection

D. Provides load calculations on both inbound and outbound traffic
A, B, D. Multilink Point-to-Point Protocol provides load balancing, re-assembles fragmented packets, and provides load calculation on both inbound and outbound traffic.

21. Basic Rate Interface in ISDN has:

A. One B channel and one D channel

B. 23 B channels and one D channel

C. Two B channels and one D channel

D. Two D channels and one B channel
C. The ISDN BRI has two B channels at 64 Kbps and one D channel at 16 Kbps.

22. In the U.S., an ISDN service provider may use:

A. 5ESS switch
B. 4ESS switch
C. MS-100 switch
D. All of the above
D. An ISDN service provider in the U.S. can use any of the switches.

23. The Primary Rate Interface in ISDN has:
A. One B channels and two D channels
B. Two B channels and one D channel
C. One B channel and 23 D channels
D. 23 B channels and one D channel
D. The Primary Rate Interface has 23 B channels and one D channel, giving it a rate of 1.536 Mbps.

24. Which statement is true of X.25?
A. It is a cell-based technology
B. It is a packet-based technology
C. It supports only PVC
B. X.25 is a packet-based technology. Although X.25 typically operates as PVC, it can also support SVC.

25. One of the parameters required for establishing an ISDN connection is:
A. SAPI (Service Access Port Identifier)
B. DN (directory number)
C. SVC number
D. CKTID (CircuitID)
B. Directory number is used in establishing an ISDN connection.

26. Which statement is true of the logical channel number (LCN) in X.25?
A. It is unique throughout the X.25 network
B. It has local significance only
C. It identifies a physical link to DTE
D. It is used by DTE
B. The LCN is a logical connection to DTE and not a physical connection. LCN has no end-to-end significance and therefore is not unique for the entire network.

27. Maximum packet size in X.25 packet can be:
A. 64 bytes
B. 128 bytes
C. 4096 bytes
D. 2048 bytes
C. The range of packet size is from 64 to 4096 bytes. The default used is typically 128 bytes.

28. In a Frame Relay network, the DLCI:
A. Identifies a pipe which leads to a layer-2 protocol address
B. Identifies a pipe which leads to a layer-3 protocol address
C. Is a network-wide identifier
D. May not change on each physical link
B. DLCI has local significance only in that it identifies a virtual circuit leading to a specific layer-3 protocol address. Therefore it is not a

network-wide identifier and can change on different physical links.

29. Local Management Interface (LMI) in Frame Relay provides:

A. The same functionality as DLCI alone

B. Less functionality than DLCI alone

C. Greater functionality than DLCI alone

D. None of the above

C. LMI was introduced to overcome limitations of DLCI. LMI provides use of Inverse ARP, flow control, and the multicasting capability.

30. In Frame Relay, which one of the following allows a station to accept or reject a frame?

A. Frame Number

B. DLCI

C. LMI

D. Frame Check Sequence (FCS)

D. When a station receives a frame where the FCS does not match the data portion, the frame is discarded.

31. The optional argument that can be supplied at the end of the ENCAPSULATION command in configuring a Frame Relay service is:

A. IETF

B. MAP

C. INT

D. ROUTE

A. The IETF parameter is optional. When specified, it changes the encapsulation method to comply with the IETF standard. Note the default for this is Cisco.

32. In the configuration command FRAME RELAY MAP IP 15.20.21.2 5 BROADCAST, number 5 represents:

A. Destination node

B. Source node

C. DLCI pipe

D. LCN

C. The number 5 indicates the DLCI pipe, at the end of which is the destination, with the IP address of 15.20.21.2

33. How many allowable standards can the LMI type in a command support?

A. one

B. three

C. five

D. four

B. LMI type can be ansi, q933a or the default Cisco.

34. ATM guarantees which of the following that Frame Relay does not?

A. Multicasting

B. Delivery

C. Error checking

D. Flow control
B. ATM guarantees delivery, which Frame Relay does not. Both Frame Relay and ATM have error checking and flow control.

35. ATM does direct broadcast.

A. True

B. False
B. False. ATM does not directly do broadcast, but it can pseudo-broadcast by replicating each broadcast packet across each VC that is set up to receive them.

36. The length of a header in an ATM cell is:

A. Three bytes

B. Five bytes
B. An ATM cell header is five bytes long.

37. For speeds of 622 Mbps or higher, the physical medium in ATM technology is generally:

A. Category 5 cable

B. Four bytes

C. Two bytes

D. Category 3 cable

E. Optical fiber

F. All of the above
C. Higher-speed ATM services use optical fiber as physical medium.

38. LANE can handle only non-routable protocols.

A. True

B. False
B. False. LANE can handle routable protocols such as TCP/IP and IPX, as well as non-routable protocols such as NetBIOS and SNA.

39. In ATM, which of the following statements is false?

A. VPI can be non-zero

B. Both VPI and VCI can be non-zero

C. VCI can be non-zero

D. VPI and VCI both can be zero
D. In ATM either VPI or VCI can be zero, but not both.

40. The configuration command ROUTER(CONFIG-LINE)#RXSPEED 38400 sets:

A. Transmit DTE rate

B. Transmit DCE rate

C. Receive DTE rate

D. Transmit DTE rate
C. RXSPEED sets the rate at which DTE can receive the data.

41. Which of the following commands is used to set up link quality monitoring (LQM) in PPP?

A. HOLD-QUEUE

B. PPP QUALITY

C. SHOW PROCESS CPU

D. PPP PREDICTOR
B. The command syntax is PPP QUALITY *percentage*, where percentage can be from 1 to 100.

42. What does a committed information rate (CIR) mean?

    A. A user is allowed to transmit data only at a fixed rate

    B. A user is guaranteed that a transmission rate will not fall below a certain threshold value

    C. A maximum rate at which a user can transmit data

    D. A fixed cost to the customer for transmission of data
    B. CIR guarantees that the rate will not drop below this value even on shared transmission links. Answer C is incorrect, because at certain peak times a user can transmit data at higher rates than CIR.

43. In Challenge Handshake Authentication Protocol (CHAP):

    A. The challenge packet contains an encrypted password

    B. The challenge is sent from the remote device to the central control router

    C. The challenge is sent from the central control router to the remote device

    D. The possibility of intrusion by an outsider is greater than in the Password Authentication Protocol (PAP)
    C. The challenge is issued by the central controller to the remote device. The response from the remote device contains an encrypted password.

44. Which of the following tells the port in an asynchronous communication in PPP to ignore specified control characters in the data stream?

    A. DSR

    B. DTR

    C. XOFF

    D. ACCM
    D. The ACCM tells the port to ignore certain control characters in the data stream via the command PPP ACCM MATCH.

45. In the command HOLD-QUEUE 100, the number 100 means:

    A. 100 incoming packets will be held in queue before the interface starts dropping packets

    B. 100 outgoing packets will be held in queue before the interface starts dropping packets

    C. 100 incoming and 100 outgoing packets will be held in queue before the interface starts dropping packets

    D. None of the above
    D. The command as given is incomplete. For incoming packets the command should be HOLD-QUEUE 100 IN and for outgoing packets the command should be HOLD-QUEUE 100 OUT.

Chapter 11 Answers

1. Which trunking protocol was developed by Cisco?

   A. LAN Emulation

   B. Inter-Switch Link (ISL)

   C. IEEE 802.10

   D. IEEE 802.1Q
   B. ISL is a trunking protocol that was developed by Cisco. Inter-Switch Link is used to exchange VLAN information, and can only be used between Cisco devices such as switches and routers.

2. VLANs operate at which layer of the OSI model?

   A. Layer 8

   B. Layer 2

   C. Layer 3

   D. Layer 5
   B. VLANs operate at Layer 2 of the OSI model. They provide Layer 2 segmentation. Communication between VLANs requires the use of a router or Layer 3 switch.

3. What are the two modes on a Catalyst switch for VLAN creation and updates?

   A. Transparent and VTP

   B. Transparent and translational

   C. Translational and source-route

   D. Forwarding and blocking
   A. The two modes on a Catalyst switch for VLAN creation and updates are transparent and VTP. Use transparent mode when you will not exchange VLAN information between switches and will configure new VLANs manually on each switch. VTP (VLAN Trunk Protocol) allows you to automatically exchange VLAN information between Cisco switches, and administer them from a central point.

4. Identify two common trunking protocols.

   A. PNNI and OSPF

   B. IEEE 802.3 and IEEE 802.5

   C. IEEE 802.1D and LAN Emulation

   D. ISL and IEEE 802.1Q
   D. ISL and IEEE 802.1Q are two common trunking protocols. ISL is the trunking protocol developed by Cisco. IEEE 802.1Q is an industry-standard trunking protocol. Note that Cisco switches will not exchange VLAN information on trunks running different trunking protocols.

5. Identify the protocol used to avoid loops in switches and VLANs.

   A. Spanning-Tree Protocol (STP)

   B. VLAN Trunk Protocol (VTP)

   C. Private Network-to-Network Interface (PNNI)

D. Border Gateway Protocol (BGP)
A. Spanning-Tree Protocol is an industry-standard protocol used to avoid bridging loops. Switches send out Bridge Protocol Data Units (BPDUs) containing information to help switches determine any potential loops in the network and place them in blocking mode.

6. Identify two advantages that VLANs provide.

A. Broadcast control

B. Increased security

C. Eliminates need for routers

D. Decreased performance
A, B. VLANs provide the flexibility to span Layer 2 broadcast domains across traditional physical boundaries. In addition, they provide increased security for users requiring privacy for network traffic.

7. What is the most common method of VLAN assignment?

A. IP address

B. MAC address

C. Port

D. Workstation type
C. Port is the most common method of VLAN assignment. VLANs can be assigned by several different methods depending on the manufacturer. Assigning VLANs by switch port is simple, very common, and the easiest to administer.

8. Identify the option that allows you to control the VLANs that are advertised over trunk ports using VTP.

A. Trimming

B. Pruning

C. Blocking

D. Shunning
C. Pruning lets you control which VLANs you want to advertise over trunk ports. This is useful for limiting the traffic passed over trunk ports, and for security. You can limit the advertisement of the Accounting VLAN to other switches, if those users will not be in other physical locations served by your network.

9. Identify the port state that a port will enter before forwarding frames:

A. Blocking

B. Forwarding

C. Disabled

D. Learning
D. A port will enter the listening and learning states before proceeding to the forwarding state. During this time, no frames will be forwarded, essentially blocking all frames. This can cause erratic connectivity issues for workstations and servers.

10. What is the switch code needed to implement industry-standard IEEE 802.1Q trunking?

    A. 2.3

    B. 3.2

    C. 4.1

    D. 1.5

    C. 4.1 is the switch code needed to implement industry-standard IEEE 802.1Q trunking. IEEE 802.1Q is the interoperable trunking protocol for exchanging VLAN information, and requires Supervisor code release 4.1 or greater.

11. The term VLAN is most commonly associated with:

    A. Routers

    B. Hubs

    C. Switches

    D. Bridges

    C. The term VLAN is most commonly associated with switches.

12. Implementation of VLAN creates a network that must be routed. This network belongs to:

    A. Layer 4

    B. Layer 3

    C. Layer 2

    D. Layer 1

    B. VLAN creates a Layer 3 type network.

13. Client-server applications providing graphical user interface created a need for:

    A. Increased bandwidth

    B. More switches

    C. Increased number of operations support systems

    D. None of the above

    A. The client-server applications providing GUI created a need for increased bandwidth. This increased bandwidth results in a complex network that may require additional switches and operations support systems.

14. A hub directs all frames to:

    A. All ports

    B. Only to the port on which the frame was received

    C. Only to a subset of ports in a multicast system

    D. All ports except the port on which the frame was received

    D. A hub repeats all frames to all ports except the port on which the frame was received.

15. A unicast frame is destined for:

    A. All ports

    B. Only one MAC address

    C. All MAC addresses

    D. A subset of MAC addresses

    B. Unicast frames are directed towards a specific MAC address.

16. Content Addressable Memory (CAM) is:

A. A Cisco product

B. A routing table

C. Updated every time the switch is turned on

D. All of the above

D. CAM is Cisco term for a forwarding table that resides in the volatile memory of the MAC addresses and is updated every time the switch is powered on.

17. If a switch does not find an address that matches the destination address, what does the switch do?

A. Copies the frame to default ports assigned for "no-match" scenario

B. Copies the frame to all ports meant for broadcasting

C. Copies the frame to all ports

D. Copies the frame to all ports meant for multicasting

C. If a switch does not find an address that matches the destination address, then the switch copies the frame to all ports

18. Switching is a term most commonly used to describe:

A. Layer 2 devices

B. Layer 1 devices

C. Layer 3 devices

D. Layer 4 devices

A. Switching is a term most commonly used to describe Layer 2 network devices that forward Ethernet and Token Ring frames based on the destination MAC address.

19. Which type of switching method allows the switch to forward traffic without receiving the entire frame?

A. store and forward

B. cut-through

C. circuit switching

D. packet switching

B. Both circuit switching and packet switching represent technologies that can use either the store and forward or the cut-through method.

20. What is the main reason a switch using the store and forward method is costlier than a switch using the cut-through method?

A. The added capability to control traffic

B. The capability to propagate damaged frames

C. The capability to switch the entire frame

D. The need for buffer space

D. The store and forward method requires provisioning of memory buffer space that adds to the cost of the switch.

21. Which is the best description of VLAN?

A. A group of end stations sharing a common physical connection

B. A group of end stations sharing a common logical connection

C. A group of end stations at the same location

D. A group of end stations on the same LAN segment
B. VLAN is a logical collection of end stations.

22. Consider the following scenario:
VLAN 1: Stations A, B, and C
Station A connected to switch A
Station B connected to switch B
Station C connected to switch C
VLAN 2: Stations D and E
Station D connected to switch A
Station E connected to switch C
A broadcast message sent by Station B will be received by:

A. Stations A and D

B. Stations C and E

C. Stations A, B, and C

D. Stations C, D, and E
C. A broadcast message sent by Station B will be received by Stations A, B, and C. Although Stations C and E are connected to the same switch, they belong to different VLANs. A broadcast message sent by station B will be received only by the stations on VLAN 1.

23. Broadcast domain is dependent upon:

A. Physical location

B. LAN media

C. Transmission rates

D. None of the above
D. Broadcast domain is independent of physical location, LAN media, and transmission rates.

24. The major benefit of VLAN is that it allows creation of workgroups based on:

A. Functions

B. Physical location

C. Switching technology

D. Transmission media
A. VLAN allows logical grouping of a workforce based on functions performed by the groups.

25. In the source-route bridging method, the path is specified by:

A. The next router on the path

B. A source station

C. A source router

D. A network broadcast
B. Source-route bridging puts the responsibility of locating the destination device on the source station.

26. The spanning-tree algorithm is used in:

A. Source-route bridging

B. Cut-through switching

C. Transparent bridging

D. Store and forward switching
C. Transparent bridging uses the spanning-tree algorithm.

27. Transparent bridging is primarily used in what environment?

A. Token Ring

B. FDDI

C. Ethernet

D. All of the above

C. Transparent bridging is used primarily in Ethernet environments.

28. A Routing Information Field (RIF) is applicable in Token Ring environments.

A. True

B. False

A. True. Token Ring frames contain a RIF, whereas Ethernet frames do not contain a RIF.

29. A Routing Information Field may contain:

A. Ring number

B. Bridge number

C. Port number

D. A and B only

E. B and C only

D. The RIF may contain a combination of bridge numbers and ring numbers.

30. The design of transparent bridging network may result in:

A. Loops

B. Broadcast frames not being received by some stations

C. Forwarding frames over and over

A, C. The design of transparent bridging network may result in looping and forwarding frames over and over. Spanning-tree algorithm is used to avoid looping by providing a blocking mechanism.

31. When might a Bridge Protocol Data Unit have to be used?

A. In a changing network topology

B. In a static network topology

C. To indicate which ports are to be opened for traffic

D. All of the above

A. BPDUs are used in a changing network topology environment to block certain ports from carrying the traffic.

32. Which of the following is not a default VLAN number for FDDI or Token Ring?

A. 1002

B. 1003

C. 1004

D. 1

D. 1002 through 1005 are default values for FDDI/Token ring. 1 is used as a default value for VLAN 1.

33. In configuring a VLAN Trunk Protocol (VTP), which of the following commands is optional?

A. SET VTP DOMAIN NAME

B. set vtp mode server

C. set vtp password

D. set vtp enable

C. SET VTP PASSWORD and SET VTP PRUNING ENABLE are optional commands.

34. For Catalyst switches, which of the following commands is used to obtain a summary of advertisements transmitted?

   A. SHOW VTP DOMAIN
   B. show vtp statistics
   C. show port status
   D. show router status
   B. The SHOW VTP STATISTICS command will provide the number of advertisements received, as well as the number of advertisements transmitted.

35. The assignments of ports to VLANS must be done in a sequential way.

   A. True
   B. False
   B. False. The ports on line cards need not be assigned in a sequential manner. For example ports 3 – 6 and 11 – 14 on card 1 could be assigned to VLAN 3, and ports 7 – 10 could be assigned to VLAN 2.

36. Which of the following commands will result in assigning ports 1 – 24 on card 6 to VLAN 1, and ports 7 – 12 on card 9 to VLAN 2?

   A. SET VLAN 1 6
   B. set vlan1 6/1-24 , set vlan 9
   C. SET VLAN 1 6 9
   D. set vlan 1 6/1-24, set vlan 2 9/7-12
   D. The correct command is SET VLAN 1 6/1-24, SET VLAN 2 9/7-12. Answers A, B, and C are not valid commands.

37. How many major states can a port have?

   A. Five
   B. Four
   C. Three
   D. Two
   A. The five states that a port can have are blocking, listening, learning, forwarding, and disabled.

38. What does the portfast option in Cisco allow?

   A. Bypassing the blocking state
   B. Bypassing the listening state
   C. Bypassing the forwarding state
   D. Bypassing the disabled state
   B. The portfast option bypasses the learning and listening states.

39. In the default configuration, the portfast settings will allow:

   A. Ping
   B. Acquiring a DHCP address consistently
   C. Enabling portfast
   D. Logging into Novell Directory Server(NDS)
   C. In a default mode portfast is disabled and will not allow ping, acquiring a DHCP address consistently, or logging into NDS. However, it is possible to enable the portfast option.

B

About the CD

CD-ROM Instructions

This CD-ROM contains a full Web site accessible to you via your Web browser. Browse to or double-click **Index (Click.htm)** at the root of the CD-ROM and you will find instructions for navigating the Web site and using the electronic book and the test bank.

Electronic Book

The CD-ROM features an electronic version of the entire book in HTML format.

Interactive Self-Study Module

An electronic self-study test bank is linked to the electronic book to help you instantly review key exam topics that may still be unclear. This module contains over 500 review questions, the same questions that appear at the end of each chapter. As you go through the self test module, you can review answers as you go, move onto the next question, and opt for further review of a question you got wrong.

C

About the Web Site

Access Global Knowledge Network

As you know by now, Global Knowledge Network is the largest independent IT training company in the world. Just by purchasing this book, you have also secured a free subscription to the Access Global Web site and its many resources. You can find it at:

http://access.globalknowledge.com

You can log in directly at the Access Global site. You will be e-mailed a new, secure password immediately upon registering.

What You'll Find There . . .

You will find a lot of information at the Global Knowledge site, most of which can be broken down into three categories:

Skills Gap Analysis

Global Knowledge offers several ways for you to analyze your networking skills and discover where they may be lacking. Using Global Knowledge Network's trademarked Competence Key Tool, you can do a skills gap analysis and get recommendations for where you may need to do some more studying. (Sorry, it just may not end with this book!)

Networking

You'll also gain valuable access to another asset: people. At the Access Global site, you'll find threaded discussions as well as live discussions. Talk to other CCIE candidates, get advice from folks who have already taken exams, and get access to Cisco instructors.

Product Offerings

Of course, Global Knowledge also offers its products here—and you may find some valuable items for purchase: CBTs, books, and courses. Browse freely and see if there's something that could help you.

Glossary

10Base2 Ethernet specification using 50-ohm thin coaxial cable and a signaling rate of 10-Mbps baseband.

10Base5 Ethernet specification using standard (thick) 50-ohm baseband coaxial cable and a signaling rate of 10-Mbps baseband.

10BaseFL Ethernet specification using fiber-optic cabling and a signaling rate of 10-Mbps baseband, and FOIRL.

10BaseT Ethernet specification using two pairs of twisted-pair cabling (Category 3, 4, or 5): one pair for transmitting data and the other for receiving data, and a signaling rate of 10-Mbps baseband.

10Broad36 Ethernet specification using broadband coaxial cable and a signaling rate of 10-Mbps.

100BaseFX Fast Ethernet specification using two strands of multimode fiber-optic cable per link and a signaling rate of 100-Mbps baseband. A 100BaseFXlink cannot exceed 400 meters in length.

100BaseT Fast Ethernet specification using UTP wiring and a signaling rate of 100-Mbps baseband. 100BaseT sends link pulses out on the wire when there is no data traffic present.

100BaseT4 Fast Ethernet specification using four pairs of Category 3, 4, or 5 UTP wiring and a signaling rate of 100-Mbps baseband. The maximum length of a 100BaseT4 segment is 100 meters.

100BaseTX Fast Ethernet specification using two pairs of UTP or STP wiring and 100-Mbps baseband signaling. One pair of wires is used to receive data; the other is used to transmit. A 100BaseTX segment cannot exceed 100 meters in length.

AAL (ATM adaptation layer) Service-dependent sublayer of the datalink layer. The function of the AAL is to accept data from different applications and present it to the ATM layer in 48-byte ATM segments.

AARP (AppleTalk Address Resolution Protocol) The protocol that maps a datalink address to an AppleTalk network address.

access list A sequential list of statements in a router configuration that identify network traffic for various purposes, including traffic and route filtering.

acknowledgment Notification sent from one network device to another to acknowledge that a message or group of messages has been received. Sometimes abbreviated ACK. Opposite of NAK.

active hub A multiport device that repeats and amplifies LAN signals at the physical layer.

active monitor A network device on a Token Ring that is responsible for managing ring operations. The active monitor ensures that tokens are not lost, or that frames do not circulate indefinitely on the ring.

address A numbering convention used to identify a unique entity or location on a network.

address mapping Technique that allows different protocols to operate together by associating addresses from one format with those of another.

address mask A string of bits, which, when combined with an address, describes which portion of an address refers to the network or subnet and which part refers to the host. (See also subnet mask.)

address resolution A technique for resolving differences between computer addressing schemes. Address resolution most often specifies a method for mapping network layer addresses to datalink layer addresses. (See also address mapping.)

Address Resolution Protocol See ARP.

administrative distance A rating of the preferability of a routing information source. Administrative distance is expressed as a value between 0 and 255. The higher the value, the lower the preference.

advertising A process in which a router sends routing or service updates at frequent intervals so that other routers on the network can maintain lists of usable routes or services.

algorithm A specific process for arriving at a solution to a problem.

ANSI (American National Standards Institute) An organization of representatives of corporate, government, and other entities that coordinates standards-related activities, approves U.S. national standards, and develops positions for the United States in international standards organizations.

AppleTalk A suite of communications protocols developed by Apple Computer for allowing communication among their devices over a network.

application layer Layer 7 of the OSI reference model. This layer provides services to end-user application processes such as electronic mail, file transfer, and terminal emulation.

ARP (Address Resolution Protocol) Internet protocol used to map an IP address to a MAC address.

asynchronous transmission Describes digital signals that are transmitted without precise clocking or synchronization.

ATM (Asynchronous Transfer Mode) An international standard for cell relay suitable for carrying multiple service types (such as voice, video, or data) in fixed-length (53-byte) cells. Fixed-length cells allow cell processing to occur in hardware, thereby reducing latency.

ATM adaptation layer See AAL.

ATM Forum International organization founded in 1991 by Cisco Systems, NET/ADAPTIVE, Northern Telecom, and Sprint to develop and promote standards-based implementation agreements for ATM technology.

AUI (attachment unit interface) An interface between an MAU and a NIC (network interface card) described in the IEEE 802.3 specification. AUI often refers to the physical port to which an AUI cable attaches.

autonomous system A group of networks under a common administration that share in a common routing strategy. Sometimes abbreviated AS.

backoff The retransmission delay used by contention-based MAC protocols such as Ethernet, after a network node determines that the physical medium is already in use.

bandwidth The difference between the highest and lowest frequencies available for network signals. The term may also describe the throughput capacity of a network link or segment.

baseband A network technology in which a single carrier frequency is used. Ethernet is a common example of a baseband network technology.

baud Unit of signaling speed equal to the number of separate signal elements transmitted in one second. Baud is synonymous with bits per second (bps), as long as each signal element represents exactly one bit.

B channel (bearer channel) An ISDN term meaning a full-duplex, 64-Kbps channel used to send user data.

bearer channel See B channel.

BECN (backward explicit congestion notification) A Frame Relay network facility that allows switches in the network to advise DTE devices of congestion. The BECN bit is set in frames traveling in the opposite direction of frames encountering a congested path.

best-effort delivery Describes a network system that does not use a system of acknowledgment to guarantee reliable delivery of information.

BGP (Border Gateway Protocol) An interdomain path-vector routing protocol. BGP exchanges reachability information with other BGP systems. It is defined by RFC 1163.

binary A numbering system in which there are only two digits, ones and zeros.

BNC connector Standard connector used to connect coaxial cable to an MAU or line card.

BOOTP (Bootstrap Protocol) Part of the TCP/IP suite of protocols, used by a network node to determine the IP address of its Ethernet interfaces, in order to boot from a network server.

bps bits per second.

BRI (Basic Rate Interface) ISDN interface consisting of two B channels and one D channel for circuit-switched communication. ISDN BRI can carry voice, video, and data.

bridge Device that connects and forwards packets between two network segments that use the same datalink communications protocol. Bridges operate at the data link layer of the OSI reference model. A bridge will filter, forward, or flood an incoming frame based on the MAC address of the frame.

broadband A data transmission system that multiplexes multiple independent signals onto one cable. Also, in telecommunications, any channel with a bandwidth greater than 4 KHz. In LAN terminology, a coaxial cable using analog signaling.

broadcast Data packet addressed to all nodes on a network. Broadcasts are identified by a broadcast address that matches all addresses on the network.

broadcast address Special address reserved for sending a message to all stations. At the datalink layer, a broadcast address is a MAC destination address of all 1s.

broadcast domain The group of all devices that will receive the same broadcast frame originating from any device within the group. Because routers do not forward broadcast frames, broadcast domains are typically bounded by routers.

buffer A memory storage area used for handling data in transit. Buffers are used in internetworking to compensate for differences in processing speed between network devices or signaling rates of segments. Bursts of packets can be stored in buffers until they can be handled by slower devices.

bus Common physical path composed of wires or other media, across which signals are sent from one part of a computer to another.

byte A series of consecutive binary digits that are operated upon as a unit, usually eight bits.

cable Transmission medium of copper wire or optical fiber wrapped in a protective cover.

cable range A range of network numbers on an extended AppleTalk network. The cable range value can be a single network number or a contiguous sequence of several network numbers. Nodes assign addresses within the cable range values provided.

carrier Electromagnetic wave or alternating current of a single frequency, suitable for modulation by another, data-bearing signal.

Carrier Detect See CD.

Category 5 cabling One of five grades of UTP cabling described in the EIA/TIA-586 standard. Category 5 cabling can transmit data at speeds up to 100 Mbps.

CCITT (Consultative Committee for International Telegraphy and Telephony) International organization responsible for the development of communications standards. Now called the ITU-T.

CD (Carrier Detect) Signal that indicates whether an interface is active.

cell The basic data unit for ATM switching and multiplexing. A cell consists of a five-byte header and 48 bytes of payload. Cells contain fields in their headers that identify the data stream to which they belong.

checksum Method for checking the integrity of transmitted data. A checksum is an integer value computed from a sequence of octets taken through a series of arithmetic operations. The value is recomputed at the receiving end and compared for verification.

CIDR (classless interdomain routing) Technique supported by BGP4 and based on route aggregation. CIDR allows routers to group routes together in order to cut down on the quantity of routing information carried by the core routers. With CIDR, several IP networks appear to networks outside the group as a single, larger entity. With CIDR, IP addresses and their subnet masks are written as four octets, separated by periods, followed by a forward slash and a two-digit number that represents the subnet mask.

CIR (committed information rate) The rate at which a Frame Relay network agrees to transfer information under normal conditions, averaged over a minimum increment of time. CIR, measured in bits per second, is one of the key negotiated tariff metrics.

circuit switching A system in which a dedicated physical path must exist between sender and receiver for the entire duration of a call. Used heavily in telephone networks.

client Node or software program, or front-end device, that requests services from a server.

collision In Ethernet, the result of two nodes transmitting simultaneously. The frames from each device cause an increase in voltage when they meet on the physical media, and are damaged.

congestion Traffic in excess of network capacity.

connectionless Term used to describe data transfer without the prior existence of a circuit.

console A DTE device, usually consisting of a keyboard and display unit, through which users interact with a host.

contention Access method in which network devices compete for permission to access the physical medium. Compare with circuit switching and token passing.

cost A value, typically based on media bandwidth or other measures, that is assigned by a network administrator and used by routing protocols to compare various paths through an internetwork environment. Cost values are used to determine the most favorable path to a particular destination—the lower the cost, the better the path.

count to infinity A condition in which routers continuously increment the hop count to particular networks. Often occurs in routing algorithms that are slow to converge. Usually, an arbitrary hop count ceiling is imposed to limit the extent of this problem.

CPE (customer premises equipment) Terminating equipment, such as terminals, telephones, and modems, installed at customer sites and connected to the telephone company network.

CRC (cyclic redundancy check) An error-checking technique in which the receiving device performs a calculation on the frame contents and compares the calculated number to a value stored in the frame by the sending node.

CSU (channel service unit) Digital interface device that connects end-user equipment to the local digital telephone loop. Often referred to together with DSU, as CSU/DSU.

datagram Logical unit of information sent as a network layer unit over a transmission medium without prior establishment of a circuit.

datalink layer Layer 2 of the OSI reference model. This layer provides reliable transit of data across a physical link. The data link layer is concerned with physical addressing, network topology, access to the network medium, error detection, sequential delivery of frames, and flow control. The data link layer is divided into two sublayers: the MAC sublayer and the LLC sublayer.

DCE (data circuit-terminating equipment) The devices and connections of a communications network that represent the network end of the user-to-network interface. The DCE provides a physical connection to the network and provides a clocking signal used to synchronize transmission between DCE and DTE devices. Modems and interface cards are examples of DCE devices.

D channel (data channel) Full-duplex, 16-Kbps (BRI) or 64-Kbps (PRI) ISDN channel.

DDR (dial-on-demand routing) Technique whereby a router can automatically initiate and close a circuit-switched session as transmitting stations demand. The router spoofs keepalives so that end stations treat the session as active. DDR permits routing over ISDN or telephone lines using an external ISDN terminal adapter or modem.

DECnet Group of communications products (including a protocol suite) developed and supported by Digital Equipment Corporation. DECnet/OSI (also called DECnet Phase V) is the most recent iteration and supports both OSI protocols and proprietary Digital protocols. Phase IV Prime supports inherent MAC addresses that allow DECnet nodes to coexist with systems running other protocols that have MAC address restrictions.

dedicated line Communications line that is indefinitely reserved for transmissions, rather than switched as transmission is required. See also leased line.

de facto standard A standard that exists because of its widespread use.

default route A routing table entry that is used to direct packets when there is no explicit route present in the routing table.

de jure standard Standard that exists because of its development or approval by an official standards body.

delay The time between the initiation of a transaction by a sender and the first response received by the sender. Also, the time required to move a packet from source to destination over a network path.

demarc The demarcation point between telephone carrier equipment and CPE.

demultiplexing The separating of multiple streams of data that have been multiplexed into a common physical signal for transmission, back into multiple output streams. Opposite of multiplexing.

destination address Address of a network device to receive data.

DHCP (Dynamic Host Configuration Protocol) Provides a mechanism for allocating IP addresses dynamically so that addresses can be reassigned instead of belonging to only one host.

discovery mode Method by which an AppleTalk router acquires information about an attached network from an operational router and then uses this information to configure its own addressing information.

distance vector routing algorithm Class of routing algorithms that use the number of hops in a route to find a shortest path to a destination network. Distance vector routing algorithms call for each router to send its entire routing table in each update to each of its neighbors. Also called Bellman-Ford routing algorithm.

DLCI (datalink connection identifier) A value that specifies a virtual circuit in a Frame Relay network.

DNIC (Data Network Identification Code) Part of an X.121 address. DNICs are divided into two parts: the first specifying the country in which the addressed PSN is located and the second specifying the PSN itself. (See also X.121.)

DNS (Domain Name System) System used in the Internet for translating names of network nodes into addresses.

DTE (data terminal equipment) Device at the user end of a user-network interface that serves as a data source, destination, or both. DTE connects to a data network through a DCE device (for example, a modem) and typically uses clocking signals generated by the DCE. DTE includes such devices as computers, routers and multiplexers.

dynamic routing Routing that adjusts automatically to changes in network topology or traffic patterns.

E1 Wide-area digital transmission scheme used in Europe that carries data at a rate of 2.048 Mbps.

EIA/TIA-232 Common physical layer interface standard, developed by EIA and TIA, that supports unbalanced circuits at signal speeds of up to 64 Kbps. Formerly known as RS-232.

encapsulation The process of attaching a particular protocol header to a unit of data prior to transmission on the network. For example, a frame of Ethernet data is given a specific Ethernet header before network transit.

end point Device at which a virtual circuit or virtual path begins or ends.

enterprise network A privately maintained network connecting most major points in a company or other organization. Usually spans a large geographic area and supports multiple protocols and services.

entity Generally, an individual, manageable network device. Sometimes called an alias.

error control Technique for detecting and correcting errors in data transmissions.

Ethernet Baseband LAN specification invented by Xerox Corporation and developed jointly by Xerox, Intel, and Digital Equipment Corporation. Ethernet networks use the CSMA/CD method of media access control and run over a variety of cable types at 10 Mbps. Ethernet is similar to the IEEE 802.3 series of standards.

EtherTalk Apple Computer's datalink product that allows an AppleTalk network to be connected by Ethernet cable.

explorer packet Generated by an end station trying to find its way through a SRB network. Gathers a hop-by-hop description of a path through the network by being marked (updated) by each bridge that it traverses, thereby creating a complete topological map.

Fast Ethernet Any of a number of 100-Mbps Ethernet specifications. Fast Ethernet offers a speed increase ten times that of the 10BaseT Ethernet specification, while preserving such qualities as frame format, MAC mechanisms, and MTU. Such similarities allow the use of existing 10BaseT applications and network management tools on Fast Ethernet networks.

Based on an extension to the IEEE 802.3 specification. Compare with Ethernet. (See also 100BaseFX, 100BaseT, 100BaseT4, and 100BaseTX.)

FDDI (Fiber Distributed Data Interface) LAN standard, defined by ANSI X3T9.5, specifying a 100-Mbps token-passing network using fiber-optic cable, with transmission distances of up to 2 km. FDDI uses a dual-ring architecture to provide redundancy. Compare with CDDI and FDDI II.

FECN (forward explicit congestion notification) A facility in a Frame Relay network to inform DTE receiving the frame that congestion was experienced in the path from source to destination. DTE receiving frames with the FECN bit set can request that higher-level protocols take flow-control action as appropriate.

file transfer Category of popular network applications that features movement of files from one network device to another.

filter Generally, a process or device that screens network traffic for certain characteristics, such as source address, destination address, or protocol, and determines whether to forward or discard that traffic or routes based on the established criteria.

firewall Router or other computer designated as a buffer between public networks and a private network. A firewall router uses access lists and other methods to ensure the security of the private network.

Flash memory Nonvolatile storage that can be electrically erased and reprogrammed as necessary.

flash update Routing update sent asynchronously when a change in the network topology occurs.

flat addressing A system of addressing that does not incorporate a hierarchy to determine location.

flooding Traffic-passing technique used by switches and bridges in which traffic received on an interface is sent out all of the interfaces of that device except the interface on which the information was originally received.

flow control Technique for ensuring that a transmitting device, such as a modem, does not overwhelm a receiving device with data. When the buffers on the receiving device are full, a message is sent to the sending device to suspend transmission until it has processed the data in the buffers.

forwarding The process of sending a frame or packet toward its destination.

fragment Piece of a larger packet that has been broken down to smaller units.

fragmentation Process of breaking a packet into smaller units when transmitting over a network medium that is unable to support a transmission unit the original size of the packet.

frame Logical grouping of information sent as a datalink layer unit over a transmission medium. Sometimes refers to the header and trailer, used for synchronization and error control, which surround the user data contained in the unit. The terms cell, datagram, message, packet, and segment are also used to describe logical information groupings at various layers of the OSI reference model and in various technology circles.

Frame Relay Industry-standard, switched datalink layer protocol that handles multiple virtual circuits over a single physical interface. Frame Relay is more efficient than X.25, for which it is generally considered a replacement.

frequency Number of cycles, measured in hertz, of an alternating current signal per unit of time.

FTP (File Transfer Protocol) An application protocol, part of the TCP/IP protocol stack, used for transferring files between hosts on a network.

full duplex Capability for simultaneous data transmission and receipt of data between two devices.

full mesh A network topology in which each network node has either a physical circuit or a virtual circuit connecting it to every other network node.

gateway In the IP community, an older term referring to a routing device. Today, the term router is used to describe devices that perform this function, and gateway refers to a special-purpose device that performs an application layer conversion of information from one protocol stack to another.

Gb (gigabit) Approximately 1,000,000,000 bits.

GB (gigabyte) Approximately 1,000,000,000 bytes.

Gbps (gigabits per second)

GBps (gigabytes per second)

GNS (Get Nearest Server) Request packet sent by a client on an IPX network to locate the nearest active server of a particular type. An IPX network client issues a GNS request to solicit either a direct response from a connected server or a response from a router that tells it where on the internetwork the service can be located. GNS is part of the IPX SAP.

half duplex Capability for data transmission in only one direction at a time between a sending station and a receiving station.

handshake Sequence of messages exchanged between two or more network devices to ensure transmission synchronization.

hardware address See MAC address.

HDLC (High-Level Data Link Control) Bit-oriented synchronous datalink layer protocol developed by ISO and derived from SDLC. HDLC specifies a data encapsulation method for synchronous serial links and includes frame characters and checksums in its headers.

header Control information placed before data when encapsulating that data for network transmission.

hello packet Multicast packet that is used by routers for neighbor discovery and recovery. Hello packets also indicate that a client is still operating on the network.

Hello protocol Protocol used by OSPF and other routing protocols for establishing and maintaining neighbor relationships.

hierarchical addressing A scheme of addressing that uses a logical hierarchy to determine location. For example, IP addresses consist of network numbers, subnet numbers, and host numbers, which IP routing algorithms use to route the packet to the appropriate location.

holddown State of a routing table entry in which routers will neither advertise the route nor accept advertisements about the route for a specific length of time (known as the holddown period).

hop Term describing the passage of a data packet between two network nodes (for example, between two routers). (See also hop count.)

hop count Routing metric used to measure the distance between a source and a destination. RIP uses hop count as its metric.

host A computer system on a network. Similar to the term node except that host usually implies a computer system, whereas node can refer to any networked system, including routers.

host number Part of an IP address that designates which node is being addressed. Also called a host address.

hub A term used to describe a device that serves as the center of a star topology network; or, an Ethernet multiport repeater, sometimes referred to as a concentrator.

ICMP (Internet Control Message Protocol) A network layer Internet protocol that provides reports of errors and other information about IP packet processing. ICMP is documented in RFC 792.

IEEE (Institute of Electrical and Electronics Engineers) A professional organization among whose activities are the development of communications and networking standards. IEEE LAN standards are the most common LAN standards today.

IGP (Interior Gateway Protocol) A generic term for an Internet routing protocol used to exchange routing information within an autonomous system. Examples of common Internet IGPs include IGRP, OSPF, and RIP.

interface A connection between two systems or devices; or in routing terminology, a network connection.

Internet Term used to refer to the global internetwork that evolved from the ARPANET, that now connects tens of thousands of networks worldwide.

Internet protocol Any protocol that is part of the TCP/IP protocol stack. (See TCP/IP.)

internetwork Collection of networks interconnected by routers and other devices that functions (generally) as a single network.

internetworking General term used to refer to the industry that has arisen around the problem of connecting networks together. The term may be used to refer to products, procedures, and technologies.

Inverse ARP (Inverse Address Resolution Protocol) Method of building dynamic address mappings in a Frame Relay network. Allows a device to discover the network address of a device associated with a virtual circuit.

IP (Internet Protocol) Network layer protocol in the TCP/IP stack offering a connectionless datagram service. IP provides features for addressing, type-of-service specification, fragmentation and reassembly, and security. Documented in RFC 791.

IP address A 32-bit address assigned to hosts using the TCP/IP suite of protocols. An IP address is written as four octets separated by dots (dotted decimal format). Each address consists of a network number, an optional subnetwork number, and a host number. The network and subnetwork numbers together are used for routing, while the host number is used to address an individual host within the network or subnetwork. A subnet mask is often used with the address to extract network and subnetwork information from the IP address.

IPX (Internetwork Packet Exchange) NetWare network layer (Layer 3) protocol used for transferring data from servers to workstations. IPX is similar to IP in that it is a connectionless datagram service.

IPXCP (IPX Control Protocol) The protocol that establishes and configures IPX over PPP.

IPXWAN A protocol that negotiates end-to-end options for new links on startup. When a link comes up, the first IPX packets sent across are IPXWAN packets negotiating the options for the link. When the IPXWAN options have been successfully determined, normal IPX transmission begins, and no more IPXWAN packets are sent. Defined by RFC 1362.

ISDN (Integrated Services Digital Network) Communication protocol, offered by telephone companies, that permits telephone networks to carry data, voice, and other source traffic.

Kb (kilobit) Approximately 1,000 bits.

KB (kilobyte) Approximately 1,000 bytes.

kbps (kilobits per second)

KBps (kilobytes per second)

keepalive interval Period of time between keepalive messages sent by a network device.

keepalive message Message sent by one network device to inform another network device that it is still active.

LAN (local-area network) High-speed, low-error data network covering a relatively small geographic area. LANs connect workstations, peripherals, terminals, and other devices in a single building or other geographically limited area. LAN standards specify cabling and signaling at the physical and datalink layers of the OSI model. Ethernet, FDDI, and Token Ring are the most widely used LAN technologies.

LANE (LAN emulation) Technology that allows an ATM network to function as a LAN backbone. In this situation LANE provides multicast and broadcast support, address mapping (MAC-to-ATM), and virtual circuit management.

LAPB (Link Access Procedure, Balanced) The datalink layer protocol in the X.25 protocol stack. LAPB is a bit-oriented protocol derived from HDLC.

LAPD (Link Access Procedure on the D channel) ISDN data link layer protocol for the D channel. LAPD was derived from the LAPB protocol and is designed to satisfy the signaling requirements of ISDN basic access. Defined by ITU-T Recommendations Q.920 and Q.921.

latency The amount of time elapsed between the time a device requests access to a network and the time it is allowed to transmit; or, amount of time between the point at which a device receives a frame and the time that frame is forwarded out the destination port.

leased line Transmission line reserved by a communications carrier for the private use of a customer. A leased line is a type of dedicated line.

link Network communications channel consisting of a circuit or transmission path and all related equipment between a sender and a receiver. Most often used to refer to a WAN connection. Sometimes called a line or a transmission link.

link-state routing algorithm Routing algorithm in which each router broadcasts or multicasts information regarding the cost of reaching each of its neighbors to all nodes in the internetwork. Link state algorithms require that routers maintain a consistent view of the network and are therefore not prone to routing loops.

LLC (Logical Link Control) Higher of two datalink layer sublayers defined by the IEEE. The LLC sublayer handles error control, flow control, framing, and MAC-sublayer addressing. The most common LLC protocol is IEEE 802.2, which includes both connectionless and connection-oriented types.

LMI (Local Management Interface) A set of enhancements to the basic Frame Relay specification. LMI includes support for keepalives, a multicast mechanism; global addressing, and a status mechanism.

load balancing In routing, the ability of a router to distribute traffic over all its network ports that are the same distance from the destination address. Load balancing increases the utilization of network segments, thus increasing total effective network bandwidth.

local loop A line from the premises of a telephone subscriber to the telephone company central office.

LocalTalk Apple Computer's proprietary baseband protocol that operates at the datalink and physical layers of the OSI reference model. LocalTalk uses CSMA/CA and supports transmissions at speeds of 230.4 Kbps.

loop A situation in which packets never reach their destination, but are forwarded in a cycle repeatedly through a group of network nodes.

MAC (Media Access Control) Lower of the two sublayers of the data link layer defined by the IEEE. The MAC sublayer handles access to shared media.

MAC address Standardized datalink layer address that is required for every port or device that connects to a LAN. Other devices in the network use these addresses to locate specific ports in the network and to create and update routing tables and data structures. MAC addresses are 48 bits long and are controlled by the IEEE. Also known as a hardware address, a MAC-layer address, or a physical address.

MAN (metropolitan-area network) A network that spans a metropolitan area. Generally, a MAN spans a larger geographic area than a LAN, but a smaller geographic area than a WAN.

Mb (megabit) Approximately 1,000,000 bits.

Mbps (megabits per second)

media The various physical environments through which transmission signals pass. Common network media include cable (twisted-pair, coaxial, and fiber optic) and the atmosphere (through which microwave, laser, and infrared transmission occurs). Sometimes referred to as physical media.

Media Access Control See MAC.

mesh Network topology in which devices are organized in a segmented manner with redundant interconnections strategically placed between network nodes.

message Application layer logical grouping of information, often composed of a number of lower-layer logical groupings such as packets.

MSAU (multistation access unit) A wiring concentrator to which all end stations in a Token Ring network connect. Sometimes abbreviated MAU.

multiaccess network A network that allows multiple devices to connect and communicate by sharing the same medium, such as a LAN.

multicast A single packet copied by the network and sent to a specific subset of network addresses. These addresses are specified in the Destination Address field.

multicast address A single address that refers to multiple network devices. Sometimes called a group address.

multiplexing A technique that allows multiple logical signals to be transmitted simultaneously across a single physical channel.

mux A multiplexing device. A mux combines multiple input signals for transmission over a single line. The signals are demultiplexed, or separated, before they are used at the receiving end.

NAK (negative acknowledgment) A response sent from a receiving device to a sending device indicating that the information received contained errors.

name resolution The process of associating a symbolic name with a network location or address.

NAT (Network Address Translation) A technique for reducing the need for globally unique IP addresses. NAT allows an organization whose addresses may conflict with others in the IP address space, to connect to the Internet by translating those addresses into unique ones within the globally routable address space.

NBMA (nonbroadcast multiaccess) Term describing a multiaccess network that either does not support broadcasting (such as X.25) or in which broadcasting is not feasible.

NBP (Name Binding Protocol) AppleTalk transport level protocol that translates a character string name into the DDP address of the corresponding socket client.

NetBIOS (Network Basic Input/Output System) An application programming interface used by applications on an IBM LAN to request services from lower-level network processes such as session establishment and termination, and information transfer.

NetWare A network operating system developed by Novell, Inc. Provides remote file access, print services, and numerous other distributed network services.

network Collection of computers, printers, routers, switches, and other devices that are able to communicate with each other over some transmission medium.

network interface Border between a carrier network and a privately-owned installation.

network layer Layer 3 of the OSI reference model. This layer provides connectivity and path selection between two end systems. The network layer is the layer at which routing takes place.

NLSP (NetWare Link Services Protocol) Link-state routing protocol for IPX based on IS-IS.

node Endpoint of a network connection or a junction common to two or more lines in a network. Nodes can be processors, controllers, or workstations. Nodes, which vary in their functional capabilities, can be interconnected by links, and serve as control points in the network.

NVRAM (nonvolatile RAM) RAM that retains its contents when a device is powered off.

OSI reference model (Open System Interconnection reference model) A network architectural framework developed by ISO and ITU-T. The model describes seven layers, each of which specifies a particular network. The lowest layer, called the physical layer, is closest to the media technology. The highest layer, the application layer, is closest to the user. The OSI reference model is widely used as a way of understanding network functionality.

out-of-band signaling Transmission using frequencies or channels outside the frequencies or channels used for transfer of normal data. Out-of-band signaling is often used for error reporting when normal channels are unusable for communicating with network devices.

packet Logical grouping of information that includes a header containing control information and (usually) user data. Packets are most often used to refer to network layer units of data. The terms datagram, frame, message, and segment are also used to describe logical information groupings at various layers of the OSI reference model, and in various technology circles.

partial mesh Term describing a network in which devices are organized in a mesh topology, with some network nodes organized in a full mesh, but with others that are only connected to one or two other nodes in the network. A partial mesh does not provide the level of redundancy of a full mesh topology, but is less expensive to implement. Partial mesh topologies are generally used in the peripheral networks that connect to a fully meshed backbone. (See also full mesh and mesh.)

ping (packet internet groper) ICMP echo message and its reply. Often used in IP networks to test the reachability of a network device.

poison reverse updates Routing updates that explicitly indicate that a network or subnet is unreachable, rather than implying that a network is unreachable by not including it in updates. Poison reverse updates are sent to defeat large routing loops.

port 1. Interface on an internetworking device (such as a router). 2. In IP terminology, an upper-layer process that receives information from lower layers. Ports are numbered, and each numbered port is associated with a specific process. For example, SMTP is associated with port 25. A port number is also known as a well-known address. 3. To rewrite software or microcode so that it will run on a different hardware platform or in a different software environment than that for which it was originally designed.

PPP (Point-to-Point Protocol) A successor to SLIP that provides router-to-router and host-to-network connections over synchronous and asynchronous circuits. Whereas SLIP was designed to work with IP, PPP was designed to work with several network layer protocols, such as IP, IPX, and ARA. PPP also has built-in security mechanisms, such as CHAP and PAP. PPP relies on two protocols: LCP and NCP.

presentation layer Layer 6 of the OSI reference model. This layer ensures that information sent by the application layer of one system will be readable by the application layer of another. The presentation layer is also concerned with the data structures used by programs and therefore negotiates data transfer syntax for the application layer.

PRI (Primary Rate Interface) ISDN interface to primary rate access. Primary rate access consists of a single 64-Kbps D channel plus 23 (T1) or 30 (E1) B channels for voice or data. Compare to BRI. (See also ISDN.)

protocol Formal description of a set of rules and conventions that govern how devices on a network exchange information.

protocol stack Set of related communications protocols that operate together and, as a group, address communication at some or all of the seven layers of the OSI reference model. Not every protocol stack covers each layer of the model, and often a single protocol in the stack will address a number of layers at once. TCP/IP is a typical protocol stack.

proxy ARP (proxy Address Resolution Protocol) Variation of the ARP protocol in which an intermediate device (for example, a router) sends an ARP response on behalf of an end node to the requesting host. Proxy ARP can lessen bandwidth use on slow-speed WAN links. (See also ARP.)

query Message used to inquire about the value of some variable or set of variables.

queue A backlog of packets stored in buffers and waiting to be forwarded over a router interface.

RAM (random-access memory) Volatile memory that can be read and written by a computer.

reassembly The putting back together of an IP datagram at the destination after it has been fragmented either at the source or at an intermediate node. (See also fragmentation.)

reload The event of a Cisco router rebooting, or the command that causes the router to reboot.

RFC (Request For Comments) Document series used as the primary means for communicating information about the Internet. Some RFCs are designated by the IAB as Internet standards.

ring Connection of two or more stations in a logically circular topology. Information is passed sequentially between active stations. Token Ring, FDDI, and CDDI are based on this topology.

ring topology Network topology that consists of a series of repeaters connected to one another by unidirectional transmission links to form a single closed loop. Each station on the network connects to the network at a repeater.

RIP (Routing Information Protocol) A routing protocol for TCP/IP networks. The most common routing protocol in the Internet. RIP uses hop count as a routing metric.

ROM (read-only memory) Nonvolatile memory that can be read, but not written, by the computer.

routed protocol Protocol that carries user data so it can be routed by a router. A router must be able to interpret the logical internetwork as specified by that routed protocol. Examples of routed protocols include AppleTalk, DECnet, and IP.

router Network layer device that uses one or more metrics to determine the optimal path along which network traffic should be forwarded. Routers forward packets from one network to another based on network layer information.

routing Process of finding a path to a destination host.

routing metric Method by which a routing algorithm determines preferability of one route over another. This information is stored in routing tables. Metrics include bandwidth, communication cost, delay, hop count, load, MTU, path cost, and reliability. Sometimes referred to simply as a metric.

routing protocol Protocol that accomplishes routing through the implementation of a specific routing algorithm. Examples of routing protocols include IGRP, OSPF, and RIP.

routing table Table stored in a router or some other internetworking device that keeps track of routes to particular network destinations and, in some cases, metrics associated with those routes.

routing update Message sent from a router to indicate network reachability and associated cost information. Routing updates are typically sent at regular intervals and after a change in network topology. Compare with flash update.

SAP (service access point) 1. Field defined by the IEEE 802.2 specification that is part of an address specification. Thus, the destination plus the DSAP define the recipient of a packet. The same applies to the SSAP. 2. Service Advertising Protocol. IPX protocol that provides a means of informing network routers and servers of the location of available network resources and services.

segment 1. Section of a network that is bounded by bridges, routers, or switches. 2. In a LAN using a bus topology, a segment is a continuous electrical circuit that is often connected to other such segments with repeaters. 3. Term used in the TCP specification to describe a single transport layer unit of information.

serial transmission Method of data transmission in which the bits of a data character are transmitted sequentially over a single channel. Compare with parallel transmission.

session 1. Related set of communications transactions between two or more network devices. 2. In SNA, a logical connection that enables two NAUs to communicate.

session layer Layer 5 of the OSI reference model. This layer establishes, manages, and terminates sessions between applications and manages data exchange between presentation layer entities. Corresponds to the data flow control layer of the SNA model. (See also application layer, datalink layer, network layer, presentation layer, and transport layer.)

sliding window flow control Method of flow control in which a receiver gives a transmitter permission to transmit data until a window is full. When the window is full, the transmitter must stop transmitting until the receiver acknowledges some of the data, or advertises a larger window. TCP, other transport protocols, and several datalink layer protocols use this method of flow control.

SNAP (Subnetwork Access Protocol) Internet protocol that operates between a network entity in the subnetwork and a network entity in the end system. SNAP specifies a standard method of encapsulating IP datagrams and ARP messages on IEEE networks.

SNMP (Simple Network Management Protocol) Network management protocol used almost exclusively in TCP/IP networks. SNMP provides a means to monitor and control network devices, and to manage configurations, statistics collection, performance, and security.

socket Software structure operating as a communications end point within a network device.

SONET (Synchronous Optical Network) High-speed synchronous network specification developed by Bellcore and designed to run on optical fiber.

source address Address of a network device that is sending data.

spanning tree Loop-free subset of a network topology. (See also Spanning-Tree Protocol.)

Spanning-Tree Protocol Developed to eliminate loops in the network. The Spanning-Tree Protocol ensures a loop-free path by placing one of the bridge ports in "blocking mode," preventing the forwarding of packets.

SPF (shortest path first algorithm) Routing algorithm that sorts routes by length of path to determine a shortest-path spanning tree. Commonly used in link-state routing algorithms. Sometimes called Dijkstra's algorithm.

split-horizon updates Routing technique in which information about routes is prevented from being advertised out the router interface through which that information was received. Split-horizon updates are used to prevent routing loops.

SPX (Sequenced Packet Exchange) Reliable, connection-oriented protocol at the transport layer that supplements the datagram service provided by IPX.

standard Set of rules or procedures that are either widely used or officially specified.

star topology LAN topology in which end points on a network are connected to a common central switch by point-to-point links. A ring topology that is organized as a star implements a unidirectional closed-loop star, instead of point-to-point links.

static route Route that is explicitly configured and entered into the routing table. Static routes take precedence over routes chosen by dynamic routing protocols.

subinterface A virtual interface defined as a logical subdivision of a physical interface.

subnet address Portion of an IP address that is specified as the subnetwork by the subnet mask. (See also IP address, subnet mask, and subnetwork.)

subnet mask 32-bit address mask used in IP to indicate the bits of an IP address that are being used for the subnet address. Sometimes referred to simply as mask. (See also address mask and IP address.)

subnetwork 1. In IP networks, a network sharing a particular subnet address. 2. Subnetworks are networks arbitrarily segmented by a network administrator in order to provide a multilevel, hierarchical routing structure while shielding the subnetwork from the addressing complexity of attached networks. Sometimes called a subnet.

switch 1. Network device that filters, forwards, and floods frames based on the destination address of each frame. The switch operates at the datalink layer of the OSI model. 2. General term applied to an electronic or mechanical device that allows a connection to be established as necessary and terminated when there is no longer a session to support.

T1 Digital WAN carrier facility. T1 transmits DS-1-formatted data at 1.544 Mbps through the telephone-switching network, using AMI or B8ZS coding. Compare with E1. (See also AMI, B8ZS, and DS-1.)

TCP (Transmission Control Protocol) Connection-oriented transport layer protocol that provides reliable full-duplex data transmission. TCP is part of the TCP/IP protocol stack.

TCP/IP (Transmission Control Protocol/Internet Protocol) Common name for the suite of protocols developed by the U.S. DoD in the 1970s to support the construction of worldwide internetworks. TCP and IP are the two best-known protocols in the suite.

throughput Rate of information arriving at, and possibly passing through, a particular point in a network system.

timeout Event that occurs when one network device expects to hear from another network device within a specified period of time, but does not. A timeout usually results in a retransmission of information or the termination of the session between the two devices.

token Frame that contains only control information. Possession of the token allows a network device to transmit data onto the network.

Token Ring Token-passing LAN developed and supported by IBM. Token Ring runs at 4 or 16 Mbps over a ring topology. Similar to IEEE 802.5. (See also ring topology.)

TokenTalk Apple Computer's datalink product that allows an AppleTalk network to be connected by Token Ring cables.

transport layer Layer 4 of the OSI reference model. This layer is responsible for reliable network communication between end nodes. The transport layer provides mechanisms for the establishment, maintenance, and termination of virtual circuits, transport fault detection and recovery, and information flow control.

twisted-pair Relatively low-speed transmission medium consisting of two insulated wires arranged in a regular spiral pattern. The wires can be shielded or unshielded. Twisted-pair is common in telephony applications and is increasingly common in data networks.

UDP (User Datagram Protocol) Connectionless transport layer protocol in the TCP/IP protocol stack. UDP is a simple protocol that exchanges datagrams without acknowledgments or guaranteed delivery, requiring that error processing and retransmission be handled by other protocols. UDP is defined in RFC 768.

UTP (unshielded twisted-pair) Four-pair wire medium used in a variety of networks. UTP does not require the fixed spacing between connections that is necessary with coaxial-type connections.

virtual circuit Logical circuit created to ensure reliable communication between two network devices. A virtual circuit is defined by a VPI/VCI pair, and can be either permanent or switched. Virtual circuits are used in Frame Relay and X.25. In ATM, a virtual circuit is called a virtual channel. Sometimes abbreviated VC.

VLAN (virtual LAN) Group of devices on one or more LANs that are configured (using management software) so that they can communicate as if they were attached to the same wire, when in fact they are located on a number of different LAN segments. Because VLANs are based on logical instead of physical connections, they are extremely flexible.

VLSM (variable-length subnet masking) Ability to specify a different length subnet mask for the same network number at different locations in the network. VLSM can help optimize available address space.

WAN (wide-area network) Data communications network that serves users across a broad geographic area and often uses transmission devices provided by common carriers. Frame Relay, SMDS, and X.25 are examples of WANs. Compare with LAN and MAN.

wildcard mask 32-bit quantity used in conjunction with an IP address to determine which bits in an IP address should be matched and ignored when comparing that address with another IP address. A wildcard mask is specified when defining access list statements.

X.121 ITU-T standard describing an addressing scheme used in X.25 networks. X.121 addresses are sometimes called IDNs (International Data Numbers).

X.21 ITU-T standard for serial communications over synchronous digital lines. The X.21 protocol is used primarily in Europe and Japan.

X.25 ITU-T standard that defines how connections between DTE and DCE are maintained for remote terminal access and computer communications in public data networks. X.25 specifies LAPB, a datalink layer protocol, and PLP, a network layer protocol. Frame Relay has to some degree superseded X.25.

zone In AppleTalk, a logical group of network devices.

INDEX

B

C

D

E

F

G

H

I

L

R

S

T

V

Z

BEFORE OPENING THE DISC PACKAGE, CAREFULLY READ THE TERMS AND CONDITIONS
WING COPYRIGHT STATEMENT AND LIMITED CD-ROM WARRANTY.

ght Statement

nis software is protected by both United States copyright law and international copyright treaty provision. Except as noted in the contents of the CD-ROM, you must treat this software just like a book. However, you may copy it into a computer to be used and you may make archival copies of the software for the sole purpose of backing up the software and protecting your investment from loss. By saying, "just like a book," The McGraw-Hill Companies, Inc. ("Osborne/McGraw-Hill") means, for example, that this software may be used by any number of people and may be freely moved from one computer location to another, so long as there is no possibility of its being used at one location or on one computer while it is being used at another. Just as a book cannot be read by two different people in two different places at the same time, neither can the software be used by two different people in two different places at the same time.

Limited Warranty

Osborne/McGraw-Hill warrants the physical compact disc enclosed herein to be free of defects in materials and workmanship for a period of sixty days from the purchase date. If the CD included in your book has defects in materials or workmanship, please call McGraw-Hill at 1-800-217-0059, 9am to 5pm, Monday through Friday, Eastern Standard Time, and McGraw-Hill will replace the defective disc.

The entire and exclusive liability and remedy for breach of this Limited Warranty shall be limited to replacement of the defective disc, and shall not include or extend to any claim for or right to cover any other damages, including but not limited to, loss of profit, data, or use of the software, or special incidental, or consequential damages or other similar claims, even if Osborne/McGraw-Hill has been specifically advised of the possibility of such damages. In no event will Osborne/McGraw-Hill's liability for any damages to you or any other person ever exceed the lower of the suggested list price or actual price paid for the license to use the software, regardless of any form of the claim.

OSBORNE/McGRAW-HILL SPECIFICALLY DISCLAIMS ALL OTHER WARRANTIES, EXPRESS OR IMPLIED, INCLUDING BUT NOT LIMITED TO, ANY IMPLIED WARRANTY OF MERCHANTABILITY OR FITNESS FOR A PARTICULAR PURPOSE. Specifically, Osborne/McGraw-Hill makes no representation or warranty that the software is fit for any particular purpose, and any implied warranty of merchantability is limited to the sixty-day duration of the Limited Warranty covering the physical disc only (and not the software), and is otherwise expressly and specifically disclaimed.

This limited warranty gives you specific legal rights; you may have others which may vary from state to state. Some states do not allow the exclusion of incidental or consequential damages, or the limitation on how long an implied warranty lasts, so some of the above may not apply to you.

This agreement constitutes the entire agreement between the parties relating to use of the Product. The terms of any purchase order shall have no effect on the terms of this Agreement. Failure of Osborne/McGraw-Hill to insist at any time on strict compliance with this Agreement shall not constitute a waiver of any rights under this Agreement. This Agreement shall be construed and governed in accordance with the laws of New York. If any provision of this Agreement is held to be contrary to law, that provision will be enforced to the maximum extent permissible, and the remaining provisions will remain in force and effect.

NO TECHNICAL SUPPORT IS PROVIDED WITH THIS CD-ROM.